A Prehistory of South America

One day I went out with some merchants to hunt in the immediate vicinity of the city.

Our sport was very poor; but I had an opportunity of seeing the ruins of one of the ancient Indian villages, with its mound like a natural hill in the center.

The remains of houses, enclosures, irrigating streams, and burial mounds, scattered over this plain, cannot fail to give one a high idea of the condition and number of the ancient population. When their earthenware, woolen clothes, utensils of elegant forms cut out of the hardest rocks, tools of copper, ornaments of precious stones, palaces, and hydraulic works are considered, it is impossible not to respect the considerable advance made by them in the arts of civilization.

Charles Darwin, 1835, near Lima, The Voyage of the Beagle

A Prehistory of South America

Ancient Cultural Diversity on the Least Known Continent

Jerry D. Moore

University Press of Colorado
Boulder

Published by University Press of Colorado
5589 Arapahoe Avenue, Suite 206C
Boulder, Colorado 80303

Printed in Canada

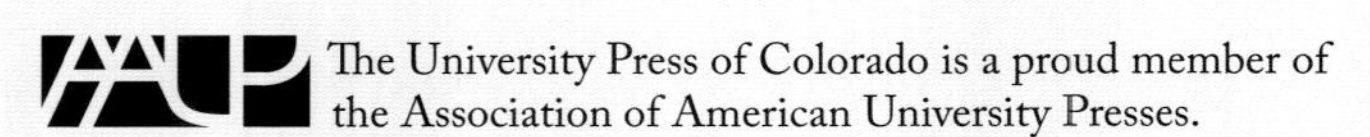
The University Press of Colorado is a proud member of the Association of American University Presses.

The University Press of Colorado is a cooperative publishing enterprise supported, in part, by Adams State University, Colorado State University, Fort Lewis College, Metropolitan State University of Denver, Regis University, University of Colorado, University of Northern Colorado, Utah State University, and Western State Colorado University.

∞ This paper meets the requirements of the ANSI/NISO Z39.48–1992 (Permanence of Paper).

Library of Congress Cataloging-in-Publication Data

Moore, Jerry D.
A prehistory of South America : ancient cultural diversity on the least known continent / Jerry D. Moore.
pages cm
Includes bibliographical references.
ISBN 978-1-60732-332-7 (pbk : alkaline paper) — ISBN 978-1-60732-333-4 (ebook)
1. Indians of South America—Antiquities. 2. Paleo-Indians—South America. 3. Prehistoric peoples—South America. 4. Cultural pluralism—South America—History—To 1500. 5. Social archaeology—South America. 6. South America—Antiquities. I. Title.
F2229.M66 2014
980'.01—dc23

2014004806

Design by Daniel Pratt

23 22 21 20 19 18 17 16 15 14 10 9 8 7 6 5 4 3 2 1

Cover illustrations: Ciudad Perdida ceremonial axis, photograph by Jerry Moore (front); Willem Janszoon Blaeu's 1635 map of the northwestern parts of South America, Lake Parima, and the route to El Dorado, public domain image courtesy of Geographicus Rare Antique Maps (background).

For Carol J. Mackey and A.M. Ulana Klymyshyn

Contents

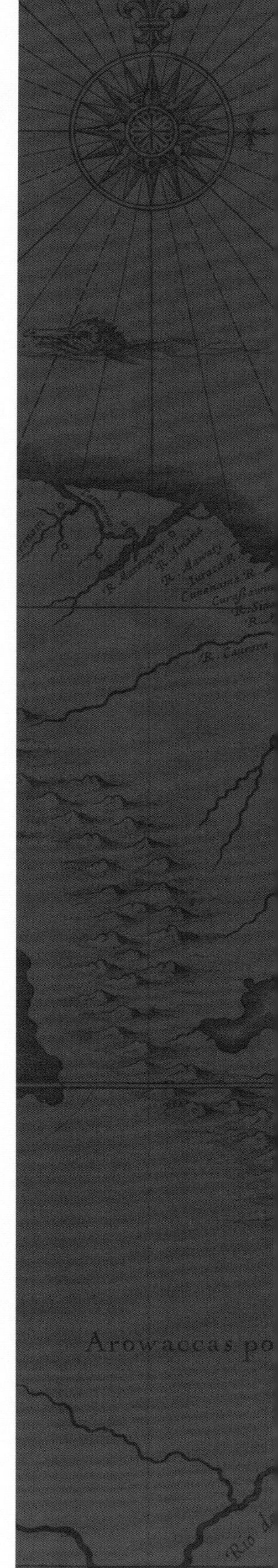

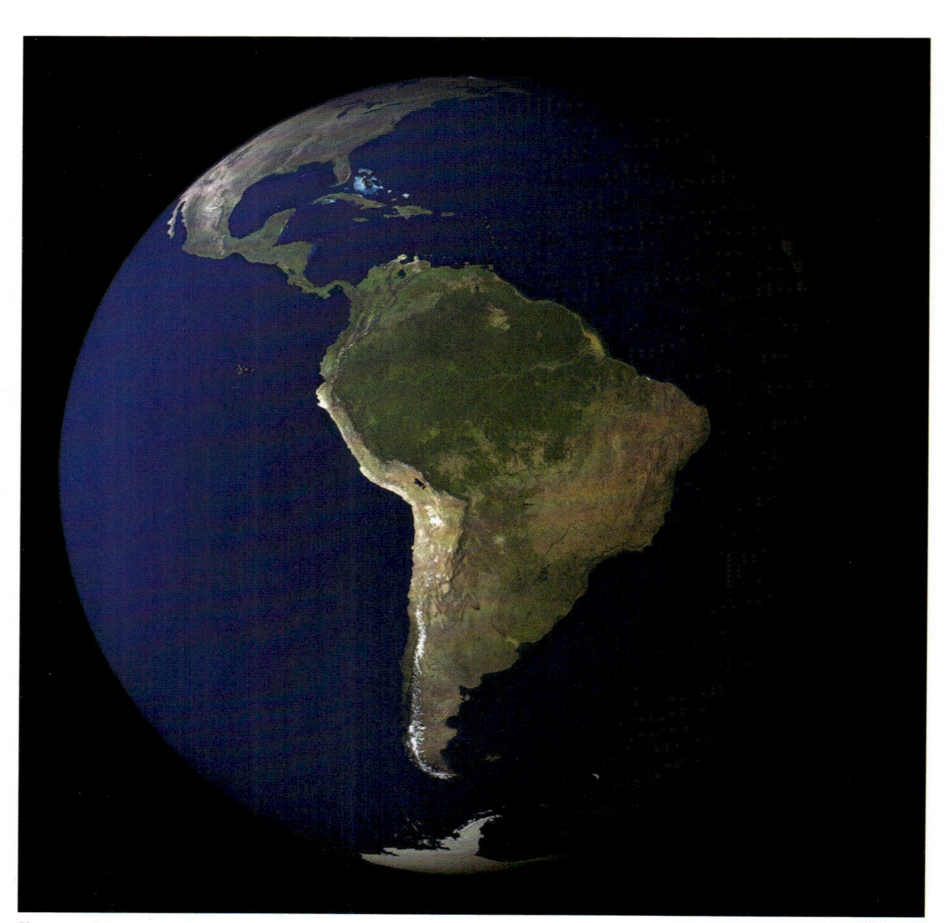

Figure 0.1 The least known continent

Preface

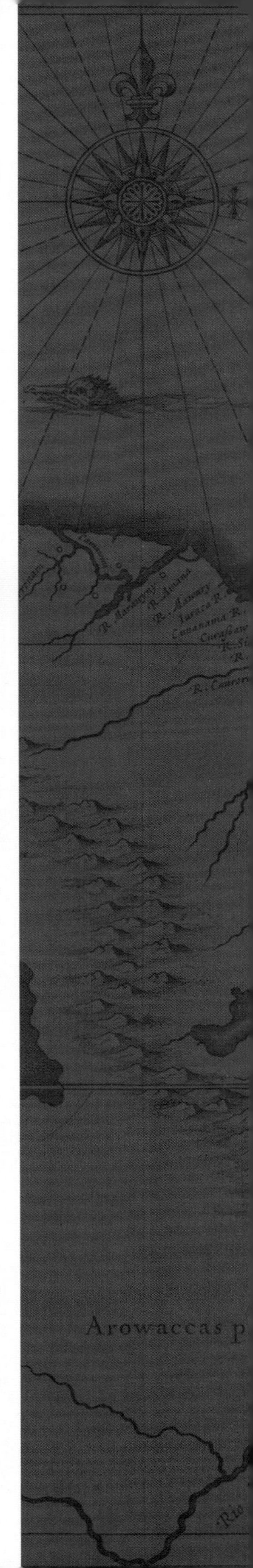

A Golden Age of South American Archaeology

You are living in a golden age of South American archaeology, a period of profound transformations in archaeological knowledge of the continent. *A Prehistory of South America: Ancient Cultural Diversity on the Least Known Continent* introduces you to the amazingly diverse achievements of ancient peoples as they populated, adapted to, and created prehistoric South America.

In the last several decades we have witnessed fundamental changes in what is known about prehistoric South America, advances on multiple fronts. Before 1970, archaeological research in South America was conducted predominantly in the western portion of the continent, particularly the Andean regions of Colombia, Ecuador, Peru, Bolivia, and Chile. Archaeological investigations in Amazonia were limited to a relatively few—although extraordinarily important—projects, generally along the navigable Amazon River. Many parts of lowland South America saw their first archaeological investigations only after the mid-1970s—such as the Llanos de Mojos in Bolivia and the Upper Xingu in Brazil—where subsequent research would uncover remarkably rich archaeological records.

Even less-remote regions were explored more thoroughly in the late twentieth century. Although the numerous prehistoric mounds along coastal Uruguay and the southern coast of Brazil had been reported since the late nineteenth century, the first systematic archaeological research did not occur there until the 1980s. Even today, vast areas of South America have seen scant or no archaeological research. Relatively little is known about the prehistories of the western Amazon and eastern slope of the Andes, a complex and vast interface that stretches down the continent. Tantalizing bits of archaeological evidence—a site here, a traded object there—suggest that the cultural interactions between the eastern Andes and western Amazonia stretched deep into antiquity. But only more research will illuminate these connections, while other discoveries are yet to be made.

(For example, when I wrote this chapter on June 28, 2013, the National Geographic Society announced the discovery of an intact Wari burial at the site of El Castillo de Huarmey on the Central Coast of Peru; see http://news.nationalgeographic.com/2013/06/130627-peru-archaeology-wari-south-america-human-sacrifice-royal-ancient-world/. Excavations directed by Miłosz Giersz and Roberto Pimentel Nita have uncovered the tombs of three noblewomen buried with sixty other individuals, a find described as a mausoleum of local elites affiliated with the Wari Empire. *Nothing like this had been discovered—until now.*)

There are other reasons this is a golden age of South American prehistory. In many parts of South America, there are regions where the first explorations occurred decades ago but were not followed by subsequent investigations. For example, in the 1930s, investigations in Tierra del Fuego by Junius Bird (discussed further in chapter 3) found tantalizing evidence for early humans who once hunted Pleistocene mammals such as now-extinct horses, ancient llamas, and ground sloths. Not until the late 1990s and early 2000s were Bird's discoveries confirmed by excavations at other archaeological sites in Patagonia. During that intervening sixty to seventy years, Bird's discoveries were dismissed or considered intriguing anomalies. Only with additional data could those discoveries be placed in a comparative perspective. This, in essence, is the archaeological problem of critical mass: when a unique discovery is made, its validity and significance may not be understood until other sites and data are available to provide a comparative perspective. Since the 1980s, the increase in archaeological surveys, excavations, and analyses has resulted in new sets of comparative data that often illuminate intriguing but poorly understood archaeological patterns.

Another reason this is a golden age of South American prehistory is the number of new projects at "well-known" sites. Numerous archaeological sites known for centuries still hold unknown secrets. An example is the site of Moche, located on the Peruvian coast near the city of Trujillo (see chapter 9). The site consists of two enormous constructions, the Huaca de la Luna and the Huaca del Sol, which sit on opposite sides of a flat sand-covered plain. Literally the size of hills, the Moche huacas have been known—and looted—for centuries. Archaeologists have studied the site of Moche, which is pockmarked by pot hunters' trenches, for more than 150 years: mapping it, studying the ceramics, calculating the volume and labor required to build the mounds, and so on. By the late twentieth century, it was thought that Moche held no more secrets.

But in 1989, looters illegally digging at the Huaca de la Luna uncovered brightly painted murals showing bizarre, fanged supernatural creatures with snake-like manes. The beauty of these murals impressed the looters who, surprisingly, contacted the authorities. A small salvage project was begun under the direction of Dr. Santiago Uceda, a young professor at the National University of Trujillo. A specialist in Paleoindian sites, Uceda immediately recognized the value of the murals and the need for an expanded and coordinated program of archaeological excavation, conservation, and community-based and international outreach. The Moche project has developed into one of the largest archaeological projects in the world, and completely unexpected discoveries are made every year. The excavations have fundamentally revised our understanding of Moche culture, sparking reassessments, scholarly disagreements, and new insights.

The work at Moche demonstrates another truth about archaeology: what we "know" about the past is subject to change. This is not only true of the site of Moche but for other "well-known" sites and regions across South America as well.

This is also a golden era for South American archaeology because different and new lines of evidence are available. Radiocarbon dating makes it possible to know the absolute age of ancient sites. Small flakes of obsidian can be analyzed to determine the combinations of trace elements that differentiate one source from another; with that information we can understand ancient patterns of trade and exchange. Animal bones can be studied to distinguish feasts from everyday meals. Sediment cores extracted from bogs and lakes can be studied for changes in pollen and thus record variations in vegetation, climate, and human impacts on the environment. The types of clay used in pottery can be analyzed to see if a vessel was locally made or imported. Microscopic grains of starch can be examined to determine whether maize or some other plant was once milled on ancient grinding tools. Human skeletons may hold the traces of diet and trauma. Ice cores drilled into high Andean glaciers contain valuable and precise data about ancient droughts. The list of these different analyses is enormous, and new techniques are being developed and applied to archaeological problems every year.

But beyond this, it is now possible to bring together a team of experts employing a variety of analyses and thus to reconstruct a fuller vision of the past. To cite just one example: in 1946 the archaeologist Junius Bird excavated a site on the coast of Peru called Huaca Prieta, where he found early evidence of preceramic sedentary villagers living on the bounty of the sea (see chapter 6). Bird excavated this site with a team of workmen and his wife, Margaret Bird, but essentially Bird did all the analysis of the materials from Huaca Prieta himself. Sixty years later, in 2006, the archaeologists Tom Dillehay and Duccio Bonavia began new excavations at Huaca Prieta but as directors of a team of nearly thirty scholars, who included specialists on radiocarbon dating, soils, ancient maize, starch grains, human skeletal remains, pollen, cordage and basketry, and numerous other materials. The wealth of data and the ability to contrast new and different lines of evidence mean that our knowledge of Huaca Prieta has dramatically expanded. And, of course, Huaca Prieta is just one of the hundreds of thousands of sites known from across South America.

So you are living in a golden age of South American archaeology. New discoveries are being made constantly. In many regions, a critical mass of data now allows for placing new discoveries in context. "Well-known" sites are being reexamined, resulting in deeper and sometimes completely unexpected insights. New analytical techniques result in diverse lines of evidence. All these factors make this an extremely exciting time to study the archaeology of South America, but these current accomplishments are very much indebted to explorations and discoveries from previous eras.

About This Book

A Prehistory of South America: Ancient Cultural Diversity on the Least Known Continent is written for undergraduate and beginning graduate students in anthropology and for the general reader interested in the peoples and cultures of ancient South America. This assumes that the reader has a basic grasp of archaeological concepts but not an extensive mastery of the field. For that reason, I have tried to write with a minimum of jargon and maximum of clarity, yet specific technical terms are used and defined throughout the text. Key sites and scholars are placed in bold print the first time their names appear in a particular chapter, as in "with his pioneering investigations at the site of **Chavín de Huántar**, the great Peruvian archaeologist **Julio Tello** (1880–1947) . . ."

Given the wide range of questions explored by archaeologists, I have had to limit the discussion to some of the most basic and fundamental domains of inquiry. Usually, these include discussions about sets of questions dealing with subsistence, economy, social and political organization, artistic creations, and worldview. Many other important topics are explored by archaeologists, ranging from detailed analyses of lithic technology to the gender implications of ancient iconographies, but the importance of such topics is best understood within a context of knowledge about the past. I believe that understanding matters of subsistence, economy, social and political organization, artistic creations, and worldview provides important frameworks for understanding other dimensions of ancient lives.

In addition to defining concepts and summarizing bodies of archaeological data, I try to show how particular sets of archaeological problems have emerged as intellectual problems. It is important to recognize that our knowledge of the past—like all forms of human knowledge—emerges from specific historical moments and builds on particular assumptions. This recursive interaction between ideas and artifacts is discussed throughout the following chapters. For example, the discussion of the archaeology of human colonization in South America is presented in the context of the history of Paleoindian studies in North America (chapter 3). The archaeological evidence of the origins of agriculture in South America is compared to earlier archaeological explorations and other assumptions about agriculture and its consequences (chapter 5). The origins of the South American states and empires are referenced to the broader archaeological literature on state-level societies elsewhere (chapter 9). In each of these cases, I try to show how a body of archaeological research has developed, to summarize what is currently known, and to identify lines for future research.

Related to this issue, I have tried to explain how specific ideas about South American archaeology have changed over the last 150 years. Many of these investigations were shaped by more general ideas about human cultures, such as Max Uhle's diffusionist hypothesis that cultures change when traits spread out from a place of origin or the notion of cultural horizons articulated by Gordon Willey and Phillip Phillips, as expressed in the terms *Archaic* (chapter 4) and *Formative* (chapter 6). Throughout this book, I try to show the connections between ideas and artifacts.

Despite my best efforts, it is obviously impossible to give complete coverage of 15,000 years of prehistory for a region as vast and diverse as the continent of South America. *A Prehistory of South America* provides a sample of archaeological cases to give the reader a sense of the varied accomplishments of South American societies. Each chapter is built around various points of comparison. Coastal settlements along the southern coast of Peru are contrasted with coastal settlements in Ecuador and Uruguay. Chiefdoms that developed in northern Colombia are compared to chiefdoms that emerged at the mouth of the Amazon River. The achievements of the Inca Empire are juxtaposed against those of earlier Andean empires, such as Chimú, Wari, and Tiwanaku. This does not imply that the prehistory of South America reflects a series of "progressive" stages, but it does recognize that similarities and important differences between ancient societies in South America are illuminated by such comparisons.

As the notes indicate, this book is based on the works of hundreds of other archaeologists whose articles are published in multiple languages. I have tried to cite relevant works published in Spanish, Portuguese, English, and French. Since these are the only languages I read, I have been unable to consult works published in other languages, which means I have not cited materials in German, Japanese, Dutch, or other languages in which South American archaeologists publish. Fortunately, most non–South American archaeologists publish in the languages of the countries in which they study, so I have been able to cite their research. Another problem is the inevitable delay between archaeological publication and scholarly publication; it is often the case that several years elapse before valuable archaeological data become widely available in scientific journals and monographs. Other important discoveries may have been reported in technical reports submitted to government agencies or grant foundations but are not broadly distributed. Undoubtedly, I have failed to cite many archaeologists' valuable research; they have my sincere apologies. However, I have made an exhaustive effort to cite relevant and recent sources, and students should examine the references at the end of each chapter as a starting place for research and additional reading.

A final note about the title, *A Prehistory of South America: Ancient Cultural Diversity on the Least Known Continent*. The first part of the title is obvious, and the reference to "diversity" is clear throughout the book—but what about the reference to "the least known continent?" I borrowed this phrase from the title of an important volume published in 1974, *Native South Americans: Ethnology of the Least Known Continent*, edited by Patricia J. Lyon. During her lengthy career as a South American anthropologist, Dr. Lyon's polymathic interests have ranged across Amazonia to the Andes, from ethnography to archaeology, and the breadth of her knowledge and contributions is inspiring. (I am also indebted to her because she published my first article on Andean archaeology in the journal *Ñawpa Pacha: Journal of Andean Archaeology*, a journal I later edited.) But when I read Dr. Lyon's volume, first as a graduate student, and re-read it at various points over the following decades, I always felt a sense of frisson about those last three words—that thrill of the possibility of discovery, of the excitement of the unknown, a place where ancient worlds await. I want you to have that sense of excitement as you read *A Prehistory of South America: Ancient Cultural Diversity on the Least Known Continent*.

Organization of the Book

The following chapters summarize the prehistory of South America in a series of thematic chapters that are roughly chronological.[1] Chapter 1, **Archaeology in South America: A Brief Historical Overview**, discusses the development of archaeological knowledge of South America, beginning with the collection of antiquities for royal museums until the creation of more professional and scholarly South American archaeology in the twentieth century. A geographical and environmental overview of South America is presented in chapter 2, **The Brave New World**. In addition to current patterns of environmental diversity, I discuss some of the general patterns of paleoenvironmental changes since the Pleistocene. Chapter 3, **The Last Ancient Homeland**, discusses current evidence for the antiquity of human presence in South America, the last continent settled by ancient humans, which is currently thought to date to approximately 15,000 to 10,000 BC. The nature of the evidence for the human presence—and the controversies surrounding this evidence—are summarized, as are current debates about the means and ways of ancient human migration. Chapter 4, **Archaic Adaptations**, presents an overview of the different ways humans adapted to South America after approximately 10,000 BC and before the development of agriculture: societies variously based on hunting high-altitude camelids (guanaco and vicuña, the wild relatives of the domesticated llama and alpaca), fishing along the coasts, or foraging in tropical rainforests. The development of agriculture is discussed in chapter 5, **Origins and Consequences of Agriculture in South America**, which summarizes data about the stunningly diverse processes that resulted in domestic plants and animals and provided the subsistence base for larger human settlements.

Chapters 6 and 7 constitute a pair of discussions dealing with the broad topic, the emergence of social complexity—one of the most important topics explored by archaeology and other social sciences. Although similar issues are explored in both chapters, they differ in geography and social forms. For example, chapter 6, **Social Complexities: Part I**, briefly introduces some of the theoretical issues surrounding the topic and a related concept of "the Formative," as used in Americanist archaeology, before looking at case studies from southern Ecuador and northern Peru, Amazonia, and the Atlantic Coast of southern Brazil and Uruguay. Chapter 7, **Social Complexities: Part II**, examines changes in settlement and architecture in three other areas—the Central Coast of Peru, the central highlands of Peru, and the Titicaca Basin—where dramatically different societies emerged between approximately 3000 and 500 BC, including the earliest cities known from South America. Chapter 8, **Regional Florescences**, is a synopsis of cultural patterns in different regions of the continent, as more complex economic networks, religious ideologies, and political innovations—including chiefdoms and early states—developed in different areas between approximately 500 BC and AD 500.

This continental perspective narrows in chapter 9, **Age of States and Empires**, focusing on the Andean region, which was—as far as we currently know—the only region where expansionistic empires emerged between AD 700–1400, as the Moche, Sicán/Lambayeque, Chimú, Wari, and Tiwanku states developed and expanded. Chapter 10, **Twilight of Prehistory**, highlights some of the broad regional patterns present between AD 1000 and 1500, contrasting the various developments across Amazonia with chiefly societies in Colombia, Ecuador, and Peru. Chapter 11, **Empire of the Four Quarters**, summarizes the unique achievements—political, architectural, religious, and social—of the Incas. Finally, chapter 12, **After Prehistory**, discusses the ways archaeology illuminates new perspectives on the changes in South America after the arrival of Europeans. Whether archaeologists investigate Spanish colonial towns, the villages of fugitive slaves, or the material remains of twentieth-century political repression, archaeology illuminates the complex and diverse cultural heritages of South America.

Note

1. Dates in the text are given either as "Before Present" symbolized by "BP," which refers to uncalibrated radiocarbon dates, or as "cal BC" or "cal AD," which refer to radiocarbon dates calibrated using the CALIB 6.0 calibration and the Southern Hemisphere calibration curve from Queen's University, Belfast, accessed at http://calib.qub.ac.uk/. Dates are reported at two sigmas, unless otherwise noted.

A Prehistory of South America

Mare antiliarum.
SEPTENTRO
peru
America
EQVINOCTIA
Canibales.
Brasilis.
Quãta orbis pars.
Terra argẽtea.
Mundus nouus.
Terra Incognita
OCCIDENS

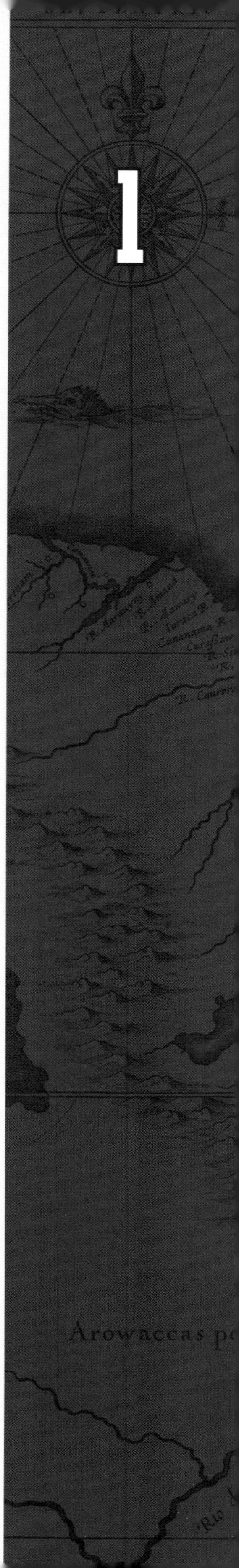

1

Archaeology in South America
A Brief Historical Overview

10.5876_9781607323334.c001

> Let us come to the rational animals.
>
> We found the entire land inhabited by people completely naked, men as well as women, without at all covering their shame. They are sturdy and well-proportioned in body, white in complexion, with long black hair and little or no beard. I strove hard to understand their life and customs, since I ate and slept with them for twenty-seven days; and what I learned of them is the following.
>
> *1502 letter from Amerigo Vespucci to his patron, Lorenzo di Pierfrancesco de' Medici*

Current archaeological knowledge builds on several centuries of interest in the antiquities and monuments of South America, although interest motivated by very different goals and practices. The first European descriptions of South American objects and sites were the by-products of conquest. Soldiers accompanying **Francisco Pizarro**'s expeditions in 1532–33—such as **Miguel de Estete** and **Pedro Pizarro**—described the towns and monuments of native kingdoms, in the process providing valuable accounts of the Inca Empire. The soldier-chronicler **Pedro de Cieza**, who arrived in America as a fourteen-year-old in the 1530s to seek the riches of the New World, was also an astute observer with an eye for detail, describing ancient road networks, fortresses, temples, and other native constructions between Colombia and Cusco. Catholic priests described the ritual artifacts and sites used by native peoples, usually to replace native religion with Christianity. Father **José de Arriaga**'s 1621 *The Extirpation of Idolatry in Peru* was a descriptive guidebook to Andean religion, listing sacred places and artifacts so local Catholic priests could recognize and eliminate pagan beliefs. A more sympathetic and extraordinarily valuable document was prepared in the early 1600s by the bilingual mestizo author **Guaman Poma de Ayala**, who wrote a 1,400-page document, *The First New Chronicle and Good Government*, in which he argued that the Spanish conquest was unjust and the colonial system cruel, supplementing his argument with hundreds of drawings illustrating Andean culture and Spanish inequities. In the early seventeenth century, Father **Bernabe Cobo** wrote detailed accounts of Inca religion and culture. Although none of these documents were focused on the scholarly study of South American cultures, they are valuable sources of information, particularly about the Incas.

A theme that emerges from these accounts, particularly in the Andean region, was the recognition that—despite the achievements of the Inca

Figure 1.1 A 1558 map of South America

Empire—some sites were the creations of earlier peoples, often vaguely described as the *huaris* (Quechua for "ancestors" or "old ones.") Some of these pre-Inca cultures had been recently assimilated by the Incas just before the Spanish conquest, and their names were still remembered. One of these cultures was the Chimú of the North Coast, who had been conquered by the Inca only a few decades before the Spaniards had conquered the Inca. Earlier cultures, however, were anonymous and unrecorded by Spanish chroniclers.

Exotic Curiosities and Cabinets of Wonder

The study of archaeological artifacts and sites had similarly indirect origins. Some objects were shipped from the New World to European monarchs as evidence of their loyal subjects' conquests, although many artifacts made from precious metals were melted into bullion without regard for aesthetics. As a by-product of Enlightenment concerns, formal collections of natural specimens and other curiosities, so-called cabinets of wonder, were established across Europe, precursors to royal collections and museums (figure 1.2).

In 1752 the Spanish natural historian and diplomat **Antonio de Ulloa** proposed establishing an Estudio y Gabinete de Historia Natural in Madrid that would house objects Ulloa and others had collected on their voyages. Not until 1771 did the Spanish king, Carlos III, establish the Real Gabinete de Historia Natural, issuing a decree to his global empire to collect and send objects of interest to Madrid. The collections included natural specimens, paintings, and other artworks, as well as antiquities. Opened in 1776 and looted by Napoleon's forces in 1813, the Real Gabinete de Historia Natural was transformed into the Real Museo de Ciencias Naturales de Madrid, the institutional ancestor of the current Museo de America.

The Spanish clergyman **Baltazar Jaime Martinez de Companion**, who served as bishop of Trujillo from 1778 to 1790 and whose diocese included the coast, highlands, and jungle regions of north-central Peru, prepared a remarkable nine-volume document known as *Trujillo del Peru*. Lavishly illustrated with watercolors portraying colonial society, documented with detailed maps and plans, and even containing musical scores of folksongs, the ninth volume of *Trujillo de Peru* was dedicated to archaeological sites and discoveries. The volume responded to a royal inquiry asking in part "if there exists some work from those times before the conquest; if it is conspicuous due to its material, form or grandeur or such vestiges of it; if, by chance, gigantic bones that appear human have been found; and if some tradition is preserved that at sometime there were giants; and also of the places from which they came, and of their duration, extinction and its causes; and about what leads to the maintenance of said tradition."[1] The good bishop replied to these and many other questions with words, images, and objects. He prepared a map of the Chimú site of Chan Chan, illustrated native mummies, and created a list of words in several non-Quechua North Coast languages. In 1788 Martinez de Companion shipped twenty-eight boxes of curiosities—dried animals, ceramics, utensils, and other objects—to the Real Gabinete de Historia Natural; these boxes have never been found. In 1790 he shipped another six boxes of the ceramics that

Figure 1.2 A 1655 cabinet of wonder—frontispiece from Museum Wormianum by Danish naturalist Ole Worm (1588–1655)

had figured in his illustrations; some of them have been found and contain nearly 200 ceramic vessels.

South American archaeology originates from the same Enlightenment-era concerns that resulted in the establishment of the first natural history and archaeological museums in Europe but also from the wave of scientific explorations that occurred in the late eighteenth and early nineteenth centuries.

Scientific Explorers, Antiquarians, and Fieldworkers

After the mid-1700s, South America saw numerous scientific expeditions, most focused on fields such as geology, botany, and zoology. For example, some of the greatest scientific explorers in South America—such as **Richard Spruce** (1817–93), **Henry W. Bates** (1825–95), **Alfred Russell Wallace** (1823–1913), and **Charles Darwin** (1809–82)—mentioned the continent's peoples and customs in passing, essentially as brief distractions from the plants, animals, and rocks these natural historians had come to study.

But **Alexander von Humboldt** was different (figure 1.3).

Alexander von Humboldt (1769–1850) was a scholar who encompassed an astounding variety of disciplines, from astronomy to zoology, from botany to political economy. His extensive explorations in tropical America from 1799 to 1804 were not primarily focused on South American antiquities—no one with his

ALEXANDER
von HUMBOLDT

polymathic tendencies could focus on any one topic—but neither did he overlook the traces of the past. Traveling in South America with **Aime Bonpland** and other companions, von Humboldt followed the major Inca roads from the high-altitude paramo near Pasto, Colombia, south through the Ecuadorian highlands and the "Avenue of the Volcanoes," and then south into the northern Peruvian provinces of Piura, Lambayeque, and Cajamarca. En route, von Humboldt studied numerous Inca fortifications, palaces, and way stations (*tambos*), taking measurements and notes that were supplemented by plans and sketches prepared by Bonpland. In summarizing Inca architecture, von Humboldt concluded, "Simplicity, symmetry, and solidity: these are the three characteristic traits that distinguish in a positive way all Peruvian buildings." This was, the Peruvian archaeologist and historian Cesar Astahuaman has noted, "the most brief, but exact, definition that has been proposed to this very day."[2]

During the nineteenth century, travelers with antiquarian interests wrote accounts of South American archaeological sites, writings more focused on archaeology but also interwoven with historical accounts, personal observations, and travelogues. The Peruvian-born mining engineer and natural historian **Mariano Eduardo de Rivero y Ustaríz** (1798–1857)—a scholar profoundly influenced by von Humboldt—also conducted archaeological and historical investigations in Peru. Rivero coauthored *Antigüedades Peruanas* with the Swiss naturalist and diplomat **Johann Jakob von Tschudi** (1818–89); published in 1851, their book was translated into English and French almost immediately.

However, the initial forays into South American archaeology were not evenly distributed across the continent. The Andean region and the Pacific coastal zones were served by steamship lines that called at multiple ports from Panama to Chile, which contributed to the number of archaeologists' and travelers' accounts from this region.

Although few authors had von Humboldt's polymathic scope, they often produced observations of archaeological interest. **William Bollaert** (1807–76), an English chemist, businessman, and writer, incorporated archaeological observations and historical research with his commercial activities in Colombia, Ecuador, and Peru—which he documented in his 1860 book, *Antiquarian, Ethnological and Other Researches in New Granada, Peru and Chile, with Observations on the Pre-Incarial, Incarial and other Monuments of Peruvian Nations*, a tome as prolix in its prose style as its title suggests. Among these nineteenth-century accounts, several classics stand out for their skill in describing and illustrating archaeological sites. The great Italian-Peruvian naturalist and explorer **Antonio Raimondi** (1824–90) incorporated numerous archaeological observations into his magisterial five-volume work, *El Perú* (published 1875–1913), based on meticulous field notes and early watercolors illustrating the weird and intriguing art style at Chavín de Huántar, including an image of the stelae that bears his name.

Another outstanding example is the work of the archaeologist, diplomat, and writer **Ephraim George Squier** (1821–88; figure 1.4).

Squier had an amazing life that ended in tragedy.[3] Encouraged in his anthropological interests by the American anthropologist Lewis Henry Morgan, Squier

Figure 1.3 Portrait of Alexander von Humboldt, 1806, painted by Fredrich George Wietsch (1758–1828)

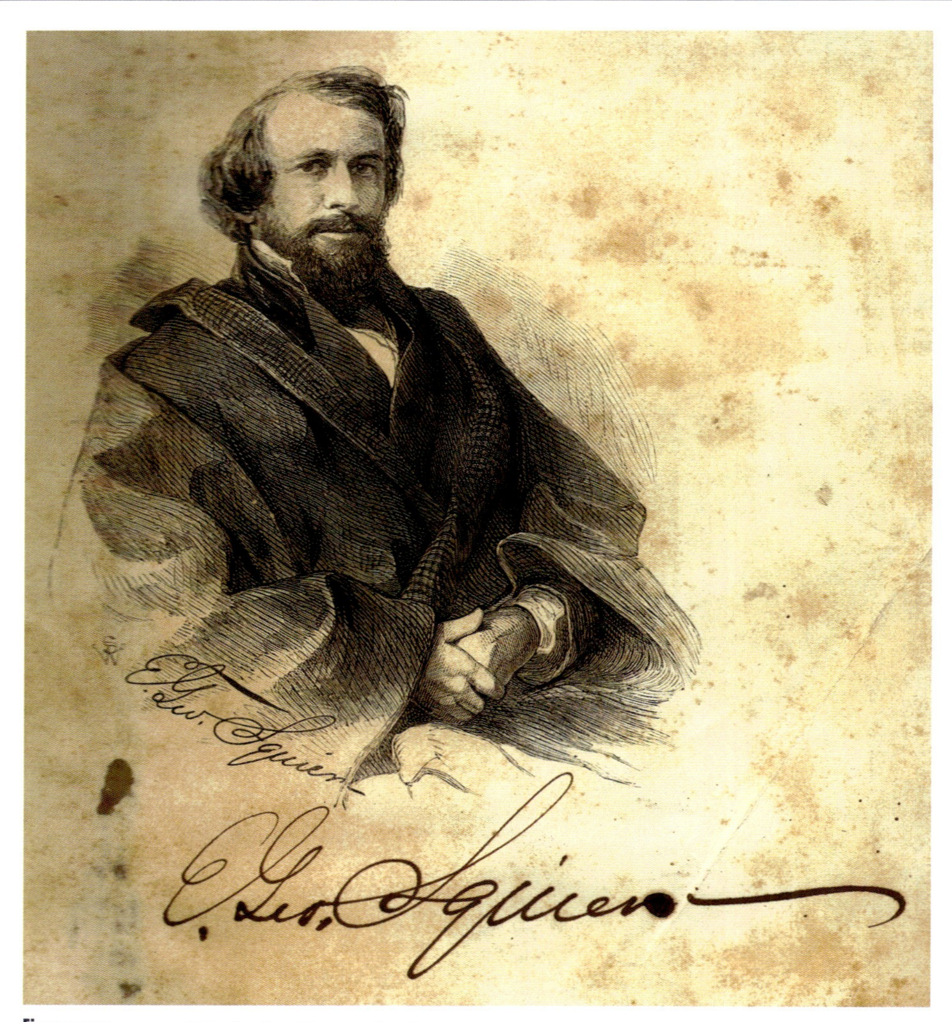

Figure 1.4 Portrait of Ephraim George Squier

began his studies in the northeastern United States. Squier's famous 1848 book, *Ancient Monuments of the Mississippi Valley: Comprising the Results of Extensive Original Surveys and Explorations,* coauthored with Edwin Davis, described hundreds of archaeological sites across the eastern United States and illustrated and classified prehistoric earthworks, concluding that such monuments had been built by cultures other than the ancestors of the Native Americans in the Northeast. Published by the Smithsonian Institution and considered the "first classic" of American archaeology, *Ancient Monuments* transformed Squier from a local newspaperman into a scholar with a national reputation. He combined careers as an editor and diplomat with his archaeological interests. Appointed the US commissioner to Peru in 1863 by President Abraham Lincoln, Squier began extensive travels in Peru in 1863–65, journeying by steamship between coastal ports and taking extended trips on horseback into the hinterland. Squier had an excellent eye

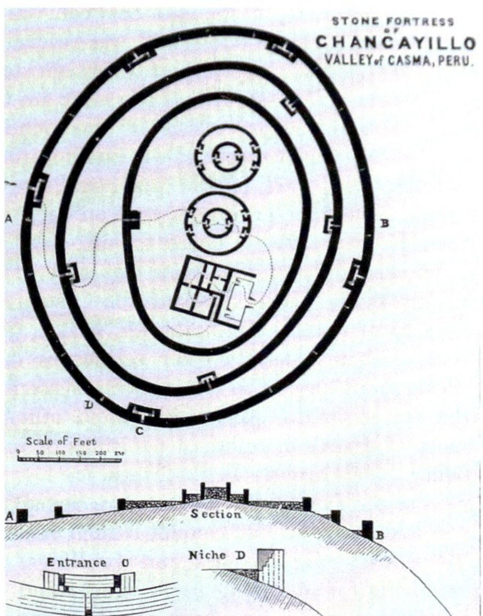

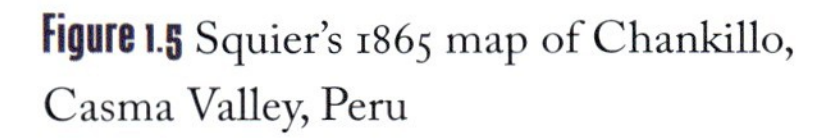

Figure 1.5 Squier's 1865 map of Chankillo, Casma Valley, Peru

Figure 1.6 NASA/IKONOS image of Chankillo, January 13, 2002

for ancient monuments, and most of his maps and plans were extremely accurate (figures 1.5, 1.6).

A notorious exception was Squier's illustration of the Gateway of the Sun, which shows an enormous portal through which a mounted horseman is about to ride (figure 1.7). In fact, the doorway is less than 2 meters (less than 7 ft) tall, and this erroneous figure was probably created as Squier descended into a lengthy illness. Nonetheless, Squier's *Incidents of Travel and Exploration in the Land of the Incas* (figure 1.8) introduced a new standard of precision and accuracy into South American archaeology.

Other scholars followed Squier's lead. The Austrian-French explorer **Charles Wiener** (1851–1913) traveled extensively in the southern Peruvian Andes and Bolivia in 1875–77. His lavishly illustrated 1880 book, *Pérou et Bolivie: Récit de voyage suivi d'études archéologiques et ethnographiques et de notes sur l'écriture et les langues des populations indiennes*, presents a remarkable visual record of archaeological sites and artifacts, as well as of daily life in the nineteenth-century Andes (figure 1.9). Wiener went on to work extensively on the shell mounds of coastal Brazil with the Museu Royal in Rio de Janeiro (discussed below).

One of the most dedicated field investigators was the Swiss-American anthropologist **Adolph Bandelier** (1840–1914). Bandelier had a well-established body of research in the Southwest, having conducted both ethnographic and archaeological research in New Mexico, Arizona, and Sonora. In 1892 Bandelier went to South America, traveling to the remote region of Chachapoyas where he carefully mapped the ruins at the site of Kuelap (figure 1.10).

Figure 1.7 Squier at the Gateway of the Sun, Tiwanaku

Figure 1.8 Alphons Stübel at the Gateway of the Sun, 1877

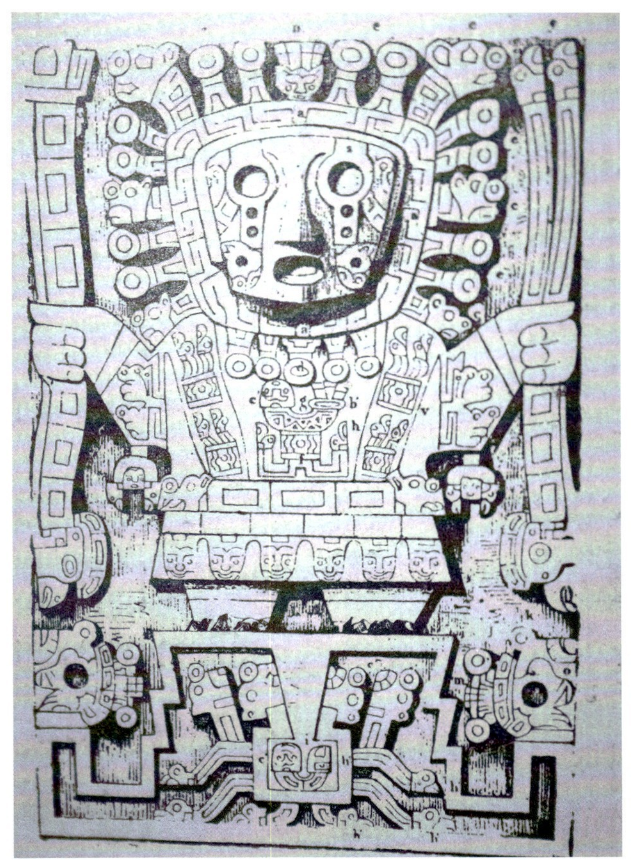

Figure 1.9 Charles Wiener's 1880 drawing of the Staff God at Tiwanaku

Bandelier's notes and plans demonstrate what an energetic and careful field-worker he was. In 1894 Bandelier and his bride, Fanny Ritter Bandelier, went to southern Peru and Bolivia, where they spent the better part of two years conducting archaeological and ethnographic research (including a three-month stint on the Island of the Sun, when they were cut off from the outside world because of civil war in Peru). In addition to extensive and detailed ethnographic observations on the local Aymara, the Bandeliers mapped the site of Tiwanaku, climbed to 13,000 feet on Mt. Illimani where they found archaeological sites, and made an extensive survey of archaeological sites on the Island of the Sun. Bandelier collected a broad array of artifacts and other objects, including a sample of human skulls that showed trephination and cranial modifications. In the course of this study, Bandelier distinguished between Inca-style ceramics and architecture and the local Chullpa styles of pottery and buildings, although it is not clear that he recognized that the Tiwanaku ceramics he photographed were from a pre-Inca culture. Prehistoric chronology would be a major issue for the next 100 years.

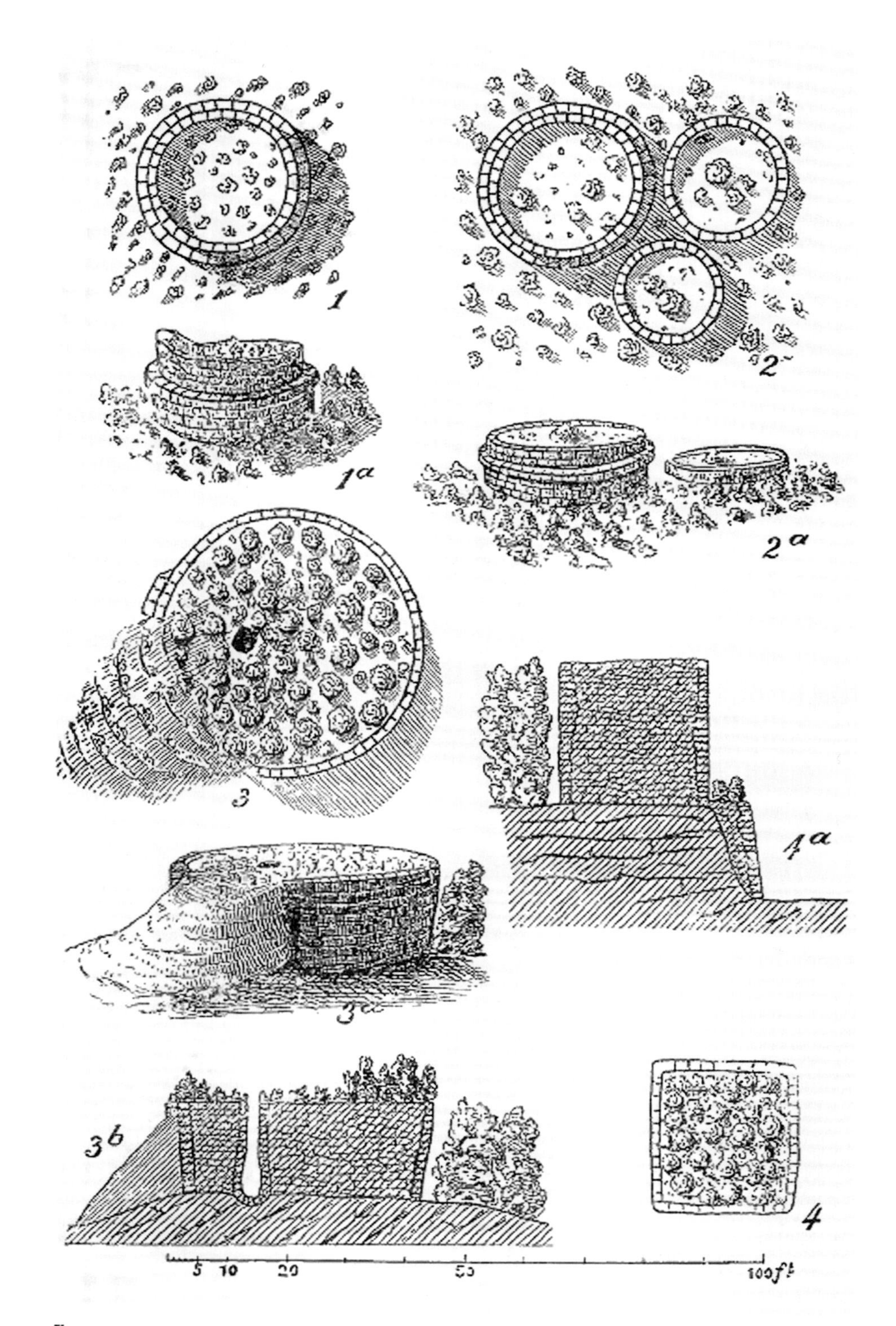

Figure 1.10 Adolph Bandelier's 1893 plans of structures at Kuelap, Chachapoyas

National Museums, National Identities, and Early Archaeologists

The establishment of museums across South America stimulated other investigations, although with somewhat mixed results. However, a factor common to all these institutions was their perceived role in establishing new national identities as Spanish colonies became South American states. Maria Margaret Lopes and Irina Podgorny have written, "The museums of natural history established in Buenos Aires (1812/1823), Rio de Janeiro (1818), Santiago de Chile (1822), Bogota (1823), Mexico (1825), Lima (1826), and Montevideo (1837) were all framed in the process of building new nation states; national museums were founded as former colonies became independent. In the New World, museums were the loci of institutionalization of natural history. But as a standard measure by which to test the scientific culture of a country, they also became symbols of national identity."[4]

In 1822 the newly independent government of Peru decreed that a national museum be established to house "the venerable relics that remain to us of the arts possessed by the subjects of the Empire of the Incas, that are worthy of being brought together in such an institution, before they have been exported away from our territory, as has been done until now, because it is in Spain's interest to erase the vestiges of that ancient and grand civilization."[5] Despite this early and explicit link between archaeology and national destiny, Peru's national museum in Lima did not open until 1826, and it floundered through much of the nineteenth century. The museum lacked focus and stature until the early twentieth century, when **Max Uhle** (1856–1944) was appointed co-director in 1906 (a position he occupied until 1911).[6] It continued to flourish under the leadership of **Julio Tello** (1880–1947), appointed head of the Archaeology Section[7] of the Museo de Historia Nacional in 1913. In 1924 Tello became the director of the newly established Museo de Arqueología Peruana, a post he occupied on two occasions (1924–30, 1937–45) and which was the institutional base for his numerous archaeological investigations (discussed below).

A national museum was established in Colombia as one of the first acts of the independent congress in 1823 and opened in 1824.[8] In 1826 Rivero y Ustaríz, the future author of *Peruvian Antiquities*, was contracted by Colombia to direct the museum, an institution that occupied different buildings before coming to rest in a massive converted prison in the heart of Bogota in 1948. Although the museum's founding collections contained antiquities, only during the second half of the nineteenth century did the collections begin to focus on the prehispanic cultures of Colombia, such as San Agustin, Muisca, and Quimbaya. In the early twentieth century, excavations by **Konrad Theodor Preuss**[9] in San Agustin (1913–14) and by **J. Alden Mason**[10] in the Tairona region (1922–23) resulted in pieces that were displayed in the National Museum of Colombia and in museums overseas.

Brazil's Museu Nacional do Rio de Janeiro (which had its origins as the Museu Real, founded in 1818 when the Portuguese monarch João VI fled Napoleon's armies and reestablished his throne in Brazil) was reorganized in 1876 into a major scientific research center, including anthropology and archaeology.[11] The Museu published archaeological reports on the shell mounds (*sambaquis*) near the mouth of the Amazon River and on the artifacts they contained.[12] A number of foreign naturalists and scientists were invited to Brazil by the subsequent emperor, Don Pedro II, overthrown in 1889.[13] Similarly, numerous museums were established in the late nineteenth century in Argentina and Chile, public institutions that articulated national worldviews in the selection of objects to display.[14] In these situations it was not uncommon to contrast archaeological objects of "obvious" skill and artistry with the "culturally impoverished" native societies then present in South America—an ethnocentric contrast that led some to suggest that archaeological marvels had been created by "lost civilizations" (much as Squier had concluded regarding the mound builders of the Ohio Valley in the United States).

In Chile, the Museo Nacional de Historia Natural was founded in Santiago in 1830. Like many of its counterparts, it faced numerous challenges in obtaining funding and political support. Initially designed to focus on "the principal vegetal and mineral products of the territory," an Anthropology Section was not established until 1910, shortly before Max Uhle was hired to conduct excavations in 1912 at the site of Chunchurí, near Calama in the Atacama Desert.[15]

In Argentina, the development of national museums stalled as independent provinces seesawed between different forms of government and fought civil wars from 1814 to 1876. National unity was achieved only after the military leader, Julio Argentino Roca (1843–1914), gained control of the presidency after 1880. Roca's popularity was based on his successful conclusion of the "Conquest of the Desert," an expansionistic and genocidal project that extended Argentina's control into Patagonia at the expense of the indigenous peoples who lived in the region. This was hardly a political environment in which archaeology or ethnography would receive government support, and paleontology and other fields of natural history were more significant disciplines in many of Argentina's nineteenth-century museums. Ironically, this emphasis on paleontology led the eminent Argentine scholar Florentino Ameghino (1854–1911) to argue that South America, specifically Argentina, was the place where humans first evolved in his 1878 book, *The Antiquity of the Peoples of La Plata*.

Nonetheless, various Argentine museums sponsored initial archaeological investigations, such as the Museo de la Plata's 1890 report on "Archaeological Explorations in the Province of Catamarca" in which the museum's director, **Francisco Pascasio Moreno**, summarized some archaeological discoveries of ceramics and petroglyphs and argued for the importance of archaeological research from a pan-continental perspective, pointing out that "we should not forget that current geographical divisions are not the same [ones] that separated the ancient precolombian societies"—an observation still relevant more than a century later.[16] These sophisticated archaeological materials contrasted with the "limited" material culture of the Yahgan and Alakaluf indigenous communities, leading Moreno to infer that a lengthy period of cultural decay was suggested by the archaeological materials. Additional work in Argentina was conducted by the Swedish-Argentine archaeologist **Eric Boman** (1867–1924), whose two-volume 1908 book, *Antiquités de la Région Andine de la République Argentine*, combined ethnographic and archaeological data.

Elsewhere, archaeological investigations were undertaken by scientific and historical societies, usually groups of historians and scholarly amateurs who were often members of the well-educated upper classes. **Jacinto Jijón y Caamaño** (1890–1950) was the scion of a wealthy Quito family and heir to Ecuador's largest fortune, who combined a career as diplomat and politician with a passionate interest in archaeology and history.[17] In 1909 Jijón y Caamaño directed excavations on his family's haciendas in Imbabura Province, northern Ecuador, and in 1916 he excavated at Manteño sites in coastal Ecuador such as Cerro Jaboncillo (discussed in chapter 10). In 1918 he conducted surveys and excavations in the southern highlands in the province of Chimborazo, documenting his discoveries in the two-volume, abundantly illustrated monograph, *Puruhá: Contribución al conocimiento de los aborígenes de la provincial del Chimborazo de la República del Ecuador*.[18] In 1919 Jijón y Caamaño invited Max Uhle to excavate in Ecuador. After a 1925 revolution, Jijón y Caamaño went into exile in Peru where he met Julio Tello and Alfred Kroeber and excavated at the multi-phase Maranga site near Lima.[19] He returned to Ecuador, where he was increasingly engaged as a politician—including an unsuccessful presidential candidacy. Jijón y Caamaño's magnum opus, *Antropología prehispánica del Ecuador*, was published posthumously in 1952.

An early attempt at synthesizing South America's prehistory was **Thomas A. Joyce**'s 1912 *South American Archaeology: An Introduction to the Archaeology of the South American Continent with Special Reference to the History of Peru*.[20] Joyce's book was an ambitious overview of the prehistories of a largely unknown continent, an uneven body of data that Joyce acknowledged as such but nonetheless attempted to summarize. A curator at the British Museum, Joyce drew extensively on Spanish, Portuguese, and French chronicles by explorers and priests, summarized the writings of nineteenth-century antiquarians, and mentioned some of Max Uhle's initial excavations. Joyce illustrated the book with engravings and photographs of artifacts from different museum collections (particularly of the British Museum), illustrations he organized based on their nations and regions of origin.

Joyce's work highlights a pivotal problem facing late-nineteenth- and early-twentieth-century archaeology in South America: the uncertainty about time. The distinctive traits of Inca material culture were well-known, such as Inca architecture with its monumental masonry constructions marked by trapezoidal doorways and niches and Inca pottery with polychrome on buff surface decorations or the distinctive jug with a bell-shaped spout referred to as an *aryboloid*. It was also obvious that other classes of architecture and pottery were definitely not Inca. Less clear were the temporal relationships between Inca and non-Inca sites and objects. Were these other types of archaeological materials different from, but contemporary with, the Inca? Did these non-Inca materials pre-date the Inca? If it was known from the Spanish chronicles that the Inca originated in the Cuzco Valley in the southern Peruvian Andes and spread north and south through much of the Andes, where did these other cultures originate? Were they earlier South American cultures or intrusive societies from elsewhere, such as Egypt, China, or Mesoamerica? When Joyce wrote *South American Archaeology*, these questions were very much unresolved.[21]

Issues of chronology and origins were central matters for South American archaeology during most of the first half of the twentieth century. These fundamental questions—How old is it? Where did it come from?—remain essential queries, especially in poorly studied regions but also in zones that have seen significant archaeological research. However, from the 1890s, when some of the first systematic excavations were conducted, until the 1960s—when radiocarbon dating, invented in 1949, became more commonly applied to South American sites—chronology and origins were the two overriding issues archaeologists faced. Two archaeologists who addressed these issues were Max Uhle and Julio Tello.

Max Uhle and Julio Tello, Pioneers in South American Archaeology

As noted, Max Uhle (1856–1944) conducted archaeological investigations for various museums, both in Latin America and abroad (figure 1.11).[22]

Trained in historical linguistics, Uhle had worked as a research assistant to the German geologist and naturalist Alphonse Stübel (1835–1904), and Uhle wrote an account of the site of Tiwanaku based on Stubel's photographs, notes, and maps made in 1876–77—the first systematic study of this important site).

Uhle was also involved in publishing archaeological studies based on collections housed in various German museums, essential training for his South American fieldwork. Uhle's first South American investigations occurred in 1892 with an expedition to Argentina and Bolivia, under the auspices of the Königliches Museum für Völkerkunde (the Royal Museum of Ethnology) in Berlin. Over the next decades, Uhle's investigations were supported by an uncertain chain of patrons, sometimes supporting his research for several years in a row, at other times leaving him nearly penniless.[23] Despite the vagaries of funding, Uhle maintained an active program of fieldwork, working in Argentina, Bolivia, Chile, Peru, and Ecuador over the course of four decades until he retired from fieldwork at age seventy-five. The American archaeologist John H. Rowe observed, "Uhle did more field work in western South America than anyone else who has ever lived."[24] Seventy years later, that may still be true.

Figure 1.11 Max Uhle, 1907

In 1896 Uhle excavated at the site of Pachacamac, near Lima, fieldwork that was initially under the auspices of the University of Pennsylvania Museum and later conducted for the University of California Berkeley. The work at Pachacamac was pivotal for understanding the chronological sequence of prehispanic cultures in the Andes, with broad implications for the archaeology of South America (figure 1.12).

In principle, the process of creating a cultural sequence is simple: different sets of distinctive cultural traits are identified and a relative order is established; Culture A came before Culture B, which came before Culture C, and so on. In practice, the process of creating a cultural sequence can be extremely difficult, especially prior to the development of radio-

Figure 1.12 Mummies from Max Uhle's excavations at Pachacamac

carbon dating and other types of absolute dating techniques. At Pachacamac, Uhle approached the problem of building a cultural sequence by applying two methods, *stratigraphy* and *seriation*. First, Uhle recognized that a stratigraphic sequence—a series of layers in which lower and earlier levels are capped by upper and subsequent levels—provides a relative chronology, a well-established concept in geology that had been applied to archaeological investigations elsewhere.[25] Further, Uhle applied the method of seriation, in which variations in the frequency of different cultural traits—such as stylistic traits or artifacts—are used to create a relative sequence of variations that may reflect changes over time. Uhle did not invent either method, but he was one of the first archaeologists to apply these methods to South American prehistory, a breakthrough that has led some to call him "the father of Andean archaeology."[26]

In 1896 at Pachacamac, Uhle excavated a trench at the base of the monumental constructions, the Old and New Temples (figure 1.13).[27]

It was obvious from the profile exposure that the Old Temple (a) had preceded and been covered by the New Temple (b). In front of the Old Temple was a cemetery (c) that in turn was covered by a sloping layer of debris (d) that contained burials later covered by the extension of the New Temple (b). In front of the terraces of the New Temple was another deposit (e) that had been built up after the terraces were constructed. These observations led to a relative sequence based on stratigraphy, from oldest to most recent, of a → c → d → b → e.

Figure 1.13 Uhle's stratigraphic section from Pachacamac

But Uhle made another set of observations: the different burials contained different types of artifacts, specifically distinct types of pottery. The burials in the oldest cemetery (c) contained pottery similar to what Uhle had observed at Tiwanaku—polychrome vessels in brown, buff, black, and white. The burials found in the debris layer d (which occurred after the construction of the Old Temple but before the New Temple expansion) contained pottery decorated with red and black designs over a white slip. Finally, the burial found in the latest deposit, stratum e, only contained Inca ceramics. Combining the stratigraphy with this seriation, Uhle concluded that the relative chronology from oldest to most recent pottery was polychrome Tiwanaku-style ceramics → red and black on white ceramics → Inca ceramics. In other excavations at Pachacamac, Uhle found some burials that had exclusively blackware ceramics, others that had mostly Inca ceramics but a few blackware ceramics, and other burials with only Inca ceramics. This led him to propose that at Pachacamac these blackwares came after the red and black on white ceramics but before the exclusively Inca ceramics.

Traveling north to the Moche Valley, Uhle excavated at Chan Chan and at the Huacas del Sol and de la Luna at Moche. In these excavations, Uhle determined that the blackwares were older than the Inca wares, and he found a polychrome pottery style at the site of Moche. Uhle concluded: "A practical result of these discoveries was the finding that the Huaca del Sol, near Moche, commonly attributed to the Incas, had been constructed at about the third older period [i.e., the polychrome period he associated with Tiwanaku] and had probably become a ruin at the time of the Chimus, as none of their relics nor those of the Incas were found upon this venerable monument. In fact, I observed four distinct and successive cultures in the valley of Trujillo."[28]

This discovery had several important implications. First, not only had Uhle provided a relative chronology, but, given that Pachacamac and the Moche Valley are more than 500 km (311 miles) apart, the relative chronology appeared applicable to sites over a broad area of the coast of Peru. This would become extraordinarily important for later Andean chronologies that envisioned the past as consisting of periods of "horizons," in which specific cultures had wide impacts across the Andes, versus "intermediate periods," in which cultural developments were seen as regional manifestations (see chapter 8). Second, Uhle could argue that, contrary to historical accounts and modern legends that attributed all ancient monuments to the Inca Empire, impressive sites pre-dated the Inca, suggesting that Andean prehistory was ancient and deep.

But the depth of the past was unknown. In the early twentieth century, the antiquity of human existence was essentially uncertain in South America. Not only were there no absolute dating techniques that could be applied to ancient sites, but neither were there hominid fossils that suggested a deep antiquity of humanity. In the Americas, the general view among archaeologists was that prehistory was relatively brief, perhaps a matter of a few thousand years at most.[29] Uhle wrote, "It is learned that the process of development and succession of periods of old Peruvian culture has been a long one. Stratum was laid over stratum during thousands of years. Were we to assign four hundred to five hundred years to each of the cultures heretofore discovered, generally four to five in each valley, we should find in this way alone that the development of the old cultures in Peru must have spanned two thousand years at least."[30] His estimate was wrong by at least 11,000 years.

This led to another supposition: the earliest Andean cultures Uhle found were not rude and underdeveloped but rather sophisticated societies who built monuments and crafted elegant and well-decorated pottery. In this, South American cultures seemed similar to the "high" cultures of Mesoamerica—the Maya of the lowlands of Central America and the Aztecs and Teotihuacanos of central Mexico—advanced New World cultures that might have developed from a common, ancestral culture.

The Ecuadorian archaeologist **Jorge Marcos** has observed that Uhle viewed South American cultures as derived from waves of diffusion, in which innovations in one region spread to neighboring areas.[31] Diffusionist theories were influential in the late nineteenth and early twentieth centuries, broadly held by archaeologists in Europe and North America as a theoretical alternative to cultural evolution. Decades after his excavations at Pachacamac and based on his excavations in Ecuador, Uhle would argue that the prehistoric cultures of the highlands of Ecuador were proto-Maya in origin.[32] To repeat, these inferences were made without accurate dates and based on perceived similarities in artifact styles. Further, Uhle correctly identified possible trade items linking northern South America and Mesoamerica. Yet, current data demonstrate that Uhle's idea that South American civilizations were derived from Mesoamerican cultures is incorrect.

Figure 1.14 Julio Tello (1880–1947), standing center

Uhle's hypothesis of Central American origins of Andean civilizations was forcefully rejected by Julio Tello (1880–1947). Tello's life story is compelling (figure 1.14).[33]

Born to a poor family in the sierra of Huarochiri east of Lima, Tello was of "near-pure" Indian blood, a fact that put him at an extreme disadvantage in the racial hierarchies of Peru. Through chance opportunities and diligence matched with intelligence, Tello overcame these obstacles and obtained an education in Lima and later in the United States. He was educated at the Universidad Nacional Mayor de San Marcos—the oldest university in the Americas—where he obtained a degree in medicine in 1908 while also working in the Museo Raimondi and the Biblioteca Nacional del Peru. Tello's dissertation was on the origins of syphilis in Peru, arguing that evidence for prehispanic cranial surgery suggested that the surgery was performed to treat this disease (still a controversial hypothesis). Tello's research on prehistoric skeletal materials came to the attention of Uhle, and Tello's thesis was published to great acclaim, leading to a two-year fellowship to study abroad. Tello chose to study anthropology at Harvard University, where he worked under the Mayanist **Alfred Tozzer** and the ethnographer **Roland Dixon** and obtained an MA degree in 1911. His time at Harvard was followed by a grant for travel in Europe where he toured libraries and museums, bringing this knowledge back to Peru. Tello returned to Lima in 1913. Soon thereafter, Tello was named director of the Museo de Arqueología y Antropología. From this institutional base, Tello conducted archaeological surveys and excavations throughout the Peruvian coast and sierra. In 1918 Tello began to teach courses at the Universidad San Marcos, where he obtained his doctorate in natural sciences that same year. In 1919 Tello conducted archaeological research in the Department of Ancash, including at the important site of Chavín de Huántar—research that would be pivotal for South American archaeology.

Tello's archaeological research articulated with an intellectual movement in Peru, *indigenismo*, an influential position that argued that Peru's national identity had to draw on its indigenous Andean traditions and not solely on postcolonial European legacies. Expressed across a broad array of the literary and visual arts, as well as in political discourse, indigenismo created an appreciative intellectual environment for the development of Andean archaeology.

In this context, it is not surprising that Tello rejected Uhle's notion that Andean civilizations had been derived from Mesoamerican antecedents. The archaeologists Cesar Astahuaman and Richard Daggett write:

> In 1921 Tello published *Introduction to the Ancient History of Peru*, a synthesis of the results of the 1919 expedition and an important theoretical work where for the first time he described Chavín as an advanced civilization with Amazonian origins . . . He proposed the autochthonous and non-imported nature of this Peruvian civilization, which had extended from the east to the west, from the montaña to the coast. Tello's ideas were opposed to the proposals by Uhle, developed between 1904 and 1914, regarding the connections between the cultures of Central America and South America . . . Uhle's ideas and previous diffusionist hypotheses had been welcomed by the dominant ethnic minority [i.e., non-indigenous "whites"] to justify their supposed superiority and foreign origins and to propose that historically indigenous peoples were dependent and without the capacity to develop their own civilization; that they were, further, a problem [inhibiting] the development of the nation, which was necessary to resolve.[34]

Tello's archaeological research resonated at multiple levels. At the scientific level, his hypothesis regarding the indigenous origins of Andean civilizations has been substantiated by decades of archaeological research, while Uhle's idea of Mesoamerican origins has been disproved. This does not imply that no connections or interchanges occurred between Mesoamerica and the Andes but rather that complex societies—including states and empires—developed independently in these two regions. Tello's hypothesis that Chavín was the first complex society in Peru has proved incorrect (as discussed in chapter 7), although his ideas about the connections between Amazonia and other regions of South America remain intriguing but incompletely proven. Also, the investigations and ideas of Uhle and Tello occurred within political and intellectual contexts in which archaeology was incorporated into debates about national identity (a topic returned to in chapter 12.) Finally, Uhle's work was fundamental for the breadth of its scope, the multiple regions in which he worked, and his development of an archaeological program for looking at cultural changes over time.

Twentieth-Century Archaeologies: Chronologies, Culture History, and Shifting Paradigms

The problems of chronology shaped many of the major archaeological projects conducted in the twentieth century. A great deal of archaeological effort was focused on the north and Central Coast of Peru. **Alfred Kroeber** (1876–1960) and colleagues such as **William D. Strong** (1899–1962) and **Anna H. Gayton** (1899–1977) studied the Uhle collections housed at the University of California Berkeley, a study summarized as designed "to group the graves according to type of artifacts represented in them; to assume that graves containing artifacts of identical type belong to the same period, and that those containing artifacts of consistently different types belong to different periods; and then, from the overlapping of types and whatever other evidence, direct or indirect, may be available, to attempt to establish a sequence of the periods."[35] In a related study, Kroeber and Strong reanalyzed the Uhle collections from the south coast Peruvian valley of Ica, where they recognized a sequence of pottery styles from the Inca conquest of Ica and another half-dozen earlier ceramic styles that Kroeber and Strong thought dated to AD 50–650. Their estimates were based on assumptions about the rate of cultural change: more similar pottery styles implied relatively brief periods of time, while dissimilar styles indicated greater lapses. Kroeber and Strong's ceramic analyses of Uhle's collections led them to accept not only "all the culture phases and periods announced by him, but [also] the establishment of finer subdivisions. In other words, intensive, first-hand re-examination of [Uhle's] evidence both corroborates and extends his conclusions."[36] Subsequent work by **John H. Rowe** (1918–2004) and **Dorothy Menzel** (1924–) refined the Ica sequence and resulted in the extremely influential chronology based on cultural horizons and intermediate periods.[37]

The pace of archaeological research accelerated as the twentieth century progressed. A number of foreign museums sponsored excavations, many with an eye to obtaining objects to display in their galleries. Some of these excavations involved practices that would be illegal or controversial today. In 1906–08, the American archaeologist **Marshall H. Saville** collected an enormous assemblage of stone sculptures—including massive stone thrones from Manteño sites on the coast of Ecuador—for the Heye Museum of the American Indian in New York City, a private museum containing over a million Native American objects later incorporated into the Smithsonian Institution's Museum of the American Indian.[38] In 1911 the Yale University historian **Hiram Bingham** was guided to the site of Machu Picchu by local farmers. He returned in 1912 and 1915, with the support of Yale University and the National Geographic Society (NGS), to excavate and map this most iconic of South American sites, the first archaeological project supported by the NGS. Bingham's "discovery" of Machu Picchu was preceded by several earlier visitors to the site, and the collections he removed to Yale University were the objects of bitter controversy between Yale and the government of Peru, a dispute only recently resolved.[39]

Although many archaeological investigations focused on the acquisition of museum-quality artifacts, other investigators were concerned with defining the temporal and spatial contours of prehispanic South American cultures. A synopsis of archaeological research in 1934–36 mentions research on Tairona sites in Santa Marta and on the San Agustin sculptures in Colombia, research on the similarity between urns collected from the Ecuadorian coast and those reported from

Marajó Island on the mouth of the Amazon, excavations of Tiwanaku-style burials near San Pedro de Atacama in northeastern Chile, the definition of a cultural complex in northern Argentina, an introduction to the archaeology of Bolivia, and extensive excavations at the site of Tiahuanaco, Bolivia, and in various valleys along the coast of Peru.[40]

The author of the review article, **Wendell Bennett** (1905–53), was one of the preeminent American archaeologists of the mid-twentieth century, who conducted archaeological and ethnographic fieldwork in Hawaii and northern Mexico before focusing on the Andes.[41] A curator at the American Museum of Natural History, Bennett excavated at Tiahuanaco and Chiripa in the Titicaca Basin, at Chavín de Huántar and other sites in the Callejon de Huaylas region of the Central Andes of Peru, in the Lambayeque and Moche Valleys on Peru's North Coast, and in the Ecuadorian highlands, Venezuela, and Colombia.[42] In his more substantial monographs—for example, his works on Tiwanaku, Chavín de Huántar, and the North Coast of Peru—Bennett's field investigations were prominently concerned with matters of chronology. A similar concern with chronology was seen in a research project Bennett helped establish, the Virú Valley project.

Bennett was one of the US archaeologists involved in the massive *Handbook of South American Indians*, a five-volume encyclopedic overview under the editorship of **Julian H. Steward** (1902–72) that was begun in 1939, completed in 1945, but not published until 1946–50.[43] The *Handbook of South American Indians* was supported by grants from the US Department of State; as World War II ignited and spread, the US government wanted information about different areas of the world, including Latin America. The volume on cultures in the Andes was shaped by Bennett's ideas, with chapters by him devoted to an introduction to the Andean highlands, the archaeology of the Central Andes, and the archaeology of Colombia—nearly 20 percent of the total text. In addition, Bennett was the volume's major editor, assisted by a slightly younger American archaeologist, **Gordon Willey** (1913–2002).[44]

Bennett, Willey, and Steward were the principal organizers of an archaeological research team that focused on a single valley on the coast of Peru, the Virú Valley, a relatively small region 40 km (about 25 miles) south of the Moche Valley.[45] This 1946 project involved the archaeologists Bennett, Willey, William D. Strong, James A. Ford, Clifford Evans, Junius Bird, John Corbett, and Donald Collier, in addition to the ethnographer Alan Holmberg and the geographer F. Webster McBryde. The Virú Valley project was an intensive archaeological study that resulted in a number of classic research reports, most of which addressed the issues of chronology. Willey explained that "it was recognized that two basic field jobs needed intensive study. One was the relative chronology of the Valley and the other the distribution of archaeological sites, by periods, throughout the Valley area."[46] The goal of the research, Ford wrote, "was to reconstruct the cultural prehistory of a North Coast valley as completely as possible through the application of archaeological techniques, and to examine the present culture of the valley and relate it to the past" (see figure 1.8). Reconstructing the cultural prehistory essentially meant identifying the sequence of prehistoric cultures present in the Virú

Valley. In the late 1940s (before the application of 14C dating), "the principal basis for reconstructing Peruvian prehistory must remain a relative scale in which time is measured by cultural change. This means, principally, ceramics."[47]

In addition to the ceramic analysis, project members tackled other problems. Bennett excavated at the site of Gallinazo, Bird excavated at preceramic sites, Strong and Evans worked on the earlier ceramic periods, and Collier focused on the later ceramic periods.[48] Ford developed the ceramic sequence for the valley based on surface collections of ceramics, while Willey studied the various types of settlements present at different periods, a settlement pattern survey.

The Virú Valley project deserves this extended commentary for several reasons. First, it was a significant piece of archaeological research, a coordinated program in which multiple lines of evidence collected by different scholars were used to illuminate key research problems. Second, the results were pivotal: the chronological sequence was fundamental not only for the North Coast of Peru but also for the development of sequences for the Central Andes. Third, the Virú Valley project simultaneously expressed the dominant mid-twentieth-century archaeological perspective known as "cultural history" while hinting at the shift to "problem-oriented" archaeological research.

In their history of Americanist archaeology, Gordon Willey and Jeremy Sabloff characterize the ideas and assumptions of culture history:

> The central theme of the Classificatory-Historical Period in American archaeology was the concern for chronology . . . Stratigraphic excavation was the primary method in the drive for chronological control of the data . . . The principle of seriation was allied to stratigraphy, and, also serving chronological ends, it developed alongside, and in conjunction with, stratigraphic studies. Typology and classification . . . now became geared to stratigraphic and seriational procedures. Whereas earlier classifications of artifacts had been merely for the purpose of describing the material, they were now seen as devices to aid the plotting of culture forms in time and space.
>
> Beyond the immediacy of stratigraphic, seriational and classificatory methods, the ultimate objectives of American archaeology in the Classificatory-Historical Period were culture-historical syntheses of New World regions and areas. For the most part, they tended to be mere skeletons of history—pottery types or artifact sequences and distributions. Some archaeologists did attempt to clothe these skeletons in more substantial cultural contexts . . . But prior to 1940, these trends were barely in the making; only later did they come into prominence.[49]

This form of culture history was tremendously important throughout Latin America. The Argentine archaeologist **Gustavo Politis** has written:

> In Latin America, culture history was almost the exclusive approach until the 1960s and remains the dominant paradigm structuring archaeological inquiry in the region . . . The North American culture-historical approach had a direct impact on the archaeology practiced in every country of Latin America.

> Archaeological finds were organized into a temporal framework of cultures, periods and phases. Technological divisions, such as those focused on ceramics and lithics, placed sherds and artifacts in seriation sequences, compartmentalized styles, technological complexes, and industries. This work was done mainly by North American archaeologists . . . but in some cases with the collaboration of local archaeologists. The framework for the reconstruction of the past has been, and remains, a complex mosaic in which regional sequences, sites, and interpretive units of integration, such as periods, traditions, subtraditions, and horizons, are articulated within a culture-history dominated approach. Most local archaeologists followed trends established by the dominance of North American culture-history paradigm.[50]

To place this in a different perspective, the culture history approach was the dominant theoretical position well into the 1960s, when a variety of other points of view—such as cultural evolution, cultural ecology, processualism, Marxist archaeology, and post-processualism—gained various followings. The dominance of culture history is implicit in the early works by Uhle and Tello and is clearly evident in the Virú Valley project and beyond. This does not mean that archaeologists from Latin American nations were imitating their North American counterparts, although, as Politis notes, "certainly archaeological practices have adopted theoretical questions and methods from foreign intellectual traditions. This is simply because, as with any research in the Western world, Latin American archaeologists are engaged as part of open scientific communities, exposed to intellectual movements generated in other countries."[51] Thus, the Virú Valley project, on the one hand, was firmly entrenched in the culture history model while Willey's explorations of settlement patterns would serve as a model of more explicitly problem-focused research programs.

These shifting paradigms were accompanied by a variety of new analytical techniques, including 14C dating, a broad array of faunal and floral analyses, and other methods discussed throughout this book. Further, archaeological projects and the development of archaeological projects across South America led to new insights and the revision of long-held assumptions. In turn, the development of university programs in archaeology in Latin America resulted in distinctive research agendas in different nations, producing varied perspectives on the past.

Notes

1. Quoted in P. Cabello Carro, "Pervivencias funerarias prehispánicas en época colonial en Trujillo del Perú: nueva interpretación de los dibujos arqueológicos de Martínez Comapañón," *Anales de Museo de América* 11 (2003): 10, my translation.

2. C. Astahuaman, "La Arquitectura Inca," in *Alexander von Humboldt: From the Americas to the Cosmos*, ed. R. Erikson, M. Font, and B. Schwartz (New York: City University of New York, 2004), 66, my translation.

3. For an excellent biography, see T. Barnhard, *Ephraim George Squier and the Development of American Anthropology* (Lincoln: University of Nebraska Press, 2005).

4. M. M. Lopes and I. Podgorny, "The Shaping of Latin American Museums of Natural History, 1850–1990," *Osiris* 15 (2000): 109–110.

5. Quoted in C. Arellano Hoffmann, "El Museo nacional de arqueología, antropología e historia como espejo de la historia y sociedad peruana," *Revista Museos* 30 (2011): 26, my translation.

6. T. Hempe Martínez, "Max Uhle y los orígenes del Museo de Historia Nacional (Lima, 1906–1911)," *Revista Andina* 31, no. 1 (1998): 161–182.

7. Peru's National Museum of History was organized in four sections: Archaeology, Colony and Republic, Savage Tribes, and Indians of the Sierra.

8. The following is based on information at http://www.museonacional.gov.co/el-museo/historia/Paginas/Historia.aspx (accessed July 19, 2012).

9. See entry on Preuss at http://www.banrepcultural.org/blaavirtual/publicacionesbanrep/bolmuseo/1986/bol15/boao.htm.

10. See L. Satterthwaite, "Obituary: John Alden Mason, 1885–1967," *American Anthropologist* 71 (1969): 871–874.

11. For a succinct critical analysis of the history and development of archaeology in Brazil, see P. Paulo, A. Funari, and L. Menezes Ferreira, "A Social History of Brazilian Archaeology: A Case Study," *Bulletin of the History of Archaeology* 16, no. 2 (2006): 18–27, at http://www.archaeologybulletin.org/article/view/bha.16203 (accessed July 18, 2012).

12. C. Hart, "Contribuições para a ethnologia do valle do Amazonas," *Archivos do Museu Nacional do Rio de Janiero* 6 (1885): 1–174; J. De Lacedra, "O Homen dos Sambiquis," *Archivos do Museu Nacional do Rio de Janiero* 6 (1885): 175–203; L. Neto, "Investigações sobe a Archeologia Brazileira," *Archivos do Museu Nacional do Rio de Janiero* 6 (1885): 257–260. For a brief early account in English, see O. Derby, "The Artificial Mounds of the Island of Marajo, Brazil," *American Naturalist* 13, no. 4 (1879): 224–229.

13. J. Anderman, "The Museu Nacional at Rio de Janeiro," in *Relics and Selves: Iconographies of the National in Argentina, Brazil and Chile, 1880–1890,* exhibit curated by J. Andermann and P. A. Schell (London: Birkbeck College, 2000), at http://www.bbk.ac.uk/ibamuseum/texts/Andermann01.htm (accessed July 18, 2012).

14. See, for example, I. Podgorny, "Vitrinas y administración: Los criterios de organización de las colecciones antropológicas del Museo de La Plata entre 1897 y 1930," in *Relics and Selves: Iconographies of the National in Argentina, Brazil and Chile, 1880–1890,* exhibit curated by J. Andermann and P. A. Schell (London: Birkbeck College, 2000), at http://www.bbk.ac.uk/ibamuseum/texts/Podgorny01.htm (accessed July 18, 2012).

15. Information from the museum's website, at http://www.mnhn.cl/Vistas_Publicas/publicContenido/contenidoPublicDetalle.aspx?folio=3906&idioma=O (accessed February 27, 2014), my translation.

16. F. Moreno, "Exploración arqueológica de la provincia de Catamarca: Primero dato sobre su importancia y resultados," *Revista del Museo de la Plata* 1 (1890–91): 9, my translation.

17. For a brief discussion of Jijón y Caamaño's life and interactions with Uhle, see K. Bruhns, "A Series of Unfortunate Events, or the Best Intentions Thwarted: A Brief History of Archaeological Time in the Northern Andes," *Ñawpa Pacha* 29 (2008): 179–190. For a more detailed biographical account, see "Arqueologico Jacinto Jijón

Caamaño" (1890–1950), at http://www.colejacintojijon.edu.ec/Proyectos/jacintoarque ologo.pdf (accessed November 3, 2013).

18. The studies originally appeared as separate publications between 1921 and 1924 in three volumes of the *Boletín de la Academia Nacional de Historia* (Quito) but were reissued under this title in 1927 by the Sociedad Historica de Estudios Historicos, Quito. Also see Jijón de Caamaño's posthumously published *Antropología Prehispánica del Ecuador* (Quito: La Prensa Católica, 1945).

19. Jijón y Caamaño's 1949 publication on Maranga was reviewed by Gordon Willey in *American Anthropologist* 53 (1951): 112–114.

20. https://archive.org/details/soamericanarchaeoojoyc (accessed July 28, 2012).

21. As an example of this uncertainty, see Joyce's discussion in chapter 8, "Peru: The Sequence of Cultures," in which he ponders the possible similarities in stone reliefs found at Chavín de Huántar and Maya stela in the Yucatan (176–177) or the chronological relationship between press-molded blackware ceramics and subsequent Inca pottery along the North Coast of Peru (184–186). Given the absence of data from other regions, Joyce limits his chronological discussion to Peru and Bolivia (i.e., Tiwanaku).

22. A detailed biography of Uhle is beyond the scope of this chapter. The essential source in English is the biographical sketch and intellectual assessment by J. Rowe, *Max Uhle, 1856–1944: A Memoir of the Father of Peruvian Archaeology*, University of California Publications in American Archaeology and Ethnology 46 (Berkeley: University of California Press, 1954). An excellent collection of Uhle's articles, accompanied by essays by archaeologists and historians, is *Max Uhle y el Perú Antiguo*, ed. Peter Kaulicke (Lima: Pontifica Universidad Catolica, 1998). Additional essays on Uhle's archaeological contributions across South America are found in the collection "Estudios Andinos: Max Uhle, su obra, y su repercussion," *Indiana* 15 (1998), at http://www.iai.spk-berlin .de/es/publicaciones/indiana/numeros-publicados/indiana-%E2%80%9315.html. For a biographical sketch of Uhle and links to images of his original field maps and other visual documentation, view the information at the Ibero-American Institute in Berlin, which houses more than 150 manuscripts, 175 notebooks, 2,150 letters, 95 plans, and nearly 5,000 photographs by Uhle, at http://www.iai.spk-berlin.de/en/library/papers -manuscripts/individual-collections/uhle-max%E2%80%931856%E2%80%931944.html (accessed August 1, 2012). The site also provides links to Uhle materials and publications at other universities and libraries. A series of monographs analyzing the collections Uhle made for the Hearst Museum at UC Berkeley is available at http://dpg.lib .berkeley.edu/webdb/anthpubs/search?all=&journal=1&volume=21.

23. Rowe, *Max Uhle, 1856–1944*, 3–12.

24. Ibid., 1.

25. For an overview, see R. Lyman and M. O'Brien, "Americanist Stratigraphic Excavation and the Measurement of Culture Change," *Journal of Archaeological Method and Theory* 6, no. 1 (1999): 55–108.

26. Rowe, *Max Uhle, 1856–1944*.

27. M. Uhle, "Types of Culture in Peru," *American Anthropologist* 4, no. 4 (1902): 753–759.

28. Ibid., 757.

29. For a discussion of this so-called flat-past perspective among North American archaeologists, see D. Meltzer, "The Antiquity of Man and the Development of American Archaeology," *Advances in Archaeological Method and Theory* 6 (1983): 1–51; D. Meltzer, "North American Archaeology and Archaeologists, 1879–1934," *American Antiquity* 50 (1985): 249–260.

30. Uhle, "Types of Culture in Peru," 728.

31. J. Marcos, "Max Uhle y la arqueología del Ecuador: precursorm investigador y profesor," *Indiana* 15 (1998): 197–215, at http://www.iai.spk-berlin.de/fileadmin/dokumentenbibliothek/Indiana/Indiana_15/IND_15_Marcos.pdf (accessed February 27, 2014).

32. M. Uhle, "Influencias mayas en el alto Ecuador," *Boletín de la Academia Nacional de la Historia* (1922): 205–240.

33. A recent overview of Tello's life consisting of several excellent essays and English translations of selected writings is *The Life and Writings of Julio C. Tello, America's First Indigenous Archaeologist*, ed. R. Burger (Iowa City: University of Iowa Press, 2009). Samuel Lothrop's obituary, "Julio C. Tello, 1880–1947," appeared in *American Antiquity* 14, no. 1 (1948): 50–56. An especially insightful biographical and intellectual overview is C. W. Astuhuamán Gonzáles and R. E. Daggett, "Julio César Tello Rojas: Arqueólogo: Una biografía," in *Julio C. Tello, Paracas primera parte* (Lima: Museo de Arqueología y Antropología de la Universidad Nacional Mayor de San Marcos, 2005), 17–61.

34. Astahuaman and Daggett, "Julio César Tello Rojas," 27, my translation.

35. A. Kroeber and W. Strong, "The Uhle Collections from Chincha," *University of California Publications in American Archaeology and Ethnology* 21, no. 1 (1924): 5.

36. A. Kroeber and W. Strong, "The Uhle Collections from Ica," *University of California Publications in American Archaeology and Ethnology* 21, no. 3 (1924): 98.

37. See J. Rowe, "Stages and Periods in Archaeological Interpretation," *Southwestern Journal of Anthropology* 18, no. 1 (1962): 40–54; D. Menzel, "Style and Time in the Middle Horizon," *Ñawpa Pacha: Journal of Andean Archaeology* 2 (1964): 1–105; D. Menzel, *The Archaeology of Ancient Peru and the Work of Max Uhle* (Berkeley: Lowie Museum of Anthropology, University of California, 1977).

38. M. Saville, *The Antiquities of Manabi, Ecuador: Final Report,* Contributions to South American Archaeology 2 (New York: Heye Foundation, 1910); C. McEwan and F. Delgado-Espinoza, "Late Prehispanic Polities of Coastal Ecuador," in *Handbook of South American Archaeology*, ed. H. Silverman and W. Isbell (New York: Springer, 2008), 505–535.

39. See K. Roman, "Peru-Yale Center for the Study of Machu Picchu and Inca Culture Opens," *Yale News* (October 2011), at http://news.yale.edu/2011/10/06/peru-yale-center-study-machu-picchu-and-inca-culture-opens (accessed August 2, 2012).

40. Wendell C. Bennett, "Archaeological Work in South America, 1934 to 1936," *American Antiquity* 2, no. 4 (1937): 248–259.

41. For biographical sketches, see Alfred Kidder II, "Wendell Clark Bennett (1905–1953)," *American Anthropologist* 56 (1956): 269–273; G. Willey, *Portraits in American Archaeology: Remembrances of Some Distinguished Americanists* (Albuquerque: University of New Mexico Press, 1988), 121–145.

42. Bennett's monographs were published in the Anthropological Papers of the American Museum of Natural History, available online at http://digitallibrary.amnh.org/dspace.

43. The history of the *Handbook of South American Indians* has been discussed by H. Silverman, "Continental Introduction," in *Handbook of South American Archaeology*, ed. H. Silverman and W. Isbell (New York: Springer, 2008), 3–26. A brief biographical sketch of Steward is R. Manners, "Julian Haynes Steward, 1902–1972," *American Anthropologist* 75 (1973): 886–903. Willey's reminiscence of his work with Steward is found in *Portraits in American Archaeology: Remembrances of Some Distinguished Americanists* (Albuquerque: University of New Mexico Press, 1988), 219–237.

44. Gordon Willey would go on to make significant contributions to the archaeology of the Andes and Mesoamerica. See J. Sabloff, "Gordon Randolph Willey," *Proceedings of the American Philosophical Society* 148, no. 3 (2004): 405–410.

45. G. Willey, "The Virú Valley Program in Northern Peru," *Acta Americana* 4, no. 4 (1946): 224–238.

46. G. Willey, *Prehistoric Settlement Patterns in the Virú Valley, Peru*, Smithsonian Institution Bureau of American Ethnology, Bulletin 155 (Washington, DC: Smithsonian Institution, 1953), xviii.

47. J. Ford, "Cultural Dating of Prehistoric Sites in Virú Valley, Peru," in *Surface Survey of the Virú Valley, Peru,* ed. J. Ford and G. Willey, Anthropological Papers of the American Museum of Natural History 43, no. 1 (New York: American Museum of Natural History, 1949), 31.

48. W. Bennett, *The Gallinazo Group, Viru Valley, Peru*, Yale University Publications in Anthropology 43 (New Haven, CT: Yale University Press, 1950); J. Bird, "Preceramic Cultures in Chicama and Viru," *Memoirs of the Society for American Archaeology* (1948): 21–28; W. Strong and C. Evans, *Cultural Stratigraphy in the Virú Valley, Northern Peru: The Formative and Florescent Epochs*, vol. 4 (New York: Columbia University Press, 1952); D. Collier, *Cultural Chronology and Change as Reflected in the Ceramics of the Virú Valley, Peru* (Chicago: Field Museum of Natural History, 1955).

49. G. Willey and J. Sabloff, *A History of American Anthropology* (San Francisco: W. Freeman, 1974), 88.

50. G. Politis, "The Theoretical Landscape and the Methodological Development of Archaeology in Latin America," *American Antiquity* 68 (2003): 246.

51. Ibid., 246–247.

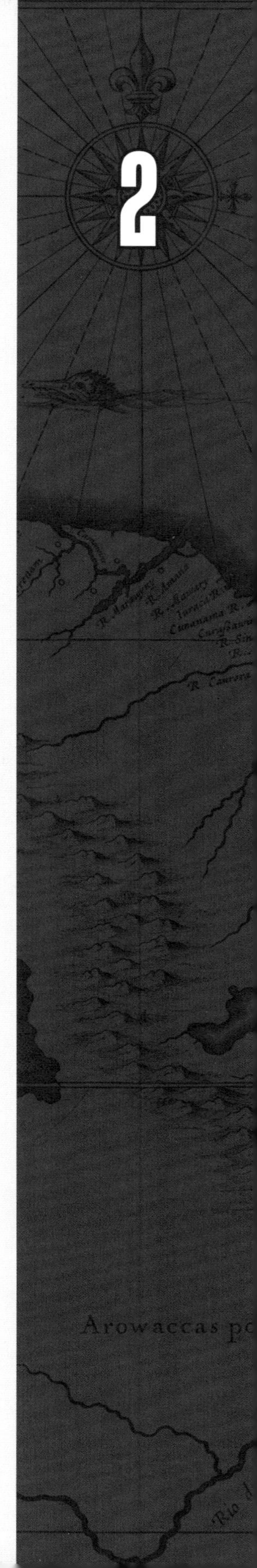

The Brave New World

Environmental Diversity in South America

10.5876_9781607323334.c002

> But during these tempests of sea and sky, so numerous and so violent, the Most High was pleased to display before us a continent, new lands, and an unknown world.
>
> *Amerigo Vespucci, 1503,* Mundus Novus

South America is characterized by diversity, as measured on every conceivable dimension.

From the Isthmus of Panama to Tierra del Fuego, the continent stretches between the latitudes of 12° N and 55° S and the longitudes of 35° and 80° W. It encompasses more than 17.8 million km^2 (6.87 million square miles), approximately one-eighth of the Earth's dry land. Of all the continents on the planet, South America has the greatest latitudinal reach, extending from the humid tropics to the frigid, windswept headlands of the Straits of Magellan.

South America is similarly varied in terms of biological diversity.[1] Conservation International identifies five **biodiversity hotspots** in South America, areas with marked species diversity of plants and animals that are under threat. The tropical Andes are the most biodiverse region on Earth, containing about 17 percent (one-sixth) of all plant species in about 1 percent of the planet's landmass. The northwest coast of South America contains the Choco-Magdalena-Tumbes biodiversity hotspot, a region of coastal mangroves, dry forests, and other habitats that is home to 2,750 endemic plant species. The Atlantic Forest hotspot ranges along the coasts of Brazil and Uruguay, extending inland to Paraguay; distinct from the Amazonian tropics, the Atlantic Forest hotspot contains 20,000 plant species—8,000 endemic species—yet 90 percent of the forest has been destroyed for modern agriculture. The savannas of the Brazilian Plateau form the Cerrado hotspot, covering more than 20 percent of Brazil. The Cerrado hotspot contains more than 4,000 endemic plant species, is the largest extent of dry forest and savanna in South America, and is threatened by deforestation and cattle ranching. Finally, and far to the south along the central-northern coast of Chile and the far western edge of Argentina, the Chilean Winter-Rainfall–Valdivian Forest hotspot contains more than 1,950 endemic plant species, as well as endemic—and threatened—species of birds, mammals, and amphibians. These are just five of the most diverse and endangered regions in the continent, an indication of the great biodiversity across South America.

This biodiversity reflects the stunning variations in geography and climate of the South American continent and coastlines (figure 2.2).

The **Andes** are South America's spine (figure 2.3).

Figure 2.1 South America from space

Figure 2.2 South America: major environmental zones

Second only to the Himalayas in average height among the world's mountains, the Andes run the length of the continent for more than 8,800 km (5,500 miles).[2] Peaks rise to more than 6,000 m (22,000 ft) at various points along this mountainous chain. From north to south, the cordillera both divides and intertwines. In northern Colombia the mountains form three chains separated by rift valleys but fuse into a single massif in southern Colombia and Ecuador. In Peru

Figure 2.3 The Andean cordillera

and Bolivia the Andes divide into two cordilleras separated by the high grasslands of the altiplano before rejoining into a single, complex chain in Argentina and Chile that continues southward into Patagonia, at which point the Andes dip under the ocean.

The Andes hug the western margins of South America. Mt. Aconcagua, at 6,960 m (22,834 ft) the tallest peak in the Americas, is less than 140 km (about 85 miles) from the Pacific Ocean near Mendoza, Argentina. Similarly, Peru's Cerro Huascarán (elevation 6,768 m [22,204 ft]) is less than 100 km (60 miles) from the Pacific Coast. Numerous mountains are volcanic cones, as in the "Avenue of the Volcanoes" in the highlands of Ecuador.

East of the Andes, South America is lower in elevation and less abrupt in relief. The **Guiana Highlands** are in the northeastern corner of the continent. They are made from crystalline rocks eroded down to an average elevation of less than 250 m (800 ft) but with isolated granite knobs or mountains (inselbergs) rising more than 600 m (2,000 ft). The center and eastern portion of the continent is dominated by the **Brazilian Plateau**, an area of more than 1,508,000 km^2 (580,000 square miles) with an average height of 914 m (3,000 ft).

The Andes, the Guiana Highlands, and the Brazilian Plateau are separated from each other by distinct and vast lowland zones (figure 2.4).

The Guiana Highlands and the northern Andes are divided by the **Orinoco Basin**, which covers 945,350 km^2 (365,000 square miles) and runs for 2,152 km (1,337 miles) before emptying into the Gulf of Paría and the Atlantic Ocean. The Southern Andes and the Brazilian Plateau flank the enormous drainage basin

Figure 2.4 South America: major river systems

created by the **Paraná**, **Paraguay**, and **Uruguay** Rivers, which drain a vast area covering 41–44 million km² (1.6–1.7 million square miles) before flowing into the **Rio de la Plata**, a gulf that empties into the south Atlantic (figure 2.5). But by far the largest lowland zone is drained by the **Amazon River** and its tributaries.

The Amazon River and its more than 1,000 tributaries form the largest river system on Earth. It drains 40 percent of the South American continent. At more

Figure 2.5 Complex channels of the Lower Paraná River, Argentina

than 6,400 km (4,000 miles), the Amazon River is second in overall length only to the Nile among the world's rivers, and its discharge is greater than that of any other river. An incredible 20 percent of all the flowing water on Earth flows out of the mouth of the Amazon. Originating as a stream trickling from a glacier at approximately 5,600 m (18,360 ft) in the central Peruvian Andes, the river begins as the **Rio Marañon** and is joined by numerous rivers flowing from Peru (such as the **Rio Ucayali**), Ecuador (including the **Rio Napo**), and Colombia (the **Rio Putumayo**). Curving east, the Amazon begins a gradual descent toward the Atlantic Ocean and is joined by the **Rio Negro** and other tributaries from the Brazilian highland (figure 2.6). Branching into numerous canals that snake around islands—including **Marajó Island**, which is the size of Switzerland—the Amazon River eventually empties into the Atlantic Ocean.

Along its course, the Amazon varies in width from 1.6 km (1 mile) to 10 km (6.2 miles), although it swells to 48 km (30 miles) or more during rainy seasons. Different rainy seasons in Ecuador (March to July) and Peru (October to January) produce alternating floods in the drainage basin's upper reaches. Iquitos, located on the Amazon about 125 km (78 miles) below the junction of the Marañon and Ucayali Rivers and more than 3,000 km (1,864 miles) from the Atlantic Ocean, is less than 106 m (350 ft) above sea level; Manaus, more than 1,600 km (1,000 miles) downstream, is only 92 m (306 ft) above sea level. The river's breadth, depth, and low relief means that the Amazon is navigable for much of its length; large ships can sail to Manaus, smaller ocean-going vessels can cruise to Iquitos, and still smaller vessels can motor hundreds of kilometers further upstream.

Figure 2.6 Confluence of the Rio Negro and the Amazon River near Manaus, Brazil

Coastal Environments

Bathed by the eastern Pacific Ocean, the western Atlantic Ocean, and the Caribbean Sea, South America has more than 30,000 km (18,000 miles) of coastline.[3] The coasts differ in terms of sea temperatures, water depths, coastal topographies, and biota (figure 2.7).

The warm (22°–29° C /71.6°–84.2° F) waters of the **Caribbean** flow counterclockwise along the coasts of Venezuela and Colombia and through the arc of the Antilles Islands before turning into the Gulf of Mexico and pouring into the Gulf Stream. The tropical region of the **western Atlantic Ocean** extends from the plains of the Orinoco River delta southward along the coasts of Venezuela, Guyana, Surinam, and French Guiana to northern Brazil. Like the Caribbean, the tropical West Atlantic region has warm sea surface temperatures (27°–28° C/80.6°–82.4° F), and both regions are characterized by highly diverse marine life. Further south, the Brazilian shelf runs for nearly 7,500 km (4,500 miles), with a continental shelf varying from a narrow 8 km (4.8 miles) in the northeast to a broad 300 km

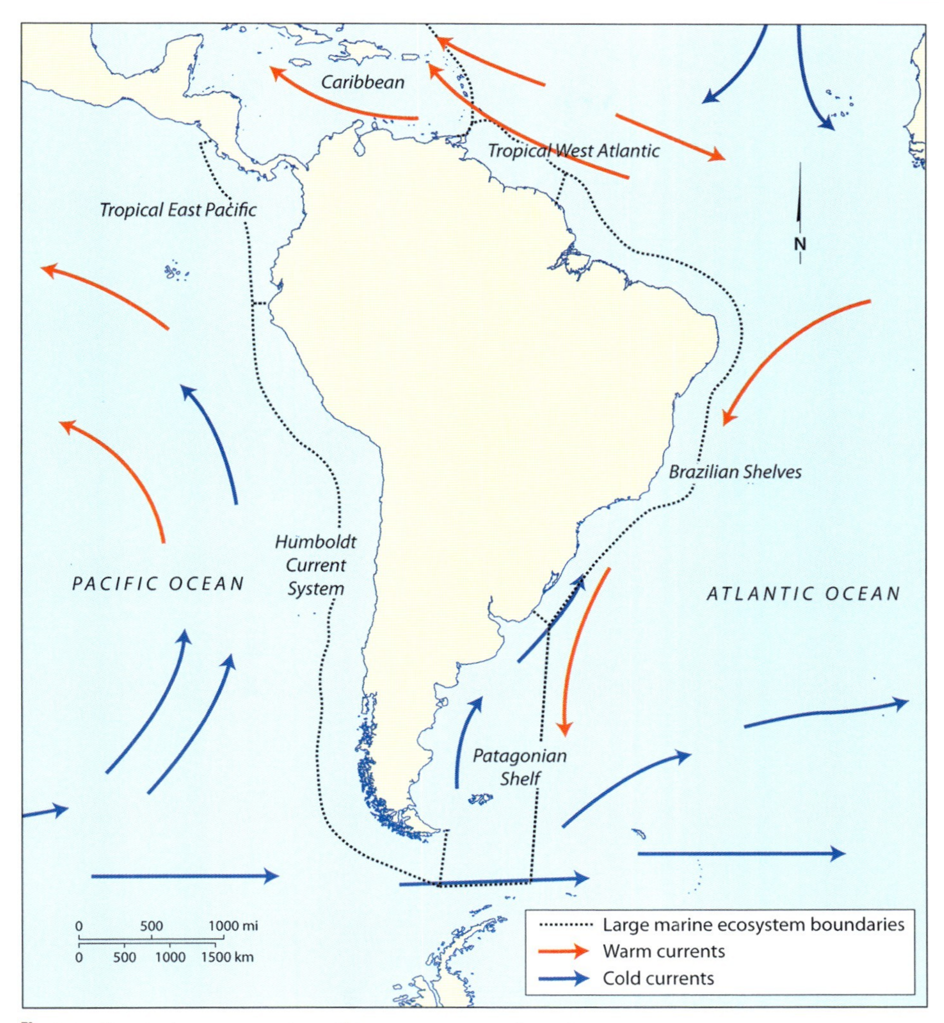

Figure 2.7 South America: major offshore currents and marine ecosystems

(180 miles) near the mouth of the Amazon. The submarine topography contains seamounts and ridges, deep-sea canyons, and abyssal plains, while the coastal marine ecosystem is a heterogeneous mix of sandy beaches, rocky coasts, coral and rocky reefs, lagoons, salt marshes, estuaries, and extensive stands of mangroves (figure 2.8).

Offshore of Brazil's coastline that juts the furthest into the Atlantic, oceanic current systems diverge in direction and temperature. The warmer **Northern Brazil Current** flows north and the Brazil Current trends south, where it mixes with the colder **Malvinas Current** before flowing east into the southern Atlantic.

From northern Uruguay to the southern tip of South America, nutrient-poor warm waters from coastal Brazil mix with nutrient-rich cold waters from Antarctica in the Patagonian shelf, forming a convergence zone of high biotic productivity.

The coastline is marked by sandy beaches interrupted by rocky headlands and coasts. The large gulf formed by the Rio de la Plata contributes an enormous volume of freshwater to the coastal zone, creating a unique bio-geographic region that is home to more than one-third of all the species of marine mammals known in the world, including the La Plata River dolphin, the Austral dolphin, orcas, and the southern right whale.

Rounding Cape Horn, the Pacific Coast of South America is dominated by the Peruvian or **Humboldt Current**. This northward-flowing current is named for the great Enlightenment-period naturalist and savant Alexander von Humboldt, who discovered the current's most salient feature: it is consistently cold. Even as the current approaches the Equator, sea surface temperatures range between 14° and 18° C (58°–64° F), approximately 10° C (18° F) colder than normal for these latitudes. The cold current is created by northeasterly winds that blow from the eastern Pacific and trigger upwelling in which colder waters from lower depths are brought to the surface. Nutrients are swept from dark depths to the upper 50 m (164 ft) of the ocean, where sunlight penetrates and plankton photosynthesize. Rich blooms of phytoplankton support anchovies and other schooling fish, making the Humboldt Current the most productive marine ecosystem on Earth. The Humboldt Current flows to far-northern Peru, where it meets the warm waters of the Equatorial Counter Current and turns west to bathe the Galapagos Islands.

Along the northwestern coast of South America, from far-northern Peru to Panama, a complex set of warm-water currents produces one of the wettest places on Earth, with some regions receiving 10 m (33 ft) of annual rainfall. The coastline is variable. Larger rivers form deltas fringed by mangrove forests, such as at the **Gulf of Guayaquil** in southern Ecuador and the **Bahia de Buenaventura** in western Colombia (figure 2.8). Elsewhere, the coast consists of high cliffs and hills that run near the ocean, interspersed with small beaches in coves and fronted by rocky reefs and promontories.

Climatic Complexities

Latitude, topography, oceanic systems, and global patterns of air circulation intersect to form complex climates across South America. For example, the Köppen-Geiger system is one of the most broadly applied schemes for classifying world climate, based on five major classes—tropical climates, arid and semiarid climates, temperate climates, continental climates, and polar climates (including tundra and alpine climates)—that are further subdivided into twenty-eight distinct types of climate. South America contains them all.

It is not surprising that this complex climate pattern is directly reflected in vegetation and land use. Southern Chile varies from a cool coastal climate to coniferous forests that receive more than 2.5 m (100 inches) of rainfall per year. The cold waters of the Humboldt Current inhibit near-shore precipitation, producing a coastal desert that stretches from central Chile (the **Atacama Desert**) to northern Peru (the **Sechura Desert**) (figure 2.9).

Figure 2.8 Inside manglares, Tumbes, Peru

Figure 2.9 The Atacama Desert, northern Chile

Rainfall in the Andes either runs west by way of relatively short river valleys to the Pacific Ocean or flows into the Atlantic Ocean via the Amazon, Paraguay-Paraná, Orinoco, or other lesser drainage systems. The abrupt topographic relief of the Andes results in the tight overlap of multiple habitats. In the Southern Andes, the high peaks create a rain shadow and a dry, cold climate in **Patagonia** (figure 2.10).

The lower summits of the Ecuadorian Andes allow moisture from the tropical Pacific to enter the western Amazon. The cold, treeless plateau of the **Bolivian altiplano** drops east to the **Llanos de Mojos**, a vast, relatively flat area of seasonally flooded savannas between the Andean foothills and Amazonia (figure 2.11). Vast regions of tropical forests cover Amazonia, where modern communities are connected by rivers, airstrips, and rare roads. This complex pattern has changed over time.

Climate Variations: Short-Term and Long-Term

Short-term climate variations had significant impacts in South America's prehistory. Some of the most notable variations are caused by **El Niño/Southern Oscillations** (ENSO) and its counterpart, **La Niña**, quasi-periodic phenomena associated with fluctuations in the Earth's orbit, changes in sea surface temperatures, and the placement of the **Inter-Tropical Convergence Zone** (**ITCZ**, discussed below; figure 2.12).

Named for "the [Christ] child" because its effects often occur around Christmas, El Niño is associated with global climate variations, whose impacts vary in different

Figure 2.10 Patagonian steppe, Argentina

Figure 2.11 Lake Titicaca viewed from the Isla del Sol

Figure 2.12 The Inter-Tropical Convergence Zone marked by clouds in the eastern Pacific Ocean and northern South America

places on Earth. Although a global phenomenon, ENSO events have pronounced consequences in South America. Changing wind patterns in the Pacific Ocean result in an anomalous buildup in warm waters along the west coast of South America, increasing sea temperature and dislodging the Humboldt Current. This dampens upwelling, decimates temperature-sensitive plankton and much of the marine food web, and triggers torrential rain along the normally arid coastal deserts.

The consequences of major El Niño events can be catastrophic. During 1997–98, *ten times the average precipitation* fell in Peru and Ecuador, causing extensive flooding and billions of dollars in damage.[4] The northern Peruvian city of Piura normally receives about 6 cm (2.4 inches) of rainfall each year; in 1997–98, *178 cm* (*5.8 ft*) of rain fell. In the nearby hyper-arid Sechura Desert, a massive lake formed that was 145 km (90 miles) long, 30 km (20 miles) wide, and 3 m (10 ft) deep, the second-largest lake in Peru; it is now—and normally—completely dry. Floods washed away houses, bridges, roads, and agricultural harvests. Irrigation systems were destroyed and farmlands devastated. Conversely, normally barren deserts bloomed with seasonal vegetation, and stands of algarobbo (*Prosopsis* sp.) trees added new growth. Elsewhere in South America, El Niño–related climatic variations can cause drought in the Southern Andes and increased rainfall in eastern Brazil. Although not all El Niño events are equally severe, they often produce significant climatic variations with tremendous consequences for human societies, especially those living along the Pacific Coast and the western watersheds of the Andes.

El Niños are known to have occurred on numerous occasions in prehistory since at least the beginning of the Holocene.[5] Sediment cores from the Laguna Pallcacocha in the southern Ecuadorian Andes suggest that the frequency of major El Niño events intensified starting about 7,000 years ago, peaked about 1,200 years ago, and decreased thereafter.[6]

El Niño/Southern Oscillations are only one of the factors that create climatic variations in South America. A related phenomenon involves movement in the

ITCZ, the atmospheric band where the major trade winds of the Northern and Southern Hemispheres collide over the tropics.[7] Although the ITCZ is generally found between about 5° N and 5° S latitudes, it may fluctuate as much as 45 degrees of latitude. The latitudinal position of the ITCZ varies based on changes in sea temperatures in the Pacific and Atlantic Oceans, as well as because of local configurations and surface temperatures of landmass and oceans.

The position of the ITCZ impacts regional rainfall patterns in South America. When the ITCZ sits near its northernmost range of 5–10° latitude N, northern South America—including the Orinoco Basin—receives 1–2 m of rainfall annually.[8] When the ITCZ shifts southward to the Equator, heavier rainfall occurs in equatorial South America and the Amazon Basin, leaving northern South America and the Orinoco relatively dry. Although the ITCZ oscillates annually between latitudinal extremes, studies of deep-sea core data off the coast of Venezuela—an area into which the Orinoco River drains—suggest that the average position of the ITCZ has migrated southward since the Holocene. In northern South America, this resulted in a gradual increase in precipitation that peaked between 10,500 and 5,400 years ago, before gradually decreasing to a minimum at about 550 to 200 years ago. Conversely, the southward shift in the ITCZ starting 5,400 years ago intersected with the increased frequency of El Niño/Southern Oscillation events after 7000 BP, which suggests some of the complex interconnections that produce climatic variations. Varying in intensity and duration, these phenomena also impact environmental diversity.

Other, non-climatic phenomena also impact the environment. Repeated volcanic eruptions affect three areas of western South America: southern Colombia/northern Ecuador, southern Peru, and southern Chile.[9] More than twenty volcanoes in northern Ecuador have had major eruptions since the end of the Ice Age, and numerous archaeological sites have been found blanketed by volcanic ash and tephras (figure 2.13).

Most of the Ecuadorian sites with such pyroclastic layers lie between the Andes and the Pacific Coast; volcanic eruptions in the cordillera pushed tall plumes of ash and gases into the sky, which were carried westward. For example, the Pululahua Volcano, located 30 km (18 miles) north of Quito, erupted sometime between 752 and 182 cal BC, shooting 5–6 km^3 of ash into the air and covering a vast area encompassing 250 × 300 km of the sierra and coast of northern Ecuador but leaving southern and Amazonian Ecuador unscathed. Within the impact area, farm fields were covered with ash, especially those on relatively flat floodplains (figure 2.14).

People moved from low-lying areas to more steeply sloped zones, entirely abandoning the areas most impacted if they escaped in time. Adjacent regions felt indirect impacts as immigrants moved into occupied territories. Trade routes were disrupted. Yet, complex and different responses to this volcanic eruption resulted. Eventually, farmlands were refurbished, the mineral nutrients from the ash enriched the soils, and people reoccupied areas they had once fled in terror.

Short-term and abrupt changes in the environment can have catastrophic consequences for human societies. Whether a drought or torrential flooding

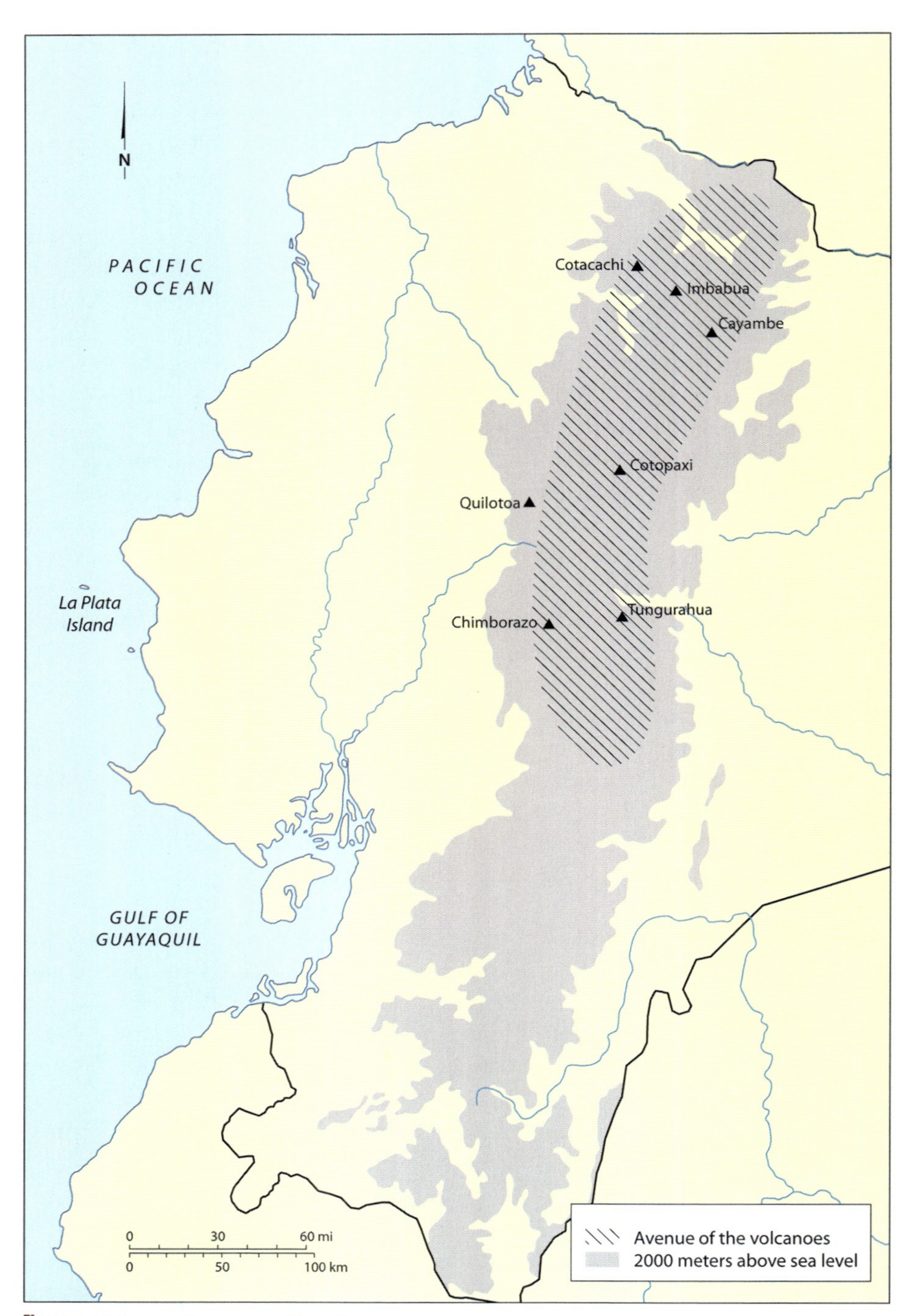

Figure 2.13 Major volcanoes in Ecuador

Figure 2.14 Road cut showing volcanic deposits in highland Ecuador

caused by an El Niño event or a volcanic explosion, catastrophes may trigger cataclysmic changes and even the collapse of civilizations. Such abrupt climatic changes have been cited as a principal cause of the collapse of the Tiwanaku state in the Southern Andes, where a prolonged drought circa AD 1100–1400 in the Titicaca Basin region led to reduced harvests, abandoned farm fields, and political collapse (chapter 9).[10] In contrast, this drought was preceded by a wetter period between 1500 BC and AD 1000 that produced greater agricultural yields and allowed for the development of larger population centers and complex societies in the Titicaca Basin. While abrupt environmental fluctuations certainly impacted ancient South Americans, the nature of the human responses varied enormously, just as the intensities and impacts of the fluctuations differed across the continent.

Climate after the Last Glacial Maximum (post-26,000–19,000 BP)

Following the **Last Glacial Maximum** (**LGM**) at about 26,000 to 19,000 years ago, climate changed dramatically at the end of the Pleistocene and into the Holocene. These changes can be readily, but incompletely, summarized in broad sweep.

Before the LGM, a combination of oscillations in the Earth's orbit around the sun, the pitch of the planet's polar axes, and the wobble of its spin resulted in higher latitudes being further from the sun and thus significantly cooler.[11] Because more of the Earth's land mass is found in the Northern Hemisphere (in contrast to the vast expanses of oceans in the Southern Hemisphere), snow accumulated on the continental landmasses of Eurasia and North America, forming vast sheets of glaciers. Since the Earth's quantity of water is effectively stable (the planet loses about the same amount of water as it gains from the fusion of hydrogen and oxygen) and since water occurs in three forms (liquid, solid, and vapor), as more moisture was frozen and captured in continental glaciers, sea levels dropped correspondingly, to 120 m (390 ft) lower than at present. New landmasses were exposed, continental temperatures cooled, and climate and vegetation patterns changed. Distinctive suites of fauna occupied different zones, including the large Pleistocene megafauna of mammoths, mastodons, ancient bison, wild horse, wooly rhinoceros, giant ground sloths, paleo-llamas, and saber-toothed cats (see chapter 3).

At about 18,000–16,000 BP, the Earth's orbital position began to shift, causing changes in the temperature and climate. As the northern latitudes tilted closer to the sun, glaciers melted, sea levels rose, dry landmasses were flooded, and habitats changed. A geologically brief cold snap—a 1,200–1,400-year period of intense cold known as the Younger Dryas Stadial—occurred between 12,800 and 11,500 years ago, but then the Earth continued to warm. Sea levels rose to near modern levels around 6,000–4,000 years ago, flooding coastal zones and the Bering Land Bridge between northeast Asia and North America. In North America and Eurasia, continental glaciers retreated toward the Arctic Circle. Similar continental-wide glaciers never covered South America, except for Patagonia, where glaciers shrank southward toward the Straits of Magellan. With warmer temperatures, vegetation communities expanded or contracted as they adapted to changing conditions. A vast number of animal species became extinct because their hard-won evolutionary adaptations to living in the frigid conditions of the Pleistocene became liabilities in this warmer new world, known as the Holocene.

If these broad contours of paleoclimate change can be summarized, the specific local consequences are difficult to state with precision, for several reasons. First, climatic phenomena are inherently complex systems, and their interconnections are difficult to estimate precisely. Second, climate change does not follow smooth trends but exhibits significant variability around a basic tendency (e.g., global temperature is rising, but this summer was colder than last). Third, changing climates are not uniformly expressed across a continent as diverse as South America; for example, increased precipitation in northern South America is associated with decreased rainfall in the Central Andes. Finally, the scientific evidence for climate change is remarkably diverse. Paleo-botanists study changes in pollen, phytoliths, and macrobotanical remains to reconstruct ancient flora. Glaciologists bore deep cores into Andean glaciers to retrieve records of prehistoric snowfalls and meltings. Archaeo-zoologists investigate faunal assemblages to look for changes in species and make inferences about habitats. Sedimentologists examine deep-sea and lake cores to identify evidence of changes in runoff. Each class of evidence reflects a different aspect of climate change, and different methods are used to date the tempo of change. For such reasons, it is challenging to present a coherent view of climate change in the Holocene in South America, as the following regional summaries indicate.

Figure 2.15 Lake Valencia, Venezuela

Northern South America and the Caribbean

As discussed earlier, climate in northern South America and the adjacent Caribbean region is regulated largely by the relative position of the ITCZ.[12] High-resolution deep-sea cores from the Cariaco Basin can be cross-indexed with sediment cores from Lake Valencia, the largest freshwater lake in Venezuela (figure 2.15).[13] The result is a detailed view of changing paleoclimate from the end of the Pleistocene to the present.

At the end of the Pleistocene, northern South America was significantly drier and cooler than it is today. In the northern Andes of Venezuela in 12,850 cal BP, temperature was an estimated 2.2° to 2.9° C (about 1.5°–2° F) cooler than at present, but it warmed dramatically after 12,300 BP—a rapid shift forced by the southward migration of the ITCZ.[14] Lake Valencia was intermittently dry and wet between 12,600 and 10,000 BP, and lower levels of rainfall and sedimentation are indicated for the Cariaco Basin.

In the Early Holocene, climate became warmer and wetter in northern South America. Water levels rose in Lake Valencia between 10,000 and 8200 cal BP. Increased sediments are also registered in the Cariaco cores. Lake levels fluctuated, however, probably in response to regional climate oscillations as registered in the sediments of Lake Valencia, a closed lake system sensitive to local fluctuations in rainfall.

Over the next five millennia, climate became even wetter and warmer. Between 8200 and 3000 cal BP, Lake Valencia filled to its highest level, its surface rising more than 27 m (88.5 ft) before spilling over the banks of the lake's basin. This period of increased precipitation characterized the circum-Caribbean region, with similar increases in moisture documented for the neo-tropical regions of Mexico, Central America, and Panama, as well as in the Cariaco Basin cores. Within this generally wetter period, two prominent drops in lake level occurred in 7600–6700 cal BP and again for a relatively brief period circa 3300–3150 cal BP.

Since 3000 cal BP, the levels of Lake Valencia have dropped, although there is debate about the pace and timing of this trend. It seems that the Little Ice Age in 500 BP was characterized by reduced rainfall in northern South America, just as glaciers expanded and climate cooled in the Central Andes.

Central Andes

Principal sources of paleoclimate data for western South America are ice cores collected from glaciers between southern Ecuador and northern Bolivia (figure 2.16).

The Quelccaya glacier, at 5,670 m (18,602 ft) above sea level in southern Peru, was cored by Lonnie Thompson of Ohio State University in 1983. The Quelccaya core produced a remarkably precise and detailed view of changing climate over the last 1,500 years.[15] The Quelccaya core was notable for three basic reasons. First, each year the glacier accumulated a new layer of ice during the wet season, separated from the previous year's ice by a thin layer of wind-borne dust laid down during the dry season. These annual dust varves produced a precisely dated sequence for the core. Second, the thicknesses of annual accumulations allowed for the calculation of snowfall (once the compression of the ice layers had been accounted for). Third, individual samples along the core could be sampled for the relative presence of two oxygen isotopes, the heavier O_{18} and the lighter O_{16}. Since the lighter O_{16} evaporates more readily from the ocean and falls as rainwater and snow, a higher ratio of O_{16} to O_{18} is a proxy for increased rainfall.

Thompson's data showed that the Southern Andes had seen higher than modern precipitation in AD 610–50, 760–1040, 1500–1720, and 1870–1984. Conversely, the data indicated drier than modern periods in AD 540–60, 570–610, 650–730, 1250–1310, and 1720–1860. Some of these fluctuations correlated with other well-known climatic events, such as the Little Ice Age of circa AD 1500–1900.[16] Other events, such as the series of droughts between AD 540 and 730, could be linked to cultural disruptions, including the collapse of the southern Moche state on the Peruvian coast.[17] But most important, the Quelccaya ice-core data demonstrated the incredible value of tropical glaciers for understanding paleoclimate in western South America and adjacent regions.

Additional ice-core samples were obtained from other glaciers in the Andes, notably Cerro Huascarán in Peru and the extinct Sajama Volcano, the highest summit in Bolivia (6,542 m [21,458 ft]; see figure 2.2).[18] At both sites, cores drilled deep into the ice retrieved detailed records of post-Pleistocene climate. Although the older cores lacked the precision of the Quelccaya core, the Huascarán and Sajama cores resulted in data on changing precipitation patterns for each of the last 250 centuries, covering all of the Holocene and the entirety of human presence

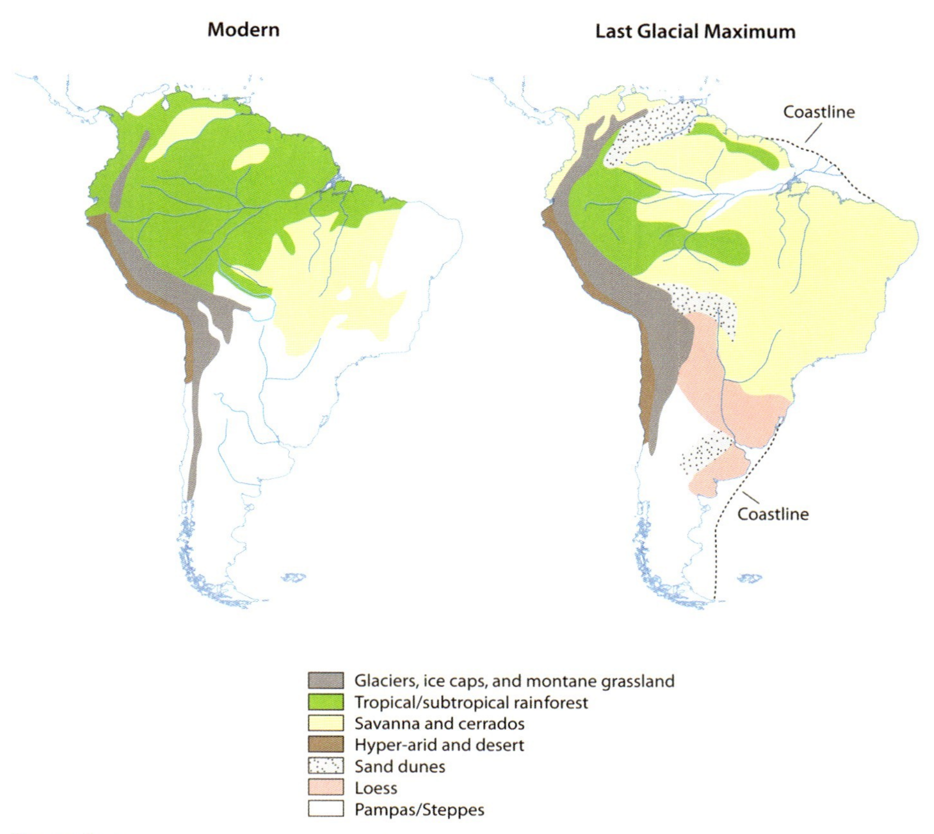

Figure 2.16 Major glaciers and sources of ice-core data

in South America (see chapter 3). Given the direction of prevailing winds from the east, the glaciers receive moisture from the Amazon Basin. Although runoff from the glaciers may flow to the Pacific Ocean (as in the case of Huascarán), their moisture originates in Amazonia, and the data are informative about a broad swath of ancient South America.

At the Last Glacial Stage (ca. 20,000–15,000 BP), the core data suggest a period in the Andes that was much cooler than today, perhaps on average as much as 8° C (~15° F) colder. Simultaneously, concentrations of airborne dust were significantly higher, suggesting a less densely forested and drier Amazonia, also indicated by lower concentrations of pollen and of nitrate, an aerosol created by plants. It seems that the Pleistocene ended as a period of intense cold, greater aridity, and sparser vegetation—at least in regions reflected in these ice cores. (The climate of the Pacific Coast is not registered by these samples.)

In circa 15,000–10,000 BP, paleoclimate began to change, and its pace accelerated in the Early and Middle Holocene. Higher ratios of O_{16} reflect increased precipitation and moisture flowing westward from Amazonia. Decreasing concentrations of airborne dust and increasing densities of nitrate suggest the spread of forest cover in Amazonia. Between 15,900 and 13,800 BP, lakes and wetlands formed in the central Atacama Desert at the western base of the Andes, south of San Pedro de Atacama.[19] These general trends were not smooth transitions but jagged variations around a mean. A major reversal occurred with a bitter cold snap in circa 14,000–11,500 BP in which glaciers advanced, temperatures plummeted, and precipitation fell—a global climatic reversal known as the Younger Dryas Reversal in North America and referred to as the Deglaciation Climate Reversal in the Andes.

After 11,500 BP, climate in the Southern Andes approached modern conditions. Vegetation communities gradually changed as climate warmed and dampened. Perhaps 2,000 years elapsed before the Amazonian forests replaced grassland savannas established in the colder and drier climates at the end of the Pleistocene. The large lakes in southern Bolivia and northern Chile evaporated, ultimately forming the blinding white, salt-encrusted lake beds of the Salar de Uyni and the Salar de Atacama. Climate was actually warmer in the Early Holocene; wetland plants sprouted around glacier lakes before being covered by ice, only to recently reemerge from thawing layers.[20] Plant remains from the melting edge of the Quelccaya glacier indicate that portions of the mountain were free of ice between 7,000 and 5,000 years ago.[21] The Andes progressively cooled, and temperatures dropped markedly during the recent Neo-glacial, or Little Ice Age, before achieving a more or less stable state, periodically interrupted by abrupt climate variations.

Since the early nineteenth century, temperature has increased dramatically, with the last century the warmest period of the last 6,000 years. The most recent warming trend was enhanced by anthropogenic factors that have led to global warming, a process destroying the tropical glaciers that bear evidence of climate change.[22]

Although the Andean ice-core data reflect changing climates that have continental and global connections, the specific nature of those connections and the changes in corresponding areas remain extremely difficult to specify. One of the most challenging regions for climatic reconstruction is the vast Amazon Basin.

Amazonia

Reconstructing the paleoclimate of the Amazon is daunting for a number of reasons. First, Amazonia is huge and the data sets are few. Nearly a decade and a half ago, Paul Colinvaux and colleagues pointed out that although the Amazon Basin is larger than Europe, only two reasonably complete pollen cores were available, leading them to comment that trying to extrapolate from these two cores was like "using a pollen diagram from Moscow to reconstruct the environmental history of Paris, an enterprise that would involve extrapolating over a comparable east-west distance. The possibility for error in such an extrapolation should be obvious."[23] Further, there are significant variations across Amazonia, along both north-south and east-west gradients, which have become more evident as more data are acquired. The impacts of El Niños are expressed in "markedly different climate responses across the [Amazon] basin."[24]

Second, sedimentary cores and pollen profiles are the two principal classes of paleoclimatic and paleoenvironmental evidence.[25] These data lack the annual or decadal resolution of ice cores; the absolute dates are usually based on radiometric samples chosen from within the cores and profiles or from adjacent layers in the sampling area. It is not uncommon for a data set spanning 13,000–14,000 years to have fewer than a dozen absolute dates along that sequence. Consequently, these data sets can identify when particular environments occurred in the past, but they seldom document the pace of change. Finally, the sediments and pollen cores may reflect variations in ancient environments that are not the product of climate changes. Changes in pollen, for example, may reflect changes in local conditions rather than regional environmental changes—such as local landslides that sweep away established species and are repopulated by aggressive newcomers—or human impacts on local environments.[26]

Paleoclimate data from southeastern Ecuador suggest that at the end of the Pleistocene, average temperatures increased above both Pleistocene and modern levels in the Early Holocene (ca. 10,000–7500 BP), before settling at near-modern levels in the mid-Holocene. In northern South America, post-glacial temperatures increased relatively abruptly, perhaps as much as 4° C (7.2° F) within a few centuries—faster than in the Southern Andes.[27] Several sediment cores from southeastern Ecuador indicate periods of higher than current precipitation in circa 8990 and 3680 cal BP, correlating with similar patterns in the Quelccaya core data.[28] Suites of plant species moved into newly available territories. After about 4000 BP, rainfall decreased, a trend punctuated by periodic droughts; however, these climatic changes apparently did not dramatically restructure the Amazonian forests. Although lake cores from southeastern Ecuador indicate a drought between circa 4200 and 3150 BP before precipitation gradually increased, the pollen from those same cores demonstrates that the same major classes of plants were always there (except for areas of local marsh species that contracted and expanded as lake levels sank and rose).[29]

The complexities of climate change in western Amazonia are demonstrated in table 2.1, which summarizes paleoenvironmental data from six locales in southeast Ecuador. Samples from highland zones exhibit the most dramatic changes; samples from lowland zones document changes in precipitation and vegetation but not wholesale replacement of habitats. Periodic droughts and floods impacted western Amazonia but never completely replaced forests with grasslands. Finally, the environment of western Amazonia changed as humans moved into the region, introducing new plant species and clearing forests with stone tools and fire.

More than 2,700 km (1,620 miles) to the east, cores from two lakes in the state of Para, in the eastern Brazilian Amazon, indicate a pattern of continuity with change.[30] Pollen and sediment cores covering the period of the last 9,200 years indicate that the Lower Amazon was forested throughout that time (figure 2.17).

Changes in the rate and composition of lake sediments indicate increased rainfall in 8500, 7400, and 6100 BP; these changes in precipitation probably reflect a combination of post-glacial increase in precipitation and local storms (El Niño

Table 2.1 Late Pleistocene to Late Holocene vegetation and climate, northern Andes and northwestern Amazonia

	Western Cordillera, Eastern Flank		*Eastern Cordillera*	*Western Edge of Amazon Basin, Andean Foothill*		
Site	*Laguna Chorreras / Palkacocha*	*Lake Surucucho (IJaviucu)*	*Cerro Toledo*	*San Juan de Bosco*	*Mera site*	*Lake Ayauch / Iago Kumpak*
Location	2° 45 minutes S, 79° 10 minutes W	3° S lat.	4° 22 minutes S, 79° 06 minutes W	3° 3 minutes S, 78° 27 minutes W	1° 28 minutes S, 78° 06 minutes W	No data / 3° 2 minutes S, 77° 49 minutes W
Elevation	3,700/4,060 m	3,180 m	3,150 m	970 m	1,100 m	500/700 m
Precipitation	East: > 2,000 mm yr–1	750 mm yr–1	Up to 6,000 mm yr–1	No data	> 4,800 mm yr–1	2,000–3,000 mm yr–1
Temperature	Daytime: 12–18° C	14° C	6.5° C	No data	20.8° C	23–24° C
Time period (yr BP)	Major vegetation changes and climate events					
Late Holocene after 4000	Moist mountain rainforest increase		Páramo expansion continued		Precipitation event northeastern Andes: 1,300–800 yr BP, flooding of western Amazonia	Dry period: 4200–3150 yr BP and 1500–800 yr BP, some taxa decline, no major forest change
Mid-Holocene ca. 7500–4000	Grass páramo expansion, Polylepis dominating the forest line		Expansion of páramo, decrease of lower mountain rainforest			Lake formation, Amazon rainforest, dry period: 4300–4800 yr BP
Early Holocene ca. 10,000–7500	Moist mountain rainforest elements remain stable		Lowest páramo and highest lower mountain rainforest distribution			
Holocene Transition ca. 11,500–10,000	Moist mountain rainforest expansion, Polylepis becomes important	Development of modern Andean forest				
Late Glacial ca. 15,000–11,500	Persistent páramo dominance	Upslope advance of forest line	Decrease of páramo, changeover to grass páramo, increase of lower mountain rainforest.			
LGM ca. 20,000–15,000	Páramo initially dominant and spread into higher elevations		Páramo dominance (moist Plantago association)			
Late Pleistocene ca. 30,000–26,000		Treeless vegetation (related to modern páramo)		Mixed lowland / mountain community	Mixed lowland / mountain community; Andean forest growth at least 700 m lower	

Source: C. Brunschön and H. Behling, "Late Quaternary Vegetation, Fire and Climate History Reconstructed from Two Cores at Cerro Toledo, Podocarpus National Park, Southeastern Ecuadorian Andes," *Quaternary Research* 72 (2009): 397.

events tend to create droughts in eastern Amazonia). These volatile storm events developed during a period of mid-Holocene climate variation across Amazonia that peaked approximately 6,200 to 4,200 years ago, in places creating vegetation communities different from those present today.[31]

Further downstream, near the mouth of the Amazon River, the Atlantic Ocean rose rapidly in the Early Holocene, reaching near-modern levels after 6500 BP.[32] Vast mud banks formed along the Brazilian coast, resulting from the enormous volume of sediment transported by the Amazon. Mangrove forests were well established between 4800 and 1100 cal BP but contracted between 1100 and 750 BP, and other plants colonized the coast. Mangroves expanded again after 750 BP and continued until the last few decades. The basic pattern of expansion of mangroves over the last eight centuries was interrupted at several points, presumably when increased runoff from the Amazon decreased the salinity of the coastal waters mangroves prefer. As drier conditions emerged and runoff decreased, mangrove forests were reestablished. Interestingly, these episodes of expansion and contraction of coastal mangroves, respectively, coincide with periods of drought and wetter than normal periods registered in the Quelccaya ice-core data.

In sum, although the different climatic regimes across Amazonia are connected, the connections are complicated. It is impossible to make sweeping generalizations across such a vast and diverse region. For example, the archaeologist Betty Meggers has argued that different ethnolinguistic groups populating Amazonia circa 4,000 to 2,000 years ago encountered an arid environment in which tropical forests were reduced to isolated patches (refugia) surrounded by open woodlands and savannas.[33] In turn, the refugia model for the Amazon had been suggested as characterizing Pleistocene vegetation at a time when global climate was colder and drier compared to today. More than four decades of research suggest that the refugia model is inaccurate. Although climates oscillated and the distribution of specific species varied, there was no wholesale replacement of tropical forests by savannas anywhere in Amazonia (figure 2.18).

As the authors of a recent review have noted, "None of the late Quaternary paleoecological records from the center of the Amazon Basin provide evidence of widespread, long-term aridity sufficient to cause the fragmentation of rainforests." In other words, there is no evidence of tropical rainforest refugia. Further, "Simple contrasts of wet versus dry, cold versus warm, cannot capture the variability of the glacial-interglacial cycles" and their impacts on Amazonian environments. Finally, the authors conclude that "simplistic notions requiring the whole of the Amazon lowlands to have a single climate subject to uniform change are bound to fail."[34]

Southern Atlantic Coast

The southeastern Atlantic Coast of Uruguay hosts a complex mosaic of habitats, including palm forests, prairies, coastal wetlands, salt marshes, and lagoons.[35] Cores containing phytoliths and pollen document changes in paleoclimate from the end of the Pleistocene (ca. 14,000–10,000 BP) to the Late Holocene (4020

Figure 2.17 (*overleaf*) Tropical forest near Santa Cruz, Bolivia

Figure 2.18 Upper Rio Pastaza flowing east toward Amazonia in Ecuador

BP, or cal BC 2600–2300). Based on the low frequency of wetland plant species, the Late Pleistocene was probably cooler and substantially drier than today. Local vegetation communities were probably temperate grasslands, with some trees and shrubs forming a thin, narrow band near the major drainages.

By 9450 BP (cal BC 8815–8536), the Early Holocene climate was wetter and warmer; the number and variety of wetland plant species indicate a habitat very similar to the modern environment, but these conditions did not last. Between approximately 6620 and 4020 BP (or cal BC 5625–5466 to cal BC 2600–2300), two millennia of unsettled climate and dramatically changing habitats are indicated. Shifts in pollen suggest an environment oscillating between drier and wetter periods over a period of 2,000 years. After 4020 BP (cal BC 2600–2300), the climate became wetter and stabilized, as indicated by a decrease in salt-tolerant amaranths and chenopods and the increase in sedges and other wetland plant species. This stable and diverse habitat provided an ideal setting for humans, who established large and relatively permanent settlements on hills and knolls above the floodplains but with immediate access to the rich and diverse resources of the coastal wetlands (see chapter 8).

Patagonia

Relatively few pollen cores or other sources of paleoclimatic data are available from southernmost South America.[36] From west to east, five principal vegetation zones exist today, their distribution structured by precipitation and elevation. West of the Andes, where as much as 400 cm (157 inches) of rain fall each year, wet moors and Magellanic Rain Forests are found.[37] At higher elevations and on the drier eastern slopes of the Andes, with 40 cm (~15–16 inches) of annual rainfall, stands of the Andean Forest contain the Antarctic beech (*Nothofagus antarctica*)—the southernmost trees on Earth. The Andean tundra is located above tree line (figure 2.19), while an area of semi-desert and the Patagonian steppe are located between the eastern slope of the Andes and the Atlantic Ocean in a zone that receives 20–40 cm (8–16 inches) of rain each year.

Today, the boundary between Andean Forest and Patagonian steppe is at the eastern base of the Andes. Not surprisingly, the situation was different in the past. A pollen core sample provides insights into changing environments over the last 13,350 years. At that earlier date, glaciers had retreated sufficiently to form a small open pond, but continued cold climate supported only a relatively thin cover of vegetation of scattered shrubs. Between 13,000 and 12,000 BP, the open pond became a small wetland with a higher density of grass pollens and charcoal, perhaps from brush fires during a warmer millennium. From 12,000 to 10,900 BP, the local environment became drier, and vegetation was dominated by drought-tolerant species. Higher amounts of rainfall occurred between 10,400 and 9900 BP, as indicated by abundant pollen from a grassland steppe and stands of Andean Forest. Arid conditions were reestablished between 9900 and 9000 cal BP, only to be replaced by wetter conditions between 9000 and 7700 cal BP, as indicated by increased quantities of *Nothofagus* pollen and other vegetation. Between 7700 and 7100 BP, the stands of Andean Forest appear to have been under stress. Pollens proliferated from open steppe plant communities at the same time *Nothofagus* pollen decreased. Further, there was increased pollen from the semi-parasitic South American mistletoe, which flourishes when Andean forests are stressed by drought. Southern Patagonia apparently suffered through a drought that was most intense circa 7400–7100 cal BP.

Although the next 2,000 years are missing from the core, possibly obliterated by a flashflood or a landslide, this detailed view of ancient climate resumes around 5350 cal BP, when wetter conditions are indicated. Based on the increase in pollen from forest species, it seems that rainfall increased and Patagonian steppe was replaced by Andean Forest, a trend toward wetter conditions indicated by the final pollen samples dating to 1800 cal BP.

Summary: Regional Climate Change since the Last Glacial Maximum

The preceding sections briefly summarize patterns of post-Pleistocene climate change for five regions of South America: northern South America and the Caribbean, the Central Andes, Amazonia, the southern Atlantic Coast, and

Figure 2.19 Antarctic beech (*Nothofagus antarctica*) trees, Patagonia

Patagonia. Other regions could be added; however, these summaries provide a set of paleoenvironmental "snapshots" of the timing, intensities, and durations of Late Pleistocene and Holocene climate change. In contrast to the broad general trend of post-Pleistocene change toward warmer and wetter environments, the regional expressions are of often quite different environmental regimes. At another level, short-term environmental variations may have sharp effects that last two centuries or less. Finally, although climatic changes and variations may be linked to continental or global processes, the different impacts were felt at the local level—which is just one reason human responses to environmental diversity and change were so varied across South America.

Conclusion: Environmental Diversity in Space and Time

South America's striking diversity fundamentally shaped the human presence in the continent. As the following chapters document, humans adapted to South America in remarkably different ways, establishing their presence in tropical forests, highland valleys and steppes, and coastal zones from the Isthmus of Panama to Tierra del Fuego. Although human cultures were never simply expressions of environmental patterns, South American societies always confronted the possibilities and constraints of their habitats. Furthermore, these environments underwent changes through time, climatic oscillations of different durations and severities. Long-term climate changes—such as the tendency toward warmer and wetter conditions after the Pleistocene—were punctuated by short-term variations, such as periods of more rainfall or drought caused by El Niño events. Even when such climatic variations were felt across broad reaches of South America, such as those associated with fluctuations in the Inter-Tropical Convergence Zone, the environmental expressions of those variations usually differed at the local level: the same factor that created drought in northern South America intensified precipitation in the Central Andes. Human responses to those changes were also varied. Relatively mobile, band societies of hunters and gatherers reacted to drought differently than did sedentary, agrarian urban civilizations. Some societies opted to narrowly adapt to a single environmental pattern, while other groups diversified and exploited multiple environmental zones.

Recognition of the importance of environmental diversity does not imply that the human experience in South America was "simply" a reflection of climate and habitat. Nothing could be further from the truth, as the following chapters demonstrate. Conversely, it is impossible to understand the achievements of human societies without acknowledging the varying dimensions of the continent they came to inhabit. Understanding these complex relationships between environment and society is essential to comprehend the cultural achievements of the peoples of South America, past and present.

Notes

1. The following is based on the Conservation International website at www.conservation.org/where/south_america/pages/overview.aspx (accessed May 5, 2014).

2. The following draws on the outstanding entry "South America," found in the 15th edition of the *Encyclopedia Britannica: Macropedia* (27: 578–595), a masterful, precise, and beautifully organized overview. For a much more detailed overview of the geographic complexities of South America, see T. Veblen, K. Young, and A. Orme, eds., *The Physical Geography of South America* (Oxford: Oxford University Press, 2007). The entries on topics ranging from Precambrian tectonics to the environmental impacts of modern urbanism are written by leading scholars and provide valuable overviews and bibliographies.

3. This discussion is based on P. Miloslavich et al., "Marine Biodiversity in the Caribbean: Regional Estimates and Distribution Patterns," *PLoS One* 5, no. 8 (2010): 1–25; "Marine Biodiversity in the Atlantic and Pacific Coasts of South America: Knowledge and Gaps," *PLoS One* 6, no. 1 (2011): 1–43. See also M. Spalding et al., "Marine Ecoregions of the World: A Bioregionalization of Coastal and Shelf Areas," *BioScience* 57, no. 7 (2007): 573–583.

4. For an excellent technical review of data about El Niño events, see C. Wang and P. Fiedler, "ENSO Variability and the Eastern Tropical Pacific: A Review," *Progress in Oceanography* 69 (2006): 239–266. For information on the impacts of the 1997–98 El Niño, see *El Niño Update* (Paris: World Meteorological Association, 1998), at http://www.wmo.int/pages/prog/wcp/wcasp/enso_background.html (accessed May 5, 2014). For the consequences of the 1997–98 El Niño along the Peruvian coast, see G. Sanchez, R. Calienes, and S. Zuta, *The 1997–98 El Niño and Its Effects on the Coastal Marine Ecosystem off Peru*, California Cooperative Oceanic Fisheries Institute Report 41 (2000): 62–86, at http://www.calcofi.org/publications/calcofireports/v41/Vol_41_Sanchez_etal.pdf (accessed February 28, 2014).

5. For an engaging overview, see B. Fagan, *Floods, Famines, and Emperors: El Niño and the Fate of Civilizations* (New York: Basic Books, 1999). The impacts of El Niños on prehispanic America are discussed in D. Sandweiss and J. Quilter, eds., *El Niño, Catastrophism, and Culture Change in Ancient America* (Washington, DC: Dumbarton Oaks, 2008). For historic data on El Niño events, see C. Caviedes, *El Niño in History: Storming through the Ages* (Gainesville: University Press of Florida, 2001); A. Hocquenhem and L. Ortlieb, "Eventos El Niño y lluvias anormales en la costa del Peru: Siglos XVI–XIX," *Bulletin de l'Institut Français d'Etudes Andines* 21, no. 1 (1982): 197–278; L. Ortlieb and J. Macharé, "Former El Niño Events: Records from Western South America," *Global and Planetary Change* 7 (1993): 181–202. For discussions of prehistoric occurrences of ENSO events, see D. Keefer, M. Moseley, and S. de France, "A 38,000-Year Record of Floods and Debris Flows in the Ilo Region of Southern Peru and Its Relation to El Niño Events and Great Earthquakes," *Palaeogeography, Palaeoclimatology, Palaeoecology* 194 (2003): 41–77; D. Sandweiss, K. Maasch, R. Burger, J. Richardson III, H. Rollins, and A. Clement, "Variation in Holocene El Niño Frequencies: Climate Records and Cultural Consequences in Ancient Peru," *Geology* 29, no. 7 (2001): 603–606; and the review article by M. Van Buren, "The Archaeology of El Niño Events and Other 'Natural' Disasters," *Journal of Archaeological Method and Theory* 8, no. 2 (2001): 129–149.

6. C. Moy, G. Seltzer, D. Rodbell, and D. Anderson, "Variability of El Niño/Southern Oscillation Activity at Millennial Timescales during the Holocene Epoch," *Nature* 420 (November 2002): 162–165.

7. For a concise summary, see A. Koutavas, P. de Menocal, and J. Lynch-Steiglitz, "Holocene Trends in Tropical Pacific Sea Surface Temperatures and the El Niño–Southern Oscillation," *PAGES News* 14, no. 3 (2006): 22–23, at https://sites.google.com/site/athankoutavas/publications (accessed February 28, 2014).

8. G. Haug, K. Hughen, D. Sigman, L. Peterson, and U. Röhl, "Southward Migration of the Intertropical Convergence Zone through the Holocene," *Science* 209 (August 2001): 1304–1308; R. Nieto, D. Gallego, R. Trigo, P. Ribera, and L. Gimeno, "Dynamic Identification of Moisture Sources in the Orinoco Basin in Equatorial South America," *Hydrological Sciences Journal des Sciences Hydrologiques* 53, no. 3 (June 2008): 602–617, at http://194.117.7.100/Ricardo/Nieto_2008_HSJ.pdf (accessed February 28, 2014).

9. The following is based on J. Zeidler and J. Isaacson, "Settlement Process and Historical Contingency in the Western Ecuadorian Formative," in *The Archaeology of Formative Ecuador*, ed. J. Raymond and R. Burger (Washington, DC: Dumbarton Oaks, 2003), 69–123.

10. M. Binford, A. Kolata, M. Brenner, J. Janusek, M. Seddon, M. Abbot, and J. Curtis, "Climate Variation and the Rise and Fall of an Andean Civilization," *Quaternary Research* 47 (1997): 235–248; M. Brenner, D. Hodell, J. Curtis, M. Rosenmeier, M. Binford, and M. Abbott, "Abrupt Climate Change and Pre-Columbian Cultural Collapse," in *Interhemispheric Climate Linkages*, ed. V. Markgraf (New York: Academic Press, 2001), 87–103. See also D. Sandweiss, K. Maasch, and D. Anderson, "Transitions in the Mid-Holocene," *Science* 283 (January 1999): 499–500. Also see discussion and literature cited in M. Van Buren, "The Archaeology of El Niño," and J. Moore, "Cul-

tural Responses to Environmental Catastrophes: Post–El Niño Subsistence on the Prehistoric North Coast of Peru," *Latin American Antiquity* 2 (1991): 27–47.

11. These long-term fluctuations in global orbits and climate were proposed by the astronomer Milutin Milankovitch. For a discussion of the key elements in the Milankovitch theory, see J. Hays, J. Imbrie, and N. Shackleton, "Variations in the Earth's Orbit: Pacemaker of the Ice Ages," *Science* 194, no. 4270 (1976): 1121–1132; A. Berger, "Milankovitch Theory and Climate," *Reviews of Geophysics* 26, no. 4 (1988): 624–657.

12. L. Peterson and G. Haug, "Variability in the Mean Latitude of the Atlantic Intertropical Convergence Zone as Recorded by Riverine Input of Sediments to the Cariaco Basin (Venezuela)," *Palaeogeography, Palaeoclimatology, Palaeoecology* 234 (2006): 97–113; see also Haug et al., "Southward Migration of the Intertropical Convergence Zone."

13. J. Curtis, M. Brenner, and D. Hodell, "Climate Change in the Lake Valencia Basin, Venezuela, ~12,600 yr BP to Present," *The Holocene* 9, no. 5 (1999): 609–619.

14. N. Stansell, M. Abbott, V. Rull, D. Rodbell, M. Bezada, and E. Montoya, "Abrupt Younger Dryas Cooling in the Northern Tropics Recorded in Lake Sediments from the Venezuelan Andes," *Earth and Planetary Science Letters* 293 (2010): 154–163.

15. L. G. Thompson, E. Mosley-Thompson, J. F. Bolzan, and B. R. Koci, "A 1500-Year Record of Tropical Precipitation in Ice Cores from the Quelccaya Ice Cap, Peru," *Science* 229 (September 1985): 971–973.

16. L. G. Thompson, E. Mosley-Thompson, W. Dansgaard, and P. M. Grootes, "The Little Ice Age as Recorded in the Stratigraphy of the Tropical Quelccaya Ice Cap," *Science* 234 (October 1986): 361–364. For an overview, see B. Fagan, *The Little Ice Age: How Climate Made History, 1300–1850* (New York: Basic Books, 2000).

17. I. Shimada, C. Schaaf, L. Thompson, and E. Mosley-Thompson, "Cultural Impacts of Severe Droughts in the Prehistoric Andes: Application of a 1,500-Year Ice Core Precipitation," *World Archaeology* 22, no. 3 (1991): 247–270.

18. L. Thompson, E. Mosley-Thompson, and K. Henderson, "Ice-Core Palaeoclimate Records in Tropical South America since the Last Glacial Maximum," *Quaternary Science* 15, no. 4 (2000): 377–394. For an overview of these and other data from the Andes, see F. Vimeux, P. Ginot, M. Schwikowski, M. Vuille, G. Hoffman, L. Thompson, and U. Shotterer, "Climate Variability during the Last 1000 Years Inferred from Andean Ice Cores: A Review of Methodology and Recent Results," *Paleogeography, Paleoclimatology, Paleoecology* 281 (2009): 229–241.

19. J. Quade, J. Rech, J. Betancourt, C. Latorre, B. Quade, K. Rylander, and T. Fisher, "Paleowetlands and Regional Climate Change in the Central Atacama Desert, Northern Chile," *Quaternary Research* 69 (2008): 343–360.

20. L. Thompson, E. Mosley-Thompson, H. Brecher, M. Davis, B. León, D. Les, P. Lin, T. Mashiotta, and K. Mountain, "Abrupt Tropical Climate Change: Past and Present," *Proceedings of the National Academy of Sciences of the United States of America* 103, no. 28 (July 2006): 10536–10543.

21. A. Buffen, L. Thompson, E. Mosley-Thompson, and K. Huh, "Recently Exposed Vegetation Reveals Holocene Changes in the Extent of the Quelccaya Ice Cap, Peru," *Quaternary Research* 72 (2009): 157–163.

22. Thompson, Thompson, and Henderson, "Ice-Core Palaeoclimate Records," 392.

23. P. Colinvaux, P. E. De Oliveira, and M. Bush, "Amazonian and Neotropical Plant Communities on Glacial Time-Scales: The Failure of the Aridity and Refuge Hypotheses," *Quaternary Science Reviews* 19 (2000): 142.

24. M. Bush, W. Gosling, and P. Colinvaux, "Climate Change in the Lowlands of the Amazon Basin," in *Tropical Rainforest Responses to Climate Change*, ed. M. Bush and J. Flenley (New York: SpringerLink, 2007), 60.

25. P. Colinvaux, M. Bush, M. Steinitz-Kannan, and M. Miller, "Glacial and Postglacial Pollen Records from the Ecuadorian Andes and Amazon," *Quaternary Research* 48 (1997): 69–78; M. Bush, B. Hansen, D. Rodbell, G. Seltzer, K. Young, B. León, M. Abbott, M. Silman, and W. Gosling, "A 17,000-Year History of Andean Climate and Vegetation Change from Laguna de Chochos, Peru," *Journal of Quaternary Sciences* 20 (2005): 703–714; P. Colinvaux, M. Frost, K. Liu, and M. Steinitz-Kannan, "Three Pollen Diagrams of Forest Disturbance in the Western Amazon Basin," *Review of Palaeobotany and Palynology* 55 (1988): 73–81; B. Hansen and D. Rodbell, "A Late-Glacial/Holocene Pollen Record from the Eastern Andes of Northern Peru," *Quaternary Research* 44 (1995): 216–227; B. Hansen, D. Rodbell, G. O. Seltzer, B. Leon, K. R. Young, and M. Abbott, "Late-Glacial and Holocene Vegetation History from Two Sides in the Western Cordillera of Southwestern Ecuador," *Palaeogeography, Palaeoclimatology, Palaeoecology* 194 (2003): 79–108.

26. For an example, see C. Brunschön, T. Haberzettl, and H. Behling, "High-Resolution Studies on Vegetation Succession, Hydrological Variations, Anthropogenic Impact and Genesis of a Subrecent Lake in Southern Ecuador," *Vegetation History and Archaeobotany* 19 (2010): 191–206.

27. M. Bush, J. Hanselman, and H. Hooghiemstra, "Andean Montane Forests and Climate History," in *Tropical Rainforest Responses to Climate Change*, ed. M. Bush and J. Flenley (New York: SpringerLink, 2007), 43–44.

28. C. Brunschön and H. Behling, "Late Quaternary Vegetation, Fire and Climate History Reconstructed from Two Cores at Cerro Toledo, Podocarpus National Park, Southeastern Ecuadorian Andes," *Quaternary Research* 72 (2009): 388–399; H. Niemann, T. Haberzettl, and H. Behling, "Holocene Climate Variability and Vegetation Dynamics Inferred from the (11,700 cal. yr BP) Laguna Rabadilla de Vaca Sediment Record, Southeastern Ecuadorian Andes," *The Holocene* 19, no. 2 (2009): 307–316; H. Neiman, "Late Quaternary Vegetation, Climate and Fire Dynamics in the Podocarpus National Park Region, Southeastern Ecuadorian Andes" (PhD diss., Georg-August-Universität Göttingen, 2008); H. Niemann and H. Behling, "Late Holocene Environmental Change and Human Impact Inferred from Three Soil Monoliths and the Laguna Zurita Multi-Proxi Record in the Southeastern Ecuadorian Andes," *Vegetation History and Archaeobotany* 19 (2010): 1–15; see also Moy et al., "Variability of El Niño."

29. M. Bush and P. Colinvaux, "A 7000-Year Pollen Record from the Amazon Lowlands," *Vegetatio* 76, no. 3 (1988): 141–154.

30. M. Bush, M. Miller, P. De Oliveira, and P. Colinvaux, "Two Histories of Environmental Change and Human Disturbance in Eastern Lowland Amazonia," *The Holocene* 10, no. 5 (2000): 543–553.

31. For a discussion from western Amazonia, see M. Bush, M. Silman, and C. Listopad, "A Regional Study of Holocene Climate Change and Human Occupation in Peruvian Amazonia," *Journal of Biogeography* 34 (2007): 1352.

32. M. Cohen, H. Behling, R. Lara, C. Smith, H. Soares Matos, and V. Vedel, "Impact of Sea-Level and Climatic Changes on the Amazon Coastal Wetlands during the Late Holocene," *Vegetation History and Archaeobotany* 18 (2009): 425–439.

33. B. Meggers, "Vegetational Fluctuation and Prehistoric Cultural Adaptation in Amazonia: Some Tentative Correlations," *World Archaeology* 8, no. 3 (1977): 287–303; B. Meggers, "Climatic Oscillation as a Factor in the Prehistory of Amazonia," *American Antiquity* 44, no. 2 (1979): 252–266.

34. Bush, Gosling, and Colinvaux, "Climate Change in the Lowlands," 57, 67.

35. This section is based on J. Iriarte, "Vegetation and Climate Change since 14,810 14C yr BP in Southeastern Uruguay and Implications for the Rise of Early Formative Societies," *Quaternary Research* 65 (2006): 20–32.

36. M. Wille and F. Schäbitz, "Late-Glacial and Holocene Climate Dynamics at the Steppe/Forest Ecotone in Southernmost Patagonia, Argentina: The Pollen Record from a Fen near Brazo Sur, Lago Argentino," *Vegetation History and Archaeobotany* 18 (2009): 225–234.

37. M. Fesq-Martin, A. Friedmann, M. Peters, J. Behrmann, and R. Kilian, "Late-Glacial and Holocene Vegetation History of the Magellanic Rain Forest in Southwestern Patagonia, Chile," *Vegetation History and Archaeobotany* 13 (2004): 249–255.

Figure 3.1 Selknam band on a beach in Tierra del Fuego, 1930s

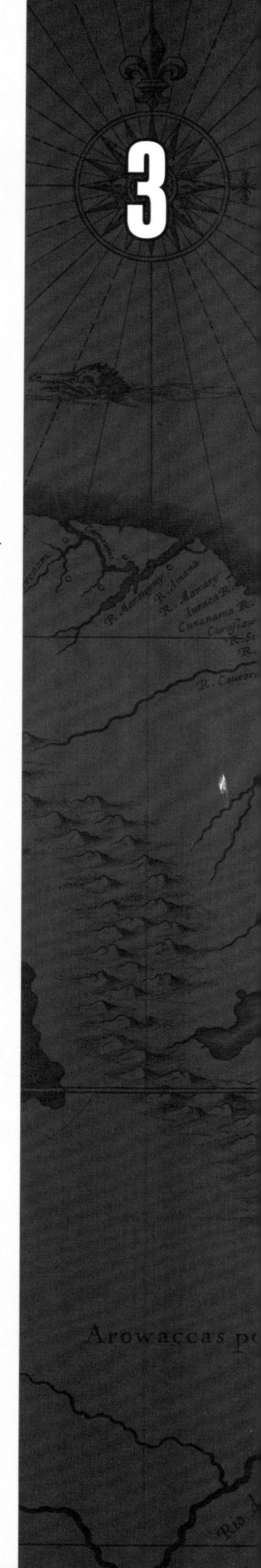

The Last Ancient Homeland

The Peopling of South America

10.5876_9781607323334.c003

> Whence have these people come? Have they remained in the same state since the creation of the world? What could have tempted a tribe of men leaving the fine regions of the North. . . to enter upon one of the most inhospitable countries in the world?
>
> —*Charles Darwin on the inhabitants of Tierra del Fuego*

In 1927, when a team of excavators at a site near **Folsom**, New Mexico, discovered an in situ projectile point between the ribs of an extinct Pleistocene species of American buffalo (*Bison antiquus*), the implication was obvious: humans had arrived in the Americas thousands of years ago.[1] The Folsom discovery led to specific inferences (figure 3.2).

First, the projectile point was obviously an *artifact*: the elegant triangular point exhibited a complex pattern of flake removal and shaping, dominated by the longitudinal channel or flute, all evidence of human action. Natural processes could not have produced such an object. Second, the Folsom site was obviously *old*, although its age was uncertain. The ancient bison was one of the numerous Ice Age species that became extinct at the end of the Pleistocene. The date of the end of the Pleistocene was a matter of debate in the 1920s, but the rib bones were clearly from an ancient animal. Finally, the artifact and the Pleistocene bison were in *association*, the Folsom point literally stuck between the animals ribs. In these ways, the Folsom site met three standard criteria for assessing claims for early antiquity of archaeological sites:

- Is it really a site? (Are the artifacts and features in the site unambiguously products of human action?)
- Is the date accurate? (Is the estimate of the site's age accurate and relatively precise?)
- Are the site and the date in association? (Is it incontrovertible that the date actually establishes the antiquity of the site rather than of some other natural processes?)

The discoveries at Folsom were followed by excavations near Clovis, New Mexico, in 1933, where larger projectile points were found with mammoth bones.

The Pleistocene megafauna were killed and butchered in a place known as **Blackwater Draw**. The finds at Blackwater Draw were extremely significant because the earliest Clovis materials were overlain by later deposits

Figure 3.2 Folsom projectile point in situ between ribs of *Bison antiquus*

containing Folsom points and later Paleoindian projectile point styles, providing an ancient cultural sequence.[2] Visited and validated by a group of archaeologists, the Clovis discoveries satisfied the same criteria as the Folsom discoveries: the projectile points were obviously artifacts in association with extinct Pleistocene megafauna and thus of considerable antiquity.

But exactly "how old" was unknown. Before the invention of radiocarbon dating by Willard Libby in the late 1940s and its first applications to archaeological sites in the 1950s, it was impossible to establish the absolute dates of early archaeological sites. The discovery of Clovis points with the remains of mammoths suggested a Pleistocene date, but only with the development of C14 dating could the precise antiquity of Clovis sites be established.

The "Clovis First" Hypothesis

By the early 1960s a number of Paleoindian sites had been radiocarbon-dated, and the results of that research were summarized in a 1964 article in *Science* magazine by the geoarchaeologist **C. Vance Haynes Jr**. In an article with the modest and unassuming title "Fluted Projectile Points: Their Age and Dispersion," Haynes proposed a bold model regarding the timing and process of the peopling of the Americas, ideas that would dominate archaeological thinking for much of the next four decades. Haynes had collected a number of radiocarbon samples, including from the Clovis and Folsom strata at Blackwater Draw Locality 1, and obtained reliable organic samples from excavators working at other sites, resulting in dates from five deposits with in situ Clovis points and from five deposits with Folsom points. After scrutinizing the stratigraphic contexts of the finds and eliminating possible sources of contamination and other errors, Haynes concluded: "From the radiocarbon evidence it appears . . . that the Folsom complex, representing bison hunters, has a relatively short time span of 1000 years between 10,000 and 11,000 years ago, and the Llano complex [i.e., Clovis], representing mammoth hunters, a span of 500 years between 11,000 and 11,500 years ago. The transition from Clovis points to Folsom points occurred during a very short period, there being few known examples that might be considered transitional."[3]

But Haynes's article was about more than simply the ages of two styles of spear points. First, Haynes observed that at each of the sites with Clovis points, there were no earlier stone tools, no crude or fumbling antecedents to Clovis points. The earliest North American projectile points were well-made and effective. While Haynes acknowledged the possibility that Siberian and Alaskan sites contained some potentially related forms, within most of North America the fluted points lacked any "indisputable progenitor." The Clovis technology appeared complete and competent.

Further, Haynes argued that Clovis points occurred across much of the southern half of North America (essentially the lower forty-eight states) at circa 11,300 BP, leading him to query, why this apparently sudden appearance? At this point in his research, Haynes did not assume that there were no North America sites earlier than Clovis but rather that there were no sites clearly antecedent to the widespread and rapid diffusion of Clovis technology. This, Haynes suggested, could be explained by factors linked to climate change during the later stages of the Ice Age.

Approximately 12,000 years ago, two major climatic factors intersected—lower sea levels and a retraction of continental glaciers (discussed in chapter 2). On the one hand, sea level was about 55 m (180 ft) lower than today. (It had been even lower about 30,000–19,000 years ago when thick glaciers covered northern Eurasia and North America and sea level was 120–130 m, roughly 400 ft, lower

Figure 3.3 Gateway to the Americas, Bering Land Bridge, National Preserve, Alaska

than at present.) During the Last Glacial Maximum, Siberia and Alaska were joined by the land bridge of **Beringia**, but the enormous glaciers presented a frigid barrier to human migration (figure 3.3).

All that changed around 12,000 years ago, when a gradually warming Earth created an **ice-free corridor** between the two major glacial systems that covered much of North America. Sea level was still low enough to allow overland travel between Eurasia and North America, but a potential route opened across North America that remained a frigid tundra but was not a frozen wasteland. Connecting Alaska, the northern Plains, and the Great Lakes region, this zone formed a conduit for humans to occupy the Americas.

The creation of this ice-free corridor, Haynes argued, explained the rapid appearance of humans using Clovis points. After moving south, people using fluted points could rapidly expand as they pursued big game—first mammoths and then ancient bison. Haynes noted that the change from Clovis to Folsom technologies was associated with the extinction of mammoths, although whether humans hunted mammoths to extinction was a matter of debate. Yet, Haynes argued that Clovis points appeared rapidly across North America without technological antecedents and that "the paucity of radiocarbon-dated sites older than 11,500 years suggests a sparse population at best." If sites earlier than Clovis were to be discovered, Haynes concluded that archaeologists "must pay closer attention to stratigraphic detail if we are to make the fullest use of radiocarbon dating."[4]

Haynes's article became the foundation of the **Clovis first hypothesis**. In essence, it argued that humans using Clovis points were the first people to inhabit North America and that they did so after circa 11,500 years ago. As tool-using predators focused on big game, humans using fluted point technology could rapidly expand throughout the Americas (figure 3.2). The archaeologist **Paul S. Martin** would subsequently argue that the extinction of mammoths and ancient bison was caused by Clovis and Folsom hunters, an idea known as the **Pleistocene overkill hypothesis**, but that issue is ancillary to Haynes's basic point.[5] The central issue from Haynes article was this: Clovis people were the First Americans.

The development of C14 dating revolutionized archaeology and contributed to dramatic reassessments of human prehistory. Yet, in North America the Clovis first hypothesis remained remarkably solid. A number of sites were suggested as being older than Clovis but failed to pass critical scrutiny. As the archaeologist **David Meltzer** has written, "What we can expect—demand, even—of a pre-Clovis site are 1) undeniable traces of humans, either their artifacts or skeletal remains, in 2) undisturbed geological deposits in proper stratigraphic position, which are 3) accompanied by indisputable radiometric ages (speared bison no longer suffice)."[6] These three criteria were essential.

Time after time, sites thought to be pre-Clovis sites failed to meet these criteria—some of them spectacularly so. One of the best-known failures was at the **Calico "site"** in southeastern California.

The Calico research was directed by **Ruth Simpson** of the San Bernardino County Museum, but the project relied on the support of paleoanthropologist **Louis Leakey**, at the height of his fame for his discoveries at Olduvai Gorge.[7] The location was chosen by Simpson and Leakey in 1963, based on Leakey's conclusion that fractured stones recovered from a backhoe trench were artifacts. Leakey obtained funding from the National Geographic Society, a major supporter of his Olduvai research. Simpson and Leakey directed excavations into the alluvial fan, recovering 170 items "unquestionably the result of human activity" and several hundred other objects "as possibly of human workmanship." Based on the geology at Calico, they estimated that the materials had "a probable age of between 50,000 and 80,000 years."

Even Leakey's wife, Mary, was unconvinced by these claims, and she took the rather extraordinary measure of urging the National Geographic Society to withdraw funding from the Calico project. Not surprisingly, C. Vance Haynes Jr. was equally unimpressed.

In a 1969 article titled "The Earliest Americans," Haynes restated his earlier hypothesis linking the expansion of humans using fluted points and the appearance of the ice-free corridor. Haynes dismissed the Calico "artifacts" as the products of natural processes and wishful thinking. Having visited Calico, Haynes argued that the entire gravel deposit contained chert gravels and igneous cobbles that would have been water-rolled, naturally producing flake scars. This natural process intersected with self-delusion, Haynes wrote, "in view of the fact that each 'artifact' has been selected from literally hundreds or thousands of individual pieces of chert." Haynes's contempt for the Calico site was obvious.[8]

In the conclusion of his article, Haynes clearly stated the criteria for discovering sites associated with the First Americans: "For establishing man's presence, the minimum requirements met for the Folsom site still apply for future excavations.

The primary requirement is a human skeleton, or an assemblage of artifacts that are clearly the work of man. Next, this evidence must lie in situ within undisturbed geological deposits in order to clearly demonstrate the primary association of artifacts with stratigraphy. Lastly, the minimum age of the site must be demonstrable by primary association with fossils of known age or with material suitable for reliable isotopic age dating."[9]

Clovis and Folsom sites met these criteria. Other sites thought to be older did not or were met with skepticism. Not all the alleged pre-Clovis sites were as implausible as Calico, but they all had skeptics. "Ambiguous artifacts, scrambled stratigraphy, dubious dates" is how David Meltzer summarized the situation. "Could the search for pre-Clovis be doomed to failure simply because there is no pre-Clovis?"[10]

Paleoindians in South America

The peopling of South America has been approached from a pan-hemispheric perspective, which is not surprising given that South America was viewed as settled by the descendants of Paleoindians who had previously migrated across Beringia into North America and moved south. Further, the archaeological evidence of the earliest South American sites was subjected to similar scrutiny as that of their North American counterparts (figure 3.4).

In 1934 the archaeologist **Junius Bird**, accompanied by his wife and colleague, **Margaret Bird**, searched for evidence of early human settlements in the southernmost tip of South America, in Tierra del Fuego (figure 3.5).[11]

The Birds conducted one of the most intrepid expeditions in the history of archaeology. For a period of thirty-two months between 1934 and 1937, they traveled by small boat and Model T searching for archaeological sites along the Straits of Magellan. Often living in the caves where prehistoric people had camped or sleeping on rocky beaches under their overturned dinghy, the Birds discovered an initial cultural sequence for this remote, wind-swept, archaeologically unknown region.

They found a series of projectile points, the earliest of which had a distinctive expanding base, a type that became known as "**fishtail**" or **Fell's Cave** points, named after the site where it was discovered (figure 3.6). These artifacts were discovered under a layer of large stones, sealed beneath boulders and rocks. Amazingly, the artifacts were found with the bones of guanaco, ancient horse, and extinct ground sloth.

In a brief article summarizing these discoveries, Junius Bird carefully distinguished between the layers above and below the rock-fall stratum: the lower and most ancient levels at Fell's Cave had horse bones, the upper levels did not. Similarly, Bird observed that while other caves' deposits contained the unburned or unbroken bones of ground sloth, Fell's Cave was the only one to have burned and butchered sloth bones together with artifacts. The other caves may have been sloth dens, and the bones were naturally deposited. But Fell's Cave, Bird argued, was an archaeological site where indisputably human-made objects existed in association with Pleistocene megafauna.

Figure 3.4 Locations of sites discussed in this chapter

Yet, three factors meant that Fell's Cave did not become South America's equivalent of Blackwater Draw. First, given the remoteness of the site, a group of archaeologists could not travel to Tierra del Fuego and independently confirm Bird's discovery, as at the Clovis sites in the United States. Second, there was the possibility that sloth and horse bones had been carried into the cave by predators

Figure 3.5 Fell's Cave, Chile

and that the early people of Tierra del Fuego simply camped on top of those layers (much in the way the Birds had pitched their tents inside caves on top of earlier archaeological deposits). None of the sloth bones had a spear point stuck into them. Finally, in 1938, C14 dating had not been invented.

Excavations at the site of **Taima-Taima**, Venezuela, challenged—but did not overturn—the Clovis first model. The site was first identified from surface artifacts recovered by **José Maria Cruxent** (1911–2005), a Spaniard who sought refuge in Venezuela in the aftermath of the Spanish Civil War. Cruxent was a major force in establishing archaeological investigations and scientific institutions in Venezuela and collaborated with numerous international researchers. The artifacts he discovered included long, lanceolate projectile points, relatively thick in cross-section and lacking the distinctive fluting of Clovis points.[12] Beginning in 1956, Cruxent had found points and other artifacts at a site near the village of El Jobo, recovering dozens of projectile points as well as scrapers and flake tools, but also modern glass, pottery, and other recent debris.[13]

The northern coast of Venezuela is an arid region covered with cactus and acacia trees; the landscape is sparsely pocked by spring-fed water holes. Cruxent excavated at the spring-fed bog at Muaco, which he argued had attracted animals and humans since the Pleistocene.[14] Excavating a trench 20 m × 12 m (65.6 ft × 39 ft) to a depth of 2.5 m (8 ft), Cruxent and his team uncovered large quantities of bones from mastodon, *Megatherium* (an elephant-sized ground sloth), and *Glyptodon* (a gigantic armadillo)—some of them cut, burned, and broken—in addition to an El Jobo point found "in situ among the animal bones," a scraper, and hammerstones but also pieces of bottle glass and other modern garbage. Radiocarbon assays run on the pieces of burned bones dated to 16, 375 ± 400 BP and 14,300 ± 500 BP—

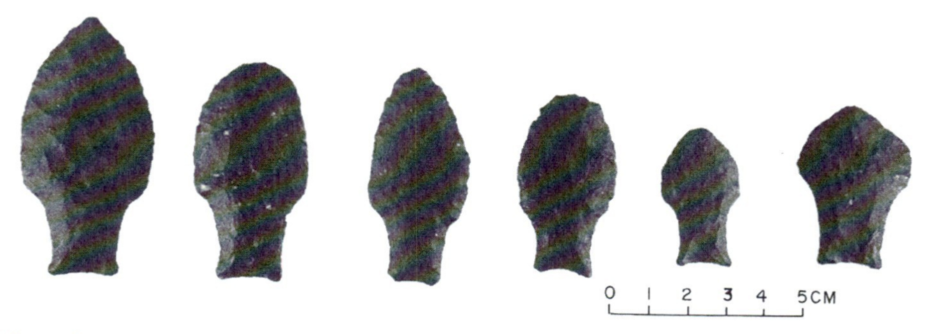

Figure 3.6 "Fishtail" projectile points from Fell's Cave

dates that might be accurate for the Pleistocene fauna but did not directly establish the antiquity of the El Jobo points.

In 1976 Cruxent invited the Canadian archaeologists Alan Bryan and Ruth Gruhn to excavate at Taima-Taima "to confirm the association of man with extinct animals and to clarify stratigraphy and dating."[15] The remains of a juvenile mastodon had been butchered, leaving cut marks on the left humerus. The midsection of an El Jobo projectile point was stuck in the mastodon's pelvis, a flake tool was next to the animal's forelimb, and a pointed cobblestone was jammed among the bones. The mastodon bones and artifacts were found on top of a natural limestone surface and covered with an undisturbed layer of gray sandy clay. Four radiocarbon dates from twigs found near the animal—thought to be the stomach contents of the mastodon's last meal—were evaluated by four different laboratories, with results ranging from 12,980 ± 85 BP to 14,200 ± 300 BP. Bryan and colleagues wrote, "The minimum radiocarbon age of the El Jobo mastodon kill is thus 13,000 years. The field data from Taima-Taima demonstrate that a big-game hunting complex of a completely different technological tradition existed in northern Venezuela at least a millennium and [a] half earlier than the well-known Clovis complex of North America."[16] The Clovis model, the excavators claimed, "is thereby refuted by field evidence."

One would think that would have settled the matter. It did not. Questions persisted about the actual association among bones, tools, and radiocarbon samples, suspicions about possible contaminations were raised, and ultimately the El Jobo discoveries did not result in the rejection of the Clovis first model.[17]

Much in the same way pre-Clovis sites in North America had been proposed, evaluated, and dismissed, the evidence for Pleistocene sites in South America was similarly discounted despite the protests of the sites' discoverers and defenders. As in North America, these putative early sites in South America failed to meet one or more of the three criteria: Is it a site? Is the date good? Are the site and date really associated?

For example, in the late 1960s the irrepressible American archaeologist **Richard Stockton "Scotty" MacNeish** (1918–2001), who had successfully directed a transformative research project in the Tehuacan Valley of central Mexico, turned his attention to the search for pre-Clovis humans in the Ayacucho region of the central Peruvian Andes. The original research project, focused on the development of human environmental adaptations, dramatically shifted its focus when MacNeish and his crew discovered at **Pikimachay Cave** a stratigraphic sequence dating to between 11,000 and 25,000 years ago, including a date of "17,650 B.C. +/–3000" [*sic*] on a sloth vertebra, associated with crude pebble and flake tools that MacNeish acknowledged were "extremely crude with the majority made from volcanic tufa that does not show evidence of man's work very clearly." Subsequent analysis indicated that the stone tools were naturally occurring flakes and battered pebbles, and the ground sloth remains were probably the unmodified remains of the naturally denning animals.[18] Pikimachay failed to meet the criteria: Is it a site? Is the date good? Are the site and date really associated?

Claims for early antiquity at the Brazilian cave site at Toca do Boqueirio da **Pedra Furada** received a similarly skeptical response.[19] A large cave site located in the state of Piaui in northeastern Brazil, the cave at Pedra Furada is one of hundreds of rock shelters found in the region's sedimentary formations. Beginning in the late 1970s, a team of French and Brazilian archaeologists led by **Niède Guidon** excavated a large area of a deep cave site with a sequence that stretched back from deposits a few thousand years old to layers that produced Pleistocene dates in excess of 32,000 years. As Guidon was later noted somewhat testily, none of the layers after circa 10,000 BP received adverse comment, but the earlier layers were met with howls of disbelief.

The skepticism was provoked for several reasons. First, the artifacts associated with the earliest dates were unconvincing. The objects were cobble and flake "tools" that could have been created when natural nodules fell from the cave's upper conglomerate strata and fractured on impact. Guidon's response was that the flake cobbles were found deep within the cave and thus had been transported there by ancient humans, but this response failed to quiet critics. Second, dating techniques applied to various portions of Pedra Furada consistently produced inconsistent results. A series of possible hearths produced inconsistent dates or were challenged as natural fires. Several pictographs at Pedra Furada and other sites, originally claimed to be as old as 35,000 BP, were re-dated at Guidon's request; the new analysis produced dates of less than 2,000 years. At Pedra Furada, bold assertions were followed by ambiguous reassessments. The site failed to meet the criteria.

By the early 1990s, the general assessment of purported pre-Clovis sites in both Americas was that the artifacts were ambiguous, the dates were problematic, or the associations were uncertain. In contrast, the antiquity and cultural reality of Clovis seemed clear: these were obviously artifacts, often found in association with extinct Pleistocene fauna, and consistently dated to after 12,000 BP. Moving through the ice-free corridor and across central North America in 11,500 BP, the descendents of these Paleoindian explorers moved into the southern reaches of South America at about 10,000 years ago and thereafter.

Or at least that is what we once thought.

Figure 3.7 A willow-leaf–shaped projectile point from Monte Verde, Chile

Monte Verde, Chile: New Discoveries and Perspectives

In the late 1970s the American archaeologist **Tom Dillehay** was teaching at Chile's Universidad Austral in Valdivia when he learned about a site exposed in a creek-side bog at a place called **Monte Verde**. Dillehay periodically dug at the site between 1977 and 1981, excavating about 120 square meters (approximately 1,292 ft^2) of the site in these early field seasons. The results were surprising and controversial (figure 3.7).

Dillehay found the remains of several mastodons in association with objects that were undoubtedly artifacts: willow-leaf–shaped projectile points, bola or sling stones with pecked grooves around their centers, two scrapers on wooden hafts, other fragments of worked wood, a "wishbone"-shaped feature of compacted gravel, sand, and branches, and a log with a groove cut down its length (figure 3.8).

Other cut bone and worked pebble tools completed the assemblage discovered in these early excavations at Monte Verde. The most surprising data were the radiocarbon dates from the cultural levels: 12,350 ± 200 BP and 13,030 ± 130 BP (uncalibrated). The cultural layers were capped by natural strata that were somewhat confusingly dated to between 11,155 ± 130 BP and 13,965 ± 250 BP (the latter date was actually older than the cultural layers below it). However, the overall pattern of radiocarbon dates led Dillehay and his colleagues to suggest that the cultural layers at Monte Verde were occupied "no less than 12,000 years ago and probably no more than 14,000 years ago."[20]

Monte Verde was older than Clovis. Or was it?

Over the next decade, Dillehay and his colleagues presented a number of relatively brief articles about their finds at Monte Verde as they also prepared a meticulous monograph documenting the geological setting, archaeological materials, and faunal and botanical materials they recovered from the site.[21] In addition, they announced the discovery of even earlier radiocarbon dates from strata below the 12,000–14,000-year-old levels, dates in excess of 33,000 BP.[22]

Figure 3.8 "Wishbone"-shaped feature at Monte Verde, Chile

Rather predictably, this triggered profound skepticism among many archaeologists, particularly the advocates of the Clovis first model. With the announcement of the 33,000 BP date, Monte Verde was placed in the same dubious category as Pedra Furada. A handful of archaeologists visited Monte Verde during the excavations, including Junius Bird, who was skeptical. Scholarly disagreements flared into heated personal attacks.[23]

Although there were personal reasons for this debate, the controversy continued for two reasons: (1) the artifact assemblage could not be dismissed as the result of natural processes (as at Calico and Pedra Furada), and (2) the implications of the 12,000–14,000 BP dates were enormous even if the 30,000 BP date was discounted.

This controversy moved toward resolution in 1997, when a group of archaeologists traveled to Chile to visit and "verify" the Monte Verde site. The group of Paleoindian specialists included archaeologists who had advocated for the existence of pre-Clovis sites in the Americas and archaeologists who were among the most consistent critics of the pre-Clovis hypothesis, including C. Vance Haynes Jr. Before traveling to Chile, the group was provided with copies of Dillehay's monograph on Monte Verde and studied collections from Monte Verde in the United States.

The target of evaluation was the upper layer (known as Monte Verde II) that had been dated to 12,000–14,000 years old. In a brief summary of their conclusions, the scholars wrote: "Although the cultural evidence is largely based on nonlithic artifacts, architectural remains, context and spatial patterns, the more traditional evidence—notably, stone tools—is nonetheless present and compelling. After looking at the collections, we have no doubt that there are genuine lithic artifacts on the MV-II surface."[24] The team turned to the stratigraphy at Monte Verde: were the layers in situ, or were they jumbled and disturbed? They wrote, "We were able to examine a number of exposures representative of the stratigraphy encountered at the main site. We saw no evidence of disturbance and no evidence of younger archaeological materials that could have become incorporated into older deposits."[25] Finally, the group looked at the dating of Monte Verde II: the archaeological strata were covered with a layer of ancient peat, which had been dated by seven separate dates to between 10,300 and 12,000 years old. The underlying (and thus older) Monte Verde II layer had been dated by eleven radiocarbon samples to around 12,500 years old. While uncertainty remained about the 33,000 BP dates from the lower levels, the Monte Verde II stratum was determined to be a cultural layer dating to 12,500 years ago.

Although this single report did not result in unanimous acceptance of the antiquity of Monte Verde, it marked a pivotal shift in the evaluation of the pre-Clovis hypothesis.[26] In turn, archaeological opinion began to change about the dynamics of migration into the Americas. Instead of the model that a small initial population of spear-using Paleoindians populated the Americas as they hunted Pleistocene megafauna, the possibility emerged that multiple populations had moved into the New World pursuing different subsistence strategies.

While these reassessments were not solely the product of Dillehay's discoveries, the acceptance of Monte Verde as a legitimate archaeological site was of tremendous importance. As the archaeologists wrote, "While the MV-II occupation is only some 1,000 years older than the generally accepted dates for Clovis, the Monte Verde site has profound implications for our understanding of the peopling of the Americas. Given that Monte Verde is located some 16,000 km (9,936 miles) south of the Bering Land Bridge, the results of the work here imply a fundamentally different history of human colonization of the New World than envisioned by the Clovis-first model and raise intriguing issues of early human adaptations in the Americas."[27]

Many of those issues are being explored today at sites across South America.

A Broadly Populated Continent

A growing number of archaeological sites across South America appear to have been coeval with the North American Clovis sites. In part, this is based on reanalysis and calibration of dates for Clovis sites, which suggest that the sites were several centuries later than previously thought. Archaeologists **Michael Waters** and **Thomas Stafford Jr.** reanalyzed reliable radiocarbon dates for Clovis sites. Using two different calibration curves, they estimate that "Clovis has a maximum possible date range of 13,250 to 12,800 calendar years BP [and] a minimum range . . . [of] 13,125 to 12,925 calendar years BP"—in other words, a duration of 200–450 years between 11,300 and 10,850 BC.[28] When we consider the widespread distribution of Clovis points in North American sites, the rapidity of their diffusion suggests either a quickly expanding population of people with Clovis points or the rapid spread and adoption of the Clovis technology by people already in North

America. (The second hypothesis would have been deemed heretical by most archaeologists two decades ago.)

Further, Waters and Stafford examined radiocarbon dates from four well-dated, unequivocal archaeological sites in southern South America: Fell's Cave in Chile (11,000 ± 170 BP) and the **Cerro Tres Tetas** (10,935 ± 35 BP), **Cuevas Casa del Minero** (10,985 ± 40 BP), and **Piedra Museo** (10,960 ± 45 BP) sites, all in Argentina. These sites are contemporary with Clovis sites in North America.

Other South American sites have similar dates.

On the desert coast of southern Peru, the site of **Quebrada Jaguay 280** was a small fishing community at the very end of the Pleistocene.[29] **Daniel Sandweiss** and colleagues excavated the dense midden of shell, fish bones, and charcoal, obtaining a series of twenty-three radiocarbon dates from between 13,250 and 11,200 calibrated years ago and a slightly later set of seven radiocarbon dates between 11,200 and 10,500 calibrated years ago: again, dates contemporary with North American Clovis sites. Instead of big-game hunters, the occupants of the Quebrada Jaguay collected surf clams and fished for croakers and drums.

Of similar antiquity but a markedly different type of archaeological deposit, the site of **Quebrada Santa Julia**, located on the now-arid coast of central Chile about 200 km (120 miles) north of Santiago, contained the base of a fluted point made from quartz crystal, other stone tools and lithic debitage, the bones of extinct horses and camelids among other animals, and three radiocarbon dates—two from charcoal in a hearth, one from a sharpened wooden artifact—of 11,090 ± 80 BP, 10,920 ± 80 BP, and 11,060 ± 80 BP. This trio of dates, when calibrated, indicates that the site was occupied between 11,400 and 10,930 BC.[30]

Further north in the Atacama Desert, **Martin Grosjean** and colleagues have reported on a relatively shallow open-air site on the eastern edge of the **Salar Punta Negra**, Chile.[31] The surface materials include the distinctive "fishtail" points like those Bird found at Fell's Cave, as well as stemmed (Punta Negra style) and roughly triangular (Tuina style) points, in addition to more than 700 scrapers, knives, and other flake tools. Although none of the projectile points were directly dated, during the excavation of a single shallow test pit, flaked artifacts were found wedged between two peat layers. Radiocarbon dates on the upper peat layer (9230 ± 50 BP) and the lower peat layer (10,470 ± 50 BP) suggest that artifacts were deposited sometime between 10,240–10,400 and 12,130–12,630 calendar years ago—not as old as Clovis, but still a very early date.

Approximately 640 km (400 miles) upstream from the mouth of the Amazon River, the region around Monte Alegre contains an extensive expanse of sandstone formations that rise to more than 300 m (984 ft) above sea level. The Monte Alegre formation contains numerous caves, including the rock shelter, or **Caverna de Pedra Pintada**, studied by **Anna C. Roosevelt** and her colleagues.[32] Named for the numerous pictographs at the site and on surrounding sandstone exposures (figure 3.9), the Caverna de Pedra Pintada is a large cave 15 m × 10 m in area (1,615 ft^2) under a 6.5 m (21 ft)-high ceiling. The shelter is located next to a permanent spring and overlooks the streams and floodplains of the Amazon River, whose main channel is about 10 km (6 miles) away.

Figure 3.9 Anna Roosevelt examining rock art at Monte Alegre, Brazil

Preliminary auger core testing encountered buried early deposits at Caverna de Pedra Pintada. Roosevelt's team excavated eleven test pits in the deepest portions of the deposit down to a maximum depth of 2.5 m (8.2 ft). The excavations exposed a complex stratigraphy with twenty different major layers that could be grouped into four main sets, from most recent to oldest: (1) Holocene/Recent layers that contained pottery, (2) a 30-cm (11.8-inch) layer of sand that contained no cultural materials, (3) an earlier cultural layer 30 cm (11.8 inches) thick that contained Late Pleistocene/Paleoindian cultural materials, and (4) a basal layer of sand and sandstone boulders that contained no cultural materials. A key point was that the Pleistocene layer, according to Roosevelt and colleagues, was sealed between two sandy layers that lacked cultural materials or organic matter that could have been mixed with the Paleoindian layer and contaminated the radiocarbon samples.

The excavators at Caverna de Pedra Pintada recovered 24 formal artifacts and more than 30,000 flakes from the earliest cultural layers, including 4 stemmed projectile points, other biface artifacts, gravers, and flake tools. To cite one example, a bifacially worked piece of chalcedony was found below a stratigraphic layer dated to 10,370 ± 70 BP, approximately cal BC 10,040 to cal BC 10,483, a very early date for human occupation in the Amazon.[33] Even earlier dates on carbonized palm seeds—important plant foods for Amazonian peoples past and present—were recorded at the base of the cave deposit and ranged from 11,145 ± 135 (cal BC 10,044 to 11,414) and 10,875 ± 295 BP (cal BC 10,044 to 11,414), which the excavators claimed marked the arrival of humans in the Lower Amazon.[34] This lowest level of Caverna de Pedra Pintada was contemporary with Clovis sites in North America.

Not surprisingly, there were criticisms of these claims.[35] Once again, C. Vance Haynes Jr. pointedly questioned the provenience and cultural nature of these early dates: for example, Haynes argued that the radiocarbon dates based on palm seeds provided good results and then suggested that the seeds had been moved into the strata by burrowing animals. Another critic argued that once the oldest dates at Caverna de Pedra Pintada were excluded as "outliers," the remaining dates from the different levels postdated Clovis by 1,000 years "and that the earliest Amazonian Paleoindians appear to have been derived from [Clovis], or from still earlier South American cultures."[36]

Roosevelt cried foul. She and her colleagues argued that the Caverna de Pedra Pintada evidence was being rejected on criteria that Clovis sites themselves could not pass. Eliminating the "outliers" missed the point that those dates were underneath a sterile layer, stratigraphically separated from the other radiocarbon samples. The palm seeds were carbonized and lacked the tooth marks animals leave on seeds. Several of the detailed criticisms were based on mistaken reading of the charts and figures that accompanied the initial article in *Science*. Nonetheless, some skeptics remained unconvinced by the increasing evidence regarding early human settlement in South America.

More Paleoindians in Brazil

A particularly robust body of data comes from Brazil, where archaeologist **Lucas Bueno** and colleagues have assembled a database of 277 carbon-14 dates between 13,000 and 8,000 BP from ninety archaeological sites.[37] The individual dates were evaluated based on the type of material sampled, the stratigraphic provenience and cultural associations of the samples, and the statistical uncertainty (i.e., "plus or minus") factors of the sample, which had to be less than 300 years. Although a few dates older than 13,000 BP had been reported, they were few and were excluded from the analysis, as were later dates when the presence of humans in South America had been well-established. The results were surprising.

Only five sites have deposits that date to the earliest time period (ca. 15,500–12,800 cal BP), but they are located in northeastern and Central Brazil. Several of the sites are along major rivers, which may have been natural routes for early migrants into the interior. Other sites are located away from the major drainages. For example, at the site of **Toca do Sítio do Meio**, a stone tool assemblage consisting of cores, scrapers, flakes, and long flaked tools known as limaces was found in good association with charcoal radiocarbon dated to 12,440 ± 240 BP; although the plus or minus factor is relatively large, the date suggests an initial human presence by around 13,000 years ago, followed by a millennium or more of very few humans in the region.

This initial "exploratory" phase was followed by a significant increase in dated archaeological sites. Between 11,000 and 10,000 years ago, there are fifty-six absolute dates from thirty-seven different sites or different cultural layers within sites. Further, the sites are more widely spread and found in different environmental zones across Brazil, with a marked increase in the Central Brazilian Plateau and even as far south as the edge of the pampa on the banks of the Uruguay River, near the modern Brazil-Uruguay border. This increase in the number of sites is paralleled by a diversification of the environments in which they are found and the resources humans used. While the Central Amazon, the savannas and cerrado of the Central Brazilian Plateau, and the pampas continued to be occupied, people also began settling the semi-deciduous forests of the Atlantic Forest. Between 9000 and 8500 BP, these different zones also saw regional variations in stone tool technologies, rock art styles, and burial practices—including multiple burials of the dead in selected caves. All these trends suggest a human population that not only had entered Brazil but that diversified into separate groups claiming specific territories and cultural practices as their own.

This study has several important implications. First, none of these Brazilian sites contain fluted projectile points, even though they are the same age as, or older than, Clovis sites in North America. (In fact, the earliest projectile points are triangular or stemmed points dating to 10,000 BP, contemporary with, but distinct from, fishtail points seen at Fell's Cave and elsewhere in western South America.) Second, the increasing frequencies of archaeological sites suggest an initial exploratory phase, followed by expansion up major river systems, followed by more local adaptations as humans settled into these different Brazilian habitats. Finally, the initial colonizers were not big-game hunters but rather practiced **broad-spectrum foraging**. Bueno and colleagues write:

> The predominance of generalist subsistence systems and the great variability of regional styles of lithic industry . . . highlight the limits of classical "overkill" and "Clovis-first" models of the peopling of the Americas. In chronological terms, archaeological excavation in the past thirty years has yielded increasingly consistent evidence of occupation in different regions of Brazil since the end of the Pleistocene, with dates at least contemporary to the Clovis Horizon in North America . . . On the other hand, the diversity of adaptive strategies suggests that the initial colonization of extra-Andean South America should be characterized as a cultural radiation with multiple dispersal trajectories. Not all areas were settled simultaneously, and there are geographical areas with little or no evidence of human exploitation throughout the Holocene.[38]

But who were these people? One possibility is that the initial forays into eastern Brazil were made by populations distinct from later arrivals. This model has been proposed by the biological anthropologist and archaeologist **Walter Neves**, a scholar who has worked in different regions of South America but given particular focus to the **Lagoa Santa** region of the Minas Gerais region in Brazil's southeastern interior.

The karstic limestone geological formations of the Lagoa Santa region are riddled with sinkholes, caverns, and rock shelters. In the mid-nineteenth century the Danish naturalist **Peter W. Lund** (1801–80) investigated the caves of the Lagoa Santa region, where he discovered the first known remains of the saber-toothed tiger and other extinct Pleistocene fauna, including specimens associated with human remains.[39] It has been suggested that the discovery of the bones of modern humans with the bones of extinct fauna was so unsettling to Lund that he stopped his investigations in 1845, although he continued to live in Lagoa Santa and to correspond with other naturalists until the end of his life.

Through the balance of the nineteenth and early twentieth centuries, the region was investigated by scientists and avocational scholars from Brazil and abroad—investigations without the benefit of carbon-14 dating.[40] Subsequent investigations in the 1970s by a French-Brazilian archaeological team, directed by **Annette Laming-Emperaire** and **André Prous,**[41] encountered a number of human skeletal remains, including the famous **Luzia.**[42] Nicknamed as the Brazilian counterpart to the famous *Australopithecus africanus* fossil "Lucy," the skeleton was discovered at **Lapa Vermelha IV** rock shelter in layers dated between 10,220 ± 220 and 11,680 ± 500 radiocarbon years BP, roughly between 11,264 and 15,145 cal BP.[43] However, the association among the dates, the skeleton, and stone artifacts and the dates' large deviations were seen as uncertain and problematic, even by Prous.[44] The situation was further muddied by an AMS date run on bone collagen that produced a minimum age of 9330 ± 60 BP, which suggested possible disturbance of the materials.[45] However, Neves and colleagues argued that Luzia represented "the oldest human remains found in the Americas, dating between 11,000 and 11,500 years B.P."[46]

But aside from the chronological issues, the most notable announcement was that Luzia was not an "Indian." As Neves and colleagues carefully stated, "Several studies concerning the extra-continental morphological affinities of Paleo-Indian skeletons, carried out independently in South and North America, have indicated that the Americas were first occupied by non-Mongoloids that made their way to the New World through the Bering Strait in ancient times." They continued, "In none of these analyses [do] the first Americans show any resemblance to either northeast Asians or modern native Americans"; rather, "*the first South Americans show a clear resemblance to modern South Pacific and African populations*" (emphasis added).[47]

This touched off a firestorm of controversy and confusion, further fueled by other debates surrounding the peopling of the Americas. First, the analyses of Luzia were announced during the long controversy over **Kennewick Man**, a disarticulated human skeleton found eroding from a riverbank along the Columbia River in southeastern Washington State. Tentatively dated to 9330–9580 cal BP, initial analyses were suspended when the US Army Corps of Engineers decided to return the remains to local Native American tribal groups, repatriation halted by a countersuit by a half-dozen eminent US physical anthropologists and archaeologists. All of this was widely reported in the US and international press. Prior to this stalemate, initial measurements of the skeleton led to the announcement that Kennewick Man was "an outlier relative to modern human populations, but . . . closer to Pacific Islanders and Ainu than to Late Prehistoric Amerinds or any other modern group."[48]

Several other strands wrapped around Luzia.[49] In the late 1990s, archaeologists **Dennis Stanford** and **Bruce Bradley** first presented their hypothesis that eastern North America was settled by coastal hunters—originally Europeans who used Solutrean-style artifacts—who ventured out on sea ice in pursuit of seals and other marine mammals during the Last Glacial Maximum. Finally, the reference to Luzia's resemblance to South Pacific and African populations led some to claim that South America had been colonized from Africa.

None of these claims were proposed by Walter Neves and colleagues; their point was more subtle and thus more difficult to splash into a headline. Neves never contended that Luzia and other Lagoa Santa hominids were immigrants from Africa or the South Pacific but rather that they exhibited characteristics more different from modern and historic Native Americans.[50] These characteristics, Neves argued, represented a suite of characteristics with greater antiquity, traits shared by the ancestral populations who occupied Australia, Melanesia—and the Americas.

The traits involved sixty-one measurements of crania morphology, which were compared to standard reference collections from other regions of the world. Multivariate analysis indicated a greater similarity between the earliest Lagoa Santa skulls and modern Australian aboriginal, Melanesian, and sub-Saharan African populations than with modern Native Americans and northern Asian populations. (For example, Australians, Melanesians, and Africans tend to have relatively broad eyes and noses, while Native Americans and northern Asians have narrower orbits and noses.) Another research team compared Neves and colleagues' data to skeletons recovered from Jōmon sites in Japan. Jōmon is a very long archaeological tradition that was older than, and contemporary with, the first settlement of the Americas. The Jōmon skulls tended to be similar to the Lagoa Santa skulls.[51]

Based on the detailed analyses of ancient skulls, it would seem that two different populations colonized the Americas—an initial population sharing traits seen among the Lagoa Santa skulls (Paleoindians) and a later population with features similar to modern Native Americans (Amerindians), two waves of immigration known as the **Dual Migration Model**.

Yet, studies of mitochondrial DNA (mtDNA) provide only limited support for this two-phase migration model. Studies of mtDNA among modern Native Americans in North and South America suggest that they share four major sets of adjacent alleles (or haplotypes) also found in Asia.[52] The genetic evidence suggests an initial immigration from Northeast Asia after the Last Glacial Maximum that resulted in the major colonization of the Americas, followed much later by the ancestors of Na-Dene groups (e.g., speakers of Tlingit, Navaho, and other Athabaskan languages) and Inuit (Eskimo). In turn, the distinctive cranial features seen in the Lagoa Santa skulls might have resulted from local variation among an isolated population (a process known as genetic drift) rather than marking ancient connections between humans in South America and other continents.

Although these different scenarios and data sets—bones and mtDNA—may seem like a confusing mess, in fact they mark an exciting moment for understanding the peopling of North and South America. If the Clovis first hypothesis no longer seems adequate, what hypothesis best covers all of the available data? In a succinct review, **Francisco Rothammer** and Tom Dillehay have summarized the Clovis first and Dual Migration models; the following points seem to be true.[53]

First, the overwhelming evidence—archaeological, osteological, and genetic—points to a North Asian origin for the first people of the Americas. Second, people using Clovis technology were not the first colonizers, although it is not known if they were preceded by earlier Paleoindians. Third, the pace of migration from north to south was apparently very rapid, with sites in southernmost South America coeval with, or nearly as old as, the earliest sites in North America. Fourth, the rapidity of the movement into South America may indicate a coastal migration as well as overland movements of people. Of course, even this scenario is an oversimplified depiction of many complex human lives (figure 3.10).

New Directions, New Controversies

The debates about the earliest sites in South America still rage and will probably continue for a decade or longer as different issues are resolved and other sites are explored (figure 3.11).

This complexity is obvious in a set of recent papers that collate and evaluate early absolute dates in different portions of South America and the Isthmus of Panama. Although a number of regions have sites that are coeval with Clovis sites in North America, research is extremely uneven across the continent. For example, despite the discovery of early sites like Fell's Cave and others in southern Patagonia, the archaeological record from northeastern Patagonia has no sites dated to older than 7200 BP and relatively few sites at all until after 3500 BP.[54] This may reflect a lack of archaeological research, destruction of earlier sites by rising sea levels along the Atlantic Coast, or perhaps increases in human population that encouraged movement into the interior portions of northern Patagonia only late in prehistory. Around 5,600 km (3,360 miles) to the north, on the Isthmus of Panama—the presumed gateway for overland migrations into South America—the archaeological patterns are similarly complex.[55] At this time, there are no archaeological sites with clearly associated pre-Clovis dates, and the projectile points indicate several different traditions including Clovis points, fishtail projectile points, and bifacial tools somewhat similar to those found at El Jobo. These sites do not appear to date before 11,050 BP (and many of the projectile points were surface finds without associated radiocarbon materials). Presumably, pre-Clovis sites lie beneath the sea, a plausible hypothesis difficult to prove.

Figure 3.10 Rock art at Cueva de las Manos, Argentina

Figure 3.11 Possible alternative routes of migrations in South America

In Peru, a massive set of radiocarbon dates indicates that there is no convincing evidence for human occupation of either the highlands or the coast before 13,000 years ago but relatively good evidence for human occupation between 13,000 and 11,500 cal BP.[56] Thirty-three radiocarbon dates from coastal sites like Quebrada Jaguay and Quebrada Tacahuay and interior sites on the north-central Peruvian coast with fishtail and other styles of projectile points indicate an early and diverse human presence. A charcoal sample from **Cueva Bautista**, Bolivia, is AMS-dated to 12,989–12,806 cal BP, but this is a single date from a single site, and other early sites date only after 9500 BP; clearly, more investigations are required.[57] In Colombia, archaeological research into the peopling of the Americas has not been a consistent priority, despite the region's pivotal location for ancient peoples moving into the continent. Stone tools associated with the bones of mastodon, horse, and deer have been found at the site of **Tibitó** and dated to 11,740 BP, thus earlier than known Panamanian sites and coeval with Clovis; there is virtually no information, however, from important parts of the country, such as the Caribbean coast (a possible route connecting to the location of El Jobo sites on the Venezuelan coast), the Pacific Coast, or Amazonia.[58] A well-dated, early archaeological site from any of these regions would fundamentally influence our understanding of the peopling of South America.

However, archaeological investigations across South America during the last three decades indicate some basic patterns in the data on first inhabitants of the continent. First, increasingly unequivocal archaeological sites in South America seem coeval with, or slightly earlier than, Clovis sites in North America, suggesting that the Clovis first model is incorrect. Second, the early archaeological sites in South America are found in a broad range of environments—temperate forests, lowland Amazonia, coastal oases, and Pleistocene lakebeds in the Atacama Desert—that suggest humans adapted to a variety of environments, using a range of tools of stone and other materials. The striking diversity of early South American lifeways becomes even more evident in later sites from the Archaic period (see chapter 4).[59] The diverse Paleoindian evidence for different human adaptations may imply the presence of even earlier colonizing populations in these different zones, although it is impossible to specify the dating for their arrivals. In addition to these basic inferences, the new data on the earliest sites in South America are leading archaeologists to map out new domains for scientific inquiry.

If we assume, for the sake of argument—and it *will* result in an argument—that South America was settled initially sometime between 12,000 and 11,000 BC, what are the implications for future archaeological research?

First, there is the issue of the timing and routes of migration.[60] Rather than envision a single population whose descendants slowly plodded south from the ice-free corridor, the earlier South American dates suggest multiple migrating populations, some possibly exploring divergent land routes and others coming on various coastal voyages. One hypothesis envisions a maritime migration south along the Pacific Coast of the Americas, a strategy that would allow for relatively rapid expansion by groups able to use the technologies of fishing and marine mammal hunting as they headed south.[61] This coastal migration hypothesis is bolstered by discoveries off the Southern California coast in the northern Channel Islands, which have been separated from the North American mainland for hundreds of thousands of years. Human skeletal remains from the **Arlington Springs** site on Santa Rosa Island have been dated to 10,960 ± 50 BP, or approximately 13,000–12,900 calibrated years ago.[62] Similarly, on nearby San Miguel Island, the "data from **Daisy Cave** suggest that the Northern Channel Islands were settled by humans by at least 11,600 cal BP, a colonization that required relatively seaworthy watercraft and a substantial economic reliance on marine resources."[63] Although some archaeologists have raised the possibility of other coastal migrations from Europe or even Australia, the most plausible current scenario is a southward expansion along the Pacific Coast, taking advantage of recently de-glaciated coastlines in Alaska and British Columbia to head south. Although a South American counterpart to Daisy Cave has not been found, very old coastal sites between southern Ecuador/southern Peru and northern Chile may suggest an earlier coastal migration (see chapter 4).

Second, the Pacific Coast migration may have been accompanied by other independent migrations from an original homeland in northeastern Asia. The overland expansion of humans indicated by the distribution of fluted projectile points in North America probably continued into South America even as new technologies (e.g., El Jobo, stemmed, or fishtail points) were developed and became widespread. It is also possible that different currents of migration moved into the western and eastern edges of South America, hugging the coasts and lowlands and initially separated by the Andes and Amazonia. In reviewing archaeological, genetic, and skeletal data for the earliest occupants of South America, Dillehay has observed that the evidence points to significant variations among South American initial populations, "probably suggesting separate migrations in the Americas from different source areas and/or [that] the first immigrants were already heterogeneous at the time of entry."[64]

Third, as additional Paleoindian sites are discovered in South America, other issues will presumably be explored. Until now, the goal of simply establishing the antiquity and legitimacy of archaeological sites has resulted in a focus on dating, artifact categories (e.g., Are the objects actually tools?), and subsistence practices (such as whether sites are associated with extinct Pleistocene fauna). Conversely, little research has focused on other aspects of life: art, ritual, residence patterns, social practices, and so on. There are exceptions. For example, the bog conditions at Monte Verde preserved not only wooden structures and stone artifacts but also the remains of plants possibly used as medicines that Dillehay notes were imported from other areas to the site. On another line of inquiry, Roosevelt and colleagues have argued that small chunks of red pigment found in the early levels of Caverna de Pedra Pintada were compositionally similar to samples from the rock art on the cave walls, images that included concentric circles and handprints from multiple phases. This may suggest that the rock art was made by Paleoindians rather than only by later Archaic peoples, but that conclusion requires actually dating the rock art. However, future archaeological investigations will undoubtedly provide new insights into Paleoindian lives in addition to issues of chronology, technology, and subsistence.

Finally, new data will result in continuous reassessments of recent hypotheses. For example, the hypothesis that there were two different coastal migrations, one down the Pacific Coast and another down the Atlantic Coast—two paths of human settlement separated by the natural barriers of the Andes and Amazonia—could be overturned by the discovery of a single, unequivocal early Paleoindian site in western Amazonia. That, in turn, would begin the process of evaluation, debate, and reassessment—just as the discoveries over the last three decades have resulted in fundamentally new insights into the peopling of South America.

Notes

1. A number of excellent overviews discuss the archaeological search for the "first Americans," particularly with an emphasis on North American archaeological sites, such as B. Fagan, *The Great Journey* (Gainesville: University Press of Florida, 2004). For a useful, brief overview of issues and controversies, see B. Fagan, *Ancient North America: Archaeology of a Continent* (New York: Thames and Hudson, 2005), 71–96. For overviews by active participants in the debates, see D. Meltzer, *First Peoples in a New World: Colonizing Ice Age America* (Berkeley: University of California Press, 2009); T. Dillehay, *The Settlement of the Americas: A New Perspective* (New York: Basic Books, 2000).

2. For a summary of the excavations at Blackwater Draw, see C. V. Haynes, "Geochronology of Paleoenvironmental Change, Clovis Type Site, Blackwater Draw, New Mexico," *Geoarchaeology: An International Journal* 10, no. 5 (1995): 317–388.

3. C. V. Haynes, "Fluted Projectile Points: Their Age and Dispersion," *Science* 145, no. 3639 (1964): 1410.

4. Ibid., 1412.

5. For a critical review of Martin's hypothesis, see D. Grayson and D. Meltzer, "A Requiem for North American Overkill," *Journal of Archaeological Science* 30 (2003): 585–593.

6. Meltzer, *First Peoples in a New World*, 9.

7. L. Leakey, D. Simpson, and T. Clements, "Archaeological Excavations in the Calico Mountains, California: Preliminary Report," *Science* 160, no. 3831 (May 1968): 1022–1023.

8. C. V. Haynes, "The Earliest Americans," *Science* 166, no. 3906 (1969): 713.

9. Ibid., 714.

10. Meltzer, *First Peoples in a New World*, 107.

11. Junius Bird (1907–82) had a long and illustrious career, and he contributed to a range of topics in South American prehistory. For his work in the tip of South America, see the engrossing account of his and Margaret Bird's expeditions in the 1930s in M. Bird and G. Willey, *Travels and Archaeology in South Chile*, ed. J. Hyslop (Iowa City: University of Iowa Press, 1988). For Bird's synopsis of the research results, see "Antiquity and Migrations of the Early Inhabitants of Patagonia," *Geographical Review* 28, no. 2 (1938): 250–275.

12. A short video with outstanding images of Cruxent's excavations has been presented by the Fundación Jose Maria Cruxent, http://www.youtube.com/watch?v=rnxg4sB9DOo (accessed November 5, 2013).

13. J. Cruxent and I. Rouse, "A Lithic Industry of Paleo-Indian Type in Venezuela," *American Antiquity* 22, no. 2 (1956): 172–179.

14. I. Rouse and J. Cruxent, "Some Recent Radiocarbon Dates for Western Venezuela," *American Antiquity* 28, no. 4 (1963): 537–540.

15. A. Bryan, R. Casamiquela, J. Cruxent, R. Gruhn, and C. Ochenius, "An El Jobo Mastadon Kill at Taima-Taima, Venezuela," *Science* 200, no. 4347 (June 1978): 1275; see also the slender but informative report on the excavations *Taima-Taima: A Late Pleistocene Paleo-Indian Kill Site in Northernmost South America—Final Reports of the 1976 Excavations*, ed. C. Ochsenius and R. Gruhn, South American Quaternary Documentation Project/Center for the Study of the First Americans (College Station: Texas A&M University Press, 1979).

16. Bryan et al., "El Jobo Mastadon," 1277.

17. See, for example, T. Lynch, "Glacial-Age Man in South America? A Critical Review," *American Antiquity* 55, no. 1 (1990): 12–36; and the response by R. Gruhn and A. Bryan, "A Review of Lynch's Descriptions of South American Pleistocene Sites," *American Antiquity* 56, no. 2 (1991): 342–348.

18. R. MacNeish, "The Early Man Remains from Pikimachay Cave, Ayacucho Basin, Highland Peru," in *The Pre-Llano Cultures of the Americas: Paradoxes and Possibilities*, ed. R. Humphrey and D. Stanford (Washington, DC: Anthropological Society of Washington, 1979); R. MacNeish, R. Berger, and R. Protsch, "Megafauna and Man from Ayacucho, Highland Peru," *Science* 168, no. 3934 (May 1970): 975–977. The quote is from R. MacNeish, "The Harvey Lecture Series: Late Pleistocene Adaptations; A New Look at Early Peopling of the New World as of 1976," *Journal of Anthropological Research* 34, no. 4 (1978): 476. For the reanalysis of the Pikimachay Cave stone "tools," see J. Rick, "The Character and Context of Highland Preceramic Society," in *Peruvian Prehistory: An Overview of Pre-Inca and Inca Society*, ed. R. Keatinge (Cambridge: Cambridge University Press, 1992), 3–40.

19. For the contentious literature surrounding this site, see N. Guidon and G. Delibrias, "Carbon-14 Dates Point to Man in the Americas 32,000 Years Ago," *Nature* 321 (1986): 769–771; D. J. Meltzer, J. M. Adovasio, and T. D. Dillehay, "On a Pleistocene Human Occupation at Pedra Furada, Brazil," *Antiquity* 68 (1994): 695–714; N. Guidon and A.-M. Pessis, "Nature and Age of the Deposits in Pedra Furada, Brazil: Reply to Meltzer, Adovasio and Dillehay," *Antiquity* 70, no. 268 (1996): 408–415. For the re-dating of rock art at Toca de Bastiana, see M. Rowe and K. Steelman, "Comment on 'Some Evidence of a Date of First Humans to Arrive in Brazil,'" *Journal of Archaeological Sciences* 30 (2003): 1349–1351. Invited by Guidon to independently test claims of rock art at Toca de Bastiana for which earlier dates were claimed to be older than 35,000 years, Rowe and Steelman replicated the analyses and re-dated the rock art, resulting in ages of less than 2,000 years. For a far-reaching and skeptical assessment of pre-Clovis sites in South America, see T. Lynch, "Glacial-Age Man in South America? A Critical Review," *American Antiquity* 55 (1990): 12–36.

20. T. Dillehay, M. Pino, E. M. Davis, S. Valastro Jr., A. Varela, and R. Casamiquela, "Monte Verde: Radiocarbon Dates from an Early-Man Site in South-Central Chile," *Journal of Field Archaeology* 9 (1982): 550.

21. T. Dillehay, *Palaeoenvironment and Site Context: Monte Verde; A Late Pleistocene Settlement in Chile*, vol. 1 (Washington, DC: Smithsonian Institution Press, 1989).

22. T. Dillehay and M. Collins, "Early Cultural Evidence from Monte Verde in Chile," *Nature* 332 (March 1988): 150–152.

23. At a cocktail party in the late 1980s, I was challenged by an eminent geoarcheologist who demanded, "do you *believe* in Monte Verde?" in an evangelical tone, as if asking if I had made Jesus Christ my personal savior.

24. D. Meltzer, D. Grayson, G. Ardila, A. Barker, D. Dincauze, C. Vance Haynes, F. Mena, L. Núñez, and D. Stafford, "On the Pleistocene Antiquity of Monte Verde, Southern Chile," *American Antiquity* 62, no. 4 (1997): 661.

25. Ibid.

26. In fact, C. Vance Haynes later still raised objections to Monte Verde in "Monte Verde and the Pre-Clovis Situation in America," *Scientific American Discovering Archaeology—Special Report: Monte Verde Revisited* (1999): 17–18.

27. Meltzer et al., "On the Pleistocene Antiquity of Monte Verde," 662.

28. M. Waters and T. Stafford Jr., "Redefining the Age of Clovis: Implications for the Peopling of the Americas," *Science* 315 (February 2007): 1122–1126.

29. D. Sandweiss, H. McInnis, R. Burger, A. Cano, B. Ojeda, R. Paredes, M. Sandweiss, and M. Glascock, "Quebrada Jaguay: Early Maritime Adaptations in South America," *Science* 281 (1998): 1830–1832; D. Sandweiss, "Terminal Pleistocene through Mid-Holocene Archaeological Sites as Paleoclimatic Archives for the Peruvian Coast," *Palaeogeography, Palaeoclimatology, Palaeoecology* 194 (2003): 23–40.

30. D. Jackson, C. Méndz, R. Seguel, A. Maldonado, and G. Vargas, "Initial Occupation of the Pacific Coast of Chile during Late Pleistocene Times," *Current Anthropology* 48, no. 5 (2007): 725–731.

31. M. Grosjean, L. Núñez, and I. Cartajena, "Paleoindian Occupation of the Atacama Desert, Northern Chile," *Journal of Quaternary Sciences* 20 (2005): 643–653.

32. A. Roosevelt, M. Lima de Costa, C. Lopes Machado, M. Michab, N. Mercier, H. Valladas, J. Feathers, W. Barnett, M. Imazio da Silveira, A. Henderson, J. Silva, B. Chernoff, D. Reese, J. Holman, N. Toth, and K. Schick, "Paleoindian Cave Dwellers in the Amazon: The Peopling of the Americas," *Science* 272, no. 5620 (April 2006): 373–384.

33. I have calibrated the radiocarbon dates presented by Roosevelt et al. using the calibration curve Intcal09 (at http://calib.qub.ac.uk/calib/), and the values are presented at two standard deviations (95% confidence level).

34. These last two sets of calibrations are considered less than certain because of the limits of the calibration curve for samples from the Southern Hemisphere that are older than 11,000 BP.

35. The objections raised by Haynes and other scholars and responses by Roosevelt and colleagues are found in "Dating a Paleoindian Site in the Amazon in Comparison with Clovis Culture," *Science*, New Series 275, no. 5308 (March 1997): 1948–1952.

36. Ibid., 1949.

37. L. Bueno, A. Schmidt Dias, and J. Steele, "The Late Pleistocene/Early Holocene Archaeological Record in Brazil: A Geo-Referenced Database," *Quaternary International* 301 (2013): 74–93.

38. Ibid., 90.

39. P. E. de Luna Filho, "Peter Wilhelm Lund: O auge das suas investigações científicas ea razaõ para o término das suas pesquisas" (PhD diss., Universidade de São Paulo, 2008).

40. For a summary, see W. Hurt Jr., "The Cultural Complexes from the Lagoa Santa Region, Brazil," *American Anthropologist* 62, no. 4 (1960): 569–585.

41. For early summaries of this research, see A. Laming-Emperaire, "Problèmes de préhistoire brésilienne," *Annales: Économies, Sociétés, Civilisations* 30e année, no. 5 (1975): 1229–1260; P. Schmitz, "Prehistoric Hunters and Gatherers of Brazil," *Journal of World Prehistory* 1, no. 1 (1987): 53–126. The French prehistorian Annette Laming-Emperaire was a remarkable scholar and individual. Trained as a Paleolithic archaeologist and a member of the French Resistance during World War II, after the war Laming-Emperaire participated in a number of archaeological expeditions in Tierra del Fuego and elsewhere in South America. She and André Prous were in the initial years of excavations in the Minas Gerais region when Laming-Emperaire was accidentally asphyxiated by a faulty gas fixture in a bathroom shower. For an obituary, see D. Lavallée, "Annette Laming-Emperaire (1917–1977)," *Journal de la Société des Américanistes* 65 (1978): 224–226. For additional background information, see B. Meggers, "Advances in Brazilian Archeology, 1935–1985," *American Antiquity* 50, no. 2 (1985): 364–373.

42. L. Rohter, "An Ancient Skull Challenges Long-Held Theories," *New York Times* (October 1999).

43. A. Araujo, W. Neves, and R. Kipnis, "Lagoa Santa Revisited: An Overview of the Chronology, Subsistence, and Material Culture of Paleoindian Sites in East Central Brazil," *Latin American Antiquity* 23, no. 4 (2012): 535.

44. See, for example, A. Prous and E. Fogaca, "Archaeology of the Pleistocene-Holocene Boundary in Brazil," *Quaternary International* 53–54 (1999): 21–41.

45. A subsequent calibration on the bone collagen date of 10,298–10,701 cal BP did not assuage the critics.

46. W. Neves, J. Powell, A. Prous, E. Ozlins, and M. Blum, "Lapa Vermelha IV Hominid 1: Morphological Affinities of the Earliest Known American," *Genetics and Molecular Biology* 22, no. 4 (1999): 463.

47. Ibid., 461.

48. J. Chatters, "The Recovery and First Analysis of an Early Holocene Human Skeleton from Kennewick, Washington," *American Antiquity* 65, no. 2 (2000): 291. For a lively overview of this and related controversies and debates, see D. Thomas, *Skull Wars: Kennewick Man, Archaeology, and the Battle for Native American Identity* (New York: Basic Books, 2001).

49. D. Stanford and B. Bradley, "The Solutrean Solution," *Discovering Archaeology*, 21, no. 1 (2000): 54–55. Expanded versions of this hypothesis are found in B. Bradley and D. Stanford, "The North Atlantic Ice-Edge Corridor: A Possible Palaeolithic Route to the New World," *World Archaeology* 36, no. 4 (2004): 459–478; and the recently published book, D. Stanford and B. Bradley, *Across Atlantic Ice: The Origin of America's Clovis Culture* (Berkeley: University of California Press, 2012).

50. See Araujo, Neves, and Kipnis, "Lagoa Santa Revisited," 546.

51. N. Seguchi, A. McKeown, R. Schmidt, H. Umeda, and C. Brace, "An Alternative View of the Peopling of South America: Lagoa Santa in Craniometric Perspective," *Anthropological Science* 119, no. 1 (2011): 21–38.

52. For a discussion, see S. Perez, V. Bernal, P. Gonzalez, M. Sardi, and G. Politis, "Discrepancy between Cranial and DNA Data of Early Americans: Implications for

American Peopling," *PloS One* 4, no. 5 (2009): e5746; H. Pucciarelli, S. Perez, and G. Politis, "Early Holocene Human Remains from the Argentinean Pampas: Additional Evidence for Distinctive Cranial Morphology of Early South Americans," *American Journal of Physical Anthropology* 143, no. 2 (2010): 298–305.

53. F. Rothammer and T. Dillehay, "The Late Pleistocene Colonization of South America: An Interdisciplinary Perspective," *Annals of Human Genetics* 73 (2009): 540–549.

54. G. Martínez, G. Flensborg, and P. Bayala, "Chronology and Human Settlement in Northeastern Patagonia (Argentina): Patterns of Site Destruction, Intensity of Archaeological Signal, and Population Dynamics," *Quaternary International* 301 (2013): 123–134.

55. R. Cooke, A. Ranere, G. Pearson, and R. Dickau, "Radiocarbon Chronology of Early Human Settlement on the Isthmus of Panama (13,000–7000 BP) with Comments on Cultural Affinities, Environments, Subsistence, and Technological Change," *Quaternary International* 301 (2013): 3–22.

56. K. Rademaker, G. Bromley, and D. Sandweiss, "Peru Archaeological Radiocarbon Database, 13,000–7000 14C B.P.," *Quaternary International* 301 (2013): 34–45.

57. J. Capriles and J. Albarracin-Jordan, "The Earliest Human Occupations in Bolivia: A Review of the Archaeological Evidence," *Quaternary International* 301 (2013): 46–59.

58. F. Aceituno, N. Loaiza, M. Delgado-Burbano, and G. Barrientos, "The Initial Human Settlement of Northwest South America during the Pleistocene/Holocene Transition: Synthesis and Perspectives," *Quaternary International* 301 (2013): 23–33.

59. For an example, see K. Stothert, D. Piperno, and T. Andres, "Terminal Pleistocene/Early Holocene Human Adaptation in Coastal Ecuador: The Las Vegas Evidence," *Quaternary International* 109–110 (2003): 23–43.

60. For an overview of archaeological and genetic studies on the peopling of the Americas, see the review articles by B. Pitblado, "A Tale of Two Migrations: Reconciling Recent Biological and Archaeological Evidence for the Pleistocene Peopling of the Americas," *Journal of Archaeological Research* (published online March 2011); T. Dillehay, "The Late Pleistocene Cultures of South America," *Evolutionary Anthropology* (1999): 206–216.

61. See, for example, T. Goebel, M. Waters, and D. O'Rourke, "The Late Pleistocene Dispersal of Modern Humans in the Americas," *Science* 310 (March 2008): 1497–1502.

62. J. Johnson, T. Stafford Jr., H. Ajie, and D. Morris, "Arlington Springs Revisited," in *Proceedings of the Fifth California Islands Symposium*, ed. D. Browne, K. Mitchell, and H. Chaney (Santa Barbara: Santa Barbara Museum of Natural History, 2002), 541–545; J. Johnson, T. Stafford Jr., G. West, and T. Rockwell, "Before and after the Younger Dryas: Chronostratigraphic and Paleoenvironmental Research at Arlington Springs, Santa Rosa Island, California" (presentation, American Geophysical Union Joint Assembly 22, Acapulco, Mexico, 2007).

63. J. Erlandson, D. Kennett, L. Ingram, D. Guthrie, D. Morris, M. Tveskov, J. West, and P. Walker, "An Archaeological and Paleontological Chronology for Daisy Cave (CA-SMI-261), San Miguel Island, California," *Radiocarbon* 38, no. 2 (1996): 370.

64. T. Dillehay, "Probing Deeper into First American Studies," *Proceedings of the National Academy of Sciences* 106, no. 4 (2009): 975.

Figure 4.1 Selknam men hunting in Tierra del Fuego, 1930s

Archaic Adaptations

10.5876_9781607323334.c004

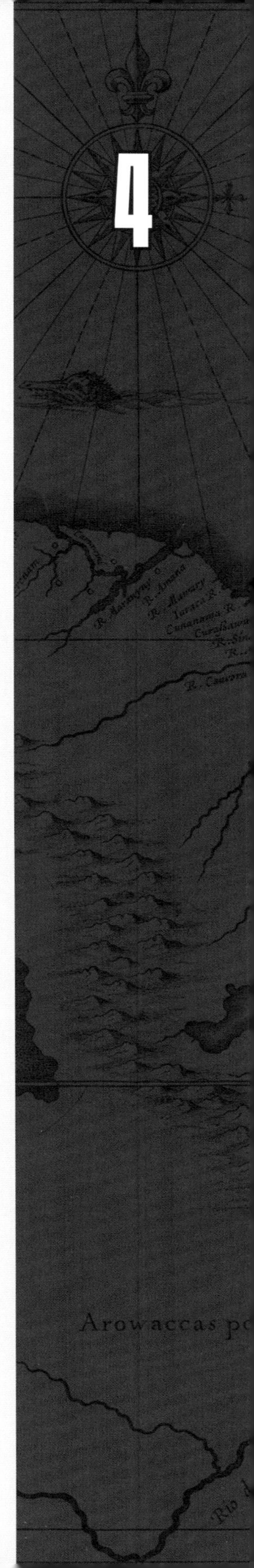

> Wherever they go, be it in the wood or near the water, they always have with them their bows and arrows. When they pass through the forest, they look straight up at the trees, now and again. Whenever they hear any noise of large birds, monkeys, or other animals that inhabit trees, they go thither and try to shoot them, and they follow until they get something. It is seldom, when one of them is out in the chase, that he returns empty-handed.
>
> *Hans Studen among the Tupi of eastern Brazil, circa 1547–55*

The term *Archaic* implies more than the word *archaic*: "antiquated," "surviving from an earlier period," or "characteristic of the past." For archaeologists working in the Americas, the Archaic refers to the period after the initial, Paleoindian occupation of the continents and before the development of settled agricultural villages.[1]

The term became widespread during the 1950s, when archaeologists **Gordon Willey** and **Phillip Phillips** presented a broad scheme for understanding the development of prehistoric societies in the New World.[2] In an impressive work of scholarship that synthesized archaeological data from across the Americas, Willey and Phillips defined the Archaic "stage" as characterized by hunting-and-gathering societies who pursued diverse game animals (smaller than the megafauna hunted by Paleoindians) and collected various plant foods but did not farm. This shift in subsistence pursuits, Willey and Phillips argued, was reflected in changing artifact assemblages: projectile points were smaller, and ground-stone tools—including manos, metates, mortars, and pestles used for preparing plant foods—became common. Ancient settlements also changed: sites were occupied for longer periods, more substantial houses were constructed, and the dead were buried in more permanent settlements. Another trend was an increasing emphasis on marine resources; in coastal regions, Archaic societies fished, collected shellfish, and hunted marine mammals. Finally, in various regions of the Americas, Willey and Phillips proposed, the first pottery appeared in Archaic sites. Although radiocarbon dating was a recent innovation and they had few absolute dates, Willey and Phillips believed the Archaic began sometime between 5000 and 2500 BC at various places in the Americas. In many places in Native America, Archaic societies developed into agricultural communities, a transition Willey and Phillips called the "Formative stage" (see chapter 6). In other places, people lived in Archaic societies until the arrival of Europeans.

For any given region of South America, aspects of Willey and Phillips's definition are true, others are not. First, the initial colonizers of the Americas hunted various game—not just Pleistocene megafauna—and they also fished, collected shellfish, and used a variety of plants (see chapter 3). Watercraft and various stone-grinding tools were used by Paleoindians, technologies Willey and Phillips considered markers of the Archaic. Finally, Archaic practices occurred much earlier than Willey and Phillips suggested.

Despite these objections, the term *Archaic* is useful shorthand for extraordinarily complex and varied human responses and innovations, such as different forms of settlements, new architectural patterns, and unprecedented forms of social practice—including emerging social distinctions and new funeral patterns among these hunting-and-gathering societies.

The archaeologist **Lewis Binford** introduced a useful model for thinking about variations in the ways hunters and gatherers organize their activities, a model envisioned as an array along a continuum.[3] At one extreme, entire groups move regularly to new areas with untapped resources—whether plants, game animals, or clams—and set up a temporary camp. Ranging out from this camp, people collect food resources and transport them back to the base camp, where the foods are prepared and consumed. This continues until locally available resources are depleted. At this point the entire group moves on, establishes a new base camp, and forages for foods—a process that is repeated. Since this foraging strategy requires the movement of the entire residential group, Binford called the practice "**residential mobility**." At the other extreme, people may live relatively permanently in one place, but work parties travel to a location where a resource occurs in a specific season, for example, a grove of nut trees that can be harvested in the fall or a rocky river rapid where salmon swim through each spring. The work party goes to that place, acquires large quantities of the seasonally available food, and transports the food back to the base camp, where it can be stored and eaten by the entire band throughout the year. Binford named this strategic acquisition of resources "**logistical mobility**."

These different approaches to hunting and gathering leave behind different suites of archaeological sites. Under residential mobility, there are two essential classes of sites: places where people live (**home bases**) and places where resources are acquired (**locations**). With logistical mobility, a greater range of sites is created: home bases, locations, seasonal camps, storage areas, specialized work camps, and so on. With residential mobility, a group's material culture tends to be relatively limited and portable. Under logistical mobility, a group's repertoire of tools and artifacts tends to be more diverse and less portable. Finally, hunters and gatherers practicing residential mobility move camps more often than the more sedentary groups engaged in logistical mobility. Again, these are not absolute categories but instead polar extremes on a conceptual continuum, useful tools for thinking about variations in hunting-and-gathering strategies during the Archaic period in South America.

Ironically, the definitional "looseness" of the term *Archaic* contributes to its utility, and an examination of Archaic societies requires us to be alert to the di-

Figure 4.2 Locations of sites discussed in this chapter

verse accomplishments of South American peoples. The following archaeological case studies range across the continent and among very different hunting-and-gathering strategies, a cross-section of some of the varied Archaic societies found in South America (figure 4.2).

The Las Vegas Culture (10,000–6,000 BP)

One hundred and twenty kilometers (74.5 miles) west of the sprawling modern metropolis of Guayaquil, Ecuador, the Santa Elena Peninsula juts into the Pacific Ocean (figure 4.2). The Santa Elena Peninsula is arid and covered with dry thorn scrub vegetation. A four-month rainy season is followed by eight dry months, unlike most of Ecuador where rain can occur throughout the year. The Santa Elena region is watered by small drainages and short rivers that flow briefly during the rainy season but shrivel once the rains cease. This area was home to one of the oldest known Archaic societies in South America, the **Las Vegas culture**. Our knowledge of the Las Vegas culture results from more than four decades of sustained research by the archaeologist **Karen Stothert**, whose broad interests in Ecuador's archaeology and ethnography are documented in numerous articles and books.[4] The Las Vegas culture originated at the end of the Pleistocene as different human groups settled along the coastlines of South America, including on the Santa Elena Peninsula. Although no sites with artifacts associated with Pleistocene megafauna have been found, a few radiocarbon dates point to human occupation between 13,820 and 11,350 calibrated years ago. These pre–Las Vegas dates are followed by a robust set of dated deposits indicating two durable phases: Early Las Vegas (10,000–8000 BP) and Late Las Vegas (8000–6600 BP).[5]

The initial Las Vegas peoples encountered diverse local habitats as environments changed in the Early Holocene. In 8000 BP, sea level was 20 m (65.5 ft) lower than today, before finally reaching near-modern levels after 6000 BP. Tectonic activity uplifted sections of the Ecuadorian coast, not regularly and simultaneously but variably along localized geological blocks. The changing coastline created a mosaic of estuaries, mangrove swamps, lagoons, rock points, and sandy beaches. The terrestrial environment was changing, although without wholesale shifts in plant species. The Santa Elena region has been a dry forest since the Late Holocene, with many of the same species as are found today. These complex and intersecting variations resulted in highly productive but changing coastal and estuarine zones.

Thus, the Las Vegas peoples adapted to a region whose environments shifted in extent and location, alternatively creating opportunities and challenges. Archaeological data from more than thirty Las Vegas sites illuminate these variations. The two largest sites, **Site 80** and **Site 67/66**, were at inland locations with access to a variety of resource zones: river bottoms, tropical forest, and coasts. Further, a sprinkling of smaller camps suggests that families or other smaller groups moved readily between different resource zones, either as the seasons changed or out of personal preference. In the Early Las Vegas period, the essential social unit was apparently a relatively small household, perhaps consisting of a nuclear family. The earliest known house was a very small, relatively flimsy hut about 2 m (6.5 ft) in diameter (figure 4.3). During the Early Las Vegas, Stothert and colleagues write, the "basic social unit of production, distribution, and consumption was the small, relatively self-sufficient family, flexibly organized for carrying out a wide variety of subsistence tasks using a few generalized tools and facilities."[6]

Figure 4.3 Traces of small hut at the Las Vegas culture site OGSE–80, Ecuador

This relatively generalized way of life seems to have changed in various ways during the Late Las Vegas period. First, there were changes in patterns of hunting and fishing. In Early Las Vegas, people hunted larger mammals (such as Virginia deer, brocket deer, and peccary) and small game (opossums, rabbits, and rats) and also fished along the estuaries, lagoons, and beaches. During Late Las Vegas, all the same animals were eaten, but fish increased in significance as small game decreased in importance. Second, there was a change in shellfish species: in Early Las Vegas, more than 80 percent of the shellfish were of a single species—the mangrove ark clam (*Anadara tuberculosa*); in Late Las Vegas, there was a greater emphasis on shellfish from rocky coasts as well as other mangrove-dwelling species, and the significance of *Anadara* decreased. Third, there was a change in the roles of settlements. During the Late Las Vegas, the dead were buried only at the two major sites, Site 80 and Site 67/66 (figure 4.4).

The graves contained primary and secondary burials, suggesting that some people had died near the site, while others were the remains of individuals who had died elsewhere on the Santa Elena Peninsula but their remains were carried to the major sites for final burial (figure 4.5).

This may suggest that new ceremonies were created during the Late Las Vegas period, rituals that connected independent households as members of a larger social group that collectively claimed specific territory.

Finally, another innovation occurred during the Late Las Vegas that would have profound implications: people began to cultivate plants. *Cultivation* refers to human actions that encourage plant growth, whether the plants are wild or domesticates. *Agriculture* is usually defined as an economic system based on domesticated

Figure 4.4 Primary burial at the Las Vegas culture site OGSE–89, Ecuador

Figure 4.5 Secondary burial at the Las Vegas culture site OGSE–89, Ecuador

plants and animals, modified species genetically distinct from their wild relatives (see chapter 5).

At Site 80, bottle gourd (*Lagenaria siceraria*) phytoliths have been found in layers dating from 9000 BP and thereafter (figure 4.6). Like many other plants,

Figure 4.6 Bottle gourd (*Lagenaria siceraria*)

bottle gourds absorb silica from the soil, which coagulates inside the cells of the plants and molds to the distinctive shapes of the cells of different plants. Phytoliths are often preserved when seeds, pollen, and other plant remains have decayed.

Phytoliths were also found from the seeds of the root crop lerén (*Calathea allouia*), a member of the arrowroot family known in English as "sweet corn root" or "guinea arrowroot." Lerén tubers can be eaten raw or dried and can be ground into a starchy flour, and the presence of grinding stones may indicate that Las Vegas people were processing lerén and other tropical root crops. Las Vegas people were also selecting and cultivating wild varieties of squash (genus *Cucurbita*). Abundant squash phytoliths were recovered from Site 80, the earliest dating to more than 10,000 BP and increasingly abundant after 9700 BP. Apparently, the people at Site 80 were selecting specific varieties of squash, causing gradual changes. Among modern squash, smaller wild plants also have smaller phytoliths; conversely, larger domesticated squash have larger phytoliths. A study of the squash phytoliths at Site 80 demonstrated that they became larger, although never as large as modern domesticated varieties but rather a semi-domesticated form. Las Vegas people selected larger squash plants and intentionally planted their seeds, a subtle process of manipulation preserved by tiny grains of silica.

But most surprising was the presence of maize phytoliths. At Site 80 maize phytoliths appeared toward the end of the Late Las Vegas period, suggesting that people had begun cultivating maize around 6,600 years ago.[7] Originating in central Mexico, maize was apparently traded down the Pacific Coast of Central America to northwestern South America and the Santa Elena Peninsula, where the people of the Late Las Vegas culture incorporated it into their lives and livelihoods.

These early cultigens were integrated into the basic Las Vegas subsistence strategy; they did not revolutionize that strategy. The Las Vegas people lived in an environment that periodically underwent shifts and stresses, a region with many different habitats within a relatively small area. Sea levels rose, coastal habitats changed, but the Las Vegas people adjusted. The complex tropical forests expanded and contracted; the Las Vegas people made do. Wild squash were collected, the seeds scattered, and larger varieties of squash gradually developed. Root crops were dug up, cuttings taken and replanted. And in some manner, a remarkable seed from Mexico found its way to the coast of Ecuador—a plant that in many ways would transform vast areas of native South America—but the Las Vegas people simply incorporated that innovative crop into their subsistence practices in their pragmatic and nonchalant manner.

San Jacinto I, Colombia: Intensive Plant Utilization in the Savanna

Approximately 80 km (49.7 miles) southeast of Cartagena and 50 km (31 miles) inland from the Caribbean, the deeply buried site of **San Jacinto I** is located in a low-lying savanna watered by seasonal drainages that flow into tributaries of the Rio Magdalena (see figure 4.2).[8] Excavated by **Augusto Oyuela-Caycedo** and **Renée Bonzani,** San Jacinto I was exposed in the stream bank of a meandering arroyo. This region of northern Colombia contains sites with very early pottery, fiber-tempered ceramics approximately 5,000 years old. San Jacinto I also contained early fiber-tempered pottery and held an extraordinary collection of botanical materials and archaeological features that provides a snapshot of the transition from food collecting to early agriculture (figure 4.7).

San Jacinto I was covered by 4 m (13 ft) of flood deposits, an overburden that protected the archaeological layers. Based on soil corings, the site covered slightly less than 350 m^2 (3,767 ft^2). The excavators exposed an area 5 m × 15 m (807 ft^2) in size, encountering sixty-eight pit ovens and forty-four open fire pits in the layers

Figure 4.7 Excavations at San Jacinto I, Colombia, showing multiple pit ovens

dating to between 6000 and 5200 BP. The ovens were large oval pits, many more than 50 cm (1.6 ft) in diameter, with a carefully built rim made from mud. A layer of fire-cracked rock and the fire-reddened walls of the pits indicated that the features held a contained and concentrated fire. In contrast, the open-fire pits were smaller, contained less fire-cracked rock, and were used for open cooking. There is an amazing density of these features at San Jacinto I, created as people intensively reused the site. A few postholes suggest that temporary windbreaks were built to protect the fires and the people tending their flames at San Jacinto I.

The dense concentration of features at San Jacinto I indicates only one aspect in the lives of food collectors in northern Colombia. The earth ovens and fire pits were used to process starch seeds from plants growing along the stream that meandered past the site: mallow, purslane, and other wild plants. The cooked seeds were probably made into a mush, which could have fermented into a mildly alcoholic drink or been ground into thick flour, rolled into a tamale-like ball, wrapped in leaves, and baked. These seeds could have been gathered only at the end of the rainy season and the beginning of the dry season—sometime between November and February in this region of northern South America.

This meant that the people of San Jacinto I carefully scheduled their presence at the site, returning each season to collect and cook these seeds. Between 6,000 and 5,200 years ago, people traveled to this area as a destination. They set up camp, collected seeds, processed them in earth ovens and fire pits, and did this year after year. Although we do not know what the people of San Jacinto I did at other times of the year and away from this place, it is clear that their seasonal movements were anchored by the sprouting of seeds along the arroyo after the rainy season. In effect, this meant that their mobility was reduced and the people of San Jacinto I were becoming more sedentary as they intensively collected the seeds. Such collecting adaptations were precursors to cultivation and agriculture. As Oyuela-Caycedo and Bonzani note, "San Jacinto I has yielded evidence of some of the preconditions expected in models on the origins of food production."[9]

Orinoco River Valley, Venezuela: Foragers in the Tropical Rainforest

The prehistory of the Orinoco Basin is relatively less-known than that of other regions in South America, and the archaeology of Archaic hunters and gatherers is even less documented than that of pottery-using villagers from later periods in Orinoquia.[10] Humans had moved into the Middle Orinoco by at least 8000 BC. Approximately 25 km (15.5 miles) downstream from the Venezuelan city of Puerto Ayacucho, the **Provincial** site is located on the east bank of the river in an open savanna edged by forest (see figure 4.2). Limited excavations at the Provincial site encountered a preceramic layer under a later ceramic stratum. The lower preceramic layer contained a small number of stone tools—a ground-stone ax, a pitted stone used for cracking nuts, a hammerstone, and a few quartzite flakes—and the remains of a hearth. Charcoal from the hearth produced a radiocarbon sample dating to 9020 ± 100 BP, which represents a human presence dating to between 8475 and 7934 cal BC.

Other sites near Puerto Ayacucho had similar preceramic layers (although unfortunately without material for radiocarbon dates). Excavations at the site of **La Culebra**, 12 km (7.5 miles) upstream from Puerto Ayacucho, exposed two distinct cultural layers. The lower layer (Atures I) contained an assemblage of scrapers and lithic debris made from locally available quartz pebbles, but no projectile points. The upper and subsequent layer (Atures II) contained several hundred flakes, a couple of scrapers, and other debitage, all made from locally available quartz, but also two distinctive projectile points—one from black chert, the other a pinkish chert—made from stones not locally available. The projectile point styles seem similar to points found at sites in Colombia situated along rivers that drain the eastern slope of the Andes and flow into the Orinoco Basin. Although the archaeological data are limited, they point to the presence of people in the Middle Orinoco who probably combined hunting and collecting palm nuts and other foods in a **broad-spectrum foraging pattern**. According to Rafael Gasson, "These findings indicate the great antiquity of two typical Orinoquia patterns: the exploitation of different ecological zones and the connection between the highlands and the lowlands."[11]

Rio Caquetá, Broad-Spectrum Foraging in the Colombian Amazon

The Rio Caquetá originates in the Colombian Andes and flows eastward for nearly 2,300 km (1,428 miles) through eastern Colombia and Brazil, coursing through numerous rapids and waterfalls before joining the Amazon River. Excavations at the site of **Peña Roja** were designed to test a hypothesis that hunters and gatherers could not live in tropical rainforests, an idea based on ethnographic cases in which tropical rainforest collectors also have access to agricultural crops.[12] The excavations at Peña Roja demonstrated that this hypothesis is false.

The excavations uncovered a series of occupational strata dating to between 9300 and 9000 BP, or approximately between 8850 and 7950 cal BC—layers beneath later levels created by pottery-using societies.[13] The earliest levels contained only stone artifacts, including cobble tools and flakes used for woodworking, and edge scrapers and blades used for butchering game and scraping hides.

But a number of objects suggested the importance of plant foods, particularly the fruits and nuts of different types of palm trees. The excavations recovered numerous seeds from the royal palm (*Maximiliana maripa*). Based on the recipes of modern people living in the Amazon, the royal palm nut and the fruit that surrounds it are thick with fat. A common recipe involves boiling the ripe fruits in water and steeping them in hot water until a rich drink forms. After the beverage is drained off, the nuts are cracked and toasted with salt. Fruits from other palms can be brewed to produce very rich beverages, as fatty as olive oil and as nutritious as mother's milk. Some palm nuts were probably milled on grinding stones; other fruits were eaten raw. All the palms from the excavations at Peña Roja were wild trees, not domesticates. The only traces of possible domesticates were phytoliths from the lerén, bottle gourd, and calabash—a set of crops also found in the Late Las Vegas sites of the Santa Elena Peninsula, Ecuador (dis-

Figure 4.8 Nukak men in camp

cussed earlier). These different lines of evidence point to an Archaic adaptation in the Colombian Amazon that was early and enduring. The Peña Roja excavations also suggest the importance of a broad-spectrum strategy for food collectors in Amazonia, a pattern characterized as "foragers who practiced small-scale domestic gardening."[14]

Drawing on his ethnographic research with modern foragers in the Amazonian regions of Colombia and western Brazil, the archaeologist **Gustavo Politis** has discussed the complex interactions involved in such a strategy.[15] Although traditional foraging societies have been impacted by modern nation-states and capitalist economies, the Nukak came into direct contact with Western society only in the early 1980s (figure 4.8).

Politis began ethnographic research in the late 1980s, and his detailed analysis of how the Nukak live in the Amazonian rainforest—and how they transform the rainforest in the process—provides intriguing insights into early human adaptations. This is not to suggest that the Nukak are a people "frozen in time" but rather that they—living in a habitat similar to that of much earlier Archaic peoples—can teach us about the strategies required to live in a lowland tropical forest.

In the late 1980s the Nukak numbered 400 to 500 people, living in several independent bands consisting of five or fewer families and twelve to forty-four people. Ranging over 10,000 km^2 (3,860 square miles), the Nukak bands are characterized by a "lack of hierarchical organization, strong solidarity patterns, and high residential mobility."[16] Less than 5 percent of the Nukak diet is based on domesticated plants. The Nukak move their camps often, occupying one place

Figure 4.9 Abandoned Nukak encampment

an average of 3.3 days, and each camp averages 7.7 km (4.8 miles) from the next (figure 4.9).

People range out from these camps to collect food resources and other forest products, usually covering an irregular loop of about 9 km (5.4 miles) and always returning to camp before nightfall. Also, the Nukak may send groups of men out from the main camp to gather canes for blow pipes that grow on a specific cluster of rocky hills; these men camp out while the rest of the band stays at the principal encampment. Otherwise, people move through the forest as members of individual bands.

In that process, the forest is subtly transformed. The Nukak use 113 species of plants; 90 of the species are uncultivated rainforest plants, and 23 species are cultivated in small gardens (most of these are recently introduced plants obtained from missionaries and other groups). But one of the most pervasive changes to the forest comes from the casual discard of wild palm seeds. The Nukak camps are scattered with edible palm nuts—collected but accidentally dropped into the soils rich in organic materials that form at the jungle campsites (figure 4.10). The human waste, charcoal, and other organic debris create anthrosols known as *terra preta,* or "dark earth" (a process that becomes even more extensive when later groups practice slash-and-burn agriculture; see chapter 5). These unintentionally modified soils create an ideal environment for plants.

Another serendipitous consequence occurs when the Nukak remove the hard shells of certain palm nuts and accidentally drop the seeds; these seeds germinate more rapidly than unshelled plants. Such processes result in clusters of valuable

Figure 4.10 Nukak women preparing palm nuts

food plants, creating "wild orchards" in the Amazonian rainforest. Politis estimates that as a band establishes between seventy and eighty campsites each year, large areas of rainforest are transformed. The Nukak also cut down palm trees to acquire the nuts, opening areas of shaded forest to sunlight and new growth. Thus, Amazonian forest dwellers modify their habitats.

The antiquity of such strategies is unknown, although the site of Peña Roja contains archaeological remains similar to those recorded for the Nukak. The large numbers of palm seeds indicate a similar reliance on tree crops. The stone tools include flake tools for woodworking and stone axes suitable for cutting large trees. It is possible that Archaic inhabitants of the Amazon manipulated plant resources long before full-scale agriculture developed.

In this broad sense, there are parallels among the Archaic practices of people during the Late Las Vegas in southwestern Ecuador, the people of San Jacinto I in northern Colombia, and the people at Peña Roja in the western Amazon. In each case, plant resources and other aspects of the environment were manipulated and modified even before the transition to full-scale agriculture and settled village life.

Coastal Adaptations in the Atacama Desert

On the far southern coast of Peru and in northern Chile, the Atacama Desert is one of the driest regions on Earth, second only to Antarctica in its aridity. Many regions have received no rainfall in recorded history. The Atacama stretches for about 1,500 km (932 miles) from southern Peru into northern Chile. The northernmost Atacama Desert has only a few, relatively small river valleys; most of the zone is covered by sand dunes and barren rock. Perhaps it is not surprising that people turned to the sea.

The Archaic patterns have antecedents in earlier Paleoindian strategies. At the site of **Quebrada Jaguay**, excavated by **Daniel Sandweiss** and colleagues, the earliest layers date to 13,000–11,000 years ago.[17] Located near the modern town of Camaná, Peru, water flows down the quebrada for a few weeks each year; it was probably wetter at the end of the Pleistocene but still essentially a desert. Today, the site is about 2 km (1.2 miles) from the Pacific; with lower sea levels at the end of the Pleistocene, the site was 7–8 km (4.2 –4.8 miles) inland. Still, the sea offered more abundant resources than the surrounding desert, and that is where the occupants of Quebrada Jaguay turned their gaze. The beach is a sandy bottom and relatively shallow portion of the continental shelf. The people of Quebrada Jaguay fished this zone with nets, collecting relatively small fish, particularly drums (*Sciaena* genus). Of the more than 6,000 animal bones recovered during the excavation, 96.5 percent were fish bones. The only terrestrial mammals were small rodents that probably died naturally and accidentally in the site. The people also collected surf clams (*Mesodesma donacium*), a mollusk about the size of a fortune cookie. Ninety-nine percent of the shellfish were of this single species (figure 4.11).

It is not surprising that a coastal settlement would collect seafood; the surprise is the singular focus of the efforts. A few strands of cordage may be fishing nets. A few fragments of gourd rinds may be containers or net floats.

At the end of the Pleistocene, the site at Quebrada Jaguay was apparently one node in a seasonal movement of food collectors, hunters and gatherers who moved from the highlands to the Pacific Ocean at specific times of the year, traveling along the drainages that were obvious routes between the sierra and the sea. When they came to the coast, they focused exclusively on coastal resources. As they descended from the sierra, they brought a few chunks of obsidian from a source in the highlands (the Alca source), 2,850 m (8,462 ft) above sea level and about 130 km (81 miles) upstream from the site at Quebrada Jaguay. Other than this, they carried little in the way of other resources. Instead, the people of Quebrada Jaguay intensively collected the easily gathered riches of the shore.

This basic pattern of incorporating coastal resources into a specific phase of an annual cycle lasted until around 10,800 to 10,500 years ago. In the Early Holocene, people established more permanent settlements along the coast. At Quebrada Jaguay, post molds and a house floor about 5 m (16.4 ft) across indicate that people were beginning to stay longer at the site (figure 4.12).

Obsidian disappears from the deposits, suggesting that people were not traveling into the sierra. Finally, Quebrada Jaguay was surrounded by other small encampments. Previously isolated in the Terminal Pleistocene, fifty-five small sites are found near Quebrada Jaguay. Seventeen sites have been radiocarbon-dated; all date to the Holocene, most between 10,900 and 8,900 years ago.

This suggests that the initial Pleistocene patterns of seasonal movements and temporary coastal encampments were replaced by more permanent coastal adaptations. As the excavators note, "Thus, building on the achievements of their

Figure 4.11 Fish bones and mollusk shells at Quebrada Jaguay, Peru

Terminal Pleistocene predecessors, the Early Holocene inhabitants of southern Peru seem to have developed a fully maritime adaptation."[18]

The adaptation to coastal zones was paralleled at similar places along the coasts of Peru and northern Chile (see figure 4.2). South of the modern Peruvian town of Ilo, the **Ring site** was a multilayer site 5 m (16.4 ft) thick dating between 11,200 and 5,900 years ago (figure 4.13).[19]

Figure 4.12 Post molds (marked by blue balloons) indicating the remains of structures at Quebrada Jaguay, Peru

Figure 4.13 Setting of the Ring site, Peru (largely destroyed by road construction after excavations)

The Ring site consisted of a circular shell midden about 25 m (82 ft) in diameter surrounding an open area or possible plaza (figure 4.14). Most of the dated layers occurred between 9,100 and 5,850 years ago, strata jammed with shells, fish

Figure 4.14 Stratigraphic profile at the Ring site, Peru

bones, the brittle carapaces and spines of sea urchins, and the white bones of sea mammals and sea birds—all indicating a focus on marine resources (figure 4.15). The only remains of terrestrial mammals were the bones of four mice. No botanical materials were preserved.

Figure 4.15 Mollusk shells, snail shells, and bird bone from the Ring site, Peru

A different kind of coastal adaptation was preserved when an ancient flash flood more than 10,500 years ago buried an open-air campsite at **Quebrada Tacahuay**, 20 km (12.4 miles) south of the Ring site.[20]

Between about 13,000 and 11,200 years ago, people intensively hunted sea birds, particularly cormorants and boobies. Fish bones, sea mammal bones, and shells were relatively rare. The sea birds were butchered—their bones scored with cut marks—and eaten. The birds were adults, possibly netted or stalked in shallow waters, rather than juveniles captured from rookeries. Thus, the broad-based maritime foraging indicated at the Ring site was only one strategy; the archaeofauna from Quebrada Tacahuay indicate that specialized hunting was also part of the human strategy along the coast.

If abundant marine resources attracted Archaic foragers to the coast, freshwater allowed them to stay. South of the Ring site and Quebrada Tacahuay, another coastal site—**Quebrada de los Burros**—has a small but permanent spring seeping out from the edge of the arroyo.[21] The site is about 150 m^2 (1,615 ft^2); it is about 2 m (6.6 ft) thick, with six distinct layers dating between 9,700 and 7,300 years ago. Postholes indicate that relatively small, semicircular huts were built. Small sardine bones imply that the inhabitants fished with nets. Other fish species were taken with hook and line; and a diverse assortment of mollusks, crabs, and sea urchins was gathered along the shoreline. As at Quebrada Tacahuay, the people of Quebrada de los Burros hunted large sea birds, but they also hunted large terrestrial game including guanaco (*Lama guanicoe*) and the now-endangered North Andean deer (*Hippocamelus antisensis*). The tools recovered from Quebrada de los Burros reflect this mix of pursuits: most of the objects relate to fishing—fishhooks, bone net weights, and harpoons—but there are also stone projectile points that indicate hunting. The lower levels of the site, dating to between 9,800 and 8,500 years ago, have fewer projectile points than the upper layers, deposited between 7,500 and 7,200 years ago; in fact, the upper layers have nearly twelve times the number of projectile points (n = 346) than the lower levels (n = 29). Large points (10–12 cm [3.9–4.7 in] long) may have been used to spear sharks or as knife blades, and smaller projectile points (5 cm [2 in] long) were used for hunting other game.

Different lines of evidence suggest changes in sedentism at Quebrada de los Burros. Approximately 1.5 km (1 mile) inland from Quebrada de los Burros, a large expanse of fog-fed vegetation—a habitat known as lomas vegetation—sprouted on hilltops during the winter. This plant community was important browse for guanaco and deer, and the people of Quebrada de los Burros hunted those animals during the austral winter, between June and September. A study of seasonal growth rings on the surf clam provides another perspective on mobility. Clams from the lower levels of the site were collected through much of the year and most intensively from October to May, thus including months when the lomas are dry. Mollusks from the upper levels imply that people were collecting clams within a shorter range of months, from September to January. Although these clams were not a major food resource (in contrast to Quebrada Jaguay), they do indicate changes in basic strategies: initially, people seem to have lived at Quebrada de los Burros most of the year, if not year-round. Later, the upper layers suggest that people were actually more mobile, moving to the coast and hunting when the lomas vegetation was damp, thick, and filled with game.

At coastal locations with more dependable water sources, people seem to have become more sedentary, and with this comes tantalizing evidence of changes in Archaic societies, such as the mummified bodies of the **Chinchorros Tradition**.[22]

Chinchorros groups were sedentary occupants of the Pacific Coast. Numerous lines of evidence point toward sedentism. Chemical isotope analysis of the skeletons indicates a high reliance on marine resources. Constant exposure to cold water and wind created bony growths in the ear canal or external auditory exostosis (a condition also known as "surfer's ear"), which caused slight deafness. By eating raw fish, the Chinchorros people ingested tapeworms that caused anemia, reflected in signs of osteoporosis in the skeletons. The Chinchorros people were also blighted by Chagas disease transmitted by reduvid bugs that live in the walls of huts, another unfortunate consequence of sedentism.

As documented by the Chilean bioarchaeologist **Bernardo Arriaza**, the Chinchorros Tradition is the earliest known example of artificial mummification, which was developed 7,000 years ago and endured for nearly four millennia.[23] In a changing set of practices that preserved and transformed the corpse, Chinchorros mummies were buried in cemeteries, which indicates a year-round presence along the Pacific Coast. The earliest form of mummification, the **Black Mummies**, involved the most elaborate modification of the body (figure 4.16).

The body was buried in a wet bog, the flesh decayed, and the bones were dug up and cleaned. The skull and other bones were reassembled, connected with reed cords to an armature of wooden poles. This frame of bones and wood was covered

Figure 4.16 Chinchorros Tradition Black Mummy

with grayish clay. Facial features and genitalia were recreated in clay. Bits of skin were patched together with animal hide. Sometimes, facial skin was removed before the body was allowed to decay, only to be reattached to the mummy. Finally, the mummy was slathered with a blue-gray layer of manganese paste, a final step in transforming the corpse into an effigy. These practices had developed by 5000 BC and decreased in popularity after 2800 BC.

The next class of Chinchorros mummies was the **Red Mummies**, which, although somewhat less elaborate in preparation than the Black Mummies, nonetheless were stunning creations. The organs and muscles were extracted from the corpse through slits slashed on the knees and ankles, shoulders, and groin. The skull was taken off. After all organs were removed, the inside of the body cavity was dried with hot coals. A supporting framework was created by sliding long poles under the skin. The empty corpse was stuffed with seabird feathers, earth, and camelid hair. The skull was topped with a shoulder-length wig fashioned from human hair and glued to the skull with manganese paste. A layer of clay left open slots for the eyes. The mouth was left ajar; the teeth gleamed. The body was then painted with red ocher pigment, except for the face and hair. Red Mummies were first created around 2000 BC and remained the principal form of Chinchorros

Figure 4.17 Reconstruction of a Chinchorros burial

mortuary treatment for the next five centuries, when Chinchorros mummies became somewhat less elaborated. **Bandage Mummies** retain the careful de-fleshing and reconstructions of the earlier mummies, but the skin was cut into strips and wrapped around the skeletons. A millennium later, mummies were wrapped in reed cords as more elaborate practices fell from favor. Another mortuary variant was **Mud-Covered Mummies**, naturally dried corpses covered with a thick paste, a treatment that first appeared around 1700 BC.

The creation of the Chinchorros mummies suggests rather complex notions by the living about the dead, although those meanings remain unclear (figure 4.17).

Minimally, there was an extensive engagement among the living, the dead, and the corpse as transformed into effigy. This suggests that the Chinchorros viewed their own mortality in something other than bilateral terms of "life" versus "death." It is possible—but far from certain—that a form of ancestor veneration is indicated. If so, it was different from later Inca mortuary practices, in which the mummy was placed in crypts where it could be extracted or feted by its descendants (see chapter 11). In contrast, the Chinchorros mummies were elaborately prepared and possibly admired but then wrapped in reed fiber shrouds and buried in cemeteries.

Figure 4.18 Location of the Kilometer 4 site, Peru

These complicated and eloquent representations of past lives contain another fascinating detail: the first Chinchorros mummies were the bodies of infants and fetuses killed by arsenic poisoning. The oldest known mummies come from the **Camarones 14 site**, located on the banks of the Rio Camarones in northern Chile, a drainage whose water naturally contains 1,000 micrograms of arsenic per liter—100 times the acceptable amount according to the World Health Organization. For pregnant women, arsenic poisoning can result in miscarriages and stillbirths. Newborns have lower birth weights, may develop cancers of the skin, liver, and bladder, and may suffer from retarded mental development. They tend to die young. At the Camarones 14 site, infant mortality was 20 percent to 25 percent, nearly double the highest rates in modern nations such as the Democratic Republic of the Congo (11.9%) and Afghanistan (14.3%). Arriaza writes that death from arsenic poisoning "threatened group survival, and as an emotional response Chinchorro people likely created artificial mummification to assuage their social grief."[24] In a bitter and deadly irony, the presence of freshwater in the Atacama, which allowed the Chinchorros people to inhabit the desert coast, contained the deadly toxins that led parents to preserve their infants' bodies in layers of clay, pigment, and skin.

But not all coastal valleys coursed with poisonous streams. The rivers of southern Peru have significantly lower levels of arsenic than the streams and oases of northern Chile.[25] The coastal region near the mouth of the Osmore Valley was the scene of relatively consistent human occupation for nearly twelve millennia.[26] For example, the **Kilometer 4 site**—named for a station on a local railroad line—contained strata spanning the entire Archaic period (figure 4.18).

Stretching over 10 hectares (22 acres) on a flat area of coastal foothills next to a now-dry spring, the Kilometer 4 site contains three cemeteries, more than seventy-five terraced residential areas, and extensive shell middens. During the Middle Archaic, Kilometer 4 was apparently seasonally occupied, but by the Late Archaic the site was a permanent settlement. Late Archaic houses were small, circular huts. The villagers of Kilometer 4 fished for anchovies and herrings, hunted game in the nearby stands of lomas vegetation, and collected a range of plant foods. They also had access to domesticated plants such as cotton. One cemetery area contained Chinchorro-style mummies, but other funeral treatments were also practiced. Excavations in a Late Archaic midden area uncovered the burial of a 45–50-year-old man, buried in a semi-flexed position in a circular pit. The man wore a fringed loincloth woven from cotton and was covered with a woven cloak. Near the corpse were several leather bags containing stone beads and other objects, including bone tubes possibly used for inhaling hallucinogenic snuff.

These complex differences in funerary practices are counterpoints to the continuities and complexities of the Archaic occupations along the coasts of southern Peru and northern Chile. At the same time the reliance on marine resources was a common aspect of life, local variations—in getting food or conceptions of the afterlife—indicate marked differences. As the evidence from the Ilo region indicates, "The degree and duration of marine exploitation suggest that regional specialization, rather than generalized forager behavior, was a characteristic of the earliest coastal settlement and endured through time."[27]

Sambaquis: Maritime Collectors and Shell Mounds on the Atlantic Coast

Sambaquis are large shell mounds found along the coast of Brazil and in northern Uruguay (figure 4.19).[28]

Some mounds are enormous, originally 50 m (164 ft) tall and 200 m × 200 m (984 ft × 984 ft) at their base, although most sambaquis are less than 5 m (16 ft) tall. Consisting of tons of mollusk shells and other materials, sambaquis are surprisingly varied—representing residential areas, burial mounds, and intentionally constructed monuments on the prehistoric landscape.

Hundreds of sambaquis are located along the seacoasts, embayments, and lagoons of the Atlantic littoral; and their distributions in time and space were influenced by post-Pleistocene fluctuations in sea level. The continental shelf is broad and relatively shallow, and now-submerged sambaquis dating to 8000 BP have been found during underwater archaeological surveys. Conversely, other sambaquis were created when the Atlantic Ocean rose above current levels during the Middle Holocene, creating lagoons in zones that are now dry. Most sambaquis were created between about 5000 and 2000 BP.

For all their essential similarity—large piles of oyster, clam, and mangrove mussel shells—sambaquis exhibit surprising variations. Studied since the late nineteenth century, sambaquis were originally interpreted as the seasonal camps of mobile fisher-folk who camped on dry knolls near lagoons and bays, stayed a

Figure 4.19 A sambaqui at the site of Santa Marta I, Santa Catarina, Brazil

while, moved on, but later returned. Today, it is clear that many sambaquis were created by sedentary food collectors.

Often strategically positioned between habitats, the people of the sambaquis acquired different sets of resources. Fish were netted in lagoons and bays, mollusks were collected in the mangroves, and occasionally dolphins and whales were hunted or scavenged.[29] Forest plants were collected—and may have been cultivated—and brought back to the settlements. At the settlements, plants were processed with mortars, metates, and anvil stones. A variety of ornaments were fashioned from polished bone and stone, including miniature "zooliths"—small ground-stone icons depicting land and sea animals such as felines, armadillos, eagles, sharks, whales, and penguins. Made with an attention to detail that scholars have called "hyper-realistic," zooliths are interpreted as "representations of entities belonging simultaneously to the material and spiritual worlds."[30]

The sambaquis were more than massive piles of food debris and abandoned artifacts. They were cultural features in a landscape in which three sets of activities intersected: the creation of living spaces, the burial of the dead, and the construction of mounds. These overlapping activities sets—what the archaeologist **Maria Dulce Gaspar** has called the "triple space association"—have been documented for more than 900 sambaquis in southern Brazil.[31] These 900 sambaquis are contemporaries of, and distinct from, other archaeological sites in the surrounding area, leading to the hypothesis that these massive mounds of shell represent a shared set of worldview and cultural practices defining a cultural group called **the Sambaquis Society**.

Excavations at the site of **Jabuticabeira II** uncovered clear evidence of this pattern. Located near the Camacho lagoon on the coast of southern Brazil, the mound is about 8 m (26.2 ft) tall and covers 90,000 m^2 (968,760 ft^2). Modern construction companies had mined the shell mound for building material (using the shell in place of gravel); the barrow cuts exposed a sequence of mounded layers. Thick strata of shells were capped by dark layers dense with organic materials and charcoal. Burials were clustered in discrete areas on top of the dark layer. The corpses were laid in shallow pits, usually tightly flexed but sometimes extended. Many of the graves held secondary burials; the individuals had died elsewhere, and their skeletons were carried to the sambaquis, possibly during a "coordinated and communal ceremony."[32] The skeletons were accompanied by everyday artifacts or jewelry made from bone or shell. Some of the bodies were covered with red pigment. Postholes encircling the burials suggest some type of windscreen or funerary scaffoldings from which offerings dangled. High densities of food refuse—the bones of fish, land mammals (tapir, monkey, and armadillo), sea mammals (whales and dolphins), and marine birds—were present and suggest feasting with the dead. At some point, large hearths were constructed; the entire mound was burned and subsequently capped with heaps of shell. The excavators write, "The ritual program of burial, feasting, and mounding of shell over a former funerary area was re-enacted over centuries, incrementally giving rise to the ultimate huge volume and monumental appearance of the sambaqui." Over a period of 800 years, an estimated 43,000 people were buried in the sambaqui at Jabuticabeira II.[33]

Other sambaquis also have dense concentrations of burials, and the paleopathologies suggest the emergence of settled Archaic lifestyles. The teeth exhibit moderate and severe occlusal wear, suggesting that dwellers of the sambaquis ingested a great deal of grit and sand. The post-cranial bones exhibit lesions produced by infectious diseases. As another group of scholars has observed, "The high positive correlation between infectious disease, population density and the level of sedentism is well known. Therefore, the disease pattern seems to indicate that these [sambaqui-dwelling] groups had low levels of mobility and relatively high population density."[34]

The largest sambaquis may have been the centers of specific territories, monumental and symbolic hubs for a set of communities sprinkled along the coasts and lagoons. Analysis of the sambaquis surrounding the major lagoon of **Santa Marta** on the southern coast of Brazil indicates that the largest sambaquis were more or less evenly spaced around the lagoon and were visible from each other. Smaller shell mounds were clustered around the larger sambaquis, producing a pattern, as **Paulo de Blassis** and colleagues have noted, in which "the territories of each group of sites are not separated but rather [have] broadly overlapping territories, pointing to patterns of interaction and articulation of these sambaquis communities surrounding the lagoon, the central place of the sambaqui economic and social universe." In turn, they write, "each of these sambaqui clusters represents the focus of a settlement nucleus—social as well as geographical—of a dense population, with marked territories, locational references, and community identities for the sambaqui communities surrounding the lagoon."[35]

In sum, the sambaquis shell mounds reflect a pattern of sedentism and emergent social complexity during the Archaic in coastal Brazil and Uruguay, although a pattern not characterized by evident social divisions. Gaspar and colleagues write, "Formalized systems of social inequality are not apparent in mortuary treatments. Funeral areas are collective and isolated burials are rare." Although some burials have slightly more elaborated treatments—a layer of painted clay placed over one body, a bit more shell mounded up over another—nothing suggests major differences of social scale. Rather, the ceremonies of secondary burial and feasting—"funeral rituals involving the offering and consumption of abundant food"—expressed a broadly shared ideology that was "decisive in [the] structuring of sambaqui society and in the development of economic and social complexity without the emergence of explicit mechanisms for rank and hierarchy."[36]

Camelid Hunters in the Pampas and the Andes

Although a number of South American game animals became extinct at the end of the Pleistocene—giant ground sloths, mastodons, and horses—the wild relatives of the llama survived (figure 4.20).

The modern South American camelids are represented by four species, two wild and two domesticated: the domesticated llama (*Lama glama*) and its wild relative, the guanaco (*L. guanicoe*), and the domesticated alpaca (*Vicuyana pacos*) and its wild relative, the vicuña (*V. vicugna*) (figure 4.21).[37] Today, the guanaco is the most widespread of the wild camelids, found from the central Peruvian Andes to Tierra del Fuego and on both sides of the Andes, literally ranging down to both the Pacific and Atlantic Coasts in the southernmost reaches of the continent. During the Pleistocene, earlier forms of paleo-llama ranged even further afield, found in northeastern Brazil in fossil and archaeological deposits dating to as late as 8,500 to 6,900 years ago.

The transitions in hunting and gathering in the Pleistocene and the Archaic were complex, varied, and nonsynchronous. For example, the vast grasslands of the pampas of southern Brazil, Uruguay, and Argentina were occupied by hunters and gatherers by the end of the Pleistocene.[38] Various game animals were hunted, including several now-extinct big-game animals such as giant ground sloth, horse, and giant armadillo, as well as camelids. In this region of South America, many of these "Pleistocene" fauna survived well into the Holocene, much longer than similar species did in North America. Further, a wide array of other game animals was hunted, including deer, capybara, peccary, and guanaco. At the site of **Arroyo Seco 2**, Gustavo Politis and colleagues uncovered a complex record of artifacts, fauna, and human burials spanning the period from approximately 12,200 to 7300 BP. Located on a low hill on the edge of a dry wash, the site was repeatedly but not continuously occupied over a period of 5,000 years. Living in an open-air base camp, the inhabitants of Arroyo Seco 2 used atlatls and bolas to hunt guanaco (the primary game animal), as well as pampean deer, armadillos, and rheas (the South American ostrich). Other artifacts such as stone scrapers, mortars, and pestles suggest a settled encampment. Arroyo Seco 2 also had a cemetery. The initial burials

Figure 4.20 (*overleaf*) Guanaco crossing a river in Torres del Paine National Park, Chile

Figure 4.21 Alpaca grazing on a boefedal, with Volcán Parinacota on the Chile-Bolivia border in the background

exhibit evidence of conflict: the first four burials were adults—an elderly male, two young adult males, and a young adult woman—found with projectile points deeply embedded in their bodies. Later burials included primary and secondary burials—totaling forty-five humans—some of whom were covered in red ocher and buried with necklaces of wolf or dog teeth. The excavators suggest that the offerings of canine teeth indicate that wolves or dogs "had a strong symbolic connotation to mediate the relation between human and supernatural spirits or beings."[39]

At various places in South America, hunting camelids seems to have become more common after 8500–5300 BP. Before then, camelid remains are found in some sites but not others and often contributed less to the diet than other game animals, such as white-tailed deer. Subsequently, camelid remains become extremely common, especially in altiplano sites as people colonized higher elevations. This shift in emphasis from deer to camelids is indicated in the central Peruvian Andes in excavations directed by **Thomas Lynch** at the site of **Guitarrero Cave**.[40] Located at an elevation of 2,580 m (8,462 ft) above sea level on a slope above the Santa River, Guitarrero Cave was first occupied about 12,000 cal yr BP as a short-term shelter for hunters but became more permanently occupied after 11,000 cal yr BP. At that point a series of superimposed layers contain a remarkably well-preserved assemblage of normally perishable objects: woven textiles, spun cordage, wooden fire drills, and a diversity of plant remains (including some possible domesticated crops, such as chilies and beans in a stratum dating to 8600–8000 BC, with maize dating sometime after 5780 BC). In addition, Guitarrero Cave showed evidence

Figure 4.22 Setting of the intermontane site of Asana, Peru

of the increasing importance of camelids in the diet, although deer remained the principal game.

A particularly detailed record of Archaic hunters comes from the southern Peruvian Andes. At an elevation of 3,400 m (11,152 ft) above sea level, the open-air site of **Asana** is located about 125 km (77.6 miles) up the Rio Osmore drainage from the coastal Ring site.[41] Intensively excavated by **Mark Aldenderfer**, Asana is located next to a spring-fed grassy area, or boefedal. The presence of this spring made the location desirable to hunters and gatherers, who repeatedly camped at various times over six millennia (figure 4.22).

These repeated encampments left traces of both shelters and ritual features, resulting in a complex series of overlapping archaeological layers. The Asana I phase dates to the Early Archaic (10,500–9800 BP). At that time, dwellings were oval huts as indicated by elliptical patterns of post molds, the remains of small huts less than 5 m^2 (54 ft^2) in area with simple floors of hard-packed sand. Hearths inside the huts were kindled for warmth; food was cooked outside. During the Middle Archaic (approximately 9800 BP), the houses at Asana were a bit larger than before—as large as 5.9 m^2 (63.5 ft^2)—and they had specially prepared floors of white clay or clay and sand sheltered by a lightweight hut covered with hides or brush. Grinding stones were used to mill seeds and to pulverize camelid and deer bones, perhaps to obtain marrow.

During the Late Archaic (5000–4400 BP), dramatic changes occurred at Asana. Dwellings became twice the size of previous huts, ovals or roughly rectangular buildings 8–12 m^2 (86–129 ft^2) in area and without specially prepared floors. Metates became common, suggesting that plants were collected when seeds formed at the end of the wet season, sometime between March and May. Since no storage pits were discovered, Late Archaic people probably did not live year-round at Asana. Nonetheless, the Late Archaic occupants of Asana invested the place with special meanings, as indicated by their construction of ritual enclosures and shrines.

The ritual enclosures date to 5000 to 4400 BP. They were specially prepared clay floors pocked with minute post molds only 2 to 5 cm (0.75–2 in) in diameter. Some post molds formed small circles of posts, as if depicting miniature huts. Other artifacts were also miniatures, including tiny spear points flaked from high-quality stone but never actually used. Other intriguing features include small pits excavated into the floor that were filled with carefully organized deposits of white clay covered with a red clay that had been mixed with water and poured into the basin as a slurry. A final, singular feature was an irregular platform of earth about 6.5 m (21.3 ft) long, which contained several rough alcoves and an odd array of pits filled with specially selected stones. At one end of this feature, a large, roughly pyramidal stone had been split, exposing the inner matrix that sparkled with shiny mineral inclusions. Just below it, a shallow pit was filled with unbroken stones of the same sparkling material and another tiny pyramidal stone of the same material but split as if to mimic the larger stone. Surrounding the earthen platform and the pyramidal stones were about 50 other pits, most 30–40 cm (9.9–15.6 in) long but only 3 cm (1.2 in) deep, which contained a chunk of red or gray stone that glittered with the same mineral inclusions in the high Andean sunlight.

It is difficult to know precisely what the Late Archaic inhabitants of Asana were enacting as they arrayed these glittering stones five millennia ago. The careful arrangements of objects are reminiscent of the modern Aymara ritual practices in which special objects—such as seashells filled with wine, candles, llama fat, and other items—are carefully placed on a poncho or cloth to create a *mesa* (table). The use of miniatures continues today in the Andean highlands in the Aymara *alasita* ceremony, in which the god of good luck, *e'eq'o*, is offered miniature versions of the objects of desire.[42] (If you want to be rich, you offer e'eq'o a tiny stack of fake $100 bills. If you want to go to Miami, you give him a tiny replica of an airplane.) Some of the shallow hearths at Asana may have been the locations where offerings were burned, the smoke rising to the ancestors or deities.

Much is uncertain about the ritual structures at Asana, but this is known: these ritual practices were created and ultimately abandoned as the relationships between people and place changed during the Archaic. In the Early Archaic, people camped at Asana in the course of regular movements between the highlands and the coast, apparently moving up from the Pacific Coast by way of the Osmore drainage to hunt camelids and deer in the highlands. By the Late Archaic, Asana was a regular encampment for hunters and gatherers who lived principally in the highlands, occasionally trading with coastal groups but living in the southern Andean sierra. After 4400 BP, the ritual structures disappeared at Asana; people continued to occupy the site, but they did so as llama herders rather than as guanaco hunters. With that change, there was an associated shift in their relation to the place by the boefedal.

Conclusion: Diverse Adaptations in a Diverse Continent

The seven regional surveys of archaeological case studies are not a comprehensive overview of the Archaic in South America, but they do provide a sense of the variations in which humans adapted in different portions of the continent. Some of those variations are obvious—people adapt to coastal zones differently than they do to tropical rainforests or high-altitude puna—but other differences and similarities are more elusive. For example, the early maritime collectors of the desert coasts of Peru and Chile apparently did not include cultivated plants in their diets, as did the people living on the Santa Elena Peninsula of southwestern Ecuador. The people of the Las Vegas culture used marine resources but did not create massive shell middens, as did their contemporaries living along the coasts of Brazil and Uruguay. The recurrent occupations at San Jacinto I were broadly similar to the repeated encampments at Asana, although the purposes and pursuits at these different places were completely different. The broad-spectrum foraging indicated for the Colombian Amazon and possibly for the Middle Orinoco was a diverse subsistence strategy like that practiced by the Las Vegas culture societies but did not produce regional "centers" like those indicated for southwestern Ecuador. And so it goes—a complex mosaic of human strategies spread across the continent.

But there are also intriguing parallels in these diverse cases. For example, these different hunting-and-gathering societies also imbued spaces with cultural meanings. It is striking to see how very different Archaic societies converted domestic spaces for the living into resting places for the dead. Whether we look at the creation of cemeteries in sambaquis, the development of collective burials at only two sites in the Santa Elena Peninsula, or the creation of elaborate mummies of the Chinchorros traditions, hunters and gatherers transformed spaces as they created worlds of meaning. More than solely responding to the availability of natural resources, hunting-and-gathering societies made their worlds—enacting rituals, burying the dead, burning offerings to the spiritual world. In these diverse gestures and acts, prehistoric people adapted to and actively constructed their environments and societies during the Archaic period in South America.

Notes

1. Some archaeologists working in Peru use the term *Preceramic* instead of *Archaic*.

2. G. Willey and P. Phillips, "Method and Theory in American Archaeology II: Historical-Developmental Interpretation," *American Anthropologist* 57 (1955): 723–819.

3. L. Binford, "Willow Smoke and Dogs' Tails: Hunter-Gatherer Settlement Systems and Archaeological Site Formation," *American Antiquity* 45, no. 1 (1980): 4–20.

4. For English-language overviews to Stothert's research, see Karen Stothert, "The Preceramic Las Vegas Culture of Coastal Ecuador," *American Antiquity* 50 (1985): 613–636; Karen Stothert, "Early Economies of Coastal Ecuador and the Foundations

of Andean Civilization," *Andean Past* 3 (1992): 43–54; Karen Stothert, "Coastal Resources and Early Holocene Las Vegas Adaptation of Ecuador," in *Trekking the Shore: Changing Coastlines and the Antiquity of Coastal Settlement*, ed. N. Bicho, J. Haws, and L. Davis (New York: Springer, 2011), 355–382; K. Stothert, D. Piperno, and T. Andres, "Terminal Pleistocene/Early Holocene Human Adaptation in Coastal Ecuador: The Las Vegas Evidence," *Quaternary International* 109–110 (2003): 23–43. For the authoritative site report, see *La Prehistoria Temprana de la Peninsula de Santa Elena, Ecuador: La Cultura Las Vegas*, Miscelánea Antropológica Ecuatoriana, Serie Monográfica 10 (Guayaquil: Museo del Banco Central de Ecuador, 1988).

5. Stothert, Piperno, and Andres, "Terminal Pleistocene/Early Holocene Human Adaptation."

6. Ibid., 33.

7. The archaeological and archaeobotanical data for the origin and diffusion of maize—and the controversies surrounding their interpretations—are discussed in chapter 5.

8. A. Oyuela-Caycedo and R. Bonzani, *San Jacinto I: A Historical Ecological Approach to an Archaic Site in Colombia* (Tuscaloosa: University of Alabama Press, 2005). See also R. Bonzani, "Seasonality, Predictability, and Plant Use Strategies at San Jacinto I, Northern Colombia" (PhD diss., University of Pittsburgh, 1995); R. Bonzani, "Learning from the Present: The Constraints of Seasonality on Foragers and Collectors," in *Advances in the Archaeology of the Northern Andes*, ed. A. Oyuela-Caycedo and J. Raymond, Monograph 39, Institute of Archaeology (Los Angeles: University of California, 1998), 20–35; A. Oyuela-Caycedo, "Sedentism, Food Production, and Pottery Origins in the Tropics: San Jacinto 1; A Case Study in the Sabana de Bolivar, Serrania de San Jacinto, Colombia" (PhD diss., University of Pittsburgh, 1993); A. Oyuela-Caycedo, "The Study of Collector Variability in the Transition to Sedentary Food Producers in Northern Colombia," *Journal of World Prehistory* 10, no. 1 (1996): 49–93; A. Oyuela-Caycedo, "Seasonality in the Tropical Lowlands of Northwestern South America: The Case of San Jacinto 1, Colombia," in *Seasonality and Sedentism: Archaeological Perspectives from Old and New World Sites*, ed. T. Rocek and O. Bar-Yosef (Cambridge, MA: Peabody Museum, Harvard University, 1998), 165–179.

9. Oyuela-Caycedo and Bonzani, *San Jacinto I*, 156.

10. R. Gassón, "Orinoquia: The Archaeology of the Orinoco River Basin," *Journal of World Prehistory* 16, no. 3 (2002): 237–311; W. Barse, "Preceramic Occupations in the Orinoco River Valley," *Science* 250 (December 7, 1990): 1388–1390; W. Barse, "El periodo arcaico en el Orinoco y su contexto en el norte de Sud America," in *Ámbito y Ocupaciones Tempranas de la America Tropical*, ed. I. Cavelier and S. Mora (Bogota: Fundación Erigaie, Instituto Colombiano de Antropología, 1995), 99–113.

11. Gassón, "Orinoquia," 266.

12. R. Bailey, G. Head, M. Jenike, B. Owen, R. Rechtman, and E. Zechenter, "Hunting and Gathering in Tropical Rain Forest: Is It Possible?" *American Anthropologist* 91, no. 1 (1989): 59–82.

13. The original radiocarbon dates are 9125 ± 250 BP, 9160 ± 90 BP, and 9250 ± 140 BP; these were calibrated using CALIB 6.0 and the Southern Hemisphere Calibration Curve.

14. J. Oliver, "The Archaeology of Forest Foraging and Agricultural Production in Amazonia," in *Unknown Amazon: Culture in Nature in Ancient Brazil*, ed. C. McEwan, C. Barreto, and E. Neves (London: British Museum Press, 2001), 59.

15. G. Politis, "Foragers of the Amazon: The Last Survivors or the First to Succeed?" in *Unknown Amazon: Culture in Nature in Ancient Brazil*, ed. C. McEwan, C. Barreto, and E. Neves (London: British Museum Press, 2001), 26–49.

16. Ibid., 32.

17. D. Sandweiss, H. McInnis, R. Burger, A. Cano, B. Ojeda, R. Paredes, M. Sandweiss, and M. Glasscock, "Quebrada Jaguay: Early South American Maritime Adaptations," *Science* 281 (September 1998): 1830–1832.

18. Ibid., 1832.

19. D. Sandweiss, "Terminal Pleistocene through Mid-Holocene Archaeological Sites as Paleoclimatic Archives for the Peruvian Coast," *Palaeogeography, Palaeoclimatology, Palaeoecology* 194 (2003): 23–40; D. Sandweiss, J. Richardson III, E. Reitz, J. Hsu, and R. Feldman, "Early Maritime Adaptations in the Andes: Preliminary Studies at the Ring Site, Peru," in *Ecology, Settlement, and History in the Osmore Drainage*, ed. D. Rice, C. Stanish, and P. Scarr, BAR International Series 545 (1989): 35–84. The Ring site has since been destroyed by road construction.

20. S. deFrance, D. Keefer, J. Richardson, and A. Alvarez, "Late Paleo-Indian Coastal Foragers: Specialized Extractive Behavior at Quebrada Tacahuay, Peru," *Latin American Antiquity* 12, no. 4 (2001): 413–426; D. Keefer, S. deFrance, M. Moseley, J. Richardson, D. Satterlee, and A. Day-Lewis, "Early Maritime Economy and El Niño Events at Quebrada Tacahuay," *Science* 281 (September 1998): 1833–1835.

21. M. Carré, L. Klaric, D. Lavallée, M. Julien, I. Bentaleb, M. Fontugne, and O. Kawka, "Insights into Early Holocene Hunter-Gatherer Mobility on the Peruvian Southern Coast from Mollusk Gathering Seasonality," *Journal of Archaeological Science* 36 (2009): 1173–1178.

22. For an excellent, brief overview, see C. Santoro, B. Arriaza, V. Standen, and P. Marquet, "People of the Coastal Atacama Desert: Living between the Dunes and the Waves of the Pacific Ocean," in *Desert Peoples: Archaeological Perspectives*, ed. P. Veth, M. Smith, and P. Hiscock (Malden, MA: Blackwell, 2005), 243–260.

23. The discussion of Chinchorros mortuary treatments is based on B. Arriaza, "Chinchorro Bioarchaeology: Chronology and Mummy Seriation," *Latin American Antiquity* 6, no. 1 (1995): 35–55; B. Arriaza, *Beyond Death: The Chinchorros Mummies of Ancient Chile* (Washington, DC: Smithsonian Institution Press, 1995); B. Arriaza, V. Standen, V. Cassman, and C. Santoro, "Chinchorro Culture: Pioneers of the Coast of the Atacama Desert," in *Handbook of South American Archaeology*, ed. H. Silverman and W. Isbell (New York: Springer, 2008), 45–58.

24. B. Arriaza, "Aresniasis as an Environmental Hypothetical Explanation for the Origin of the Oldest Artificial Mummification Practice in the World," *Chungará: Revista de Antropología Chilena* 27, no. 2 (2005): 260.

25. See M. Castro de Esparza, "The Presence of Arsenic in Drinking Water in Latin America and Its Effect on Public Health" (paper presented at International Congress Natural Arsenic in Groundwaters of Latin America, Mexico City, June 2006), 20–24.

26. The following discussion is based on S. deFrance, N. Grayson, and K. Wise, "Documenting 12,000 Years of Coastal Occupation on the Osmore Littoral, Peru," *Journal of Field Archaeology* 34 (2009): 227–246; K. Wise, N. Clark, and S. Williams, "A Late Archaic Period Burial from the South-Central Andean Coast," *Latin American Antiquity* 5 (1994): 212–227.

27. deFrance, Grayson, and Wise, "Documenting 12,000 Years," 243.

28. This discussion is based on M. Gaspar, P. DeBlasis, S. Fish, and P. Fish, "Sambaqui (Shell Mound) Societies of Coastal Brazil," in *Handbook of South American Archaeology*, ed. H. Silverman and W. Isbell (New York: Springer, 2008), 319–335; M. Bonomo, "The Use of Space in the Pampean Atlantic Coast and the Adjacent Plains (Argentina, South America): A Comparative View," in *Trekking the Shore: Changing Coastlines and the Antiquity of Coastal Settlement*, ed. N. Bicho, J. Haws, and L. Davis (New York: Springer, 2011), 333–353; J. A. Rodriguez, "Human Occupation of the Eastern La Plata Basin and the Adjacent Littoral Region during the Mid-Holocene," *Quaternary International* 132 (2005): 23–36; P. DeBlasis, A. Kneip, R. Scheel-Ybert, P. Giannini, and M. Gaspar, "Sambaquis e Paisagem: Dinâmica natural e arqueologia regional no litoral do sul do Brasil," *Arqueología Suramericana/Arqueologia Sul-americana* 3, no. 1 (2007): 29–61; P. Giannini, X. Villagran, M. Fornari, D. Rodriguesdo Nascimento Jr., P. Menezes, A. Tanaka, D. Assunção, P. DeBlasis, and P. Carvalho do Amaral, "Interações entre evolução sedimentar e ocupação humana pré-histórica na costa centro-sul de Santa Catarina, Brasil," *Boletim do Museu Paraense Emílio Goeldi: Ciências Humanas* 5 (2010): 105–128; G. Wagner, K. Hilbert, D. Bandeira, M. Tenório, and M. Okumura, "Sambaquis (Shell Mounds) of the Brazilian Coast," *Quaternary International* 239 (2011): 51–60.

29. On cetacean exploitation see P. Volkmer de Castilho, "Utilization of Cetaceans in Shell Mounds from the Southern Coast of Brazil," *Quaternary International* 180 (2008): 107–114.

30. Gaspar et al., "Sambaqui (Shell Mound) Societies of Coastal Brazil," 329.

31. Cited in Wagner et al., "Sambaquis (Shell Mounds) of the Brazilian Coast," 52.

32. Gaspar et al., "Sambaqui (Shell Mound) Societies of Coastal Brazil," 326.

33. Ibid., 327.

34. Wagner et al., "Sambaquis (Shell Mounds) of the Brazilian Coast," 57.

35. DeBlasis et al., "Sambaquis e Paisagem," 48, my translation.

36. Gaspar et al., "Sambaqui (Shell Mound) Societies of Coastal Brazil," 329.

37. G. Mengoni Goñalons, "Camelids in Ancient Andean Societies: A Review of the Zooarchaeological Evidence," *Quaternary International* 185 (2008): 59–68. See also J. Wheeler, M. Fauere, C. Guerín, and F. Parenti, "Découverte d'une mégafaune holocène à la Toca de Serrote do Artur (aire archéologique de São Raimondo Nonato, Piauí, Brésil)," *Comptes Rendus de Académie des sciences (Sciences de la terre et de planètes)* 329 (1999): 443–448.

38. For a succinct summary, see G. Politis, "The Pampas and Campos of South America," in *Handbook of South American Archaeology*, ed. H. Silverman and W. Isbell (New York: Springer, 2008), 235–260. For an overview of Pleistocene and Holocene settlements in the Pampean region, see G. Politis, P. Messineo, and C. Kaufmann, "El poblamiento temprano de las llanuras pampeanas de Argentina y Uruguay," *Com-*

plutum 15 (2004): 207–224; and for a discussion of diet and skeletal materials, see G. Politis, C. Scabuzzo, and R. Tykot, "An Approach to Pre-Hispanic Diets in the Pampas during the Early/Middle Holocene," *International Journal of Osteoarchaeology* 19 (2009): 266–280.

39. Politis, "Pampas and Campos of South America," 246.

40. T. Lynch, *Guitarrero Cave: Early Man in the Andes* (New York: Academic Press, 1980); E. Jolie, T. Lynch, P. Geib, and J. Adovasio, "Cordage, Textiles, and the Late Pleistocene Peopling of the Andes," *Current Anthropology* 52, no. 2 (2011): 285–296.

41. M. Aldenderfer, "Middle Archaic Period Domestic Architecture from Southern Peru," *Science* 241 (September 1988): 1828–1830; M. Aldenderfer, "The Archaic Period in the South-Central Andes," *Journal of World Prehistory* 3, no. 2 (1989): 117–158; M. Aldenderfer, "Continuity and Change in Ceremonial Structures at Late Preceramic Asana, Southern Peru," *Latin American Antiquity* 2 (1991): 227–258; M. Aldenderfer, "Domestic Space, Mobility and Ecological Complementarity: The View from Asana," in *Domestic Architecture, Ethnicity, and Complementarity in the South-Central Andes*, ed. M. Aldenderfer (Iowa City: University of Iowa Press, 1993), 13–24; M. Aldenderfer, *Montane Foragers: Asana and the South-Central Andean Archaic* (Iowa City: University of Iowa Press, 1998); M. Aldenderfer, "High Elevation Foraging Societies," in *Handbook of South American Archaeology*, ed. H. Silverman and W. Isbell (New York: Springer, 2008), 131–143.

42. H. Tschopik, "The Aymara of Chucuito, Peru," *Anthropological Papers of the American Museum of Natural History* 44 (1951): 137–308.

Figure 5.1 Quinoa at 3,800 m, Apurimac, Peru

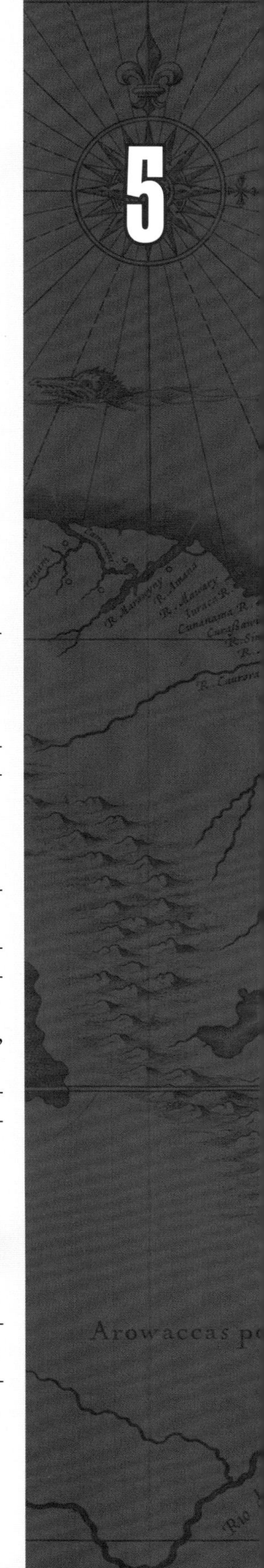

Origins and Consequences of Agriculture in South America

10.5876_9781607323334.c005

> Of provisions, besides maize, there are two other products which form the principal food of these Indians. One is called *potatoe*, and is a kind of earth nut, which, after it has been boiled, is as tender as a cooked chestnut, but it has no more skin than a truffle, and it grows under the earth in the same way.
>
> The other food is very good, and is called *quinoa*. The leaf is like a Moorish rush . . . and the plant grows almost to the height of a man, forming a very small seed, sometimes white and at others reddish. Of these seeds they make a drink, and also eat them cooked, as we do rice.
>
> *Pedro Cieza de Leon on the people of Quito*

The origin of agriculture has long been an important domain of archaeological research. Ever since the British archaeologist **V. Gordon Childe** famously defined "**the Neolithic Revolution**"—the shift from hunting and gathering to agriculture that was akin to the Industrial Revolution in its transformative consequences—archaeologists have investigated the tempo, causes, and consequences of ancient agriculture. Given the durability of hunting and gathering as a way of life for more than 90 percent of the human experience, the relatively recent emergence of agriculture over the last 10,000 years demands an explanation. Further, there is increasing evidence that the transition to agriculture occurred independently in different regions of the Earth yet at approximately the same time at the end of the Pleistocene, resulting in what has recently been called "an eerie synchronicity in the timing of the first domesticates."[1] The transition to agriculture involved different suites of plants and animals in ten different regions: East Asia, New Guinea, South Asia, the Near East, northern sub-Saharan Africa, eastern North America, Mesoamerica, and three regions in South America—northern South America, the southern Andean highlands, and western Amazonia. The three South American centers of origin resulted in domesticated crops and animals that would transform the prehispanic economies of the continent and the modern economies of the world.[2]

Key Terms and Methods

This chapter discusses the evidence for the origins of agriculture, summarizes proposed explanations for these origins, and describes some of the agrosystems found in different areas of South America. First, a few definitions are in order.[3] To start, there is the important distinction between wild and domesticated resources. **Domestication** is the process by which changes in the

Figure 5.2 Petroglyph depicting humans and camelids

morphology or genetics of plants and animals occur as a result of human interventions, often by artificially selecting species that have certain qualities (a larger fruit or a less toxic tuber). This may result in new domesticated species. Second, there are several terms relating to human involvement with plant or animal species (figure 5.2).

Wild resources can be **managed**—for example, setting controlled burns to create open browse for game animals—without resulting in domesticated species. **Cultivation** is the "intentional preparation of the soil"; this may involve either wild or domesticated species. Finally, three terms reflect the engagement of human societies with domesticates. **Farming** refers to the use of domesticated animals, plants, or both for food, fibers, transport, and other purposes. **Agriculture** refers to an economic system that is largely dependent on farming domesticated animals and plants, although hunting and gathering may continue to be pursued. **Agrosystem** refers to a particular set of domesticates and agricultural practices.

In South America, the number of domesticated plants far outnumbers the number of domesticated animals.[4] Only a few animals were originally domesticated in South America: the llama, alpaca, Muscovy duck, and guinea pig (figure 5.3, figure 5.4).

In contrast, a variety of plants first domesticated in South America became widespread cultigens, many of extraordinary importance to modern agriculture and commerce, including the potato, cotton, and specific varieties of beans, yams, squash, and chilies. For this reason, investigating the origins of South American

Figure 5.3 Guinea pigs in a market in Ecuador

agriculture requires the study of various plant remains, a field referred to as **paleoethnobotany** or **archaeobotany**.[5] **Macrobotanical remains** refer to the large items—seeds, stalks, tubers, and charcoal—that are evidence of plant use visible to

Figure 5.4 Guinea pigs on a stick, Ecuador

the naked eye. **Microbotanical remains** refer to microscopic evidence of ancient plants, which take different forms.

Palynology is the study of pollen grains, minute specks of genetic material, each with a hard exterior surface—the exine.[6] The exine is extraordinarily durable, often lasting thousands of years. Further, pollen exines exhibit radically diverse exterior geometries that are consistent at the family or genus levels, and these distinctive microscopic morphologies allow for the identification of ancient

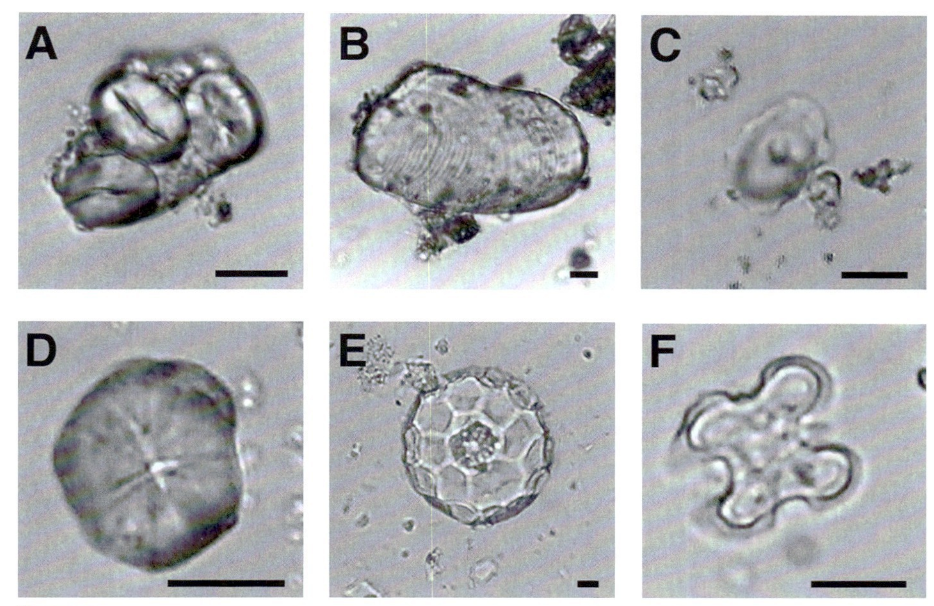

Figure 5.5 Selection of phytoliths and starch grains from the site Los Ajos, Uruguay

pollens. Pollen is dispersed in various ways—blown by the wind, carried by bats or birds that feed on the plant's fruits, or simply falling nearby. Different factors affect the preservation of pollen. Highly alkaline soils may chemically degrade the pollen grains. Some bacteria and fungi feast on certain pollens. Floods or seasonal downpours can erode the pollen. The best locations for pollen sampling are often relatively calm ponds or bogs, where the pollen settles into the sediments and can be sampled and extracted in stratigraphic cores. Pollen is also recovered from other archaeological sources, such as excavated caves and rock shelters, the surfaces of ancient storage pots or metates, and even coprolites (desiccated feces). Palynological data can indicate changes in vegetation communities, including changes caused by farming, variations in plant use, or patterns of human consumption.

Phytoliths are another class of plant remains, minute accretions of soluble silica absorbed by plants from the groundwater and earth and accumulated in the leaves and stalks (figure 5.5).[7]

Similar to pollens, phytoliths exhibit distinctive surface geometries associated with different plant species, although phytoliths from a single species can vary depending on whether they were formed in stalks, leaves, or fruit. Additional measurements, such as maximum and average length and width, are needed to identify phytoliths. For example, domesticated plants often have larger phytoliths than their wild relatives, as wild members of the squash family (*Cucurbita*) are smaller than 100 microns (0.1 mm), while phytoliths from domesticated species are larger. In a square centimeter of hard squash rind, several thousand phytoliths can occur, making them an abundant—but extremely small—source of paleobotanical data. In archaeological contexts, soil samples are collected and submitted for analysis, in which the phytoliths are bathed in a series of chemical washes to separate them from clays and organic materials, spun in a centrifuge, dried, and mounted on microscope slides for study.

Increasingly, the **study of starch grains** is an important source of paleobotanical information, especially for root crops but also for seed- or fruit-producing plants. During photosynthesis, plants produce glucose, which is preserved as granules of nonsoluble starch, a ready source of energy for the plant's next growing season. Starch is stored in the roots, rhizomes, seeds, and fruits of different plants. Different plant species have starch grains of different shapes and sizes. Remarkably durable, ancient starch grains have been recovered from small fissures and pits of grinding tools and from dental tartar of prehistoric human teeth.

The study of macrobotanical remains, pollen, phytoliths, and starch grains from well-dated archaeological contexts provides the basic data for understanding the origins of agriculture in South America and the connections between South America and other regions of the world, particularly Mesoamerica. In addition, studies of the DNA-based molecular signatures of domesticated plants and their closest nondomesticated relatives have identified potential places of origins and, in a few cases, instances in which wild plants were domesticated in two separate locales. Yet, the most interesting conclusion that emerges from these studies is the sheer diversity of plants—root crops, trees, fruits, and grains—first domesticated across South America.

Places of Origins

Based on 2013 archaeological evidence, plants and animals were domesticated in several different zones across South America (figure 5.6).[8]

Rather than a single "center" of domestication, South America contains at least three and possibly four centers in which one or more important crops were domesticated. Some of these are very broad regions—such as the Andes—where other crops first appeared. The paleobotanist **Dolores Piperno** writes, "The origins of major and now minor crops are spread from the northern parts to the southern parts of the continent, west and east of the Andes, mostly in seasonal types of lowland tropical forests for major root and seed crops but also in lowland wet forests and mid-elevation moist forest habitats."[9] Although the patterning of early domesticates is undoubtedly affected by the uneven intensities of archaeological and paleobotanical research across South America, the fact that these "centers" are in some cases separated by 1,000 km (600 miles) or more and yet had domesticated plants by 7500 BP suggests that domestication and early agriculture occurred independently in different portions of South America. There was not one center from which domesticated crops diffused across the continent. There was, however, a tendency for the wild ancestors of early domesticates to be plants from seasonal tropical forests—environments with dry seasons lasting four to seven months, annual rainfall of 120 to 180 cm (47 to 70 inches), and more fertile soils than those found in humid tropical rainforests.

The earliest South American crops were a suite of root crops, fruits, gourds, legumes, and seed plants. Arrowroot (*Maranta arundinacea*) and lerén (*Calathea

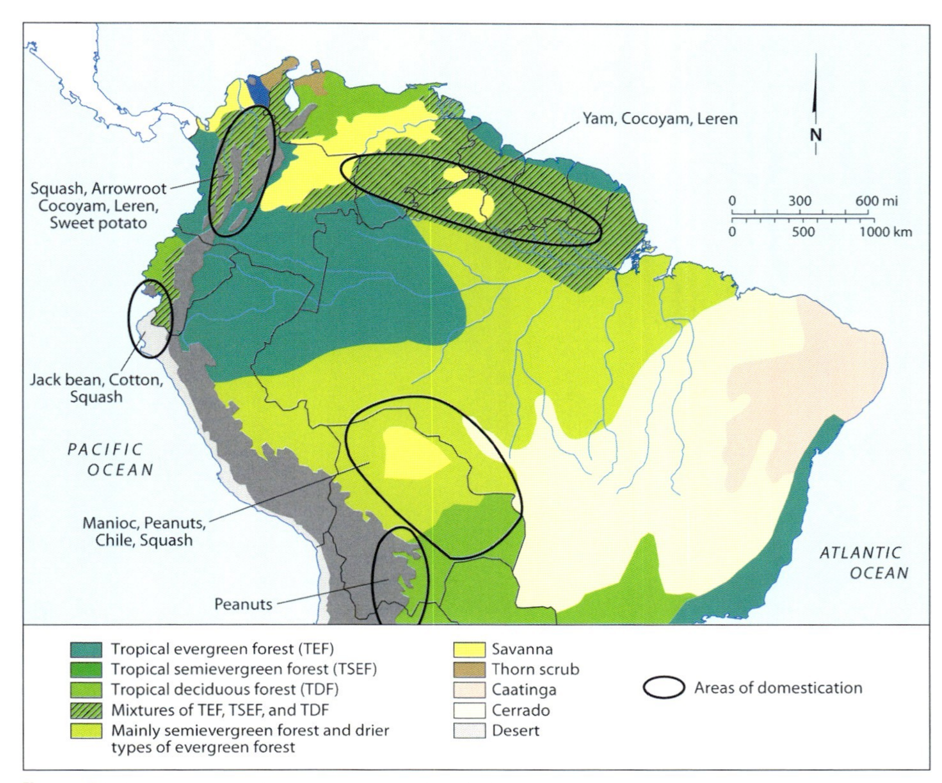

Figure 5.6 Major zones of domestication in South America

allouia) were cultivated for their starchy tubers and are found in sites in northern South America and Panama dating to 10,200 to 7600 BP, along with *Cucurbita moschata* (varieties of pumpkins and butternut squash) and bottle gourd (*Lagenaria siceraria*) (figure 5.7, figure 5.8).

After about 8500 BP, the tempo of the movement of domesticates increased. Originally domesticated in the savannas and forests of the southwestern Amazon and on the eastern foothills of the Bolivian Andes, peanuts (*Arachis hypogaea*) appeared on the North Coast of Peru after 8500 BP and were carried north to Panama by 7600 BP. Manioc (*Manihot* sp.) and peanuts may have originated in the same region, although manioc (also known as cassava or yucca) appeared in the Colombian Amazon by 5800 BP (figure 5.9).

Chili peppers, another tropical lowland genus (*Capsicum*), may have been domesticated in two or more zones in the northern and southern lowlands but were widespread by 6000–5000 BP (figure 5.10).

Two tree species also appear among the early domesticates: avocado (*Persea americana*) and pacae (*Inga feuillea*). The pacae is a leguminous tree that bears long pods whose seeds are enveloped in a sweet white pulp, leading to its other name, "the ice-cream tree."

Figure 5.7 (*above*) Arrowroot

Figure 5.9 (*below*) Manioc tubers

Figure 5.8 (*above*) Butternut squash and pumpkins

Figure 5.10 (*below*) Varieties of chili peppers

Figure 5.11 Varieties of modern corn in Peru

Two points are important. First, the original suites of domesticated plants were "neither seed, tree, nor root crop based but rather mixtures of these different elements."[10] Second, these crops were domesticated in specific locales but then very quickly moved over large areas of the New World tropics. One of the most significant of these emigrant species was maize (figure 5.11).

Based on current evidence, maize or corn (*Zea mays*) first appeared in the central Balsas Valley in the state of Guerrero, western Mexico. Receiving between 50 and 100 centimeters of rainfall between May and September, the region is the home of the native plant teocinte, the closest living relative of maize. Excavations at **Xihuatoxtla Shelter** uncovered a long sequence of occupation spanning 10,000 to 7500 BP.[11] The earliest evidence for maize consists of starch grains and phytoliths dating to 8700 BP (see figure 5.2). Interestingly, there is no evidence for exploiting teocinte from the earlier levels, suggesting that maize had been domesticated sometime before 8700 BP in the seasonal forests of southwest Mexico. It has been suggested that maize was first attractive to humans for its sugary stalks, which could be chewed or squeezed for a fermentable juice for an alcoholic drink.[12] As more seeds began to cluster on the plants, the minute cobs attracted human interest and eventually became the principal focus of artificial selection and domestication—ultimately forming multi-row ears of corn.

From its original Mexican home, maize spread widely through the Americas, reaching lower Central America by 7600 BP, the highland Cauca Valley of Colombia between 7000 and 6000 BP, and southwest Ecuador between 6000

Figure 5.12 Varieties of common beans

and 5000 BP. At that point, the southern expansion of maize is poorly understood, and recent data may be revised. Radiocarbon dates on maize cobs from the site of Huaca Prieta on the North Coast of Peru may indicate that maize was a minor crop between 6700 and 4000 BP (see chapter 6), and maize starch grains have been removed from human teeth dated to 4500 BP.[13] Based on current archaeological evidence, maize does not seem to have become a major food crop along the Peruvian coast until sometime after 4500 BP. The southward expansion of maize reached the La Plata Basin of southeastern Uruguay between 3950 and 3350 BP (4580 and 3380 cal BP), where maize was accompanied by domesticated squash (*Cucurbita* sp.), beans (*Phaseolus* sp.), and *Canna*.[14]

Other crops have such broadly distributed wild relatives that domestication may have occurred independently and repeatedly, only to be accompanied by hybridization as domesticated varieties cross-bred with wild local varieties. For example, the domestication of quinoa (*Chenopodium quinoa*), a highland seed plant, apparently occurred at various times and places in South America—in Peru around 5000 BC, in Chile at 3000 BC, and in Bolivia after 750 BC (see figure 5.1). Quinoa exhibits significant genetic variations as different varieties adapted to highland or coastal zones.[15] Different varieties of beans also have complex origins (figure 5.12).

The varieties of common bean (*Phaseolus vulgaris*)—kidney beans, pinto beans, black beans, and cranberry beans are widely available modern examples—were apparently domesticated independently in Mesoamerica and South America. In South America, varieties from the northern Andes tend to be smaller than those in the Southern Andes, forming distinctive gene pools and producing a kaleidoscopic abundance of beans. The lima bean (*Phaseolus lunatus*) and other broad beans are descendents of wild varieties found from Colombia to Argentina, resulting in a similarly flamboyant array of different cultivars, with very large broad beans found on the coast of Peru by 6500 to 5000 cal BP. The origins of the jack bean (*Canavalia* sp.) are poorly understood, as the wild relatives are widely dis-

Figure 5.13 Oca, an edible tuber from the Andes

tributed, especially in riverine and seashore zones where the wild plants produce spectacular pods of varyingly toxic seeds. Despite this daunting feature, jack beans were domesticated by 5000 cal BP along the west coast of South America.[16]

The origins of root and tuber crops are similarly diffuse. Yams (*Dioscorea* sp.) may have been domesticated in the Guinea highlands of northeastern South America, although they appear in the middle Cauca Valley of Colombia between 8000 and 6000 cal BP, accompanied by a New World member of the taro family (*Xanthosoma sagittifolium*). A rich variety of tubers and roots was cultivated in the Andean highlands, including oca (*Oxalis tuberosa*), jicama (*Pachyrrhizus ahipa*), ullucu (*Ullucus tuberosus*), and, of course, the potato (*Solanum tuberosum*) (figure 5.13, figure 5.14).

Since roots and tubers can be vegetatively propagated—a cutting from a valued plant can be replanted—it is relatively easy to artificially select for desirable characteristics, adapting plants to narrowly defined environmental niches. This process occurred over millennia in the Andes, resulting in around 2,500 varieties of potatoes from Peru alone.[17]

Of course, not all plant crops were food crops. Cotton (*Gossypium barbadense*) was grown for its fibers. A widely distributed genus consisting of fifty species found in tropical and subtropical zones around the world, cotton was independently domesticated in Africa/Asia and the Americas as prehistoric peoples discovered the value of its fibers for making cordage, textiles, and other products. Ironically, in the New World the wild variety of cotton resulted from hybridization of a native variety with another form that originated from Asia or Africa. One of cotton's distinctive qualities is its ability to survive prolonged exposure to seawater, and

Figure 5.14 Oca and potatoes at market in Pisac, Peru

"the apparent propensity for long-distance dispersal appears to be a characteristic of the entire cotton tribe."[18] This wayfaring capacity and an enthusiasm for promiscuous hybridization led to the development of the New World cottons, with domesticated forms appearing in the Zaña Valley by 6300–6000 cal BP.

Bottle gourd (*Lagenaria siceraria*) is another rambling plant (figure 5.15).

Originating in Africa, the bottle gourd was widely dispersed across Eurasia by the end of the Pleistocene and has been recovered from prehistoric sites in Japan dating to 11,700 and 10,900 cal BP.[19] Currently, two competing hypotheses explain the arrival of bottle gourds in the Americas.[20] A long-standing hypothesis

Figure 5.15 Harvest of bottle gourds

has proposed that the buoyant gourds—which grow across Africa—were carried accidentally by ocean currents across the Atlantic and established themselves naturally in South America, only to be domesticated later. In contrast, a 2005 study of the DNA sequences of ancient gourds from the west coast of South America—at sites like **Quebrada Jaguay** (see chapter 4) and others—suggested that the earliest American bottle gourds are more closely related to Asian forms than to African varieties. Rather than an accidental tourist, the bottle gourd may have been intentionally transported into the Americas by Paleoindians who brought this useful plant into the New World—although it is difficult to explain how this tropical gourd was cultivated as people moved through the cold climates of North America. However, an extensive 2014 genetic study of a large sample of specimens from archaeological sites and living plants suggests that South American plants are more closely related to African than to Asian varieties. At this writing, the prehistory of this extremely useful plant remains obscure.

Of course, man does not live by bread alone—or by maize, manioc, or quinoa, for that matter. It has been observed that "alcohol is the most ancient, the most widely used, and the most versatile drug in the world," and various plants were made into alcoholic beverages across South America.[21] Based on archaeological, historical, and ethnographic information, scholars have documented a sobering array of fermented beverages made from South American plants. The beverages are often referred to as *chicha*, a word borrowed from Arawakan languages and applied rather indiscriminately by Spaniards and traditional people to fermented

Figure 5.16 Drinking manioc chicha

drinks across the continent.[22] Most of these beverages are relatively low-alcohol, undistilled brews. In many portions of the prehispanic Andes, *chicha de maíz* was prized—a maize beer made by germinating kernels, letting them dry (i.e., malting), boiling the malted maize and other botanicals for extended periods, and fermenting the brew in large jars. Because chicha de maíz quickly turns into vinegar, it was brewed weekly—one estimate suggests that a household would consume around 46 liters (47.5 quarts) each week—and made in large quantities in advance of fiestas, communal work parties, and other group events.[23]

Another brew, also called chicha but made from manioc, is made across lowland South America (figure 5.16). Mashed manioc or manioc cakes are added to water. Several wads of the mash are chewed and spit back into the brew, thus introducing the enzyme diastase, found in saliva, that triggers the fermentation process. In a few days, a weak alcoholic drink results. Although uncommonly recorded in ethnographic literature, a number of other plants were fermented, including quinoa, cactus fruits, and the fruits of *Schinus molle*, the California pepper tree.[24]

Coca is another important non-food, domesticated plant (figure 5.17).

Despite being a broadly distributed genus containing more than 230 species across South America, only two species, *Erythroxylum coca* and *Erythroxylum novogranatense,* contain significant traces of cocaine.[25] Infamous as the source of cocaine, coca leaves are chewed throughout the Andes as a stimulant and hunger suppressant. The leaves are brewed as tea, used in folk medicines, and incorporated into rituals. Coca leaves are often chewed with a powder from burned shell, limestone, or tree bark, additives that are rich in calcium carbonate and release the alkaloids in the leaves.

Figure 5.17 Coca leaves

The ethnobotanist **Timothy Plowman** has argued that *Erythroxylum novogranatense* was a domesticate derived from the wild *Erythroxylum coca*, which grows widely along the eastern slopes of the Andes and in wetter valleys, including on the damp Pacific Coast of Ecuador but not on the dry coast of Peru.[26] Plowman suggested that hunters and gatherers may have sampled the tender leaves as an emergency food, but the stimulant properties were immediately obvious. At some point, the wild coca was artificially selected to grow in more arid environments, resulting in a new species with two varieties: *Erythroxylum novogranatense* var. *truxillense* (Trujillo coca) and *Erythroxylum novogranatense* var. *novogranatense* (Colombian coca). Trujillo coca contains the essence of wintergreen and other flavors that made it popular for flavoring medicines and beverages, including Coca-Cola. It was also esteemed in antiquity, at least by 4500 to 3700 cal BP, and was widely used in South America.[27] Colombian coca was broadly cultivated in the northern Andes and may have been traded northward into Central America.

A range of other plants—domesticated, cultivated, and managed—were valued as drugs. Of the sixty-four species of tobacco (*Nicotiana* genus) found world-wide, over half are natives of South America. Wild tobaccos grow throughout the Andean highlands, from southern Ecuador to northern Chile and eastward to the Gran Chaco. Two species, *Nicotiana rustica* and *N. tabacum,* were very early domesticates treasured for the nicotine alkaloid they contain. Northern South America is considered the original center of tobacco domestication, an addictive innovation that became more widely adopted than any other pre-Columbian domesticate—even more widespread than maize—"to the very limits of New World agriculture from Canada to Chile."[28] More commonly used as a ritual drug than a recreational one in South America, the modes of nicotine ingestion were astounding in their variety: smoking, chewing, snuff taking, drinking a thick tea or paste made from boiled tobacco leaves, or administrating it in a ritual enema.[29]

Tobacco was only one of a broad array of psychoactive and hallucinogenic plants used throughout South America. In the Amazon, the *liana* (*Banisteriopsis* spp.) is found as a wild plant, an invasive plant in abandoned gardens, and a cultigen (figure 5.18); it is the principal component in *ayahuasca*, which in Quechia means "vines of the soul."[30]

A late-twentieth-century informant describes ayahuasca's hallucinatory effect as "characterized by the sensation of flying while observing beautiful and often spectacular sights, a time when exultation sweeps the body, and all physical discomforts are forgotten. Objects and scenes are always vividly colored in bright but natural technicolor."[31] The San Pedro cactus (*Trichocereus pachanoi*), a native to the Andes found between 2,000 and 3,000 m (6,560–9,840 ft) above sea level, was used extensively as a source of mescaline during visionary quests (figure 5.19).[32] Readily propagated from cuttings, San Pedro cactus may have been cultivated prehistorically.

The floripondio shrub or angel's trumpet (*Brugmansia* spp.), now a commonly cultivated ornamental plant in the warmer zones of North America, contains an extremely toxic set of alkaloids cautiously incorporated into hallucinogenic potions and poultices by modern *curanderos* in South America (figure 5.20).[33]

The pods of the *vilca* plant (*Anadenanthera* sp.)—a managed but not domesticated tree—were ground into a hallucinogenic snuff used by traditional South American shamans to transform themselves. A modern visitor described the experience as feeling "as though the flood gates of the Universe had been thrown open."[34] In most cases the archaeological evidence for the use of hallucinogenic plants is indirect, based on finding depictions of the plants in iconography on ceramics or stelae, artifacts such as special grinding palettes and snuff tubes for preparing and ingesting drugs, and traces of psychoactive compounds recovered from well-preserved mummies.[35] Historic and ethnographic accounts demonstrate the broad use of psychoactive plants among traditional societies, information that provides insight into the ancient use of plants in prehistoric South America.[36]

From Foraging to Farming

Given the enormous variety of South American domesticates and the varied environments and societies in which they are used, it is no surprise that the transitions

Figure 5.18 Ayahuasca vine growing on tree

Figure 5.19 San Pedro cactus

to agriculture were diverse across the continent. Maize and potatoes are very different kinds of plants; their domestications were similarly diverse. Further, the ways domesticates were incorporated into ancient economies differed, resulting in a "mosaic like pattern with multiple areas of early independent agriculture [that] is reflected in the diversity shown by early food producing economies that emerged in different parts of the continent."[37]

Several points are in order. First, it has been common to emphasize the use of domesticated plants and animals as one of the defining characteristics of agriculture, which actually focuses on the *end* of the transition. As Piperno writes, "The commonplace focus on *domestication* as the preeminent event in human/plant relationships is perhaps misplaced and . . . the crucial shift we may want to understand is *the origins of plant cultivation* when people began to repeatedly sow and harvest plants in plots prepared for this purpose."[38] Second, it seems probable that the emphasis on plant cultivation was in part a response to global climate changes at the end of the Pleistocene—an inference based on the nearly synchronous development of cultivation in seven different regions of the world between 11,000 and 9,000 years ago.[39] If this is correct, then we need to understand how cultivation enhanced the breadth of resources available to human societies, decreasing the risks associated with environmental changes by broadening the range of available resources.

This was probably the case within the **Las Vegas culture** in southwest Ecuador. As discussed in chapter 4, the complex mosaic of terrestrial and coastal

Figure 5.20 Angel's trumpet

environments underwent variations in the Early Holocene, rearrangements of mangroves and beaches as well as of various plant communities. Early cultivated plants such as squash were chosen for larger and larger size, and lerén was valued as a starchy root. The use of these cultivated plants did not immediately revolutionize Las Vegas society; rather, these plants were incorporated into a broad set of subsistence pursuits that included foraging for marine and terrestrial resources.

Extensive archaeological research by **Tom Dillehay** and colleagues in the **Zaña and Nanchoc Valleys of northern Peru** provides another vista on the initial settlement of western South America and the development of agricultural societies.[40] Beginning around 11,500 BP and continuing over the next six millennia, archaeological evidence from 111 preceramic sites—37 of which were excavated—has resulted in a complex picture of these changes. The archaeobotanist **Jack Rossen** summarizes these transformations:

> During the early Preceramic El Palto phase (11,500–9,800 BP) highly mobile groups used plants as reliable supplements to their hunting lifeways, with a strong coastal focus on algarrobo pods, cactus fruits, snails and other wild foods. In the upper valley, the cultivation of squash began during this phase. The Las Pircas phase (9,800–7,800 BP) was a time of continued broad-spectrum plant collecting in much of the valley but also the local development of multiple plant cultivation and house gardening in selected areas such as the south bank of the Nanchoc River. Simple feeder ditch [irrigation] technologies may have begun during this time as well.
>
> During the following Tierra Blanca phase (7,800–5,000 BP) the intensity and nature of plant cultivation changed, with a shift from single-family house gardening to multifamily fields and canal systems. Plant use during the Preceramic phases is understood in terms of persistent hunting-gathering in much of the valley, plus a gradual adoption and proliferation of house gardening and then irrigation technology applied to community agricultural fields in the upper valley.[41]

Given this pattern of subtle integration of domesticates into a regionally focused foraging economy in this portion of northern Peru, it is striking to realize that "the early cultivated and domesticated plants documented in the Zaña Valley [archaeological] records were all introduced from elsewhere in South America . . . The crops are thus an interesting mixture of lowland and highland representatives, and they arrived from areas east and west of the Andes as well as from northern and southern South America."[42]

This suggests some interesting points. First, the presence of diverse cultigens and domesticates in the Zaña Valley from such far-flung places of origin implies the existence of relatively complex patterns of exchange and (possibly) migration during the Archaic/Preceramic period. Archaeobotanist **Christine Hastorf** has discussed some of the social interactions involving the exchange and diffusion of plants, asking "what led people to carry, trade, gift, or steal these plants?"[43] Exploring a set of decisions that "were as much cultural as economic or ecological," Hastorf argues that "although it is impossible to substantiate this claim, food probably has been the most common gift item through human (pre)history."[44] For example, among modern Amazonian horticultural societies, house gardens are principally tended by women, and desirable seeds and cuttings are exchanged between women. If women leave their birthplace through migration or marriage, they may carry seeds and cuttings to their new homes, in part as a measure of their natal identities.[45] Conversely, if societies practice matrilocal residence and grooms provide bride service by working for their future fathers-in-law before establishing their own gardens, specific varieties of crops might be given to the newlyweds as they establish their homes.[46]

Second, it is likely that different crops were exchanged through different social networks. For example, **Donald Lathrap** has argued for extensive exchange of forest products originating in the Amazon Basin, including various hallucinogenic plants such as *Anadenathera* and ayahuasca, suggesting that these psychoactive drugs would have been transported far beyond their places of origin by itinerant professional healers.[47] Evidence for such long-distance exchange of psychoactive plants includes packets of plants and snuff paraphernalia buried with a prehistoric curer and traces of coca and ayahuasca in the hair of mummies dating to AD 500–1000—evidence of psychoactive plants hundreds of kilometers from their natural habitats, suggesting the existence of "extensive trade networks in antiquity" reaching from northern Chile to as far away as Amazonia.[48]

The diversity of South American cultivated and domesticated plants, their distant centers of origin, and the tremendously varied human societies that adapted or adopted those plants strongly imply that there was no single pathway between foraging and farming. As Dillehay has noted:

> It is becoming clear that domestication and food production, social complexity, demographic aggregation, new technologies and response to environmental stress did not always form a "coherent cultural package of changes" . . . New models now view early societies independently operating at different velocities and directions of change at different places and times around the world . . . Taken together, new data and ideas have constituted a fundamental challenge to the way we think about early hunters and gatherers, the beginnings of simple and complex forager societies, plant food production and farming, social relations, and the contributions early societies made to later ones.[49]

Neolithic Revolution or Neolithic Evolution?

Based on current evidence, the cultivation of plants was simply integrated into other subsistence activities in prehistoric South America. Cultivation preceded domestication. The archaeobotanical evidence also suggests that specific genera were chosen for cultivation. For example, many members of the squash family are edible plants that regularly colonize the disturbed soils of camps and villages. The vast majority of the earliest squash are from the genus *Cucurbita*, whose wild members bear some of the largest seeds and fruits of any members of the squash family. Similarly, the family that contains lerén (*Marantaceae)* has numerous members with edible tubers, but relatively few species were collected by and cultivated tropical foragers.[50] In short, human selection was already at work long before the plants were domesticated.

The causes behind the origins of agriculture have been debated for decades. Hypotheses have been advanced and repeatedly rejected. As noted, **V. Gordon Childe** argued that domestication and agriculture occurred in the Near East when plants, animals, and humans retreated to oasis areas at the end of the Ice Age; that hypothesis has been disproven for the Near East and was never particularly relevant for tropical regions. In the late 1950s, **Robert Braidwood** argued that domestication developed from a broad-spectrum foraging adaptation in which humans gradually learned how to cultivate plants and breed animals, a transition that, Braidwood felt, did not require a causal explanation. In the 1960s, **Lewis Binford** argued that agriculture was a response to increased human population density, the result of increased population and decreased landmasses as sea levels rose at the end of the Pleistocene. The role of population growth as a cause of agriculture was further developed by **Mark Cohen** in his work, including *The Food Crisis in Prehistory*, despite the limited evidence for human population growth until after agriculture was established. All of these models posit that food collectors were forced to become farmers. An alternative set of hypotheses proposes that certain aspects of cultivated foods attracted people to become farmers. For example, one model suggests that the higher yields of agricultural foods created surpluses that were useful for the development of social elites, products that could be used in feasts or exchanged for other objects. Broadly stated, models for the origins of agriculture envision people being either forced to farm or attracted to farming, either-or models sometimes classified as "push" versus "pull" models.

In light of these long-standing debates, it is daunting to realize, as **T. Douglas Price** and **Ofer Bar-Yosef** recently wrote: "The simple fact is that we do not yet have a good grasp on the causes for the origins of agriculture. The how and the why of the Neolithic transition remain among the more intriguing questions in human prehistory. There is as yet no single accepted theory for the origins of agriculture—rather, there is a series of ideas and suggestions that do not quite resolve the question."[51] Therefore, while we can assume that the practices of cultivation and, eventually, domestication were the result of human decisions and interactions, the specific pathways to agriculture may be as divergent as the different plants and animals that became the foundations of agriculture in ancient South America.

Divergent Agrosystems

The diverse sets of cultigens and domesticates were incorporated into an array of agrosystems tailored to fit the varied environments and social settings of prehispanic South America.[52] Many of these agrosystems are still used by modern traditional farmers, and this ethnographic knowledge illuminates archaeological studies of ancient agriculture. We understand that agricultural systems are not simple reflections of the natural environment but rather are active human creations. The cultural geographer **William Denevan** has noted: "There are no environmental limitations to the development of agriculture, only cultural limitations. 'Agricultural potential' is a cultural phenomenon; it is not something inherent in nature that can be measured, that exists independent of culture. Today, with available technology, agriculture can be carried out anywhere on earth. Whether it is or not in any given habitat is dependent on whether the culture involved has the necessary technology, and whether or not there is a perceived need in relation to the costs involved (capital, material, labor)."[53]

Household Gardens

Household gardens were among the earliest agrosystems, taking advantage of the disturbed soils and enhanced fertility of previous settlements or garbage-dumped margins of seasonal encampments that created anthrosols. As discussed in chapter 4, the Nukak people of the Amazonian regions of Colombia and western Brazil collect resources from "wild orchards," taking advantage of the anthrosols that develop in their former campsites and harvesting the palms that have sprouted from seeds previously shelled but dropped. A similar situation is described by **Laura Rival** for the **Huaorani** of the Ecuadorian Amazon, who are completely aware of the role of human agency in shaping the forest (figure 5.21).

"Huaorani people daily consume a great number of cultigens that are not planted in gardens," Rival writes. "They see in their forested land the historical record of the activities of past generations. They are quite explicit about the inseparability of people and the forest, which they describe as a succession of fallows."[54] The Huaorani occupy an anthropogenic forest, combining plant resources that are wild, tended, cultivated, and domesticated. In this anthropogenic forest, "Numerous plant species are encouraged to grow outside of cultivated areas as people engage in numerous daily actions (planting, selecting, transplanting, protecting, using, and discarding) that have a direct or indirect effect on the distribution of species, be they fully domesticated or not." Interestingly, the garden plots in which the Huaorani raise manioc are overgrown, un-cleared, and unkempt spaces. The fast-growing sweet manioc the Huaorani plant is principally consumed as a feast food, manioc beer, particularly during "diplomatic" feasts when bands need to establish allies with rival groups. Since it can be planted throughout the year in plots nearly anywhere in the forest and it grows in five months, "manioc allows for the organization of large feasts to which *huarani* [i.e., "others" or "enemies"] guests can be invited."[55] In contrast, the peach palms that grow in the anthrosols of old sites "are taken to be gifts from deceased relatives."[56]

The Huaorani agricultural practice illuminates a fundamental insight into the interactions between humans and the natural realm in tropical forests, particularly in Amazonia. Since the 1980s, archaeologists, botanists, geographers, and ethnographers have realized that South American tropical forests are not wild, pristine expanses of raw nature but rather are—to varying degrees—anthropogenic landscapes.

Multiple lines of evidence point to human transformation of the landscape. Changes in pollen profiles document the prehistoric expansion of ancient cultivators.

Plant distributions reflect human interventions. Then there is the matter of *terra preta*, or dark soils.

Across Amazonia, swatches of distinctively dark soils had been observed since the late nineteenth century, but they were attributed to a variety of natural processes, such as drifts of volcanic ash or fluvial deposits. Three traits suggest their non-natural origins. First, terra preta layers are found on top of very different types of soils, including tropical soils otherwise leached of organics. Second, the terra preta soils are known from various geomorphological settings: near river-banks, in interior zones, and on hilltops—including places where organic-rich sediments were unlikely to accumulate. Finally, many of the terra preta soils contain potsherds.[57]

Since 1980, it has become obvious that the terra preta soils—also known as **Amazonian Dark Earths (ADE)**—are anthrosols and in some cases actually archaeological sites. They appeared broadly across Amazonia between 450 BC and AD 950, although there are numerous undated terra preta deposits, so these dates may be pushed earlier. No one knows how many ADE deposits there are. One estimate suggests that perhaps 0.1 percent to 0.3 percent of the Amazon Basin contains terra preta deposits, a total of roughly 6,000 to 18,000 km^2 (2,316 to 6,948 square miles) sprinkled over the forest, with a deposit every 2 km^2 (1.2 square miles). The largest deposits cover 200 to 500 ha (494 to 1,235 acres), although most are relatively small and less than 2 ha (5 acres) in size. The densest concentrations are along major rivers and their tributaries, as well as adjacent to river rapids and waterfalls, but terra preta deposits are also found in inland areas, although these deposits are smaller and generally associated with upper tributaries and streams. The terra preta vary in depth—some a few centimeters thick, others 2 or more meters—and the configurations of these soils also vary: some form linear deposits, many others are rings, while some are circular deposits. These different properties of terra preta reflect various community organizations (e.g., independent households versus large villages) and different cultural activities (e.g., garbage discarded versus intentional soil preparation).

But these different lines of evidence all suggest a fundamental model: the Amazonian rainforest is not a pristine natural landscape but rather an anthropogenic landscape, one that contains the traces of human action and interventions during (at least) the last 2,000–3,000 years. Further, Amazonia was not a resource-poor, unpopulated zone but was broadly occupied by prehistoric foragers, cultivators, and farmers who tended and reshaped the forest.

Shifting Agriculture

Shifting agriculture—also known as **slash-and-burn** or **swidden** agriculture—is another agrosystem widely used across the tropical forests of South America (figure 5.22).[58]

The basic strategy is in part an adaptation to poor soils covered by heavy vegetation. In many regions, soils lack high organic content because tropical rains have leached away the nutrients and mature tropical forests quickly recycle organic

Figure 5.21 Huaorani man with a blow gun

Figure 5.22 Canela men clearing garden plots, Ecuadorian Amazon

matter as bacteria, lichens, and fungi consume fallen plant matter. Tropical soils often lack layers of humus rich in nitrogen, phosphates, or potash. Shifting agriculture is a response to this. Farmers cut down brush and smaller trees, usually leaving the larger trees standing. After the cut brush has dried, the farmers burn the slash piles (figure 5.23).

Crops are planted in the ashes between the charred stumps. A variety of plants are raised, forming polycultural plots. Usually, it is only possible to farm a plot for a few years, as the nutrients in the ashes are exhausted and harvests decline. To have a steady food supply, farmers must clear another plot and begin planting anew. The forest reclaims the previous fields, although some domesticates may grow in a feral condition as the land lies fallow. Depending on local soil conditions, five to twenty-five years may pass before an old garden can be cleared, burned, and replanted. Thus, a shifting agriculturalist must have access to multiple plots at various stages in the process: one under cultivation, another in preparation for planting, and one or more in fallow. For this reason, shifting agriculture is considered a "space-extensive" agrosystem.

Within these broad parameters are enormous variations. For example, the ethnographer **Robert Carneiro** provided a classic account of slash-and-burn agriculture among the **Kuikuru** of Central Brazil based on his fieldwork during 1954–55.[59] The Kuikuru's swidden plots average about 1.5 acres (3.3 ha), planted principally in manioc; over a period of 18 to 20 months, 6 to 7 tons of manioc tubers are produced before the field is allowed to go fallow. Despite requiring 25 years before the field can be replanted, the Kuikuru have sufficient land that the 145 people in the community can be fed from plots less than 4 miles from the village.

Figure 5.23 Smoke from slash-and-burn farming, Upper Xingu, Brazil

A similar pattern was documented by the cultural geographer William Denevan for the **Campa** people of the Gran Pajonal (grassland plateau) living in the western Amazonian region of eastern Peru.[60] The Campa clear swidden fields 1 to 2 acres (0.5–1.5 ha) in area that are planted in manioc, maize, and other crops. In most cases, only one significant manioc harvest is obtained from a field, although other crops—such as sweet potatoes, beans, squash, peanuts, arrowroot, and pineapple—can be planted and harvested over the next two or three years. A Campa farmer clears a new field each year, ideally close to the current and previous year's fields. Abandoned fields must lie fallow for a decade or longer. Consequently, Campa households regularly establish new dwellings, although residences are also abandoned because of deaths or the lack of game animals.

The antiquity of slash-and-burn agriculture is somewhat controversial. The archaeological signature of swidden agriculture should include soil amendments (increased charcoal and higher organic material) and modified pollen and phytoliths from cultigens and invasive weeds and other plants. It is difficult to distinguish the archaeological consequences of swidden cultivation from other human impacts on the environment. The historian of fire **Stephen Pyne** has written that "frontiers are often flaming fronts . . . the violent abrasion of people against people and of people against land kindles flame," which was probably the case as humans colonized South America.[61] Cores from lake sediments in the Lower Amazon record the impacts of anthropogenic fires as early as 6,500 years ago, but the first evidence of agriculture (maize pollen) appeared several millennia later, at 3350 BP, when the frequency of fires also increased.[62]

Further, there is reason to expect that the use of swidden agriculture developed and spread sometime after the initial experiments of cultivation and domestication, whether in house gardens or tended forests. The archaeologist **Manuel Arroyo-Kalin** has analyzed anthrosols in the Central Amazon and distinguishes between *terra pretas,* the dark soils containing ceramics and organic materials discussed earlier, and *terra mulatas*, mixed soils that—although modified by humans—contain lower concentrations of charcoals and minuscule quantities of artifactual materials.[63] Samples of the terra mulatas indicated surface burnings, while the interface between the terra mulata and the underlying soils showed traces of churning that might be associated with farming. Arroyo-Kalin argues that there is a gradation among the Amazonian Dark Earths, from terra preta that have dense concentrations of organic and artifactual materials that were probably ancient and permanent settlements to terra mulata soils that bear traces of slash-and-burn farming.

Swidden agriculture may have diffused throughout South America along with three crops: bitter manioc, sweet manioc, and maize (figure 5.24).

As discussed earlier, maize spread across South America after 7000 to 6000 BP, reaching eastern Amazonia by 3000 BP and the La Plata Basin by 4000 to 3500 BP. Slash-and-burn agriculture was probably essential for maize cultivation in the tropical forest, especially in areas away from richer alluvial soils associated with rivers. Maize is frequently intercropped with sweet manioc (as the Campa do), often in relatively small plots and house gardens that might leave few archaeological traces. In contrast, bitter manioc cultivation involves more extensive burnings, leaving behind larger expanses of terra mulatas that are the archaeological evidence of ancient agriculture.

Agricultural systems in South America evolved and diversified over millennia. For example, Arroyo-Kalin provides a basic model of those changes: arboriculture in the Early to Middle Holocene became more spatially intensive through time. Earliest agriculture involved household gardens, and maize and sweet manioc were probably grown in midden heaps and household gardens very early in the Holocene by people living in tropical forests. Since bitter manioc requires drier and more open habitats, shifting agriculture may have been an effort to replicate those habitats in tropical forests, a process that also produced terra preta and terra mulata anthrosols.[64]

Given that swidden agriculture is a multi-crop agricultural strategy adapted to local conditions, it is yet another aspect of South American prehistory that would seem to resist broad generalization. Yet, a very influential—and hotly contested—hypothesis was proposed in the 1950s by the American archaeologist

Figure 5.24 Woman with manioc from her swidden, Ecuadorian Amazon

Lista 3
PSP
GLORIA LUG
CONCEJALA DE

Betty J. Meggers, which became the center of controversy over the next sixty years.[65] This hypothesis was neatly encapsulated in the title of one of her many books, *Amazonia: Man and Culture in a Counterfeit Paradise*. Meggers argued that the inherent environmental limits of the tropical forest—particularly the low soil fertility—required shifting cultivators to move frequently and precluded the development of large settlements in the ancient Amazon. In her original 1954 article Meggers wrote:

> The tribes belonging to the Tropical Forest pattern of culture occupy an environment . . . with limited agricultural potential. The introduction of slash-and-burn agriculture . . . brings a more reliable food supply, which in turn permits a denser and more sedentary population and a release of labor from subsistence activities that is reflected in an expansion of all other aspects of the culture. More time is available for the gathering and preparation of raw materials and for the process of manufacture, and this permits the introduction of pottery and loom weaving of domesticated cotton. Other new traits are woven basketry and dugout canoes. The settlement pattern consists of semi-permanent villages composed of communal or single-family houses of pole and thatch construction.
>
> Although it represents an increase in [the] security of food supply, slash-and-burn agriculture is not sufficiently productive or permanent of locale to support large concentrations of population or stable settlements.[66]

Observing that complex polities such as the Inca Empire had not penetrated the tropical forest regions and that neither the historic Spanish and Portuguese empires nor modern nation-states had been able to establish large interior cities in Amazonia, Meggers wrote: "The conclusion seems unavoidable that there is a force at work to which man through his culture must bow . . . In short, the environmental potential of the tropical forest is sufficient to allow the evolution of culture to proceed only to the level represented by the Tropical Forest culture pattern; further indigenous evolution is impossible, and any more highly evolved culture attempting to settle and maintain itself in the tropical forest environment will inevitably decline to the Tropical Forest level."[67]

The broader evidence for more complex prehistoric societies in Amazonia is discussed in chapters 8 and 10. At this point, two generalizations about shifting cultivation in South America's tropical forests are important. First, depending on the specific environmental setting in which it is employed, shifting cultivation exhibits significant variations in fallow periods, the productivity and diversity of crops planted, as well as its consequences for human settlements. For example, Carneiro's study among the Kuikuru found that although they had moved their villages, it was never because of a lack of food or adequate farmland. Similarly, Denevan found that Campa households moved their dwellings for non-agricultural reasons. Thus, there is more variation among slash-and-burn cultivators than Meggers envisioned. Second, shifting cultivation is not the only agricultural strategy used in the tropical forests, and one of the most broadly found agrosystems is known as raised bed or drained field agriculture.

Figure 5.25 Modern raised fields under cultivation, Llanos de Mojos, Bolivia

Raised Field Agriculture

Raised field agriculture—also called **drained field agriculture**—is found throughout the tropical regions of the world and in different environments in South America. This strategy is often used to reclaim seasonally flooded or boggy areas that are otherwise too wet to plant (figure 5.25).[68]

In essence, the technique involves mounding up a raised bed of earth that is flanked by furrows. Crops are usually planted on top of the raised bed. Alternatively, the fields can also function to collect water in the furrows, creating a form of passive irrigation. Prehistoric raised fields are found in different zones of South America.

A large expanse of drained fields exists in the **Rio Guayas Basin** of southwest Ecuador, where an estimated 50,000 hectares of raised fields are scattered across the low-lying and often flooded region.[69] It has been suggested that at their peak, these fields could have fed 100,000 to 150,000 people—a significant portion of the total population of the Guayas Basin, estimated at 400,000 to 500,000 in circa AD 1500.[70] The archaeologist **Florencio Delgado-Espinoza** has argued that the fields were clustered around prehispanic communities, and the construction of the intensive agricultural fields was probably at the behest and direction of local chiefs.[71]

Another set of well-studied drained fields is found in the **Venezuelan llanos**, seasonally inundated savannas that flood during the rainy season and are drained by tributaries of the Middle Orinoco River. Found in different clusters along the various drainages, the largest set studied by the archaeologist **Alberta Zucchi** and the cultural geographer William Denevan covered more than 15 km^2 (5.8 square miles), with 500 to 525 separate field complexes. The fields averaged 15.5 m (50.8 ft) wide; some fields are 1 to 2 km (0.6–1.2 miles) long.[72] Although maize cultivation in this area probably began after 1000 BC, the construction of the raised fields occurred later, at circa AD 500.[73] Pollen analyses at these and other drained fields in the llanos indicate that the fields were planted in maize, squash, chilies, arrowroot, quinoa, tomatoes, and other food crops.[74] It has been suggested that the development of these extensive agricultural systems accompanied the rise of prehispanic chiefdoms in the Middle Orinoco, an issue discussed further in chapter 8.

Raised fields are known from the **Guyanas region** of northeastern South America, which encompasses Guyana, Surinam, French Guyana, and adjacent portions of Brazil, Colombia, and Venezuela.[75]

The coastal region between the mouths of the Amazon and Orinoco has been the focus of research by the archaeologists **Stephen Rostain, José Iriarte, Doyle McKey**, and colleagues. Probably constructed between AD 1000 and 1300, the Guyanas raised fields tend to be long and narrow—around 5 to 30 m (16.4–98.4 ft) long, 1–3 m (3.3–9.9 ft) wide, and less than 1 m (3.3 ft) tall (see figure 5.4). The Guyanas raised fields are modified to fit the eccentricities of local drainage conditions: some are linear, while others are rectangular or oval-shaped. Pollen and phytolith analyses from fields identified freshwater marsh plants and grasses but also domesticated plants, principally maize, sufficient to support a large human population.[76] As Rostain notes, the raised fields of the Guyanas are only one class of human earthworks built prehistorically in this portion of coastal Amazonia.[77]

Another example of raised field agriculture is known from eastern Bolivia, in the **Llanos de Mojos region** on the southeastern headwaters of the Amazon River (figure 5.26). The environment consists of broad pampas, flat savannas with patches of palm and scrub forest, and narrow ribbons of forested riverbanks. During the rainy season, the pampas are covered with shallow floodwaters. During the dry season, water is scarce and the soils are poor. "The ancient inhabitants of the zone created an anthropogenic landscape," the archaeologist **Clark Erickson** writes, "to resolve these problems and make the area highly productive. A major part of this transformation of the environment was the construction of raised fields."[78]

Their achievement was stunning. It is estimated that a *minimum* of 10,000 km (6,210 miles) of fields with a combined area of 12,000 ha (29,640 acres) were built over an area of about 6,000 km^2 (2,316 square miles). The fields were constructed between approximately AD 900 and 1400. Although they were not built at a single time, they represent a significant investment of labor. Experimental reconstructions of raised fields indicate that they require about 600 person-days to construct a hectare, which in turn produced more than 2,000 kilograms of maize in a given harvest, as well as crops of manioc, sweet potato, mate, and other crops. Recent investigations of prehistoric fields have discovered macrobotanical remains, starch grains, and phytoliths from squash, peanuts, cotton, yams, and palms, in addition to the major staples of maize and manioc.[79] The raised fields are only one class of human modifications to the landscape in eastern Bolivia. Erickson has documented a wide array of house mounds, large mound constructions, raised causeways flanked by canals, and deep ring ditches—all of which indicate a sub-

Figure 5.26 Prehistoric raised fields, Llanos de Mojos, Bolivia

stantial human presence and transformation of the landscape. The presence of defensive walls suggests a landscape of conflict, but there is no clear evidence for the emergence of chiefdoms in the Bolivian llanos (unlike the situation suggested for the Venezuelan llanos).

High in the Andes near the frigid waters of Lake Titicaca, another experiment in raised field agriculture occurred between AD 400 and 1100, supported in part by the Tiwanaku Empire. At between 3,500 and 4,000 m (11,480–13,120 ft) above sea level, only extremely hardy crops like potato, quinoa, and other Andean tubers grow on the altiplano, and these crops can be devastated by bitter frosts. The **Pampa Koani**, near Lake Titicaca, contained more than 7,000 hectares (17,290 acres) of raised fields, a project requiring more than 2,290 person-years of effort. The Pampa Koani raised field complex, the archaeologist **Alan Kolata** observed, "is a representative portion of a vast network of similar abandoned fields that encompasses nearly the entire circumference of Lake Titicaca."[80] Based on traces of ancient fields visible in aerial photos, an estimated 70 km^2 (27 square miles) of raised fields rimmed the lakeshore. The principal reason for the fields was to reclaim waterlogged land, but a second function was to protect crops from bitter cold: cold air tends to flow away from the raised bed and down into the surrounding swales, protecting the crop.[81]

A final example of raised field agriculture comes from the Casma Valley of the North Coast of Peru.[82] There, two sets of raised fields were constructed on the opposite margins of the lower river valley. The southern, larger set covers an estimated 439 ha (ca. 1,085 acres); the fields were associated with a work camp established by the Chimú Empire, a prehispanic state (AD 900–1470) of the North Coast of Peru (see chapter 9). Stratigraphic excavations indicated that the tops of the fields, rather than the flanking furrows, were planted, and the fields were cultivated to reclaim waterlogged lands. Ironically, the challenge for agriculture in the coastal valleys of Peru is usually drought, not abundant rainfall, and the Casma Valley fields seem to have been constructed in the aftermath of a major El Niño/ Southern Oscillation (ENSO) event in the mid-AD 1300s.

This brief review of raised field agriculture makes several points. First, extensive slash-and-burn agriculture was not the only agrosystem used in lowland South America; raised fields are found in widely separated areas in the Amazon and Orinoco Basins, as well as in coastal Amazonia. Second, it seems as if the development of raised fields occurred long after the initial introduction of crops and farming, apparently in response to the need to intensify and increase agricultural surpluses. Third, the decision to invest in these agricultural projects may have been made by chiefdoms, states, and empires—and also by non-hierarchical village communities.

Canal Irrigation

As mentioned, access to water is one of the recurrent challenges for agriculture on the arid coasts of western South America, a challenge **canal irrigation systems** confront (figure 5.27).

Figure 5.27 Irrigation canal and farms, Arequipa, Peru

Figure 5.28 Terraces and irrigation farming, Colca Valley, Peru

Irrigation systems are not limited to the arid coastal zones. In the Andean highlands, irrigation systems are an integral element of the terracing systems that sculpt the mountainsides, providing the agrarian basis for ancient and modern societies (figure 5.28).

For example, the ethnographer **David Guillet**, writing about the **Colca Valley** in southern Peru, observes:

> In the semiarid environment of the Colca Valley, it is impossible to discuss terrace systems independently of their role in irrigation. Terraces provide a surface for cultivation and, more important, for the flow of water to plots. Without irrigation, the slopes would be virtually uncultivable. Precipitation is simply too low and unreliable for rainfall agriculture . . . The water that feeds the irrigation system . . . comes from the plateaus and snow-capped mountains of the puna. The snowmelts of peaks feed upland lakes and streams. Canals extract water from these sources and bring it down to the cultivated slopes, where it enters a complex system of feeder canals.[83]

In the highlands, irrigation systems transport silt along with water, resulting in deeper and richer soils. Terraces inhibit or slow erosion and allow for cultivation of less fertile soils on steep slopes (figure 5.29).[84] The irrigation networks were

Figure 5.29 Terrace farming, Pisac, Peru

created and maintained by social networks, as local communities or ancient kingdoms managed water, soil, and labor.

Vast irrigation systems were constructed in the coastal valleys of Peru; much of the resulting farmland is no longer farmed. More land was irrigated in prehistory than today, **Charles Clement** and **Michael Moseley** have observed, with perhaps 35 percent less land farmed today in Peru's coastal valleys and an astounding loss of 62 percent to 80 percent of formerly productive highland terraces.[85]

Small-scale irrigation canals have been discovered by Dillehay and colleagues in the Upper Zaña Valley, dating to at least 5,400 14 cal yr BP and possibly as old as 8040–7340 cal yr BP, making them the oldest irrigation canals currently known from South America.[86] The canals are superimposed ditches exposed in a stratigraphic profile. The entire extent of the irrigation system is unknown, but the earliest ditches seem to run less than 2 km (1.2 miles), bringing water from small tributaries of the Nanchoc River to terrace-edge farming fields. Yet, the fact that the canals are superimposed indicates that the residents of the North Coast knew how to design irrigation systems that followed the contours of the western Andean foothills. The earliest ditches were 50 to 70 cm (19.5–27.3 in) wide and 20 to 30 cm (7.8–11.7 in) deep, gravity-fed systems with very subtle slopes, just enough to move water.

From these modest beginnings, people living in the valleys of the Peruvian coast created some of the largest hydraulic projects known in the ancient world. For example, on the Central Coast of Peru there is evidence for extremely early monumental constructions dating between circa 3000 and 1800 BC (see chapter 6), a period of explosive growth of human settlements that subsisted on marine resources and domesticated plants—maize, squash, beans, chilies, and other crops—farmed either through floodwater agriculture or using relatively small irrigation systems.[87] Although irrigation systems did not "cause" this early demographic increase and monumental constructions, the development of large inland settlements along the river valleys strongly suggests the significance of these agrosystems.

The significance of irrigation agriculture is clear for later prehispanic societies along the Peruvian coast (figure 5.30).

In the **Moche Valley**, the archaeologist **Brian Billman** has studied the development of irrigation systems over time.[88] Between 1800 and 400 BC, the middle Moche Valley became a focus of settlement and farming. Several dozen relatively short canals (less than 3.7 km [2.3 miles] long) and a handful of larger canals (as long as 7 km [4.3 miles]) carried water to 4,100 ha (10,127 acres) of farmland. Over the next four centuries (during the Salinar phase, circa 400 to 1 BC), new zones in the lower valley were farmed as new canals were built and irrigated 6,750–7,300 ha (16,673–18,031 acres) of farmland. At this point the growth of irrigation apparently paused until AD 200–900, when more canals were built by the Moche state (discussed in chapter 9). Major canals, several 30 km (18 miles) or longer, carried water to farmlands far from the Rio Moche. These canal projects required significantly more human effort than previous canals and nearly doubled the total

Figure 5.30 Middle Moche Valley, Peru

Figure 5.31 Andean maize agriculture as illustrated by Felipe Guaman Poma

amount of irrigated land in the Moche Valley, to an estimated 12,550–13,200 ha (30,999–32,604 acres).

Yet, even this was insufficient for the later Chimú Empire (AD 900–1470), which developed canal systems to irrigate more than 19,000 ha (46,930 acres) of farmland. The Chimú expanded the irrigation networks within the Moche Valley and constructed a 70 km (42 miles)-long canal to carry water from the neighboring Chicama Valley to the Moche Valley. This enormous hydraulic project probably required a crew of 1,000 laborers working for a generation, but with this colossal project the Chimú seem to have overreached. Some archaeologists argue that the inter-valley canal never worked because of design errors; other archaeologists suggest that it functioned but was rendered unusable by an ENSO event in the 1300s, tectonic uplift, or the lack of rainfall.[89] Nonetheless, the expansive canal systems on the North Coast are yet another archaeological example of how ancient humans modified landscapes and constructed their lives in prehistoric South America (figure 5.31).

Conclusion: The Myth of the Pristine Landscape

Multiple lines of archaeological, botanical, and ethnographic evidence indicate the diverse ways in which humans modified South American environments over the last 12,000 years (figure 5.31). Plants were cultivated long before they were domesticated, and they were integrated into foraging economies. This gradual integration occurred very early in the Holocene and took place independently at various locales across the continent. In turn, domesticated innovations were exchanged broadly, raised in areas far from the ranges of their wild ancestors. As humans integrated a remarkable array of plants into their lives—as foodstuffs, fibers, containers, or drugs—they created cultures of stunning diversity. In these varied processes, ancient South Americans created tended forests, cut down and burned jungles, drained and farmed waterlogged lands, terraced mountainsides, and channeled water to desert lands. In the process, they left behind an impressive archaeological legacy.

The cultural geographer William Denevan has written about the "pristine myth" of the landscape of the Americas, the vision that native peoples lived in nature that was not disturbed until the arrival of Europeans. This vision is false, Denevan writes: "By 1492, Indian activity had modified vegetation and wildlife, caused erosion, and created earthworks, roads, and settlements throughout the Americas. This may be obvious, but the human imprint was much more ubiquitous than is usually realized. The historical evidence is ample, as are data from surviving earthworks and archaeology."[90] The transformations of nature, including the evolution of agriculture, were expressed in the multiplicity of cultural traditions across the South American continent.

Notes

1. T. Douglas Price and Ofer Bar-Yosef, "The Origins of Agriculture: New Data, New Ideas—An Introduction to Supplement 4," in *The Origins of Agriculture: New Data, New Ideas*, Wenner-Gren Symposium Supplement 4, *Current Anthropology* 52 (2011): S169.

2. For recent overviews of plant domestication, see D. Pearsall, "Plant Domestication and the Shift to Agriculture in the Andes," in *The Handbook of South American Archaeology*, ed. H. Silverman and W. Isbell (New York: Springer, 2008), 105–120; D. Piperno, "The Origins of Plant Cultivation and Domestication in the New World Tropics: Patterns, Process, and New Developments," in *The Origins of Agriculture: New Data, New Ideas*, Wenner-Gren Symposium Supplement 4, *Current Anthropology* 52 (2011): S453–S470.

3. Price and Bar-Yosef, "Origins of Agriculture," S165.

4. For an overview of animal domestication, see P. Stahl, "Animal Domestication in South America," in *The Handbook of South American Archaeology*, ed. H. Silverman and W. Isbell (New York: Springer, 2008), 121–130.

5. For a thorough overview of the field, see C. Hastorf, *Current Paleoethnobotany: Analytical Methods and Cultural Interpretations of Archaeological Plant Remains* (Chicago: University of Chicago Press, 1988). In addition, examine relevant chapters in E. Anderson, D. Pearsall, E. Hunn, and N. Turner, eds., *Ethnobiology* (Hoboken, NJ: John Wiley & Sons, 2011).

6. For overviews of palynology, see V. Bryant Jr. and R. Holloway, "The Role of Palynology in Archaeology," *Journal of Archaeological Method and Theory* 6 (1983): 191–224.

7. For a thorough overview, see D. Piperno, *Phytoliths: A Comprehensive Guide for Archaeologists and Paleoecologists* (Lanham, MD: AltaMira, 2006); see also D. Piperno, "Identifying Crop Plants Phytoliths (and Starch Grains) in Central and South America: A Review and an Update of the Evidence," *Quaternary International* 193 (2009): 146–159.

8. The following discussion is based on Piperno, "Origins of Plant Cultivation."

9. Ibid., S455.

10. Ibid., S450.

11. A. Ranere, D. Piperno, I. Holst, R. Dickau, and J. Iriarte, "The Cultural and Chronological Context of Early Holocene Maize and Squash Domestication in the Central Balsas River Valley, Mexico," *Proceedings of the National Academy of Sciences* 106, no. 13 (March 31, 2009): 5014–5018.

12. J. Smalley and M. Blake, "Sweet Beginnings: Stalk Sugar and the Domestication of Maize," *Current Anthropology* 44, no. 5 (2003): 675–703; M. Blake, "Dating the Initial Spread of Zea Mays," in *Histories of Maize: Multidisciplinary Approaches to the Prehistory, Biogeography, Domestication, and Evolution of Maize*, ed. J. Staller, R. Tykot, and B. Benz (New York: Elsevier, 2009), 45–62. See also J. Staller, *Maize Cobs and Cultures: History of* Zea Mays *L* (New York: Springer, 2009).

13. A. Grobman, D. Bonavia, T. Dillehay, D. Piperno, J. Iriarte, and I. Holst, "Preceramic Maize from Paredones and Huaca Prieta, Peru," *Proceedings of the National*

Academy of Sciences (2012): 1755–1759; D. Piperno, "Northern Peruvian Early and Middle Preceramic Agriculture in Central and South American Contexts," in *From Foraging to Farming in the Andes: New Perspectives on Food Production and Social Organization*, ed. T. Dillehay (Cambridge: Cambridge University Press, 2011), 279.

14. J. Iriarte, I. Holst, O. Marozzi, C. Listopad, E. Alonso, A. Rinderknect, and J. Montaña, "Evidence for Cultivar Adoption and Emerging Complexity during the Mid-Holocene in the La Plata Basin," *Nature* 432 (December 2, 2004): 614–617.

15. C. Heiser Jr. and D. Nelson, "On the Origin of the Cultivated Chenopods (Chenopodium)," *Genetics* 78 (1974): 503–505; E. Fuentes, E. Martinez, P. Hinrichsen, E. Jellen, and P. Maughan, "Assessment of Genetic Diversity Patterns in Chilean Quinoa (*Chenopodium Quinoa* Willd.) Germplasm Using Multiplex Fluorescent Microsatellite Markers," *Conservation Genetics* 10 (2009): 369–377.

16. J. Sauer and L. Kaplan, "Canavalia Beans in American Prehistory," *American Antiquity* 34, no. 4 (1969): 417–424; Pearsall, "Plant Domestication and the Shift," 108; Piperno, "Origins of Plant Cultivation," S458.

17. Information from International Potato Center website http://cipotato.org/ (accessed November 29, 2011).

18. J. Wendel and R. Cronn, "Polyploidy and the Evolutionary History of Cotton," *Advances in Agronomy* 78 (2003): 155.

19. G. Crawford, "Advances in Understanding Early Agriculture in Japan," *Current Anthropology* 52, no. S4 (2011): S341.

20. See L. Kistler, http://www.pnas.org/search?author1=Logan+Kistler&sortspec=date&submit=Submit; A. Montenegro, http://www.pnas.org/search?author1=%C3%81lvaro+Montenegro&sortspec=date&submit=Submit; B. Smith, http://www.pnas.org/search?author1=Bruce+D.+Smith&sortspec=date&submit=Submit; J. Gifford, http://www.pnas.org/search?author1=John+A.+Gifford&sortspec=date&submit=Submit; R. Green, http://www.pnas.org/search?author1=Richard+E.+Green&sortspec=date&submit=Submit; L. Newsom, http://www.pnas.org/search?author1=Lee+A.+Newsom&sortspec=date&submit=Submit; B. Shapiro, "Transoceanic Drift and the Domestication of African Bottle Gourds in the Americas," *Proceedings of the National Academy of Sciences* 111, no. 8 (February 10, 2014): 2937–2941, at http://www.pnas.org/search?author1=Beth+Shapiro&sortspec=date&submit=Submit (all accessed March 8, 2014).

21. J. Jennings and B. Bowser, "Drink, Power and Society in the Andes: An Introduction," in *Drink, Power and the Andes*, ed. J. Jennings and B. Bowser (Gainesville: University Press of Florida, 2009), 1.

22. For additional discussion, see D. Goldstein, R. Coleman Goldstein, and P. Williams, "You Are What You Drink: A Sociocultural Reconstruction of Pre-Hispanic Fermented Beverage Use at Cerro Baul, Moquegua, Peru," in *Drink, Power and the Andes*, ed. J. Jennings and B. Bowser (Gainesville: University Press of Florida, 2009), 133–166. In the same volume, also see the articles by T. Bray, "The Role of Chicha in Inca State Expansion: A Distributional Study of Inca *Aríbalos*," in *Drink, Power and the Andes*, ed. J. Jennings and B. Bowser (Gainesville: University Press of Florida, 2009), 108–132; K. Anderson, "Tiwanaku Influence on Local Drinking Patterns in Cochabamba, Bolivia," in *Drink, Power and the Andes*, ed. J. Jennings and B. Bowser (Gainesville: University Press of Florida, 2009), 167–199; F. Hayashida, "*Chicha* Histo-

ries: Pre-Hispanic Brewing in the Andes and the Use of Ethnographic and Historical Analogies," in *Drink, Power and the Andes*, ed. J. Jennings and B. Bowser (Gainesville: University Press of Florida, 2009), 232–256.

23. Weekly estimate by J. Jennings and M. Chatfield, "Pots, Brewers, and Hosts: Women's Power and the Limits of Central Andean Feasting," in *Drink, Power and the Andes*, ed. J. Jennings and B. Bowser (Gainesville: University Press of Florida, 2009), 214; see also J. Moore, "Prehispanic Beer in Coastal Peru: Technology and Social Context of Prehistoric Production," *American Anthropologist* 91 (1989): 682–695.

24. Goldstein et al., "You Are What You Drink," 137–157.

25. S. Bieri, A. Brachet, J. Veuthey, and P. Christen, "Cocaine Distribution in Wild *Erythroxylum* Species," *Journal of Ethnopharmacology* 103 (2006): 439–447.

26. T. Plowman, "The Origin, Evolution, and Diffusion of Coca, *Erythroxylum* spp., in South and Central America," in *Pre-Columbian Plant Migration*, ed. D. Stone (Cambridge, MA: Harvard University Press, 1984), 125–165.

27. M. Rivera, A. Aufderheide, L. Cartmell, C. Torres, and O. Langsjoen, "Antiquity of Coca-Leaf Chewing in the South Central Andes: A 3,000 Year Archaeological Record of Coca-Leaf Chewing from Northern Chile," *Journal of Psychoactive Drugs* 37, no. 4 (2005): 455–458.

28. J. Wilbert, *Tobacco and Shamanism in South America* (New Haven, CT: Yale University Press, 1987), 6.

29. Ibid., 9–132; see also J. Wilbert, "Does Pharmacology Corroborate the Nicotine Therapy and Practices of South American Shamanism?" *Journal of Ethnopharmacology* 32, nos. 1–3 (1991): 179–186.

30. R. Schultes and R. Raffauf, *Vine of the Soul: Medicine Men, Their Plants and Rituals in the Colombian Amazonia* (Oracle, AZ: Synergistic Press, 1992); see also M. Dobkindel Rios, *Visionary Vine: Psychedelic Healing in the Peruvian Amazon* (San Francisco: Chandler, 1972). For detailed chemical analyses of the active ingredients in modern ayahuasca brews, see D. McKenna, G. Towers, and F. Abbiot, "Monoamine Oxidase Inhibitors in South American Hallucinogenic Plants: Tryptamine and P-carboline Constituents of Ayahuasca," *Journal of Ethnopharmocology* 10 (1984): 195–223. For a stunning collection of photographs taken by Richard Schultes in the course of his ethnobotanical research, see R. Schultes, *Where the Gods Reign: Plants and Peoples of the Colombian Amazon* (Oracle, AZ: Synergistic Press, 1990).

31. F. Flores and W. Lewis, "Drinking the South American Hallucinogenic Ayahuasca," *Economic Botany* 32, no. 2 (1978): 156.

32. D. Sharon, "The San Pedro Cactus in Peruvian Folk Healing," in *Flesh of the Gods: The Ritual Use of Hallucinogens*, ed. Peter Furst (New York: Praeger, 1972), 114–135; D. Sharon, *Shamanism and the Sacred Cactus: Ethnoarchaeological Evidence for San Pedro Use in Northern Peru*, San Diego Museum Papers 23 (San Diego: San Diego Museum, 2000); D. Sharon and C. Donnan, "The Magic Cactus: Ethnoarchaeological Continuity," *Archaeology* 30, no. 6 (1977): 374–381.

33. V. de Feo, "The Ritual Use of Brugmansia Species in Traditional Andean Medicine in Northern Peru," *Economic Botany* 58, Supplement (2004): S221–S229.

34. Quoted in R. Burger, "What Kind of Hallucinogenic Snuff Was Used at Chavín de Huantar? An Iconographic Identification," *ÑawpaPacha* 31, no. 2 (2011):

135. See also C. Torres and D. Repke, *Anadenanthera Visionary Plant of Ancient South America* (Binghamton, NY: Hawthorn, 2006).

35. See, for example, A. Cordy-Collins, "Chavín Art: Its Shamanistic/Hallucinogenic Origins," in *Pre-Columbian Art History: Selected Readings*, ed. A. Cordy-Collins and J. Stern (Palo Alto, CA: Peek, 1977), 353–362; C. Donnan, *Moche Art and Iconography* (Los Angeles: UCLA Latin American Center Publications, 1976); C. Donnan, *Moche Art of Peru: Precolumbian Symbolic Communication* (Los Angeles: Museum of Culture History, UCLA, 1978); P. Furst, "Hallucinogens in Precolumbian Art," in *Art and Environment in Native America*, ed. M. E. King and I. R. Traylor (Lubbock: Museum of Texas Technological University, 1974), 50–101; P. Knobloch, "Wari Ritual Power at Conchapata: An Interpretation of *Anadenantheracolubrina* Iconography," *Latin American Antiquity* 11, no. 4 (2000): 387–402; A. Llagostera, C. Torres, and M. A. Costa, "El complejo psicotrópico Solcor-3 (San Pedro de Atacama)," *Estudios Atacameños* 9 (1988): 61–98; C. Torres, "Chavín's Psychoactive Pharmacopoeia: The Iconographic Evidence," in *Chavín: Art, Architecture, and Culture*, ed. W. Conklin and J. Quilter, Monograph 61 (Los Angeles: Cotsen Institute of Archaeology, UCLA, 2008), 239–259; C. Torres, D. Repke, K. Chan, D. McKenna, A. Llagostera, and R. E. Schultes, "Snuff Powders from Pre-Hispanic San Pedro de Atacama: Chemical and Contextual Analysis," *Current Anthropology* 32, no. 5 (1991): 640–649.

36. There is an enormous literature on this topic, but the essential overview remains R. Schultes and A. Hofmann, *Plants of the Gods: Their Sacred, Healing and Hallucinogenic Powers* (Rochester, NY: Healing Arts, 1979). For classic ethnographies dealing with specific societies, see N. Chagnon, *Yanomamo: The Last Days of Eden* (Orlando: Harcourt Brace Jovanovich, 1992); M. Harner, *The Jivaro: People of the Sacred Waterfalls* (Berkeley: University of California Press, 1972); G. Reichel-Dolmatoff, *The Shaman and the Jaguar* (Philadelphia: Temple University Press, 1975). For two excellent and eminently readable perspectives on ethnographic research focused on traditional plant use, see W. Davis, *One River: Explorations and Discoveries in the Amazon Rain Forest* (New York: Simon and Schuster, 1996); M. Plotkin, *Tales of a Shaman's Apprentice: An Ethnobotanist Searches for New Medicines in the Amazon Rainforest* (New York: Penguin Books, 1993).

37. J. Iriarte, "Narrowing the Gap: Exploring the Diversity of Early Food-Production Economies in the Americas," *Current Anthropology* 50, no. 5 (2009): 677.

38. Piperno, "Origins of Plant Cultivation," S464, emphasis added.

39. An interesting hypothesis regarding this synchronicity and its linkage to global climate change is articulated by P. Richerson, R. Boyd, and R. Bettinger, "Was Agriculture Impossible during the Pleistocene but Mandatory during the Holocene? A Climate Change Hypothesis," *American Antiquity* 66, no. 3 (2001): 387–411, and briefly restated by the same authors, "Constraints on the Development of Agriculture," *Current Anthropology* 50, no. 5 (2009): 627–631.

40. T. Dillehay, ed., *From Foraging to Farming in the Andes: New Perspectives on Food Production and Social Organization* (Cambridge: Cambridge University Press, 2011).

41. J. Rossen, "Preceramic Plant Gathering, Gardening, and Farming," in *From Foraging to Farming in the Andes: New Perspectives on Food Production and Social Organization*, ed. T. Dillehay (Cambridge: Cambridge University Press, 2011), 177.

42. D. Piperno, "Northern Peruvian Early and Middle Preceramic Agriculture in Central and South American Contexts," in *From Foraging to Farming in the Andes: New Perspectives on Food Production and Social Organization*, ed. T. Dillehay (Cambridge: Cambridge University Press, 2011), 275.

43. C. Hastorf, "Domesticated Food and Society in Early Coastal Peru," in *Time and Complexity in Historical Ecology*, ed. W. Balee and C. Erickson (New York: Columbia University Press, 2006), 97.

44. Ibid., 102.

45. Ibid., 98–99.

46. For a detailed ethnographic study among manioc cultivators in Surinam, see M. Elias, L. Rival, and D. McKey, "Perception and Management of Cassava (*Manihot esculenta Crantz*) Diversity among Makushi Amerindians of Guyana (South America)," *Journal of Ethnobiology* 20, no. 2 (2000): 239–265; L. Rival and D. McKey, "Domestication and Diversity in Manioc (*Manihot esculenta Crantz* ssp. *esculenta*, Euphorbiaceae)," *Current Anthropology* 49, no. 6 (2008): 1119–2228.

47. D. W. Lathrap, "The Antiquity and Importance of Long-Distance Trade Relationships in the Moist Tropics of Pre-Columbian South America," *World Archaeology* 5, no. 2 (1973): 170–186. For an ethnographic account of modern traditional Aymara healers, see J. Bastien, *Healers of the Andes: Kallawaya Herbalists and Their Medicinal Plants* (Salt Lake City: University of Utah Press, 1987).

48. S. Wassen, "A Medicine-Man's Implements and Plants in a Tiahuanacoid Tomb in Highland Bolivia," *Etnologiska Studier* 32 (1972); quote from J. Ogalde, B. Arriaza, and E. Soto, "Identification of Psychoactive Alkaloids in Ancient Andean Human Hair by Gas Chromatography/Mass Spectrometry," *Journal of Archaeological Science* 36 (2009): 471.

49. Dillehay, *From Foraging to Farming in the Andes*, 2, 4.

50. Piperno, "Origins of Plant Cultivation," S466.

51. Price and Bar-Yosef, "Origins of Agriculture," S168.

52. For a brief, though dated, review, see R. Matheny and D. Gurr, "Variation in Prehistoric Agricultural Systems of the New World," *Annual Review of Anthropology* 12 (1983): 79–103. For an encyclopedic overview by one of the leading scholars, see W. Denevan, *Cultivated Landscapes of Native Amazonia and the Andes* (New York: Oxford University Press, 2001), a book that informs much of this section.

53. W. Denevan, "Hydraulic Agriculture in the American Tropics: Forms, Measures, and Recent Research," in *Maya Subsistence: Studies in Memory of Dennis E. Puleston*, ed. K. Flannery (New York: Academic Press, 1982), 181.

54. L. Rival, "Domestication as a Historical and Symbolic Process: Wild Gardens and Cultivated Forests in the Ecuadorian Amazon," in *Advances in Historical Ecology*, ed. W. Balée (New York: Columbia University Press, 1998), 237.

55. Ibid., 241.

56. Ibid., 239.

57. For an early discussion of the anthropogenic origins of terra preta soils, see N. Smith, "Anthrosols and Human Carrying Capacity in Amazonia," *Annals of the Association of American Geographers* 70, no. 4 (1980): 553–566. For archaeological investigations of terra preta soils, see M. Eden, W. Bray, L. Herrera, and C. McEwan, "Terra

Preta Soils and Their Archaeological Context in the Caquetá Basin of Southeast Colombia," *American Antiquity* 49 (1984): 125–140; E. Neves, J. Peterson, R. Bartone, and C. da Silva, "Historical and Socio-Cultural Origins of Amazonian Dark Earths," in *Amazonian Dark Earths: Origin, Properties, Management*, ed. J. Lehmann, D. C. Kern, B. Glaser, and W. I. Woods (Norwell, MA: Kluwer Academic, 2003), 29–49; J. Petersen, E. Neves, and M. Heckenberger, "Gift from the Past: *Terra Preta* and Prehistoric Amerindian Occupation in Amazonia," in *Unknown Amazon: Culture in Nature in Ancient Brazil*, ed. C. McEwan, C. Barreto, and E. G. Neves (London: British Museum Press, 2001), 86–105. For an outstanding summary, see C. Erickson, "Historical Ecology and Future Explorations," in *Amazonian Dark Earths: Origin, Properties, Management*, ed. J. Lehmann, D. C. Kern, B. Glaser, and W. I. Woods (Norwell, MA: Kluwer Academic, 2003), 455–500. For an engaging popular account, see C. Mann, *1491: New Revelations of the Americas before Columbus* (New York: Vintage Books, 2005).

58. There is an enormous literature on shifting cultivation, as it is practiced around the world and studied by geographers, ecologists, agronomists, anthropologists—and archaeologists. For a succinct overview of South American swidden systems, see D. Dufour, "Use of Tropical Rainforests by Native Amazonians," *BioScience* 40, no. 9 (1990): 652–659. For ethnographic studies in addition to those cited below, see D. Harris, "The Ecology of Swidden Cultivation in the Upper Orinoco Rain Forest, Venezuela," *Geographical Review* 61, no. 4 (1971): 475–495; N. Flowers, D. Gross, M. Ritter, and D. Werner, "Variation in Swidden Practices in Four Central Brazilian Indian Societies," *Human Ecology* 10, no. 2 (1982): 203–217; M. Eden and A. Andrade, "Ecological Aspects of Swidden Cultivation among the Andoke and Witoto Indians of the Colombian Amazon," *Human Ecology* 15, no. 3 (1987): 339–359.

59. R. Carneiro, "Slash-and-Burn Cultivation among the Kuikuru and Its Implications for Cultural Development in the Amazon Basin," in *Native South Americans: Ethnography of the Least-Known Continent*, ed. P. Lyons (Boston: Little, Brown, 1974), 73–91.

60. W. Denevan, "Campa Subsistence in the Gran Pajonal, Eastern Peru," *Geographical Review* 61, no. 4 (1971): 496–518.

61. S. Pyne, "Missouri Compromise" at http://web.missouri.edu/~guyetter/missouri_comp2.pdf (accessed March 9, 2014); see also Pyne's outstanding book, *Fire: A Brief History* (Seattle: University of Washington Press, 2001).

62. For example, see M. Bush, M. Miller, P. De Oliveira, and P. Colinvaux, "Two Histories of Environmental Change and Human Disturbance in Eastern Lowland Amazonia," *The Holocene* 10, no. 5 (2000): 543–553.

63. M. Arroyo-Kalin, "Slash-Burn-and-Churn: Landscape History and Crop Cultivation in Pre-Columbian Amazonia," *Quaternary International* 249 (2012): 4–18.

64. Ibid., 11.

65. See, as examples, B. Meggers, "The Continuing Quest for El Dorado: Round Two," *Latin American Antiquity* 12, no. 3 (2001): 304–325; B. Meggers, M. Heckenberger, and colleagues in "Revisiting Amazonia circa 1492," *Science* 302 (2003): 2067–2070.

66. B. Meggers, "Environmental Limitation on the Development of Culture," *American Anthropologist* 56, no. 5 (1954): 807.

67. Ibid., 809.

68. The classic introduction to raised field agrosystems is W. Denevan, "Aboriginal Drained-Field Cultivation in the Americas," *Science* 169, no. 3946 (1970): 647–654.

69. J. Parsons, "Ridged Fields in the Río Guayas Valley, Ecuador," *American Antiquity* 34 (1969): 76–80; K. Matthewson, "Estimating Labor Inputs for the Guayas Raised Fields: Initial Considerations," in *Prehispanic Agricultural Fields in the Andean Region*, ed. W. Denevan, K. Matthewson, and G. Knapp, British Archaeological Reports International Series (Oxford: British Archaeological Reports, 1987), 359.

70. Matthewson, "Estimating Labor Inputs," 331.

71. F. Delgado-Espinoza, "Intensive Agriculture and Political Economy of the Yaguachi Chiefdom of Guayas Basin, Coastal Ecuador" (PhD diss., University of Pittsburgh, 2002).

72. A. Zucchi and W. Denevan, *Campos Elevados e Historia Cultural Prehispánica de los Llanos Orientales de Venezuela* (Caracas: Universidad Católica Andrés Bello, 1979), 26.

73. A. Zucchi, "Prehistoric Human Occupations of the Western Venezuelan Llanos," *American Antiquity* 38, no. 2 (1973): 182–190. For a more recent brief introduction and bibliography for the region, see R. Navarrete, "The Prehistory of Venezuela—Not Necessarily an Intermediate Area," in *The Handbook of South American Archaeology*, ed. H. Silverman and W. Isbell (New York: Springer, 2008), 429–458.

74. C. Spencer, E. Redmond, and M. Rinaldi, "Drained Fields at la Tigra, Venezuelan Llanos: A Regional Perspective," *Latin American Antiquity* 5, no. 2 (1994): 119–143.

75. S. Rostain, "Agricultural Earthworks on the French Guiana Coast," in *The Handbook of South American Archaeology*, ed. H. Silverman and W. Isbell (New York: Springer, 2008), 217–233; S. Rostain, "Pre-Columbian Earthworks in Coastal Amazonia," *Diversity* 2 (2010): 331–352; D. McKey, S. Rostain, J. Iriarte, B. Glaser, J. Birk, I. Holst, and D. Renard, "Pre-Columbian Agricultural Landscapes, Ecosystem Engineers, and Self-Organized Patchiness in Amazonia," *Proceedings of the National Academy of Sciences* 107, no. 17 (2010): 7823–7828; J. Iriarte, B. Glaser, J. Watling, A. Wainwright, J. Birk, D. Renard, S. Rostain, and D. McKey, "Late Holocene Neotropical Agricultural Landscapes: Phytolith and Stable Carbon Isotope Analysis of Raised Fields from French Guianan Coastal Savannahs," *Journal of Archaeological Science* 37 (2010): 2984–2994.

76. Iriarte et al., "Late Holocene Neotropical Agricultural Landscapes," 2993.

77. Rostain, "Pre-Columbian Earthworks in Coastal Amazonia," 340–344.

78. C. Erickson, "Raised Fields as a Sustainable Agricultural System from Amazonia" (paper presented at the symposium Recovery of Indigenous Technology and Resources, Bolivia, 18th International Congress of the Latin American Studies Association, Atlanta, March 10–12, 1994). Among Clark Erickson's numerous publications, see also C. Erickson, "Archaeological Perspectives on Ancient Landscapes of the Llanos de Mojos in the Bolivian Amazon," in *Archaeology in the American Tropics: Current Analytical Methods and Applications*, ed. P. Stahl (Cambridge: Cambridge University Press, 1995), 66–95; C. Erickson, "The Domesticated Landscapes of the Bolivian Amazon," in *Time and Complexity in Historical Ecology: Studies in the Neotropical Lowlands*, ed. W. Balée and C. Erickson (New York: Columbia University Press, 2006), 235–278.

Erickson's work is also profiled in the excellent popular book by Charles Mann, *1491: New Revelations of the Americas before Columbus* (New York: Vintage, 2006).

79. R. Dickau, M. Bruno, J. Iriarte, H. Prümers, C. Betancourt, I. Holst, and F. Mayle, "Diversity of Cultivars and Other Plant Resources Used at Habitation Sites in the Llanos de Mojos, Beni, Bolivia: Evidence from Macrobotanical Remains, Starch Grains, and Phytoliths," *Journal of Archaeological Science* 39 (2012): 357–370.

80. A. Kolata, "The Agricultural Foundations of the Tiwanaku State: A View from the Heartland," *American Antiquity* 51, no. 4 (1986): 758. See also C. T. Smith, W. M. Denevan, and P. Hamilton, "Ancient Ridged Fields in the Region of Lake Titicaca," *Geographical Journal* 134, no. 3 (1968): 353–367; C. Erickson and K. L. Candler, "Raised Fields and Sustainable Agriculture in the Lake Titicaca Basin of Peru," in *Fragile Lands of Latin America: Strategies for Sustainable Development*, ed. J. Browder (Boulder, CO: Westview, 1989), 230–248.

81. A. Kolata and C. Ortloff, "Thermal Analysis of Tiwanaku Raised Field Systems in the Lake Titicaca Basin of Bolivia," *Journal of Archaeological Science* 16, no. 3 (1989): 233–263.

82. T. Pozorski, S. Pozorski, C. Mackey, and A. Klymyshyn, "Pre-Hispanic Ridged Fields of the Casma Valley, Peru," *Geographical Review* 73, no. 4 (1983): 407–416; J. Moore, "Prehistoric Raised Field Agriculture in the Casma Valley, Peru," *Journal of Field Archaeology* 15, no. 3 (1988): 265–276; J. Moore, "Cultural Responses to Environmental Catastrophes: Post–El Niño Subsistence on the Prehistoric North Coast of Peru," *Latin American Antiquity* 2 (1991): 27–47.

83. D. Guillet, "Terracing and Irrigation in the Peruvian Highlands," *Current Anthropology* 28, no. 4 (1987): 412.

84. For a detailed study, see M. Goodman-Elgar, "Evaluating Soil Resilience in Long-Term Cultivation: A Study of Pre-Columbian Terraces from the Paca Valley, Peru," *Journal of Archaeological Science* 35, no. 12 (2008): 3072–3086.

85. C. Clement and M. Moseley, "The Spring-Fed Irrigation System of Carrizal, Peru: A Case Study of the Hypothesis of Agrarian Collapse," *Journal of Field Archaeology* 18, no. 4 (1991): 425–443.

86. T. Dillehay, H. Eling Jr., and J. Rossen, "Preceramic Irrigation Canals in the Peruvian Andes," *Proceedings of the National Academy of Sciences* 102, no. 47 (November 22, 2005): 17241–17244.

87. J. Haas and W. Creamer, "Crucible of Andean Civilization: The Peruvian Coast from 3000 to 1800 BC," *Current Anthropology* 47, no. 5 (2006): 753–754.

88. B. Billman, "Irrigation and the Origins of the Southern Moche State on the North Coast of Peru," *Latin American Antiquity* 13, no. 4 (2002): 371–400. See also M. Moseley and E. Deeds, "The Land in Front of Chan Chan: Agrarian Expansion, Reform, and Collapse in the Moche Valley," in *Chan Chan: Andean Desert City*, ed. M. E. Moseley and K. C. Day (Albuquerque: University of New Mexico Press, 1982), 25–54; C. Ortloff, R. Feldman, and M. Moseley, "Hydraulic Engineering and Historical Aspects of the Pre-Columbian Intravalley Canal Systems of the Moche Valley, Peru," *Journal of Field Archaeology* 12 (1985): 77–98.

89. For this debate, see T. Pozorski and S. Pozorski, "Reassessing the Chicama-Moche Intervalley Canal: Comments on 'Hydraulic Engineering Aspects of the

Chimu Chicama-Moche Intervalley Canal,'" *American Antiquity* 47 (1982): 851–868; I. Farrington, "The Design and Function of the Intervalley Canal: Comments on a Paper by Ortloff, Moseley, and Feldman," *American Antiquity* 48, no. 2 (1983): 360–375; cf. C. Ortloff, M. Moseley, and R. Feldman, "The Chicama-Moche Intervalley Canal: Social Explanations and Physical Paradigms," *American Antiquity* 48, no. 2 (1983): 375–389.

90. W. Denevan, "The Pristine Myth: The Landscape of the Americas in 1492," *Annals of the Association of American Geographers* 892, no. 3 (2005): 379.

Figure 6.1 Shell midden, southern Ecuador

Social Complexities
Part I

10.5876_9781607323334.c006

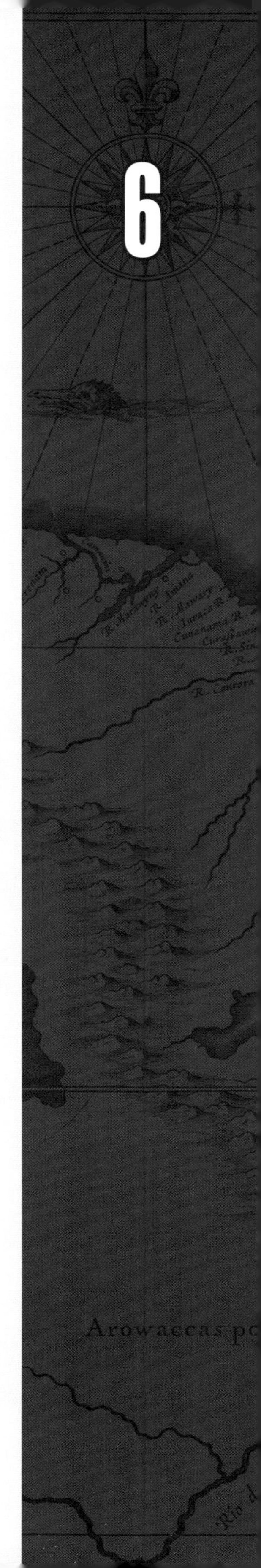

> These Indians raised works both for the convenience and veneration of posterity. With these the plains, eminences, or lesser mountains, are covered; like the Egyptians, they had an extreme passion for rendering their burial-places remarkable.
>
> . . . the Indians having laid a body without burial in the place it was to rest in, environed it with stones and bricks as a tomb; and the dependents, relations, and intimate acquaintance of the deceased, threw so much earth on it as to form a tumulus or eminence which they called *guaca*.
>
> *Antonio de Ulloa, 1772*

This chapter and chapter 7 present a continental overview of archaeological cases relating to the multifaceted topic "the origins of social complexity." This topic has a long history in social theory, from Enlightenment philosophers such as Jean-Jacques Rousseau and Thomas Hobbes to nineteenth-century social thinkers such as Karl Marx and Emile Durkheim, twentieth-century social scientists such as Talcott Parsons and Anthony Giddens, and more recent analyses dealing with resiliency, chaos theory, agent-based modeling, and other approaches to complex systems. Despite these centuries of theoretical ponderings, many of the questions remain the same or unanswered.

If, as Rousseau famously declared in his 1762 *The Social Contract*, "Man is born free, and everywhere he is in chains," more recent theoretical questions, the Mesoamericanist **David Carballo** and colleagues have written,

> have multiplied as they have also become more refined: Why did people relinquish portions of their productive and decision-making autonomy for the economic and political arrangements that characterize complex societies? Why did many accept that wealth and power was wielded by a few? Why did they settle in early cities when the transition to urban life meant more work and shorter life spans for a majority of the population? Why does the nature of human groupings have many cross-cutting parallels across time and space, and yet also highly significant differences and specific features? How can we understand both the diversity of human social formations and why have they coalesced, disaggregated, and recalibrated numerous times across human history?[1]

Even this brief statement glosses a huge array of social configurations, ranging from small, mobile hunting-and-gathering communities to densely populated and socially stratified urban societies. Archaeologists are interested in the varieties of the human social experience, contrasting the lives of small groups of mobile hunters and gatherers with the challenges and advantages of urban life. Understanding the origins and trajectories of social complexity is one of the central questions archaeology addresses,[2] and this is true for archaeologists investigating prehistoric South America.

The initial stages in these transitions are among the most difficult to discern. The ethnographer **Polly Wiessner** has written, "Perhaps the dimmest areas that remain in studies of political 'evolution' are the initial stages in which inequalities beyond those of age, ability, and gender emerged, grew, and became institutionalized . . . the onset and dynamics of the institutionalized inequality remain concealed by sparse archaeological evidence. What is apparent, however, is that the process was often protracted and punctuated by booms and crashes . . . The emergence of institutionalized inequality is considered to be a threshold in political evolution when deeply rooted orientations of small-scale societies were overcome, paving the way for the development of complex polities."[3]

In a review of recent archaeological literature, **Jennifer Kahn** notes that "current studies of social complexity focus to a great extent on the transformative nature of the process, identifying the rate and scale of sociopolitical and economic change, in addition to the resulting effects. There is also a widespread recognition of the local contingencies and historical nature of the process. Researchers come at the question of long-term change from a variety of theoretical stances and methodological approaches, making this theme one of the most variable."[4]

Among archaeologists working in the Americas, the initial development of complex societies is often referred to as the "Formative" or "the Formative transition," roughly the New World equivalent of the term *Neolithic* used by archaeologists working in Europe and Asia. The concept of the Formative emerged from the mid-twentieth-century research of New World archaeologists, including scholarly projects and archaeological fieldwork. For example, in 1955 **Gordon Willey** and **Phillip Phillips** offered this definition of Formative writing: "The establishment of an agricultural, settled village type of life in nuclear America has been variously referred to as 'Archaic,' 'Developmental,' 'Formative,' 'Pre-Classic' and 'Food-producing.' We think that *Formative* is particularly apt, as it implies the 'formation' of the American village-agricultural pattern, and because this pattern is 'formational' to later and more advanced developments."[5]

A number of archaeological research programs crystallized around the concept of the Formative, but its most fervid advocate was the American archaeologist **James A. Ford** (1911–68).[6] Drawing on his extensive field experience in South America and the southeastern United States, Ford argued that the Formative was a widespread cultural horizon, archaeologically marked by the first pottery. Ford's posthumously published magnum opus, *A Comparison of Formative Cultures in the Americas: Diffusion or the Psychic Unity of Man,* was primarily a comparative study of ceramic assemblages from the Andes to the Mississippi Valley. However, Ford included other cultural practices in his concept: "It is preferable to define the Formative more loosely as the 3000 years (or less in some regions) during which the elements of ceramics, ground stone tools, handmade figurines, and manioc and maize agriculture were being diffused and welded into the socioeconomic life of the people living in the region extending from Peru to the eastern United States. At the start of this span of years, all these people had an Archaic economy and technology; at its end they possessed the essential elements for achieving civilization."[7]

Ford argued that these traits were spread by seafaring coastal groups who migrated from northern South America to Central America and the southeastern United States in a process he referred to as the "Colonial Formative."[8] Over the last fifty years, an enormous quantity of archaeological research and thousands of absolute dates have indicated that Ford's model was fundamentally incorrect.

The oldest pottery Ford knew of—the Valdivia ceramics of coastal Ecuador, discussed below—is not, in fact, the oldest in South America.[9] Pottery developed in multiple locations across the Americas, leading **John Hoopes** to conclude "that independent invention played a greater role in the adoption and development of ceramics than the widespread diffusion of technologies and style."[10] Pottery developed independently in lowland Brazil, northern Colombia, coastal Ecuador, and the Central Coast of Peru, as well as in Panama, southern Mesoamerica, and the central and southeastern regions of the United States. If the origins of pottery were more complex and diverse than Ford envisioned, it is no surprise that other traits and practices associated with his model—such as the development of ring villages (see below), the adoption of agriculture, and the creation of monumental mounds—have more complex origins than he proposed.

Which leads one to ask: Why is the term *Formative* still used at all? In many regions of South America, it is not. For example, the American archaeologists **John Rowe** and **Dorothy Menzel** developed an alternative chronology for the Central Andes, essentially contrasting periods of broad cultural integration ("horizons") with periods characterized by regional developments ("intermediate periods")—oscillations largely expressed in the spatial and temporal spread of styles of pottery, architecture, and art motifs.[11] In the Guianas, the chronological framework visualizes a progress shift from mobile hunters and gatherers to semi-sedentary coastal foragers to slash-and-burn agriculturalists, but the chronological phases were based on stylistic suites of lithic tools and pottery, such as "Sipaliwini," "Ronquin," and "Saladoid."[12] A conceptually similar, but otherwise utterly distinct, chronology for northern Chile is based on a series of cultural groupings (Alto Ramirez I, Alto Ramirez II, Alto Ramirez III), designating localized cultural variations that do not imply major reorganizations in human societies.[13] But in other regions of South America the term *Formative* is still used, if not in Ford's specific sense. For example, in the Central Andes, the very influential text *The Peoples and Cultures of Ancient Peru*, by Peruvian archaeologist **Luis Lumbreras**, explicitly adopted the concept of Formative as defined by Willey and Phillips.[14]

In essence, "Formative" serves as an archaeological shorthand for the changes in social complexity that resulted in settled village life, with its various attendant aspects: the emergence of craft specialization, the development of public architecture, the origins of social differences and inequalities, the evolution of more complex political systems, the expansion of long-distance trade, and the creation of new religious concepts and worldviews. Although sometimes presented as a precursor to urbanism and complex state-level societies, these fundamental transformations were not uniform, contemporary, or continental in scope. These broad social changes occurred for a range of reasons and were differently expressed at distinct times in various parts of South America. Rather than constantly repeating the complete list of different transformations listed in the previous sentences, the word *Formative* neatly—but messily—signifies those complex and fascinating transformations in South American prehistory.

Within these very broad parameters of inquiry, the present chapter and chapter 7 discuss archaeological examples of the Formative transition. This chapter examines one of the earliest known examples of the Formative in South America, the discoveries in southwestern Ecuador associated with Valdivia culture, and contrasts that evidence from two nearby regions—in northern Peru and southeastern Ecuador—where very different Formative societies developed at the same time (figure 6.2).

Following a discussion of Late Formative societies in the highlands of Ecuador, the focus shifts to Amazonia, with a brief consideration of early village societies in western and Central Amazonia and then a summary of recent—and spectacular—finds in southwest Amazonia. This chapter concludes with a summary of new and much-debated research into the origins of village life along the Atlantic Coasts of southern Brazil and Uruguay, initial archaeological investigations that promise to illuminate the origins of social complexity in this little-known region of South America.

Chapter 7 deals with archaeological sites from three better-known regions of western South America: the Central Coast and highlands of Peru and the Titicaca Basin. As discussed in chapter 2, extensive archaeological research has been conducted in these areas, with important implications regarding the origins of settled village life, emergent social inequalities, and the development of ceremonial centers and the first cities. These two chapters introduce the reader to an amazing array of archaeological cases that reflect the complex expressions of social complexity in Formative societies in South America.

Divergent Formative Transitions in Ecuador and Northern Peru

Valdivia Culture

One of the first regions in which the Formative was studied was southwest Ecuador (see figure 6.2).[15] The mangrove-rimmed islands and coastlines of the Pacific Coast were explored by the Ecuadorian businessman and archaeologist **Emilio Estrada**, who, in turn, interested **Clifford Evans** and **Betty Meggers** in the region. Their research led to the discovery and definition of the Formative culture known as **Valdivia**. Subsequent investigations by many other archaeologists have resulted in a detailed body of archaeological data on the Valdivia complex.[16]

Figure 6.2 Locations of sites discussed in this chapter

Initial excavations near the coastal village of Valdivia recovered Valdivia ceramics and the definition of this Formative culture (figure 6.3).

Limited test excavations in 1956–57 and 1961 by Estrada, Meggers, and Evans recovered stone, bone, and shell artifacts but most significantly thousands of potsherds and stylized depictions of women made from stone or pottery dubbed "Venus figurines" (figures 6.4, 6.5).

Figure 6.3 Valdivia ceramics

The potsherds from bowls, plates, and cooking pots were coil-built ceramics whose unpainted surfaces were variously smoothed or incised, pricked, and jabbed with bone awls or indented with the fingernails of ancient potters. The seriation of the ceramics from the Valdivia site and nine neighboring sites led to a relative sequence in which four periods were defined (A through D), as was a partially overlapping and subsequent ceramic complex, the Machalilla phase. Cross-dated with uncalibrated radiocarbon samples of charcoal and shell, the earliest Valdivia ceramics were dated to 5,000–4,300 years ago, the latest to 3,400–3,000 years ago.[17]

When first discovered, the Valdivia ceramics had no known South American antecedents. The investigators suggested that the pottery had come from prehistoric cultures located elsewhere.[18] Controversially, Meggers and colleagues argued that the origins of this intrusive culture were derived from the pre-agricultural Jōmon culture of Japan, writing that the comparison of Valdivia and Jōmon pot-

Figure 6.4 Valdivia figurine

tery "showed the early Valdivia Phase to share a larger number of traits with Early and Middle Jōmon than with any New World area or complex."[19] This hypothesis of the trans-Pacific introduction of ceramics to South America sparked a heated controversy that lasted several decades. Current archaeological data do not support the hypothesis.[20]

Figure 6.5 Venus figurines from Real Alto, Ecuador

Subsequent archaeological surveys and excavations resulted in data about Valdivia chronology, settlement patterns, domestic architecture, and subsistence practices. Central to this expanding knowledge were excavations begun in the mid-1970s and directed by **Donald Lathrap** and **Jorge Marcos** at the site of **Real Alto**. Additional perspectives on Valdivia society came from excavations in the 1980s at the interior Valdivia site of **Loma Alta**, as well as from regional surveys. This research led to refinements of the Valdivia chronology by **Elizabeth Hill**

Figure 6.6 Setting of Real Alto, Ecuador

and Jorge Marcos, excavations in domestic architecture by **James Zeidler** and **Jonathan Damp**, and the analysis of subsistence changes by **Deborah Pearsall** and **Peter Stahl**—only a few of the major studies regarding different aspects of Valdivia society.

Over a period of 3,000 years, Valdivia society underwent significant shifts in the organization of settlements and architecture. Valdivia sites were four to ten times larger and more dispersed than Archaic Las Vegas sites (see chapter 4), with Valdivia communities occupying different river valleys or separated by 10 km (6 miles) or more.[21]

Real Alto is located approximately two km (1.2 miles) inland from the Gulf of Guayaquil on the dry hills and low valleys of the Santa Elena Peninsula (figure 6.6).

In 4400–3300 BC, the initial community at Real Alto consisted of 50–60 people living in a dozen or so small dwellings encircling an open area or plaza. Houses were small, flimsy huts, less than 2 m (6.6 ft) across.[22] A few centuries later, at 3000 BC, Real Alto was transformed into a village of 90–100 substantial dwellings occupied by an estimated 600–1,100 people. Houses were significantly larger after 3000–2400 BC, 10 to 12 m (32.8–39.4 ft) long and 7 to 9 m (23–29.5 ft) wide, similar to dwellings built by traditional societies in the western Amazon.[23] By circa 2700–2600 BC, the spatial pattern at Real Alto had changed again, to a roughly rectangular arrangement of dwellings surrounding a plaza 16 ha (39.5 acres) in area. In addition, the first examples of nondomestic "public" architecture appeared.

Archaeologists often consider the creation of "nondomestic" or "public" architecture an index of emergent complexity.[24] For example, the appearance of buildings requiring more labor than an average home suggests new sets of cultural considerations beyond those of shelter and family.[25] Elaborate funeral constructions may signal new conceptions of death or the "above-average" status of the deceased. Various kinds of religious constructions may mark the public nature of religion, the emergence of ritual specialists, or the existence of religious sodalities. Elaborate houses may indicate the development of elites, an initial divergence that may develop into distinct classes or castes. Thus, the appearance of public architecture is an important topic for archaeologists working in South America and elsewhere.

In this light, the public buildings at Real Alto are significant when compared with other Valdivia buildings. Four nonresidential mounds were built in the plaza at Real Alto, the two largest mounds at the plaza's northern end. Of these two, the larger mound was 125 m × 40 m (410 ft × 131 ft) at its base and 1.8 m (5.9 ft) tall. It was topped by an elliptical building that held the remains of a mature woman buried in a pit lined with broken grinding stones. Another pit nearby contained the partial remains of seven individuals: six prepubescent individuals and the secondary burial of an adult male. It is not clear if these other people were buried when the adult woman died or sometime later. Nonetheless, the attention given to the woman's burial suggests she was of high status. Jorge Marcos named this the "Charnel House."

Opposite the Charnel House was another mound, 50 m × 37 m (164 ft × 121 ft) at its base and 1.4 m (4.6 ft) tall, that had evidence of recurrent feasts and rituals, including smashed drinking bowls and the remains of rare and valued foods—rock crab, sea turtle, and deer. Dubbed "the Fiesta Mound," Marcos suggested that this mound was analogous to the men's houses found in traditional lowland Amazonia societies.

In approximately 2400–1800 BC, Real Alto shrank in population, although it still served as a ceremonial center for the surrounding region.[26] Sites with Valdivia ceramics became more widespread in Ecuador after 1800 BC, and large Valdivia sites with monumental architecture were constructed, such as at **San Isidro** in the Jama Valley, 200 km (120 miles) north of Real Alto, and **La Emerenciana,** 170 km (102 miles) to the southeast. Zeidler describes this process as "colonization . . . when large inland ceremonial centers with satellite communities appear in the wetter environments to the north, east, and south, where they became more heavily reliant on agricultural production."[27] On the Santa Elena Peninsula, only small hamlets existed during the Late Valdivia phases. In 1900 BC a massive volcanic eruption from the highlands blanketed western Ecuador with ash, and some zones—including the Jama Valley where the Late Valdivia center of San Isidro was located—were abandoned for centuries.[28]

The Santa Elena Peninsula and the Valdivia sequence have been the principal vantage point from which the Formative developments in Ecuador have been viewed. However, more recent discoveries in southern Ecuador and far northern Peru suggest that Valdivia was only one of several Formative developments in this region of South America.

Figure 6.7 Santa Ana–La Florida, Ecuador—excavations in progress

Santa Ana–La Florida, Southeastern Ecuador

The site of **Santa Ana-La Florida** is in the southeastern portion of Ecuador in the province of Zamora-Chinchipe (figure 6.6).

Excavated by **Francisco Valdez** and colleagues, Santa Ana–La Florida is on the eastern slope of the Andes, in a transitional zone between the highlands and the lowland jungles in a narrow river valley that flows into the Rio Marañon.[29] The archaeology of this remote area is poorly known, but Santa Ana–La Florida is surprisingly old and complex. Multiple radiocarbon samples indicate a lengthy occupation from circa 3000 to 200 BC, but with major construction occurring from 2600 to 1700 BC. The occupation at Santa Ana–La Florida overlaps with Real Alto, although it is definitely *not* a Valdivia site.

Santa Ana–La Florida contains two principal zones covering approximately a hectare (figure 6.7).

A circular cobble-lined walkway surrounds a plaza about 40 m (131.2 ft) in diameter and leads to a terraced hillside rising 3–4 m (10–13 ft). In each quadrant of the plaza is a rectangular cobblestone pavement that may be a floor or building foundation. The functions of these four constructions are unknown, but they do not appear to be dwellings, and the plaza lacks residential midden. However, surrounding this area are the remains of ten to fifteen elliptical structures, probably houses, each about 4–6 m (13–19.7 ft) in diameter. It is not absolutely certain that these dwellings were contemporary with the other ceremonial architecture at the site.

Figure 6.8 Santa Ana–La Florida, Ecuador—circular hearth and spiral walls

The second area at Santa Ana–La Florida contains spiraling stone walls that coil inward to form a ceremonial hearth (figure 6.8).

This hearth contained offerings of greenstone beads and fragments of human bone. Other poorly preserved burials and offerings of polished stone, bones, and turquoise beads were found between the coiled concentric walls. Another shaft tomb was found next to the ceremonial hearth. This tomb contained the remains of at least two individuals with a rich trove of offerings: four stirrup-spout bottles, other fine ceramics, stone bowls and a mortar in the shape of a bird, greenstone pendants and beads—some probably originally sewn onto garments—and a conch shell (*Strombus*), that had been divided between the two individuals. These artifacts are extraordinary and intriguing. The stirrup-spout vessels include a double-sided bottle showing two different versions of the same human emerging from the opened valves of a *Spondylus* shell, perhaps an image of a shaman. Another ceramic vessel is a four-legged creature with a human-like head whose bulging cheek probably depicts coca chewing. The fine stone bowls were engraved with stunning and mysterious motifs. One bowl depicts the blunt triangular heads of smiling serpents, a motif found later at archaeological sites in the highlands and coast of Peru at Huaca Prieta and La Galgada (chapter 7). This bowl also portrays a human head with a bird's body, perhaps a shaman being transformed into avian form.

The architectural and artifactual data have led Valdez to interpret Santa Ana–La Florida as an early ceremonial center that combined funerary offerings and other rituals. Further, the presence of *Strombus* shells and other exotic items suggests the interaction between the people of Santa Ana–La Florida and populations to the west. Valdez summarizes the implications of the materials from Mayo-Chinchipe:

> The social implications of these processes are evident in the Mayo-Chinchipe culture, particularly in reference to craft specialization (ceramics, lithics, textiles, etc.) and in the development of a broad network of short and long-distance interactions. The architectural and mortuary evidence from the site of Santa Ana–La Florida appears to be an early example of the expression of social inequality and evidence of the complexity and antiquity of such societies. It is relevant to consider that there are increasingly more indications for the appearance of social complexity at different latitudes from the third millennium before Christ, wherein interregional interactions stand out as an extremely important mechanism in the development of social complexity. In this sense, it is clear that the Mayo-Chinchipe culture was a participant in the development of cosmological concepts that characterize Andean civilization.[30]

Formative Transitions in Far Northern Peru

Another—and very different—perspective on Formative village life comes from the Department of Tumbes in far northern Peru (see figure 6.2).[31] Although this region has not seen the intense archaeological research of the Santa Elena Peninsula, recent excavations have uncovered prehistoric occupations coeval with Real Alto and the Valdivia sequence. The earliest dates come from **El Porvenir**, a small (100 m × 300 m [328 ft × 984 ft]) hamlet consisting of a half-dozen houses surrounding a plaza. El Porvenir is located 8 km (4.8 miles) inland on a terrace overlooking the Zarumilla River floodplain (which today marks the border between Peru and Ecuador). The initial dates for El Porvenir are from the end of the Archaic

Figure 6.9 El Porvenir, Peru—post molds from dwelling dating circa 4750–4320 BC

period, at 4750 to 4320 cal BC. The residents of El Porvenir lived in elliptical pole and thatch dwellings (figure 6.9) 18–20 m^2 (194–215 ft^2) in area, larger than Early Valdivia houses at Real Alto.

The El Porvenir villagers relied on marine resources, particularly shellfish. From about 4000 to 1200 BC, El Porvenir was abandoned as families moved to other zones before returning to the site. During this hiatus at El Porvenir, the site of **Santa Rosa** was occupied.

Figure 6.10 Santa Rosa, Peru—circular hearth dating to 3350–2910 BC

Approximately 30 km (18 miles) southwest of El Porvenir, between 3500 and 2900 cal BC, Santa Rosa was a small hamlet and funerary site on the Tumbes River. A large elliptical pole and thatch dwelling made from substantial upright posts and covering 120 m^2 (1,292 ft^2) may have been the residence of an extended family. Santa Rosa's inhabitants collected a variety of shellfish, hunted deer, and collected wild squash, but there is no clear evidence for agriculture or pottery at this time. Santa Rosa, however, was the scene of elaborate funeral rites. The people of Santa Rosa constructed large circular hearths, creating clay-lined basins more than 2 m (6.6 ft) across (figure 6.10).

Algarobbo wood and other fuel was placed in the basin and set on fire, leaving a thick layer of brick-red burned earth and a dense cap of grayish ash. A scatter of skeleton fragments indicates some form of funeral rite. The bodies were not cremated—the bones lack the crazings that form when flesh burns on bone—but rather were "exposed" to fire. The bones were then retrieved and placed in low cairns of stones and mud, accompanied by offerings of *Spondylus* shells.

In the Zarumilla Valley just 1.2 km (0.8 miles) from El Porvenir, the site of **Uña de Gato** presents another vista on emergent social complexity in far northern Peru. The core of the site covers 225 m × 175 m (738 ft × 574 ft) and consists of a possible plaza surrounded by four artificial mounds; this central area is surrounded by a much larger 300 m × 500 m (984 ft × 1,640 ft) area of domestic debris and shell midden. The oldest occupation dates to 2200–1890 BC, but the settlement became prominent after about 1400–1100 BC, when mound construction began. Although

Figure 6.11 Uña de Gato, Peru—excavations at base of Mound I

Uña de Gato's mounds have been partially destroyed, the largest, Mound I, was at least 40 m × 30 m (131 ft × 98.4 ft) at its base and stood 6–7 m (19.7–23 ft) high (figure 6.11).

Mound I was built in four stages between 1100 and 800 BC. From its inception, Mound I was a unique construction. In the first stage it was a platform mound made from hand-modeled "bread-loaf"–shaped adobes carefully mortared with gray clay. The initial mound was topped with a gray clay floor, and its sides were covered with red stucco. As it grew taller and longer over subsequent constructions, Mound I was a special form of public architecture, at the time unique in the Zarumilla Valley.

It is important to restate that the level of archaeological detail available from the Santa Elena Peninsula, Zamora-Chinchipe, and Tumbes varies enormously. There is every reason to expect that major discoveries will occur over the next decades that could substantially revise our current understanding. That said, it seems clear that very different developments were happening at roughly the same time in these three zones within a radius of 150 km (90 miles). For example, the large resident population that coalesced at Real Alto was not present at Santa Ana–La Florida, and the resident population at El Porvenir and Santa Rosa was much smaller than the one at Real Alto. The creation of special funerary spaces occurred at Real Alto, Santa Ana–La Florida, and Santa Rosa, but the nature of the burial treatments was markedly different. Ceremonial hearths were created at Santa Ana–La Florida and Santa Rosa but again were very different types of constructions. The fine lapidary tradition from Santa Ana–La Florida was not present at Real Alto or the Tumbes sites, and well-developed Valdivia ceramics were absent from the Early and Middle Formative contexts in Tumbes and Zamora-Chinchipe. Finally, the creation of nonresidential, public architecture varies among these three cases. Special-purpose platform mounds were built at Real Alto and Uña de Gato, but the purposes of those mounds were different. As of this writing, the spiraling constructions of Santa Ana–La Florida are unique.

Formative Societies in Highland Ecuador

Despite the very early development of complex societies on the Santa Elena Peninsula of southwest Ecuador and in the Zamora-Chinchipe region of southeast Ecuador, the development of more complex societies in the nearby highlands of Ecuador is poorly understood. As **Karen Bruhns** has discussed, despite the existence of Paleoindian sites in the Ecuadorian highlands, there are no known sites until after about 1500 BC, and only a small number of those have been excavated.[32] There seem to be two basic reasons for this. First, highland settlements were often dispersed individual hamlets and homesteads rather than large communities (figure 6.12). Such dispersed household sites are difficult to discover. Second, the Ecuadorian highlands were repeatedly blasted by volcanic eruptions, which caused the periodic abandonment of regions and covered archaeological sites with deep layers of volcanic ash and tephras.

As discussed in chapter 2, the region of southern Colombia and northern Ecuador has experienced dozens of large-scale volcanic eruptions since the end of the Ice Age. A review of major volcanic eruptions for which absolute dates are available indicates a series of events, at 13,000–9000 BP, 8600–8200 BP, 7700–5700 BP, 4500 BP, 4050–2900 BP, 2400 BP, and 980–810 BP.[33] The volcanologists **Minard Hall** and **Patricia Mothes** observe, "In each of these periods there is a large . . . eruption or a series of events whose overall impact was severe. In most of these events, it was not the event itself that may have affected the inhabitants or

Figure 6.12 Modern landscape in highland Ecuador, with dispersed homesteads and farmlands

provoked their leaving the area, but more likely it was a secondary impact, such as a widespread covering of pumice and ash that made the area inhospitable for decades or hundreds of years."[34]

These prehistoric eruptions were major events in highland Ecuador, and the volcanic events had human consequences (figure 6.13).

Located north of Quito and flanked by volcanoes, the archaeological site **Cotocollao** was discovered when roads and trenches for a housing development cut through the volcanic ash covering the site. Initial test excavations were followed by a massive salvage project that exposed several archaeological components, including the Late Formative farming village. Cotocollao began as a sprinkling of household clusters on a hillside between 1500 and 1100 BC. The settlement contained an estimated twenty-seven to thirty-seven rectangular houses made from pole and thatch that were 4–5 m (13–16 ft) wide and 6–8 m (19.7–26.2 ft) long. Around 160 to 260 people may have lived in these dwellings.[35] There was no overall plan to the community, nor was there any obvious monumental architecture. The houses contained a basic repertoire of artifacts: pottery, bone awls, stone mortars and metates, stone axes, chipped-stone tools made from obsidian, basalt, and flint, and modest ornaments of shell and crystal. The only evidence of ceremonial space was a cemetery containing primary and secondary burials, whose treatments were sufficiently varied that they suggest status differences among the living.[36] Between 1100 and 500 BC, Cotocollao gradually became a community of more than 100 houses and over 600 inhabitants. Cotocollao was a basic farming village until the

Figure 6.13 Volcán Cotopaxi, Ecuador

Pululahua Volcano exploded, covering the settlement in pyroclastic debris and causing the abandonment of the village.

Other regions of Ecuador were unscathed by the eruptions. Even in those regions, though, there is little evidence for the development of complex regional centers in the highlands of Ecuador. In the southern Ecuadorian highlands, the archaeological evidence points to relatively small, dispersed communities linked by craft exchange. Bruhns writes, "In the highlands there are apparently no large sites or readily identifiable special purpose architecture. The historic situation of a population scattered in farmsteads or hamlets without urban centers and no architecturally differentiated ceremonial centers appears to have had a considerable time depth in the southern highlands."[37]

For example, the site of **Challuabamba**, located on the Rio Tombebamba on the outskirts of the city of Cuenca, has absolute dates as old as 2000 BC but with an upper level dating to 1450–1400 BC.[38] Challuabamba is one of the few highland Formative sites to have received focused investigations.[39] Covering approximately 7 ha (15.5 acres), Challuabamba has remains of structures with cobblestone foundations; a few fragments of clay with stick impressions suggest the walls were wattle and daub, but only the foundations and floors of the structures remain.[40] Although **Terence Grieder** and colleagues have dubbed one of the structures they excavated at Challuabamba a "noble house," there is little evidence for major social differences within the community.[41] Rather, Challuabamba seems to have been a wealthy community deeply involved in craft production and exchange. **Dominique Gomís** has documented that the ceramics from Challuabamba are elegant bichrome vessels, with a principal type consisting of red slipped bands and other motifs over buff-colored pottery, "which is characterized by the production of finely made objects, with polished surfaces, [showing] the high control of the firing."[42] Ceramic production was followed in importance by textile production, based on the number of artifacts associated with spinning and weaving.[43] The residents of Challuabamba had access to *Spondylus* shells from the coast and exotic game from the Pacific Coast and the Amazonian lowlands (ocean catfish, crocodile, agouti, and paca), as well as to meaty haunches of deer. In addition to this evidence for exchange among coast, sierra, and jungle, the presence of ceramics with stylistic elements similar to pottery found in northern Peru also suggests north-south trade routes.

In its involvement in craft production and exchange, Challuabamba was not unique. At the site of **Pirincay**, 20 km (12 miles) away on the Paute River, Karen Bruhns and colleagues found numerous workshops where beads were manufactured from quartz crystal. The occupation at Pirincay began at 1500–1400 cal BC and continued to 400–300 BC. "The remains of over fifty workshops have now been found," Bruhns writes, as indicated by "debitage, quartz hammers and drills, and the remains of beads broken during their manufacture."[44] Each of these workshops was relatively small, "suggesting artisanal production of the beads by individuals, rather than large-scale production."[45] Since Pirincay was 15 km (9 miles) away from the rock crystal source, other settlements probably controlled access to raw material and traded it to Pirincay. In addition, the occupants of Pirincay had access to fine thin-walled ceramics, and the community was also involved in exchange with coastal zones, as indicated by shells from marine mollusks such as *Spondylus*. Salt was also a probable coastal import, although not preserved in the archaeological deposits.

At the site of **Putushio** in the southern Ecuadorian highlands, **Mathilde Temme** has documented the existence of Late Formative gold working dating to after approximately 1212–775 cal BC.[46] Located on a ridge overlooking the head-

Figure 6.14 Putushio, southern Ecuador; large boulders were used to grind mineral ores

waters of the Rio Jubones—a natural corridor that flows southwest to the Pacific Ocean—Putushio was a sparse settlement spread over a larger area of about 400 ha (880 acres) (figure 6.14).

Dwellings were wattle and daub walls on cobblestone foundations. The ceramic styles show clear connections with those from Challuabamba, Pirincay, and other highland sites to the north. What is distinctive about Putushio is the evidence for metallurgy. The site has large, flat boulders that were shaped into milling stones for crushing ore. Fragments of ceramic molds were recovered, as were minute flecks and droplets of gold. The minute traces of gold—most less than a millimeter in size—were natural gold rather than alloys. At the end of the Formative period, silver was added to the gold, as were small quantities of copper. Metal working continued at Putushio after the Formative but shifted to an increased use of copper-gold alloys. In the Ecuadorian highlands, Putushio is the only known Formative site with gold metallurgy.

In sum, the Late Formative evidence from the southern Ecuadorian highlands suggests a different pattern of social complexity, one without clear evidence of centralization. Community-level craft production complemented agriculture, as different settlements manufactured different goods for trade. This trade may have resulted in modest differences among households but not in major social distinctions or classes. Exactly how goods were exchanged is somewhat unclear, although the evidence for trade among coast, sierra, and jungle and between the Ecuadorian highlands and northern Peru is indisputable. Finally, these complex interactions did not result in the development of key central places with ceremonial architecture.

The Formative developments in Ecuador and northern Peru exhibited some broad parallels—the development of settled villages, creation of public spaces, and elaboration of different technologies—but were marked by striking regional differences. It is simply incorrect to think that cultural practices that first appeared on the Santa Elena Peninsula spread to adjacent regions—as James Ford suggested—or even indirectly stimulated parallel developments. Rather, these developments associated with the Formative were marked by regional variations, even within a relatively small area. Not surprisingly, even greater variations existed across the broad swath of South America.

The Formatives of Amazonia

Manuel Arroyo-Kalin has observed that "Amazonia sits uncomfortably within [the] American account of the Neolithic Revolution" referred to as the Formative.[47] As with much of the prehistory of the Amazon, current archaeological knowledge is partial, fragmentary, and inconclusive. The evidence for early plant domestication and widespread movement of crops across the continent (see chapter 5) apparently did not stimulate the development of sedentism and village life across Amazonia.

For example, in the western Amazon, **Ernesto Salazar** has studied a number of archaeological sites with mound complexes in the **upper Upano Valley** of eastern Ecuador (see figure 6.2).[48] Although earlier researchers had proposed a sequence whose initial phase dated to 2200–1100 BC, more recent excavations and more numerous calibrated dates suggest that the establishment of villages began no earlier than 700 BC. Villages with mounds developed at 500–200 BC, becoming more extensive settlements over the subsequent centuries and perhaps organized into chiefdoms. At circa AD 400–600 the region was blanketed by ash from a volcanic eruption and only resettled after circa AD 800 to 1200 by a low density of small communities that reoccupied the earlier mounds.[49] Significantly, although the upper Upano Valley was less than 300 km (180 miles) from the third millennium BC agricultural towns at Real Alto, it seems as if settled village life occurred much later in western Amazonia.

A similar gap appears elsewhere in Amazonia. Despite the presence of Early Holocene age sites at Peña Roja in the western Amazon (see chapter 4) and very early sites at Pedra Pintada and other sites near Santarem on the Lower Amazon (see chapter 3), there is little evidence for significant population in the intervening 2,000+ km (1,200 miles). **Eduardo Góes Neves** notes that, based on his archaeological investigations in the Central Amazon, "evidence of human occupation from 5700 to 500 BC is absent, despite the identification of more than 100 archaeological sites in a 900 km^2 research area."[50] Given current data, there seems to be a gap in the human presence across much of Amazonia until 500 BC, with a major upsurge in human occupation after circa AD 500.[51] This relatively late appearance of settled agricultural villages seems indicated by the chronology of terra preta

Figure 6.15 Excavations at Belém Mound, Camutins Stream, Marajó Island

soils (see chapter 5). For example, Arroyo-Kalin notes that regarding the terra preta soils found in the Central Amazon project, near Manaus, "the vast majority of occupations associated with their formation begin around or after 0 AD."[52]

This relatively late development seems broadly true for the middle and Lower Amazon Basin. For example, on **Marajó Island** (see figure 6.1), an island the size of Switzerland in the mouth of the Amazon River, a sequence of pottery styles is thought to mark the initial occupation of the island and the emergence of chiefdoms after approximately AD 400, according to archaeologist **Denise Schaan** (figure 6.15).

Although Anna Roosevelt and colleagues collected pottery with absolute dates from 8050 to 7500 BC at the Taperinha shell midden 500 km (300 miles) upstream from Marajó Island,[53] and coastal *sambaquis* in the state of Pará have ceramics dating to between 2800 and 1000 BC, the oldest ceramic level on Marajó Island is associated with the Ananatuba phase, dated roughly to 1500–1000 BC.[54] Schaan describes these societies as "small villages of pottery producers—probably incipient farming communities—[who] appeared 3,500 years ago in the north, center, and southeast" of Marajó Island and who "probably lived by hunting, fishing and gathering, as well as by small-scale cultivation."[55] Not for another 1,900 years would more complex societies emerge on Marajó Island (see chapter 8). The establishment of pottery-using, agricultural communities did not immediately result in more complex societies on Marajó Island.

A similar situation characterized the archaeology of Central Brazil, a region of dry savannas, seasonally flooded lowlands, and tropical forests—drier habitats than found in the rainforest zones of Amazonia. As **Irmhild Wüst** and **Cristina**

Barreto have documented, this zone saw the creation of very large prehistoric settlements, including large ring villages covering 20 to 90 ha (44 to 198 acres), with populations of 600 to 1,000 people.[56] **Ring villages** refer to a settlement pattern in which houses surround an open plaza that may have a men's house or other special building in the center, a community plan still used. Famous from ethnographic studies, such as the French anthropologist Claude Lévi-Strauss's analysis of the social space of the Bororo, archaeological ring villages are either circles or horseshoe arrays of dwellings around a plaza.[57] Yet, these large settlements were late prehistoric developments. Although the earliest Archaic sites from the region date to 9000 BC and maize agriculture was present from 850 BC, human settlement in Central Brazil intensified only after AD 800, when ring village sites appeared throughout the region (see chapter 8). Wüst and Barreto write, "The emergence of ring villages seems to have occurred suddenly and late in the lengthy history of human occupation in Central Brazil."[58]

In sum, there seems to be a basic pattern across Amazonia in which Archaic period sites, even those with early cultigens, were followed by a long delay in the development of settled village life, often a gap of a millennium or longer. Recently, Neves asked, "How should we interpret these hiatuses?"[59] It is very possible that the scarcity of mid-Holocene sites in the Amazon Basin reflects the lack of archaeological research, although such gaps appear in relatively well-studied zones. It has been suggested that climatic fluctuations—such as extended periods of drought—may have stressed human populations, resulting in the hiatuses. However, there are relatively few paleoclimatic reconstructions for such an enormous area as the Amazon (see chapter 2). In short, the reasons for this apparent hiatus are unknown, and their clarification awaits future archaeological research.

Monumental Earthworks in the Southwestern Amazon

One of the most intriguing recent discoveries in South America is of hundreds of ditch enclosures and other earthworks located in the southwestern Amazon.[60] These modifications of the landscape take different forms, including canals, causeways, mounds, and raised fields (see chapter 5). Although most of these features appear to date roughly to AD 500–1500 (see chapter 8),[61] a distinctive and potentially older set of earthworks has been studied in western Brazil, enigmatic geometric earthworks that are at least 2,000 years old.

The geometric earthworks are ditched enclosures that form circles, ellipses, squares, and rectangles, and there are a surprisingly large number of them. For example, Denise Schaan and colleagues have documented 281 enclosures over a 25,000 km^2 (9,650 square-mile) area in the state of Acre, in western Brazil. Another 80 enclosures are known from adjacent areas of Brazil and Bolivia.[62] The earthworks enclose areas of 1 to 3 ha (2.47 to 7.41 acres), defined by ditches averaging 11.5 m (37.7 ft) wide and 1.4 m (4.6 ft) deep. The ditch is often flanked on the outside by an embankment, usually about a half meter tall.

At this writing, only a few of the ditch enclosures have been dated, but the results are surprising. Schaan and colleagues have excavated at three enclosure sites.

Figure 6.16 Geometric earthworks at Severino Calazans, Acre, western Brazil

The oldest dates associated with enclosure construction come from the **Severino Calazans** site, a 230 m (750 ft)-long and 12 m (39 ft)-wide rectangular ditch; the earliest date that may be associated with earthwork construction is 1211–942 cal BC, although two other dates indicate construction between approximately 170 BC and AD 25 (figure 6.16).

Another site, **Fazenda Colorada**, is a more complex set of enclosures including a circular enclosure, a rectangular enclosure, and a U-shaped double-ditch enclosure associated with more than a dozen mounds—apparently house mounds based on the pottery and burned clay fragments found during the excavations (figure 6.17). The radiocarbon dates from Fazenda Colorada point to a consistent occupation of the site from AD 25–342 until AD 675–869 and perhaps much later, until the fourteenth century AD.

A third site, **Jaco Sá**, consists of (1) a northern rectangular enclosure, 140 m (459 ft) on each side, that surrounds a circular ditch 100 m (328 ft) in diameter; (2) a southern rectangular enclosure 160 m (525 ft) on each side, associated with an ancient roadway; and (3) a much smaller (80 m × 60 m [262 ft × 197 ft]) rectangular embankment positioned between the northern and southern complexes. The road associated with the southern enclosure was walled, 40 m (131 ft) wide, and ran westward for more than 400 m (1,310 ft). Radiocarbon dates from the northern and southern enclosures suggest that they were built between circa AD 545 and 960. Unlike Fazenda Colorada, Jaco Sá lacks clear evidence of a habitation zone.

It must be remembered that these 3 Brazilian sites have been only partially excavated and are only 3 of the 281 sites known in the project area. Other, apparently similar geometric earthworks are known from Bolivia. Future research will modify understanding of these features, but a few obvious inferences can be made. First, the earthworks point to major modifications of the environment. The

Figure 6.17 Geometric earthworks at Fazenda Colorada, Acre, western Brazil

constructions only became visible following modern deforestation, but the region must have been cleared of trees when the earthworks were constructed. Second, although the enclosures vary in size, they all represent group effort. To give a rough sense of the effort involved, consider the northern square enclosure at Jaco Sá, which has a ditch 640 m long (140 m × four sides), 11 m wide, and 3.5 m deep.[63] Assuming a roughly triangular ditch in cross-section, the total volume of earth excavated was approximately 12,320 m^3. Based on ethnographic figures showing that a man with hand tools can excavate about 2.6 m^3 daily, the northern ditch enclosure would require about 4,740 person-days of effort—roughly three months' work for a crew of forty workers—and the rectangular northern enclosure at Jaco Sá was only one of the site's constructions.[64] Thus, the enclosures almost certainly reflect the collective efforts of social groups.

But what *are* they?

The enclosures in Acre are located away from major rivers—in some cases more than 30 km (18 miles) away—which suggests that they are not floodwater features (like the canals and causeways **Clark Erickson** has documented in the Llanos de Mojos of Bolivia [see chapter 5]), although they are often associated with a source of water such as a spring or stream. The ring ditches may have been defensive moats, although they are often very shallow, and there is little evidence of palisades as indicated by post molds from upright timbers. The archaeological evidence points to two major classes of ditch enclosures: enclosures that contain areas with pottery and other domestic debris and enclosures that have few or no artifacts. The enclosures with residential debris, as **John Walker** has written of ring ditches in the Llanos de Mojos, "divided and organized space . . . However else pre-Columbian Mojeños used their ring ditches, they permanently marked a line between the interior and the exterior. [In addition,] creating a ring ditch and defining a cultural space clearly marks a group of people."[65]

A different social statement may be associated with the enclosures that lack interior artifacts, which Schaan and colleagues interpret as ceremonial and ritual enclosures. They write: "The enclosed flat areas and the roads were usually devoid of cultural debris. This distribution of archaeological materials seems to suggest that the centers of the earthworks were kept clean, as if they were public areas, central plazas for gatherings and festivities, as is customary among modern indigenous communities in Amazonia."[66]

Although much remains unknown about the ditch enclosures and the people who built them, the archaeological data strongly suggest that this portion of southwestern Amazonia was occupied by many more prehistoric communities than previously thought. Further, those communities were widely distributed across the landscape, not tethered to major river systems. Finally, the enclosures suggest that communities were organized and labor groups could be mobilized to create these earthworks. As **Sanna Saunaluoma** and Schaan note, "The cultural tradition of monumental earthwork construction in the southwestern Amazonian lowlands began around 1000 BC, maybe even centuries earlier. Since monumental architecture contributes significantly to making new social, political, and economic formations stronger, the emergence and extension of geometric earthwork sites

Figure 6.18 Southeastern Uruguay, one of the largest mounds in the region, 7 m high, 50 m long

in eastern Acre suggest growing complexity among the region's Formative-stage societies."[67]

The Formative of Coastal Uruguay

Along the Atlantic Coast of Uruguay and southern Brazil, hunters and gatherers occupied the areas around resource-rich wetlands and estuaries after 8000 BP and incorporated domesticated plants into their subsistence practices by 4000 cal BP (see chapter 5). After approximately 4500 BP, the coastal zone was dotted with hundreds of artificial mounds, known locally as *cerritos de indios* in Uruguay (figure 6.18).

The number of these sites is staggering. For example, the archaeologist **Robert Bracco** and his colleagues estimate that around 1,500 mounds are located within 30,000 km^2 (11,580 square miles) in the southern, Uruguayan portion of the **Merin Basin**.[68] The mounds are between 20 m and 40 m (65.6–131 ft) in diameter and may reach heights of 7 m (23 ft), although most are 0.5 to 2.0 m (1.5–6 ft) in height. Individual sites have as many as 50 mounds.[69]

There are several competing interpretations regarding these mounds, sparking a surprisingly heated debate. Bracco and colleagues have marshaled a wealth of detailed paleoenvironmental data to reconstruct the changing configurations of the Merin Basin and adjacent wetlands. To oversimplify, Bracco and colleagues argue that environmental factors explain the spatial distribution of the mounds, interpreting the cerritos de indios as either (1) gradual midden accumulations from families living on higher natural knolls in swampy zones or (2) accumulations of midden into mounds located near fertile farmlands. Bracco notes that "the settlement pattern privileged those spaces where today swamps are more extensive, the hydraulic network is densest, and today the soil fertility is highest."[70]

An alternative perspective is that the cerritos de indios were residential mounds clustered around a plaza, similar to the "ring villages" discussed earlier.[71] This "settled village" interpretation is advanced by **José Iriarte**, who conducted excavations at the site of **Los Ajos** (figure 6.19).

Figure 6.19 Los Ajos, Uruguay: panorama of mound village

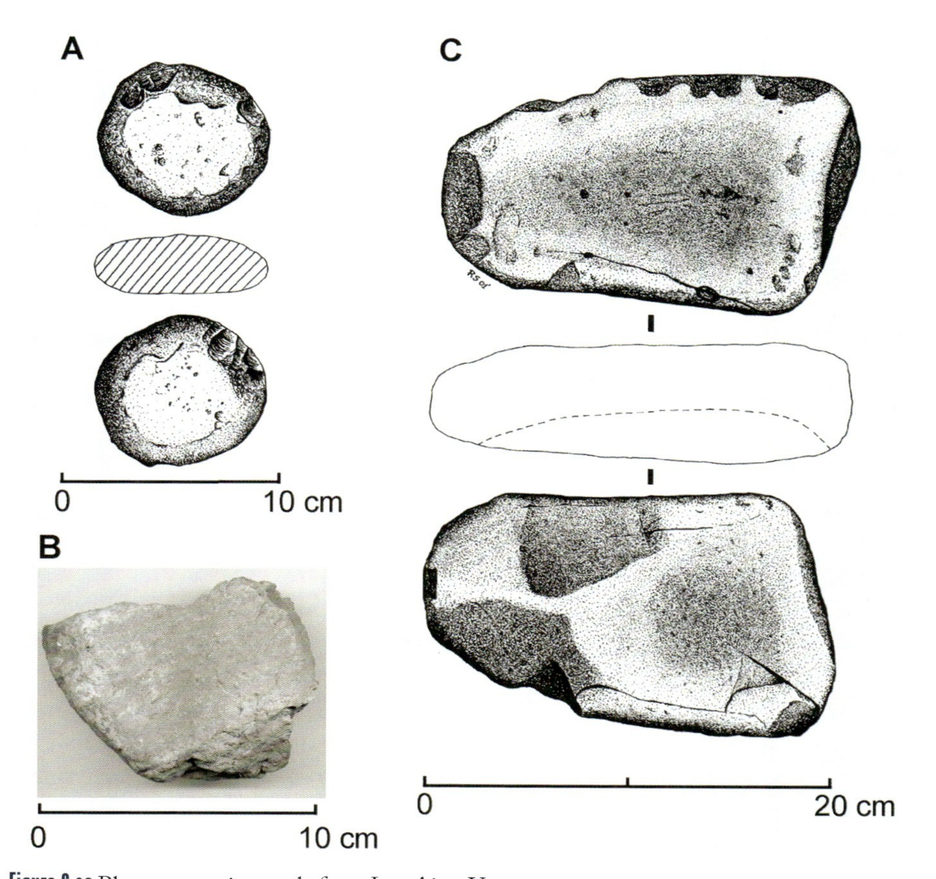

Figure 6.20 Plant-processing tools from Los Ajos, Uruguay

Excavations there suggested that settled villages and mound constructions began at 2890–2210 BC (4840–4160 cal. BP).[72] Los Ajos covers 12 ha (29.6 acres); the site has a half-dozen mounds arrayed in a horseshoe pattern around an open plaza. The 1.75 m to 2.5 m (5.7–8.2 ft)-tall mounds are roughly quadrangular, flat-topped accumulations of household debris—charred food remains, ash lenses, stone tools and debitage, and chunks of burned clay (figure 6.20).

Despite the fact that no post molds, house floors, or other traces of dwellings were uncovered, Iriarte interprets the mounds as domestic debris surrounding an open central plaza. He writes:

> Los Ajos inhabitants began to live in a circular village, partitioning the site into a number of functionally discrete areas. During this time, Los Ajos witnessed the creation of an open plaza area flanked by accretional, circular, dome-shaped residential mounds closely arranged in a circular format. This initial stage of village formation evidences the incorporation and centralization of a clearly demarcated communal space into the overall geometric village layout. Significantly, starting shortly after the beginning of the Preceramic Mound Period, Los Ajos phytolith and starch grain data mark the earliest occurrence of at least two domesticated crops in the region: *Zea mays* and *Cucurbita* spp.[73]

Archaeologists disagree as to whether the mounds were residential architecture or intentional constructions. Bracco and his colleagues have argued that in addition to lacking archaeological traces of residential architecture (such as post molds or floors), the Los Ajos mounds lack other classes of archaeological materials that might suggest permanent settlements and village life (such as storage features, elaborated artifact traditions suggesting craft specialization, or milling stones associated with agriculture).[74] Bracco and colleagues also argue that Iriarte's block excavations in 2 of Los Ajos's 6 mounds surrounding the plaza may not be representative of the 50 mounds at the site or of the 150 mounds located within a 2-km (1.2-mile) radius of Los Ajos.[75]

A third hypothesis about the cerritos de indios is advanced by **José López Mazz**, who attempts to account for diachronic changes *and* synchronic variations in mound construction and function.[76] Between 4000 and 2500 BP, López Mazz argues, the mounds demarcated the territories of distinct groups of mobile hunters and gatherers—essentially serving as camping spots within a specified range. The use of non-local raw materials for chipped-stone artifacts suggests that these groups were wide-ranging, while the faunal materials point to a local focus, with deer and rodent bones at interior sites and fish and marine mammal remains at coastal sites. Palm fruits were an important plant food. The dead were rarely buried in these mounds. Pottery appeared in the region around 3000 BP. According to López Mazz, the settlement pattern changed at about 2500 BP: there were many more mounds, and the mounds became larger as more soils were transported to build them up. Rather than a mobile strategy, people apparently shifted to a more logistic strategy, with some mounds occupied relatively permanently and others as short-term or ephemeral encampments. This was accompanied by the intensification of hunting and fishing, as well as an increasing emphasis on agriculture. In this later phase, the mounds were frequently used to bury the dead.

López Mazz contends that, contra Bracco, the mounds were not located in areas subject to flooding; nor do they have clear evidence for living floors or other domestic architecture, as Iriarte suggests. Rather, López Mazz argues that the category "mounds" includes several different classes of constructions, including (1) cemetery mounds, (2) platform mounds, (3) low surfaces (*microrelieves*) that are low artificial surfaces associated with domestic occupations, and (4) earthworks characterized by the importation of artificial fill. The burial mounds are interesting: they have the remains of primary and secondary burials but also food remains associated with feasts marking the final journey of the deceased, a meal in which the living also participated. Some burial mounds have multiple construction levels, discrete layers of earth capped by a hard-fired surface with small indentations left by circular arrangements of tiny poles, placements from repeated rituals.

These contradictory hypotheses reflect the limited archaeological knowledge available for Uruguay. As **Gustavo Verdesio** notes, systematic investigations of the cerritos de indios only began in 1986.[77] This lack of archaeological research intersected with a narrative of national identity that viewed the indigenous cultures of Uruguay as insignificant and backward. Exacerbated by the dictatorship of 1973–84 and the lack of research funding and academic support, it is not surprising that current archaeological understanding of the prehistory of Uruguay is confusing—especially regarding the thousands of cerritos that are known. In cases like these, when research is in its infancy and few sites have been studied, conflicting archaeological hypotheses are common.

But some patterns seem evident for the Formative transitions in Uruguay, changes that are paralleled in other regions of South America.[78] First, the introduction of domesticated crops did not immediately change subsistence and settlement; rather, first, domesticates were incorporated into a foraging practice (similar to cases known from coastal Peru and lowland Colombia [see chapter 5]). Second, more permanent settlements were associated with changing relationships between people and landscape. For example, the development of burial mounds capped by burned surfaces where rituals were subsequently conducted is broadly analogous to the development of the Charnel House at Real Alto, constructions where the dead are commemorated and marked on the landscape. These are very loose analogies at best, which future research may resolve and refine.

Conclusion

This brief and selective overview suggests that very different paths led to the emergence of social complexity. For example, early villages appeared on opposite sides of South America in coastal Ecuador and coastal Uruguay, but currently there is little evidence for the establishment of villages in the Central Amazon Basin or in western Amazonia until much later. There is good evidence for the gradual increase in the size of settlements in southwest Ecuador and northern Peru but no evidence for Early Formative villages or towns in the nearby highlands of Ecuador. Thus, settlement patterns varied significantly.

There are similar variations in the scale and scope of nondomestic, "monumental" constructions. For example, the variations among the cerritos de indios are sufficiently subtle that it is difficult to distinguish house mounds from cemetery mounds or other earthworks. Conversely, at Real Alto there are clear differences among the Charnel House, the Fiesta House, and Valdivia dwellings. At Santa Ana–La Florida a relatively elaborate ceremonial and funerary complex seems excessively elaborate to serve a community of ten–fifteen families. The ditch enclosures at Severino Calazans did not surround a resident community when the severely geometric earthwork was made between 1211 and 942 BC. On the opposite side of the continent, public constructions such as platform mounds covered with red stucco were being built at the site of Uña de Gato in far northern Peru.

We see analogous variations in other dimensions archaeologists often consider as indicating the emergence of more complex societies. For example, the archaeological indications for inter-regional trade at Santa Ana–La Florida and for craft specialization and exchange in the later settlements of Pirincay, Challuabamba, and Putushio in the highlands of Ecuador have not been found at coeval sites in the Tumbes region, the Central Amazon Basin, or southwestern Amazonia. To date, there is little evidence for warfare, unless some of the geometric enclosures in southwestern Amazonia may prove to have been defensive structures. There are few clear signs of social distinctions and none that might indicate clear social classes.

In short, the different cases discussed in this chapter suggest that the processes leading to social complexity were varied and subtle. Although we might—with no small measure of false certainty—define "complex societies," the archaeological data remain intriguingly elusive about the initial transformations in human societies that produced them. In this sense, the questions raised by Carballo and colleagues at the beginning of this chapter remain incompletely answered, a situation that only becomes more complicated when we look at the social complexities in other regions of South America in chapter 7.

Notes

1. D. Carballo, P. Roscoe, and G. Feinman, "Cooperation and Collective Action in the Cultural Evolution of Complex Societies," *Journal of Archaeological Method and Theory* 21, no. 1 (2014): 99.

2. For an insightful comment on archaeology's role in the exploration of complexity, see the video interview of Jeremy Sabloff, "Emergence of Social Complexity," YouTube video, 6:00, posted by Santa Fe Institute, September 20, 2012, http://www.youtube.com/watch?v=RMK_FwQHpHQ. A well-known Mesoamerican archaeologist, Sabloff is the president of the Santa Fe Institute.

3. P. Wiessner, "Vines of Complexity: Egalitarian Structures and the Institution of Inequality among the Enga," *Current Anthropology* 43, no. 2 (2002): 233.

4. J. Kahn, "Anthropological Archaeology in 2012: Mobility, Economy, and Transformation," *American Anthropologist* 115, no. 2 (2013): 253.

5. G. Willey and P. Phillips, "Method and Theory in American Archeology II: Historical-Developmental Interpretation," *American Anthropologist* 57 (1955): 729.

6. C. Evans, "James Alfred Ford 1911–1968," *American Anthropologist* 70 (1968): 1161–1167.

7. J. A. Ford, *A Comparison of Formative Cultures in the Americas: Diffusion or the Psychic Unity of Man?* (Washington, DC: Smithsonian Contributions to Anthropology, 1969), 5.

8. Ford accepted the hypothesis, proposed by Clifford Evans and Betty Meggers, that the Early Formative ceramics of coastal Ecuador had been introduced by trans-Pacific voyagers from Japan who brought with them Jōmon pottery; this issue is discussed below.

9. H. Bischoff and J. Viteri Gamboa, "Entre Vegas y Valdivia: La Fase San Pedro en el suroeste de Ecuador," *Bulletin de l'Institut Français d'Études Andines* 35 (2006): 361–376; A. Roosevelt, R. Housley, M. Imazio da Silveira, S. Maranca, and R. Johnson, "Eighth Millennium Pottery from a Prehistoric Shell Midden in the Brazilian Amazon," *Science* 254 (December 13, 1991): 1621–1624.

10. J. Hoopes, "Ford Revisited: A Critical Review of the Chronology and Relationships of the Earliest Ceramic Complexes in the New World, 6000–1500 B.C.," *Journal of World Prehistory* 8 (1994): 42.

11. J. Rowe, "Stages and Periods in Archaeological Interpretation," *Southwestern Journal of Anthropology* 18, no. 1 (1962): 40–54; D. Menzel, "Style and Time in the Middle Horizon," *Ñawpa Pacha: Journal of Andean Archaeology* 2 (1964): 1–105.

12. S. Rostain, "The Archaeology of the Guianas: An Overview," in *Handbook of South American Archaeology*, ed. H. Silverman and W. Isbell (New York: Springer, 2008), 279–302.

13. M. Rivera, "The Archaeology of Northern Chile," in *Handbook of South American Archaeology*, ed. H. Silverman and W. Isbell (New York: Springer, 2008), 963–977.

14. L. Lumbreras, *The Peoples and Cultures of Ancient Peru*, trans. Betty Meggers (Washington, DC: Smithsonian Institution Press, 1974). The English version of Lumbreras's *De los pueblos, de las culturas y las artes del Antiguo Perú* (1969) was translated by Dr. Betty Meggers, an advocate for the concept of the Formative.

15. For example, see E. Ishida *Andes: The Report of the University of Tokyo Scientific Expeditions to the Andes in 1958* (Tokyo: Bijutsu Shuppan Shu, 1961); S. Izumi and K. Terada, *Andes 3: Excavations at Pechiche and Garbanzal, Tumbes Valley, Perú 1960* (Tokyo: Kadokawa, 1966).

16. For an introduction to this literature, see J. Damp, "Architecture of the Early Valdivia Village," *American Antiquity* 49 (1984): 573–585; D. Lathrap, D. Collier, and H. Chandra, *Ancient Ecuador: Culture, Clay and Creativity, 3000–300 BC* (Chicago: Field Museum of Natural History, 1975); D. Lathrap, J. Marcos, and J. Zeidler, "Real Alto: An Ancient Ceremonial Center," *Archaeology* 30 (1977): 2–13; J. Marcos, "The Ceremonial Precinct at Real Alto: Organization of Time and Space in Valdivia Society" (PhD diss., University of Illinois, Urbana-Champaign, 1978); J. Marcos, *Real Alto: la Historia de un Centro Ceremonial Valdivia*, Biblioteca Ecuatoriana de Arqueología 4, Primera and Segunda Partes (Quito: Corporación Editorial Nacional, 1988); J. Marcos, "A Reassessment of the Chronology of the Ecuadorian Formative," in *El Área Septrentrional Andina: Arqueología y Etnohistoria*, ed. M. Guinea (Quito: Biblioteca Abya-Yala, 1998), 295–346; J. Marcos, "A Reassessment of the Ecuadorian Formative," in *The Archaeology of Formative Ecuador*, ed. J. S. Raymond and R. Burger (Washington, DC: Dumbarton Oaks, 2003), 7–32; J. Marcos and A. Michczynski, "Good Dates and Bad Dates in Ecuador: Radiocarbon Simples and Archaeological Excavation: a Commentary on the 'Valdivia Absolute Chronology,'" *Proceedings of the Third Latin American Congress of the University of Varsovia, Varsovia and Biskupin-Wenecja* (Warsaw: Andean Archaeological

Mission of the Institute of Archaeology, Warsaw University, 1996); J. Zeidler, "The Ecuadorian Formative," in *Handbook of South American Archaeology*, ed. H. Silverman and W. Isbell (New York: Springer, 2008), 459–488.

17. B. Meggers, C. Evans, and E. Estrada, *Early Formative Period of Coastal Ecuador: The Valdivia and Machalilla Phases* (Washington, DC: Smithsonian Institution, 1965); for excavation information, see 16–17; for ceramic descriptions, see 42–94; for Venus figurines, see 95–107; for dating, see 147–152.

18. Ibid., 157.

19. Ibid., 158. See also "News of Science: Smithsonian Ecuadorian Expedition," *Science* 125, no. 3251 (April 19, 1957): 729–730; E. Estrada, B. Meggers, and C. Evans, "Possible Transpacific Contact on the Coast of Ecuador," *Science* 135, no. 350 (February 2, 1962): 371–372.

20. For information regarding this hypothesis and controversy, see G. McEwan and D. Dickson, "Valdivia, Jomon Fishermen, and the Nature of the North Pacific: Some Nautical Problems with Meggers, Evans, and Estrada's (1965) Transoceanic Contact Thesis," *American Antiquity* 43, no. 3 (1978): 362–371; R. Daggett, "The Life Cycle of an Idea: Transpacific Voyages and American Archaeology," *Journal of the Virgin Islands Archaeological Society* 6 (1978): 13–22.

21. J. Raymond, "Social Formations in the Western Lowlands of Ecuador during the Early Formative," in *The Archaeology of Formative Ecuador*, ed. J. Raymond and R. Burger (Washington, DC: Dumbarton Oaks, 2003), 42.

22. J. Damp, "Better Homes and Gardens: The Life and Death of the Early Valdivia Community" (PhD diss., University of Calgary, Alberta, 1979); J. Damp, "Architecture of the Early Valdivia Village," *American Antiquity* 49 (1984): 573–585.

23. J. Zeidler, "Social Space in Valdivia Society: Community Patterning and Domestic Structure at Real Alto, 3000–2000 B.C." (PhD diss., University of Illinois, Urbana-Champaign, 1984).

24. For an introduction to this literature, see E. Abrams, "Architecture and Energy: An Evolutionary Perspective," *Journal of Archaeological Method and Theory* 1 (1989): 47–87; E. Abrams, *How the Maya Built Their World* (Austin: University of Texas Press, 1994); R. Rosensweig and R. Burger, "Considering Early New World Monumentality," in *Early New World Monumentality*, ed. R. Burger and R. Rosensweig (Gainesville: University Press of Florida, 2012), 3–22.

25. J. Moore, *The Prehistory of Home* (Berkeley: University of California Press, 2012).

26. Marcos, "Reassessment of the Ecuadorian Formative," 18; F. Schwarz and J. S. Raymond, "Formative Settlement Patterns in the Valdivia Valley, SW Coastal Ecuador," *Journal of Field Archaeology* 23, no. 2 (1996): 205–224.

27. Zeidler, "Ecuadorian Formative," 464.

28. J. Zeidler and J. Issacson, "Settlement Process and Historical Contingency in the Western Ecuadorian Formative," in *The Archaeology of Formative Ecuador*, ed. J. S. Raymond and R. Burger (Washington, DC: Dumbarton Oaks, 2003), 69–123.

29. F. Valdez, "Inter-zonal Relationships in Ecuador," in *Handbook of South American Archaeology*, ed. H. Silverman and W. Isbell (New York: Springer, 2008), 865–888; F. Valdez, J. Guffroy, G. De Saulieu, J. Hurtado, and A. Yepes, "Découverte d'un site cérémonial formatif sur le versant oriental des Andes," *Compte Rendus Paleovol* 4 (2005): 369–374.

30. F. Valdez, "Arqueología en la Cuenca Mayo—Chinchipe," in *Antiguas civilizaciones en la frontera de Ecuador y Perú: Una propuesta binacional para la integración andina*, ed. Quirino Olivera Núñez (Chiclayo: Asociación Amigos del Museo de Sipán, 2010), 21, my translation.

31. J. Moore, "Architecture, Settlement and Formative Developments in the Equatorial Andes: New Discoveries in the Department of Tumbes, Peru," *Latin American Antiquity* 21, no. 2 (2010): 147–172; J. Moore, "Making a Huaca: Memory and Praxis in Prehispanic Far Northern Peru," *Journal of Social Archaeology* 10, no. 3 (2010): 531–555.

32. K. Bruhns, "Social and Cultural Development in the Ecuadorian Highlands and Eastern Lowlands during the Formative," in *Archaeology of Formative Ecuador*, ed. J. S. Raymond and R. L. Burger (Washington, DC: Dumbarton Oaks, 2003), 125–174.

33. M. Hall and P. Mothes, "Volcanic Impediments in the Progressive Development of Pre-Columbian Civilizations in the Ecuadorian Andes," *Journal of Volcanology and Geothermal Research* 176 (2008): 352–353.

34. Ibid., 353.

35. M. Villaba, *Cotocollao: Una Aldea Formativo del Valle de Quito*, Miscelánea Antropología Ecuatoriana, Serie Monográfica 2 (Quito: Museos del Banco Central del Ecuador, 1988), 64–74.

36. Ibid., 103–109.

37. Bruhns, "Social and Cultural Development," 148.

38. T. Grieder, J. Farmer, D. Hill, P. Stahl, and D. Ubelaker, *Art and Archaeology of Challuabamba, Ecuador* (Austin: University of Texas Press, 2009), 20–23.

39. J. Idrovo Urigüen, "El Formativo en la sierra ecuatoriana," in *Formativo Sudamericano, una reevaluación*, ed. P. Legerberger (Quito: Ediciones Abya-Yala, 1999), 114–123; D. Gomís, "La cerámica formativa tardía de la sierra austral del Ecuador," in *Formativo Sudamericano, una reevaluación*, ed. P. Legerberger (Quito: Ediciones Abya-Yala, 1999), 139–159; D. Gomís, "El territorio austral: durante el formativo tardío," in *Reconocimiento y Excavaciones en el Austro Ecuatoriano*, ed. D. Collier, J. Murra, and B. Malo Vega (Núcleo de Azuay: Casa de la Cultura Ecuatoriana, 2007), 291–328; P. Stahl, "Selective Faunal Provisioning in the Southern Highlands of Formative Ecuador," *Latin American Antiquity* 16, no. 3 (2005): 313–328.

40. There is some dispute about the size of the site: Gomís and Idrovo state the site is 7 hectares, Grieder and Stahl estimate it at 70 hectares.

41. T. Grieder, J. Farmer, A. Carrillo, and B. Jones, "Art and Prestige among Noble Houses of the Equatorial Andes," in *Andean Archaeology II: Art, Landscape, and Society*, ed. H. Silverman and W. Isbell (New York: Kluwer Academic/Plenum, 2002), 157–177.

42. Gomís, "El territorio austral," 306–307, my translation.

43. Ibid., 300.

44. Bruhns, "Social and Cultural Development," 165.

45. Bruhns, "Patrones de asentamiento, rutas de comunicación y mercancías de intercambio de larga distancia en el Formativo Tardío del Austro Ecuatoriano," *Bulletin de l'Institut Français d'Études Andines* 39, no. 3 (2010): 690, my translation.

46. M. Temme, "El Formativo Putushío—Sierra Sur de Ecuador," in *Formativo Sudamericano, una reevaluación*, ed. P. Legerberger (Quito: Ediciones Abya-Yala, 1999), 124–138.

47. M. Arroyo-Kalin, "The Amazonian Formative: Crop Domestication and Anthropogenic Soils," *Diversity* 2 (2010): 474.

48. E. Salazar, "De vuelta al Sangay: Investigaciones arqueológicas en el Alto Upano, Amazonia Ecuatoriana," *Bulletin de l'Institut Français des Etudes Andines* 27, no. 2 (1998): 213–240; E. Salazar, "Pre-Columbian Mound Complexes in the Upano River Valley, Lowland Ecuador," in *Handbook of South American Archaeology*, ed. H. Silverman and W. Isbell (New York: Springer, 2008), 263–278.

49. S. Rostain, "Between Sierra and Selva: Landscape Transformations in Upper Ecuadorian Amazonia," *Quaternary International* 249 (2012): 31–42. See also S. Rostain, "Secuencia arqueológica en montículos del valle del Upano en la Amazonia Ecuatoriana," *Bulletin de l'Institut Français des Etudes Andines* 28, no. 1 (1999): 53–89.

50. E. Góes Neves, "Ecology, Ceramic Chronology and Distribution, Long-Term History, and Political Change in the Amazonian Floodplain," in *Handbook of South American Archaeology*, ed. H. Silverman and W. Isbell (New York: Springer, 2008), 363.

51. M. Heckenberger and E. Góes Neves, "Amazonian Archaeology," *Annual Review of Anthropology* 38 (2009): 255–258.

52. Arroyo-Kalin, "Amazonian Formative," 476.

53. A. Roosevelt, I. Housley, M. Imazio da Silveira, S. Maranca, and R. Johnson, "Eighth Millennium Pottery from a Prehistoric Shell Midden in the Brazilian Amazon," *Science* 254 (1991): 1621–1624.

54. The discussion of Marajó chronology is based on D. Schaan, "The Camutins Chiefdom: Rise and Development of Social Complexity on Marajó Island, Brazilian Amazon" (PhD diss., University of Pittsburgh, 2004); D. Schaan, "The Nonagricultural Chiefdoms of Marajó Island," in *Handbook of South American Archaeology*, ed. H. Silverman and W. Isbell (New York: Springer, 2008), 339–357; D. Schaan, "Long-Term Human Induced Impacts on Marajó Island Landscapes, Amazon Estuary," *Diversity* 2 (2010): 182–206.

55. Schaan, "Long-Term Human Induced Impacts," 189.

56. I. Wüst and C. Barreto, "The Ring Villages of Central Brazil: A Challenge for Amazonian Archaeology," *Latin American Antiquity* 10, no. 1 (1999): 3–23.

57. See C. Lévi-Strauss, "Contribution à l'étude de l'organisation sociale des Indiens Bororo," *Journal de la Société des Américanistes* 28, no. 2 (1936): 269–304; for a brief discussion, see also Lévi-Strauss, *Tristes Tropiques*, trans. J. Russell (New York: Criterion Books, 1961), 202–206.

58. Wüst and Barreto, "Ring Villages of Central Brazil," 5.

59. Neves, "Ecology, Ceramic Chronology and Distribution," 363–364.

60. M. Pärssinen, M. D. Schaan, and A. Ranzi, "Pre-Columbian Geometric Earthworks in the Upper Purus: A Complex Society in Western Amazonia," *Antiquity* 83 (2009): 1084–1095; S. Saunaluoma, "Pre-Columbian Earthworks in Riberalta, Bolivian Amazon," *Amazonica* 2 (2010): 86–113; S. Saunaluoma and D. Schaan, "Monumentality in Western Amazonian Formative Societies: Geometric Ditched Enclosures in the Brazilian State of Acre," *Antiqua* 2, no. 1 (2012): 1–11.

61. See J. Walker, "Social Implications from Agricultural Taskscapes in the Southwestern Amazon," *Latin American Antiquity* 22, no. 3 (2011): 275–295; J. Walker, "Ama-

zonian Dark Earth and Ring Ditches in the Central Llanos de Mojos, Bolivia," *Culture, Agriculture, Food and Environment* 33, no. 1 (2011): 2–14.

62. D. Schaan, M. Pärssinen, S. Saunaluoma, A. Ranzi, M. Bueno, and A. Barbosa, "New Radiometric Dates for Pre-Columbian (2000–700 B.P.) Earthworks in Western Amazonia, Brazil," *Journal of Field Archaeology* 37, no. 2 (2012): 132–142; Saunaloma and Schaan, "Monumentality in Western Amazonian Formative Societies," 1.

63. Schaan et al., "New Radiometric Dates," 138.

64. The labor estimate is based on the classic article by C. Erasmus, "Monument Building: Some Field Estimates," *Southwestern Journal of Anthropology* 21 (1965): 277–301.

65. J. Walker, "Pre-Columbian Ring Ditches along the Yacuma and Rapulo Rivers, Beni, Bolivia: A Preliminary Review," *Journal of Field Archaeology* 33, no. 4 (2008): 423.

66. Schaan et al., "New Radiometric Dates," 139.

67. Saunaluoma and Schaan, "Monumentality in Western Amazonian Formative Societies," 9.

68. R. Bracco, L. del Puerto, H. Inda, and C. Castiñeira, "Mid-Late Holocene Cultural and Environmental Dynamics in Eastern Uruguay," *Quaternary International* 132 (2005): 37–45.

69. J. M. López Mazz, "Las estructuras tumulares (cerritos) del litoral atlántico uruguayo," *Latin American Antiquity* 12 (2001): 231–255.

70. R. Bracco, "Montículos de la cuenca de la Laguna Merín: Tiempo, Espacio y Sociedad," *Latin American Antiquity* 17 (2006): 515, my translation.

71. I. Wüst and C. Barreto, "The Ring Villages of Central Brazil: A Challenge for Amazonian Archaeology," *Latin American Antiquity* 10 (1999): 3–23.

72. J. Iriarte, "Mid-Holocene Emergent Complexity and Landscape Transformation: The Social Construction of Early Formative Communities in Uruguay, La Plata Basin" (PhD diss., University of Kentucky, 2003); J. Iriarte, "Landscape Transformation, Mounded Villages and Adopted Cultigens: The Rise of Early Formative Communities in South-Eastern Uruguay," *World Archaeology* 38 (2006): 644–663; cf. Bracco, "Montículos de la cuenca de la Laguna Merín."

73. Iriarte, *Mid-Holocene Emergent Complexity*, 5.

74. R. Bracco Boksar, L. del Puerto, H. Inda, and F. García-Rodríguez, "Un Aporte Crítico a Partir de 'Comentarios Sobre Montículos de la Cuenca de la Laguna Merín: Tiempo, Espacio y Sociedad,'" *Latin American Antiquity* 19 (2008): 329.

75. Ibid., 329–330.

76. López Mazz, "Las estructuras tumulares"; J. M. López Mazz and C. Gianotti, "Construcción de espacios ceremoniales públicos entre pobladores prehistóricos de las tierras bajas de Uruguay: El estudio de la organización especial en la localidad arqueológica Rincón de Los Indios," *Revista de Arqueología* 11 (1998): 87–105.

77. G. Verdesio, "From Erasure to the Rewriting of Indigenous Pasts: The Troubled Life of Archaeology in Uruguay," in *Handbook of South American Archaeology*, ed. H. Silverman and W. Isbell (New York: Springer, 2008), 1115–1126.

78. Bracco, "Montículos de la cuenca de la Laguna Merín," 511, argues that even using the term *Formative* implies "importing models developed for other cultures with [apparently] similar but unequivalent mounds"; my translation.

Figure 7.1 Feline sculpture, Chavín de Huántar

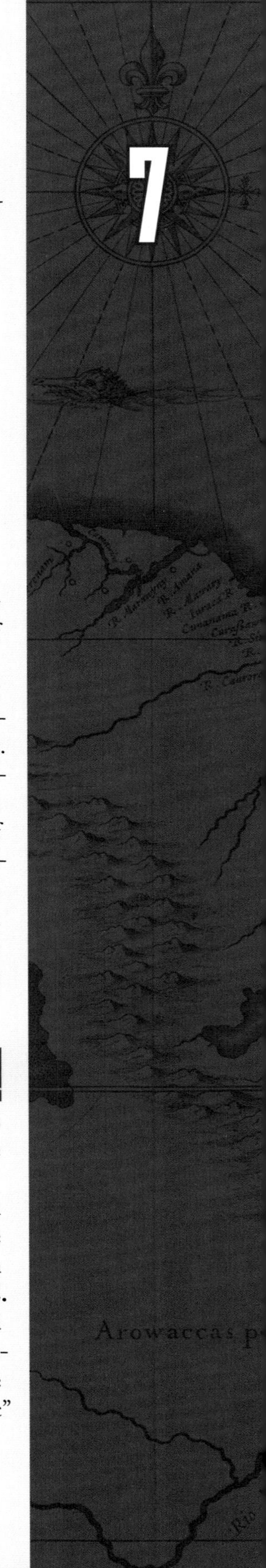

Social Complexities
Part II

7

10.5876_9781607323334.c007

> Near this village of Chavín there is a large building of huge stone blocks very well wrought; it was a guaca, and one of the most famous of the heathen sanctuaries, like Rome or Jerusalem with us; the Indians used to come and make their offerings and sacrifices, for the Devil pronounced many oracles for them here, and so they repaired here from all over the kingdom.
>
> *Antonio Vasquez de Espinosa, 1622*

This chapter continues the discussion of the emergence of social complexity begun in chapter 6 but shifts to an examination of three regions: the coast of Peru, the Central Andean highlands, and the Titicaca Basin (figure 7.2).

As discussed in chapter 1, these regions have been the focus of a great deal of archaeological research over the past 150 years; nonetheless, much remains unknown, and some topics are subjects of heated archaeological debate. The basic issues are not minor quibbles. Is agriculture essential for permanent settlements and complex societies? When did the first cities develop in South America? Are monumental constructions necessarily the products of state-level political systems, or can other social forms produce great buildings? What causes such changes in human societies? In the midst of these heated debates, the only point of consensus among archaeologists working in South America is that simplistic models of social evolution are inadequate for explaining the social complexities that emerged in the Peruvian coast, the Central Andes, and the Titicaca Basin after 2000 BC.

Formative Villages on the Coast of Peru

The arid coast of Peru is fronted by extremely rich coastal waters, and this fundamental environmental feature shaped the development of settled village life (figure 7.3).

Relatively permanent settlements of coastal foragers were present from early in the Archaic period at sites like Quebrada Jaguay and the Ring site (see chapter 4), reflecting non-agrarian, maritime sedentism. This pattern led to the **maritime hypothesis**, proposed by the archaeologist **Michael E. Moseley**, who posited that marine resources along the coasts of Peru and Chile were sufficiently abundant and predictable that sedentary and increasingly complex societies developed before agriculture was adopted. People in these permanent communities began to construct nondomestic "public"

Figure 7.2 Locations of sites discussed in this chapter

architecture: mounds, religious buildings, and other special spaces. The foundations of civilization preceded farming. Further, settled villages also developed before ceramics were adopted in the region; thus, early settled villages were neither agricultural nor pottery-using—two criteria usually associated with the Formative (see chapter 6).

Figure 7.3 Fishing boats on the coast of Peru

Huaca Prieta

The existence of preceramic settlements on the coast was documented by **Junius Bird** in his 1946 excavations at the large mound site of **Huaca Prieta**, located near the mouth of the Chicama Valley on the North Coast (figure 7.2).[1] Huaca Prieta is a large mound, 125 m × 50 m (410 ft × 166 ft) at its base and 12 m (39.4 ft) tall. Bird uncovered evidence of small rectangular one- or two-room structures with cobblestone walls at the site. Huaca Prieta consisted of layers of cobblestone walls and dark midden blackened with organic materials, which gives the mound its name. Bird estimated that several hundred people once lived at Huaca Prieta. The abundant remains of fish scales, sea urchin spines, and shells were accompanied by several domesticated plants—cotton, bottle gourd, chili peppers, achira, and

Figure 7.4 Junius Bird examining textiles and vegetal material at Huaca Prieta, Peru

beans—but no staples such as maize or manioc. Although the inhabitants practiced "rudimentary agriculture," the principal foodstuffs were collected plants and marine resources. The residents of Huaca Prieta also made reed mats and basketry, constructed cotton twine fishnets with bottle gourd floats, and incised and engraved gourd bowls and containers (figure 7.4).

Carbon-14 samples from Huaca Prieta were the first dated from any archaeological site in South America. The earliest charcoal sample Bird collected from Huaca Prieta resulted in an uncalibrated C14 date of 4298 ± 230 BP, a sample with a midpoint age of 3385 BC.[2] Based on later ceramic styles in the uppermost levels, Bird thought the occupation at Huaca Prieta continued until approximately 500–200 BC.

Sixty years later, another multiyear research project was initiated at Huaca Prieta by **Tom Dillehay**, **Duccio Bonavia**, and colleagues.[3] Beginning in 2006, Dillehay, Bonavia, and a large team of archaeologists and other specialists re-excavated areas where Bird had worked and opened new excavations in the Huaca Prieta mound and nearby archaeological sites. The initial results of this research have recently been published; the findings are very surprising. First, the initial occupation at Huaca Prieta was much older than thought previously. The initial human presence in the immediate vicinity has been dated to between 13,720 and 13,260 cal BP (roughly 11,770 to 11,310 BC).[4] Because these strata are deeply buried, the areal extent of this early occupation is unknown, although it is clear that these initial inhabitants made stone tools, hunted sea lions, and fished. Settlement at Huaca Prieta itself began at circa 8979 to 7500 cal BP (approximately 7030 to 5500 BC), even before the actual mound was created. In this early phase, maritime foragers who also engaged in casual gardening lived around the small brackish lagoon.

Mound building began at circa 7572 to 6538 cal BP, when a mound about 25 × 25–35 m (82 ft × 82–115 ft) at its base and about 5 m (16.4 ft) tall was built along a natural terrace. A few postholes and cane fragments may indicate that small perishable structures were built on the mound. The Huaca Prieta mound was intentionally and gradually built; it was not just a big heap of midden. Low retention walls of cobblestones were built and filled in, slowly raising the mound. "The mound building phases," Dillehay and colleagues write, "did not develop from a gradual accumulation of occupation midden but from deliberate and gradual, planned mounding over a period of ~3000 years."[5]

Over these millennia, the Huaca Prieta mound was transformed in size, form, and function. Between about 6538 and 5308 cal BP (4588 to 3358 BC), more layers were added, raising the mound to 8 m to 10 m (26–33 ft) and approximately 85 m (279 ft) at its base. Stone-walled rooms were built on terraces on the mound's east and west slopes, and cobblestone berms and retention walls were used to create a **sunken circular court**—a distinctive feature of ceremonial architecture in the Central Andes (discussed below.) Between 5308 and 4107 BP (3358 to 2157 BC), a 25 cm (9.75 in)-thick layer of yellowish clay was spread over most of the mound. A ramp was added on the east side of the mound, an extension 40 m (131.2 ft) long and 35 m (114.8 ft) wide. Stepped structures were constructed in the sunken plaza. Mound building stopped in the final and fifth phase, 4107 to 3455 cal BP (3358 to 1505 BC), although people built cobblestone burial chambers on the rim of the sunken court and on the peak of the mound. Huaca Prieta continued in use as a religious place after the Formative, as people from subsequent cultures—including the Incas (see chapter 11)—conducted rituals and buried their dead on the mound, enacted recognitions of the enduring sacredness of this black mound by the sea.

In addition to the sequence of very early mound construction, Dillehay, Bonavia, and colleagues found a surprising discovery: maize. Although maize phytoliths and starch grains dating to approximately 7000 to 5500 cal BP were known from southwestern Ecuador and by 4580 to 3380 cal BP had reached the southeastern coast of South America, the earliest maize from coastal Peru had been dated to after 3800 BP (see chapter 5). Maize starch grains removed from the teeth of a human burial had been dated to 4500 BP, but this was slender evidence for the adoption of maize by societies along the coast of Peru. Notably, the absence of domesticated staple plants at Huaca Prieta and other coastal sites—places where organic materials are well-preserved—had stimulated the "maritime hypothesis."

Instead, the materials from Huaca Prieta and the nearby site of Paredones suggest that maize was a minor food crop by 6700 to 4000 cal BP. The dates were from charcoal from intact floors that bracketed the maize samples, as well as AMS dates based on the maize cobs themselves. The dates are not without problems: some samples produced dates that were out of sequence or were clearly contaminated, but the overall dating appears correct. Further, the maize cobs and phytoliths indicated two different types of maize, with small (less than 6 cm long) cobs of primitive popcorn and a somewhat later flour corn with larger kernels. The presence of maize ears, stalks, and husks suggests that the maize was grown nearby rather than simply imported to the coast of Peru. And yet, the excavators note, "The maize remains appear only intermittently . . . suggesting that this crop was not a primary element of the diet in comparison with other faunal and floral resources, which included fish, shellfish, seaweed, sea lions, wild plants, squash, beans, chili peppers, and other cultigens."[6]

Based on the current evidence, the development of initial complex societies on the coast of Peru did not require or even eagerly embrace agriculture once new crops were introduced. Agriculture was apparently integrated into previous subsistence patterns rather than revolutionizing economy and society. The adoption of maize would have significant consequences for coastal societies after approximately 2500 BC, but the initial impacts were minor and subtle.[7]

La Paloma

Robert Benfer excavated at the site of **La Paloma** (see figure 7.2) and documented the existence of sedentary maritime populations over three broad time periods: circa 6600 to 4000 cal BC (the Luz phase), 4000–3800 cal BC (the Encanto Temprano phase), and 3800 to 3400 cal BC (Encanto 1 phase).[8]

In each of these levels, Benfer and his research team uncovered the remains of multiple houses built from willow and cane frames and covered by reed mats. From the earliest levels, the Paloma houses were densely packed dwellings in a settlement without a plaza or other evidence of community planning. Analysis of more than 200 burials from Paloma identified some fascinating changes in the population over two millennia. Life expectancy increased, and fewer infants and children died. Diet improved, male and female stature increased, the rate of anemia decreased, and the reduction of tooth wear suggests a high-quality rather than a coarse diet. The people of Paloma ate a variety of wild plants as well as beans and squash; they also hunted sea mammals, collected shellfish, and fished. The differences between male and female body stature and robustness (sexual dimorphism) decreased over time; Benfer suggests this is because men and women were engaged in similar subsistence activities—collecting mollusks or pulling in fishnets—that indicate a more sedentary maritime lifestyle. However, men had a higher occurrence of auditory exostoses—bony growths in the ear canal caused by exposure to cold wind and water, known as "surfer's ear"—which suggests that men went diving for subtidal shellfish in the cold waters of the Humboldt Current.

Aspero

Aspero, located near the mouth of the Rio Supe (see figure 7.2), was first studied by **Gordon Willey** and **John Corbett** in 1941, reexamined by Michael Moseley and Willey in 1971, and extensively excavated by **Robert Feldman** in 1973–74.[9] A relatively large midden of 12 ha (about 26 acres) suggests a relatively permanent population at the site, but the pivotal discovery was of seven artificial mounds—one containing a burial of an infant and adult (Huaca de los Sacrificios) and the other with a mound-top ceremonial structure (Huaca de los Idolos). The oldest and latest dates for Huaca de los Sacrificios are 3135–2023 cal BC (4260 ± 150 BP) and 2762–1957 cal BC (3950 ± 150 BP); similarly bracketing dates for Huaca de los Idolos are 4052–3337 cal BC (4900 ± 160 BP) and 2780–2023 cal BC (3970 ± 145 BP).

The burials on Huaca de los Sacrificios were intriguing in that the adult was unaccompanied by grave goods whereas the infant was buried with numerous objects: elaborate textiles and more than 500 shell, bone, and stone beads. On Huaca de los Idolos, a nested set of rooms with increasingly narrow doors restricted access to small inner rooms, possibly the place for a shrine (see figure 7.4). Dedicatory caches in the floor of Huaca de los Idolos include carved wooden sticks, "ojos de dios"–like objects made from string and canes, worked red and yellow feathers, and an offering of small human figurines made from unbaked clay—with males and females dressed in long robes and flattop tasseled hats.

Neither of these mounds was colossal in scale. Huaca de los Idolos was 32 m × 22 m (105 ft × 72.2 ft) at its base, and although it appears more than 10 m (33 ft) tall, only 3.5 m (11.5 ft) is from artificial fill. Two points are clear, however. The Aspero mounds were special architecture, nondomestic spaces where ceremonies were held. Further, the people at Aspero, as Moseley and Willey noted, engaged in maritime "subsistence [that] supported a sedentary style of life, with communities of appreciable size" who built "corporate labor structures which do not appear to be ordinary residences," suggesting that "communities were changing from an egalitarian to a non-egalitarian form of organization."[10] Moseley and Willey hypothesized that the social institutions that produced preceramic nonresidential architecture—corporate work groups, some form of coordination, and incipient distinctions in power and prestige—may have been precursors of later social developments once agriculture was established. Thus, the developments at Aspero may be seen, according to Moseley and Willey, as a "pre-adaptation" to later Andean civilizations.

Huaynuná

The site of **Huaynuná** is on a small bay north of the mouth of the Rio Casma (see figure 7.2).[11] The preceramic component dates to 2900–2501 cal BC (4200 ± 80 BP) and 1880–1527 cal BC (3450 ± 65 BP), somewhat later than, but overlapping with, the occupations at Aspero and Caral. The preceramic midden at Huaynuná covers 8 ha (17.6 acres) and contained potato, achira, sweet potato, and cotton as well as dense layers of fish bones and shell. Since there is no arable land at the site, the people of Huaynuná either tilled gardens elsewhere or traded with inland communities for food crops. The traces of seven small huts indicate a sedentary or semi-sedentary population. Another small building, 3 m × 2.5 m (9.8 ft × 8.2 ft) in size, had a well-plastered floor and a distinctive **ventilated hearth with a sub-floor flue**. These sub-floor ventilation systems bring outside air to the hearth and are prominent in the Mito and Kotosh ceremonial architecture of the Central Andes; they also occur at various locations at Caral (discussed below). At Huaynuná this feature is dated to 2463–2122 cal BC (3860 ± 60 BP). In addition, the people of Huaynuná modified a hillside to create a ritual space, making four terraces bisected by a staircase. A small circular room built from beach cobbles and plaster stood on top of the terrace. Lacking traces of domestic use, both the room with the hearth and the terraced slope seem to be ritual spaces and "public" architecture.

After about 3000 BC, communal work and the creation of public constructions became abundant along the Central Coast of Peru, but that was not the only place where Formative societies built large artificial mounds. As discussed in chapter 4, large artificial mounds were built by Archaic societies living along the coast of Brazil and Uruguay, who constructed *sambaquis*. As described in chapter 6, ritual mounds were constructed by Formative societies at the site of Real Alto in southwest Ecuador, and ceremonial complexes were built at Santa Ana–La Florida. Somewhat later, numerous *cerritos de indios* were erected in coastal Uruguay, some of which apparently were religious-ceremonial in purpose.

Although the coast of Peru was not the only place where monumental constructions occurred, some factors—not all of which are understood—made this region a particular center for the development of complex architecture, experiments in cultural landscapes that by 3000 to 2000 BC were expressed in monumental centers. First, as Moseley had suggested, the rich resources of the Humboldt Current were key to supporting sedentary villages, and there is abundant archaeological evidence for the maritime adaptations. Second, it seems that coastal populations increased significantly after 6000 BP (or 6850 cal BP, 4900 cal BC). In a classic 1987 paper, **John Rick** analyzed the then-available radiocarbon dates from the coast of Peru, examining the frequency of dates for different time periods (figure 7.5).[12]

Assuming that frequencies of radiocarbon dates reflect human populations, populations increased dramatically on the coast, a maritime equivalent of a "Neolithic Demographic Transition," in which populations increased as societies became more sedentary.[13] The dietary trends documented at Paloma and Huaca Prieta appear part of a larger trend, one that gave additional importance to cultigens. As agriculture grew in significance, coastal communities tended to concentrate near river valleys. These valleys are the principal sources of freshwater along the desert coast, and communities shifted to these verdant swaths, effectively increasing population densities.

Social Complexity and Early Urbanism: The Norte Chico and Caral

In the Supe and neighboring Huaura, Pativilca, and Fortaleza River Valleys—a region known as the **Norte Chico**—dozens of sites that date to 3100–1800 BC,

Figure 7.5 Mound excavations at Caral, Peru

including Aspero, reflect similar evidence for emerging social complexities as seen at Aspero (see figure 7.2).

For example, research directed by **Jonathan Haas**, **Winifred Creamer**, and **Alvaro Ruiz** has documented the presence of a dozen sites in the Pativilca and Fortaleza Valleys that have radiocarbon dates indicating occupations between 3100 and 1800 cal BC.[14] Their important and ongoing research illuminates other investigations in the region, including the pivotal excavations at the site of **Caral** directed by **Ruth Shady Solís**.[15]

Located 23 km (13.8 miles) inland on the southern margin of the Supe Valley, Caral has a 66-ha (145-acre) monumental center, with a ceremonial precinct of massive mounds, sunken circular courts, and plazas surrounded by a residential zone (figure 7.5).

Shady Solís has argued convincingly that Caral represents an urban center, perhaps the oldest city known in the Americas. A suite of radiocarbon dates points to major constructions occurring at Caral between 2876 and 2339 cal BC (4090 ± 90) and 2046–1767 cal BC (3640 ± 50).[16]

Caral has at least thirty-two public buildings, including six large mounds. The large mounds include the massive **Great Temple**, measuring 170.8 m × 149.7 m (560 ft × 491 ft) at its base and 29.9 m (98 ft) in maximum height.

Figure 7.6 Sunken circular plaza, Caral, Peru

The Great Temple is fronted by a large sunken circular court whose staircases articulate with the stairs that climb the principal facade of the Great Temple (figure 7.6). Sunken circular courts are prominent architectural features at coastal ceremonial centers and at some highland sites like Chavín de Huántar (discussed below).

Opposite and across the plaza is the Temple of the Amphitheater, a complicated building with multiple rooms attached to a circular sunken plaza approximately 31.5 m (103.3 ft) in diameter. Excavators recovered more than thirty whistles made from condor and pelican bones, suggesting that ceremonies took place inside these spaces. Again, the staircases of the amphitheater are aligned with the access to the building complex. In both cases, the articulation of sunken courts and mounded constructions suggests processionals or at least movements between mounds and sunken courts. These were important, religiously significant places.

Shady Solís argues that Caral was the center of a settlement network consisting of eighteen sites within the Supe Valley. An estimated 200,000 m^3 of constructions are found at Caral. Caral and Pueblo Nuevo, an incompletely studied site located downstream, are the largest and most densely constructed settlements among a central cluster of Supe Valley sites. Caral, Pueblo Nuevo, and three other sites (Miriaya, Era de Pando, and Lurihuasi) contain more than 75 percent of the constructions in the valley. Much smaller sites away from this mid-valley cluster represent villages and hamlets sprinkled along the banks of the Supe Valley.

The Caral and Supe Valley settlement data have important implications. First, there are obvious differences in size and scale between these settlements. They are not similar communities in terms of populations, the elaborateness of architecture, or the labor invested in the constructions. Second, the Supe Valley sites formed a network of interacting settlements rather than isolated and independent communities. These communities apparently had different roles within this network. The archaeological traces of some activities are widespread: fishing, cultivation (of achira, cotton, squash, beans, bottle gourd, sweet potato, avocado, and other tree fruits, supplemented later by maize), stone tool making, and other household crafts. Other activities were restricted. Mural painting, fine mason work, and complex architectural planning are present at the larger sites, absent from more modest settlements. In addition, Shady Solís argues, coastal and inland settlements were linked through exchange of the differing productions of the sea and the river valley.

Beyond this, Caral and the other Supe Valley settlements were articulated to even larger networks based on religion and commerce. For example, Caral and several other Supe Valley sites have special chambers with sub-floor ventilation ducts like those in Huaynuná or at Huaricoto and Kotosh (described below). Even further afield, the people of the Supe Valley had access to the highly prized *Spondylus* shells, a warm-water mollusk that lives more than 1,200 km (720 miles) away along the coasts of northernmost Peru and Ecuador. Therefore, it seems that Caral and the Supe Valley communities were articulated into a network that, in turn, was connected to other networks of communities in the prehistoric Andes.

Based on these data from the Norte Chico, it seems that a tremendous transformation occurred between 3000 and 2000 BC. For example, the Great Pyramid at Caral is 170.8 m × 149.7 m (560.2 ft × 491 ft) at its base and between 19.3 m (63 ft) and 29.9 m (98.1 ft) tall, making it more than *ninety times* the volume of Huaca de los Idolos. Shady Solís calculates that of all the labor invested in prehistoric constructions in the Supe Valley, more than one-fourth (27.8%) was invested at Caral, while less than 2 percent was invested at Aspero. These are somewhat crude measures, as they do not take into account the different phases of construction or the specific chronologies of remodeling. But they make an obvious point: a fundamental change occurred in this region between 3000 and 2000 BC.

There are major disagreements among archaeologists about the timing, nature, and causes of these transformations.[17] Did public constructions occur as early as 3100 BC or only later, between 2300 and 2000 BC? Are the radiocarbon dates based on samples that actually date construction phases, or are they from earlier deposits that were scavenged for fill and incorporated into later constructions? Did the emergence of large-scale public works occur when prehistoric subsistence was principally dependent on marine resources or only after the introduction and acceptance of agriculture, particularly maize? Do these large mounds represent centralization based on religious authority, complex chiefdoms, or state-level societies? All these questions remain points of contention.

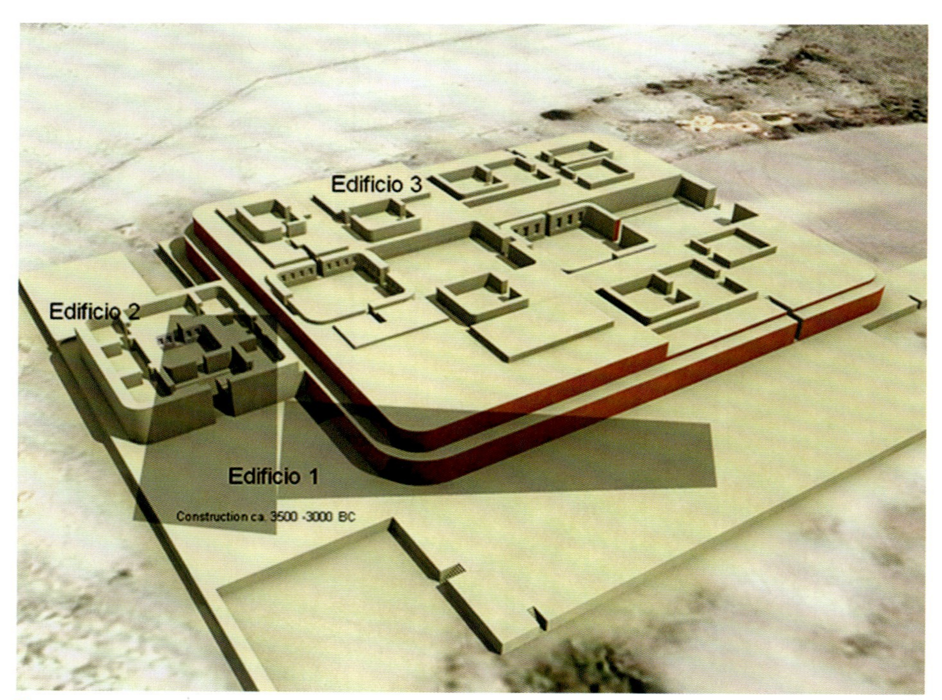

Figure 7.7 Sechin Bajo, Peru—reconstruction of major building phases

Complex Societies in the Casma Valley: Sechin Bajo, Cerro Sechin, and Sechin Alto

The Norte Chico was a pivotal region for the development of complex societies along the Peruvian coast, but it was not the only one or even the earliest. Monumental constructions in the Casma Valley, about 180 km (108 miles) north of Supe, are actually older (see figure 7.2).[18]

Archaeological investigations into the development of complex societies in the Casma Valley began in the 1930s with the work of the great Peruvian archaeologist **Julio Tello** (see chapter 2) and continue with ongoing investigations by the US archaeologists **Thomas** and **Shelia Pozorski** and multinational excavation teams directed by the German archaeologist **Peter Fuchs**. From these sustained investigations, a general picture of the development of social complexity has emerged.

On the north side of the Casma Valley, about 12 km (7.2 miles) inland, the site of **Sechin Bajo** contains a sequence of massive and impressive ceremonial architecture—sequentially constructed and reconstructed, anchored to the same pivotal location that spans the Archaic-Formative transition (figure 7.7).[19] Sechin Bajo's inland location suggests that subsistence was no longer principally dependent on marine resources but that agriculture may have become a significant part of the economy.

Figure 7.8 Sechin Bajo, Peru—multiple constructions of sunken circular plazas

Covering approximately 37 ha (81.4 acres), Sechin Bajo presents an archaeological kaleidoscope of multiple constructions that Fuchs and his colleagues have defined as three broad remodeling phases (figure 7.8).

The Primer Edificio was a large, 2 m (6.5 ft)-tall platform built from stones and adobe bricks, covered with a well-made floor, and associated with a sequence of sunken circular plazas. The dates for the Primer Edificio range from 3712–3514 cal BC (4891 ± 49 BP) to 2943–2866 cal BC (4333 ± 28 BP). Beginning as a 16 m × 16 m (52.5 ft × 52.5 ft) platform, the Primer Edificio was remodeled and expanded at least five times. Multiple sunken circular plazas were constructed, filled in, and reconstructed in one portion of the building; their entrances and staircases were repeatedly placed in the same location (figure 7.9).

At one phase in the remodeling, a rectangular sunken court (15.5 m × 15.5 m [50.8 ft × 50.8 ft]) was built, and its floor and walls were plastered. Later, a sunken circular plaza was built in the rectangular court, then yet another circular court was built on the previous one, only to have the entire Primer Edificio filled with clean gravel and capped with a layer of mud.

At this point, construction at Sechin Bajo apparently paused as another site, **Cerro Sechin**, became a major ceremonial site in the Casma Valley (figure 7.9).[20]

Although early deposits date from 9600 to 7500 BP, the major construction at Cerro Sechin began between 2300 and 2000 BC (2348–2022 cal BC; 3830 ± 50 BP; and 2115–1944 cal BC; 3740 ± 40 BP). Cerro Sechin was a major ceremonial center for the next 1,500 years, until approximately 500 BC (figure 7.10).

Figure 7.9 (*overleaf*)Cerro Sechin, Peru—reliefs of stacked decapitated heads

Figure 7.10 Cerro Sechin, Peru—relief of a trophy head

As **Henning Bischof** notes, "In the Casma Valley, the central platform of Cerro Sechin is the best-known edifice of its time. Without doubt, it was constructed for ritual purposes because on its walls scenes of bloody sacrifices are depicted . . . The building is marked, from its earliest phase, by a wide inventory of standardized architectural features. From a wide vestibule, a central chamber with curved corners allowed the actors to remain hidden as they carried out a spectacular *mise en scene* as required by a ritual script."[21] Surrounded by murals portraying fantastic anthropomorphic felines and crocodiles, for centuries the ritual chambers of Cerro Sechin echoed with the pomp of ceremonies and screams of sacrifices.

After a long gap, there was a renewed explosion of construction at Sechin Bajo. When construction resumed, the builders oriented their monuments directly toward the principal entrance at Cerro Sechin, less than 2 km (1.2 miles) away on the other side of the valley. Builders shifted their energies to the Segundo Edificio, a quadrangular complex of mound-top rooms 39 m × 35 m (128 ft × 114.8 ft) in area. Constructions in this area took place between 1611 and 1443 cal BC (3304 ± 27 BP) and 1411–1209 cal BC (3097 ± 28 BP). The Segundo Edificio was followed immediately by an extensive, multi-phase construction between 1886 and 1501 BC (3386 ± 80 BP) and 1411–1208 cal BC (3097 ± 30 BP), a complex dubbed the "Tercer Edificio." This complex extended the Segundo Edificio and covered sections of the Primer Edificio, raising the entire complex by 6 m (19.7 ft). Built in two phases, the Tercer Edificio initially contained two large patios that were subsequently subdivided into four smaller plazas of different sizes, linked by staircases. A distinctive set of rooms with curved interior corners, finely plastered walls painted in red and white, and niches in the walls are similar to rooms known from the Casma Valley and elsewhere.

At various places along the building walls, molded reliefs and paintings suggest the special religious focus of the Sechin Bajo complex. For example, the Crocodile Deity—a complex combination of reptilian and anthropomorphic motifs—appears as graffiti inscribed on the outside of the Segundo Edificio. Similar motifs are known from the site of Cerro Sechin, as well as later art at the site of Chavín de Huántar. As crocodiles did not live along the Central Coast of Peru, the image is usually seen as connecting the coast with the distant jungle zones to the east. In another location, fronting a plaza, a trio of reliefs depicts feline anthropomorphic figures. The figures face forward, their fanged lips snarling, holding a knife in one hand and a hanging sphere (possibly a trophy head) from which snakes dangle.

This complex process of building, filling, and rebuilding at Sechin Bajo was not some frenetic construction effort but rather a process of "ritual interment." Fuchs and colleagues observe, "It is important to note that the construction of each one of these buildings with their respective remodelings and internal changes signifies the ritual burial of preceding architecture until the site was completely abandoned. With few exceptions, the previous structures were respected and the new buildings were raised on top of them, simultaneously resulting in the vertical and horizontal growth of the complex."[22] As Fuchs and colleagues note, similar evidence of ritual burial is known from Caral, as well as from the site of Kotosh in the Central Andean highlands (discussed below). When Sechin Bajo was finally

Figure 7.11 Principal mound at Sechin Alto, Peru

Figure 7.12 Conical adobes at Sechin Alto, Peru

abandoned, it continued to be used as a cemetery, its special nature resonating over the following millennia.

For example, a major urban complex evolved in the lower Casma Valley, where **Sechin Alto** was the center of a multi-settlement polity incorporating several large communities (see figure 7.2, figure 7.11). Located near the junction of the Sechin and Casma Valleys, the principal mound at Sechin Alto was a staggering 300 m × 250 m (984 ft × 820 ft) at its base and 35 m (114.8 ft) tall, making it the largest construction in the Americas when it was built (figure 7.12).[23]

Excavations by Shelia and Thomas Pozorski have recovered radiocarbon dates ranging from 1600 to 1400 cal BC, although these samples were derived from the upper portion of the mound, and another 20 m (65.6 ft) of construction underlies the dated layers. This suggests that the bulk of the mound was built between 2150 and 1400 BC, when approximately 1.3 million m^3 (1.7 million $yards^3$) of the mound was constructed. Built from conical mud bricks and stone blocks (figure 7.13), the front of the mound was cut by a wide staircase that passed through two atria to the peak of the mound. The mound is at the western end of a line of plazas extending 1.4 km (0.8 miles) to the east, with several sunken circular courts aligned to the central axis of the site. The excavators estimate the site's population as approximately 18,000 inhabitants.

Further, Pozorski and Pozorski argue that Sechin Alto represents the earliest state-level society in the Andes. They write: "A number of characteristics of Sechin Alto site and the polity it headed argue convincingly for the emergence of state-level political organization in the Casma Valley by Initial Period times. The sheer magnitude of construction involving building phases represented by hundreds of thousands of m^3 of stones and earth documents the leaders' capacity to mobilize and support a huge labor force drawn from a sizable population." They interpret the evidence for site planning, in which mounds and other structures were aligned, as evidence of "a preconceived plan [that] argues for a lineage of rulers who maintained their hegemony across many generations. The 'master plan' conceived by these rulers was executed with precision." In turn, the Pozorskis view Sechin Alto and other Casma Valley sites as constituting a "clear five-level hierarchy in the settlement pattern," with Sechin Alto as the capital.[24] Absent from the archaeological evidence are other indications of hierarchy and centralization. There is little evidence for the existence of elites and commoners, scant indication of economic specializations, and no indication of military expansions.

For such reasons, there is debate about whether Sechin Alto and its related communities actually represent a state-level society. **Charles Stanish** has written, "In short, the Initial period cultural landscape was populated with thousands of corporate buildings on hundreds of sites of varying sizes and complexity. The evidence suggests the existence of local polities with little regional integration with no single site that can be described as a political center of a multivalley polity."[25] He concludes that "the model that best characterizes" Central Andean societies before circa AD 500 "is a series of autonomous and semiautonomous polities without any evidence of complexity beyond that of a chiefdom society."[26]

Yet, it is undeniable that such monumental constructions indicate significant changes in the social order. More complex, permanent settlements developed at various points along the coast of Peru between approximately 3000 and 2000 BC. These developments mark the transition from early coastal villages of sedentary marine foragers and horticulturalists to the creation of much larger settlements with monumental constructions and nonresidential architecture. Given that so many of these sites show evidence of repeated occupations and modifications, it is reasonable to infer that these new cultural creations were made by resident and growing communities. The creation of similar architectural features, such as sunken circular courts or hearths with sub-floor ventilation shafts, and the use of similar motifs—such as the Crocodile Deity—suggest that these different coastal communities were in contact and drew upon a shared cultural repertoire and iconography.

Finally, between 1600 and 900 BC, numerous large settlements developed in the different valleys along the coast of Peru—in the Lurin Valley, the Rimac Valley, the Chillón Valley, the Pativilca Valley, and as far north as the Chao Valley.[27] These different expressions of social complexity exhibit similar patterns of monumental architecture. Thomas and Shelia Pozorski have summarized these similarities and their implications:

> Communication among Early Formative coastal settlements is indicated by important commonalities. Truly monumental architecture makes its first appearance during the Early Formative, and sites which reflect this phenomenon share other important traits. All have as their largest structure(s) one or more large platform mounds which are consistently bilaterally symmetrical and usually U-shaped. Commonly associated with these mounds are one or more rectangular and/or circular plazas, and the resultant mound/plaza layout frequently results in a linear plan for the site—the site axis coinciding with the centerline of a major mound. Many of the major U-shaped mounds face up valley with the open end of their "U" oriented toward the source(s) of rivers and irrigation water . . . In addition to monumental construction, iconographic representations appear closely linked to the sudden proliferation of inland sites [in contrast to coastal, maritime-focused communities] and, by extension, to the adoption of irrigation agriculture.[28]

Despite these similarities in architectural forms, there were significant variations in other dimensions of social complexity. For example, while many of these large settlements developed inland near agricultural lands, some monumental sites retained their coastal settings, depended on marine resources, and exchanged with farming communities for cultivated foods. Some settlements consisted principally of ceremonial mounds, while other sites had large resident populations in addition to the monumental architecture. Additional archaeological investigations are necessary to clarify these differences and further our knowledge of this dynamic and diverse period of cultural developments on the coast of Peru.

Hearths, Temples, and Pilgrimage Centers in the Central Andean Highlands

Between approximately 3000 and 1500 BC, a varied array of social formations developed in the Central Andes, emergent complex societies that created distinctive types of public architecture focused on religion and ceremonies. While the coast of Peru witnessed the development of monumental centers and arguably the first cities in South America, communities in the Andean highlands created very different places and spaces. In general, these early highland sites contained architecture that was smaller in scale and more intimate in experience. Rather than the enormous mounds and expansive plazas of the coast, highland communities initially constructed smaller chambers in which attention focused on the interiors. Initially, these spaces were associated with relatively small social groups, but some became

Figure 7.13 Mito-style chamber found at Chavín de Huántar, Peru

important ceremonial centers for regions or even vast zones of the Central Andes. Based on current evidence, these centers were religious or theocratic in their focus rather than capitals of chiefdoms or states.

Ritual Chambers in the Central Andean Highlands

The curious combination of small chambers and central fire pits ventilated by a flue that runs under the floor was an important and recurrent element in rituals in the Central Andes over two millennia (figure 7.13). These chambers with ventilated hearths were not dwellings; they lacked domestic debris, the chambers were constructed to a specific repertoire of architectural elements, and they are found in ceremonial zones rather than residential areas in archaeological sites.

The oldest of these chambers date to 2700–2100 cal BC and are known at five different sites (see figure 7.2): Huaricoto[29] (2696–2118 cal BC; 3970 ± 110 BP), La Galgada[30] (2351–2015 cal BC; 3820 ± 60 BP), Huaynuná[31] (2345–2014 cal BC; 3810 ± 50 BP), Piruru[32] (2294–1926 cal BC; 3770 ± 60 BP), and Caral[33] (2288–1981 cal BC; 3730 ± 70 BP and 2046–1767 cal BC; 3640 ± 50 BP). Interestingly, these sites are found over an area of approximately 300 km × 200 km (180 miles × 120 miles) in the highlands and along the coast of Peru. Further, these chambers apparently served as a conceptual model for subsequent and more elaborated chambers at the site of Kotosh (ca. 2500 BC–AD 1) and were incorporated into the highland pilgrimage center of Chavín de Huántar as late as ~850–750 BC.[34] Thus, these odd chambers have a remarkably widespread and enduring presence in the Central Andes for more than 1,300 years.

One could accuse archaeologists of seeing patterns when none existed, except for the unique architectural features and artifacts associated with these chambers. First, the presence of a central hearth and ventilation shafts is uniquely associated with the small chambers. Second, there is evidence of careful treatments of the floor surrounding the hearth; in many cases, the surrounding floor has been carefully made of red or yellow clays. Third, the objects found in the hearth indicate special uses; they contain quartz crystals, obsidian flakes, chili pepper seeds, or imported shells. The hearths do not appear to be simply fire pits for cooking or warmth.

These chambers appear to reflect a suite of ceremonial practices known as the **Kotosh Religious Tradition**, named after the site of Kotosh. As defined by **Richard Burger** and **Lucy Salazar-Burger**, this religious practice was focused on burning offerings in small chambers, ceremonies that could only be witnessed by a small group of participants. This simple-seeming practice seems to have cross-cut communities and ethnic groups, given its wide distribution. Further, the essential folk-religion practice is alternatively incorporated in more formalized settings, as at Kotosh, or coexisted with other ritual performances, as at Chavín de Huántar.

Kotosh

Located at about 2,000 m (6,560 ft) above sea level on a tributary of the upper Huallaga River, **Kotosh** is one of the most important sites in Andean prehistory (see figure 7.2). Despite covering less than 1.2 ha (2.96 acres), the site was intensively constructed and reconstructed over six major phases that span the years 2500 BC to AD 1. This resulted in a complex jumble of more than a hundred structures that were built, used, carefully entombed, and built upon again.

During the initial Mito phase, the constructions were small rectangular chambers with split-level floors forming a sunken rectangular space in the middle of the room surrounded by a bench. A hearth in this lower floor was fanned by a sub-floor ventilation shaft. This hearth and the surrounding floor anchored ritual practice; the archaeologist **Elisabeth Bonnier**, for example, argued that the clay floor itself was "a stretch of sacred ground . . . a sacrosanct surface."[35] At Kotosh, these chambers were large and elaborate. For example, the **Templo de las Manos Cruzadas** was about 9.5 m × 9.3 m (31.2 ft × 30.5 ft) in area, with 2 m-thick (6.5 ft) stone walls set in mud mortar and plastered. A wide door on the south wall led into the room. The walls were covered with niches and clay reliefs, including two sets of crossed arms that give this temple its name. At some point the roof of the Templo de las Manos Cruzadas was removed, the crossed arms were carefully covered with black sand, the door was sealed, and the temple was filled with cobblestones and capped with a layer of red clay—only to have another temple built right on top of it. This temple, the **Templo de los Nichitos**, 9.5 m × 8.5 m (31.2 ft × 27.9 ft) in size, was configured similar to its predecessor, although with many small niches for which the temple is named. In turn, the Templo de los Nichitos was carefully sealed and built upon.

This process of intentionally filling a ritual chamber has been called "ritual entombment." The archaeologist **Yoshio Onuki** observed that the process of entombment and renovation was "the most notable characteristic of the early ceremonial life in Peru. One may propose that temple renovation was the first impetus for the sociocultural development that promoted the dynamic process during the late Preceramic and the Formative."[36]

This impetus was apparently shared among a small set of communities in the vicinity of Kotosh. For example, the site of **Shillacoto** (largely buried under the modern city of Huanuco, Peru) also contains a Kotosh-style temple measuring 15 m × 15 m (49.2 ft × 49.2 ft) in area with 3 m (9.8 ft)-tall well-plastered and decorated walls. In addition, artifacts at Shillacoto include fine ceramics (including bowls and figurines decorated with elegant modeled depictions of humans, monkeys, and felines), intricately carved bone tubes and other objects, and mirrors polished from jet, a coal-black gemstone. Similar ceramics were found at other nearby sites, as was evidence for intentional renovation and reconstruction of these monuments. Onuki argues that the local evidence for renovation implies the existence of new social interactions, both within the upper Huallaga and between the sierra and the coast.

The specific contours of this interaction are unclear. For example, the wide distribution of chambers with sub-floor ventilation shafts probably indicates a shared but fundamental cultural concept rather than a trait introduced from the sierra. Ceramic styles suggest connections among the highlands, the coast, and possibly the western Amazon.

Onuki writes, "The renovation of ceremonial constructions is notable from the Preceramic until the end of the Formative. Although the motives for the renovations are unknown, it is possible to infer that—given the need for more and more manpower—they resulted in larger and larger quantities of food and drink, increasingly complicated organization of work, and more and more laborious elaborations and decorations of architecture. Overall, the renovation promoted economic, technological, and ideological development, as well as the exchange between the coast and the sierra."[37]

Other inferences are possible. Sites like Kotosh and Shillacoto were unique settlements, as indicated not by their size but as foci of human efforts that made them disproportionally important. Second, there was evidence for specialization. Not only did these sites contain ritual complexes and elaborated buildings that were the products of specialized skills, but the occupants had access to crafts made by specialists: potters, weavers, and mirror grinders. Third, these settlements did not exist in isolation but rather as powerful nodes in far-reaching networks based on religion and commerce.

Some aspects of these religious practices were enduring, while other new forms of society and culture are also indicated. For example, at Shillacoto, the only evidence found for ceremonial activities was two burial chambers on top of the earlier temples. After 1500–1000 BC, a burial crypt was constructed directly above an earlier chamber's central hearth, leading Onuki to suggest that it was designed to put out the earlier ceremonial fire. Another crypt was constructed later at Shillacoto, a stone-lined crypt that held a single skull; although the other bones may have disintegrated, Onuki considers that this crypt was designed for one person's head.

Thus, after circa 1500–1000 BC, there seems to have been a change in ceremonial architecture, religious practice, and social order in the Upper Huallaga. Rather than ceremonial chambers that were ritually entombed and reconstructed—a progressive sequence of temples that pivoted around a sacred axis—the mounds were converted into places for distinctive tombs.

La Galgada

Interestingly, a broadly similar transformation occurred at the site of **La Galgada**.[38] Located on the western slope of the Andes at 1,100 m (3,608 ft) above sea level, La Galgada is on a year-round tributary of the westward-flowing Santa River in an arid region with a sparse forest of thorny acacia, cacti, and other desert species (see figure 7.2).

Excavated by **Terence Grieder** and colleagues, the site consists of two major mounds (the larger "North Mound" and the "South Mound") and a circular plaza about 18 m (59 ft) across, all surrounded by small (less than 14 m^2 [150.4 ft^2]) elliptical houses. Construction at the North Mound began in 2460–2100 cal BC, with subsequent remodeling and additions over the next five centuries. The North Mound contains a fascinating record of architectural transformations built in rough masonry.

Over a period of three to four centuries, the North Mound contained gradual accumulations of small chambers, usually less than 3 m × 3 m (10 ft × 10 ft) in area. These chambers had features seen elsewhere in north-central Peru at this time: central hearths with sub-floor ventilation flues, walls with curving interior corners, sunken rectangular spaces in the middle of the chamber, and small niches in the walls. The chambers were transformed into burial crypts, sealed, and filled over; new chambers were constructed in those upper levels. With a single exception, the burial crypts held groups of bodies—from three to twenty-seven individuals—often males and females and of different ages, from newborns to mature adults. The burials were accompanied by grave goods and subjected to specific programs of preparation. The earliest burials had their hair cut short, and tufts of hair were placed around the corpses. Later burials also exhibited a concern with hair, as decorated hairpins were found with the bodies, along with jewelry, textiles, gourds, and stone vessels. These differences in burial treatment indicate a "community [that] remained egalitarian and fragmented in its ceremonial organization, but the things which accompany the later burials were unique or rare, represented much more labor, and not everyone had equal amounts or equal quality."[39]

La Galgada exhibits some patterns in common with Kotosh and Shillacoto, such as the construction of relatively small ritual chambers, the transformation of ritual chambers into burial crypts, and repeated constructions anchored to a specific place. Yet, after circa 2000 cal BC, La Galgada underwent another transformation: the tell-like accumulation of small structures was sheathed in tiered

Figure 7.14 View of the "Castillo," Chavín de Huántar, Peru

masonry, the masonry was surrounded by massive revetments, a prominent staircase was erected on the west side of the North Mound, and a set of small chambers was constructed on top of the mound.

In effect, this architectural transformation included changes from small, intimate, multiple chambers with central hearths that were converted into burial crypts to a single monumental mound, accessed by way of a prominent staircase and topped by ritual chambers that lacked central hearths. In turn, these architectural changes suggest changes in social order. Grieder writes that with these later modifications of the North Mound, "A person could occupy the position at the top of the central stairs at La Galgada and hold the only unique and unrivaled position, a position of authority which had no antecedent in Preceramic design."[40]

Chavín de Huántar: Pilgrimage Center in the Central Highlands

Chavín de Huántar is one of the most important archaeological sites in the Andes, long viewed as the center of a religion revered across a broad swath of the Central Andes (see figure 7.2).[41] Located at 3,150 m (10,330 ft) elevation on the eastern slope of the Cordillera Blanca, Chavín de Huántar sits at the junction of two rivers—the Huascheca and the Mosna—that flow eastward toward the Amazon Basin by way of the Marañon (figure 7.14).

Western observers have known about the site since the Colonial era. Visited by numerous travelers, Chavín de Huántar first became prominent in the archaeological literature through the work of the Peruvian archaeologist Julio C. Tello. Tello made two essential discoveries: first, in 1919 he studied the ruins at the site itself, and second, over the next decades Tello recognized that the distinctive motifs incorporated into Chavín de Huántar's architecture and artifacts were found at sites and collections from a broad region of the sierra and coast of central Peru (figure 7.15).

These distinctive motifs include feline figures with curving fangs and claws, snakes with flicking tongues, and raptors, among other elements, that form a unique stylistic set (figure 7.16).

As he recognized similar traits on ceramic vessels, incised stone bowls, gold plaques, and architectural reliefs in collections and sites along the coast of Peru, Tello concluded:

> Within the domain of the Andes, no civilization has such well defined and peculiar features as the Chavín civilization. Its most important center is the upper Marañon basin, and its widespread area of dispersion crosses the frontiers of the northern Andes. Where remains are found, whatever the example of building or handicraft, or whatever the material employed—stone, metal, bone, clay or any other that

Figure 7.15 Feline and snake motifs, Chavín de Huántar, Peru

> has withstood the action of the weather—there appear the vigorous unmistakable architectural, sculptural or pictorial creations of an extraordinary race. Its name and recollection have been erased from man's memory with the passage of centuries, but it has left behind undeniable traces of a civilization of such peculiarity and originality that it has no equal in other South American prehistoric cultures.[42]

The broad distribution of artifacts and monuments with Chavín-style motifs led to the idea of a **horizon**, a period in which a coherent set of material culture was found widely in the Peruvian Andes, suggesting some form of cultural integration (figure 7.17).

The spread of the Chavín style marked the Early Horizon in the chronological framework devised by **John Rowe** and **Dorothy Menzel** that envisioned a series of horizons—characterized by broadly influential cultural practices—interspersed by intermediate periods, which were defined by regional developments.[43] Unlike later empires such as the Inca, who had constructed fortresses and other imperial installations, these Chavín sites and iconography seemed religious in purpose. That, coupled with Colonial accounts of the site's role as an oracle, suggested that Chavín de Huántar was the center of a pilgrimage network whose impact was felt over a region approximately 800 km (480 miles) from north to south and 200 km (120 miles) from the sierra to the coast. Chavín represented, as Tello famously dubbed it, "**la cultural matriz**," the "mother culture" of Andean civilizations.

The site of Chavín de Huántar covers approximately 50 ha (123.5 acres), with a 10-ha (24.7-acre) core of ceremonial architecture surrounded by a residential zone, most of which lies underneath the modern town of Chavín. Most excavations have focused on the ceremonial core, with the notable exceptions of Richard Burger's 1975 and 1976 excavations in the residential area and surrounding hamlets in the valley and excavations conducted by **John Rick**, **Daniel Contreras**, and **Matthew Sayre** in a domestic zone known as "La Banda" between 2003 and 2005. Combined with the earlier investigations by Tello in 1919, 1934, and 1940, extensive excavations in the 1960s and 1970s directed by **Luis Lumbreras**, **Hernan Amat**, and **Rosa Fung**; ongoing investigations by John Rick that began in 1995, and investigations by numerous other archaeologists mean that "Chavín de Huántar has become one of the best documented archaeological sites in Peru."[44]

Figure 7.16 The Raimondi Stela, Chavín de Huántar, Peru

The public architecture consists of massive flattop buildings that sit on terraces overlooking three distinctive plazas. The mounds—also referred to as "temples" and "castillos"—were built from well-cut stones, and they have exterior walls built from large blocks of stone and decorated with three-dimensional sculpted stone heads portraying felines. The mounds are massive volumes of solid fill interspersed with passageways (*galerias*), rooms, ventilation shafts, and drainage canals. Inside the mound and hidden from public view, one chamber held the principal religious object at the site—the 4.5 m (14.8 ft)-tall Lanzón, a granite stela that depicts a fanged anthropomorphic feline, the principal deity of Chavín religion. The Lanzón was integral to the building—it cannot be removed without dismantling the entire temple—and yet it could only be approached single-file through a narrow corridor that led to the small room in which it stands.

The Lanzón was not for the general public, and the interior spaces of the temples were probably restricted to small numbers of priests and initiates. Iconography depicts at least two different psychotropic plants—the mescaline-containing San Pedro cactus and the vilca tree (*Anadenathera colubrine*), whose seeds are made into a hallucinogenic snuff—which were probably ingested by initiates and priests. A spectacular cache of twenty conch shell trumpets (*Strombus galeatus*) inside the mounds strongly suggests that sounds were incorporated into the ritual, and the discovery of small mirrors may indicate that reflected light illuminated rituals in the subterranean darkness.

Outside in the bright Andean daylight, three plazas were open to the sky. A sunken circular plaza 21 m (68.9 ft) in diameter was an architectural form also known from other archaeological sites (e.g., Sechin Bajo, Pampa de las Llamas-Moxeke, and Caral). Two sunken rectangular courts—one 20 m × 20 m (65.6

ft × 65.6 ft) in size, the other 105 m × 85 m (344.5 ft × 278.8 ft)—may have been used for ceremonies, assemblies of pilgrims, or feasts. The sunken circular plaza was decorated by a curving display of incised reliefs depicting a procession of jaguars on the lower levels and a march of anthropomorphic supernaturals or costumed ritual specialists carrying staffs of San Pedro cactus or blowing conch shell trumpets.

The iconography displayed on Chavín sculpture and other objects is otherworldly, intriguing, and resistant to easy interpretation. A number of the motifs—jaguars, snakes, caimans, and raptors—depict fearful animals of power that do not normally live in the high Andes but rather come from the Amazonian lowlands. Some of the objects—San Pedro cactus, maize cobs and other crops, shell trumpets, thorny oyster (*Spondylus* spp.) shell—are readily interpreted. John Rowe suggested that the sculptors of Chavín were deploying visual metaphors, while Donald Lathrap pointed to the Amazonian elements as indicating the lowland origins of highland civilization in the Andes. But it is the combination of these elements and the unsettling order of their presentation that makes the art distinctive. It may be that some of the figures are of *amarus*, literally, composite figures or chimeras that exist only in their sculptors' worldview.

More recently, anthropologist **Gary Urton** has observed that "underlying all fascination with Chavín art is the perception that a considerable degree of artistic skill is represented in the composition, design, and execution of most works rendered in this style," while "we are often simultaneously repelled and attracted by the absence of a clearly identifiable focal subject . . . The eye immediately encounters a profusion of complex, interlocking forms with no easily discernible central image and with no clearly defined figure/ground relation among the various parts of the clusters of images. It is as though one is viewing a very complex, highly stylized jigsaw puzzle, but as to whether or not the pieces are all in their proper places, and if so what the image in the puzzle is supposed to be 'about,' one cannot say with certainty."[45]

Another fundamental point of uncertainty is the antiquity of the site itself, both in the relative stages of its construction and its absolute dating. For three decades, the essential model of construction at Chavín de Huántar was articulated by John Rowe and envisioned three construction stages. Rowe's model was based on an examination of the exterior seams in the monumental construction—surfaces where differences in construction techniques, materials, or other architectural treatments mark different phases of construction. Based on the patterns in the exterior seams, Rowe suggested that (1) a U-shaped, east-facing "Old Temple" with lateral mounds to the north and south was followed by (2) the construction of a "New Temple" formed by additions and new buildings stretching east from the Old Temple and (3) final constructions of mounds flanking the large sunken rectangular plaza. This basic three-stage model was also expressed in changes in art styles that Rowe identified. Based on his excavations in domestic zones, Richard Burger suggested that ceramics could be divided into three styles, which he cross-dated using radiocarbon dating: the Urabarriu phase (850–460 BC), the Chakianani phase (460–390 BC), and the Janabarriu phase (390–200 BC). In turn,

Figure 7.17 Chavín-style stirrup-spout bottle

Burger argued that these phases generally correlated with the three phases of construction at Chavín de Huántar.

Several significant implications were derived from these details of construction, ceramics, and chronology. First, the notion of Chavín as the "mother culture" of Andean civilization was disproved because Chavín de Huántar was constructed after the large coastal sites with "Chavin-like" architectural and artifactual styles, such as Sechin Alto and Pampa de las Llamas-Moxeke. Instead of the original source of civilization, Chavín de Huántar was constructed toward the end of the first development of complex societies in the Andes. Second, the occupation and construction at Chavín de Huántar were relatively brief compared with sites like Kotosh and La Galgada that have sequences lasting millennia. In particular, the construction of the New Temple and its additional renovations occurred over a period of less than three centuries. Finally, the radiocarbon dates from Chavín de Huántar suggested that the site's significance—possibly as an oracular shrine and pilgrimage center—increased as the fortunes of large coastal settlements waned.

The phasing and absolute dating of construction at Chavín de Huántar have been questioned by more recent research, as have the implications they suggested. Much of this research has been directed by John Rick and his students. For example, **Sylvia Kembel** conducted extensive research on building seams at Chavín, but instead of only considering the exterior seams, Kembel examined the building seams visible inside the gallerias and other interior spaces of the monumental constructions—in effect, studying how the building was put together from the inside out. Precise measurements with laser transits were the basis for computer-based digital reconstructions of Chavín de Huántar. New seams were discovered and interior spaces were correlated. This research produced the first three-dimensional view of the interior of the monumental construction and resulted in several new insights.

First, the construction sequence was more complex than previously thought, with a minimum of fifteen construction phases rather than three. Second, there was a fundamental change in architectural objectives, with earlier constructions that emphasized large volume with small spaces (such as the tiny chamber in the massive building that holds the Lanzón) to large-space/low-volume constructions (such as the large plazas). Based on this, it is reasonable to suggest a shift in the purposes of the ceremonial architecture, from small select groups of initiates to larger congregations of people. Third, the sequence of construction at Chavín de Huántar and the occupation of the site seem much older than previously thought. Based on her work and then-available radiocarbon dates, Kembel suggested that most of the monumental construction at Chavín de Huántar had been completed by 750 BC and that the monumental center had fallen into decline and disuse between 500 and 400 BC. In a 2009 article, Rick and colleagues presented data from dozens of radiocarbon dates and other chronometric techniques, leading them to conclude: (1) the initial occupation in the vicinity of Chavín de Huántar dates to at least 2200 BC, (2) monumental construction began by 1200 BC, (3) a change in use of the monumental architecture occurred between 800 and 500/400 BC, and (4) use of the monumental constructions ended sometime around 500–400 BC.[46]

The chronological revisions at Chavín de Huántar do not imply that Chavín was, in fact, the "mother culture" of Andean civilizations. Rather, these new data suggest new questions. First, it seems as if the motifs, especially the significance of the felines and supernaturals bearing staffs, draw on a widely distributed Central Andean tradition rather than one that originated at Chavín de Huántar. Second, quite different social and political processes seem to be exemplified at different stages of the site's development. Finally, the decline of early forms of complex societies in the Central Andes—including the abandonment of large ceremonial centers on the coast and in the highlands—requires further attention to the variations and different causes behind these processes.

The Formative in the Titicaca Basin

Over 3,800 m (12,464 ft) above sea level and straddling the boundary between Peru and Bolivia, the Titicaca Basin was home to emerging village societies beginning around 2000 to 1500 BC (see figure 7.2).[47] Preceded by Late Archaic foraging societies, the Early Formative (ca. 2000 to 1000/800 BC) hamlets and small villages, Charles Stanish notes, "were undifferentiated settlements of probably no more than a few dozen households: the sites were small, similar to each other and had little internal variation." Observing that "virtually everywhere that survey and reconnaissance have been conducted within a few km of [Lake Titicaca], a few Early Formative sites have been found," Stanish suggests that "the Early Formative lifeway developed out of the Late Archaic period one around 2000 BC."[48] The Formative period ended circa AD 300–500, as Pukara waned as a regional polity in the northern basin and Tiwanaku in the southern basin emerged as a state-level society, ultimately becoming a dominant political power in the Southern Andes (see chapter 9).[49]

Recent investigations in the southern Titicaca Basin have focused on the development of early village societies on the **Taraco Peninsula**, a 20 km (12 mile)-long spur that juts into the shallower southern shores of Lake Titicaca (figure 7.18).[50]

Unlike other areas of the Titicaca Basin, the Taraco Peninsula did not have a significant Archaic occupation, but that changed dramatically in the Early and Middle Formative period. As **Matthew Bandy** has discussed, the Early Formative settlements on the Taraco Peninsula consisted of relatively small villages, about 3.5 ha (8.6 acres) in size and housing ten families or so.[51] In the Middle Formative, a few villages grew somewhat larger, upward of 5 ha (12.4 acres), with perhaps as many as forty families, although most villages were the same size as those in the Early Formative. Based on survey data, Bandy and colleagues estimate that average population density was approximately seven to eight persons per km^2 (eighteen to twenty-one people per square mile)—significantly denser than other regions surveyed in the Titicaca Basin. Early Formative settlements consisted of small villages and even smaller hamlets.[52] These communities subsisted on a combination of fish and other lake resources, small-scale herding camelids, and limited cultivation of gardens that contained both domesticated quinoa and its wild, weedy relative

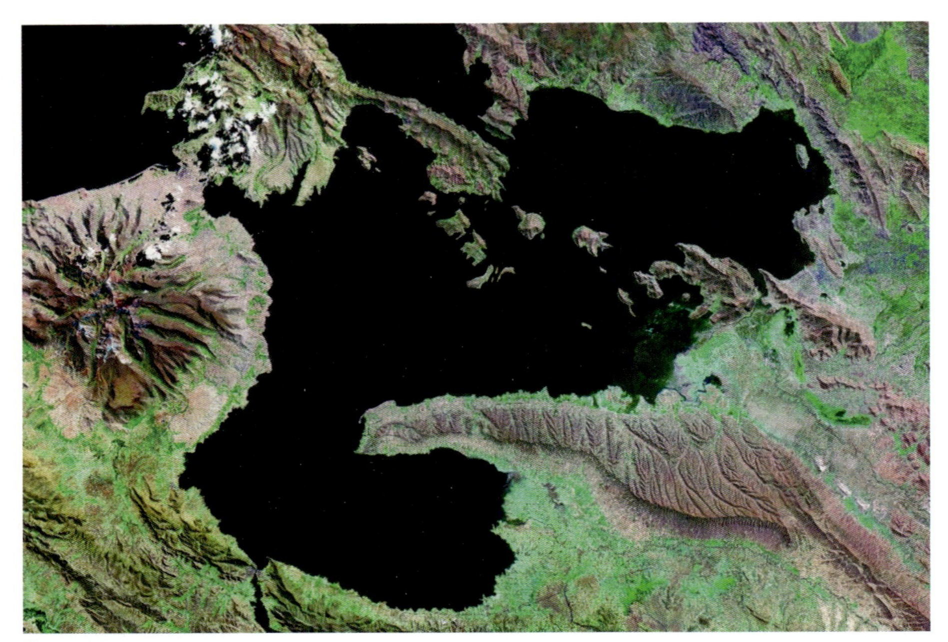

Figure 7.18 Satellite image of the Taraco Peninsula, Lake Titicaca

quinoa negra—both of which were eaten. Only later, during the Middle Formative after 800 BC, is there evidence that Taraco Peninsula farmers became "more meticulous cultivators of quinoa."[53]

The Early Formative villages on the Taraco Peninsula were not stable but apparently grew to a certain size and fissioned.[54] As communities became more populous, conflicts intensified, ultimately erupting in a community's division. There was no absolute threshold for these breakups, and during the Middle Formative communities grew larger and tolerated those conflicts longer as the Taraco Peninsula filled up with people and unoccupied land became scarce. The last example of village fissioning occurred before 800 BC, replaced by other means of addressing community conflicts. By the Middle Formative (ca. 800–300 BC), these new social institutions included the creation of ceremonial centers and new forms of religion.

Chiripa and Huatacoa: Sunken Courts and Stela

One of these centers emerged at the site of **Chiripa**, which had been occupied during the Early Formative and developed into one of the largest communities on the Taraco Peninsula. This emergence was associated with the development of a set of religious practices known as the **Yaya-Mama Religious Tradition**. The Quechua name of this tradition refers to the male (*yaya* = father) and female (*mama* = mother) aspects combined in the depiction of a deity carved into a stone stela. This tradition was initially defined through the research of **Sergio Chávez** and **Karen Mohr Chávez**, who wrote: "The Yaya-Mama Religious Tradition, named after

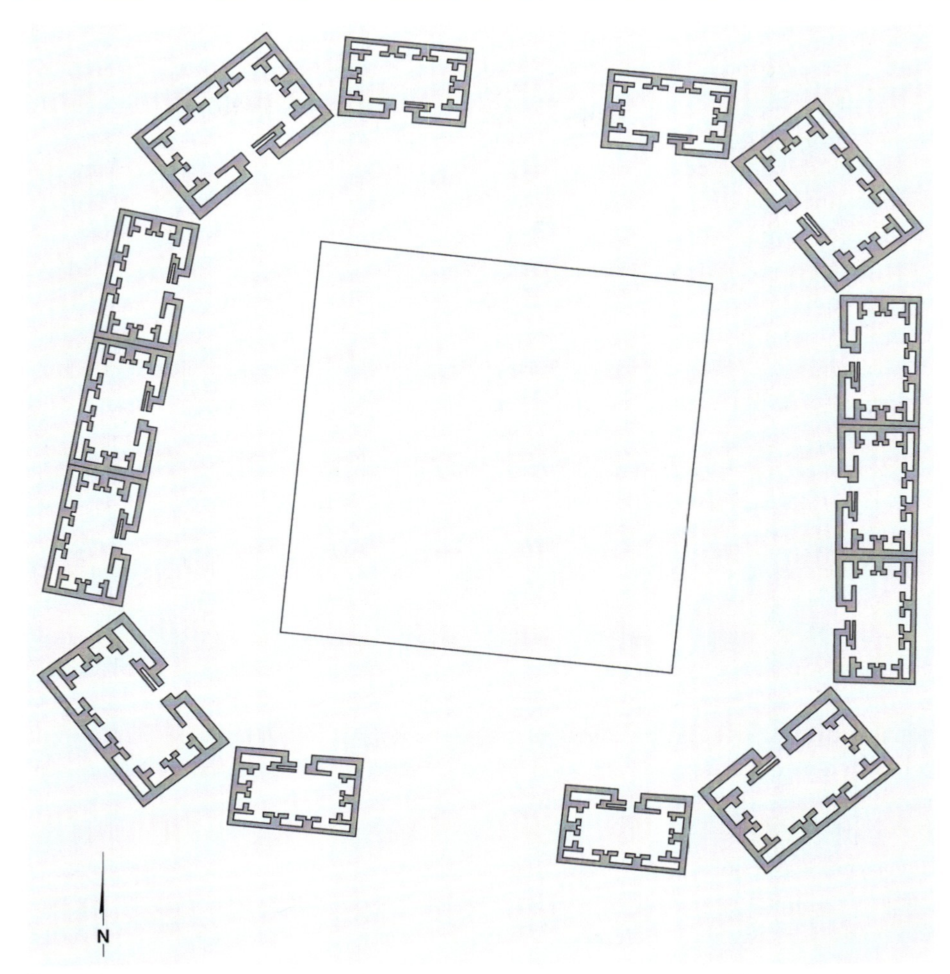

Figure 7.19 Reconstruction of the sunken patio and associated structures at Chiripa, Bolivia

the style of associated stone sculpture, was characterized by: 1) temple-storage centers such as at Chiripa, 2) Yaya-Mama style stone sculpture having supernatural images, associated with the temples, 3) ritual paraphernalia including ceramic trumpets and ceremonial burners, and 4) a supernatural iconography including heads having rayed appendages and vertical divided eyes."[55] This tradition did not emerge as a complete and coherent set of artifacts, motifs, and practices but rather is an amalgamation of elements that emerged or were introduced into the Titicaca Basin at different points in prehistory, coalescing by the Late Formative.[56]

Excavations at Chiripa in the 1930s had documented the presence of sunken courts, 20 m × 30 m (65.5 ft × 98.4 ft) across, surrounded by rectangular adobe and field stone structures and thus forming a rectangular or trapezoidal enclosed complex (figure 7.19). Subsequent research documented the presence of similar sunken court complexes at sites surrounding Lake Titicaca, and excavations exposed their origins.[57] During the Early Formative, two sites were known to have sunken courts: **Huatacoa** on the north side of the basin and Chiripa on the opposite, south side of the basin. In the Middle Formative these features proliferated, as did other forms of nondomestic architecture. These architectural forms marked a shift "from architectural spaces intended for public, open performances to spaces intended for restricted, closed events."[58] In her excavations at Huatacoa, **Amanda Cohen** uncovered a sequence of superposed sunken courts.[59] The earliest layers held an open plaza with a specially prepared yellow clay floor that was then covered by an initial sunken court; these two ceremonial constructions date to 1350 BC. Sometime after 800 BC, these lower levels were covered by an intriguing complex that combined an effigy mound depicting a local deity and a sunken court 85 m^2 (914 ft^2) in area. Another modification took place in which dedicatory offerings of artifacts and human burials were placed on the effigy mound, and the entire mound was covered in yellow clay; the sunken mound continued to be used without significant modifications. The final construction was of a much larger rectangular sunken court, covering 225 m^2 (2,422 ft^2) and creating a distinctive and exclusive space. These transformations of architectural spaces, Cohen argued, reflect increasing formalized ritual spaces and ceremonial activities, harbingers of the Yaya-Mama tradition.

The Yaya-Mama tradition was clearly evident at Chiripa, where the sunken rectangular court was surrounded by special storage buildings that effectively screened the court from casual viewers. Within this segregated space, evidence of ritual activities includes incense braziers, ceramic pan pipes, hallucinogenic snuff tubes, and evidence for feasting. **Christine Hastorf** interprets these developments as reflecting changes in the notions and practices of Formative communities in the southern Titicaca Basin, in which "ceremonial gatherings . . . called upon the ancestors, while uniting the participants. This social glue periodically reformed a communal memory and provided a framework for community cohesion."[60] Further, the participants in these ceremonies were not exclusively residents of Chiripa but included inhabitants of other communities on the Taraco Peninsula.[61] It is intriguing that as the Yaya-Mama Religious Tradition developed, village fissioning ceased, leading Bandy to suggest that this religious tradition created a new modality of community integration.[62] This transformation, however, did not lead to Chiripa's ascendance or domination over the region. Rather, Bandy argues, Chiripa became one of several settlements integrated into a polity that encompassed the Taraco Peninsula, a regional system whose centers shifted between communities and was not exclusively centered at Chiripa.[63] This peninsular political network may have covered 100 km^2 (38.6 square miles) and had 5,000 people. Ultimately, this polity came into rivalry with another emerging political center at Tiwanaku, a settlement that would become ascendant in the Titicaca Basin and the Southern Andes (see chapter 9).

Conclusion

Much remains unknown about the development of complex societies in ancient South America. However, from the cases discussed in this chapter and in chapter

6, two points seem obvious: (1) there was no single place where "civilization" developed, and (2) there are numerous forms of "social complexity."

An emerging—and theoretically challenging—body of archaeological data indicates some of the divergent trajectories that led to social complexity. As Dillehay and colleagues note,

> A growing body of evidence [indicates] that the Early to Middle Holocene period in the Central Andes was a complex mosaic of different economies and social forms . . . Additional research will continue to reveal that the origins of Andean civilization have several interrelated regional roots, each characterized by different social and economic conditions. In our perspective, a critical threshold was crossed when these societies moved beyond the domestic context to include planned sedentary communities and a formalized and structured public life. Not only did these societies establish social complexity and public monuments, but they also initiated important environmental changes such as extensive landscape modification and the domestication and spread of plants and animals that eventually led to the development of early states in the Andes.[64]

Just as this appears true for the Central Andes, similarly diverse and intriguing routes to social complexity were traversed at different times and places across prehistoric South America. Understanding these different trajectories is among the most important and complicated topics explored by archaeologists working in South America.

Notes

1. J. Bird, "Preceramic Cultures in Chicama and Virú," in *A Reappraisal of Peruvian Archaeology*, ed. I. Rouse (Menasha, WI: Memoirs of the Society for American Archaeology 4, 1948), 21–28; J. Bird, J. Hyslop, and D. Skinner, "The Preceramic Excavations at the Huaca Prieta, Chicama Valley, Peru," *Anthropological Papers of the American Museum of Natural History* 62, no. 1 (1985). For a charming home movie of the Bird family working at Huaca Prieta, see "Junius Bird Excavation at Huaca Prieta, Peru, 1946," YouTube video, 6:16, posted by "greenuptime," August 6, 2011, http://www.youtube.com/watch?v=PdMdor74aUU (accessed March 20, 2014).

2. This date has been calibrated using the ShCal 04 calibration program for the Southern Hemisphere; for a discussion of early radiocarbon dating at Huaca Prieta, see Bird, Hyslop, and Skinner, "Preceramic Excavations at the Huaca Prieta," 52–58.

3. T. Dillehay, D. Bonavia, S. Goodbred, M. Pino, V. Vasquez, T. Rosales Tham, W. Conklin, J. Splitstoser, D. Piperno, J. Iriarte, A. Grobman, G. Levi-Lazzaris, D. Moreira, M. Lopéz, T. Tung, A. Titelbaum, J. Verano, J. Adovasio, L. Cummings, P. Bearéz, E. Dufour, O. Tombret, M. Ramirez, R. Beavins, L. DeSantis, I. Rey, P. Mink, G. Maggard, and T. Franco, "Chronology, Mound-Building and Environment at Huaca Prieta, Coastal Peru, from 13,700 to 4000 Years Ago," *Antiquity* 86 (2012): 48–70; A. Grobman, D. Bonavia, T. Dillehay, D. Piperno, J. Iriarte, and I. Holst, "Preceramic Maize from Paredones and Huaca Prieta, Peru," *Proceedings of the National Academy of Sciences* 109, no. 5 (2012): 1755–1759.

4. These early dates fall beyond the current range of calibration curves available for the Southern Hemisphere; all the subsequent dates are calibrated based on the ShCal curve at https://c14.arch.ox.ac.uk/oxcal/OxCal.html.

5. Dillehay et al., "Chronology, Mound-Building and Environment at Huaca Prieta," 65.

6. Grobman et al., "Preceramic Maize from Paredones and Huaca Prieta," 1.

7. For these later consequences, see J. Haas, W. Creamer, L. Huamán Mesía, D. Goldstein, K. Reinhard, and C. Vergel Rodríguez, "Evidence for Maize (Zea mays) in the Late Archaic (3000–1800 B.C.) in the Norte Chico Region of Peru," *Proceedings of the National Academy of Sciences* 110, no. 13 (2013): 4945–4949.

8. R. Benfer, "The Preceramic Period Site of Paloma, Peru: Bioindications of Improving Adaptation to Sedentism," *Latin American Antiquity* 1, no. 4 (1990): 284–318; see also R. Benfer, "Challenges and Rewards of Sedentism: The Preceramic Village of Paloma, Peru," in *Paleoanthropology at the Origins of Agriculture*, ed. M. Cohen and G. Armelagos (New York: Academic Press, 1984), 531–558; J. Quilter, *Life and Death at Paloma: Society and Mortuary Practices in a Preceramic Peruvian Village* (Iowa City: University of Iowa Press, 1989).

9. G. Willey and J. Corbett, *Early Ancón and Supe Culture: Chavin Horizon Sites of the Central Peruvian Coast* (New York: Columbia Studies in Archaeology and Ethnology 3, 1954); M. Moseley and G. Willey, "Aspero, Peru: A Reexamination of the Site and Its Implications," *American Antiquity* 38, no. 4 (1973): 452–468; R. Feldman, "Aspero, Perú: Architecture, Subsistence Economy, and Other Artifacts of a Preceramic Maritime Chiefdom" (PhD diss., Harvard University, Cambridge, MA, 1980); R. Feldman, "Preceramic Corporate Architecture: Evidence for the Development of Non-Egalitarian Social Systems," in *Early Ceremonial Architecture in the Andes*, ed. C. Donnan (Washington, DC: Dumbarton Oaks, 1985), 71–92; R. Feldman, "Architectural Evidence for the Development of Non-egalitarian Social Systems in Coastal Peru," in *The Origins and Development of the Andean State*, ed. J. Haas, S. Pozorski, and T. Pozorski (Cambridge: Cambridge University Press, 1987), 9–14.

10. Mosley and Willey, "Aspero, Peru," 466.

11. T. Pozorski and S. Pozorski, "Huaynuná: A Late Cotton Preceramic Site on the North Coast of Peru," *Journal of Field Archaeology* 17 (1990): 17–26.

12. J. Rick, "Dates as Data: An Examination of the Peruvian Preceramic Radiocarbon Record," *American Antiquity* 52, no. 1 (1987): 55–73.

13. For a discussion of this widespread phenomenon, see J. Bocquet-Appel and O. Bar-Yosef, eds., *The Neolithic Demographic Transition and Its Consequences* (New York: Springer, 2008).

14. J. Haas, W. Creamer, and A. Ruiz, "Dating the Late Archaic Occupation of the Norte Chico Region in Peru," *Nature* 432 (2004): 1020–1023; J. Haas, W. Creamer, and A. Ruiz, "Power and the Emergence of Complex Societies in the Peruvian Preceramic," in *Foundations of Power in the Ancient Andes*, ed. K. Vaughn, D. Ogburn, and C. Conlee (Arlington, VA: American Anthropological Association, 2005), 37–52; J. Haas and W. Creamer, "Crucible of Andean Civilization: The Peruvian Coast from 3000 to 1800 BC," *Current Anthropology* 47, no. 5 (2006): 745–775; J. Haas, W. Creamer, L. Huamán Mesía, D. Goldstein, K. Reinhard, and C. Vergel Rodríguez, "Evidence for Maize

(*Zea mays*) in the Late Archaic (3000–1800 B.C.) in the Norte Chico Region of Peru," *Proceedings of the National Academy of Sciences* 110, no. 3 (2013): 4945–4949.

15. R. Shady Solís, "America's First City? The Case of Late Archaic Caral," in *Andean Archaeology III: North and South*, ed. W. Isbell and H. Silverman (New York: Springer, 2006), 28–66; R. Shady Solís, *La Ciudad Sagrada de Caral-Supe* (Lima: Museo de Arqueología e Antropología, Universidad Nacional Mayor de San Marcos, 1999); R. Shady Solís, J. Haas, and W. Creamer, "Dating Caral, a Pre-ceramic Site in the Supe Valley of the Central Coast of Peru," *Science* 292 (2001): 723–726.

16. Shady Solís, "America's First City?" 60; these dates approximately bracket the construction of the Great Pyramid at Caral.

17. For an introduction to these debates, see the comments and responses in Haas and Creamer, "Crucible of Andean Civilization," 756–769.

18. S. Pozorski and T. Pozorski, "Recent Excavations at Pampa de las Llamas-Moxeke, a Complex Initial Period Site in Peru," *Journal of Field Archaeology* 13 (1986): 381–401; S. Pozorski and T. Pozorski, *Early Settlement and Subsistence in the Casma Valley, Peru* (Iowa City: University of Iowa Press, 1987); S. Pozorski and T. Pozorski, "Early Civilization in the Casma Valley, Peru," *Antiquity* 66 (1992): 845–870; S. Pozorski and T. Pozorski, "La Dinámica del Valle de Casma durante el Periodo Inicial," *Boletin de Arqueología PUCP* 2 (1998): 83–100; S. Pozorski and T. Pozorski, "Temple, Palais ou Entrepot? La Centralisation du Pouvoir dans le Perou Prehistorique," in *La Ville et le Pouvoir en Amérique: Les formes de l'autorité*, ed. J. Monnet (Paris: Edition L'Harmattan, 1999), 87–110; J. C. Tello, *Arqueología del Valle de Casma: Culturas: Chavín, Santa o Huaylas Yunga y Sub-Chimú* (Lima: Universidad Nacional Mayor de San Marcos, 1956).

19. P. Fuchs, R. Patzschke, G. Yenquec, and J. Briceño, "Del Arcaico Tardío al Formativo Temprano: las investigaciones en Sechín Bajo, valle de Casma," *Boletín de Arqueología PUCP* 13 (2009): 55–86.

20. L. Samaniego, E. Vergara, and H. Bischoff, "New Evidence on Cerro Sechín, Casma Valley, Peru," in *Early Ceremonial Architecture in the Andes*, ed. C. Donnan (Washington, DC: Dumbarton Oaks, 1985), 165–208; L. Samaniego, E. Vergara, and H. Bischoff, "Nuevos datos arquimétricos para la historia de ocupación de Cerro Sechín-Periodo Lítico al Formativo," in *Arquitectura y Civilización en los Andes Prehispánicos*, ed. E. Bonnier and H. Bischoff (Mannheim: Reiss-Museum, 1997), 145–161; H. Bischof, "Los periodos Arcaico Tardío, Arcaico Final y Formativo Temprano en el valle de Casma: evidencias e hipótesis," *Boletin de Arqueologia PUCP* 13 (2009): 9–54.

21. Bischof, "Los periodos Arcaico Tardío," 13–14, my translation.

22. Fuchs et al., "Del Arcaico Tardío al Formativo Temprano," 73, my translation.

23. T. Pozorski and S. Pozorski, "Architecture and Chronology at the Site of Sechín Alto, Casma Valley, Peru," *Journal of Field Archaeology* 30, no. 2 (2005): 143–161.

24. Ibid., 159.

25. C. Stanish, "The Origin of State Societies in South America," *Annual Review of Anthropology* 30 (2001): 51.

26. Ibid., 56.

27. For more detailed discussions, consult W. Alva Alva, "Investigaciones en el Complejo Formativo con Arquitectura Monumental de Purulén, Costa Norte, del Perú," *Beiträge zur Allgemeinen und Vergleichenden Archäologie* 8 (1986): 283–300; R.

Burger, "The U-Shaped Pyramid Complex, Cardal, Peru," *National Geographic Research* 3 (1987): 363–375; R. Burger and L. Salazar-Burger, "The Second Season of Investigations at the Initial Period Center of Cardal, Peru," *Journal of Field Archaeology* 18 (1991): 275–296; W. Creamer, A. Ruiz, and J. Haas, "Archaeological Investigation of Late Archaic Sites (3000–1800 B.C.) in the Pativilca Valley, Peru," *Fieldiana Anthropology* 40 (2007): 1–78; J. Haas and W. Creamer, "Crucible of Andean Civilization: The Peruvian Coast from 3000–1800 B.C.," *Current Anthropology* 47, no. 5 (2006): 745–775; K. Makowski, "Andean Urbanism," in *Handbook of South American Archaeology*, ed. H. Silverman and W. Isbell (New York: Springer, 2008), 633–657; S. Pozorski and T. Pozorski, "Early Cultural Complexity on the Coast of Peru," in *Handbook of South American Archaeology*, ed. H. Silverman and W. Isbell (New York: Springer, 2008), 607–631; J. Quilter, "Architecture and Chronology at El Paraíso, Peru," *Journal of Field Archaeology* 12 (1985): 279–297; R. Ravines and W. Isbell, "Garagay: Sitio Ceremonial temprano en el valle de Lima," *Revista del Museo Nacional* 41 (1975): 253–275; M. Tellenbach, *Die Ausgrabungen in der formativzeitlichen Siedlung Montegrande, Jequetepeque-Tal, Nord-Peru = Las excavaciones en el asentamiento formativo de Montegrande, valle de Jequetepeque en el Norte del Perú* (Munchen: C. H. Beck, 1986); C. Williams, "A Scheme for the Early Monumental Architecture of the Central Coast of Perú," in *Early Ceremonial Architecture in the Andes*, ed. C. Donnan (Washington, DC: Dumbarton Oaks, 1985), 227–240.

28. T. Pozorski and S. Pozorski, "Early Complex Society and Ceremonialism on the Peruvian North Coast," *SENRI Ethnological Studies* 37 (1993): 48.

29. R. Burger and L. Salazar-Burger, "Ritual and Religion at Huaricoto," *Archaeology* (November-December 1980): 26–32; R. Burger and L. Salazar-Burger, "The Early Ceremonial Center of Huaricoto," in *Early Ceremonial Architecture in the Andes*, ed. C. Donnan (Washington, DC: Dumbarton Oaks, 1985), 111–138; R. Burger and L. Salazar-Burger, "Early Organizational Diversity in the Peruvian Highlands: Huaricoto and Kotosh," in *Andean Archaeology: Papers in Memory of Clifford Evans*, ed. R. Matos M., S. Turpin, and H. Eling Jr., Monograph of the Institute of Archaeology 27 (Los Angeles: Institute of Archaeology, University of California, 1986), 65–82.

30. T. Grieder and A. Bueno Mendoza, "Ceremonial Architecture at La Galgada," in *Early Ceremonial Architecture in the Andes*, ed. C. Donnan (Washington, DC: Dumbarton Oaks, 1985), 93–110; T. Grieder, A. Bueno Mendoza, C. E. Smith Jr., and R. Malina, *La Galgada, Peru: A Preceramic Culture in Transition* (Austin: University of Texas Press, 1988).

31. T. Pozorski and S. Pozorski, "Huaynuná, a Late Cotton Preceramic Site on the North Coast of Peru," *Journal of Field Archaeology* 17, no. 1 (1990): 17–26; T. Pozorski and S. Pozorski, "Ventilated Hearth Structures in the Casma Valley, Peru," *Latin American Antiquity* 7, no. 4 (1996): 341–353.

32. E. Bonnier, "Arquitectura Preceramica en la Cordillera de los Andes, Piruru frente a la diversidad de los datos," *Anthropologica* 6 (1987): 335–361; E. Bonnier, "Preceramic Architecture in the Andes: The Mito Tradition," in *Archaeologica Peruana 2*, ed. E. Bonnier and H. Bischof (Alemana, Mannheim: Sociedad Arqueologica Peruano, 1997), 120–144; E. Bonnier and C. Rozenberg, "Del santuario al caserío: Acerca de la neolitización en la Cordillera de los Andes Centrales," *Boletín del Instituto Francés de Estudios Andinos* 17, no. 2 (1988): 23–40; M. Montoya V., "Arquitectura en la tradición

'El Mito' en el valle medio de Santa: Sitio El Silencio," *Boletín del Instituto Francés de Estudios Andinos* 36, no. 2 (2007): 199–220.

33. R. Shady and C. Leyva, *La Ciudad Sagrada de Caral-Supe: Los orígenes de la civilización andina y la formación del Estado pristino en el antiguo Perú* (Lima: Instituto Nacional de Cultura, 2003).

34. D. Contreras, "A Mito-Style Structure at Chavín de Huántar: Dating and Implications," *Latin American Antiquity* 21, no. 1 (2010): 1–19.

35. Bonnier, "Preceramic Architecture in the Andes," 125.

36. Y. Onuki, "Las actividades ceremoniales tempranas en la Cuenca del Alto Huallaga y algunos problemas generales," in *El mundo ceremonial andino*, ed. L. Millones and Y. Onuki (Lima: Editorial Horizante, 1993), 83, my translation.

37. Ibid., 92–93, my translation.

38. T. Grieder, A. Bueno Mendoza, C. Smith Jr., and R. Malina, *La Galgada, Peru: A Preceramic Culture in Transition* (Austin: University of Texas, 1988).

39. Ibid., 197.

40. Ibid., 212.

41. A very large literature discusses Chavín; a partial listing of sources includes W. Bennett, *The North Highlands of Peru: Excavations in the Callejón de Huaylas and at Chavín de Huántar,* Anthropological Papers, vol. 39, part 1 (New York: American Museum of Natural History, 1944); E. Benson, ed., *Dumbarton Oaks Conference on Chavín* (Washington, DC: Dumbarton Oaks, 1971); R. Burger, "The Radiocarbon Evidence for the Temporal Priority of Chavín de Huántar," *American Antiquity* 48 (1981): 592–602; R. Burger, *The Prehistoric Occupation of Chavín de Huántar, Peru,* University of California Publications in Anthropology 14 (Berkeley: University of California Press, 1984); R. Burger, "Concluding Remarks: Early Peruvian Civilization and Its Relation to the Chavín Horizon," in *Early Ceremonial Architecture in the Andes*, ed. C. B. Donnan (Washington, DC: Dumbarton Oaks, 1985), 269–289; R. Burger, "Unity and Heterogeneity within the Chavín Horizon," in *Peruvian Prehistory*, ed. R. Keatinge (Cambridge: Cambridge University Press, 1988), 99–144; R. Burger, *Chavín and the Origins of Andean Civilization* (London: Thames and Hudson, 1992); R. Burger, "The Chavín Horizon: Stylistic Chimera or Socioeconomic Metamorphosis?" in *Latin American Horizons*, ed. D. S. Rice (Washington, DC: Dumbarton Oaks, 1993), 41–82; R. Burger, "Chavín de Huántar and Its Sphere of Influence," in *Handbook of South American Archaeology*, ed. H. Silverman and W. Isbell (New York: Springer, 2008), 681–703; S. Kembel, "Architectural Sequence and Chronology at Chavin de Huantar" (PhD diss., Stanford University, 2001); S. Kembel, "The Architecture of the Monumental Center of Chavín de Huántar: Sequence, Transformation, and Chronology," in *Chavin: Art, Architecture, and Culture*, ed. W. Conklin and J. Quilter (Los Angeles: Cotsen Institute of Archaeology, University of California, 2008), 35–81; S. Kembel and J. Rick, "Building Authority at Chavin de Huantar: Models of Social Organization and Developments in the Initial Period and Early Horizon," in *Andean Archaeology*, ed. H. Silverman (Malden, MA: Blackwell, 2004), 51–76; L. Lumbreras, "Towards a Re-evaluation of Chavín," in *Dumbarton Oaks Conference on Chavín*, ed. E. Benson (Washington, DC: Dumbarton Oaks, 1971), 1–28; L. Lumbreras, *The Peoples and Cultures of Ancient Peru* (Washington, DC: Smithsonian Institution Press, 1974); L. Lumbreras, "Excavaciones en el templo antiquo de Chavín

(sector R): informe de la sexta Campaña," *Ñawpa Pacha* 15 (1977): 1–38; L. Lumbreras, *Chavín de Huántar en el Nacimiento de la Civilización Andina* (Lima: Instituto Andino de Estudios Arqueológicos, 1989); L. Lumbreras, *Chavín: Excavaciones Arqueológicas* (two volumes) (Lima: Universidad Alas Peruanas, 2007); W. Conklin and J. Quilter, eds., *Chavin: Art, Architecture and Culture* (Los Angeles: Cotsen Institute of Archaeology, University of California, 2008); J. Rick, "The Evolution of Authority and Power at Chavín de Huántar, Perú," in *Foundations of Power in the Prehispanic Andes*, ed. K. J. Vaughn, D. E. Ogburn, and C. A. Conlee, Archaeological Papers of the American Anthropological Association 14 (Arlington, VA: American Anthropological Association, 2005), 71–89; J. Rick, "Context, Construction, and Ritual in the Development of Authority at Chavín de Huántar," in *Chavín: Art, Architecture and Culture*, ed. W. Conklin and J. Quilter, Monograph 61 (Los Angeles: Cotsen Institute of Archaeology, University of California, 2008), 3–34; J. Rick, C. Mesia, D. Contreras, S. Kimbel, R. Rick, M. Sayre, and J. Wolf, "La cronología de Chavín de Huántar y sus implicancias para el Periodo Formativo," *Boletin de Arqueologia PUCP* 13 (2009): 87–132; J. Rowe, *Chavín Art: An Inquiry into Its Form and Meaning* (New York: Museum of Primitive Art, 1962); J. Rowe, "Form and Meaning in Chavín Art," in *Peruvian Archaeology: Selected Readings*, ed. J. Rowe and D. Menzel (Palo Alto: Peek Publications, 1967), 72–103; M. Sayre, "Life across the River: Agricultural, Ritual, and Production Practices at Chavín de Huántar, Perú" (PhD diss., University of California, Berkeley, 2010); J. Tello, "Discovery of the Chavín Culture in Peru," *American Antiquity* 9, no. 1 (1943): 135–160.

42. Tello, "Discovery of the Chavín Culture in Peru," 154.

43. One of the basic chronologies used in Peruvian archaeology, the Rowe-Menzel chronology consisted of these stages: Paleoindian, Preceramic, Initial Period, Early Horizon, Early Intermediate Period, Middle Horizon, Late Intermediate Period, and Late Horizon.

44. Burger, "Chavín de Huántar and Its Sphere of Influence," 683.

45. G. Urton, "The Body of Meaning in Chavin Art," in *Chavin: Art, Architecture and Culture*, ed. J. Quilter and W. Conklin (Los Angeles: Cotsen Institute of Archaeology, 2008), 215–216.

46. J. Rick et al., "La cronología de Chavín de Huántar."

47. For slightly divergent chronologies, see C. Hastorf, "The Formative Period in the Titicaca Basin," in *Handbook of South American Archaeology*, ed. H. Silverman and W. Isbell (New York: Springer, 2008), 545–561; C. Stanish, *Ancient Titicaca: The Evolution of Complex Society in Southern Peru and Northern Bolivia* (Berkeley: University of California Press, 2003).

48. Stanish, *Ancient Titicaca*, 100–101.

49. C. Stanish and A. Levine, "War and Early State Formation in the Northern Titicaca Basin, Peru," *Proceedings of the National Academy of Sciences* 108, no. 34 (August 23, 2011): 13901–13906.

50. The Taraco Archaeological Project was directed by Christine Hastorf and Matthew Bandy.

51. M. Bandy, "Early Village Society in the Formative Period in the Southern Lake Titicaca Basin," in *Andean Archaeology III: North and South*, ed. W. Isbell and H. Silverman (New York: Springer, 2006), 210–236.

52. Stanish, *Ancient Titicaca*, 123–125.

53. M. Bruno and W. Whitehead, "Chenopodium Cultivation and Formative Period Agriculture at Chiripa, Bolivia," *Latin American Antiquity* 14, no. 3 (2003): 339.

54. M. Bandy, "Fissioning, Scalar Stress, and Social Evolution in Early Village Societies," *American Anthropologist* 106, no. 2 (2004): 322–333.

55. K. Mohr Chávez, "The Significance of Chiripa in Late Titicaca Basin Developments," *Expedition* 30, no. 3 (1989): 17–26. See also S. Chávez and K. Mohr Chávez, "A Carved Stela from Taraco, Puno, Peru, and the Definition of an Early Style of Stone Sculpture from the Altiplano of Peru and Bolivia," *Ñawpa Pacha* 13 (1975): 45–84.

56. A. Roddick and C. Hastorf, "Tradition Brought to the Surface: Continuity, Innovation, and Change in the Late Formative Period, Taraco Peninsula, Bolivia," *Cambridge Archaeological Journal* 20 (2010): 157–178.

57. See, for example, M. Bandy, C. Hastorf, L. Steadman, K. Moore, M. Elgar, W. Whitehead, J. L. Paz, A. Cohen, M. Bruno, A. Roddick, K. Frye, M. Soledad Fernandez, J. Capriles Flores, and M. Leighton, *Taraco Archaeological Project Report on 2003 Excavations at Kala Uyuni* (Berkeley: University of California Archaeological Research Facility, 2004).

58. R. Beck, "Platforms of Power: House, Community, and Social Change in the Formative Lake Titicaca Basin (Bolivia)" (PhD diss., Northwestern University, Evanston, IL, 2004), 340. See also R. Beck, "Architecture and Polity in the Formative Lake Titicaca Basin, Bolivia," *Latin American Antiquity* 15, no. 3 (2004): 323–343.

59. A. Cohen, "Ritualization in Early Village Society: The Case of the Lake Titicaca Basin Formative," in *Becoming Villagers: Comparing Early Village Societies*, ed. M. Bandy and J. Fox (Tucson: University of Arizona Press, 2010), 81–99. See also A. Cohen, "Ritual and Architecture in the Titicaca Basin: The Development of the Sunken Court Complex in the Formative Period" (PhD diss., University of California, Los Angeles, 2010).

60. C. Hastorf, "Sea Changes in Stable Communities: What Do Small Changes in Practices at Çatalhöyük and Chiripa Imply about Community Making," in *Becoming Villagers: Comparing Early Village Societies*, ed. M. Bandy and J. Fox (Tucson: University of Arizona Press, 2010), 156.

61. C. Hastorf, "Community with the Ancestors: Ceremonies and Social Memory in the Middle Formative at Chiripa, Bolivia," *Journal of Anthropological Archaeology* 22 (2003): 327.

62. Bandy, "Fissioning, Scalar Stress, and Social Evolution," 330.

63. Ibid., 229–232. Cf. Stanish, *Ancient Titicaca*, 115–117.

64. Dillehay et al., "Chronology, Mound-Building and Environment at Huaca Prieta," 68–69.

Figure 8.1 *Inhabitants of Tierra del Fuego*, illustration from Captain James Cook's first voyage, 1768–1771

Regional Florescences

10.5876_9781607323334.c008

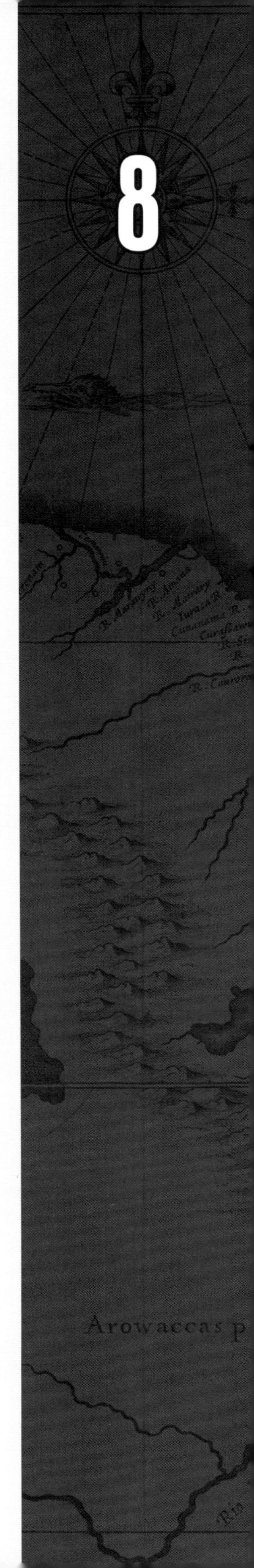

> We entered a port to pass the winter, and remained there two whole months without ever seeing anybody. However, one day, without anyone expecting it, we saw a giant, who was on the shore of the sea, quite naked, and was dancing and leaping and singing, and whilst singing he put the sand and dust on his head . . .He was so tall that the tallest of us only came up to his waist . . . He had a large face, painted red all round, and his eyes were also painted yellow around them, and he had two hearts painted on his cheeks; he had but little hair, and it was painted white.
>
> *Antonio Piagafetta, 1519, encounter with a Patagonian*

As noted repeatedly, the prehistory of South America is characterized by diversity, and that continued to be the case even after the development of sedentism and agricultural economies. There is a tendency to view South American prehistory as if the development of agrarian states and empires was inevitable and universal. Nothing could be further from the truth: a broad array of small-scale societies based on hunting and gathering, gardening, or shifting agriculture existed over much of the continent when Europeans arrived. Many of those societies had developed remarkably enduring cultures.

It is also sometimes assumed that because South America was one of the regions where cities developed independently in world prehistory, the emergence of urbanism became the dominant and successful lifestyle. False again; urbanism—although it developed very early along the coast of Peru (ca. 3000–2000 BC; see chapter 7)—proved a very fragile accomplishment. Rather than the case of "the city triumphant," current data indicate that urbanism in prehispanic South America was limited to the Central Andes and appears to have arisen, collapsed, and been reinvented on multiple occasions (see chapter 9). Nor was the restricted extent of urbanism the simple product of environmental limits. While stark regions in South America—such as the cold, windswept fjords of Tierra del Fuego—were not promising locales for the emergence of prehispanic cities, other regions—such as the Paraná–la Plata Delta and the temperate highland valleys of Ecuador and Colombia—pose no obvious limits on permanent residence, settlement size, or social complexity. Understanding these different developments requires looking at individual cases and cultural trajectories.

This chapter discusses some of these variations among prehistoric South American societies, with a broad temporal focus of approximately 200 BC to AD 1000 (figure 8.2).

Figure 8.2 Locations of sites and regions discussed in this chapter

These chronological limits are intentionally loose, providing more of a temporal target than firmly dated beginnings and ends. The archaeological cases discussed were chosen to include often overlooked examples. What follows is a brief tour of the continent, spanning from the southernmost tip of Tierra del Fuego to the northernmost tropical zones of South America, and ranging from highly mobile and sedentary hunters and gatherers to examples of agrarian and non-agrarian chiefdoms, each of which flourished in a particular region.

A final note: although the different cultural patterns discussed in this chapter were "regional" in scope, this does not imply that they were backward. If a culture's artistic production is one measure of its achievement, then societies like Majaoara and the Nasca created some of the most sophisticated objects made in all of human history. If the ability to muster human labor to create public works is an indirect measure of social achievement, then the vast causeways of the Venezuelan llanos, the aquaculture networks of Marajó, and the mysterious lines of Nazca are constructed testaments of ancient achievement. Finally, if the ability of societies to endure and thrive is an index of the human spirit, then we see the archaeological evidence of that human spirit across the length of South America, from the Orinoco to Cape Horn.

Patagonia: Hunting-and-Gathering Variability in the Uttermost Part of the Earth

In Patagonia, temperature and precipitation limit agriculture, and hunting and gathering were the major subsistence pursuits from the Pleistocene until the late nineteenth and early twentieth centuries. Covering more than 1 million km^2 (386,000 square miles), the rugged Andean cordillera fractures into a convoluted coastline of fjords and channels (figure 8.3).

Extensive ice fields and glaciers of the cordillera give way to Patagonian steppes in the east. Climate is structured by two different gradients: a decrease in rainfall from west to east and a decline in temperature from northeast to southwest. Although sheep were introduced in the late nineteenth century and the northernmost zones of Patagonia have wheat farms, hunting and gathering was the major economic system throughout prehistory.[1]

This does not mean the hunting-and-gathering adaptations were static or that foraging adaptations across Fuego-Patagonia were identical. As **Juan Barceló** and colleagues have discussed, it has been suggested that groups living in Fuego-Patagonia were exemplars of a subantarctic or **southern circumpolar adaptation** shared with groups living in Tasmania, southern New Zealand, and elsewhere.[2] This model holds that the preindustrial occupants of frigid archipelagos and icy waters were limited by similar environmental factors, and the food supply was limited by factors beyond human control. Terrestrial resources were scarce, so people sought coastal resources such as shellfish, marine birds, fish, and occasionally fur seals—resources that could be easily and reliably obtained from many places along the coast, offering little opportunity for intensification and scant reason for storage and accumulation. Not only did this result in a limited subsistence technology, but human populations were sparse, dispersed, and mobile. The natural environment, this hypothesis posits, selected against wealth accumulation, the creation of social differences, and conflict or warfare. An environment in which coastal resources were widespread, available, and not densely concentrated selected for small egalitarian bands that foraged along the coast, forgoing warfare and social

Figure 8.3 (*overleaf*) Coastal environments along Beagle Channel

complexity and exploiting the cold shores with a basic and unchanging "conservative" material culture.

Not surprisingly, this model is incomplete, overlooking the variations within Fuego-Patagonia and other subantarctic regions. In fact, different regions in southernmost South America have distinct environmental zones adapted to with different hunting-and-gathering strategies throughout prehistory. Having occupied Patagonia since the Early Holocene (see chapter 3), humans adapted to the varying climatic regimes by the Late Holocene after 4,500 years ago until the arrival of Europeans in the sixteenth century. In the sixteenth century, the indigenous nations of Patagonia included the **Mecharnuekenk** of central Patagonia; the **Aónikenk** (Southern Tehuelche) of southern Patagonia; the **Selk'nam** (Ona) and **Haush** (Mannekenk), who respectively occupied the northern and southern parts of Tierra del Fuego; the **Yámana** (Yahgan), who lived on the islands and coasts of southern Tierra del Fuego; and the **Kawésar** (Alakaluf) and **Chonos**, who occupied the southern and northern Pacific Coasts of Patagonia.[3] These ethnic groups are sometimes referred to as the "canoe Indians" (Yámana, Kawésar, and Chonos) versus the "foot Indians" (Mecharnuekenk, Aónikenk, Selk'nam, and Haush), which still fails to capture the cultural variations at contact or the differences among late prehistoric populations.

In discussing the archaeological record of historic adaptations in Tierra del Fuego, **Maria Estela Mansur** and **Raquel Piqué** have written:

> When the first European settlers established themselves in Tierra del Fuego, the island was inhabited by hunter-gatherer societies that had developed two different strategies for resource exploitation. One was specialized in littoral and marine resources, whereas the other relied principally on the exploitation of the hinterland but with complementary use of the Atlantic littoral. The former . . . comprised two main groups: the Yámana, who lived on the southern coasts, including Beagle Channel and the islands and islets stretching towards the south, and the Kawesqar, who occupied the islands and coasts of the western sector of the Magellan Strait. In order to exploit maritime resources they had developed an elaborate technology including harpoons, canoes, and other navigation and sea-hunting equipment. Subsistence was based on hunting the two most common types of pinnipeds (*Arctocephalus australis* and *Otaria lavescens*), but they complemented their diet by collecting mussels and other shellfish, catching fish and birds, collecting eggs, mushrooms, and berries, and occasionally hunting guanaco (*Lama guanicoe*) or exploiting accidentally beached whales. Families formed relatively independent units that periodically moved, sailing by canoe along the coasts. This strategy was highly dependent on the exploitation of forest resources, as most of the technology required the availability of wood for the manufacture of canoes, long harpoon shafts, etc. Archaeological investigations have revealed that this strategy already existed along the Beagle Channel coasts at least 6,000 years ago . . .
>
> The second strategy corresponds to two groups who occupied most of the territory of the island: the Selknam and the Haush. They had developed gener-

Figure 8.4 Sea lions on Beagle Channel

alized strategies combining terrestrial mammal and bird hunting, collection of a wide variety of terrestrial and littoral resources, fishing, etc. The central and northern regions were the territory of the Selknam, while the Haush occupied the easternmost part of the island.[4]

Within these broad patterns, further variations are indicated by the archaeological record. First, there seems to have been a significant increase in archaeological sites during the Late Holocene, marking a growth in human populations in late prehistory.[5] Faunal data from sites on the islands and shores of the southern and western coasts of Patagonia indicate that marine resources made up as much as 55 percent to 95 percent of the diet (figure 8.4).[6]

Within a 50 to 90 km (30–54 mile)-wide zone into the interior, diet was based on a mix of terrestrial and marine resources. Further inland, guanaco hunting was a principal pursuit, although more complex than once thought. For example, staple isotope analysis of human skeletons of thirty-two individuals dating from 2600 to 300 cal BP, recovered from sites in the Lago Salitroso region of central Patagonia, suggests that the expected reliance on guanaco was supplemented with plants but also with occasional consumption of marine resources. This finding is remarkable since the Lago Salitroso region is more than 330 km (198 miles) from the Atlantic and 210 km (130 miles)—*and on the other side of the Andes*—from the Pacific Ocean. **Augusto Tessone** and colleagues note cautiously that "it is possible to propose that marine resources were incorporated into the diet in small proportions by the end of the Late Holocene, obtained either directly or through exchange. This implies that at the more recent phases of this period the range of mobility may have included the Atlantic and/or Pacific Coasts although intermittently."[7] Another indicator of mobility and interaction is the presence of obsidian at sites in Tierra del

Fuego that came from the Pampa del Asador source located 600 km (360 miles) north of the Straits of Magellan.[8]

A study of stable isotopes from late prehistoric (1500–500 BP) skeletal materials indicates that the basic differences in subsistence practices of interior and coastal groups, as documented for historic groups, also characterized the recent past, although with some changes.[9] For example, some pre-contact Yámana groups may have relied more on guanaco and other game than exclusively collecting shellfish, as the historic accounts suggest. The extermination of guanaco and other game by ranchers in Patagonia may have reduced the post-contact Yámana to a diet of marine resources.

Another source of variation was contact between Patagonian societies and populations to the north and west. **Francisco Mena** has noted that in the archaeological record after 1000 BP, there were "pronounced cultural differentiation and interesting cultural changes," in part as a result of contact between groups in northern Patagonia with populations in the Andes and the pampas.[10] For example, ceramics appeared in central Patagonia after about 1200 BP, probably as a result of contact with groups living in the Rio de la Plata hinterland. These relatively crude and extremely rare ceramics did not replace the more traditional containers used by mobile hunters and gatherers, such as baskets and armadillo shells, and the ceramics may have been used as ceremonial or prestige items or been made locally and used as utilitarian cooking items.

Ceramics also suggest another axis of interaction between the peoples of Patagonia and the Mapuche of Chile. Some of the earliest pottery appeared on the eastern cordillera of northern Patagonia by the eleventh century, although the Mapuche made greater inroads after the seventeenth century, essentially absorbing the hunting-and-gathering groups (see chapter 12).[11] Intriguingly, some of these ceramics incorporate geometric motifs also seen at rock art sites in Patagonia. These motifs are widely found from northern to south-central Patagonia, appearing also on ceremonial stone axes and on ceremonial guanaco-hide cloaks made by the northern Tehuelche (Gununa'Kena). Mena observes that the broad distribution of such motifs and their appearance in diverse media "reflects the great mobility of historic hunters in Patagonia, including the massive displacement of populations and frequent long-term incursions."[12] Such widespread cultural traits indicate that even relatively small hunting-and-gathering bands did not exist in isolation but may have had contacts that extended over hundreds of miles in this, the "uttermost part of the earth."[13]

Despite such evidence for variations across time and space in Patagonian prehistory, artifact assemblages from specific regions show some striking continuities. For example, excavations directed by **Ernesto Piana** and **Luis Orquera** at **Túnel I** uncovered a series of base camps that span from 6680 ± 210 to 450 ± 60 BP (see figure 8.2).[14] The site is on a steep, rocky shore on the northern coast of the Beagle Channel. It was used repeatedly as a base camp where stone tools were made and maintained, hides and bones were worked, and a variety of game was consumed: fur seals, sea lions, small cetaceans, large whales, guanacos, cormorants, penguins, sardines, and huge quantities of shellfish. These animals were killed and butchered with various tools—bone harpoons, awls, flaked stone scrapers, and projectile points—many of which appear in the earliest strata and were still used thousands of years later. At Túnel I and other sites dating between circa AD 600 and 1700, the most significant technological innovation was the adoption of the bow and arrow, as indicated by the appearance of relatively small projectile points. Except for this innovation, the artifact assemblage and the faunal remains point to a remarkably stable adaptation.

Although there were variations in the specific artifacts and changes in the relative importance of game species (and in the cuts of meat that were used), Piana and Orquera write that the overall pattern of "the littoral adaptation in the Beagle Channel region may be characterized as generically stable,"[15] the result of several intersecting factors:

> (1) The very oceanic environment, with the abundance and even distribution of the resources, privileged simple means of resource exploitation over the complex ones. (2) There were no major environmental changes over the period under discussion [i.e., after ca. 6500 BP]. (3) The geographical location (between sea and mountains) limited the possibilities of pressure from neighboring groups. (4) The relationships between the Fuegian sea-nomads and their staples were sustainable. The sex and age composition of the hunted pinnipeds . . . suggests that the Beagle Channel inhabitants benefited by a constantly renewed influx of sea mammals born in locations beyond human reach and fed into the highly productive waters that surround the southernmost tip of South America. The hunting pressure exercised mainly on pre-reproductive males and the few captures of females practically eliminated the risk of overexploitation. Something comparable occurred with guanacos and mussels.[16]

Yet, this extraordinarily stable adaptation contained a single flaw: the need for the Yámana to acquire fat. Given the harsh environment and their rigorous lives, the inhabitants of Beagle Channel consumed large quantities of fat to meet their bodies' high metabolic requirements. That essential fat came from eating seals and other pinnipeds. In the late 1800s, western sealers discovered the pinniped breeding colonies and hunted the animals to near extinction. With that vital food supply gone, the Yámana were forced to shift to shellfish and fish that contained less fat, and this less nourishing diet contributed to the elimination of their way of life after more than seven millennia of success.

From the Pampas to the Paraná—Diversification and Intensification

The pampas are part of vast grasslands that extend from southern Brazil across Uruguay and into the northern half of Argentina, covering approximately 700,000 km^2 (270,200 square miles).[17] Bordered by the woodlands of the Uruguayan and Brazilian boreal forests to the north[18] and various xerophytic forests to the west and south, the pampas are divided into the western "dry" pampas and the eastern "wet" pampas. The wet pampas are created by the floods and flow of the Paraná and Uruguay Rivers, which empty into the Atlantic by way of the Rio de la Plata—

Figure 8.5 Lower Paraná delta, Argentina

forming a large delta of lagoons and wetlands exploited by Late Holocene hunters and gatherers, as well as by earlier populations (see chapter 6.) (figure 8.5)

Across this environmental gradient, humans adopted different subsistence strategies, whose collective success is indicated by an increase in the overall number of archaeological sites during the Late Holocene.[19] This was accompanied by two fundamental trends: diversification and intensification. Prehistoric occupants of the pampas deployed a greater range of food-collecting strategies. For example, the groups living near the deltas of the Paraná–la Plata and other rivers exploited a range of pampaean and estuarine resources.[20]

Shellfish—the freshwater pearly mussel (*Diplodon*)—and fish, especially various species of catfish, were reliable year-round resources, collected by men and women using hooks, harpoons, or nets. For example, the granulated catfish (*Pterodoras granulosus*) can weigh nearly 9 kg (20 pounds). It is estimated that during the summer months, there may be more than eighty-five fish in a cubic meter of lake.[21] The nutria (*Myocastor coypus*) is a semi-aquatic, herbivorous rodent that lives in swamps throughout the Americas, including in the US Gulf Coast (figure 8.6). Weighing up to 9 kg (20 pounds), nutria live in dense colonies and can be trapped or hunted. The wild Brazilian guinea pig (*Cavia aperea*) is a small (1 kg) rodent widely found and easily caught. In short, hunters and gatherers who lived in the estuaries had a variety of game animals—mussels, catfish, nutria, and guinea pigs—that were abundant and easily obtained, a risk-reducing strategy (figure 8.6).

Figure 8.6 Brazilian nutria (*Myocastor coypus*)

Gustavo Martinez and **Quentin Mackie** observe, "Places in the landscape associated with riverine and lagoon environments became the location of residential, multi-purpose and long-lasting settlements, frequently used and re-used through time. These changes were part of an increasing process of cultural complexity that included intensification."[22]

This increased hunting of small game during the Late Holocene has been interpreted as evidence of intensification, a trend not limited to delta regions and estuaries. In summarizing their study of changing settlement and subsistence practices at sites in the low hills of the Sierra del Tandil in the wet pampas south of the Paraná-Plata delta, where hunters increasingly caught guinea pigs and large lizards, **Carlos Adrián Quintana** and colleagues write:

> The function of base camps can be inferred based on numerous and diverse lines of evidence: decorated ceramics (that appear for the first time in the local archaeological record), mineral pigments, bone and shell artifacts, lithic objects (in particular, small triangular stemmed projectile points), [and the use of] local lithic materials (quartzite, quartz, and chert) and . . . a stone exotic to the region (obsidian). These trends in subsistence strategies characterized by intensification and diversification in the use of small [game] species are accompanied by technological innovations that exhibit changes in the ways of life of late [prehistoric] indigenous societies, which suggest less mobile settlement systems and increases in demographic growth comparable to the process that in Europe and the Near East is called "**broad spectrum revolution**."[23]

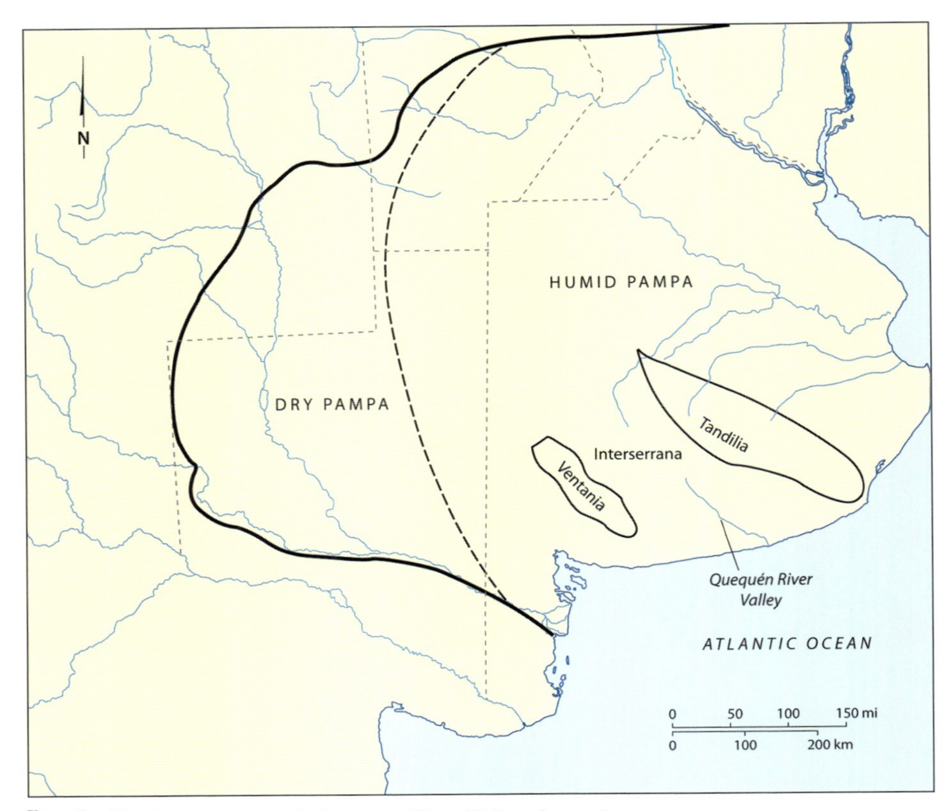

Figure 8.7 The Interserrana and Quequén River Valley, Argentina

This process appears to have begun approximately 3,000 years ago. **Gustavo Politis** and colleagues report on the presence of ceramics from the site of **Zanjon Seco 2**, located in the Interserrana region of the dry pampas (figure 8.7), where pottery has been recovered from layers dating to 3070 BP ± 40 and 3080 BP ± 40—dates that calibrate to approximately 1400–1150 BC. Although only a few potsherds were recovered from the Zanjon Seco sites, the ceramics were from open bowls that were smoothed and burnished before being decorated with incisions, punctations, and zigzag lines. These pottery motifs occur at other sites in adjacent regions of the pampas and northern Patagonia; it is possible that ceramics first appeared in the southeastern pampas and in northern and northeastern Uruguay between 3000 and 2500 BP, spread to the northeastern pampas and the littoral zone of the Rio de la Plata at approximately 1700–1500 BP, and finally appeared in northernmost Patagonia between 1500 and 1200 BP. These dates might suggest the gradual diffusion of ceramic technology across the Southern Cone, and the presence of ceramics is paralleled by other changes that suggest a process of intensification among the hunters and gatherers of the pampas.

One indication of intensification is the increasing importance of plant resources, indicated by a marked increase in mortars and other milling tools seen at archaeological sites across the pampas. Similarly, the study of stable isotopes indicates that while deer and guanaco were principal game animals for hunters and gatherers of the pampas, small game such as armadillo and freshwater and marine fish became more important in the Late Holocene.[24] Further, some foraging groups regularly migrated between interior and coastal zones, incorporating marine resources into their diet as part of a planned and scheduled annual cycle.

Martinez and Mackie discuss another interesting form of "intensification" for the Interserrana zone of the pampas along the Quequén River Valley. They document not only a dramatic increase in the use of mortars but also an intriguing strategy in which supplies of raw lithic materials were stockpiled across the otherwise stone-less pampa. Different types of stone were transported significant distances—50 km to 70 km (30–42 miles)—from their sources in the hills flanking the Interserrana and cached at various locations, a strategy that made "a heterogeneous lithic resource environment more homogeneous: a system of artificial quarries was established by the placement of large numbers of large cores across the landscape."[25] In this sense, the hunters and gatherers constructed the landscape, another form of intensification.

Intensification involves more than small game, plant resources, or caches of stone, however; it also reflects and reinforces changes in social relations. As Politis and colleagues write: "The increase in innovations and/or the acquisition of technologies, as in the case of ceramics, are not explicable exclusively in terms of factors solely linked to changes in economy and subsistence; their introduction and assimilation within specific cultural contexts depends on the social and historical characteristics of such contexts, where the retention or incorporation of traits are, in part, socially mediated. From this point of view, in the Pampean region, the process of intensification was the product of a minimum of three aspects: the use of specific spaces, production, and social relations."[26]

Although the archaeological data pointing to intensification of the use of spaces and in production (particularly subsistence and craft production) are relatively straightforward, the evidence for changes in social relations is somewhat indirect.

In the upper delta of the Paraná—a zone on the northeastern periphery of the humid pampas—Politis and colleagues recently described their research into late prehispanic mounds in the **Los Tres Cerros** locality, discussing it as an anthropogenic landscape. Excavation trenches across the mounds exposed not a geological sequence but a series of artificial remodelings as the mounds were built up from repeated occupations and intentional mounding. Radiocarbon dates point to initial occupation around AD 1100, with an increase in population between AD 1280 and 1400. The pottery—unpainted wares decorated with incisions and occasionally molded into zoomorphic forms—is associated with the **Goya-Malabrigo** pottery assemblage in which surface treatments, vessel forms, and manufacturing techniques were combined in "an intricate mix of inventions, borrowed elements, and manipulations that display an amazing propensity to redefinition by individual and local groups."[27] Despite such redefinitions, the Goya-Malabrigo ceramics were distinct from **Tupi-Guarani ceramics** found in adjacent regions of the Paraná delta and northeastern pampas, a point returned to later.

The mounds in the Upper Paraná delta suggest alternate hypotheses regarding forms of socio-political organization at different scales. Looking at a specific site, the mounds' existence may imply "some sort of consolidated leadership able to organize the communal work," although ethnographic cases of mound building conversely suggest that "the mounds are built through the cooperation of the extended family group," and "the building of earthen mounds can be performed by societies without any marked hierarchical divisions, in which the organization of the collective building process is based on interlacing social relationships."[28] At the regional scale of analysis, while most mounds are either isolated or perched on natural landforms above seasonal floodwaters, some sites—such as the Los Tres Cerros locality—have clusters of mounds, a different kind of settlement reflecting other social or political factors. Politis and colleagues suggest "the hypothesis that in the Paraná Delta . . . differences, a hierarchy of settlements may have existed that could be a reflection of social distinctions of some sort (i.e., a ranked society)."[29]

Finally, these recent archaeological investigations across the pampas regions indicate that by AD 1000–1200, some of the ethnic and cultural diversity described by Europeans in the sixteenth and seventeenth centuries already existed. "Ethnohistorical sources show the Delta as a heterogeneous area of multiethnic confluence, with a marked population turnover," Politis and colleagues write, and this seems to have been broadly true five centuries before contact.[30] The Goya-Malabrigo ceramic styles were apparently used by the Chaná-Timbú and related ethnic groups who lived in the Paraná delta at the beginning of the European conquest. The Chaná-Timbú are described as emphasizing nutria hunting and other estuarine pursuits in the Upper Paraná delta, but in the lower delta they tilled gardens in which they raised maize, beans, and squash.[31] In contrast, the Tuipiguarani archaeological tradition—as defined by pottery, polished stone axes, and urn burials—is thought to be associated with the Guarani ethnolinguistic groups, some of whom occupied the Lower Paraná delta (see chapter 10). Overlaying these archaeological traditions and the proposed ethnolinguistic affiliations, variations in subsistence practices—specifically the significance of agriculture—resulted in a complex archaeological pattern.

This mosaic of ethnicity, language, and subsistence pursuits present in the northeastern pampas along the Paraná River was less evident across the grasslands of the pampas. Although the broad trends of diversification and intensification are similar, they were differently expressed. This general pattern of broad-spectrum foraging (which in places also incorporated agriculture), the creation of anthropomorphic landscapes (whether lithic caches or mound building), and the development of new, although incompletely understood, forms of socio-political organization apparently occurred across the broad reach of the pampas. Additional archaeological research will clarify and modify current understanding of those patterns.

Marajoara—Non-Agricultural Chiefdoms in the Amazon AD 300–1350

At its mouth, the Amazon River fractures into a complex delta of islands and channels before emptying into the Atlantic Ocean. The largest island in the delta, Marajó Island, covers 50,000 km^2 (19,300 square miles; figure 8.8).

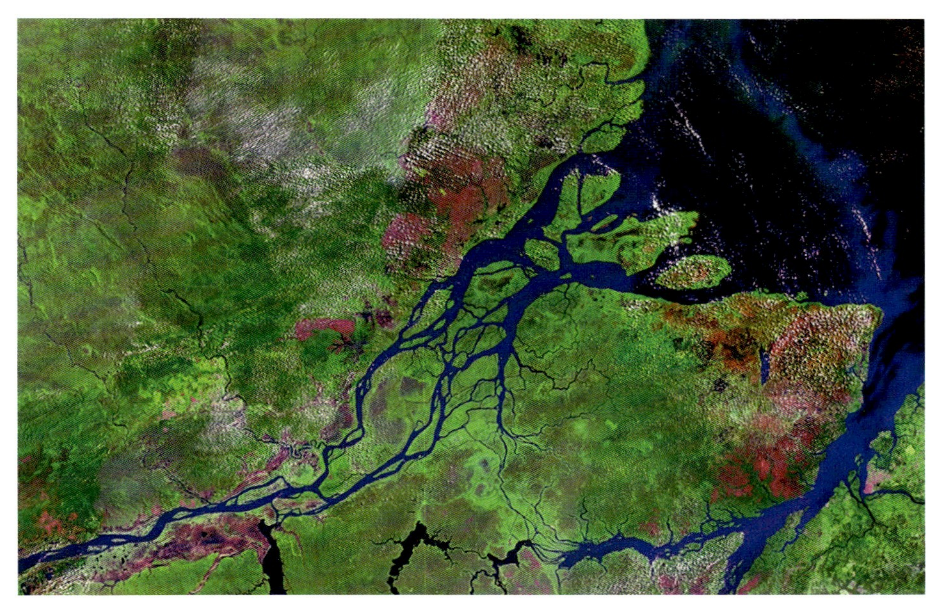

Figure 8.8 Mouth of Amazon River; Marajó Island is approximately the size of Switzerland

For almost a millennium, the island was the home of the **Marajoara chiefdom. Anna Roosevelt** has written:

> The Marajoara culture was one of the outstanding nonliterate complex societies of the world. Apparently a chiefdom, it had an enormous geographic domain that dwarfs those of some famous, old-world civilizations. Like many early complex societies, the Marajoara occupied the alluvial floodplain of a major river, the Lower Amazon. During its reign, from about A.D. 400–1300, the society made great achievements in earthen constructions and ritual ceramic art. It was responsible for the erection of hundreds of monumental earthen mounds that served as platforms for numerous large and small settlements and urn cemeteries. The society developed an intensive subsistence system that maintained large population centers for almost 1000 years.[32]

Roosevelt's synopsis summarizes a complex hypothesis, some elements of which have been validated while others are less certain. First, Marajoara was apparently a chiefly society with a broad geographic range that endured for nearly a millennium. Second, Marajoara groups constructed large earthworks and produced elegant and complex ceramics, although these efforts may not have been the result of centralized authority, as the word *reign* suggests. Finally although it is true that the people of Marajoara developed "an intensive subsistence system" rather than one based on agriculture, it seems that Marajoara culture was a chiefly society based on aquatic resources.

The archaeologist **Denise Schaan** has argued that Marajoara aquaculture was a unique adaptation reflecting the ebb and flow of the Amazon delta.[33] The low-lying islands, never more than 10 m (33 ft) above sea level, have two major environmental zones—tropical rainforests and savannah grasslands—intercut by channels edged by gallery forests and swatches of mangrove swamps. During the rainy season (January–June), low landforms are flooded, leaving only high ground dry. In the peak of the dry season (September–December), vast areas emerge from the floodwaters. These alternating flood and dry seasons create varying opportunities for humans. In the dry season, aquatic resources—fish, turtles, and reptiles—are limited to the river channels, but in the wet season they swim into the inundated grasslands as the Amazon floods. As the fish spread over Marajó Island they are harder to catch, creating an ironic situation in which fish are scarce when they are most abundant. In contrast, terrestrial game are driven onto small promontories as the floodwaters rise, only to disperse as the dry season returns. This rich and varying environment was occupied from at least 5,500 years ago, but the distinctive Marajoara culture appeared after AD 300.

The archaeological sites of Marajó Island were first observed by travelers in the late nineteenth century. Systematic archaeological excavations were conducted in the late 1940s by **Betty Meggers** and **Clifford Evans**, who defined Marajoara and other ceramic styles in the course of surveys and excavations. They interpreted the archaeological sites as indicating a **Tropical Forest culture**, a phrase indicating "both a cultural area and a level of cultural development." Derived from the *Handbook of South American Indians*, edited by Julian Steward, the Tropical Forest culture type was envisioned as based on shifting cultivation of manioc and other root crops, which required regular movements of settlements (see discussion in chapter 5). In a cultural evolutionary scheme, Meggers and Evans wrote, Tropical Forest societies were intermediaries "between the Marginals [*sic*], nomadic hunters and gatherers of wild foods, and the class-divided, occupationally specialized Circum-Caribbean and Andean peoples living by permanently productive agriculture."[34]

In reality, the Marajoara chiefdom was a rare South American example of a non-agricultural chiefdom. The Marajoara chiefdom was distinct in that socio-political complexity was based on *aquaculture* rather than *agriculture*. Although complex societies based on fishing and other marine resources are known from the Pacific Coast of North America, after the Archaic period non-agricultural complex societies were relatively rare in South America.

The evidence for Marajoara social complexity consists of settlement systems, public projects in the form of fishponds and other earthworks, craft specialization, and differential burial treatments. Numerous mounds are found across Marajó Island. While some of these were simple residential mounds perched above the high-water mark of floods, others were ceremonial and funerary mounds reaching heights of 8–10 m (26.2–33 ft). Schaan interprets these clusters of residential, ceremonial, and funerary mounds as reflecting "distinct settlement systems, some small chiefdoms of perhaps 1000 to 3000 inhabitants each."[35]

Schaan focused on one settlement system of thirty-seven mounds stretched along a 10-km (6-mile) stretch of the Camutins River (figure 8.9).

The largest ceremonial mounds in the **Camutins Chiefdom** were clustered near large fishponds. The two largest ceremonial mounds—**M-1**, covering 13,493

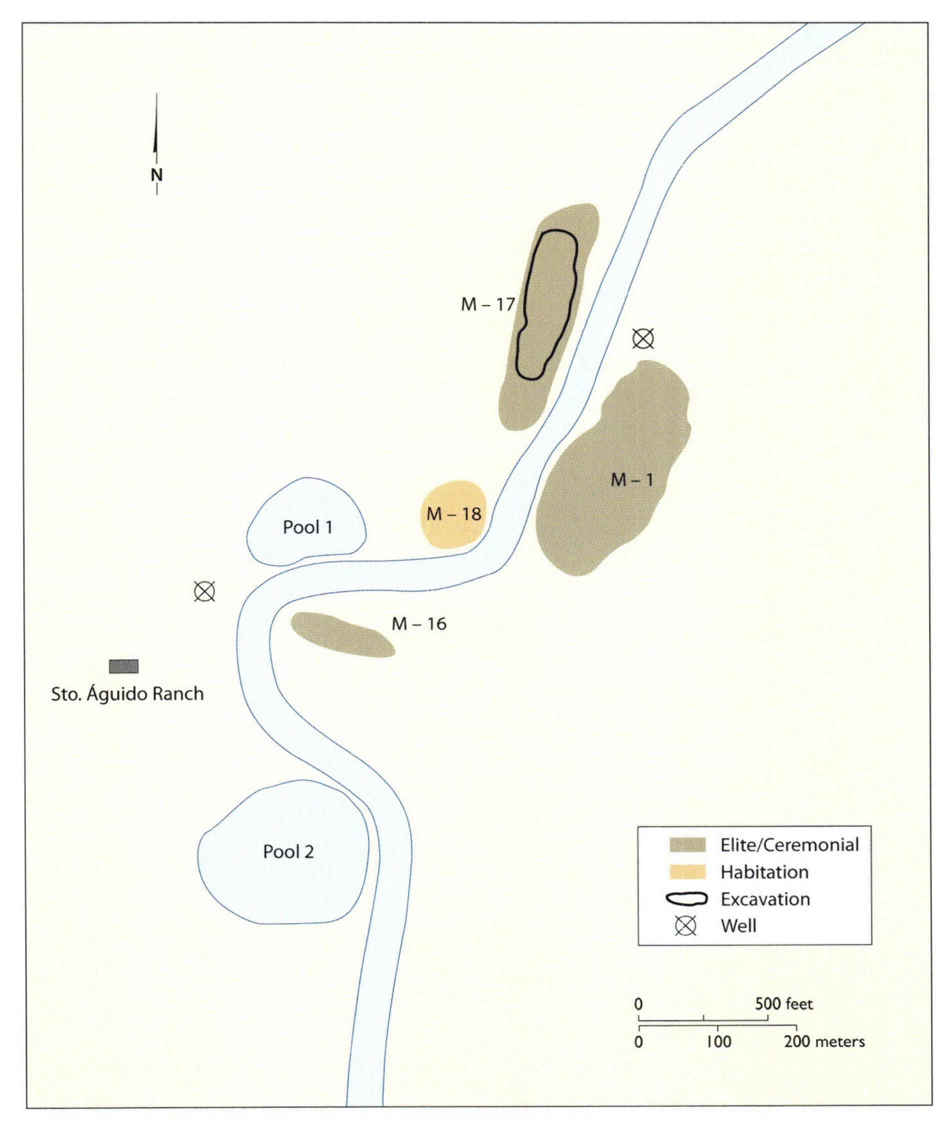

Figure 8.9 Os Camutins Mound Group, Marajó Island, Brazil

m² (145,239 ft²) and standing 11 m (33 ft) tall, and **M-17**, 6,000 m² (64,584 ft²) at its base and 6.4 m (21 ft) tall—were significantly larger than the residential mounds. Most residential mounds were only large enough for a single house, perhaps occupied by an extended family. The fishponds were large, roughly four to eight times the volume of an Olympic swimming pool. The ponds required significant labor to excavate but relatively modest effort to maintain. When rivers overflowed during the rainy season, the pools filled and fish were channeled into the ponds with weirs and canals. As the dry season advanced and the rivers dropped, the ponds were cut off from the river, creating a separate fish-filled pool that provided protein during the dry season when other game dispersed. It was a process of "moving earth to manage water."[36]

Schaan argues that this pragmatic innovation was bolstered by ritual and ideology. The ceremonial mounds adjacent to the fishponds were places where the dead were buried. Schaan writes:

> Excavations of Marajoara funerary structures have revealed variation in size, form and decoration of funerary vessels and associated grave goods both in the horizontal and vertical dimensions, indicating that mortuary practices varied between individuals, as well as geographically and chronologically . . . Clustered urn burials found in the highest mounds are a sign that only a small part of the total population deserved such special treatment. The fact that the burials were clustered in a special area of the mound and personal wealth was not emphasized suggests that group membership was more important than individual identity. Ancestor worship ceremonies in these mounds were likely performed as part of a strategy to justify elite access to resources.[37]

The people of Marajoara displayed complex iconographies on ceramic vessels, decorating vessels by excision, incision, modeling, and painting—often combining these techniques with the use of white and red slips (figure 8.10).[38]

While plainware utilitarian ceramics for domestic use were probably made in various households, the skill and expertise of the highly decorated wares minimally suggest the work of part-time specialists. Stylistic variations suggest the existence of several groups of specialists. The highly decorated ceramics include funerary urns, as well as bowls, plates, bottles, and vases used in communal rituals such as initiation rites or funerals (figure 8.11). The highest densities of fineware sherds are on the tallest and largest ceremonial mounds.

The decorative elements on the Marajoara finewares, Schaan argues, leave "no doubt that their imaginative world was inhabited by beings that share many recognizable characteristics with the local fauna but also reveal supernatural attributes."[39] Along with depictions of caimans, lizards, scorpions, owls, king vultures, monkeys, turtles, jaguars, manatees, ducks, and other birds, snakes are the most common motifs. According to Schaan, "Realistic and stylized snakes, snake heads, and snake skin patterns are the most recurrent figures and designs on Marajoara ceramics."[40] The Marajoara may have seen themselves, Schaan suggests, as "the People of the Snake."

The prominence of snakes recalls the various traditional myths widespread across Amazonia. They included myths that the ancestors arrived in a large anaconda canoe and tales that linked snakes with the abundance of fish. Schaan writes:

> Double-headed and paired snakes are widely represented in Marajoara iconography and are probably inspired by recurrent Amazonian myths of an ancestral snake. The Marajoara "mythical" snakes with their triangular-shaped heads show marked similarities to two species of the *Bothrops* genus (*B. atrox* and

Figure 8.10 Marajoara incised cylinder urn

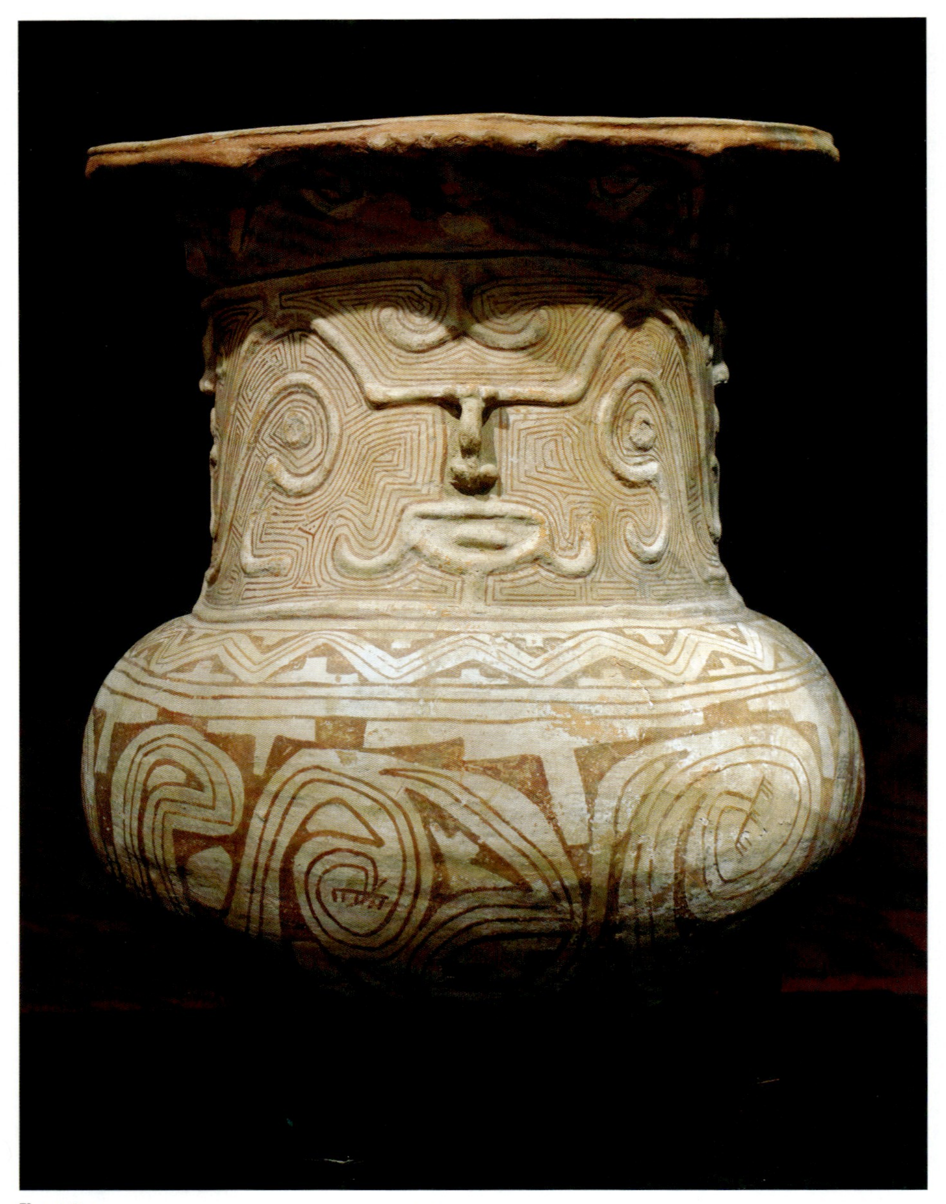

Figure 8.11 Marajoara anthropomorphic burial urn

B. majaronesis) popularly known as *jararaca*, both of which are very poisonous. These species are still common on Marajó, and it is worth noting that during the rainy season animals, including snakes, migrate to the shrinking areas of habitable dry land where they are forced into close proximity with people . . . It is possible that as a symbol of regeneration and life (e.g., the periodic shedding of their skins), as well as being potentially deadly, snakes in general came to be associated with the world of the dead and therefore with funerary urns.[41]

The people of Marajó Island buried their dead in various ways, depending in part on the social status of the deceased. Elite burials received more elaborated funerary treatments and were buried with a richer array of grave goods, including larger urns. The corpses of elite individuals were given secondary burials in which the body was de-fleshed, either by boiling portions of the body or allowing it to decompose naturally, and then the bones were painted with red paint. These secondary burial treatments assisted the dead person's transition into the spirit world by removing the traces of corporal existence. The skull was placed in the bottom of the urn, followed by the rest of the bones. Other objects were placed among the bones, such as ceramic stools, snuff tubes, miniature ceramic vessels, stone axes, jewelry, and the distinctive artifact called the *tanga*. The tanga was a triangular ceramic pubic covering worn by women. In some cases, elaborately decorated tangas are found in burial urns. Further, large quantities of sherds from different-sized tangas are found on the ceremonial mounds, suggesting that female initiation ceremonies also occurred on these mounds.

Non-elites were buried in smaller urns and with fewer or no grave goods. Elite burials were also accompanied by non-elite burials, leading Schaan to suggest that the "concentration of multiple burials at certain locations may imply that the death of a great chief was accompanied by the sacrifice of slaves and servants, who were buried in smaller, simpler urns around him."[42]

The archaeological evidence from Marajó Island points to the existence of permanent communities organized into networks equivalent to "simple chiefdoms," although the nature of the relationship between elites and non-elites and the details of political organization remain unclear. Schaan envisions a situation in which "the fact that the ceremonial area, elite residence, craft production, funerary rituals, and feasting were all concentrated in the same physical setting next to resources resulted in the centralization of the political economy. This should not be understood, however, as absolute power."[43] Rather, Schaan argues, "The relation between elite and commoners was likely one of cooperation, rather than overt social coercion."[44] Although "the data point to the existence of social hierarchies and differential access to resources," Schaan concludes that "the absence of social coercion in the archaeological record suggests a relation of mutual obligations between people of unequal social rank. Accordingly, commoners would contribute with labor and possibly other products such as starch"—for example, manioc—"over which [the] elite likely did not have direct control. The elite would reciprocate with protection and protein resources, due to their 'generosity' and special relation to the gods."[45]

Ultimately, however, the chiefdoms of Marajoara did not endure. Sometime between AD 1000 and 1350 the creation of large mounds and earthworks ended, although the region was not abandoned. The reasons for these changes are unclear. Historical sources from the sixteenth and seventeenth centuries indicate that 40,000 people occupied Marajó Island, comprising several different ethnolinguistic groups who fiercely defended their territories. Within these boundaries, settlements consisted of relatively small and independent villages, with no major ceremonial mounds. So, although Marajó Island continued to be occupied, the

Marajoara chiefdoms disappeared before Europeans sailed into the mouth of the Amazon.

Agricultural Chiefdoms of the Western Llanos of Venezuela

As mentioned in chapter 5, the llanos of western Venezuela were worked into extensive complexes of prehistoric raised fields, agricultural projects adapted to the cycles of flood and ebb of the tributaries of the Orinoco River. The archaeology of these agricultural complexes and the organization of the prehistoric societies who created them are matters of some controversy, requiring a brief detour into the divergent points of view in Venezuelan archaeology.

The earthworks of the Western Llanos have long been known. Alexander von Humboldt, traveling across the llanos in March 1800, observed the presence of "bancos . . . which are in reality shoals in the basin of the steppes, rising some 4 to 5 feet above the plains [which] can reach some 3 to 4 leagues in length" (roughly 10 miles).[46] It is not clear that Humboldt understood that these earthworks were manmade; nor did he recognize them as prehistoric constructions. Despite these early observations and excavations by Venezuelan archaeologists in the late nineteenth century, archaeological research did not gain momentum until the twentieth century when several archaeologists affiliated with major US research institutions—**Wendell C. Bennett**, **Cornelius Osgood**, and **A. V. Kidder II**—were invited to conduct excavations at several sites in the 1930s.[47] In 1941, Osgood returned to Venezuela with **George D. Howard**, and their work resulted in the first archaeological overview of Venezuela.[48] Subsequently, Howard published a broader study of ceramics from lowland Amazonia that drew on his own excavations at the site of **Ronquín** in the Middle Orinoco. The study compared those results with archaeological collections from elsewhere in Venezuela and in the adjacent regions of lower Central America, the islands of the Caribbean, and northern South America.[49]

It is interesting to contrast this research with then-contemporary investigations by American archaeologists in the Central Andes. At approximately the same time, US archaeologists working in the highlands and coastal valleys of Peru had developed extensive and sustained research programs, including the Virú Valley project.[50] The Central Andean investigations built on several decades of earlier archaeological knowledge of Uhle, Tello, and many others—investigations that had resulted in a broad chronological framework for the Andes. In contrast, Venezuela in the 1930s and 1940s was virtually an archaeological terra incognita. Fewer archaeologists worked in the larger lowlands of South America than in the Central Andes. For example, in 1937 Wendell Bennett published an eleven-page report on archaeological investigations in South America that reported on work during the previous two years, 1934–36.[51] In contrast, **Irving Rouse** published a 1961 synopsis of archaeological investigations in lowland South America and the Caribbean, *a report with fewer than six pages of text that covered the period 1935–60.*[52] One of these brief reports covered two years of investigations; the other described twenty-five years of fieldwork.

Finally, these different twentieth-century archaeological projects incorporated distinct assumptions about their respective regions' connections to other areas. In the Virú Valley, the essential assumption was that cultural patterns had developed and were expressed at the regional scale—that is, the North Coast of Peru. Although influenced by developments in other areas, these patterns were essentially local expressions of prehistoric cultures. In contrast, the prehistory of Venezuela was seen, to overstate the argument slightly, as basically "derivative," influenced by migrations and diffusions that originated elsewhere but left their traces in passing.

For example, Osgood and Howard proposed a basic model that envisioned these influences as occurring along three lines: a north-south axis along the Pacific Coast from Central America to northern South America, another north-south axis along the Atlantic Coast from the Caribbean to northern South America, and an east-west axis between the northern Andes and the lower Orinoco. These three lines of diffusion visually resembled an "H" and strongly implied that cultural innovations occurred elsewhere, outside of Orinoquia. Thus, in their discussion regarding "the place of Venezuela in American prehistory," Rouse and José Cruxent determined the region to be "intermediate."[53] Venezuela's prehistory was poorly understood, barely investigated, and seen as derivative.

To further complicate this situation, the seminal work by Rouse and Cruxent applied a scheme for classifying archaeological materials that assumed that sets of traits—usually on ceramic styles—corresponded to archaeological "complexes," which implicitly involved distinct cultures. Essentially, a specific set of traits would define an archaeological complex, a supposedly coherent set of artifacts made by separate groups of humans who shared a body of cultural knowledge, including the ways they made artifacts.[54] The archaeologist's task was to define those sets of shared traits and document their spread through time and space with stratigraphic excavations and systematic surveys.

Rouse and Cruxent defined a sequence of ceramic complexes as a "series."[55] For example, the **Barrancoid series** was marked by thick, heavy, coarse paste used to form bowls and double-spout bottles; the surfaces were smoothed and decorated by carving, modeling, appliqués, and incising. Barrancoid styles originated around 1000 BC and continued in use for the next millennium. They were followed by the **Saladoid series**, a set of ceramic styles broadly characterized by red on plain or white on red cross-hatched lines painted on thin, fine-paste wide-mouth bowls. The Saladoid ceramic complex appeared between 1000 BC and AD 500 in the Orinoco region, Rouse and Cruxent believed, spreading to the coast of Venezuela and into the West Indies between AD 300 and 1000. A third ceramic series, the **Arauquinoid series**, consisted of pottery tempered with the spicules of freshwater sponges, sharp siliceous rods that provide structure to the soft-bodied invertebrate and strengthen the clays in ceramic vessels. Arauquinoid ceramics were decorated with incised parallel lines and appliquéd lugs, including distinctive "coffee-bean" eyes.[56] Arauquinoid ceramics developed in the llanos around AD 500–700 and appeared in the Orinoco drainage after AD 1000.

If the Rouse and Cruxent stylistic approach was applied to the development of different archaeological cultures in time and space—essentially laying out contours of innovation, diffusion, and migration in a cultural-historical framework—it was theoretically isolated from the Marxist-based archaeology of **Mario Sanoja** and **Iraida Vargas**. Despite methodological similarities with Cruxent and Rouse in the classification of artifacts, Sanoja and Vargas rejected the concepts of "series" or "phases" and instead embraced the "modo de vida," or "modes of life." For example, Sanoja wrote, "The modes of life have a spatial dimension in that they represent the social response of a human group to the objective conditions of a specific environment, but at the same time they are dialectical in that the contradiction between the social group and the environment is resolved within the historical conjunctures that depend on the internal dynamics of the group and its relation with other similar groups." Sanoja argued that an archaeological approach that emphasized stylistic ceramic traits, such as practiced by Rouse and Cruxent, "ignored the problems presented by the comparison of different contexts" as it ignored the variations between different modes of life.[57]

The archaeologist **Samuel Wilson**, who has conducted research in the Caribbean, notes that "the picture that has been emerging since the early 1980s is that the Orinoco basin was a zone of intensive cultural contact and interaction for thousands of years, and particularly so in the last 2500 years" (essentially the point Rouse, Cruxent, Osgood, and Howard were exploring decades earlier). However, rather than progressive waves of migrating cultures, Wilson emphasizes the roles of trade and exchange in the spread of cultural traits, writing, "given the substantial influences coming in from outside the region, from both the river systems [i.e., Orinoco and Amazon] and Llanos to the west and the Amazon basin to the south . . . the Middle and Lower Orinoco formed the crucible in which Saladoid, Barrancoid, and many other archaeological cultures developed, and there was usually a high degree of interaction, even over large distances, among the many groups living there."[58]

In sum, rather than seeing the Orinoco region as an isolated recipient of cultural innovations developed elsewhere, current archaeological evidence points to a complex topography of change in which combinations of migrations, exchange and trade, local innovations, and dynamic interactions occurred between the Orinoco region and the northern Andes, Amazonia, and the Caribbean.

One expression of these dynamic changes was the emergence of complex chiefdoms in the Western Llanos after approximately AD 650, when a number of sites with large mound constructions emerged. This process is best known through two different long-term research projects, directed respectively by the archaeologist **Alberta Zucchi** and by the archaeologists **Elsa Redmond** and **Charles Spencer**.[59]

In the late 1960s, Zucchi excavated large mounds and studied earthworks (*calzadas*) at the site **Hato de la Calzada** in the province of Barinas in western Venezuela. The overall site is large, covering a minimum of 15 ha (33 acres) of artificial mounds connected by causeways.[60] Zucchi's excavations cross-sectioned a major mound (Mound 1), 11.8 m (38.7 ft) tall and 60–80 m (197–262 ft) in diameter. Her excavations exposed a complex series of construction episodes. Originally built on a low natural knoll, the lower strata consist of midden with shells and ceramics capped by two burned layers, which may have been the remnants of a perishable building or could have been intentionally set for a ceremonial or architectural purpose. The three layers immediately above the burned strata are interesting. Each deposit consists of a distinct soil dug from different places around the mound; each layer is homogeneous and distinct and created a flat, mound-top surface. Above these three layers, the shape of the mound is less distinct. The function of the mound is unknown, although the absence of skeletal remains or burial pits suggests it was not a funerary mound. Based on a sequence of radiocarbon dates, Zucchi argued that Mound I at Hato de la Calzada was begun at circa AD 450–550, with construction continuing after AD 650.

Archaeological survey in the Barinas region in the late 1970s by the archaeologist **Adam G. Garson**, a Yale doctoral student, documented some of the fourteen causeways radiating out from Hato de la Calzada—raised linear surfaces up to 2 m (6.5 ft) tall and 10–12 m (33–39.6 ft) wide, with different spurs running from 300 m to 5,000 m (984–16,400 ft) in length.[61] Some causeways connected the main mounds at Hato de la Cazada to other mound groups, while others linked habitation areas to streams or were built within settlements. The combination of large mounds and linked causeways suggests that relatively large, permanent communities occupied the Western Llanos between AD 650 and 1200.

These patterns were not limited to Hato de la Cazada and its immediate vicinity but rather are found over a broader region, as demonstrated by the work of Redmond, Spencer, and colleagues.[62] Their survey in the Llanos de Barinas recorded thirty-two archaeological sites that were clearly different in size, forming primary (n = 1), secondary (n = 5), and tertiary (n = 26) settlements. Settlement patterns with such ranked hierarchies are often associated with chiefdoms, with the largest site the primary center of a paramount chief.

The principal settlement was **El Gaván** (figure 8.12).

Covering 33 ha (73 acres) and with an estimated population of 670–1,000 residents, El Gaván was not only the largest of the sites but was also a well-organized site.[63] The entire site is encircled by a calzada 6–8 m (19.7–26.2 ft) wide on top and 20–25 m (65.6–82 ft) wide at its base. Excavations on the calzada uncovered a line of post molds that suggests El Gaván was encircled by a log palisade. Two large mounds—one 12 m (39 ft) tall, the other 10 m (33 ft) tall—sit opposite each other across a 500 m (1,640 ft)-long plaza flanked by more than 134 smaller residential mounds. The taller mound in the eastern part of the site was climbed using an 80 m (262.4 ft)-long ramp or staircase that extended into the plaza.

The residential mounds differed in size and associated artifacts, possibly indicating variations among the families of El Gaván. For example, excavations on a meter-tall house mound (Area A) uncovered post molds of a rectangular pole and thatch house covering 27.9 m^2 (300 ft^2), with a well-made floor, and a small annex or storeroom just outside the house. Excavations at another, lower mound (Area D) exposed another rectangular pole and thatch house, but smaller (16.6 m^2 [179 ft^2]) and lacking an annex. Assuming that each mound housed a different family, the variations in mound height and house size hint at social variations among the residents of El Gaván.

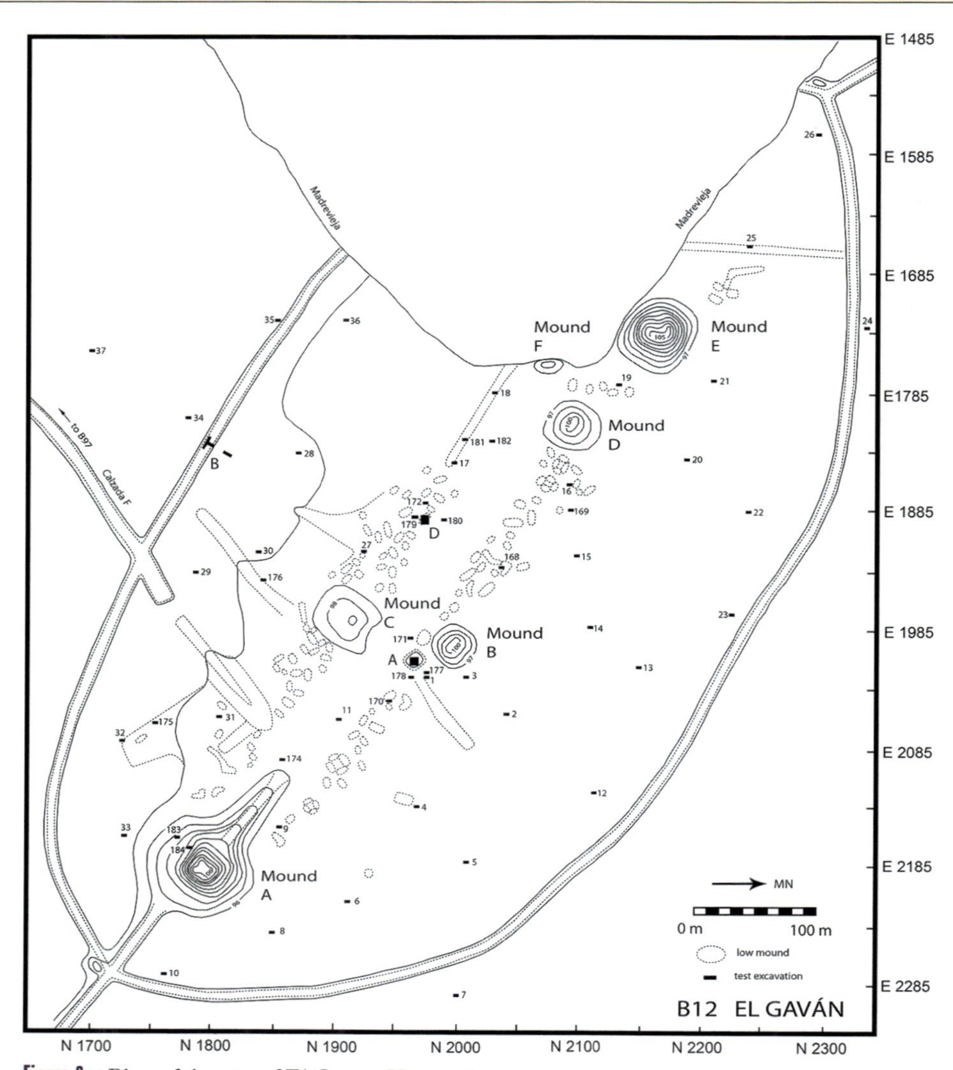

Figure 8.12 Plan of the site of El Gaván, Venezuela

There is other evidence for social variations at El Gaván. Partial skeletons were placed in pits in the plaza or at the base of the large mound, either secondary burials or butchered bodies that Spencer and Redmond interpret as "possibly represent[ing] captives or sacrificial victims whose bodies were dismembered and interred in the mound fill of public constructions."[64] In contrast, other individuals were buried in their houses, placed in carefully laid-out, extended burials. Two burials were found under the larger house mound, Area A, interred with pots as offerings. One burial had a greenstone-malachite bead that probably came from the Andes of Ecuador or southern Colombia. Redmond and colleagues write, "The differences in location, height, and size of the two exposed house mounds, as well as the funerary—and exotic—accompaniments associated with certain members of the Area A household, signal the latter's higher social position in El Gaván society and their participation in long distance prestige-good exchange."[65]

Not only was El Gaván distinct in size and formal plan, but the primary center sat at the hub of multiple causeways linking it to the secondary centers, physically connecting these nodes in a network. Secondary centers emulated the architectural layout of El Gaván, though at a smaller scale, with pairs of large mounds on opposite sides flanked by smaller residential mounds (although fewer than at El Gaván) and with additional calzadas on their peripheries. Such constructions were not present at the tertiary residential settlements. This network of causeways linked about two-thirds of the region's population and was a major instrument and reflection of political authority. Redmond and Spencer write, "The regional causeway network would have facilitated the alliances between the paramount chief at B12 [El Gaván] and the local village chiefs that are established and maintained through feasting and exchange, among other strategies of chiefly control. One expression of those alliances on the local level might have been the mobilization of labor for the construction of monumental earthworks at the regional center. Another strategy might have involved the production and mobilization of agricultural surpluses from subordinate villages to chiefly granaries."[66]

Some of this agricultural surplus undoubtedly came from the extensive set of raised fields nearby.[67] The **La Tigra drained fields** cover 35 ha (86.5 acres). Pollen samples indicate that maize was the principal staple crop, along with other domesticated plants ranging from chilies to tomatoes. These farmlands could produce a large surplus, more than six times the maize required by the small community that probably worked the fields. Since this small village and the La Tigra fields were directly connected by causeways to the primary center at El Gaván, it is likely that surplus crops were used by the El Gaván chiefdom, a powerful source of economic power.

Another source of power was the ability to muster a force of warriors. The evidence for warfare at El Gaván is indirect but intriguing. First, there is the evidence of a palisaded enclosure at El Gaván, which suggests the need for defense. Second, the causeways were built wider than needed for simple pedestrian traffic but broad enough so ranks of warriors could quickly march to defend the primary and secondary centers from attack. The final evidence for warfare marks the end of the El Gaván chiefdom. Redmond and colleagues write:

> The abandonment of the regional center seems to have been precipitated by a violent conflagration, when both the high-status residence in Area A and the defensive palisade were destroyed by fire, along with most of the other structures at the site. The two thermoluminescence dates associated with the burned residence in Area A have midpoints of A.D. 760 ± 120 and A.D. 900 ± 120, and suggest that the final attack and abandonment of El Gavan occurred not long after A.D. 760–900. Accompanying the destruction and abandonment of the regional center was the widespread abandonment of all the secondary centers and villages that made up the El Gavan polity.[68]

Nasca: Ceremonial Centers and Ceramics on the South Coast of Peru

On the South Coast of Peru, the Nasca culture developed over eight centuries, from approximately 200–150 BC until AD 600–640 (see figure 8.2).[69] As a broad cultural pattern, Nasca styles exhibit continuities and connections with the earlier Paracas culture and were fundamentally reshaped by the expansion of the Wari Empire. In the intervening centuries a complex and, in many ways, mysterious cultural tradition developed.

The geographic core of the Nasca culture was the branching network of drainages known as the Rio Grande de Nazca and the Ica Valley (figure 8.13).

The Rio Grande de Nazca is a candelabra of ten slender rivers that alternately flow as surface water and sink underground, creating chains of oases rather than continuous bands of irrigable land. (Note that "Nasca" refers to the archaeological culture, while "Nazca" refers to the region.) Yet, Nasca society was dependent on agriculture, raising maize, beans, squash, manioc, sweet potatoes, jicama, potatoes, chilies, and cotton. Combined with the resources of the nearby sea, agriculture and fishing were the subsistence basis of Nasca village life.

These village economies also supported craft production, probably by part-time specialists who created objects of stunning beauty. In general, these crafts were made using relatively simple technologies but sparked by human creativity to produce marvelous objects. By twisting cotton fibers and camelid wool on drop spindles, Nasca weavers created magnificent textiles using simple back-strap looms, painting images on the fabrics with pigments made from the roots of herbs or elaborating borders with intricate embroideries using just needle and thread (figures 8.14 and 8.15).

Similarly, Nasca potters used basic ceramic techniques such as coiling and paddling to make most vessels. Simple brushes with bristles of human hair were used to paint amazingly complex figures and motifs, the meanings of which archaeologists and art historians still debate (figure 8.16). Although there were clear continuities in motifs, a basic change occurred from more naturalistic forms to elaborate visual kaleidoscopes of images. Finally, the most famous creations for which the potters are known, the geoglyphs called "the Nazca lines," are simply paths in which dark surface stones have been swept away, exposing the white sands of the desert (figure 8.17). In all these cases, relatively simple technologies were used to express the complex creative visions of the Nasca people.

As with many other aspects of Andean archaeology, changes in Nasca ceramic designs were first recognized by **Max Uhle** (see chapter 1). Additional fieldwork in the Nasca region during the 1920s by **Julio Tello** and **M. Toribio Mejia Xesspe** led to the discovery of the earlier Paracas culture and also to documentation of numerous Nasca sites.[70] Uhle's collections from the Rio Grande de Nazca were sent to the Hearst Museum at the University of California, Berkeley, where they were studied by **Alfred Kroeber** and **Anna Gayton** and later, in the 1950s, by **Lawrence Dawson**.[71] Dawson arrived at a nine-phase sequence, which, although Dawson never published a full description of the seriation himself, was used by

Figure 8.13 Nazca lines from space, also showing the Panamerican Highway, Peru

other US archaeologists working in the region, including **John Rowe** and **Dorothy Menzel**.[72] The Dawson sequence treated individual pots as exhibiting constellations of traits and artistic themes that could be seriated individually, resulting in a detailed and nuanced approach to Nasca pottery. Each of the nine phases in the Dawson sequence was originally thought to last a century, but radiocarbon dating demonstrated that some phases were longer than others and some phases were essentially contemporary. Further, phase 9 ceramics are so heavily influenced by Wari styles that they are not really "Nasca" pots, despite being found in the Nazca Valley.

More recently, excavations directed by **Markus Reindel** and **Johnny Isla** at Nasca sites in the Palpa Valley, one of the main drainages of the Rio Grande de Nazca system, have recovered more than 150 absolute dates from seventeen sites.[73] These dates result from standard radiocarbon dating on wood and charcoal and AMS dates from very small samples, such as bits of straw extracted from adobe

Figure 8.14 The *Paracas Mantle*, an elegant Nasca textile

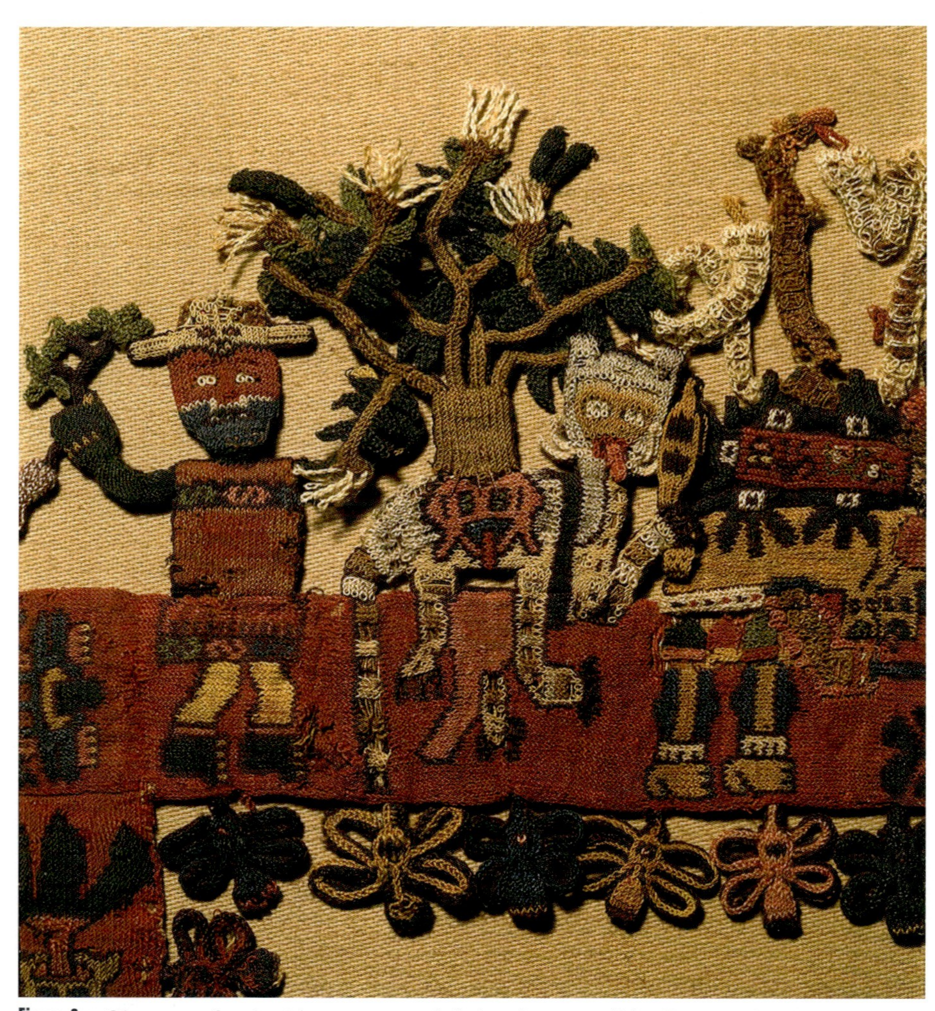

Figure 8.15 Close-up of embroidery on upper-left-hand corner of the *Paracas Mantle*

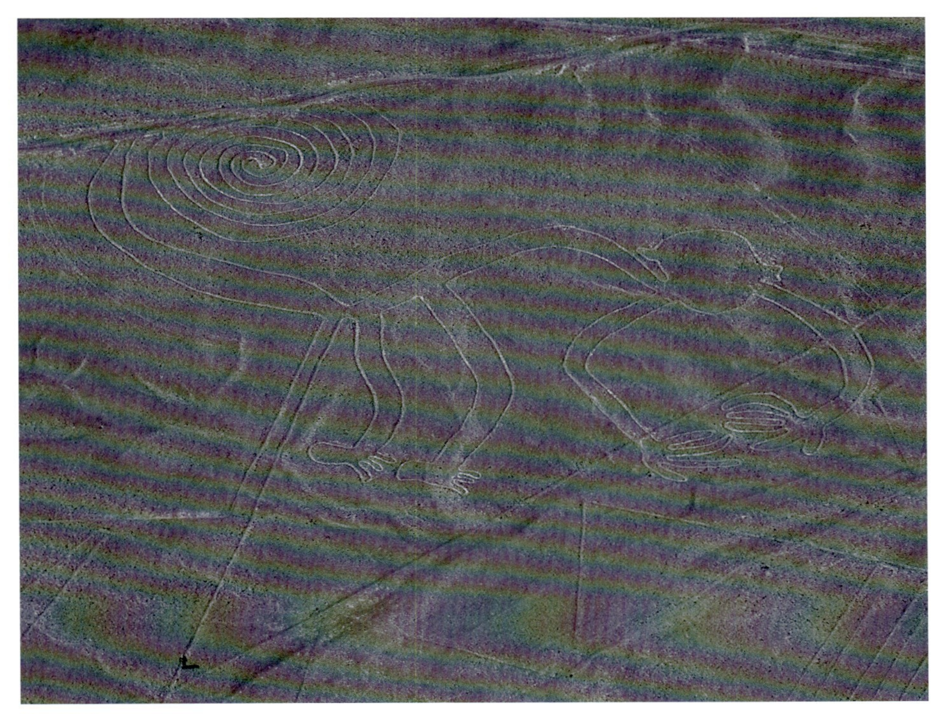

Figure 8.16 Depiction of a monkey, Nasca lines, Peru

bricks. Their analysis provides very precise absolute dates for the major Nasca phases (table 8.1).

These different phases saw significant variations through time and space in settlement patterns, social orders, and other dimensions. For example, **Donald Proulx** conducted archaeological surveys in the lower portions of the Rio Nasca and Rio Grande, recording data on 128 archaeological sites, 79 of which had ceramics that could be identified to a specific phase in the Nasca sequence.[74] Of these, the vast majority of the sites (86%; n = 68) had Nasca 3 ceramics, many had Nasca 5 ceramics (43%; n = 34), but other phases were scarcely represented (Nasca 1: n = 2, Nasca 2: n = 4, Nasca 4: n = 0, Nasca 6: n = 9, Nasca 7: n = 7, Nasca 8: n = 6).

The settlement patterns changed over time. During the Early Nasca period, sites were located either in the lower drainages where water flowed on the surface or in the upper sierra where there was limited rainfall but not in the intervening middle valley that lacked surface water and rain. This middle valley sector was occupied only after Nasca 5, when subterranean wells and galleries—or **puquios**, discussed below—were built.

Similarly, the upper drainages of the Rio Grande de Nazca had significant occupation during the Early Nasca period (Nasca phases 2–4), with numerous sites recorded during surveys directed by **Katharina Schreiber**. For example, **Kevin Vaughn** and **Mosés Linares** reported on excavations of the Early Nasca village of **Upanca**. Located 1,600 m (5,248 ft) above sea level near a small but reliable

Table 8.1 Major Nasca phases

Years	Periods	Cultures	Phases	Ceramic Styles
1500	Late Horizon	Inca/Ica		Inca/Ica
1400				
1300		Ica		Ica
1200	Late Intermediate Period			
1100				
1000				
900				
800				
700	Middle Horizon	Wari		Chakipampa, Loro
600				
500			Late Nasca	Nasca (6?), 7
400				
300	Early Intermediate Period	Nasca	Middle Nasca	Nasca 4, 5
200				
AD 100			Early Nasca	Nasca 2, 3
0±	Transition	Initial Nasca		Nasca 1
BC 100				Ocucaje 10
200				
300			Late	Ocucaje 8, 9
400				
500	Early Horizon	Paracas	Middle	Ocucaje 5, 6, 7
600				
700			Early	Ocucaje 3, 4
800				

water source, Upanca had been occupied since the Archaic period (ca. 3000 BP in this region). By the Early Nasca period, Upanca was a 5-ha (12.4-acre) village of self-sufficient farmers who may have raised coca on nearby rain-fed terraced fields. Living in relatively small circular houses and patio groups scattered along a cactus-covered ridge above a quebrada, the Early Nasca people of Upanca had lives of rustic domesticity.[75] Except for their fineware pottery.

Based on counts of pottery rims, finewares comprised 60 percent and plainwares 40 percent of the Early Nasca pottery at Upanca. Fineware pottery was not made at the site. There may have been minor differences in social status among the Upanca households but no major presence of elites. Commoners had access to fine Nasca pottery.

Vaughn documented this same pattern at another Early Nasca village community, the site of **Marcaya**. A village of about seventy structures consisting of

Figure 8.17 Polychrome double-spout bottle portraying a Nasca anthropomorphic mythical being

Figure 8.18 Nasca ceremonial center of Cahuachi, Peru

dwellings and patios, Marcaya was occupied during Nasca phases 3 and 4, a relatively brief occupation sometime between AD 110 and 410. At Marcaya, fineware ceramics made up 56 percent of the assemblage. There were some differences among the Marcaya households, with some families having access to goblets that depict humans wearing turbans, so-called headjars. Vaughn discovered this pattern at other Early Nasca villages, documenting that Early Nasca rural villagers had access to fine pottery they did not make.[76]

It seems that the fine pottery came from the site of **Cahuachi** (figure 8.18). Cahuachi is the largest known Nasca site, sprawling along the south bank of the Rio Nasca for about 2 km (1.2 miles) and covering 150 ha (370.5 acres). Cahuachi was the preeminent settlement during the Early Nasca period, with most construction ending after Nasca 3, an abrupt end interpreted as marking a "collapse."[77]

The site was investigated in 1926 by Alfred Kroeber, who recognized its monumentality and special role within the Nasca settlement system.[78] In 1952–53, **William D. Strong** mapped and excavated at Cahuachi, addressing issues of relative chronology in stratigraphic excavations that recovered changing styles of pottery.[79] Strong applied methods used in the Virú Valley project, where excavations through domestic debris recovered different types of pottery, resulting in a ceramic sequence. Cahuachi contained ceramics from the earlier Paracas phases and the entire Nasca sequence (as then understood); however, Strong commented that "the Middle Nazca cultural phase represents the climax of the famous Nazca culture," a peak in development that refers to both "polychrome ceramic techniques and art style as well as to size and complexity of architectural units"[80] (figure 8.19). For example, excavations in the largest mound, the Great Temple, contained predominantly Middle Nazca ceramics (figure 8.20).

The site consists of around forty mounds, either entirely artificial or modified natural hills. About 85 percent of Cahuachi consists of open areas without mounds,

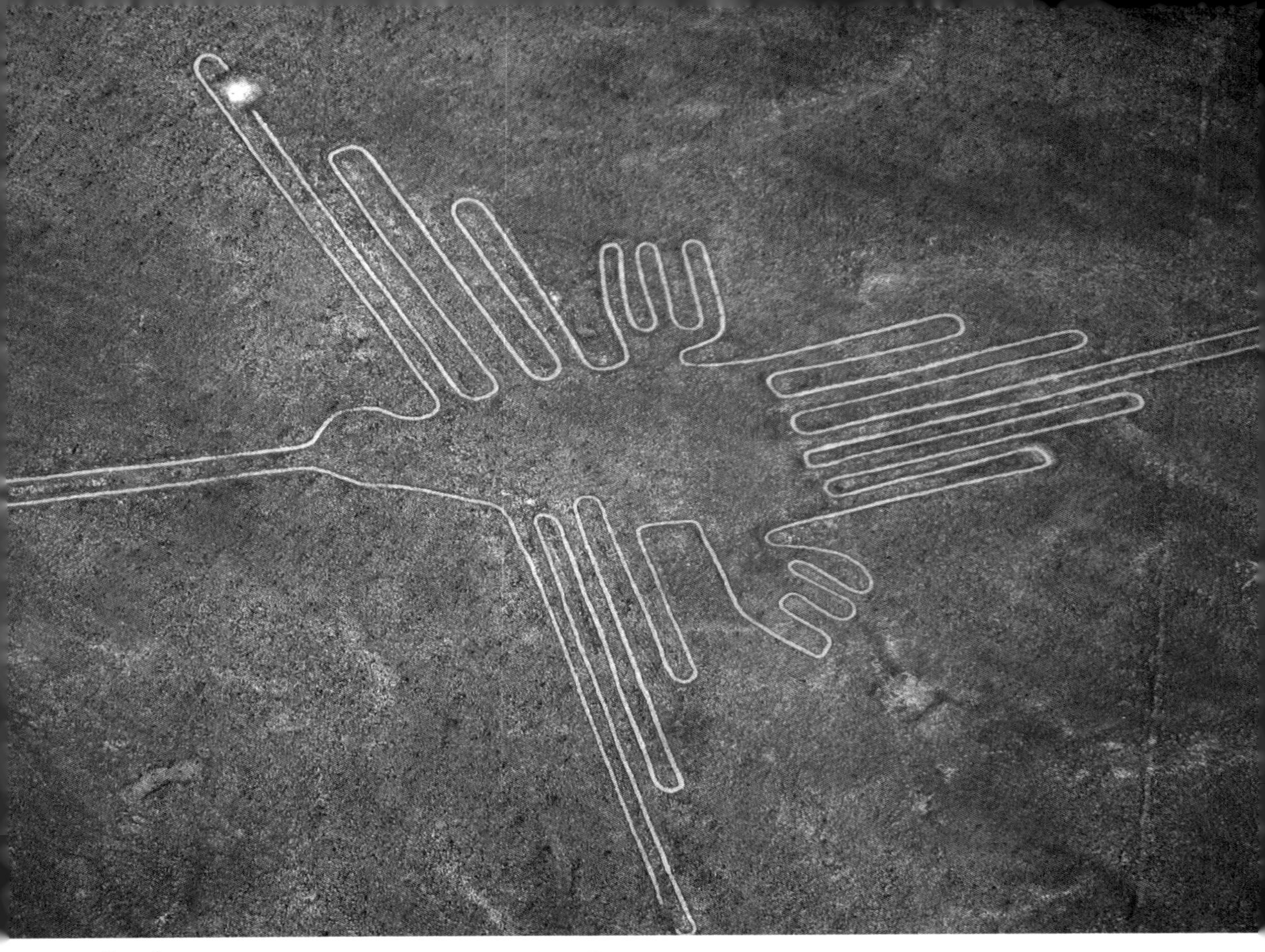

Figure 8.19 Depiction of a hummingbird, Nasca lines, Peru

some with cemeteries and others that may have enclosures bordered by low walls. Intriguingly, what was absent was evidence for extensive population living at the site.

The large mounds of dense domestic debris at Cahuachi suggested to Strong the existence of a resident population, and Cahuachi was classified as an urban center. As the largest Nazca urban center, Cahuachi was interpreted as the capital of a Nazca state.

Yet, excavations by **Helaine Silverman** at Cahuachi indicated no clear evidence for a large resident population. In multiple excavations across the site, Silverman found domestic debris but little evidence for actual dwellings.[81] The domestic debris seems to have been used for architectural fill rather than constituting the in situ trash of an urban population. Importantly, during twenty-five years of subsequent excavations, the Italian archaeologist **Giuseppe Orefici** has not found extensive residential areas at Cahuachi, leading him to conclude that "we can affirm that during our investigations we did not produce discoveries indicating habitation zones in Cahuachi."[82]

This led Silverman to propose that Cahuachi was a pilgrimage center, permanently occupied by a small community of shamans or priests and episodically crowded by throngs of the devout who traveled to Cahuachi from the region surrounding Ica and the Rio Grande de Nazca.

Figure 8.20 Nasca double-spout and bridge bottle

This hypothesis has been supported by a recent study of human skeletons from Cahuachi in which the oxygen isotope values found in the bones indicated that these people were pilgrims from the surrounding river valleys rather than people who had been born and raised at Cahuachi.[83]

Other bones found at Cahuachi and at other Nasca sites point to a different mode of death, as these skulls were used as trophy heads. **Kelly Knudson** and colleagues have written that, throughout the Nasca phases, "trophy heads were an important part of Nasca lifeways."[84] Although trophy heads have been found elsewhere in the Andes and are depicted in the iconography of various prehispanic cultures, the largest number of known trophy heads is associated with Nasca culture.[85] The large opening (foramen magnum) at the base of the

Figure 8.21 Top of bottle (see figure 8.20) showing warriors with trophy heads

skull was widened so brains and other soft tissues could be removed. The hair and skin of the face was sometimes left in place, the eyes and lips permanently pinned together with algarobbo thorns. A distinctive trait of Nasca trophy heads is that a hole was drilled in the center of the forehead so a rope could be threaded through the skull.

Trophy heads are shown as elements on Nasca fine-line vessels—as objects held by deities, as objects placed in tombs, and as "headjars" depicting heads (figure 8.21).[86]

The Nasca actively cut off peoples' heads. A single cache of forty-eight skulls was found at the Early Nasca site Cerro Carapo in the Palpa Valley, all from robust males between twenty and forty-five years of age, except for a single individual between twelve and fifteen whose gender could not be determined.[87] The skulls were not sun-bleached white, indicating that they were buried still covered with skin.

This implies that trophy heads were not ancestors but displays of war victims. Although it has been argued that Nasca warriors raided and killed foreign rivals in neighboring regions, this may not be correct. Knudson and colleagues analyzed strontium, carbon, and oxygen isotopes in the tooth enamel from Nasca trophy heads collected by Kroeber; this analysis indicated that the skulls were those of people from the Nasca basin. They write, "Our data do not support the hypothesis that Nasca trophy heads were taken from enemy warriors from foreign locales. Although trophy heads of individuals perceived as local or foreign could have important ritual functions, we argue that transforming local Nasca individuals into trophy heads highlights their ritual role."[88]

The nature of this ritual is unclear. Ceremonial decapitations may have been part of agricultural rituals, criminal executions, or brutal displays of power. But whatever the cultural rationale, men were killed, blood flowed, and heads were removed for display.[89]

Taking all these different lines of archaeological evidence into consideration—from dwellings to ceremonial centers, from fine pottery to trophy heads—a wide variety of issues surrounds and confounds current understanding of the sociopolitical organization of Nasca society and its changes over eight centuries. These debates revolve around several key questions. What are the different properties and functions of Nasca sites? To what extent were these settlements integrated or interacting? What is the evidence of public works and the ability to coordinate labor? What is the evidence for social distinctions? Was Nasca a state, a chiefdom, a religion—or what?

For example, Johnny Isla and Markus Reindel argue that other sites in the Nasca region were intermediate between Cahuachi and Nasca villages in size and function—specifically that other sites, although smaller than Cahuachi, had architecturally similar features and also contained burials of elites.[90] Isla and Reindel interpret these sites as on a separate tier, between regional centers and rural villages, of a state-level society.

Approaching the problem from a different tack, Katharina Schreiber and **Josué Lancho Rojas** have studied prehispanic waterworks known as *puquios*, used in areas where the rivers flow underground.[91] These systems involve excavating a wide vertical well into the ground and then tunneling a horizontal shaft to intersect the subsurface flow of water. Based on the dates of villages and hamlets surrounding the fields once watered by puquios, Schreiber and Lancho Rojas argue that they were constructed when Cahuachi was at its peak influence. Given the amount of work required to construct the puquios—and the danger inherent in such desperate measures—Schreiber and Lancho Rojas contend that a state-level society must have been involved.

Different interpretations also cluster around funeral treatments. It is obvious that different individuals in Nasca society had very different funerals, strongly suggesting that social differences existed. But do such differences imply the existence of social classes, as Isla and Reindel conclude, or do they imply variations in individuals' social rankings but not a stratified society?[92]

In broad terms, the debates coalesce into three positions. One model envisions Cahuachi as a pilgrimage center maintained by a small cadre of religious specialists who lived there but without an urban population. As a pilgrimage center, Cahuachi was a catalyst for people living throughout the Rio Grande de Nazca and Ica Valleys, whose participation in this larger social network is indicated by access to fineware ceramics. Some of these communities may have been local chiefdoms, but there was no overarching state-level society.

Conversely, the same data are used to argue that Cahuachi was the primary center in the Nazca region; larger settlements elsewhere in the region were secondary centers ruled by local elites, and rural communities formed a third tier in the settlement system. The creation of public works (such as the puquios) and the exchange of fine craft products (such as ceramics and textiles) indicate a level of coordinated efforts associated with state-level societies.

Finally, there is a temporal position: it may be that Nasca society was a loose coalition of chiefdoms and communities until the Middle Nasca–Phase 5 period of circa AD 450–550, when construction at Cahuachi ceased and it was no longer a major ceremonial center. At this point, major changes in settlement patterns—perhaps triggered by a sustained drought—marked a turning point in Nasca prehistory. After this transformative era, Nasca society became more centralized and hierarchical until the region was subsumed into the Wari Empire (see chapter 9).

Cahuachi's decline and shifts in settlement systems may be correlated with evidence for environmental degradation, as documented by **David Beresford-Jones** and colleagues. Working in the lower Ica Valley, this team of archaeologists and archaeobotanists documented the importance of forests of algarobbo trees (*Prosopis*) in coastal desert habitats. This deep-rooted and long-living tree, Beresford-Jones and colleagues write, "was the ecological 'keystone' species in this desert region, fixing nitrogen and enhancing soil fertility and moisture, ameliorating desert extremes in the microclimate beneath its canopy and underpinning the floodplain with one of the deepest root systems of any tree known."[93] People gradually destroyed the algarobbo forest for fuel and building materials and to open up new lands for farming. This deforestation had unintended consequences in which El Niño (floods) and La Niña (droughts) were tipping points. Over centuries, the algarobbo deforestation "undermined the multiple ecological influences of the genus Prosopis in this environment, and in particular the protection it affords in an environment of high-energy, episodic flood events and of one of the world's strongest and most persistent wind regimes."[94] With diminished protection from flooding, canal systems were destroyed by floods and left "high and dry" as the main river cut deeper into the earth. Once-fertile fields were covered by wind-blown sand, and by the Middle Horizon people had reverted to an earlier, essentially Archaic, subsistence regime, collecting marine resources from the distant sea and eating more wild plants than domesticated crops.

There are major disagreements among the models of Nasca society, but several points are clear. First, there was a set of art styles broadly shared across the region.

Rural villagers in distant communities had access to finewares, as did the elites at Cahuachi and elsewhere. Second, there were significant social differences between individuals in Nasca society, although it is not clear that rigid social classes existed. Third, the puquios seem to represent major investments in the agricultural infrastructure of Nasca society, projects designed to bring water to fields in the dry deserts of southern Peru.

Conclusion

The archaeological cases discussed in this chapter represent different kinds of prehistoric South American societies, varying in numerous dimensions. These peoples lived in starkly different environments—the cold coasts of Tierra del Fuego, the tropical rainforests of Orinoquia, and the narrow strips of arable land on the coast of Peru. These different communities deployed distinct technologies, producing elegant stone projectile points, elaborate ceramic urns, and stunning textiles. They pursued very different economic strategies: fishing, hunting marine mammals, pursuing guanaco and deer, creating riverine aquaculture, developing slash-and-burn agriculture, creating extensive raised agricultural fields, or building large irrigation projects. Based on current archaeological data, these communities varied from highly mobile bands, simple chiefdoms, more complex and hierarchical chiefdoms, and perhaps to social forms such as ritual-based pilgrimage networks or states. One might wonder why such different archaeological cases should be discussed in a single chapter.

Several interesting points make this comparison useful. First, these different societies existed at approximately the same time across South America. When Cahuachi was at its peak at AD 100–450, guanaco hunters roamed the pampas and people using Saladoid ceramics appeared in the Orinoco region. At the same time Marajoara chiefdoms thrived, between AD 400 and 1300, chiefdoms also developed in the Western Llanos of Venezuela. As people built mounds and population increased in the Upper Paraná between AD 1100 and 1280–1400, distant groups camped at the Túnel I site along the Beagle Channel. Of course, other South American societies lived other, very different types of lives (as discussed in chapters 9–11).

In addition to their rough contemporaneity, each of these cases represents examples of societies that are fully realized. A glance at the embroidery on a Nasca fabric or a studied examination of the iconography on a Nasca pot reveals a stunning human mastery of media, but the toolkit used for millennia at Túnel I also represents an enduring and masterful human adaptation to a challenging environment. The clever design of raised fields and causeways in the Western Llanos marks a society that has reached a critical plane of achievement. The intelligent projects that "domesticated" Amazonian floodwaters, routing flopping fish into ponds for the dry season, mark a mastery of the environment by the Marajoara, while the intricate ceramics designs of their pottery convey a deep concern with the cosmos. The planning involved in hauling stone out to key locations on a stone-less pampa is another example of the stunning human ability to solve problems, as are the wells and adits of puquios excavated to bring buried water to surface crops. These archaeological cases provide just a few examples of the different ways human societies flourished in the diverse regions of prehistoric South America.

Notes

1. The archaeological literature on Patagonia has tended to focus either on evidence for Paleoindian occupations or on the extension of ethnohistoric patterns into prehistory. For an overview of the literature on hunting-and-gathering adaptations in South America, see V. Scheinsohn, "Hunter-Gatherer Archaeology in South America," *Annual Reviews in Anthropology* 32 (2003): 339–361. For an introduction to Patagonia, its prehistory, and its ethnography, see the chapters in C. McEwan, L. Borrero, and A. Prieto, eds., *Patagonia: Natural History, Prehistory and Ethnography at the Uttermost End of the Earth* (Princeton, NJ: Princeton University Press, 1997). For early sites see L. Borrero, "Early Occupations in the Southern Cone," in *Handbook of South American Archaeology*, ed. H. Silverman and W. Isbell (New York: Springer, 2008), 59–77. For an overview of theoretical issues, see M. del Castillo Bernal, L. Mamelu, and J. Barceló, "La arqueología patagónica y la reconstrucción de la historia indígena," *Revista Española de Antropología Americana* 41, no. 1 (2011): 27–50.

2. J. A. Barceló, M. F. del Castillo, L. Mameli, E. Moreno, and B. Videla, "Where Does the South Begin? Social Variability at the Southern Top of the World," *Arctic Anthropology* 46, nos. 1–2 (2009): 51.

3. L. Borrero, "The Origins of Ethnographic Subsistence Patterns in Fuego Patagonia," in *Patagonia: Natural History, Prehistory, and Ethnography at the Uttermost End of the Earth*, ed. C. McEwan, L. Borrero, and A. Prieto (Princeton, NJ: Princeton University Press, 1997), 60–81. Various groups were given names by their neighbors or by Europeans (in parentheses), terms different from what they called themselves.

4. M. Mansur and R. Piqué, "Between the Forest and the Sea: Hunter-Gatherer Occupations in the Subantarctic Forests in Tierra del Fuego, Argentina," *Arctic Anthropology* 46, nos. 1–2 (2009): 144–146.

5. F. Morello, L. Borrero, M. Massone, C. Stern, A. García-Herbst, R. McCulloch, M. Arroyo-Kalin, E. Calás, J. Torres, A. Prieto, I. Martinez, G. Bahamonde, and P. Cárdenas, "Hunter-Gatherers, Biogeographic Barriers and the Development of Human Settlement in Tierra del Fuego," *Antiquity* 86 (2012): 71–87.

6. Barceló et al., "Where Does the South Begin?" 53.

7. A. Tessone, F. Zangrando, G. Barrientos, S. Valencio, H. Panarello, and R. Goñi, "Isótopos estables del carbón en Patagonia Meridional: Datos de la cuenca del Lago Salitroso (Provincia de Santa Cruz, República Argentina)," *Magallania* 33, no. 2 (2008): 27, my translation.

8. Morello et al., "Hunter-Gatherers, Biogeographic Barriers," 81–83.

9. D. Yesner, M. Figuerero Torres, R. Guichon, and L. Borrero, "Stable Isotope Analysis of Human Bone and Ethnohistoric Subsistence Patterns in Tierra del Fuego," *Journal of Anthropological Archaeology* 22 (2003): 279–291.

10. F. Mena, "Middle to Late Holocene Adaptations in Patagonia," in *Patagonia: Natural History, Prehistory and Ethnography at the Uttermost End of the Earth*, ed. C.

McEwan, L. Borrero, and A. Prieto (Princeton, NJ: Princeton University Press, 1997), 56–57.

11. As discussed in L. Orquera, "Advances in the Archaeology of the Pampa and Patagonia," *Journal of World Prehistory* 1, no. 4 (1987): 392–393.

12. Mena, "Middle to Late Holocene Adaptations," 57.

13. The phrase comes from the title of the 1951 book with the same title by Lucas Bridges; E. Lucas Bridges, *Uttermost Part of the Earth: The First History of Tierra del Fuego and the Fuegian Indians* (New York: Overlook/Rookery, 2007).

14. E. L. Piana and L. A. Orquera, "The Southern Top of the World: The First Peopling of Patagonia and Tierra del Fuego and the Cultural Endurance of the Fuegian Sea-Nomads," *Arctic Anthropology* 46, nos. 1–2 (2009): 103–117.

15. Ibid., 112.

16. Ibid., 113.

17. G. Politis, "The Pampas and Campos of South America," in *Handbook of South American Archaeology*, ed. H. Silverman and W. Isbell (New York: Springer, 2008), 235–236.

18. For a discussion of the archaeology of this region, see A. S. Dias, "Hunter-Gatherer Occupation of South Brazilian Atlantic Forest: Paleoenvironment and Archaeology," *Quaternary International* 256 (2012): 12–18.

19. G. Martinez and Q. Mackie, "Late Holocene Human Occupation of the Quequén Grande River Valley Bottom: Settlement Systems and an Example of a Built Environment in the Argentine Pampas," *Before Farming* 1 (2003–2004): 4.

20. The following is based on D. Loponte and A. Acosta, "Late Holocene Hunter-Gatherers from the Pampean Wetlands, Argentina," in *Zooarchaeology of South America*, ed. G. Mengoni Goñalons, British Archaeological International Series (Oxford: BAR, 2004), 39–57.

21. Ibid., 40.

22. Martinez and Mackie, "Late Holocene Human Occupation," 4. For a critical and alternative point of view, see M. Alvarez, "Subsistence Patterns during the Holocene in the Interserrana Area (Pampean Region, Argentina): Evaluating Intensification in Resource Exploitation," *Journal of Anthropological Archaeology* 34 (2014): 54–65.

23. C. Quintana, F. Valverde, and D. Mazzanti, "Roedores y lagartos como emergentes de la diversificación de la subsistencia durante el Holoceno Tardío en sierras de la región pampeana Argentina," *Latin American Antiquity* 13, no. 4 (2002): 470, my translation.

24. G. Martínez, A. Zangrando, and L. Prates, "Isotopic Ecology and Human Palaeodiets in the Lower Basin of the Colorado River, Buenos Aires Province, Argentina," *International Journal of Osteoarchaeology* 19 (2009): 281–296.

25. Martinez and Mackie, "Late Holocene Human Occupation," 14.

26. G. Politis, G. Martínez, and M. Bonomo, "Alfarería Temprana en Sitios de Cazadores—Recolectores de la Región pampeana (Argentina)," *Latin American Antiquity* 12, no. 2 (2001): 177, my translation.

27. Quoted in ibid., 86.

28. Ibid.

29. Ibid.

30. Ibid., 76.

31. Ibid., 86.

32. A. Roosevelt, *Moundbuilders of the Amazon: Geophysical Archaeology on Marajo Island, Brazil* (San Diego: Academic Press, 1991), 1.

33. Schaan has produced a number of outstanding studies on the Marajoara culture. For a synopsis, see D. Schaan, "The Nonagricultural Chiefdoms of Marajó Island," in *Handbook of South American Archaeology*, ed. H. Silverman and W. Isbell (New York: Springer, 2008), 339–357; D. Schaan, "Into the Labyrinths of Marajoara Pottery: Status and Cultural Identity in Prehistoric Amazonia," in *Unknown Amazonia: Culture in Nature in Ancient Brazil*, ed. C. McEwan, C. Barreto, and E. Neves (London: British Museum Press, 2001), 108–133; D. Schaan, "The Camutins Chiefdom: The Rise and Development of Social Complexity on Marajó Island, Brazilian Amazon" (PhD diss., University of Pittsburgh, 2004); D. Schaan, *Cultura Marajoara* (Rio de Janeiro: Senac Nacional, 2009). Another recent article is D. Schaan, "Long-Term Human Induced Impacts on Marajó Island Landscapes, Amazon Estuary," *Diversity* 2 (2010): 182–206.

34. B. Meggers and C. Evans, *Archaeological Investigations at the Mouth of the Amazon*, Bureau of Ethnology Bulletin 167 (Washington, DC: Smithsonian Institution, 1957), 17–18.

35. Schaan, "Nonagricultural Chiefdoms of Marajó Island," 341.

36. Ibid.

37. Schaan, "Camutins Chiefdom," 361.

38. Schaan, "Into the Labyrinths of Marajoara Pottery," 113.

39. Ibid.

40. Schaan, "Camutins Chiefdom," 360.

41. Schaan, "Into the Labyrinths of Marajoara Pottery," 116.

42. Ibid., 113.

43. Schaan, "Camutins Chiefdom," 391.

44. Ibid., 390.

45. Ibid.

46. A. von Humboldt, *Personal Narrative of a Journey to the Equinoctial Regions of the New Continent*, trans. J. Wilson (London: Penguin Classics, 1995 [1814–15]), 163. A "league" is the distance a traveler can cover in an hour, varying as to terrain and whether the traveler is on foot or horseback. Therefore, the distance of the bancos is a very rough estimate.

47. W. Bennett, "Excavations at La Mata, Maracay, Venezuela," *Anthropological Papers of the American Museum of Natural History* 36, no. 2 (1937): 69–137; C. Osgood, "Excavations at Tocorón, Venezuela," *Yale University Publications in Anthropology* 29 (1943); A. Kidder II, *Archaeology of Northwestern Venezuela*, Papers of the Peabody Museum of American Archaeology and Ethnology 26, no. 1 (Cambridge, MA: Harvard University, 1944). The invitation was arranged by the doctor, businessman, and aficionado of archaeology Dr. Rafael Requena (1879–1946), then the personal secretary to the Venezuelan president and caudillo, Dr. Juan Vicente Gómez (1857–1935; final term as president 1931–35). Despite his conviction of the reality of the myth of Atlantis, Requena was instrumental in the development of Venezuelan archaeology; for a brief overview of his role, see R. Gasson and E. Wagner, "Los otros 'vestigios de la Atlántida' o el

surgimiento de la arqueología moderna en Venezuela y susconsecuencias," in *Tiempos de Cambio: La Ciencia en Venezuela 1936–1948*, ed. Y. Freites and Y. Arna (Venezolana, Caracas: Fondo Editorial Acta Científica, 1992), 215–240.

48. C. Osgood and G. Howard, *An Archaeological Survey of Venezuela*, Yale University Publications in Anthropology 27 (New Haven, CT: Yale University Press, 1943).

49. G. Howard, *Excavations at Ronquín, Venezuela*, Yale University Publications in Anthropology 28 (New Haven, CT: Yale University Press, 1943); G. Howard, *Prehistoric Ceramic Styles of Lowland South America, Their Distribution and History*, Yale University Publications in Anthropology 37 (New Haven, CT: Yale University Press, 1947). Also see Anna Roosevelt's excellent monograph and discussion of Venezuelan ceramic chronology, *The Excavations at Corozal, Venezuela: Stratigraphy and Ceramic Seriation*, Yale University Publications in Anthropology 83 (New Haven, CT: Yale University Press, 1997).

50. For an anecdotal history of these developments, see G. Willey, *Portraits in American Archaeology: Remembrances of Some Distinguished Americanists* (Albuquerque: University of New Mexico Press, 1988).

51. W. Bennett, "Archaeological Work in South America, 1934 to 1936," *American Antiquity* 2, no. 4 (1937): 248–259. Although this report included nations with territories in Amazonia and Orinoquia, no investigations in lowland regions are mentioned.

52. I. Rouse, "Archaeology in Lowland South America and the Caribbean, 1935–60," *American Antiquity* 27, no. 1 (1961): 56–62.

53. I. Rouse and J. Cruxent, in *Venezuelan Archaeology* by Irving Rouse, José M. Cruxent (New Haven, CT: Yale University Press, 1963), 6, classified Venezuela as in the Intermediate zone, despite distancing themselves from Osgood's idea of the passive role of the region in receiving developments from afar.

54. For an extended discussion of Rouse's view on how his and Cruxent's research employed concepts such as styles, complexes, and traditions, see I. Rouse, "The Place of 'Peoples' in Prehistoric Research," *Journal of the Royal Anthropological Institute of Great Britain and Ireland* 95, no. 1 (1965): 1–15.

55. The following discussion is based on Rouse and Cruxent, *Venezuelan Archaeology*, 81–95, 112–129.

56. Ibid., 92.

57. M. Sanoja Obediente, *Las Culturas Formativas del Oriente de Venezuela: La Tradición Barrancas del Bajo Orinoco* (Caracas: Biblioteca de la Academia Nacional de la Historia, 1979), 15–16, my translation.

58. S. Wilson, *The Archaeology of the Caribbean* (Cambridge: Cambridge University Press, 2007), 63.

59. A. Zucchi, "Human Occupations of the Western Venezuelan Llanos," *Latin American Antiquity* 38, no. 2 (1973): 182–190; E. Redmond and C. Spencer, *Archaeological Survey in the High Llanos and Andean Piedmont of Barinas, Venezuela*, Anthropological Papers of the American Museum of Natural History 86 (New York: American Museum of Natural History, 2007).

60. Zucchi suggested the site covered 8 km^2 (3.09 square miles). The smaller estimate is based on Garson's subsequent survey cited in Redmond and Spencer, *Archaeological Survey in the High Llanos*, 79.

61. Cited in W. Denevan, "Prehistoric Roads and Causeways of Lowland Tropical America," in *Ancient Road and Settlement Hierarchies in the New World*, ed. C. Trombold (Cambridge: Cambridge University Press, 1991), 238–239.

62. C. Spencer and E. Redmond, "Prehispanic Causeways and Regional Politics in the Llanos of Barinas, Venezuela," *Latin American Antiquity* 9, no. 2 (1998): 95–110.

63. C. Spencer and E. Redmond, "Prehispanic Chiefdoms of the Western Venezuelan Llanos," *World Archaeology* 24, no. 1 (1992): 134–157.

64. Ibid., 149.

65. E. Redmond, R. Gasson, and C. Spencer, "A Macroregional View of Cycling Chiefdoms in the Western Venezuelan Llanos," in *Complex Polities in the Ancient Tropical World*, ed. J. Bacus and L. Lucero, Archaeological Papers of the American Anthropological Association 9 (Arlington, VA: American Anthropological Association, 1999), 118.

66. Redmond and Spencer, *Archaeological Survey in the High Llanos*, 325.

67. C. Spencer, E. Redmond, and M. Rinaldi, "Drained Fields at la Tigra, Venezuelan Llanos: A Regional Perspective," *Latin American Antiquity* 5, no. 2 (1994): 119–143.

68. Redmond, Gasson, and Spencer, "Macroregional View of Cycling Chiefdoms," 120.

69. An extensive literature exists regarding different aspects of Nasca society. A comprehensive and clear overview is H. Silverman and D. Proulx, *The Nasca* (Malden, MA: Blackwell, 2002). Also see D. Proulx, "Paracas and Nasca: Regional Cultures on the South Coast of Peru," in *Handbook of South American Archaeology*, ed. H. Silverman and W. Isbell (New York: Springer, 2008), 563–585. Alternative considerations are raised in K. Schreiber, "Regional Approaches to the Study of Prehistoric Empires: Examples from Ayacucho and Nasca, Peru," in *Settlement Pattern Studies in the Americas: Fifty Years since Virú*, ed. B. R. Billman and G. M. Feinman (Washington, DC: Smithsonian Institute Press, 1999), 160–171; K. Schreiber, "The Wari Empire of Middle Horizon Peru: The Epistemological Challenge of Documenting an Empire without Documentary Evidence," in *Empires*, ed. S. E. Alcock, T. N. D'Altroy, K. D. Morrison, and C. M. Sinopoli (Cambridge: University of Cambridge Press, 2001), 70–92.

70. J. Tello and M. Toribio Mejia Xesspe, *Paracas: Segunda Parte; Cavernas y Necropolis* (Lima: Universidad Nacional Mayor de San Marcos, 1979); R. Shady Solís, ed., *Arqueología del Rio Grande de Nasca*, Cuadernos de Investigación del Archivo Tello 3 (Lima: Museo de Arqueología e Antropología, Universidad Nacional Mayor de San Marcos, 2002).

71. Uhle's collections were not the result of his own excavations but instead a set of 660 vessels looted from various sites in the Rio Grande de Nazca region, which he purchased in 1905.

72. For an outstanding historical overview of Nasca studies, see D. Proulx, *A Sourcebook of Nasca Ceramic Iconography* (Iowa City: University of Iowa Press, 2006).

73. I. Unkel, M. Reindel, H. Gorbahn, J. Isla Cuadrado, B. Kromer, and V. Sossna, "A Comprehensive Numerical Chronology for the Pre-Columbian Cultures of the Palpa Valleys, South Coast of Peru," *Journal of Archaeological Science* 39 (2012): 2294–2303.

74. D. Proulx, *Settlement Patterns and Society in South Coastal Peru: Report on a Survey of the Lower Rio Nasca and Rio Grande, 1998* (Donald A. Proulx private collection, 2007).

75. K. Vaughn and M. Linares, "3,000 Years of Occupation in Upper Valley Nasca: Excavations at Upanca," *Latin American Antiquity* 17, no. 4 (2006): 595–612; K. Vaughn, "Households, Crafts, and Feasting in the Ancient Andes: The Village Context of Early Nasca Craft Consumption," *Latin American Antiquity* 15, no. 1 (2004): 61–88; H. Van Gijseghem and K. Vaughn, "Regional Integration and the Built Environment in Middle-Range Societies: Paracas and Early Nasca Houses and Communities," *Journal of Anthropological Archaeology* 27 (2008): 111–130.

76. K. Vaughn and H. Neff, "Moving beyond Iconography: Neutron Activation Analysis of Ceramics from Marcaya, Peru, an Early Nasca Domestic Site," *Journal of Field Archaeology* 27 (2000): 75–90; K. Vaughn and H. Neff, "Tracing the Clay Source of Nasca Polychrome Pottery: Results from a Preliminary Raw Material Survey," *Journal of Archaeological Science* 31 (2004): 1577–1586.

77. For example, Silverman and Proulx, *The Nasca*, 249.

78. A. Kroeber and D. Collier, *The Archaeology and Pottery of Nazca, Peru: Alfred Kroeber's 1926 Expedition*, ed. P. Carmichael (Walnut Creek, CA: Altamira, 1998).

79. W. Strong, "Paracas, Nazca, and Tiahuanacoid Cultural Relationships in South Coastal Peru," *Memoirs of the Society for American Archaeology* 13 (1957): 1–48.

80. Strong, "Paracas, Nazca, and Tiahuanacoid Cultural Relationships," 28.

81. These arguments are presented by H. Silverman, "Cahuachi: Non-Urban Cultural Complexity on the South Coast of Peru," *Journal of Field Archaeology* 15, no. 4 (1988): 403–430; H. Silverman, *Cahuachi in the Ancient Nasca World* (Iowa City: University of Iowa Press, 1993); H. Silverman, "The Archaeological Identification of an Ancient Peruvian Pilgrimage Center," *World Archaeology* 26 (1994): 1–18; H. Silverman, *Ancient Nasca Settlement and Society* (Iowa City: University of Iowa Press, 2002). For a recent stimulating theoretical discussion regarding pilgrimage, see J. Kantner and K. Vaughn, "Pilgrimage as Costly Signal: Religiously Motivated Cooperation in Chaco and Nasca," *Journal of Anthropological Archaeology* 31 (2012): 66–82.

82. G. Orefici, "Cahuachi, el centro ceremonial en adobe más grande del mundo," in *Nasca: El Desierto de los Dioses de Cahuachi/Nasca: The Desert of the Cahuachi Divinities*, ed. G. Orefici (San Isidro, Peru: Graph Ediciones, 2009), 40, my translation. See also Orefici's magisterial and beautiful two-volume book *Cahuachi: Capital Teocrática Nasca* (Lima: Universidad de San Martin de Porras, 2012), a magnificent publication.

83. E. Webb, C. White, and F. Longstaffe, "Exploring Geographic Origins at Cahuachi using Stable Isotopic Analysis of Archaeological Human Tissues and Modern Environmental Waters," *International Journal of Osteoarchaeology* 23, no. 6 (2013): 698–715.

84. K. Knudson, S. Williams, R. Osborn, K. Forgey, and P. Williams, "The Geographic Origins of Nasca Trophy Heads using Strontium, Oxygen, and Carbon Isotope Data," *Journal of Anthropological Archaeology* 28 (2009): 245. See also S. Williams, K. Forgey, and E. Klarich, *An Osteological Study of Nasca Trophy Heads Collected by A. L. Kroeber during the Marshall Field Expeditions to Peru* (Chicago: Field Museum of Natural History, 2001).

85. For an excellent overview of head-taking and its varied social and political contexts in South America, see D. Arnold and C. Hastorf, *Heads of State: Icons, Power, and Politics in the Ancient and Modern Andes* (Walnut Creek, CA: Left Coast Press, 2008).

86. For a review of the ritual use of trophy heads, see D. Proulx, "Ritual Uses of Trophy Heads in Ancient Nasca Society," in *Ritual Sacrifice in Ancient Peru*, ed. E. Benson and A. Cook (Austin: University of Texas Press, 2001), 119–136.

87. D. Browne, H. Silverman, and R. García, "A Cache of 48 Nasca Trophy Heads from Cerro Carapo, Peru," *Latin American Antiquity* 4, no. 3 (1993): 274–294.

88. Knudson et al., "Geographic Origins of Nasca Trophy Heads," 253.

89. For two nuanced discussions of the meaning of trophy heads in Early Nasca and Late Nasca societies, respectively, see L. DeLeonardis, "The Body Context: Interpreting Early Nasca Decapitated Burials," *Latin American Antiquity* 11 (2000): 363–386; C. A. Conlee, "Decapitation and Rebirth: A Headless Burial from Nasca, Peru," *Current Anthropology* 48, no. 3 (2007): 438–445.

90. See, for example, J. Isla and M. Reindel, "Burial Patterns and Sociopolitical Organization in Nasca 5 Society," in *Andean Archaeology III*, ed. H. Silverman (New York: Springer, 2006), 374–400.

91. K. Schreiber and J. Lancho Rojas, "The Puquios of Nasca," *Latin American Antiquity* 6 (1995): 229–254; K. Schreiber and J. Lancho Rojas, "El control del agua y los puquios de Nasca/Water and Aqueduct Control in Nasca," in *Nasca: El Desierto de los Dioses de Cahuachi/Nasca: The Desert of the Cahuachi Divinities*, ed. G. Orefici (San Isidro, Peru: Graph Ediciones, 2009), 132–151.

92. P. Carmichael, "Nasca Burial Patterns: Social Structure and Mortuary Ideology," in *Tombs for the Living: Andean Mortuary Practices*, ed. T. Dillehay (Washington, DC: Dumbarton Oaks, 1995), 161–187.

93. D. Beresford-Jones, O. Whaley, C. Alarcón Ledesma, and L. Cadwallader, "Two Millennia of Changes in Human Ecology: Archaeobotanical and Invertebrate Records from the Lower Ica Valley, South Coast Peru," *Vegetation History and Archaeobotany* 20 (2011): 290. See D. Beresford-Jones's remarkable book, *The Lost Woodlands of Ancient Nasca: A Case Study in Ecological and Cultural Collapse* (Oxford: Oxford University Press, 2011). See also D. Beresford-Jones, S. Arce T., O. Whaley, and A. Chepstow-Lusty, "The Role of Prosopis in Ecological and Landscape Change in the Samaca Basin, Lower Ica Valley," *Latin American Antiquity* 20, no. 2 (2009): 303–332.

94. Beresford-Jones et al., "Two Millennia of Changes in Human Ecology," 290.

Figure 9.1 Gold funerary mask from the North Coast of Peru

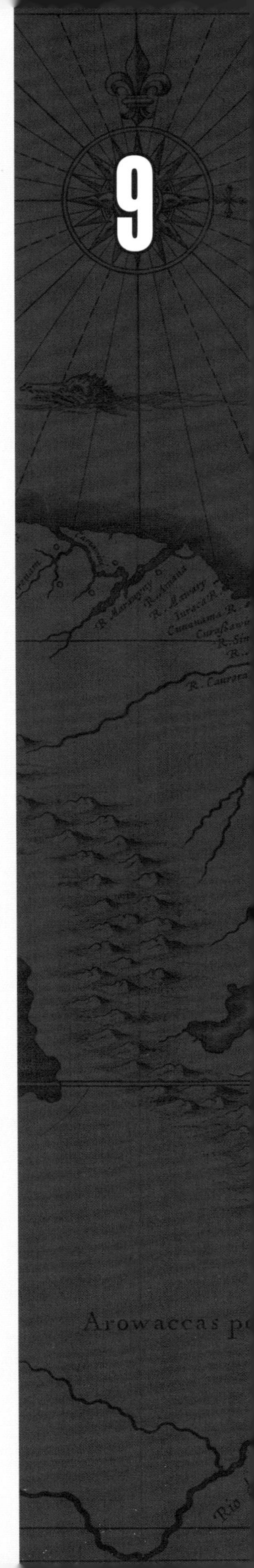

Age of States and Empires

10.5876_9781607323334.c009

> Some Indians relate that, in ancient times, before the Yncas extended their sway so far, there was a powerful lord in this valley, who was called Chimu, as the valley is now. He did great things, was victorious in many battles, and built certain edifices that even now, though so ancient, clearly appear to have been very grand.
>
> *Pedro Cieza de Leon, 1532–50,* Chronicle of Peru

When Spaniards invaded western South America in the early sixteenth century, they encountered one of the most impressive civilizations in the ancient world: the Inca Empire. Francisco Pizarro and his men captured the Inca king, Atahualpa, and began the process of conquest. Although the fall of the Inca Empire was not immediate and the consequences of conquest still reverberate across the Andes, the Spanish conquest and colonization of the Incas was a transformative clash between worlds, with multiple layers of consequence (discussed further in chapters 10 and 11).

Because of the enormous impact of the Inca Empire, both on the native peoples of the Andes and on the development of Andean archaeology, there has been a tendency to view the Incas and their empire as the culmination of earlier South American political systems and cultural patterns. This can only be true in a very limited sense, however, because the development of prehistoric South American empires occurred in a limited range in space and time.

As far as we know, empires developed in three regions of western South America: the **North Coast** of Peru, the **Central Andes**, and the **Titicaca Basin** (figure 9.2).

Further, these empires emerged in a relatively defined period between circa AD 500 and 1500. This millennium of Andean empires contrasts, for example, with the presence of empires in the circum-Mediterranean beginning in ancient Egypt in the fifteenth century BC and continuing until today in some manner. This caveat does not diminish the impressive accomplishments of Andean empires but rather places them within contexts of space and time. From a continental perspective, empires were the anomalies in South American prehistory, with chiefdoms more widespread and recurrent forms of socio-political complexity (as discussed in chapters 6, 7, and 8).

Some definitions are in order. **Empires**, the archaeologist **Carla Sinopoli** succinctly and usefully defines, "are large states with heterogeneous ethnic and cultural composition. They are formed through conquest or coercion, including both the application and/or the threat of force, through which powerful states incorporate less powerful polities and regions."[1] This definition delineates the social and political terrains in which empires emerge. First, empires

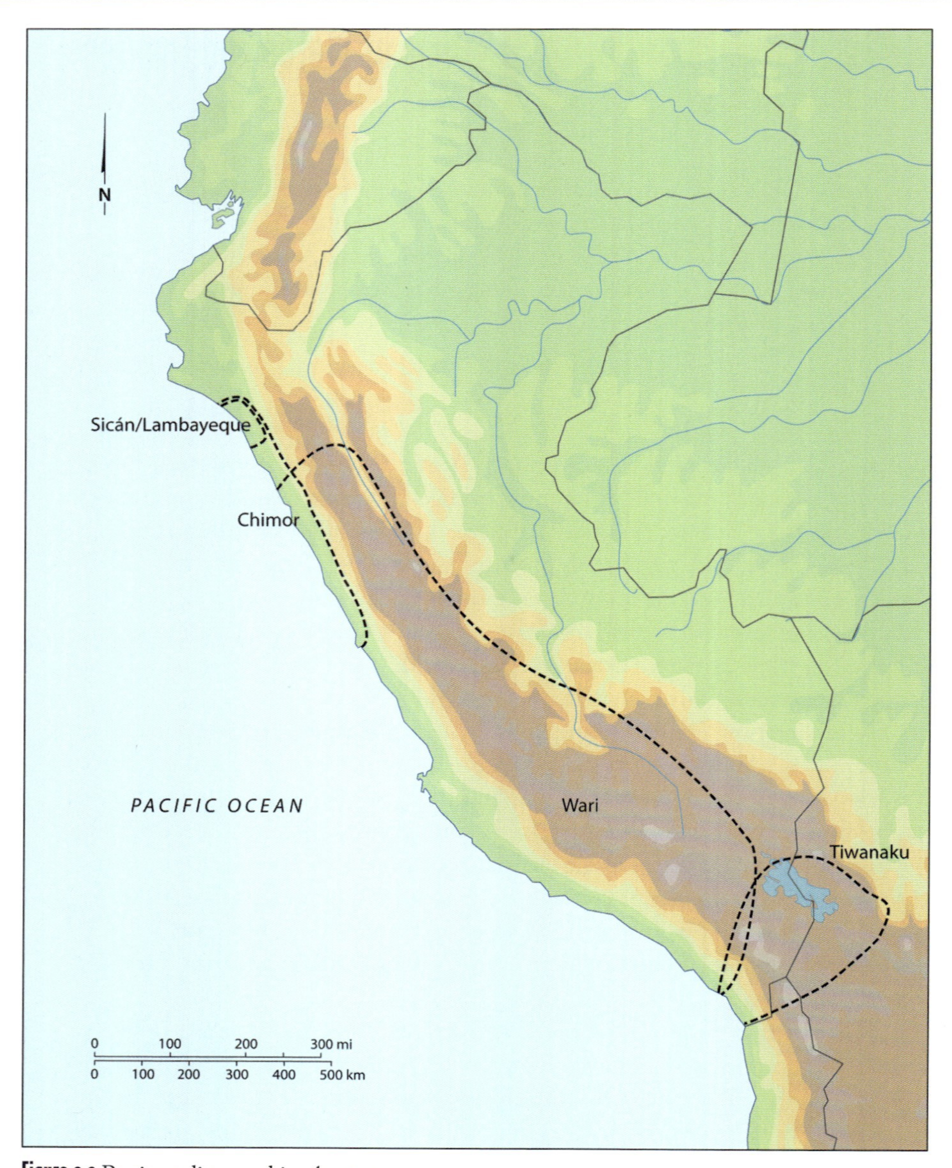

Figure 9.2 Regions discussed in chapter 9

are derived from preexisting **states**, political entities **Kent Flannery** has defined as "huge, politically centralized, socially stratified societies."[2] This definition is intentionally brief, encompassing, and relative. States encompass larger populations and territories than chiefdoms. States are often reflected in settlement hierarchies in which there are four levels (such as capital/cities/towns/villages). The largest settlements, or "primary centers," exhibit evidence for specific or unique functions; they may be the only places with royal palaces, principal temples, or major markets. Similarly, different settlements contain evidence for the differential mobilization of labor, with primary centers often having monumental architecture (such as temples or pyramids) or large public works (such as road systems, planned communities, or waterworks) not found in smaller settlements. Finally, state-level societies exhibit clear differences among people, with divisions based on wealth, caste, ethnicity, or some combination reflected in myriad ways—whether by dwelling, clothing, or burial practices. Within these broad parameters, there are enormous variations among states.

Despite such variations, states are the building blocks of empires, and empires emerge from landscapes of conflict. Empires develop when ascendant states exert their control over other peoples and polities, a process usually met with covert or overt resistance. This necessarily means that empires vary in stability and duration. Empires may last for centuries (such as the Roman and Ottoman Empires) or only for a single ruler's lifespan. Empire building requires more than military conquest; it involves multiple and overlapping spheres, including the manipulation of ideology, attempts to achieve legitimacy, the ability to integrate and administer people and territory, and efforts to obtain the resources required to rule. These complex problems are seldom "solved." Empires are rarely stable. Sinopoli writes, "Empires are not created out of whole cloth, but change throughout their histories in structure, organization, composition, and cultural content. An understanding of any empire thus requires an understanding of its historical trajectory and the nature of and reasons underlying changes in its structure and content." She adds, "The extent to which more coherent strategies are developed within particular empires may relate to (1) a polity's duration (and vice versa), (2) whether or not stable infrastructures are created (including administrative structures, military structures, transport networks), and (3) whether unifying ideological or belief systems are successfully fostered."[3]

The North Coast: Moche, Lambayeque, and Chimú

The North Coast of Peru is approximately 400 km (240 miles) long, extending roughly from the Huarmey Valley north to the Piura Valley and the Sechura Desert (figure 9.3).[4]

As discussed in chapter 2, the region is an arid, relatively narrow coastal plain sliced by a series of river valleys that have their headwaters in the Andean cordillera. These well-watered valleys contrast starkly with the barren deserts that border them; it is not surprising that they were the locations for human occupations throughout prehistory. Several of these valleys were centers for the development of Andean states and empires.

The **Moche** developed in different coastal valleys at different times in the centuries between AD 200 and 800 (see figure 9.2). This polity developed in two zones, a southern sphere in the **Moche and neighboring Chicama Valleys** and a northern sphere centered in the lower **Lambayeque Valley** that at various times extended to the **Jequetepeque and Piura Valleys**. As discussed below, archaeological understanding of Moche is very much in flux, and even a seemingly simple statement about "where the Moche lived" glosses over complex interpretations.

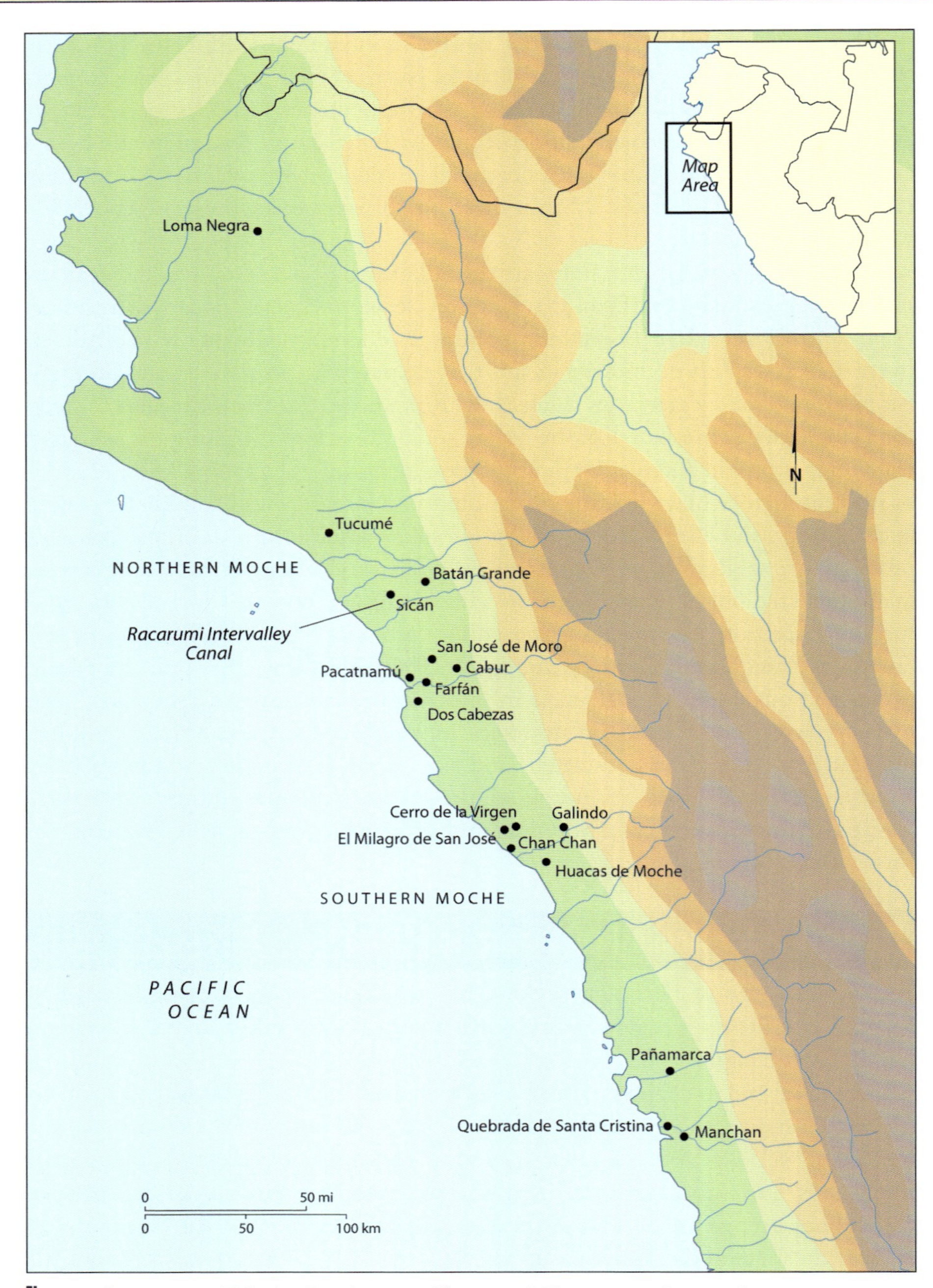

Figure 9.3 Locations of Moche, Lambayeque/Sicán, and Chimú sites discussed

The **Lambayeque or Sicán culture** (ca. AD 750–1375) (not surprisingly) developed in the Lambayeque Valley, but by the Middle Sicán period (ca. AD 900–1100) it had established a cultural presence in the Jequetepeque Valley, as well as having some interaction with the Tumbes region in far northern Peru.

Figure 9.4 Huaca de la Luna (*foreground*), Huaca del Sol, and the modern city of Trujillo, Peru, in the distance

Finally, the **Chimú Empire** (ca. AD 900–1470) spread out from the Moche Valley in a multi-stage process of imperial expansion that ultimately encompassed most of the valleys of the North Coast, in the process creating the largest polity conquered by the Inca Empire. These three cultural traditions and varying political systems interacted in complex ways.

The Mochicas (ca. AD 200–850)

The Moche culture (ca. AD 200–850) is one of the most intensively studied of the archaeological cultures in South America.[5] There has been a tremendous increase in archaeological research into Moche culture since the mid-1980s.[6] The reasons for this tardy expansion in understanding are somewhat baffling. The enormous mounds at the **site of Moche** are looming prominences on the landscape of the lower Moche Valley that attracted looters and collectors since the Colonial era (figure 9.4).

The major constructions at the site of Moche, **Huaca del Sol** and **Huaca de la Luna**, were mentioned by Eduardo de Rivero y Ustaríz in 1841 and were the destination of a day's visit by Ephraim George Squier, who lavished much more attention on the ruins and artifacts of the Chimú capital, Chan Chan (see chapter 1). By the late nineteenth and early twentieth centuries, Moche ceramics were in European museums and private collections, yet there was a level of uncertainty about Moche's place within Central Andean prehistory. In part, this was a result of early historical accounts that recalled the existence of the Chimú but were mute about the much earlier Moche.

In 1895 and again in 1899–1900, **Max Uhle** conducted two excavation campaigns at the site, digging at the base of Huaca de la Luna where he uncovered

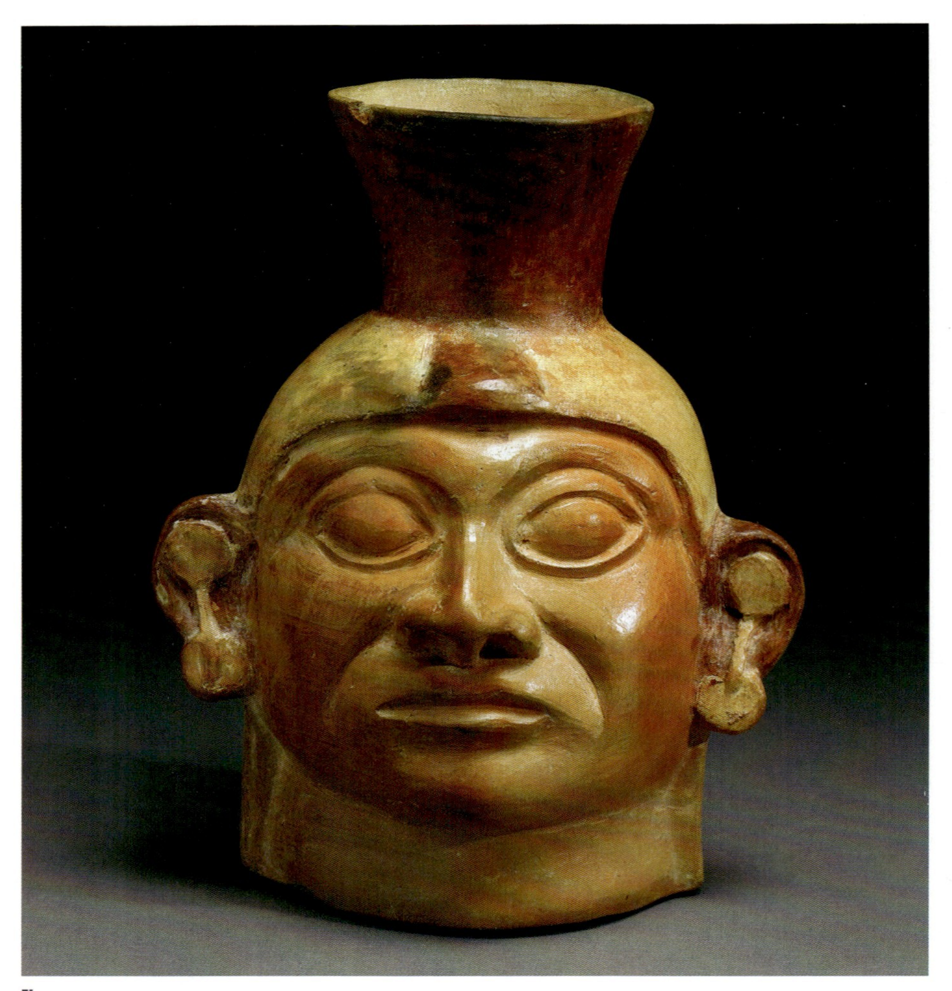

Figure 9.5 Mold-made Moche portrait vessel

spectacular mold-made polychrome ceramics that antedated the blackware pottery he had encountered in his earlier excavations at **Pachacamac** (see chapter 1). At Pachacamac, Uhle had uncovered superimposed burial lots that allowed for the construction of a rough relative chronology, with the late Inca materials underlain by earlier blackwares and even earlier polychromes he associated with Tiwanaku (later determined to be Wari pottery; see below).[7] At Moche, other polychrome vessels (obviously *not* Tiwanaku ceramics) were discovered beneath Chimú blackwares (figure 9.5).

Uhle classified these North Coast mold-made polychromes as "Proto-Chimu." Writing about the Uhle collections, the American anthropologist **Alfred Kroeber** observed, "Proto-Chimu pottery is the well-known red and white ware of the northern Peruvian coast, the most freely and best, modeled in Peru; bearing loop or stirrup handles which are also spouts; usually flat-bottomed; and tem-

Figure 9.6 Moche feline effigy vessel

pered, baked, and polished with consistent skill. There are some mediocre pieces among the 600 from Moche sites [in Uhle's collections,] but scarcely any poor ones, technologically."[8]

That was an understatement.

The Mochicas created some of the most spectacular pottery known from the ancient world (figure 9.6).

In addition to a broad array of utilitarian wares, the Moche devised two major classes of exquisite vessels: mold-made pottery and vessels covered with fine-line paintings with amazing accuracy and artistic control. The mold-made pottery depicts the world of the Mochicas. Pots portray plants, animals, buildings, warriors, kings, sacrificial victims, and deities. The pots also depict a variety of human activities: child rearing, warfare, and exuberant sex. Many of these vessels are more sculptures than pots. For example, one class of mold-made pots called "portrait vessels" literally depicts different faces, almost all of men. The Moche expert **Christopher Donnan** has observed, "Only a few ancient civilizations actually developed true portraiture, showing the anatomical features of a person with such accuracy that the individual could be recognized without reliance on accompanying symbols or texts. Of all the civilizations that developed in the Americas prior to European contact, only one perfected true portraiture and produced it in quantity."[9] That, of course, was the Moche.

Moche potters also made fine-line vessels, which were decorated with intricate scenes painted in black or brown pigments. Many scenes were painted on stirrup-spout vessels, the imagery scrolling around the bottle's globe, although plates and other vessels also had fine-line decorations. The themes of fine-line vessels were just as diverse as those of the mold-made pottery—women weaving on back-strap looms, caravans of load llamas, lords receiving tribute, and war victims tortured by their executioners.

In addition to the aesthetic elegance and the fascinating (and sometimes horrifying) scenes depicted on Moche pots, these artifacts are significant for two profound reasons. First, the variations in Moche ceramics—particularly in the forms of stirrup-spout vessels—provided the first basis for a relative chronology for the Moche. Second, we now understand that some scenes displayed on Moche pots really happened.

Moche artifacts were desired not only by foreign museums and antiquarians, but Peruvian collectors also amassed enormous collections. Preeminent among them was **Rafael Larco Hoyle** (1901–66).[10] A member of a wealthy family from the Chicama Valley, Larco Hoyle was educated in Peru and the United States, pursuing university studies at Cornell and New York University in agriculture and business administration—training for his future in commerce. Throughout his life, Larco Hoyle managed and diversified his family's sugar plantation and commercial interests, but he also devoted significant effort (and wealth) to acquiring archaeological collections and engaging in serious study of the materials. This led to the establishment of the Museo Larco in 1926, housed in a separate building at the family's Hacienda Chiclín, in the Chicama Valley. Not only did Larco Hoyle dramatically increase the collections (e.g., buying thousands of objects from hacienda owners in other coastal valleys during the Depression) but he also engaged in survey, site recording, and excavations.

Larco Hoyle's investigations resulted in several important insights for archaeology of the North Coast. First, Larco Hoyle identified and defined North Coast cultures before the Moche, the archaeological complexes of **Cupisnique** (ca. 1000–50 BC)—a style that showed strong affinities with Chavín culture (see chapter 7)—and **Salinar** (400 BC–AD 1). Second, Larco Hoyle proposed a five-stage relative chronology for the Moche defined by changes in the forms of stirrup-spout vessels. This five-stage chronology spanned the period of about AD 100–700 and was the major chronological framework for the next fifty years.

Related to this chronological framework, Larco Hoyle proposed an influential model of the organization of Moche society and polity. The leading scholars of Moche studies, **Luis Jaime Castillo** and **Santiago Uceda**, provide a succinct summary of Larco Hoyle's model:

> Rafael Larco Hoyle . . . conceived of the Mochicas as [a] single, unified and centralized society that originated in the Moche and Chicama valleys . . . The Mochicas had a single capital, the Huaca del Sol–Huaca de la Luna site, with an urban center between the two monuments, and from which an omnipotent elite ruled the entire north coast, combining coercion and conviction, military power and a powerful ideology based on elaborate religious liturgy, temples, and ceremonial artifacts that legitimated the dominant regime. A unified Mochica society could only have had a single developmental sequence, in which the extension of the state first grew steadily to control the valleys north and south, and then declined[,] losing control of these territories until finally it was subsumed by a foreign power. A unified developmental sequence would also translate into increasing complexity of its intuitions, scope, and use of technologies.[11]

This basic model of a unitary Moche polity whose capital was at Huaca de la Luna–Huaca del Sol remained the essential perspective until the late 1980s, when discoveries in northern Peru triggered a reexamination of the ceramic chronology and of Moche's unitary nature. The best-known of these discoveries was the fabulous **Tomb of the Lord of Sipán** in the Lambayeque Valley.[12]

Although 350 Moche tombs have been excavated scientifically on the North Coast of Peru, many more have been sacked by looters searching for fine artifacts to sell. In 1987 the tombs at Sipán nearly suffered the same fate, as local looters dug into one of the smaller pyramids. The looting was halted by the police, who confiscated some of the objects and notified the Peruvian archaeologist **Walter Alva Alva** of the Bruning Museum in the city of Lambayeque.

Police officers armed with machine guns cordoned off the Sipán pyramid, and Alva and his team began a salvage excavation at the site. Traces of superimposed constructions exposed in the looters' pits showed at least six building stages. Alva and his team cleared the grave robbers' trenches and tunnels and—amazingly—recovered spectacular artifacts the looters had overlooked, including a meter-long, elaborately modeled royal scepter.[13] These objects immediately posed a problem for Larco's unitary model of the Moche: If the site of Moche was the capital of a unified state, then why was a royal scepter in the Lambayeque Valley?

But Sipán held even more surprises.

Alva Alva and his colleagues continued cleaning up after the looters, finally arriving at an intact, undisturbed surface. Excavating into an adobe-lined chamber in the mound, they exposed seventeen wooden beams laid across the chamber. These roof beams were intact, and underneath them was the tomb of the Lord of Sipán (figure 9.7).

A thirty-five- to forty-five-year-old adult male, the Lord of Sipán was accompanied by a dazzling wealth of objects. The Tomb of the Lord of Sipán is the richest burial excavated by archaeologists anywhere in the Americas. Over a thousand ceramic vessels were in the tomb. The body was in a coffin made from

Figure 9.7 Reconstruction of the royal tombs at Sipán

wooden planks (a rare commodity on the desert coast), held together by straps of beaten copper. There were broad collars (pectorals) of *Spondylus* shell beads, thousands of minuscule disks each smaller than a lentil. The body was attired in a knee-length tunic appliquéd with gilded copper platelets; a necklace with gold and silver beads shaped like peanuts, the largest more than 3½ inches long; and another silver necklace that depicted a coil of human heads. The lord had four metal nose ornaments, half-moon sheets of beaten gold. His head was covered with a large sheet of hammered gold, shaped to fit the contours of his face, his features permanently defined by a gilded set of artificial eyes, nose, and mouth. The Lord of Sipán was buried with several gold crowns and several sets of ear spools: elegant disks made from hammered gold and turquoise that portrayed preening ducks, prancing deer, and a Moche king flanked by warriors. Among the numerous rich offerings was a golden back-flap, a distinctive Moche object that dangled behind from a warrior's belt.

The Lord of Sipán was a warrior-king. This was a royal grave.

He did not go to his grave alone. Six other individuals flanked the lord's coffin: two adult men, three young adult females, and a nine- to ten-year-old child. One man may have been a bodyguard; the other man's status is unknown. The women had died long before the lord's death, and their disarticulated bones were carefully wrapped in textiles and placed in the tomb. When the child died is unknown. These six bodies had lain with the Lord of Sipán for seventeen centuries.

The Sipán discovery had a clear implication: if this was a royal burial of a Moche king, then it strongly suggested that the site of Moche was not the single capital of a unified state. Even if he had died during an inspection tour of the north, presumably the Lord of Sipán would have been carried back to Moche if it were the only royal capital.

Other reconsiderations of Larco Hoyle's model were based on more than a single excavation. The discovery of **Moche ceramics in the northern Piura Valley**, along with ceramics of the **Vicús style**, indicated a distinctive stylistic blend, a Moche-Vicús culture marked in its earliest phases by sophisticated and beautiful ceramics followed by simpler and coarser ceramics—a ceramic sequence not anticipated by Larco Hoyle's model. In 1983 investigations of Moche burials from the site of **Pacatnamú** in the Jequetepeque Valley documented another ceramic sequence that did not follow Larco's five-stage chronology. Excavations at the site of **San Jose del Moro**, also in the Jequetepeque Valley, documented these variations.[14] In these northern sites, the ceramic sequence was not a five-stage sequence but a three-phase chronology, roughly corresponding to Moche I, III, and V but with additional differences between the northern Lambayeque and Jequetepeque Valleys and the Moche Valley and neighboring valleys to the south (see figure 9.5).

These archaeological reassessments have led to a fundamental revision in models of the spread and political organization of Moche culture. Rather than a single, monolithic, and centralized polity, Castillo and Uceda write, "it seems more likely that the rise of the Mochicas was a case of multiple origins, happening in several different locations of the north coast, at different moments and most likely generated by different preconditions." Descending from local predecessors, Moche culture developed "first as an elite tradition" that diversified. Diversification was accompanied by "the extension of agricultural fields due to better and more reliable irrigation technologies . . . [that] would have produced higher agricultural yields and thus opportunities for personal enrichment. A new and wealthier elite could easily develop in this environment, creating opportunity and need for social differentiation, as well as a higher dependency on culturally produced resources. Ceremonialism, the need for bigger and more elaborate temples, and the development of more refined ritual objects and paraphernalia all materialized an ideology that needed to emphasize social division and status differentiation . . . The Mochicas developed at this time, under these opportunities and circumstances." This rich elite culture influenced craft workers and eventually "trickled down to lower social strata, eventually to influence and shape all aspects of society," but the process varied in different regions.[15]

Currently, the strongest evidence for a centralized Moche state comes from the southern valleys, where the site of Moche was the largest urban center, covering more than a square kilometer between Huaca de la Luna and Huaca del Sol. On the south side of the site, Huaca de la Luna was a vast complex of temples and plazas, perched at the base of Cerro Blanco (figure 9.8).

The product of multiple construction stages, the east side of Huaca de la Luna was a stepped platform that loomed over a large walled plaza. The facades of each

Figure 9.8 Huaca de la Luna at the foot of Cerro Blanco

tier were covered with larger-than-life murals depicting sinuous dragons with feline heads, lines of male dancers, warriors on parade, and neck-bound prisoners being led to executions. Inner walls of the temple were covered with checkerboard murals of a fanged deity (figure 9.9).

Another spectacular mural depicted a complex scene of warriors and priests, monkeys and parrots, suns and stars, fishermen on rafts, and dozens of other motifs. It is a sophisticated mural whose meaning is unknown but whose narrative structure is indisputable (figure 9.10).

Huaca de la Luna was a multi-layer complex, an enormous stack of plazas, patios, temples, and enchanting artworks where rituals were accompanied by the screams of human sacrifice.

Human sacrifice is commonly depicted on Moche fine-line pottery and documented by the traces of violent death on skeletons. The archaeologist **Steven Bourget** uncovered the remains of seventy-five human sacrifices in one courtyard of Huaca de la Luna, individuals executed over five separate episodes.[16] Analysis of dental traits among the dead suggests that they came from multiple populations from outside the Moche Valley, perhaps war captives brought to Huaca de la Luna for sacrifice.[17] The skeletons were in one of the side areas in Huaca de la Luna, a smallish plaza with 8 m (26 ft)-tall walls enclosing a large boulder outcropping from the lower flanks of Cerro Blanco. The skeletons were covered in layers of clay that had eroded from the adobe walls, perhaps runoff during torrential El Niño rains. The skeletons exhibited multiple signs of trauma—knife-slashed temporal

Figure 9.9 "Checkerboard" relief, Huaca de la Luna

lobes, club-crushed crania, and throats slashed, leaving cut marks on cervical vertebrae—brutal deaths like those depicted in sacrifice scenes on fine-line ceramics. Even in death, these victims found no peace: their bodies were pulled apart, the lower jaws yanked out, their faces flayed. The bodies were then left unburied, exposed to the sun and wind. When excavated, the skeletons were covered with hundreds of egg casings from muscoid flies, buzzing insects that quickly discovered the dead, settled over the bodies, laid eggs that grew to larvae, and ultimately reemerged as adult flies that swarmed away to new sources of decay. Bourget suggests, "The departure of hundreds of new flies would have signaled the end of the sacrificial ceremony."[18]

These discoveries point to some of the complexities of Moche society. The Moche were amazing craftsmen, creators of some of the most elegant objects ever produced by humans. The Moche also engaged in acts of cruelty and torture, among the darkest acts of brutality known in human history. And they built great monuments.

A half-kilometer to the north, Huaca del Sol was one of the largest constructions built in prehispanic South America (figure 9.11).

Originally 228 m × 136 m (748 ft × 446 ft) at its base, over 40 m (131 ft) tall, and constructed in at least eight different phases, Huaca del Sol contained an estimated 130 million adobe bricks. Many of the bricks were marked by imprinted lines, divots, and other signs thought to be **makers' marks**, signifying the hundreds of corvée labor groups responsible for providing the bricks (figure 9.12).[19]

Figure 9.10 Complex, possibly narrative, mural, Huaca de la Luna

Figure 9.11 Adobe construction exposed in the upper portion of Huaca del Sol

Figure 9.12 Adobes with makers' marks

On the flat plain between the two huacas were densely packed barrios of workshops and dwellings that covered about 100 ha (247 acres). This urban core was defined by a grid of roads and alleys running north-south and east-west that demarcated blocks.[20] Within each block, combinations of rooms, patios, and storage bins were used in different workshops that produced ceramics, metal objects, semi-precious stone ornaments, and textiles. Craft production was specialized and organized at Moche.

Various lines of evidence and inference suggest that the southern Moche was a state. The southern region exhibits a primary center (the site of Moche) and other affiliated settlements in the Moche, Chicama, Virú, and Nepeña Valleys. The evidence for social divisions is compelling. There is indisputable evidence for the mobilization of human labor and the creation of public works, including the expansion of irrigation canals in the Moche Valley (see chapter 5).[21] The Moche used military power. Although the southern Moche polity was apparently more centralized than the northern kingdoms, there were significant variations as the heyday of Moche culture ended.[22] In the south, the Moche state seems to have undergone changes in the late AD 700s and early 800s. While it was previously thought that the site of Moche was abandoned during Moche IV and the mid-valley site of **Galindo** became the Moche V center in the valley, the current picture is more complicated. The site was not abandoned, the Moche IV and Moche V styles temporally overlapped in use, and Huacas de Moche continued to be occupied into the early 800s. In the northern valleys, Moche styles were used and elites retained their positions well into the ninth century, interacting

Figure 9.13 Lambayeque effigy bottle

with the expansionistic Wari Empire (discussed later) until they were dislodged by highland chiefdoms based in Cajamarca. Neither the development nor the "collapse" of the Moche was uniform or monolithic. The trajectories of decline of the Mochicas were just as complex as their pathways to florescence.

Lambayeque/Sicán (AD 750/800–1375)

The cultural tradition referred to as **Lambayeque** or **Sicán** is unevenly known, with specific aspects understood in detail and other swaths of knowledge vaguely documented (figure 9.13).

The core region of this society was a cluster of river valleys—the Motupe, La Leche, Reque, Lambayeque, and Zaña Rivers and their tributaries—that today is one of the largest farming regions in Peru, although a breadbasket dependent on irrigation.[23]

A seventeenth-century legend recalled the arrival of a Lord Ñamlap from a distant land who established a royal house and dynasty in the valley that bears his name.[24] According to the legend, Ñamlap was accompanied by his queen and a retinue of courtiers: a cook, a brewer, someone responsible for his clothing and face paints, and "a Preparer of the Way" who sprinkled the pink and white powder of ground *Spondylus* shells in the ruler's path (figure 9.14).

Ñamlap sired many children and lived a long life, but as death approached Ñamlap retired to his palace, where he died hidden from his subjects. So the legend became that he had flown from his palace and taken immortal form. Ñamlap's dynasty continued and, as with Ñamlap, the deaths of his heirs were concealed from commoners, although the royal burial mounds were recognized as sacred huacas for centuries.

Despite being sacred and noble, these large mounds have been the targets of some of the most intense and organized looting in South America.[25] For decades, Lambayeque Valley sites have been destroyed by grave robbers seeking gold (figure 9.15).

Vast quantities of artifacts were dug up and sold to collectors and museums. For example, between the 1930s and the 1970s, the site of **Batan Grande** was looted systematically in grave-robbing campaigns organized by the owner of the hacienda on which the huacas stood. Recent estimates are that more than 100,000 looters' pits pockmark the site, which has been termed "a mecca" of grave looting.[26]

Excavations directed by **Izumi Shimada** have dramatically contributed to archaeological knowledge of the Sicán polity.[27] Based on radiocarbon dates and significant shifts in cultural practices, three phases are recognized: Early Sicán (AD 750/800–900), Middle Sicán (AD 900–1100), and Late Sicán (AD 1100–1375). Shimada describes Early Sicán ceramics as having a characteristic black polished surface; these ceramics have been found between Moche V and Middle Sicán layers at **Huaca del Pueblo Batan Grande** and at the site of **Sicán**. Polished blackware ceramics continue into later phases. The Early Sicán ceramics exhibit a "prototype" of depictions of the **Sicán Deity** and the **Sicán Lord**, according to Shimada the "hallmark icons" of Middle Sicán art.[28] Despite this stylistic continuity, there were major differences between the periods. For example, the Early Sicán apparently did not build corporate architecture, whereas the Middle Sicán built some of the largest pyramids on the North Coast of Peru.[29]

The Middle Sicán period was characterized by monumental constructions, the development of extensive metallurgical production, and the creation of distinctive blackware pottery—including a double-spout and bridge bottle. Shimada argues that this phase was marked by the development of a state-level society whose capital was at Sicán, a site with over a dozen monumental mounds associated with tombs. The site's Great Plaza (500 m × 250 m [1,640 ft × 820 ft]) was flanked by a large mound complex called **Huaca Loro**, a truncated pyramid 80 m × 80 m (262 ft × 262 ft) at its base and 35 m (114.8 ft) tall, joined to a 150 m (492 ft)-long multi-level platform on its north side. Huaca Loro and the surrounding

Figure 9.14 Lambayeque funerary tunic

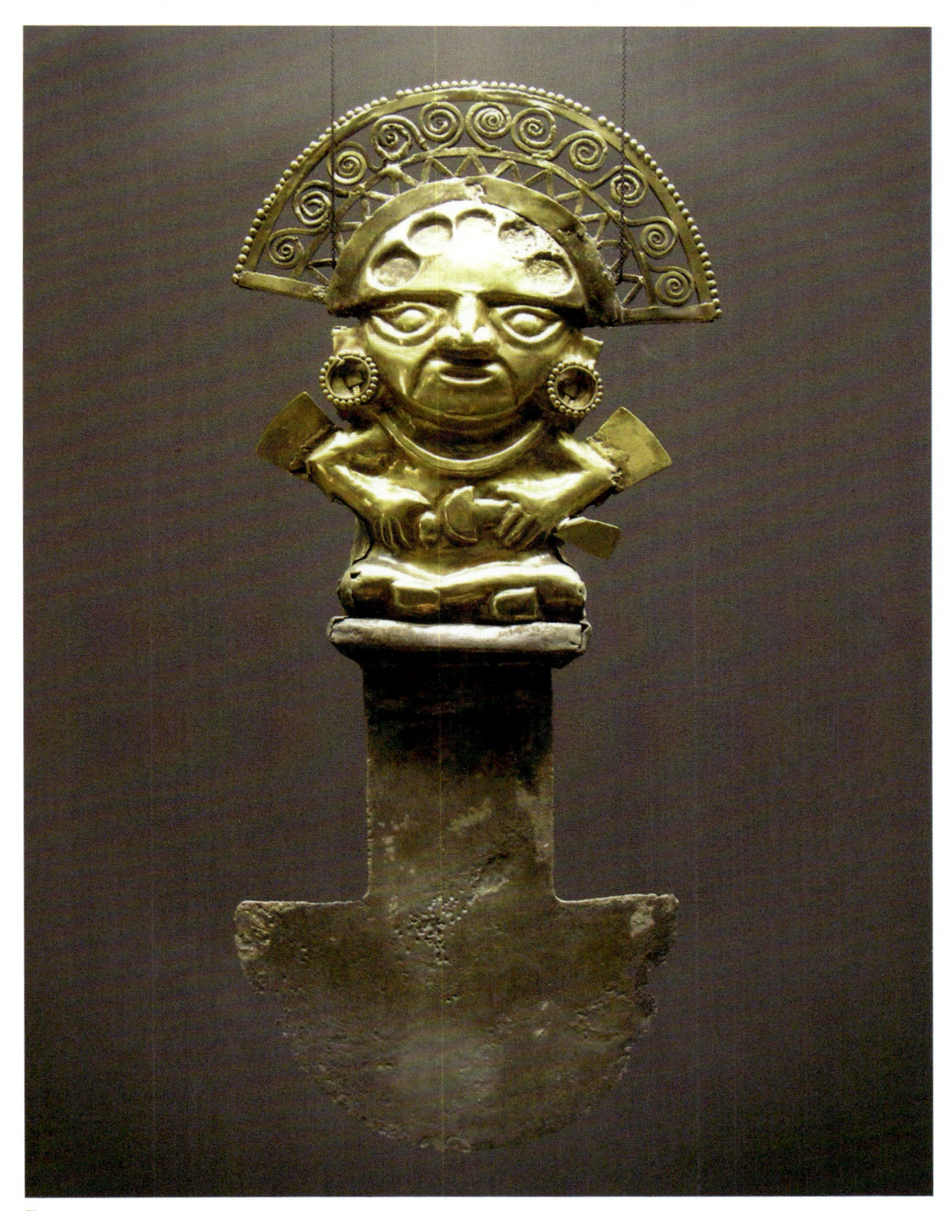

Figure 9.15 Lambayeque gold tumi

mounds at Sicán were topped with colonnaded temples decorated by polychrome murals. Extensive offerings of *Spondylus* shells, copper-arsenic bronze artifacts, and human sacrifices were placed in the huacas. The builders used **chamber and fill construction**, in which large rectangular cells of adobe brick retaining walls were filled with rubble, household debris, and other materials and then capped by a layer of adobe bricks and built upon again.[30] The bricks varied in size, and diagonal and curving lines, dots, footprints, or other impressions marked many adobes. As at the site of Moche (see figure 9.12), these impressions are interpreted as makers' marks, and the bewildering array of marks in a single wall or chamber may indicate that builders obtained their adobes from multiple producers, perhaps from different territories, or from communities controlled by different local elites. Thus, the huacas at Sicán and other Lambayeque sites suggest the centralized control of labor, as large projects drew on and coordinated the work of people from various communities.

Production and labor were organized to produce tremendous quantities of metal objects (see figure 9.1).[31] Metallurgy involved both crafting of exquisite gold alloy objects for elites and mass production of copper-arsenic bronze for more common objects, such as needles, tumi knives, hoe blades, digging stick tips, and flat I-shaped sheets of copper that were exchange items and may have been used as a form of money.[32] Gold alloy objects ranged from 1 to 21 karats, composed of gold, silver, and copper selected by Lambayeque metalsmiths for their various physical qualities. Hammered sheets of gold alloy—0.03–0.05 millimeters thin—were worked by cutting, engraving, or joining multiple pieces into complex objects. Copper objects were mass-produced in metalworking shops, specialist areas separated from dwellings, again suggesting some form of centralized control.

The volume of this metallurgical output is astonishing. For example, Shimada describes the metal objects recovered from the intact East Tomb at Huaca Loro, a 3 m × 3 m (9.8 ft × 9.8 ft) chamber that held the skeletons of the principal adult male, two women, and two juveniles. More than *1.2 tons of grave goods were in the tomb*, including fifteen bundles of copper objects weighing more than 200 kg (440 lbs) and 2,000 small sheets of gold foil once sewn to garments. The principal male had gold ear spools, a pair of gold gauntlets each nearly a meter long, and a face mask made from sheet gold measuring 46 cm × 29 cm with inlaid eyes—the whites from silver alloy, irises of amber, and pupils of emeralds. The mask, Shimada remarks justifiably, was "a masterpiece of Sicán goldsmithing."[33]

The Lambayeque polity also organized pottery production in ceramics and engaged in long-distance exchange. Sicán potters made very distinctive mold-made, blackware bottles with double spouts flared like horns and a complex bridge piece often crowned by the image of the "Lord of Sicán." The Lord of Sicán is distinguished by his double-peaked hat or crown and his large ear spools, and he may depict Ñamlap. Although archaeologists easily confuse blackware sherds from Lambayeque vessels with later Chimú ceramics, indisputable Middle Sicán ceramics are reported as far north as the Piura Valley and Ecuador's Isla de Plata and as far south as **Pachacamac** and **Ancon** on the Central Coast of Peru (see chapter 10). The presence of these ceramics strongly points to long-distance exchange networks, in which copper and ceramics were traded north to obtain products from the northern Andes, such as *Spondylus* shells, amber, and emeralds.

In addition to organizing production of metal objects and pottery, the Lambayeque polity expanded agricultural production. As with the Moche and later Chimú, irrigation systems were essential elements of the agricultural infrastructure for Lambayeque society. Although many Sicán/Lambayeque canals have been destroyed by subsequent agriculture, a well-preserved and impressive segment is the 50 km (30 miles)-long **Racarumi Intervalley Canal** that diverted water from the Chancay/Lambayeque drainage and irrigated the **Pampa de Chaparrí**. Geoarchaeological studies and AMS dates indicate that the Pampa de Chaparrí Canal was built during the Middle Sicán period and was used until the early Colonial era. An archaeological survey demonstrated that the earliest sites associated with the canal date to the Middle Sicán period; these sites were very small hamlets and communities, not administrative centers where water was controlled. Based on investigations of the Pampa de Chaparrí, **Frances Hayashida** has suggested that the maintenance and administration of Middle Sicán canals may have been the responsibility of local kin groups (*parcialidades*, as known in Colonial documents) rather than directly maintained by a "state authority." However, the Pampa de Chappari and its agricultural production were vital to the expansion of the Lambayeque polity. Hayashida writes, "The development of the Pampa de Chaparrí from desert to irrigated farmlands coincided with the rapid and dramatic growth of the Middle Sicán state, as seen in the construction of monumental adobe mounds at the nearby Sicán capital, marked differentiation between social classes, and the production, accumulation and trade of wealth items (e.g., objects of arsenical bronze and precious metal alloys) on an unprecedented scale. While water management may not have required the guiding hand of the state, the growth of irrigation agriculture is inseparable from the rise of the Sicán polity."[34]

Current debates about Sicán/Lambayeque's political organization stem from contrasting sets of archaeological data from the Lambayeque region and the Jequetepeque Valley. Since the 1990s, research in the Jequetepeque Valley has identified ruins once thought to be Chimú sites as actually earlier Lambayeque sites. Although the extent and depth of the Lambayeque presence in the Jequetepeque Valley are incompletely known, major sites clearly have Lambayeque occupations. For example, **Pacatnamú,** the largest Lambayeque site in the region, covers a square kilometer on a wedge-shaped bluff near the Pacific Ocean. Pacatnamú contains one of the largest concentrations of ceremonial architecture on the North Coast of Peru, including fifty-three truncated pyramids with mound-top structures surrounded by the enclosing walls of compounds.[35] These mound-compound complexes combine ceremonial spaces, burial structures, and residential areas. Originally considered a Moche site, Pacatnamú flourished during the Lambayeque period and may have been the Lambayeque "capital" in the Jequetepeque Valley.

Similarly, **Carol Mackey's** excavations at the site of **Farfan**—initially classified as a Chimú-period site—have shown that the site was originally built during the Lambayeque period, although with extensive Chimú and Inca occupations as well.[36] Located at a strategic crossroads between the coast and the highlands and controlling canal systems and access to farmland, Farfan was a small administrative center of walled compounds, a small village of dwellings, a ceramic workshop, and a cemetery with a few burials containing Lambayeque double-spout vessels and copper artifacts—although most individuals lacked such exotic items. **William Sapp** documented the residence of a local-level lord at the site of **Cabur**, consisting of a 10 m (32.8 ft)-tall truncated mound built using the Sicán-style chamber and fill Lambayeque technique but surrounded by compounds that followed local architectural styles.[37] Further, excavations at the smaller village sites suggest that Lambayeque cultural practices influenced even rural populations away from monumental centers in the Jequetepeque Valley.[38]

Several possible interpretations emerge from this incompletely understood archaeological record. One position, articulated by Shimada, is that Lambayeque was a state by the Middle Sicán period—an interpretation based on the scale of monumental construction, metallurgy, the emergence of exalted elites, and the evidence for long-distance exchange. This model envisions an expansionistic state, centered in the Lambayeque Valley, that incorporated adjacent regions and influenced distant zones. An alternative model proposes distinct spheres of Lambayeque culture—somewhat like the northern Moche/southern Moche pattern discussed earlier—with different regions sharing cultural elements but politically independent, a form of "peer-polity interaction."[39] A final view sees Lambayeque as an influential art style, whose ceramics and architectural forms were varyingly adopted by people elsewhere but without political integration.

In sum, the evidence for the centralization of power and production seems clear for the Lambayeque region during the Middle Sicán period, with the possible existence of a four-tier settlement hierarchy in the Jequetepeque Valley that may or may not reflect the southward expansion of the Lambayeque/Sicán polity. It has been suggested that the center of the Lambayeque polity shifted to the site of **Túcume** in the lower valley, although this is not absolutely clear (figure 9.16).

The Chimú occupied Túcume and extensively remodeled the site, obscuring the extent and nature of the earlier Sicán occupation.[40] Drawing on a comparative analysis of Middle Sicán and Late Sicán iconography, **Justin Jennings** has proposed that a catastrophic El Niño triggered a cosmological crisis and that "Late Sicán cosmology might best be understood as the result of a revitalization movement that sought to revive a 'traditional' cosmology that had been neglected"—a plausible but uncertain possibility.[41] A great deal remains unknown about the end of Sicán. Although there is no clear consensus about the organization of Lambayeque society, we do know that it was conquered by an emergent state from the south, the Chimú.

The Chimú (ca. AD 900–1470)

The Chimú developed an empire that extended from the Moche Valley to impose its authority on the Peruvian coast from the Lambayeque Valley to the Casma Valley, a distance of more than 400 km (240 miles; see figure 9.3).[42] The empire was ruled from the capital city of **Chan Chan**, sprawling over 20 km^2 (7.72 square miles), with a dense urban core of 6 km^2 (2.3 square miles) and a population estimated at 30,000–40,000 inhabitants—one of the largest urban settlements known in prehistoric South America (figure 9.17).

Only 7 km (4.6 miles) from the earlier Moche center at Huaca de la Luna and Huaca del Sol—a site that continued to be venerated by the Chimú—Chan Chan was a very different place.

Figure 9.16 Eroded walls and mounds, Túcume, Peru

Figure 9.17 Chan Chan, ruins of adobe-walled ciudadelas

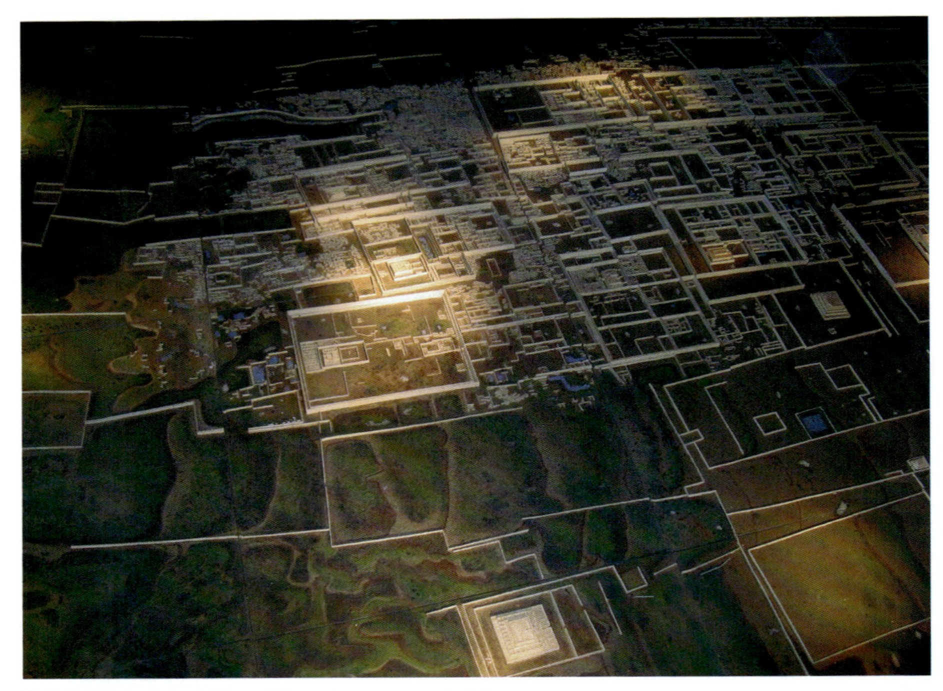

Figure 9.18 Model of Chan Chan showing ciudadelas

Although the site had been studied and looted since the Colonial period (see chapter 1), a major research project directed by Michael Moseley and Carol Mackey between 1969 and 1974 resulted in significant advances in archaeological knowledge of Chan Chan and the Chimú Empire. Chan Chan's built environment was dominated by ten enormous walled enclosures, called *ciudadelas* or "little cities," which were the palaces of the Chimú rulers (figure 9.18).

Surrounded by thick walls up to 9 m (29.5 ft) tall, the ciudadelas enclosed 67,300 to 212,000 m^2 (724,417 to 2,281,968 ft^2).[43] Within these walls were a variety of architectural spaces and features: large plazas with ramps and platforms, banks of storerooms, three-sided structures with niches known as *audiencias*, kitchen areas, and burial platforms. These last features are particularly distinctive, limited to nine of the ten ciudadelas at Chan Chan, one possible example in the Virú Valley, and two other sites outside the Moche Valley associated with the northern expansion of the Chimú, Farfan, and Túcume.[44] The size of the ciudadelas and their distinctive architectural features clearly identify them as elite architecture associated with the rulers of the Chimú state. Finally, access to the ciudadelas was tightly restricted. In most cases, a single door gave entrance to the vast complex of rooms and corridors, and baffled entrances controlled the movements of people within the ciudadelas and tightly regulated any encounters between a king and his subjects (figure 9.19).[45]

Chan Chan's ciudadelas were surrounded by other barrios of non-royal residences. Some dwellings contained "scaled-down" architectural elements seen in

Figure 9.19 Friezes on ciudadela walls, Chan Chan

the ciudadelas—smaller ramps and benches, fewer audiencias, and modest storerooms—interpreted as the residences of non-royal elites. More widespread were the barrios of cane-walled dwellings and workshops of Chan Chan's commoner classes. Excavations documented the presence of copper-working, spinning and weaving, and woodworking workshops in these barrios. These archaeological and architectural patterns reflect significant differences in economic activity, control of resources, and power within Chan Chan and, by extension, within the Chimú Empire. Interestingly, these material indications of social distinctions are paralleled by a creation myth about the Chimú recorded centuries later that involves pairs of stars: elites were from one pair of stars, commoners from another. As **John Rowe** has commented, "Evidently differences between social classes were great and immutable on the north coast, for the creation legend . . . relates that two stars gave rise to the kings and nobles and two others to the common peoples" (figure 9.20).[46]

Surrounding the metropolis of Chan Chan, a number of rural settlements were integrated into the Chimú state.[47] Nearby farming communities raised maize, cotton, and scores of other crops; villagers' houses had large storage bins, bigger than a single family would need and suggesting production for Chan Chan's urban population. For example, the site of **Cerro de la Virgen**, about 5 km (3 miles) northwest of Chan Chan, was occupied by around 1,000 people who fished, produced textiles and other crafts, and farmed cotton and other crops, presumably for export to Chan Chan. The occupants of another site, **El Milagro de San Jose**,

Figure 9.20 Chimú silver beaker (*kero*)

oversaw the agricultural fields watered by an important branch of the Chimú-constructed irrigation system. The site contained a small compound with courtyards, niched rooms, and audiencias that have been interpreted as architectural expressions of Chimú administration. In these and other ways, the Chimú controlled the Moche Valley.

Chimú expansion and political integration occurred principally in the coastal zones and lower valleys. **Brian Billman** has documented how the Chimú consolidated and expanded earlier irrigation systems built by the Moche (see chapter 5). In the southern portion of the Moche Valley, previous canals were maintained and expanded to irrigate more than 37 km^2 (9,143 acres) of farmland; however, the northern Moche Valley had the greatest expansion of irrigation networks. The **La Cumbre Intervalley Canal** was the largest of these projects, an ambitious hydraulic endeavor that channeled water more than 70 km (42 miles) from the neighboring Chicama Valley and diverted it to fields on the north side of the Moche Valley. At a minimum, the La Cumbre Intervalley Canal would have required 1,000 workers laboring for a generation (about twenty-six years). Significant amounts of new farmland were brought into production, although crop yields were limited by recurrent water shortages and some new fields were probably planted only during years of above-average rainfall and runoff in the sierra. Nonetheless, the Chimú substantially increased the extent of agricultural lands in the Moche Valley, to roughly 30–40 percent more land than is under cultivation today. In this process, the Chimú integrated the adjacent Moche and Virú Valleys into their expanding state—a process that may have required 250 years—ruling those areas directly from Chan Chan.[48]

In the 1300s the Chimú launched a program of expansion and deployed new patterns of imperial integration. Mackey has argued that this occurred in several stages. First, by AD 1320 the Chimú had expanded north to the Jequetepeque Valley, claiming the Lambayeque/Sicán site of Farfan for their own and converting it into a provincial center. The Chimú then spread south to the Casma Valley, where they co-opted and expanded the regional center of **Manchan** and absorbed local elites into their imperial project. Third, the Chimú expanded north from their holdings in Jequetepeque to conquer the Lambayeque Valley and polity, establishing a regional capital at Túcume. These expansionist moves seem to mark the maximum extent of territory directly controlled by the Chimú, although their influence was felt at much greater distances.

Within these territories, the Chimú imposed a form of imperial control in which communities of different sizes formed distinct nodes in the administrative framework. With Chan Chan as the undisputed primary center, provincial centers such as Farfan, Manchan, and Túcume were outposts of imperial control, while smaller communities formed additional levels of empire.

The Chimú Empire's expansion was met with different responses. According to legend, the Chimú thrust into the Jequetepeque Valley, led by General Pacatnamú, was violently resisted by the Lambayeque lords of the valley. The Chimús' response has been corroborated by Mackey's excavations at Farfan. The Chimú razed their defeated enemies' buildings, leveling the walls to their foundations and building a new Chimú compound on top of them, dominating people and places. Two other Chimú compounds were built on bare earth. The violent conquest at Farfan did not result in political or cultural reconstructions across the Jequetepeque Valley. Mackey writes, "Thus far, the evidence suggests that the Lambayeque traditions persisted in local communities and it does not appear that Chimú cultural traditions permeate down to the local level."[49] Similarly, **Edward Swenson** observes, "Despite the undeniable economic colonization of the region, the Chimú empire did not attempt to radically alter the distinctive political landscape of the Jequetepeque Valley."[50]

Southward in the Casma Valley, where Chimú expansion was not resisted militarily, accommodation was the imperial strategy. Research by Mackey and **A. M. Ulana Klymyshsyn** demonstrated that Manchan, the Chimú provincial center, exhibited two classes of elite architecture: large, open compounds built in the local Casma Valley style, and five free-standing compounds that more closely followed Chimú architectural style, similar to the buildings occupied by non-royal elites in Chan Chan. With barrios of self-sufficient commoners who combined farming and fishing with part-time craft production, Manchan was the principal Chimú settlement in the Casma Valley, but there is little evidence for dramatic change in the surrounding countryside. An exception was the site of **Quebrada Santa Cristina**, a camp of workers supported by the Chimú state who built an extensive area of raised agricultural fields in the aftermath of a major El Niño/Southern Oscillations event in the mid-fourteenth century, a project that reflects the Chimú Empire's sustained interest in agricultural production in coastal valley zones.[51]

Far to the north, the Chimú captured the Lambayeque center of Túcume, a cluster of truncated and walled compounds on the flanks of Cerro La Raya covering more than 220 ha (484 acres) (figure 9.16).

The Chimú modified preexisting constructions at Túcume, leaving most of the pyramids intact and presumably integrating Lambayeque elites into the Chimú imperial project—a pattern seen elsewhere at sites in the Lambayeque Valley system. **Daniel Sandweiss** and **Alfredo Narvaez** write, "In the Chimú Period, Túcume continued to grow. In the monumental sector, Huaca 1 (and presumably the other pyramids) continued in use, with a major remodeling sometime during the Chimú occupation. At Huaca Larga, the free-standing pyramid of the Lambayeque Period was converted into the long, massive platform still visible today; the investment in labor must have been tremendous."[52] The Chimú strategy in the Lambayeque Valley seems to have incorporated local elites into the imperial administration.

In the course of their imperial expansion, the Chimú implemented different policies and stratagems. Like all empires, the Chimú organized labor and production, whether directed to the production of stunning artworks in precious metals or feathered textiles or to the less impressive but no less important excavation of canal ditches (figure 9.21). The Chimú also manipulated religion and ideology, incorporating and modifying deities known from earlier cultural traditions—particularly venerating the Sea and the Moon, powerful icons fundamentally distinct from the later solar cults of the Inca (figure 9.22).

Figure 9.21 Chimú ceremonial tumi

The Inca conquered the coast of Peru around AD 1470, defeating the Chimú on the battlefield, dismantling the imperial administration at Chan Chan, and occupying the provincial centers of Manchan, Farfan, and Túcume (see chapter 11). These conquests in the fifteenth century fundamentally changed the political landscape of the North Coast of Peru, which had developed and changed over the previous millennium.

Figure 9.22 (*overleaf*) Chimú or Chimú/Inca figurine made from wood, *Spondylus* shell, and other materials

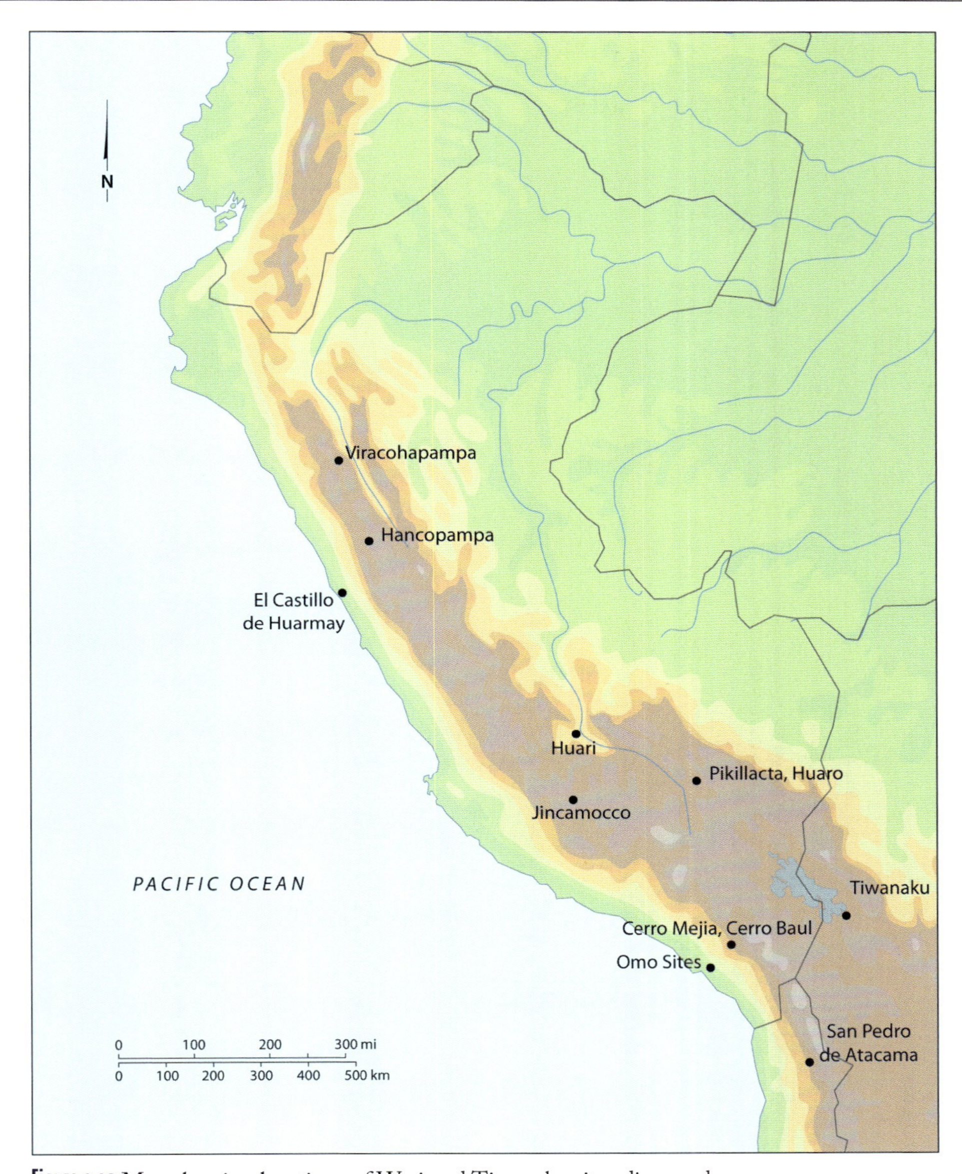

Figure 9.23 Map showing locations of Wari and Tiwanaku sites discussed

The Central Andes: Wari Empire (AD 750–1000)

The Wari Empire is known only through archaeological evidence (figure 9.23).[53] Originally, Wari ceramics were confused as coastal variants of Tiwanku ceramics because both pottery complexes include polychromes with similar color palettes of browns, bluffs, black, and cream (figure 9.24).[54]

During the mid-twentieth century, it became evident that there were two interacting but distinct stylistic spheres, one centered in the Titicaca Basin in southern

Figure 9.24 (*overleaf*) Figurine depicting a Wari dignitary

Peru, Bolivia, and northern Chile and the other spreading from the Ayacucho Valley through the Peruvian Andes. This latter pattern is associated with development and expansion of the Wari Empire, which began at about AD 550–600 and continued until about AD 1000.[55]

Archaeological knowledge about the Wari has developed erratically. **Julio C. Tello** investigated the site of **Huari** in 1931 but only published a brief newspaper article discussing his finds. A relatively short report was published in 1950 by John Rowe, **Gordon Willey**, and **Donald Collier**, based on a visit of "a little over an hour."[56] This report recognized the enormity of the site of Huari, its distinctive architecture consisting of impressive multi-story walls of rough fieldstone set in mud mortar that surrounded large (50 × 50 m [150 × 150 ft]) compounds. This distinctive building style was present across much of the site and, Rowe and colleagues wrote, was also similar to "two sites at opposite ends of Peru: **Viracochapampa** near Huamachuco and **Pikillacta** near Cuzco."[57] These two sites, more than 900 km (540 miles) apart, suggested the extent of the Wari Empire.

The recognition of Wari ceramics and architectural styles did not immediately lead to a consensus about the existence of a Wari state and empire.[58] However, **Katharina Schreiber** has argued convincingly that the spatial extent of Wari architecture indicates the ability not only to mobilize labor but also to impose a form of architecture, "whether at the capital city or at the provincial centers, [that] was designed to keep people out. Wari sites are characterized by large formidable stone enclosures, sometimes three stories tall, with few entries and no windows." Wari religious art was inscribed on portable objects, such as ceramic vessels and cloth, rather than on fixed surfaces, public stelae, or sculptures. In Wari imperial centers, Schreiber writes, "there was no central place to which people needed to travel to appreciate these religious monuments and symbols . . . Wari was an empire that established political and economic sovereignty over vast regions and large populations"[59](see figure 9.24).

Prior to the Wari, the Ayacucho Valley region was occupied by the **Huarpa culture**, an archaeological complex known principally from its ceramic assemblages. The Ayacucho Valley was an agriculturally fertile region, and maize was widely consumed by people from all walks of life, before and after the emergence of the Huari state.[60] It has been suggested that Huarpa had several large settlements that coalesced into the site of Wari, although it is not clear if these predecessors were state-level societies or if Wari "the state and empire arose as part of the same process."[61] Despite this uncertainty, all of the major architecture at the capital pertains to the Wari era, so if the area was previously occupied, it was extensively remodeled.

Huari is one of the largest sites in the Andes (see figure 9.23). Its central urban core covers 2.5 km^2 (1 square mile), surrounded by over 15 km^2 (5.8 square miles) of less monumental buildings, residences, and household middens. The architecture at Huari and other Wari sites, **William Isbell** observes, "favor[ed] labyrinthine enclosures" over large volumes, such as pyramids or mounds. These compounds "were carefully planned, beginning with foundations and drains, up through doorways and roofs," and were subdivided into grids.[62] A common design

Figure 9.25 Walls and corridor at the site of Pikillacta, Peru

was a central open patio flanked on three or four sides by long, narrow (about 2 m [6.5 ft]-wide) rooms or halls with one to three stories, forming "apartment-like" residences for the occupants of a compound. In addition, circular or D-shaped buildings served as religious buildings. Wari buildings were built from fieldstone, sometimes covered with white plaster, while carefully cut and fitted masonry was used in temples and other special constructions.

At Huari, buildings underwent transformations. The largest excavated sector, named **Vegachayoc Moqo**, was initially a royal compound with a roofed, U-shaped, terraced platform mound overlooking an open patio or assembly area. Subsequently, a D-shaped temple was built in the patio—possibly a royal mortuary monument—and finally a long wall with niches containing a jumble of human bones, animal sacrifices, pottery, and other offerings associated with commoner burials.[63]

Despite the changing uses of buildings, Wari constructions began with a rigid plan. This is exemplified by the site of Pikillacta, located in the southern portion of the Valley of Cusco (figure 9.25).

Pikillacta is a geometric masterpiece, a gridwork of walls and plazas covering a little more than a square kilometer.[64] Pikillacta is defined by a large rectangular enclosure approximately 745 m × 630 m (2,444 ft × 2,067 ft) in size delineated by fieldstone walls that in places remain 12 m (39.4 ft) tall. The tight patterning is even more impressive when one visits the site and realizes that these straight walls stretch over an undulating landform.

In addition to architecture, the Wari Empire was symbolized in its pottery.[65] Wari ceramics often exhibit intricate polychrome designs and motifs (figure 9.26). Among the most spectacular of these vessels are large ceremonial urns Tello excavated at **Conchapata.**[66] These urns are 1–1.5 m (3.2–4.5 ft)-tall vessels, whose spouts narrow to depict human heads, some with distinctive turbans or hats. The figures "wear" a tunic or poncho decorated with depictions of Staff Gods, sometimes distinguished as male and female, well-known from the Gateway of the Sun in Tiwanaku but also from much earlier Andean sites, such as Chavín de Huántar. The more obvious and temporally close connection to Tiwanaku led **Dorothy Menzel** to propose that religious pilgrims had traveled there and returned with the religious beliefs and iconography linked to the Staff Gods.[67] In contrast, **Anita Cook** has argued that these motifs were selected by emerging elites at Conchapata and the Ayacucho region, who drew upon "a selective cultural lexicon," whereas William Isbell has argued that the depiction of such icons at Tiwanaku and Wari sites simultaneously drew on a shared iconography found in the Southern Andes.[68] Regardless of the specific origins of their icons, these vessels clearly depict Wari elites and exemplify fine craft production in ceramics, textiles, and other media (figures 9.27, 9.28, and 9.29).

Yet, despite the striking beauty and intriguing iconography of Wari ceramics, portable artifacts are less certain markers of empire than is the creation of an imperial infrastructure: compounds, storerooms, and roads.[69] For example, Viracochapampa, located in the Huamachuco Valley in north-central Peru, clearly exhibits the rigid geometries of Wari architecture, even though the site was abandoned before the compounds were completed and may have never been used.[70] This may indicate, as **Terence D'Altroy** and Katharina Schreiber suggest, "that the infrastructure and communication abilities of the fledgling empire were overextended in this region, 800 km (480 miles) distant from the capital, or local resistance may have prevented it from establishing control there."[71] Wari influence and prestige can be seen elsewhere in northern Peru, especially in the spread of stylistic elements in pottery, but this does not suggest actual Wari imperial control.[72]

Elsewhere, the presence of different levels in a settlement hierarchy suggests the existence of state-level control.[73] Schreiber has detailed the impacts of empire in the Carahuarazo Valley in southern Peru.[74] Before the arrival of the Wari, residents lived in a handful of villages and hamlets. Seven modest villages were more or less evenly spaced and surrounded by agricultural lands used for raising potatoes and other tubers and for camelid herding. When the Wari moved into the region at circa AD 600–800, two high-elevation villages were abandoned and new settlements were established at lower elevations, possibly marking an increased emphasis on maize farming. Agricultural terraces were expanded when the Wari arrived. The Wari also built the local administrative center **Jincamoco**, demolishing an earlier village to do so. A classic Wari walled compound, Jincamoco sat

Figure 9.26 (*overleaf*) Wari vessel depicting a dignitary

Figure 9.27 Wari-style poncho

astride the Wari road that connected the central highlands and the Nazca Valley. Over time, Jincamoco was enlarged until it covered approximately 15 ha (33 acres). Three other smaller Wari compounds were also constructed, positioned near maize fields and roads.

The Carahuarazo case exemplifies one imperial strategy. For the Cotahuazi Valley, Justin Jennings and **Wily Yépez Álvarez** have suggested an alternative pattern; it seems that local elites modified buildings to imitate Wari constructions. Although extremely tall walled compounds only appear during the period of Wari influence, the internal buildings follow local architectural patterns, leading Jennings and Yépez Álvarez to write that "the sites are local sites made to look Wari and not Wari sites built by locals." The tall walled compounds were "imposing in form and restrictive in nature; the enclosure wall was probably a daunting

Figure 9.28 (*overleaf*) Wari object, a hand with inlay

Figure 9.29 Wari feathered textile

symbol that the power of the new paramount chief was based in something neither personal nor local."[75]

Other expressions of Wari power far from its capital are the hilltop sites of **Cerro Baul** and **Cerro Mejia**, located in the Moquegua Valley of southern Peru.[76] About 600 km (360 miles) from the Ayacucho Valley, Cerro Baul is prominently located on a 600 m (1, 968 ft) summit. From the valley floor, it takes about an hour to climb to the site. The valley bottom was occupied by farming communities affiliated with the Tiwanaku state (discussed below). Cerro Baul was one of three hilltop Wari outposts in the Moquegua region, along with Cerro Mejia and Cerro Petroglifo. Excavations by Michael Moseley, **P. Ryan Williams**, **Donna Nash**, and others have documented that Cerro Baul covered about 3 ha (6.6 acres). Cerro Baul's architecture includes fieldstone masonry compounds and buildings, two D-shaped temples, an elite residence, and a massive brewery where a beverage was made from the small fruits of the Peruvian pepper tree (*Schinus molle*), a distinctly Wari brew. Another brewery was located on nearby Cerro Mejia, which also had an elite residential compound and patio, among the various constructions spread along the hilltop.

The nearly impregnable locations of these sites contrast with the evidence of brewing and feasting. Moseley and colleagues have suggested that Cerro Baul "was an embassy-like enclave established atop a sacred natural bastion to emphasize political prowess regardless of economic impracticalities."[77] In addition to the defensive locations, Williams and Nash argue, these mountaintop settlements presented views of distant sacred mountain peaks.[78] The relationship between these Wari enclaves and the communities below may have changed over time, perhaps as local elites interacted with Wari elites. However, by about AD 1030, Cerro Baul and Cerro Mejia were abandoned, the sites symbolically "closed" with ceremonies involving final banquets, offerings of Andean condor and other birds, the smashing of elegant polychrome vessels, and burning the hilltop buildings.[79]

The Wari deployed varying strategies of empire, resulting in what Schreiber has called "a mosaic of control."[80] Future archaeological research will further our understanding of these complex and varied ways the Wari expanded their territory, incorporated new populations, and interacted with neighboring polities, especially Tiwanaku.

Figure 9.30 Gateway of the Sun, Tiwanaku, Bolivia

Lake Titicaca and Beyond: Tiwanaku (AD 400–1100)

In the Titicaca Basin, the **Tiwanaku polity** emerged as a contemporary rival of the Wari state (see figure 9.23).[81] The site of **Tiwanaku** has been visited since the Colonial period, and detailed travelers' accounts describe the impressive and enigmatic stone architecture and art at the site (figure 9.30).

Tiwanaku was studied by nineteenth-century archaeologists, including Ephraim George Squier, Adolph Bandelier, Max Uhle, and others (see chapter 2). Excavations at Tiwanaku and surrounding sites by Wendell Bennett and excavations and reconstructions by **Carlos Ponce Sanguines** resulted in a relative chronology for the Tiwanaku sequence.[82] Multiple projects since the 1970s have resulted in a dramatic expansion of archaeological knowledge—investigations that have included excavations at Tiwanaku and other sites, regional surveys, and paleoenvironmental reconstructions.[83]

The capital of Tiwanaku, as **Charles Stanish** observes, was a "vast, planned urban capital [that] sprawled over the altiplano landscape."[84] The city emerged in the center of a broad plain at 3,840 m (12,595 ft) above sea level, flanked by mountain ranges and Lake Titicaca. An extensive midden area of approximately 4–6 km^2 (1.5–2 square miles) surrounds the urban core of pyramids, sunken plazas, and fine masonry constructions. Widely varying population estimates have been suggested for the city, with a thin consensus suggesting 15,000–25,000 residents.[85] Today, the site is a combination of what **Jean-Pierre Protzen** and **Stella Nair** have described as "several eroded mounds, outlines of court-yard structures, weathered uprights, the so-called Gateway of the Sun . . . some statues . . . foundation stubbles, and jumbles of building stones—but not a single standing original building."[86]

The initial ritual construction was a **Semi-Subterranean Temple**, a 28 m × 26 m (91.8 ft × 85.3 ft) sunken court entered through a single doorway and faced with fine-cut stone with tenoned stone heads (figure 9.31).

This sunken court clearly has antecedents in earlier ritual architecture in the Tiwanaku Basin (see chapter 7). As part of the Tiwanaku city, the Semi-Subterranean Temple held monumental monoliths and stelae, forming what **Paul Goldstein** has called "the single greatest concentration of Tiwanaku sculpture found at any site . . . a collection of important icons."[87] During the third and fifth centuries AD, the **Kalasasaya** was constructed—a slightly elevated, walled enclosure measuring 130 m × 120 m (426 ft × 394 ft) and containing a small (28 × 26 m [91.8 ft × 85.3 ft]) sunken court, which "probably replaced the Semi-subterranean Temple as the primary focus of the emerging ritual city."[88] After AD 500, another building phase culminated in the construction of the **Akapana Mound**, which became the ritual focus of the city (figure 9.32).

Standing 18 m (59 ft) tall and 257 m × 197 m (843 ft × 646 ft) at its base, the Akapana is a stone-faced, terraced pyramid that has been interpreted as an architectonic metaphor for a sacred mountain.[89] The Akapana may have contained a system of drains and fountains that captured rainwater and threaded it through the mound's terraced surfaces. Although aspects of its construction remain unclear, after AD 700 the Akapana was undoubtedly the major monument at Tiwanaku.[90]

The capital's urban landscape restated a socio-religious gradient. The elite residential compound, known as the **Putini**, is due west of the Kalasasaya and was constructed from well-cut stone block and adobe bricks. Entered through an elaborate doorway, the buildings of the Putini complex surrounded a large plaza. The surrounding buildings were intricate warrens of dwellings and kitchens, containing evidence of daily food preparation and more elaborate feasts. An adjacent, much-looted burial area contained offerings—imported turquoise beads, fineware keros, and hallucinogenic snuff trays—that suggest the elite status of the dead.[91]

Pilgrims arriving from the west would have first encountered the **Pumapunku complex**, which William Isbell and **Alexei Vranich** have written "acted as the official entrance to Tiwanaku, channeling visitors in their eastward quest toward snowcapped Illimnai," a revered sacred mountain that dominates the physical and conceptual landscape.[92] The Pumapunku was a complicated hive of buildings, plazas, stairways, platforms, and courtyards stretching over a half-kilometer—a construction Vranich has argued represents the center of the Andean world.[93]

While most of the center's population lived in scores of dense settlements that stretched from the architectural core of Tiwanaku to the edge of Lake Titicaca,[94] the center of Tiwanaku housed elite residences, elaborate architecture, and sacred spaces.[95] For such reasons, **Alan Kolata** characterized Tiwanaku as an architectural expression of a cosmological model, "the principal template, conceived by elites, for Tiwanaku's social and moral order, and a public expression of its social values."[96]

Tiwanaku's development was also based on controlling labor and enhancing agricultural production. An impressive result was the construction of raised agricultural fields (see chapter 5). In the Titicaca Basin, raised fields were built-up

Figure 9.31 (*overleaf*) Tiwanaku—Semi-Subterranean Plaza

Figure 9.32 Tiwanaku—statue with Akapana Mound in background

earthen mounds between 5 m and 20 m (16.4–65.6 ft) wide and as long as 200 m (656 ft). Kolata has estimated that approximately 190 km^2 (4,693 acres) of raised fields were cultivated, writing, "This specialized, intensive form of agricultural production was the cornerstone of Tiwanaku's agrarian economy."[97] Experimental plantings on renovated fields produced extremely large yields of potatoes, although modern yields may have been greater than prehispanic harvests.[98] Approximately 100,000 people could have been fed by the Titicaca Basin raised fields.[99] The expanse of raised fields increased as Tiwanaku coalesced and expanded, suggesting the role of the state in organizing agricultural production.[100]

Moving out of the Titicaca Basin, Tiwanaku's impact was felt to the west and the south, but in different ways. For example, archaeological sites near the oasis of **San Pedro de Atacama**, located in the hyper-arid desert of northern Chile, contain artifacts that display Tiwanaku motifs and styles (figure 9.33). These objects include fine textiles, hats, metal objects, and wooden trays used for inhaling psychoactive snuffs (figure 9.34).[101] The archaeologists **Mauricio Uribe Rodríguez** and **Carolina Agüero Piwonka** have written, "Such symbols of power iconographically linked local populations to the metropolis in the altiplano [i.e., Tiwanaku]. In this manner, the circulation of objects and icons from the core to distant places imprinted a sense of cohesion on those populations related to Tiwanaku but in highly differentiated and dispersed ways given the vast distances and culturally diverse regions, contributing to the creation and maintenance of regular and predictable ideological ties . . . that varied according to the organization of each population, privileging elites and with little circulation [of objects and icons] among commoners."[102]

A different pattern is present on the South Coast of Peru, where Tiwanaku established a direct and sustained presence in the Moquegua Valley—particu-

Figure 9.33 The oasis of San Pedro de Atacama, Chile

larly in the upper drainage of the Osmore Valley—creating new settlements and incorporating preexisting communities. For example, Paul Goldstein notes that even everyday objects used in Moquegua were very similar to those used in the Tiwanaku core, demonstrating "the maintenance of an explicitly Tiwanaku identity in a territory fully annexed to the Tiwanaku state system."[103] A cluster of sites from overlapping phases known as the **Omo Site Group**, at 38 ha (83.6 acres) the largest known Tiwanaku complex outside Bolivia, was the locus of Tiwanaku's initial colonization and later presence in the Moquegua Valley.[104] Initially, about a dozen sites with Tiwanaku and Tiwanaku-related ceramics were found in the region, a number that increased until there were more than forty-five settlements with a total area of about 42 ha (92.4 acres) by AD 1000.[105]

The upper Moquegua Valley was the region closest to Tiwanaku in which coastal products—maize, cotton, and coca—could be raised. Despite being 270 km (162 miles) apart, the route connecting the upper Moquegua and Tiwanaku was a relatively straightforward corridor linking colony and center.[106] The Tiwanaku presence is indicated not only by everyday objects but also by the construction at **Omo M-12** of a small temple that replicates Tiwanaku architecture. The Omo temple contains a small, sunken rectangular court, fronted by several patios and flanked by complexes of small rooms. Access to the patio was restricted, and it was designed as an exclusive space rather than a broad arena for public displays. Further, the construction of this temple marks a fundamental shift in the Tiwanaku presence on the coast. Paul Goldstein writes: "The definition of a Tiwanaku sunken-

Figure 9.34 Tiwanaku-style hallucinogenic snuff tray

court temple complex at Omo, 300 kilometers [180 miles] southwest of the site of Tiwanaku, is the first confirmation of this characteristic architectural type outside of the Lake Titicaca basin. In contrast to the household-centered ritual that integrated Omo phase colonial communities, the appearance of a specialized complex for state-centered ceremony and administration underscores the explosive expansion of the Tiwanaku state during Tiwanaku V (A.D. 725–1000) and the transformation of a loosely integrated string of colonies to a centrally governed provincial system."[107]

Despite the evidence of this imperial presence, the Moquegua region was rather loosely braided into the Tiwanaku state. Stanish and colleagues conducted an archaeological survey in the high puna on the pass between the upper Moquegua drainage and the Titicaca Basin, covering more than 100 km (60 miles) of modern and prehistoric roads and trails.[108] Of the 182 sites found, 28 had Tiwanaku ceramics, much fewer than sites with Late Intermediate Period (n = 120), Inca-phase (n = 125), or even Colonial-era (n = 54) components. The Tiwanaku presence in these critical mountain passes is described as "light but continuous," although there was no evidence of Tiwanaku architecture or the creation of roadside constructions (*tambos*) like those found associated with Inca roads (see chapter 11) or new local administrative centers such as Schreiber identified with the Wari conquest of the Carahuarazo Valley (discussed earlier). These archaeological data "support a model of an informal Tiwanaku exchange system characterized by caravan trips made by many disparate people moving goods [and] differ from what we would expect from a formal type of state-sponsored trade."[109]

The current evidence suggests that Tiwanaku was an extremely influential but relatively fragile political system. Its iconography was revered, its textiles and ceramics esteemed by distant elites, but there is little current evidence for a major political presence outside the Titicaca Basin except in the Moquegua Valley.

When the end came, it was quick and devastating. At about AD 950–1100, a persistent period of abrupt climatic change associated with the Medieval Climatic Period produced a significant drought in the Southern Andes.[110] The drought was so severe that a major sub-basin of Lake Titicaca, known as Lago Wiñaymarka, actually emptied as lake levels fell. Raised fields were left high and dry, lacking sufficient water to keep plants from wilting as salts built up on desiccated fields. In the Moquegua Valley, this drought period was associated with "a drastic social upheaval" and collapse.[111] Tiwanaku itself went into dramatic decline. Monumental constructions ceased. Offerings at the Akapana halted. Many monoliths—the stone representations of Tiwanaku deities or ancestors—were defaced. The population shrank away from the sacred core, occupying a small bluff on the western margin of the city, a faint remnant of its once-glorious past.

Conclusion

The emergence of states and empires in western South America was not the result of uniform causes; nor were these states and empires identical expressions of social and political organization. There are certain common aspects, however. Each of these prehistoric states and empires had a principal center significantly larger and more elaborate than any other site in the cultural tradition: Moche, Sicán, Chan Chan, Huari, and Tiwanaku. These sites stand out in terms of their overall size, the extent and elaborateness of monumental architecture, the evidence for craft production, and evidence for elites. Further, the presence of these major centers was felt in their respective surrounding hinterlands. For example, the subsistence demands of Moche, Chan Chan, and Tiwanaku placed demands on people living in the rural regions surrounding these centers; in each case, significant efforts were invested in expanding and changing agricultural production. In the case of Wari, reorganization of agricultural production in the Ayacucho Valley is not clear, although significant expansions of agricultural terraces in the Carahuarazo Valley occurred when the Wari Empire conquered this region. As for the Lambayeque/Sicán polity, the evidence for major restructuring of agriculture is unclear, although existing agriculture was expanded.[112]

Less clear is evidence for the extent and depth of imperial expansion. For example, the Moche and the Sicán/Lambayeque seem to have had their greatest impact on their respective neighboring valleys, and it is unclear how deeply those states controlled or reorganized the rural hinterlands. The impact of the Chimú Empire was apparently larger and occasionally profound, as in the brutal restructuring of Farfan, but even then it is uncertain how far the empire's impact penetrated into rural areas—and there is little evidence for the profound restructurings we know from the Inca Empire (see chapter 11). The Wari Empire's impact was far-reaching (affecting such distant areas as the Huamachuco Valley, the Moquegua Valley, and the Valley of Cusco) and in some places imposing, as suggested by the rigid geometries of Pikillacta. Less clear are the impacts of the Wari on intervening areas, although future investigations may clarify this. Of all the proposed Andean empires, Tiwanaku is the most curious. On one hand, there is clear evidence of the sophistication and prestige of the center at Tiwanaku, expressed by the elegance of carved stone and buildings but also by the rugged pragmatism of potato fields. Further, there is clear evidence that Tiwanaku cultural practices were prestigious, adopted, and emulated away from the Titicaca Basin, in the Moquegua Valley and farther south at San Pedro de Atacama. Nonetheless, the interconnections between Tiwanaku and its distant nodes of influence remain vague and uncertain—yet another intriguing and unresolved problem in understanding the archaeology of ancient states and empires in South America.

Notes

1. C. Sinopoli, "Empires," in *Archaeology at the Millennium: a Sourcebook*, ed. G. Feinman and T. D. Price (New York: Springer-Verlag, 2007), 444. For an excellent overview of theoretical issues and empirical evidence of two Andean empires, the Wari and the Inca, see T. D'Altroy and K. Schreiber, "Andean Empires," in *Andean Archaeology*, ed. H. Silverman (Malden, MA: Blackwell, 2004), 255–79.

2. K. Flannery, "Process and Agency in Early State Formation," *Cambridge Archaeological Journal* 9, no. 1 (1999): 3.

3. Sinopoli, "Empires," 450.

4. "The North Coast" refers to an archaeological culture area, not the modern geo-political border.

5. There is an enormous—and constantly growing—literature on the Moche. For assessments of changing perspectives on the Moche, see L. Castillo and S. Uceda, "The Mochicas," in *Handbook of South American Archaeology*, ed. H. Silverman and W. Isbell (New York: Springer, 2008), 707–29; C. Chapdelaine, "Recent Advances in Moche Studies," *Journal of Archaeological Research* 19 (2011): 191–231; J. Quilter, "Moche Politics, Religion, and Warfare," *Journal of World Prehistory* 16, no. 2 (2002): 145–95.

6. For brief historical overviews of Moche studies, see E. Benson, *The Worlds of the Moche on the North Coast of Peru* (Austin: University of Texas Press, 2012), 7–21; J.

Quilter, *The Moche of Ancient Peru: Media and Messages* (Cambridge: Harvard Peabody Museum Press, 2011); S. Uceda and E. Mujica, "Moche Propuestas y Perspectivas," in *Moche Propuestas y Perspectivas*, ed. S. Uceda and E. Mujica (Lima: Travaux de l'Institut Français de'Etudes Andines), 11–27.

7. M. Uhle, "Types of Culture in Peru," *American Anthropologist* 4, no. 4 (1902): 753–59.

8. A. Kroeber, "The Uhle Pottery Collections from Moche," *University of California Publications in American Anthropology and Archaeology* 21, no. 5 (1925): 199.

9. C. Donnan, *Moche Portraits from Ancient Peru* (Austin: University of Texas Press, 2003), 3. Donnan is the leading expert on Moche ceramics, research he has documented in numerous publications; see C. Donnan, *Moche Art of Peru: Pre-Columbian Symbolic Communication* (Los Angeles: UCLA Museum of Cultural History, 1978); C. Donnan, *Ceramics of Ancient Peru* (Los Angeles: UCLA Fowler Museum of Cultural History, 1992); C. Donnan and D. McClelland, *Moche Fineline Painting: Its Evolution and Its Artists* (Los Angeles: UCLA Fowler Museum of Cultural History, 1999).

10. The following is based on the obituary written by Clifford Evans, "Rafael Larco Hoyle: 1901–1966," *American Antiquity* 33, no. 2 (1968): 233–36.

11. L. Castillo and S. Uceda, "The Mochicas," in *Handbook of South American Archaeology*, ed. H. Silverman and W. Isbell (New York: Springer, 2008), 710. These authors refer to R. Larco Hoyle, *Los Mochicas—Pre-Chimu de Uhle and Early Chimu de Kroeber* (Buenos Aires: Sociedad Geográfica Americana, 1945).

12. The following is based on W. Alva Alva and C. Donnan, *Royal Tombs of Sipán* (Fowler Museum of Culture History, University of California, Los Angeles, 1993).

13. Ibid., 49.

14. For additional discussion, see L. Castillo Butters, "Moche Politics in the Jequetepeque Valley: A Case for Political Opportunism," in *New Perspectives on the Political Organization of the Moche*. Actas del Congreso "Nuevas Perspectivas en la Organización Política Mochica" (Lima, 6 al 8 de Agosto del 2004), ed. Luis Jaime Castillo and Jeffrey Quilter, 2–24 (Pontificia Universidad Católica del Perú, Dumbarton Oaks, and Museo Arqueológico Rafael Larco Herrera, 2008); I. Shimada, *Pampa Grande and the Mochica Culture* (Austin: University of Texas Press, 1994).

15. Castillo and Uceda, "The Mochicas," 713–14.

16. S. Bourget, "Las excavaciones en la Plaza 3A de la Huaca de la Luna," in *Investigaciones en la Huaca de la Luna 1995*, ed. S. Uceda, E. Mujica, and R. Morales (Trujillo: Universidad Nacional de La Libertad, 1997), 51–59; S. Bourget, "Rituals of Sacrifice: Its Practice at Huaca de la Luna and Its Representation in Moche Iconography," in *Moche Art and Archaeology in Ancient Peru,* ed. J. Pillsbury (New Haven: Yale University Press, 2001), 89–110. For additional discussions, see J. Millaire, "The Manipulation of Human Remains in Moche Society: Delayed Burials, Grave Reopening, and Secondary Offerings of Human Bones on the Peruvian North Coast," *Latin American Antiquity* 15, no. 4 (2004): 371–88; J. Verano, "War and Death in the Moche World: Osteological Evidence and Visual Discourse," in *Moche Art and Archaeology in Ancient Peru*, ed. J. Pillsbury (New Haven, CT: Yale University Press, 2001), 111–25.

17. R. Sutter and R. Cortez, "The Nature of Moche Human Sacrifice: A Bio-Archaeological Perspective," *Current Anthropology* 46, no. 4 (2005): 521–49.

18. Bourget, "Rituals of Sacrifice," 105.

19. M. Moseley, "Prehistoric Principles of Labor Organization in the Moche Valley, Peru," *American Antiquity* 40, no. 2 (1975): 191–96; C. Hastings and M. Moseley, "The Adobes of Huaca del Sol and Huaca de La Luna," *American Antiquity* 40, no. 2 (1976): 196–203.

20. For more detailed discussions, see C. Chapdelaine, "La ciudad de Moche: urbanismo y estado," in *Moche: hacia el final del milenio: actas del Segundo Coloquio sobre la Cultura Moche*, ed. S. Uceda and E. Mujica (Lima: Fondo Editorial, Pontificia Universidad Católica del Perú, 2003), 247–285; C. Chapdelaine, "Tumbas y clases sociales en la zona urbana del sitio Huacas de Moche, costa norte del Perú," in *Desarrollo arqueológico costa norte del Perú*, Tome I, ed. L. Valle Alvarez (Peru: Ediciones Sian Trujillo, 2004), 177–188; H. van Gijseghem, "Household and Family at Moche, Peru: An Analysis of Building and Residence Patterns in a Prehispanic Urban Center," *Latin American Antiquity* 12, no. 3 (2001): 257–73.

21. The expansion of Moche irrigation systems has been extensively studied by B. Billman, "Irrigation and the Origins of the Southern Moche State on the North Coast of Peru," *Latin American Antiquity* 13, no. 4 (2002): 371–400; see chapter 5 for discussion.

22. A recent, excellent overview is C. Chapdelaine, "Recent advances in Moche archaeology," *Journal of Archaeological Research* 19 (2011): 191–231. For a skeptical review of Moche as a state, see J. Quilter and M. Koons, "The Fall of the Moche: A Critique of Claims for South America's First State," *Latin American Antiquity* 23, no. 2 (2012): 127–43, a provocative and well-argued essay that I find unconvincing.

23. P. Kosok, *Life, Land, and Water in Ancient Peru* (New York: Long Island University Press, 1965).

24. C. Donnan, "An Assessment of the Validity of the Naymlap Dynasty," in *The Northern Dynasties: Kingship and Statecraft in Chimor*, ed. M. Moseley and A. Cordy-Collins (Washington, DC: Dumbarton Oaks, 1990), 243–74.

25. For a synopsis of looting at the site, see http://traffickingculture.org/encyclopedia/case-studies/batan-grande/.

26. I. Shimada, "The Batan Grande-La Leche Archaeological Project: The First Two Seasons," *Journal of Field Archaeology* 8, no. 4 (1981): 405.

27. I. Shimada, "Cultural Continuities and Discontinuities on the Northern North Coast of Peru, Middle-Late Horizons," in *The Northern Dynasties: Kingship and Statecraft in Chimor*, ed. M. Moseley and A. Cordy-Collins (Washington, DC: Dumbarton Oaks, 1990), 297–392; I. Shimada, "Late Prehispanic Coastal States," in *The Inca World: the Development of Pre-Columbian Peru, AD 1000–1534*, ed. L. Laurencich-Minelli (Norman: University of Oklahoma Press, 2000), 49–100.

28. Shimada, "Late Prehispanic Coastal States," 51.

29. J. Jennings, "Catastrophe, Revitalization and Religious Change on the Prehispanic North Coast of Peru," *Cambridge Archaeological Journal* 18, no. 2 (2008): 177–94.

30. R. Cavallaro and I. Shimada, "Some Thoughts on Sican Marked Adobes and Labor Organization," *American Antiquity* 53, no. 1 (1988): 75–101; I Shimada and R. Cavallaro, "Monumental Adobe Architecture of the late prehispanic Northern North Coast of Peru," *Journal de la Société des Américanistes* 71 (1988): 41–78.

31. I. Shimada, S. Epstein, and A. Craig, "Batán Grande: A Prehistoric Metallurgical Center in Peru," *Science* 216, no. 4549 (May 28, 1982): 952–59.

32. D. Hosler, H. Lechtman, and O. Holm, *Axe-Monies and Their Relatives* (Washington, DC: Dumbarton Oaks, 1990).

33. Shimada, "Late Prehispanic Coastal States," 56. See also L. Nordt, F. Hayashida, T. Hallmark, and C. Crawford, "Late Prehistoric Soil Fertility, Irrigation Management, and Agricultural Production in Northwest Coastal Peru," *Geoarcheology* 19 (2004): 21–46; M. Ertsen, "Structuring Properties of Irrigation Systems: Understanding Relations between Humans and Hydraulics through Modeling," *Water History* 2 (2010): 165–83.

34. F. Hayashida, "The Pampa de Chaparrí: Water, Land, and Politics on the North Coast of Peru," *Latin American Antiquity* 17, no. 3 (2006): 257.

35. C. Donnan and G. Cock, eds., *The Pacatnamu Papers*, vol. 1 (Los Angeles: Museum of Cultural History, University of California Los Angeles, 1986).

36. C. Mackey, "The Persistence of Lambayeque Ethnic Identity: The Perspective from the Jequetepeque Valley," in *From State to Empire in the Prehistoric Jequetepeque Valley, Peru*, ed. C. Zori and I. Johnson, BAR International Series 2310 (Oxford: Archaeopress, 2011), 149–68.

37. W. Sapp, "Lambayeque Norte and Lambayeque Sur: Evidence for the Development of an Indigenous Lambayeque Polity in the Jequetepeque Valley," in *From State to Empire in the Prehistoric Jequetepeque Valley, Peru*, ed. C. Zori and I. Johnson, BAR International Series 2310 (Oxford: Archaeopress, 2011), 93–104.

38. For example, see R. Cutright, "Food for the Dead, Cuisine of the Living: Mortuary Food Offerings from the Jequetepeque Valley, Perú," in *From State to Empire in the Prehistoric Jequetepeque Valley, Peru*, ed. C. Zori and I. Johnson, BAR International Series 2310 (Oxford: Archaeopress, 2011), 83–92.

39. A classic example of peer-polity interaction are the various Classical Greek city-states, which shared language, deities, and other cultural traits but remained fiercely independent; for definition, discussion, and examples, see C. Renfrew and J. Cherry, eds., *Peer Polity Interaction and Socio-Political Change* (Cambridge: Cambridge University Press, 1986).

40. T. Heyerdahl, D. H. Sandweiss, and A. Narváez, *Pyramids of Túcume: The Quest for Peru's Forgotten City* (London: Thames and Hudson, 1995).

41. J. Jennings, "Catastrophe, Revitalization and Religious Change on the Prehispanic North Coast of Peru," *Cambridge Archaeological Journal* 18, no. 2 (2008): 189.

42. There is an extensive literature on the Chimú. For a 2008 review, see J. Moore and C. Mackey, "The Chimú Empire," in *Handbook of South American Prehistory*, ed. H. Silverman and W. Isbell (New York: Springer, 2008), 783–807. Essential collections include M. Moseley and K. Day, eds., *Chan Chan: Andean Desert City* (Albuquerque: University of New Mexico Press, 1982); M. Moseley and Alana Cordy-Collins, eds., *The Northern Dynasties: Kingship and Statecraft in Chimor* (Washington, DC: Dumbarton Oaks, 1990).

43. To put this in perspective, the US Defense Department's Pentagon—the modern world's largest office building—covers approximately 600,000 square meters.

44. Moore and Mackey, "Chimú Empire," 707; for identification of a burial platform at Virú-124, see G. Willey, "Prehistoric Settlement Patterns in the Viru Valley, Peru" *Bureau of American Ethnology Bulletin* 155 (1953): 324–29.

45. J. Moore, *Architecture and Power in the Ancient Andes: the Archaeology of Public Buildings* (Cambridge: Cambridge University Press, 1996), 179–219.

46. J. Rowe, "The Kingdom of Chimor," *Acta Americana* 6 (1948): 47.

47. R. Keatinge, "Chimú Rural Administrative Centers in the Moche Valley, Peru," *World Archaeology* 6 (1974): 66–82; R. Keatinge, "Urban Settlement Systems and Rural Sustaining Communities: An Example from Chan Chan's Hinterland," *Journal of Field Archaeology* 2, no. 3 (1975): 215–27. Salvage excavations in 2011 at Cerro de la Virgen suggest that fishing was also an important activity, with the surplus catch provided to Chan Chan. It may also be that limited access to irrigation water restricted cotton cultivation at the site (Brian Billman, electronic communication, January 28, 2012).

48. C. Mackey, "Chimú Statecraft in the Provinces," in *Foundations of Andean Civilization: Papers in Honor of Michael E. Moseley*, ed. J. Marcus, C. Stanish, and P. R. Williams (Los Angeles: Cotsen Institute of Archaeology: University of California, 2009), 325–49.

49. Mackey, "Persistence of Lambayeque Ethnic Identity," 157.

50. E. Swenson, "Architectural Renovation as Ritual Process in Late Intermediate Period Jequetepeque," in *From State to Empire in the Prehistoric Jequetepeque Valley, Peru*, ed. C. Zori and I. Johnson, BAR International Series 2310 (Oxford: Archaeopress, 2011), 132.

51. C. Mackey and A. Klymyshyn, "The Southern Frontier of the Chimu Empire," in *The Northern Dynasties: Kingship and Statecraft in Chimor*, ed. M. Moseley and A. Cordy-Collins (Washington, DC: Dumbarton Oaks, 1990), 195–226; J. Moore, "Prehispanic Raised Field Agriculture in the Casma Valley: Recent Data, New Hypotheses," *Journal of Field Archaeology* 15 (1988): 265–76; J. Moore, "Cultural Responses to Environmental Catastrophes: Post-El Niño Subsistence on the Prehistoric North Coast of Peru," *Latin American Antiquity* 2 (1991): 27–47.

52. D. Sandweiss and A. Narvaez, "Túcume Past," in *Pyramids of Túcume: the Quest for Peru's Forgotten City*, ed. T. Heyerdahl, D. Sandweiss, and A. Narváez (London: Thames and Hudson, 1995), 194.

53. This discussion draws on several excellent overviews on the Wari: W. Isbell, "Huari Administration and the Orthogonal Cellular Administrative Horizon," in *Huari Administrative Structure: Prehistoric Monumental Architecture and State Government*, ed. W. Isbell and G. McEwan (Washington, DC: Dumbarton Oaks, 1991), 293–315; W. Isbell, "Wari and Tiwanaku: International Identities in the Central Andean Middle Horizon," in *Handbook of South American Prehistory*, ed. H. Silverman and W. Isbell (New York: Springer, 2008), 731–59; K. Schreiber, *Wari Imperialism in Middle Horizon Peru*, Anthropological Papers of the Museum of Anthropology 87 (Ann Arbor: University of Michigan, 1992); K. Schreiber, "The Wari Empire of Middle Horizon Peru: The Epistemological Challenges of Documenting an Empire without Documentary Evidence," in *Empires: Perspectives from Archaeology and History*, ed. S. Alcock, T. D'Altroy, K. Morrison, and C. Sinopoli (Cambridge: Cambridge University Press, 2001), 70–92. Also, following Isbell's suggestion, "Wari" refers to the culture and polity, whereas "Huari" refers to the major site in the Ayacucho Valley.

54. J. Tello, "Las ruinas de Huari," in *100 Años de Arqueología en el Perú: Fuentes e Investigaciones para la Historia del Perú*, ed. R. Ravines (Lima: Instituto de Estudios Peruanos, 1970 [1931]), 519–25.

55. For a recent discussion of chronological issues for Wari, see W. Isbell and A. Korpisaari, "Burial in the Wari and the Tiwanaku Heartlands: Similarities, Differences, and Meanings," *Diálogo Andino* 39 (2012): 91–122, especially 92–94.

56. J. Rowe, D. Collier, and G. Willey, "Reconnaissance Notes on the Site of Huari, near Ayacucho, Peru," *American Antiquity* 16, no. 2 (1950): 122.

57. Ibid., 123.

58. See, for example, R. Shady and A. Ruiz, "Evidence for Interregional Relationships during the Middle Horizon on the North-Central Coast of Peru," *American Antiquity* 44, no. 4 (1979): 676–84, who argued that Wari cultural styles could have been spread through exchange networks.

59. Schreiber, "Wari Empire of Middle Horizon Peru," 92.

60. B. Finucane, "Maize and Sociopolitical Complexity in the Ayacucho Valley, Peru," *Current Anthropology* 50, no. 4 (2009): 535–45.

61. Schreiber, "Wari Empire of Middle Horizon Peru," 81; see also, Isbell, "Wari and Tiwanaku," 745.

62. Isbell, "Wari and Tiwanaku," 750.

63. E. Bragayrac, "Archaeological Excavations in the Vegachayoq Moqo Sector of Huari," in *Huari Administrative Structure: Prehistoric Monumental Architecture and State Government,* ed. W. Isbell and G. McEwan (Washington, DC: Dumbarton Oaks, 1991), 75.

64. G. McEwan, "Archaeological Investigations at Pikillacta, a Wari Site in Peru," *Journal of Field Archaeology* 23, no. 2 (1996): 169–86; G. McEwan and N. Couture, "Pikillacta and its Architectural Typology," in *Pikillacta: The Wari Empire in Cuzco*, ed. G. McEwan (Iowa City: University of Iowa Press, 2005), 11–27.

65. There is an enormous literature on Wari ceramics and related styles, with Dorothy Menzel's article a fundamental and technical text: D. Menzel, "Style and Time in the Middle Horizon," *Ñawpa Pacha: Journal of Andean Archaeology* 2 (1964): 1–105.

66. A. Cook, "The Middle Horizon Ceramic Offerings from Conchapata," *Ñawpa Pacha: Journal of Andean Archaeology* 22-23 (1984–1985): 49–90; W. Isbell, "Conchapata, Ideological Innovator in Middle Horizon 1A," *Ñawpa Pacha*: *Journal of Andean Archaeology*, 22-23 (1984–1985): 91–126.

67. Menzel, "Style and Time in the Middle Horizon," 67.

68. Cook, "Middle Horizon Ceramic Offerings," 70; Isbell, "Conchapata, Ideological Innovator in Middle Horizon 1A," 732.

69. This argument has been convincingly made by Katharina Schreiber; see Schreiber, *Wari Imperialism in Middle Horizon Peru*, "The Wari Empire of Middle Horizon Peru."

70. See J. Topic, "Huari and Huamachucho," in *Huari Administrative Structure: Prehistoric Monumental Architecture and State Government*, ed. W. Isbell and G. McEwan (Washington, DC: Dumbarton Oaks, 1991), 141–64; for additional discussion, see J. Thatcher, "Early Intermediate Period and Middle Horizon 1B Ceramic Assemblages of Huamacucho, North Highlands, Peru," *Ñawpa Pacha: Journal of Andean Archaeology* 10–12 (1972–1974): 109–27.

71. D'Altroy and Schreiber, "Andean Empires," 274.

72. For an excellent example of Wari stylistic influence on late Moche ceramics at San Jose de Moro, see L. Castillo B., J. Rucabado Y., M. del Carpio P., K. Bernuy Q., K. Ruiz R., C. Rengifo Ch., G. Prieto B., and C. Fraresso, "Ideología y poder en la consolidación, colapso y reconstitución del Estado Mochica del Jequetepeque: El Proyecto Arqueológico San José de Moro (1991–2006)," *Ñawpa Pacha: Journal of Andean Archaeology* 29 (2008): 1–86.

73. This argument was applied by Isbell and Schreiber, "Was Huari a State?" *American Antiquity* 43 (1978): 372–89.

74. K. Schreiber, "Conquest and Consolidation: A Comparison of the Wari and Inka Occupations of a Highland Peruvian Valley," *American Antiquity* 52, no. 2 (1987): 266–84. In addition to discussing the changes Wari brought to the Carahuarazo, Schreiber contrasts those patterns with the subsequent Inca Empire, which although imposing a new set of imperial institutions, placed different demands on the people of the region.

75. J. Jennings and W. Yépez Álvarez, "Architecture, Local Elites, and Imperial Entanglements: The Wari Empire and the Cotahuasi Valley of Peru," *Journal of Field Archaeology* 28, nos. 1–2 (2001): 154, 155. For additional discussion of interpretations of Wari imperial administration, see the provocative article by J. Jennings, "Understanding Middle Horizon Peru: Hermeneutic Spirals, Interpretative Traditions, and Wari Administrative Centers," *Latin American Antiquity* 17, no. 3 (2006): 265–85; N. Craig and J. Jennings, "Politywide Analysis and Imperial Political Economy: The Relationship between Valley Political Complexity and Administrative Centers in the Wari Empire of the Central Andes," *Journal of Anthropological Archaeology* 20 (2001): 479–502.

76. M. Moseley, D. Nash, P. Williams, S. de France, A. Miranda, and M. Ruales, "Burning down the Brewery: Establishing and Evacuating an Ancient Imperial Colony at Cerro Baúl, Peru," *Proceedings of the National Academy of Sciences of the United States of America* 102, no. 48 (2005), 17264–71; D. Nash and P. R. Williams, "Architecture and Power: Relations on the Wari-Tiwanaku Frontier," in *The Foundations of Power in the Prehispanic Andes*, ed. K. Vaughn, C. Conlee, and D. Ogburn, Archaeological Papers of the American Anthropological Association 14 (2004), 151–74; D. Nash and P. R. Williams, "Wari Political Organization on the Southern Periphery," in *The Foundations of Andean Civilization, Works in Honor of Michael E. Moseley*, ed. J. Marcus, C. Stanish, and P. R. Williams (Los Angeles: Cotsen Institute of Archaeology Press, 2009), 257–76; P. Williams, "Cerro Baul: A Wari Center on the Tiwanaku Frontier," *Latin American Antiquity* 12, no. 1 (2001): 67–83.

77. Moseley et al., "Burning down the Brewery," 17264.

78. P. R. Williams and D. Nash, "Sighting the *apu*: A GIS Analysis of Wari Imperialism and the Worship of Mountain Peaks," *World Archaeology* 38, no. 3 (2006): 455–68.

79. Moseley et al., "Burning down the Brewery," 17269.

80. Schreiber, *Wari Imperialism in Middle Horizon Peru*, 69.

81. J. Janusek, *Identity and Power in the Ancient Andes: Tiwanaku Cities through Time* (New York: Routledge, 2004); J. Janusek, *Ancient Tiwanaku* (Cambridge: Cambridge University Press, 2008).

82. W. Bennett, "Excavations at Tiahuanaco," *Anthropological Papers of the American Museum of Natural History* 34, no. 3 (1934): 359–494; W. Bennett, "Excavations in Bolivia," *Anthropological Papers of the American Museum of Natural History* 35, no. 4

(1936); W. Bennett, "A revised sequence for the south Titicaca Basin," in *A Reappraisal of Peruvian Archaeology (Memoirs of the Society for American Archaeology, No. 4)*, ed. Irving Rouse (Washington, DC: Society for American Archaeology, 1948), 90–93; C. Ponce Sanguines, *Tiwanaku: Espacio, Tiempo y Cultura. Ensayo de Síntesis Arqueologica* (La Paz: Academia Nacional de Ciencias, 1972).

83. For an authoritative overview of archaeological research in the region, see C. Stanish, *Ancient Titicaca: The Evolution of Complex Society in Southern Peru and Northern Bolivia* (Berkeley: University of California Press, 2003).

84. Ibid., 172.

85. Example: Isbell, "Wari and Tiwanaku"; A. Kolata, *Tiwanaku and Its Hinterland: Archaeological and Paleoecological Investigations of an Andean Civilization* (Washington, DC: Smithsonian Institution Press, 2003); cf. Stanish, *Ancient Titicaca*.

86. J.-P. Protzen and S. Nair, "On Reconstructing Tiwanaku Architecture," *Journal of the Society of Architectural Historians* 59, no. 3 (2000): 358.

87. P. Goldstein, "Tiwanaku Temples and State Expansion: A Tiwanaku Sunken-Court Temple in Moquegua, Peru," *Latin American Antiquity* 4, no. 1 (1993): 25.

88. A. Vranich, "The Construction and Reconstruction of Ritual Space at Tiwanaku, Bolivia (A.D. 500–1000)," *Journal of Field Archaeology* 31, no. 2 (2006): 122.

89. L. Manzanilla, *Akapana: Una Pirámide en el Centro del Mundo* (Ciudad Universitario, Mexico: Instituto de Investigaciones Antropológicas, Universidad Nacional Autónoma de México, 1992).

90. On problems with reconstruction, see Protzen and Nair, "On Reconstructing Tiwanaku Architecture," note 60.

91. N. Couture and K. Sampeck, "Putini: A History of Palace Architecture in Tiwanaku," in *Tiwanaku and Its Hinterland: Archaeology and Paleoecology of an Andean Civilization*, vol. 2, ed. A. Kolata, (Washington, DC: Smithsonian Institution Press, 2003), 226–63.

92. W. Isbell and A. Vranich, "Experiencing the Cities of Wari and Tiwanaku," in *Andean Archaeology*, ed. H. Silverman (Malden, MA: Blackwell, 2004), 171.

93. A. Vranich, "Interpreting the Meaning of Ritual Spaces: The Temple Complex of Pumapunku, Tiwanaku, Bolivia" (PhD diss., University of Pennsylvania, Philadelphia, 1999).

94. J. Albarracin-Jordan, "Tiwanaku Settlement System: The Integration of Nested Hierarchies in the Lower Tiwanaku Valley," *Latin American Antiquity* 7, no. 3 (1996): 183–210.

95. A. Kolata and C. Ponce Sanguines, "Tiwanaku: The City at the Center," in *The Ancient Americas: Art from Sacred Landscapes*, ed. R. Townsend (Chicago: Art Institute of Chicago, 1992), 317–33.

96. Kolata, *Tiwanaku and Its Hinterland*, 176.

97. A. Kolata, "The Technology and Organization of Agricultural Production in the Tiwanaku State," *Latin American Antiquity* 2, no. 2 (1991): 101; see also A. Kolata, "The Agricultural Foundations of the Tiwanaku State: A View from the Heartland," *American Antiquity* 51, no. 4 (1986): 748–62; J. Janusek and A. Kolata, "Top-Down or Bottom-Up: Rural Settlement and Raised Field Agriculture in the Lake Titicaca Basin, Bolivia," *Journal of Anthropological Archaeology* 23 (2004): 404–30.

98. M. Bandy, "Energetic Efficiency and Political Expediency in Titicaca Basin Raised Field Agriculture," *Journal of Anthropological Archaeology* 24 (2005): 271–96. Bandy strongly criticizes previous estimates of the fields' productivity.

99. C. Stanish, "Agricultural Intensification in the Titicaca Basin," in *Seeking a Richer Harvest: The Archaeology of Subsistence Intensification, Innovation, and Change,* ed. T. Thurston and C. Fisher (New York: Springer, 2007), 125–39.

100. For an alternative view, see C. Erickson, "The Social Organization of Prehispanic Raised Field Agriculture in the Lake Titicaca Basin," in *Economic Aspects of Water Management in the Prehispanic New World,* ed. V. Scarborough and B. Isaac (Greenwich, CT: JAI, 1993), 369–426; C. Erickson, "Neo-Environmental Determinism and Agrarian Collapse in Andean Prehistory," *Antiquity* 73 (1999): 634–42; C. Erickson, "Intensification, Political Economy, and the Farming Community: In Defense of a Bottom-Up Perspective of the Past," in *Agricultural Strategies,* ed. J. Marcus and C. Stanish (Los Angeles: Cotsen Institute, 2006), 233–265.

101. For descriptions of snuff trays, see C. Torres, "Imágenes legible: la iconografía Tiwanaku como significante," *Boletin del Museo Chileno de Arte Precolombino* 9 (2004): 55–73. For discussion of textiles, see A. Rodman, "Textiles and Ethnicity: Tiwanaku in San Pedro de Atacama, North Chile," *Latin American Antiquity* 3, no. 4 (1992): 316–40. For data indicating an indirect Tiwanaku presence in San Pedro de Atacama, rather than colonization, see K. Knudson, "Tiwanaku Influence in the South Central Andes: Strontium Isotope Analysis and Middle Horizon Migration," *Latin American Antiquity* 19, no. 1 (2008): 3–23; C. Torres-Rouff, "The Influence of Tiwanaku on Life in the Chilean Atacama: Mortuary and Bodily Perspectives," *American Anthropologist* 110, no. 3 (2008): 325–37.

102. M. Uribe Rodríguez and C. Agüero Piwonka, "Iconografía, Alfarería y textileria Tiwanaku: elementos para una revisión del Periodo Medio en el norte grande de Chile," *Chungara, Revista de Antropología Chilena,* Volumen Especial (2004): 1055–68, at http://www.scielo.cl/scielo.php?script=sci_arttex¬t&pid=S0717-73562004000400041&lng=en&nrm=iso&tlng=en (accessed March 26, 2014), my translation.

103. P. Goldstein, "Tiwanaku Temples and State Expansion: A Tiwanaku Sunken-Court Temple in Moquegua, Peru," *Latin American Antiquity* 4, no. 1 (1993): 30.

104. Ibid.

105. P. Goldstein, "Exotic Goods and Everyday Chiefs: Long-Distance Exchange and Indigenous Sociopolitical Development in the South Central Andes," *Latin American Antiquity* 11, no. 4 (2000): 335–61.

106. B. Owen, "Distant Colonies and Explosive Collapse: The Two Stages of the Tiwanaku Diaspora in the Osmore Drainage," *Latin American Antiquity* 16, no. 1 (2005): 50.

107. Goldstein, "Tiwanaku Temples and State Expansion," 42.

108. C. Stanish, E. de la Vega, M. Mosle, P. Williams, C. Chavez, B. Viing, and K. LaFavre, "Tiwanaku Trade Patterns in Southern Peru," *Journal of Anthropological Archaeology* 29 (2010): 524–32.

109. Ibid., 530.

110. M. Binford, A. Kolata, M. Brenner, J. Janusek, M. Seddon, M. Abbot, and J. Curtis, "Climate Variation and the Rise and Fall of an Andean Civilization," *Quaternary Research* 47 (1997): 235–48.

111. B. Owen, "Distant Colonies and Explosive Collapse: The Two Stages of the Tiwanaku Diaspora in the Osmore Drainage," *Latin American Antiquity* 16, no. 1 (2005): 7.

112. S. Téllez and F. Hayashida, "Campos de cultivo prehispánicos en la pampa de Chaparrí," *Boletín de Arqueología PUCP* 8 (2004): 378–90.

Figure 10.1 Sinú effigy vessel of Mother and Child

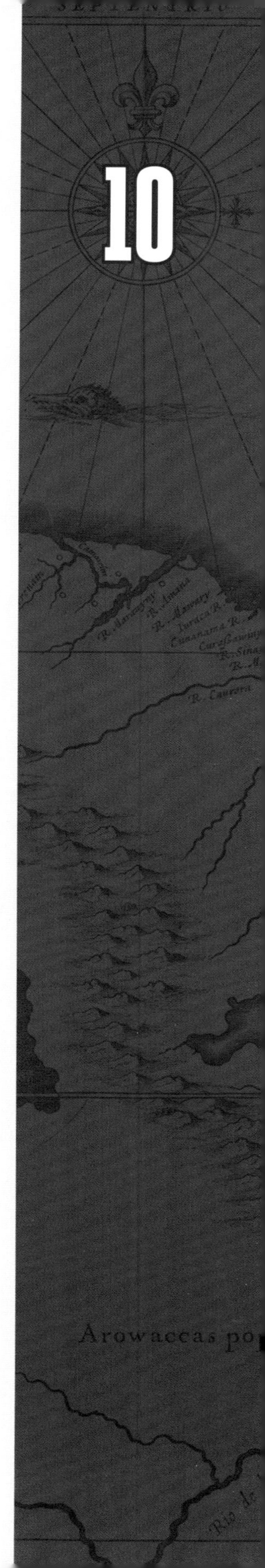

10 Twilight of Prehistory

10.5876_9781607323334.c010

> Twenty-two leagues from the first settlement of Yorimán, is the site of the largest village that we met with on the whole river, its houses covering a length of more than a league and a half.
>
> A single family does not live in one house, as is usually the case in Spain, but the smallest number that are contained under one roof are four or five, and very often more, from which circumstance the great number of people in this village may be imagined.
>
> *Fr. Cristobal de Acuña, 1639,* A New Discovery of the Great River of the Amazons

The last five centuries of South American prehistory were marked by fundamentally different social and political experiences across the continent, a previously unseen disparity in the scales of social life (figure 10.2). For example, along the coast of Tierra del Fuego, groups of mobile hunters and gatherers—the immediate ancestors of the historic Yámana—lived on marine resources, with seals, fish, shellfish, and other seafood comprising from 55 percent to 95 percent of the diet, supplemented by guanaco and other terrestrial resources (see chapter 8).[1] Their adaptive strategy was remarkably successful and stable, with only minor variations in artifact types over thousands of years and no discernible changes in types of sites, most being short-term camps and shell middens. Along the Beagle Channel region, **Luis Orquera** and **Ernesto Piana** have observed, basic resources were evenly distributed "in time and space," and when food supplies "declined in the immediate surroundings of a camp, it was more convenient to move to a less exploited patch than to intensify their exploitation."[2] This had other consequences: "There were no great opportunities or reasons to control access to resources, accumulate individual wealth (giving occasion for social inequalities), or recognize leadership beyond personal prestige to coordinate collective tasks" such as hunting sorties or annual initiation ceremonies.[3] A basic strategy that emerged soon after people arrived at the southernmost tip of South America and produced a stable, resilient way of life for thousands of years is a remarkable example of human resiliency and success.

About 3,000 miles to the north, a completely different configuration emerged and expanded from the Andean Valley of Cusco. Beginning in the fifteenth century, a regional chiefdom successfully defended itself from enemy attack, vanquishing its rivals and beginning more than a century of explosive military conquests and political domination. Consolidating its core, the chiefdom drove south to conquer the Titicaca Basin, the place from whence the Creator God Viracocha had come, creating men by blowing his breath

Figure 10.2 Regions discussed in chapter 10

into stones. Having conquered this southern realm, the kingdom's rulers turned north and west, consolidating the Peruvian coast and marching into the northern Andes. These conquered peoples and territories were fused into an imperial project at whose peak sat a divine emperor descended from the Sun. The wealth of empire flowed into the capital city, adorning temples and palaces and provisioning armies, artisans, and nobles. This society would be known as the Incas (see chapter 11).

Thus, in the last five centuries before the arrival of Europeans, South American societies achieved amazingly different forms of social complexity, political organization, and centralization—all accompanied by remarkably distinct cosmologies, artistic traditions, and ideologies. In this chapter, a cross-section is presented of different South American societies in these last centuries before contact (see figure 10.1). As always, this sample of case studies is incomplete, but it does give the reader a sense of the diverse cultural traditions that existed during this twilight of prehistory.

The Amazons: Languages, Settlements, Ceramics, and Worldviews

Although it is common to think of the Amazon as a single environmental unit, the Brazilian archaeologist **Helen Pinto Lima** has posed the question "Which Amazon?," writing that "our perspective is that 'the Amazons' we see today are the result of the combined agency of nature and human societies. The old myth of the pristine forest has fallen."[4] In addition to the myth of the pristine forest (see chapter 5), another long-held notion has been discredited—namely, that the tropical forests were insufficiently productive to support permanent settlements and complex societies. The archaeologist **Eduardo Góes Neves** has observed, "In the case of Amazonia and the northern part of South America, the ethnographic and ethnohistoric literature is filled with evidence that in the sixteenth century, and in some places until today, local indigenous groups were regionally integrated into multiethnic networks that included specialized production and exchange, mobilization for warfare, and the periodic concentrations of chiefly social formations. These formations were multi-linguistic, a phenomenon that sometimes was accompanied by the development of *linguas francas* (pidgins) in light of patterns generated by exchange networks. It is probable that many of the Amazonian social forms in the five centuries preceding the European conquest had this same general structural pattern."[5]

There are several intertwined issues in this quotation. The first two points are obvious: (1) the Amazon was a diverse landscape influenced by human actions, and (2) pre-contact societies from circa AD 1000–1500 were larger, more complex, and more integrated than previously thought. A third point is less obvious. The complex patterns of exchange, periodic mobilizations, the development of chiefdoms, and the creation of lingua francas imply that cultural traditions were not static, stable sets.

This has particular relevance for understanding the last 500 years of Amazonian prehistory, as there is ethnolinguistic evidence for similar, but widely separated, languages, a pattern interpreted as evidence of multiple migrations and intrusions (figure 10.3) Even taking into account the disruptions and dislocations caused by European conquest—including population decline, cultural exterminations, and enslavements that continued well into the twentieth century—it is still obvious that these language distributions were the product of complex migrations and interactions.[6]

"The Amazon basin," the linguists **R. M. Dixon** and **Alexandra Aikhenvald** write, "is the least known and least understood linguistic region in the world.

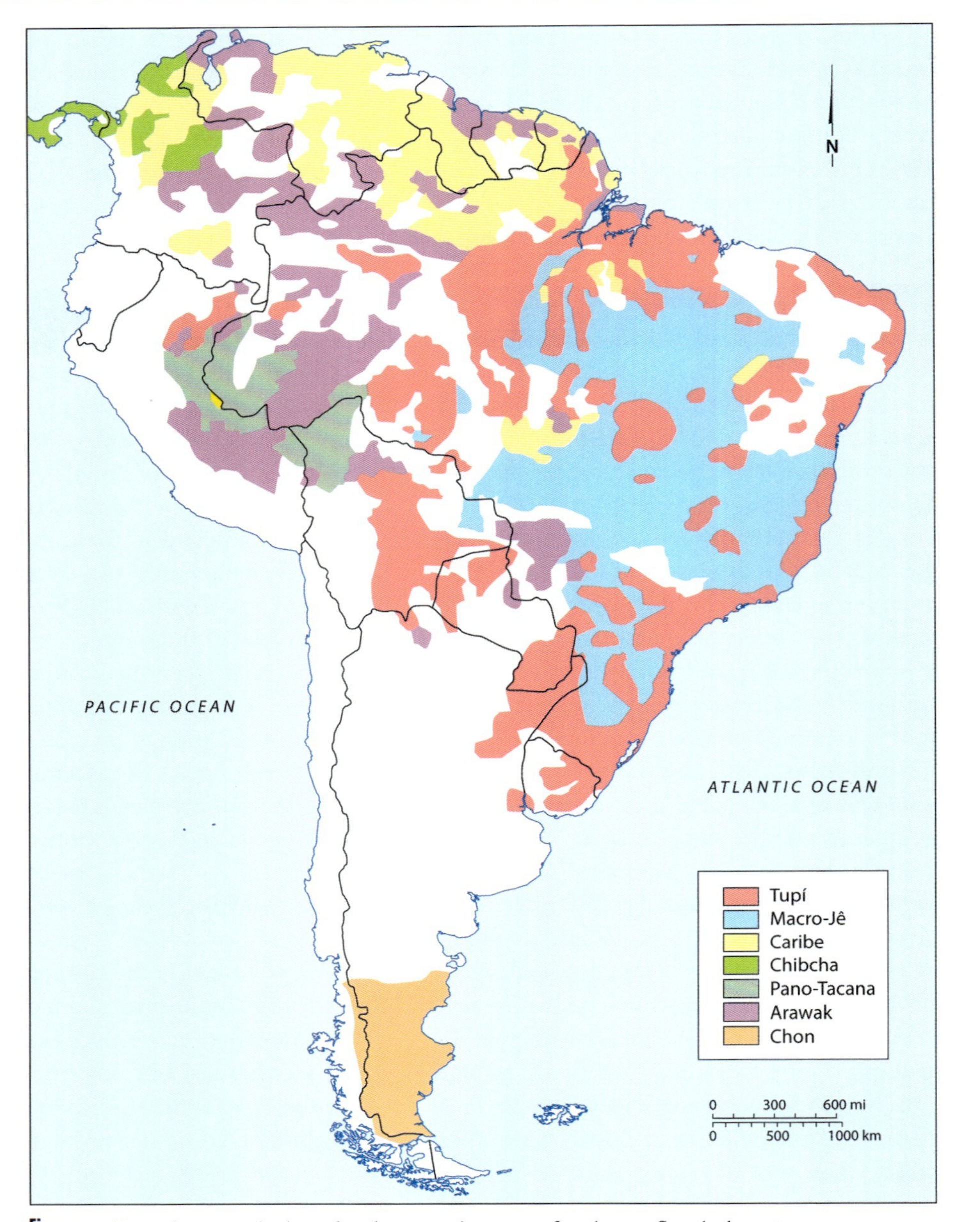

Figure 10.3 Distribution of selected indigenous language families in South America

Maps of the language families of South America (with one color for each genetic group) purvey an impression of anarchy—there are dabs of yellow and blue and red and orange and brown mingled together like a painting by Jackson Pollack . . . In fact, the major language families all have markedly discontinuous distributions (more than is found in any other part of the world)."[7]

An estimated 1,500 languages were spoken at contact; 350 indigenous languages are still used in South America (see figure 10.2).[8] In northern South America, various **Chibchan languages**—such as Muisca in northern Colombia (discussed later)—are related to other languages found in Panama, Costa Rica, and Nicaragua. Various **Carib languages** are found in northern South America, particularly north of the Amazon River in northern Brazil, the Guianas, Venezuela, and lowland Colombia. The **Macro-Gê languages** tend to be located in the interior regions of eastern Brazil. Speakers of Pano and Tukano languages tend to be found in the western Amazon on the headwaters of some of the major drainages. Finally, there are two widely dispersed language families: **Tupi-Guarani** and **Arawak**.

Tupi-Guarani Expansions

Tupi-Guarani includes ten major language families, nine of which are in the Brazilian Amazon south of the Amazon River, while the tenth (Tupi-Guarani) is found along the Atlantic Coasts of Brazil and Uruguay and in interior zones of Uruguay, Paraguay, and Bolivia. **Francisco Silva Noelli** writes, "Today a consensus exists on the following two points. First, there was a common center of origin, from which the Tupi fanned out. Second, the Tupi differentiated through distinct historic and cultural processes. But there is no consensus as to *where* the Tupi center was located and *where* their routes of expansion passed."[9]

Not only is there no consensus about the paths of Tupi expansion, but even to use the term *expansion* in contrast to *migration* invokes a controversy, as Noelli writes, because "the term migration means a moving from one place to another, a leaving of the original region." That term might appropriately describe the situation when Tupi-Guarani speakers tried to escape other peoples, such as Europeans after AD 1500, but it inadequately describes "those Tupian peoples who moved in other ways, possibly for other reasons . . . expanding to new territories without abandoning old ones . . . The better term for these population shifts is expansion, meaning distention and spreading, a conquering of new regions without abandoning previous ones."[10]

Other points of controversy include the pace, paths, and forms of expansions. For example, **Robert Walker** and colleagues have argued that variations among different Tupi languages point to an original core in western Brazil, followed by a northeastern expansion toward the Amazon, followed by further expansions, including a southwestern movement and expansion to the Atlantic Coast (figure 10.4).[11] (Note: the lines in figure 10.4 do not represent the paths of migration but instead the relative connections between speakers of different modern Tupi languages.) An analysis comparing genetic differences and linguistic variations among modern Tupi speakers and Je speakers conducted by **Virginia Ramallo** and colleagues suggests that the Tupi spread by having communities split, migrating to new areas, and establishing new populations—separate colonies, as it were—while Je speakers interacted with other populations, resulting in "an intricate and non-linear mode of dispersion."[12]

Some idea of the timing of this expansion is indicated by radiocarbon dates at the **Morro Grande site** on the coast of Brazil. As discussed by **Rita Scheel-Ybert** and her colleagues, Brazilian archaeologists commonly associate the appearance

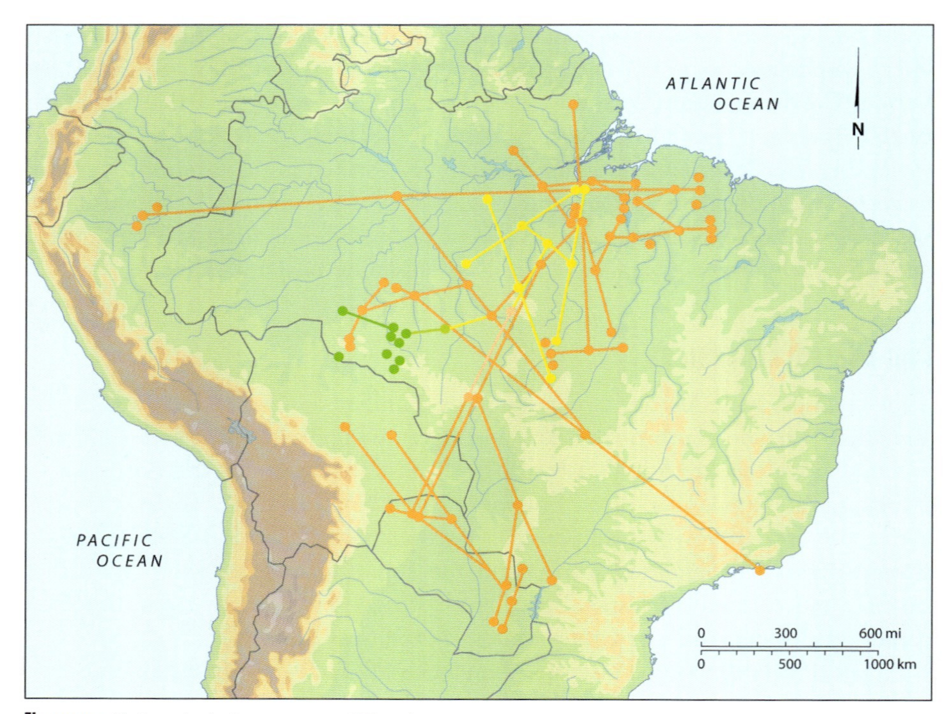

Figure 10.4 Cultural phylogenetics of Tupi languages

of polychrome pottery with the arrival of Tupi speakers on the Atlantic Coast, based on similarities between those ceramics and ceramics used by historic Tupi-Guarani groups.[13] In addition to ceramics, another element connects the Morro Grande site to later Tupi-Guarani cultural practices: the use of fire in mortuary ritual. "Fire," **Mariana Beauclair** and colleagues write, "performed an essential role in Tupinamba funerary rituals. It was one of the necessary elements to grant the soul a successful journey to the Guajupia[,] the place of the afterlife[,] which was conceived as a place of pleasure, beyond the mountains, where the souls would meet their ancestors and live eternally in joy."[14] At Morro Grande, selected burnings of tree bark surrounded a polychrome burial urn; they resulted in radiocarbon dates 2600 ± 160 BP (1050–351 cal BC), while charcoal from a utilitarian hearth produced a date of 2920 ± 70 BP (1262–890 cal BC). If, in fact, polychrome urn burials and fire rituals were associated with Tupi speakers, this suggests their arrival on the Atlantic Coast sometime between 1200 and 500 BC, with the initial Tupi-Guarani expansions out of western Brazil preceding this at some unknown time.

A linguistic group, a genetic population, and a set of cultural practices are very different phenomena. Languages, genes, and cultural practices spread through different mechanisms—new vocabulary is adopted, gene pools vary through genetic drift or genetic isolation, and cultural practices may change through innovation, diffusion, or adaptations. There is no reason to think that language, genes, and culture will appear in a single discrete package. That said, current evidence suggests that Tupi speakers began to expand from western Brazil sometime before 3,000–2,000 years ago—perhaps as early as 5,000 years ago, as Noelli has suggested—and were not a late prehistoric expansion as once thought.[15]

The Arawak Diaspora from Northwestern Amazonia to the Antilles and the Upper Xingu

Arawak refers to another South American language family, and its expansion is as complicated as that of Tupi. As with Tupi, the very name used to describe its expansion invokes controversy. **Michael Heckenberger** has suggested the term *diaspora* as "a simple gloss for a very complex set of processes of cultural change and diversity associated with the dispersal of early agriculturalists and their technologies across the humid lowlands of South America after circa 300 B.P.," a term chosen "to avoid more agency-neutral terms such as expansion, dispersion, or radiation."[16]

Whatever the process, the result was that Arawak languages are more widespread than any other indigenous South American language family, found across lowland South America with a northward expansion through the arc of islands that frame the eastern edge of the Caribbean Sea, from Grenada to Cuba. Because the earliest European explorers first landed in these New World islands, Arawak words were adopted quickly into Spanish and later English: *canoe*, *maize*, *tobacco*, *hammock*, *hurricane*, and *barbeque,* to name just a few.

Based on current reconstructions, the Arawak languages originated in the northwest Amazon, along the rivers between the Rio Solimões in Brazil and the Middle Orinoco in Venezuela.[17] Current estimates suggest that Arawak languages began to diverge as groups spread out sometime before 3,000 years ago, moving northward along the Orinoco drainage and southward to the confluence of the Rio Solimões and the Rio Negro between approximately 1000–500 BC. The pace of expansion continued with speakers of Arawak languages moving down the Amazon as well as upstream along the Amazon's major tributaries, such as the Ucayali in the Peruvian Amazon, by AD 500.

Migration into the Caribbean islands began around 400–200 BC, as the ancestors of the **Taino** (the first native people Columbus encountered) moved from Trinidad into the Antilles. With a confidence rarely encountered in the anthropological literature, **Julian Granberry** has written: "From our language data we know with certainty that the Taino spoke a Northwest Maipurán Arawak language," linked to languages spoken in western Venezuela and northeastern Colombia.[18] The Venezuelan archaeologist **Alberta Zucchi,** drawing on her research in the Venezuelan llanos and Middle Orinoco (see chapter 8), has proposed that the expansion of Northern Maipurán speakers was marked archaeologically by the appearance of a distinctive pottery style (called Cedeñoid) characterized by finely incised, parallel lines etched into their surfaces.[19] This pottery shares similarities in vessel form and pottery tempers with other archaeological complexes in six different portions of South America—the Middle Orinoco and Llanos, Central

Amazon, the Rio Negro Basin, Guyana, Brazilian Guyana, and the Western Antilles—present in these regions between 1000 BC and AD 1800.

These ceramics, in turn, are often included in the **Saladoid-Barrancoid** ceramic traditions, which Heckenberger summarizes as "composed of cooking griddles and a variety of pots decorated with incised line, punctuation, appliqué, modeling, and monochrome painting (usually white or black) on buff or red slips, and tempered with grit and sponge spixule (cauixi)."[20] Developing on the Middle Orinoco at circa 1000–500 BC, these ceramic styles were predecessors of later prehistoric ceramic traditions.

But more than pottery styles accompanied the spread of Arawak languages. Heckenberger has argued that speakers of Arawak languages had "a very clear settlement pattern . . . organized around a central plaza or other central sacred space" (although non-Arawak Gê speakers also have circular villages; discussed later).[21] Heckenberger's model envisions a rather extensive set of Arawakan characteristics, "a constellation of cultural features" including populous and permanent villages laid out as concentric circles with designated public and sacred central plazas; villages linked in socio-political networks through extensive and regular exchanges (trade, inter-marriage, feasts, and ceremonies); intensive agriculture with manioc as a staple; the use of aquatic resources; well-defined social ideologies emphasizing "regional sociality rooted in shared substance or heritage, (kinship), geography (territory) and an ideology of 'in-ness' in a regional moral community," counterbalanced by "non-predatory" ideologies and accommodations with neighbors while preparing for potential attacks by building defensive structures.[22] These social patterns were accompanied by specific types of material culture: bull-roarers, sacred flutes, masks, hammocks, ballgames, and idols. Finally, Heckenberger argues, Arawak societies tended to have a social hierarchy in which elites and commoners were recognized, with elite status based in part on heredity, primogeniture, and metaphorical kinship with mythic ancestors.[23] Despite variations between Arawak groups and these features' presence among non-Arawak groups, "the broad cultural schema, glossed here as an ethos of settled village life, regionality, and social hierarchy, is present in most historically known Arawak."[24]

This complex model is derived from Heckenberger's archaeological research in the Upper Xingu. Based on archaeological survey and excavations in a 1,000 km^2 (386 square mile) research area, a basic sequence has been established. The earliest known occupations are marked by sites with incised pottery dating to AD 800–1250, part of the initial Arawak expansion into this portion of southern Amazonia and a phase known as **Early Ipavu**. Population grew over those four-and-a-half centuries, leading to a period of village nucleation and structural elaboration between AD 1250 and 1650, the **Late Ipavu** phase, during which large fortified villages become prominent. In turn, specific large villages became centers of multi-village clusters, large settlements linked physically to smaller hub settlements by trails and raised causeways (figure 10.5).

Principal villages had a variety of earthworks: ditches (as much as 3 m [9.8 ft] deep, 15 m [49.2 ft] wide, and 2,500 m [8,200 ft] long), mounds, raised causeways and roads 20–50 m (65.6–164 ft) wide, canoe ports, reservoirs, and fish ponds. In

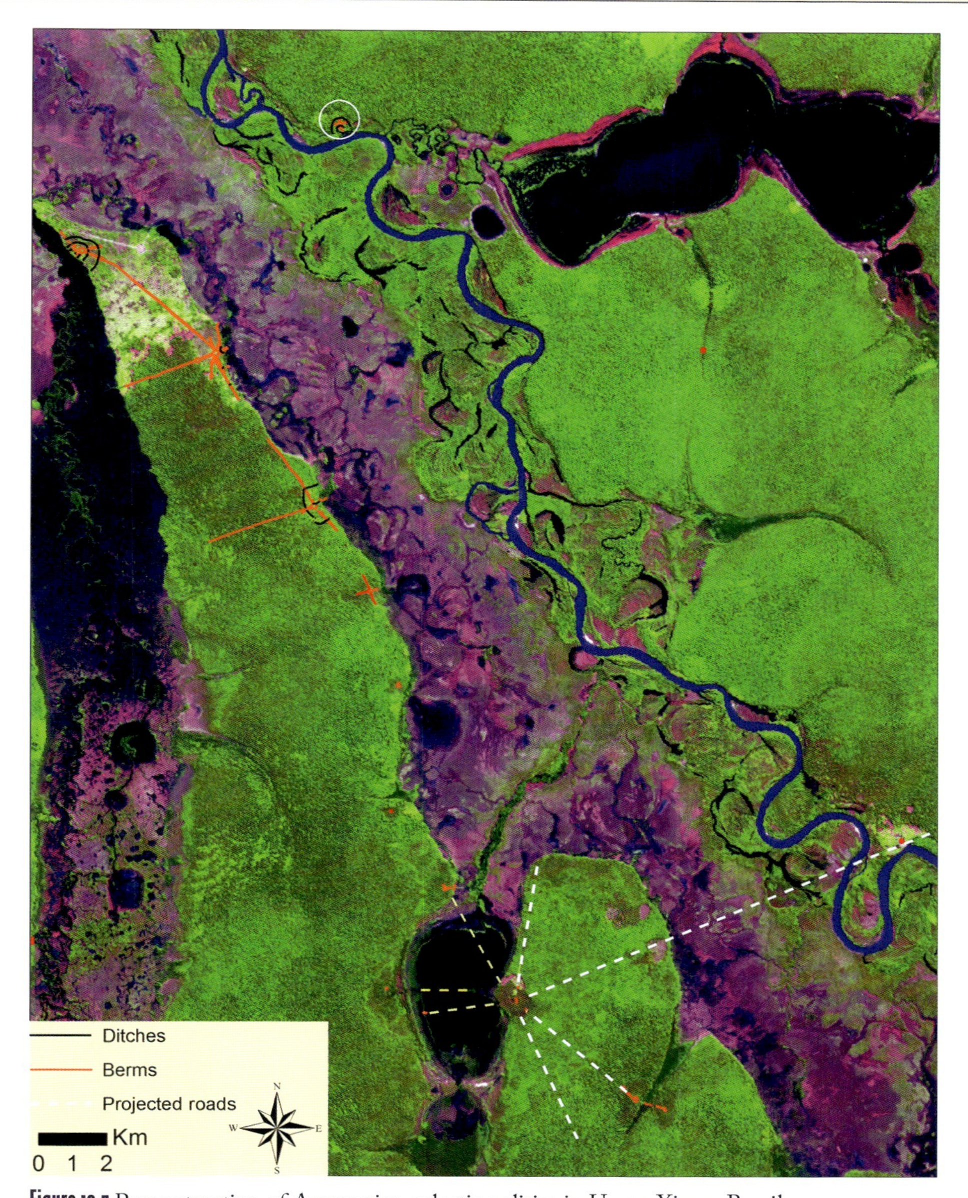

Figure 10.5 Reconstruction of Amazonian galactic polities in Upper Xingu, Brazil

many ways, these earthworks are similar to those known from other regions in lowland South America (see chapters 3 and 8), archaeological expressions of concentrations of people and public effort not predicted by the Tropical Forest model.

On the Upper Xingu, according to Heckenberger, these clusters of villages formed "**galactic polities**," a term the anthropologist **Stanley Tambiah** applied to traditional kingdoms of Southeast Asia, where the centripetal force of the center was based as much on ritual and tradition as on centralized political, military, or economic power.[25] The anthropogenic features of the Upper Xingu landscape, Heckenberger contends, "were constructed and functioned for some time as part of an integrated architectural scheme, which articulated with (in fact can be considered the 'core' of) a broader culturally constructed landscape, including areas of intensive terra firme gardening, intricate pathways and satellite sites."[26] Built between AD 1250 and 1650, these settlements are thought to reflect chiefdoms. During these four centuries, the Arawak of the Upper Xingu came into increasing contact with neighboring Tupian- and Gê-speaking groups, although the Xinguano villages seem to have relied on a defensive strategy in contrast to their more bellicose neighbors. Further, there is some possibility that the eastward expansion of the Inca Empire into the regions bordering Amazonia resulted in indirect repercussions that intensified conflict (see chapter 11).

However, these developments were cut short by the arrival of Europeans in South America. Disease advanced ahead of actual settlements. By the early 1600s, Portuguese had established sustained contact with the Lower Xingu, and a combination of epidemics, slave raiding, and punitive expeditions well into the twentieth century resulted in devastating decline in the Upper Xingu. For example, the 3,000 people living in the Upper Xingu in the 1890s—a much reduced population from pre-contact—were further decimated to around 500 people in 1950.[27] It is little wonder that twentieth-century ethnographers observed a social and political system fundamentally different from the galactic polities that developed in the Upper Xingu at AD 1250–1650.

Central Brazil: Ring Villages and Macro-Gê Communities

Over 400 km (240 miles) to the south, a different archaeological pattern has been documented in territory occupied by the Bororo, speakers of a non-Arawak, Macro-Gê language. Long-term ethnoarchaeological and archaeological investigations by **Irmhild Wüst**, **Cristina Barreto**, and others have documented the appearance of "ring villages" in Central Brazil in the fourth–eighth centuries AD. Ring villages were well established by AD 800, at which point "this form of community came to be widespread and well-established in all of Central Brazil" (figure 10.6).[28]

Although it has been suggested that ring villages were the products of the dislocations caused by European colonization, this type of settlement predates the sixteenth century. "Instead," Wüst and Barreto write, "archaeological evidence points to the emergence of ring villages as a largely local development. Their rapid and sudden onset, their large size, and the concentric ring layout suggests [*sic*] that other pressures in the area promoted a rapid organization of population into larger and more structured communities."[29]

The ring villages form separate communities, unconnected into larger networks as in the Upper Xingu. Rather, the ring villages were independent social units with dwellings encircling a plaza that often contained a men's house. Settlements may have had as many as three concentric rings of dwellings, forming sites as large as 500 m (1,640 ft) in diameter with estimated populations of as many

Figure 10.6 Modern Amazonian ring village: a Kuikuru village in the Upper Xingu

as 1,000 people.[30] Drawing on analogies with ethnographic groups, the residents may have been organized into exogamous moieties, in which (to oversimplify) people belonged to one of two different kin groups that intermarried.[31]

Wüst has carefully argued that one must be careful in drawing simple analogies between archaeological sites and ethnographic practices. Nonetheless, ring villages associated with exogamous moieties, Barreto notes, "promote stability: a relative social equality among different domestic units is mirrored in the equidistant spacing houses have from the center of political decision-making (the plaza or men's house), which reduces internal conflicts and augments cohesion . . . A residence pattern based on equality and complementarity functions to integrate [the community] and reduce conflicts."[32]

A recent increase in archaeological research may lead to a reassessment of the chronology and interpretations of ring settlements in Central Brazil, although much recent work has been done in response to environmental impact analyses rather than being motivated by specific research agendas.[33] Nonetheless, available archaeological data suggest several points. First, the ring villages were not ephemeral or shifting small communities, as the Tropical Forest model proposed by Steward and others suggested. They were substantial, often large settlements. Second, ring villages were not the product of post-contact disruptions and migrations but rather appeared in Central Brazil by circa AD 800 and continued as a major settlement form into the Colonial era and well into the twenty-first century. Third, no current evidence suggests an overarching, supra-community form of political order. Ring villages were not parts of coalitions or building blocks of larger

Figure 10.7 Archaeological fieldwork at Açutuba, Central Brazil

states but instead fiercely independent communities whose encircled dwellings marked an internally coherent community distinct from neighbors and enemies.

Central Amazon Basin: Incised Pottery, Polychrome Pottery, and Palisade Villages

In the Central Amazon Basin near the modern Brazilian city of Manaus, Eduardo Góes Neves and colleagues have conducted an extensive program of archaeological survey and excavation near the confluence of the Rio Negro and Rio Solimões, the main channel of this segment of the Amazon River (figure 10.7). An intriguing pattern emerges from their investigations. Despite early occupations documented downstream in the Lower Amazon—including hunters and gatherers at Pedra Pintada by 9200 BC and 3500 BC shell middens at the mouth of the Amazon (see chapter 4)—and large mound sites constructed by the third millennium BC in the upper Upano of Ecuador (see chapter 5), there is scant evidence for early occupations in the Central Amazon region. Rather, Neves writes, "in the central Amazon . . . evidence of human occupation from 5700 to 500 BC is absent, despite the identification of more than 100 archaeological sites in a 900 km^2 research area."[34]

Neves interprets the rarity and small size of pre–1000 BC sites as indicating the limited significance of domesticated plants and agriculture in the Central Amazon. By AD 1000, this pattern had fundamentally changed: sedentary agricultural societies, often farming *terra preta* (dark earth) soils, lived in larger, more permanent, and thus more archaeologically "visible" settlements.[35] Although the rea-

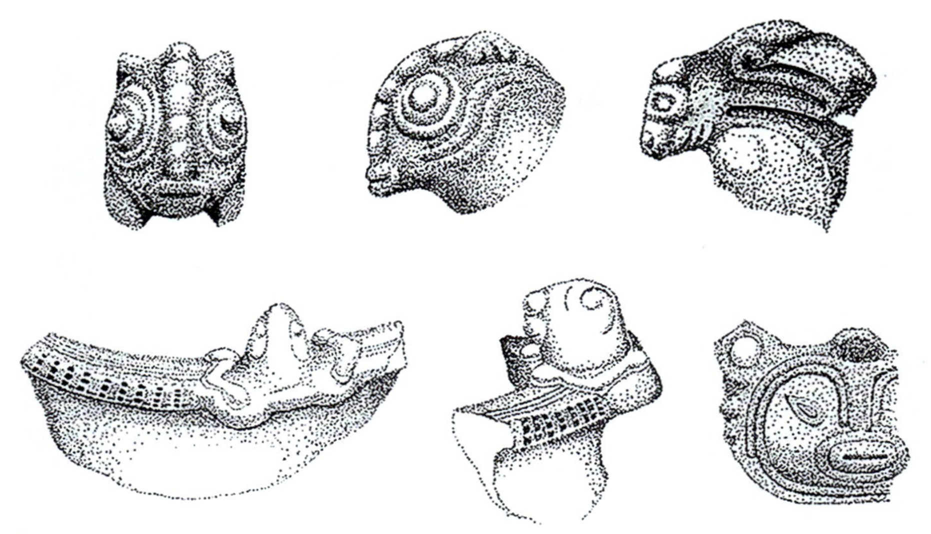

Figure 10.8 Açutuba ceramics

sons behind the apparent absence of earlier settlements are unclear, the increased presence of larger settlements between circa AD 500 and 1000 seems undeniable.

Archaeological research directed by Neves has documented 378 archaeological sites in the Central Amazon project study area, resulting in a basic chronology. The earliest phase with pottery, the **Açutuba phase** (ca. 200 BC to AD 300), is marked by ceramics with wood bark temper added to the paste and pots variously decorated with curvilinear incisions or zoomorphic figures, alternatively covered with red or white slip and in some cases covered in polychrome paint (figure 10.8).[36] The **Axinim phase** (ca. AD 1–800) had elaborate, almost baroque ceramic styles, with sophisticated technologies employing incisions and excisions to highlight different fields on the slipped surfaces of the pottery, creating a unique ceramic tradition. The **Manacapuru phase** (AD 300–700) is marked by the use of *cauixí* temper to the ceramic paste, a few predominant vessel forms, and various decorations consisting of incised lines, punctations, zoomorphic appendages, flanged rims, and red slip (figure 10.9). A major change in ceramics occurred during the **Paredão phase** (AD 700–1250), in which well-made and highly fired ceramic vessels were created in an array of forms—vessels with pedestals, vessels with handles, and funerary urns—and were elaborately decorated with fine-line incisions, delicate painted lines, and stylized anthropomorphic appliqués. Finally, the **Guarita phase** (AD 700–1500) was marked by ceramics with reinforced rims, polychrome painting over white or red slips, and anthropomorphic funerary urns.[37]

Behind these details of pots and dates, a basic pattern emerges: there was a clear florescence in Central Amazon ceramic technologies associated with changes in social and political patterns. One hypothesis is that there was a correlation between ceramics decorated with incising (the "Incised Border Tradition"; in this case, the Açutuba, Axinim, Manacapuru, and Paredão phases) and the spread of speakers of Arawak languages contrasting with the well-made ceramics decorated

Figure 10.9 Manacapuru ceramics

by painting and, later, with polychrome designs and speakers of Tupi languages (in this case, during the Guarita phase). The abrupt appearance of polychrome ceramics in the Central Amazon, according to this hypothesis, may be associated with migrations of Tupi speakers into the region.

The shifts in ceramic styles and ethnolinguistic groups in the Central Amazon were accompanied by changes in settlement plans and architecture, particularly after polychrome pottery became common. At the beginning of the Paredão phase,

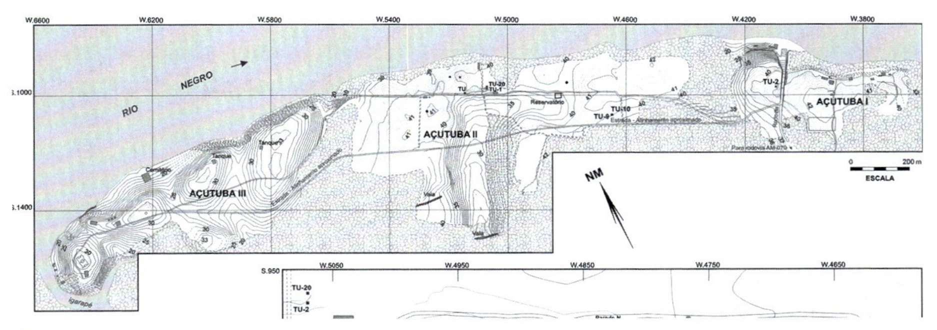

Figure 10.10 Site map of Açutuba Locality

ring villages appeared in which houses were built on top of artificial mounds. A few earlier settlements had been circular, but ring villages became the dominant settlement pattern during the Paredão phase. Toward the end of the Paredão phase, some house mounds were used as burial sites, with the dead interred in ceramic urns in the floors of the dwellings. For example, at the **Antonio Galo** site, located at the confluence of the Rio Negro and Rio Solimões, a dozen house mounds surround a circular plaza, covering about 1 ha (2.47 acres). Toward the end of the occupation, people began using the house mounds for sepulchers, burying their dead in ceramic urns in the floors of their dwellings.

Settlements grew larger. The Antonio Galo site expanded from 1 ha (2.47 acres) during the Paredão phase to 14 ha (36.6 acres). The **Açutuba Locality** consists of a trio of settlements stretching over 3 km (1.8 miles) on the south bank of the Rio Negro, about 38 km (22.8 miles) upstream from Manaus (figure 10.10). The actual occupation area covers at least 30 ha (74.5 acres), although less dense deposits of cultural materials are found over 50 ha (123.5 acres).[38] At the central site area, **Açutuba II**, there were two major components, with Model Incised Ceramics dating to AD 250–1000 followed by Guarita ceramics at AD 1050/1100–1450 (see figure 10.4). Açutuba II also had a large plaza, a rectangular space running perpendicular to the riverbank and covering 450 m × 100 m (1,476 ft × 328 ft). The settlements are also associated with terra preta soils and suggest the existence of intensive agriculture at this time in the Central Amazon.

There is also evidence of conflict. During the first millennium AD, some artificial mounds were surrounded by palisades. At Açutuba, a gully that served as a natural moat was supplemented by a defensive ditch and wall that ran for 150 m (492 ft).[39] Large post molds from palisade walls and deep ditches point to a concern with defense; Moraes and Neves write that defensive constructions began between AD 850 and 1250 and were associated with the Guarita expansion.[40] These scholars draw a parallel between these earlier settlements and later Amazonian chiefdoms described by early European chroniclers, in which regional chiefdoms formed alliances to battle common enemies.[41]

The archaeological data point to communities of 1,000 or more inhabitants, permanently settled in specific locations, and part of linked, complex alliances.

However, there is no evidence for prehispanic states in Central Amazonia, and even anthropological models of chiefdoms probably fail to capture, as Eduardo Neves and colleagues stated, "the rich political dynamics of these social formations."[42]

Polychrome Ceramic Complexes in Amazonia

A number of archaeological complexes along the Lower Amazon are characterized by their spectacular painted pottery, examples of the **Polychrome Ceramic Tradition**, which contrasts with another widespread suite of ceramic styles known as the **Incised-Punctated Tradition** (figure 10.11).[43] In general, Incised-Punctated Tradition ceramics are older, with stylistic similarities to even earlier pottery found at sites such as **San Jacinto I** and **Puerto Hormiga** in Colombia and **Valdivia** in coastal Ecuador (see chapter 6).[44] In the Middle Orinoco, pottery in the Incised-Punctated Tradition has the added trait of being tempered with the spicules of freshwater sponges (*cauixi*). *Cauixi*-tempered pottery appeared in the Middle Orinoco after AD 400 and in the Guyanas by AD 600; it was still in use when Europeans arrived. Incised-Punctated ceramics are found within a 300-km (180-mile) radius from the confluence of the Tapajos and Amazon Rivers, near the modern Brazilian city of Santarem. One hypothesis is that these late types of Incised-Punctated ceramics were spread by people who spoke Carib languages, expanding from the northern Guyana plateau and occupying the Santarem region.

After AD 800, polychrome pottery was widely used in Amazonia, with nearly identical pottery styles found from the mouth of the Amazon River to the Central Amazon and as far west as the Rio Napo in Ecuador (figure 10.12). The earliest polychrome pottery is found on the Upper Madeira River, a major tributary that flows from the Bolivian lowlands to join the Rio Amazonas downstream from Manaus. In the **Mojo de Llanos region** of the Bolivian lowlands, **John Walker** has identified similarities between the local **San Juan Polychrome** and the Guarita polychromes of the Central Amazon, with the San Juan Polychrome dating to AD 490–540.[45] Intriguingly, the San Juan Polychromes were associated with raised field agriculture (although not with *all* raised fields in the Mojo de Llanos region). After AD 500, polychrome pottery appeared in the Lower Amazon on Marajó Island and was in the Central Amazon around AD 900. By AD 800, a stylistically related polychrome was present in sites along the Rio Caquetá in the Amazonian region of southeastern Colombia, where it continued in use until the 1600s.[46]

In their path-breaking research along the Rio Napo in the Ecuadorian Amazon, **Clifford Evans** and **Betty Meggers** were among the first archaeologists to recognize the widespread distribution of polychrome pottery; they published two radiocarbon dates that suggest the polychromes were in use by AD 1150–1325.[47] Intriguingly, similar polychromes were not found by **Geoffroy de Saulieu** and **Carlos Duche Hidalgo** on the Pastaza River, a smaller tributary of the Amazon that is also in the Ecuadorian Amazon.[48] Thus, polychrome ceramics were widespread but not universal. Assuming that these ceramics spread by way of the river systems that are the corridors of transport in native Amazonia, Polychrome Tradition Ceramics spread over more than 3,500 km (2,100 miles).[49]

Figure 10.11 Modern Amazonian polychrome pottery, Ecuador

The similarities in the intricate motifs are striking. **Claide de Paula Moraes** and Eduardo Góes Neves write, "There existed common codes impressed in the forms and decorations of the ceramics that were shared by, and probably significant to, people living from the middle Madeira [River drainage] to the Rio Napo region in Ecuador."[50] Several possible explanations may account for this distribution. The spread of polychrome ceramics may mark the expansion of an ethnolinguistic group in late prehistory, although this is doubtful given the ethnic diversity of Amazonia by AD 1400.[51] It is also possible that craft specialists in different regions were in contact and the polychrome styles spread through exchange, diffusion, and imitation. It may be that as more intensive forms of agriculture were practiced, human populations increased and moved into new regions, transporting polychrome ceramics and the knowledge of their manufacture into new zones.

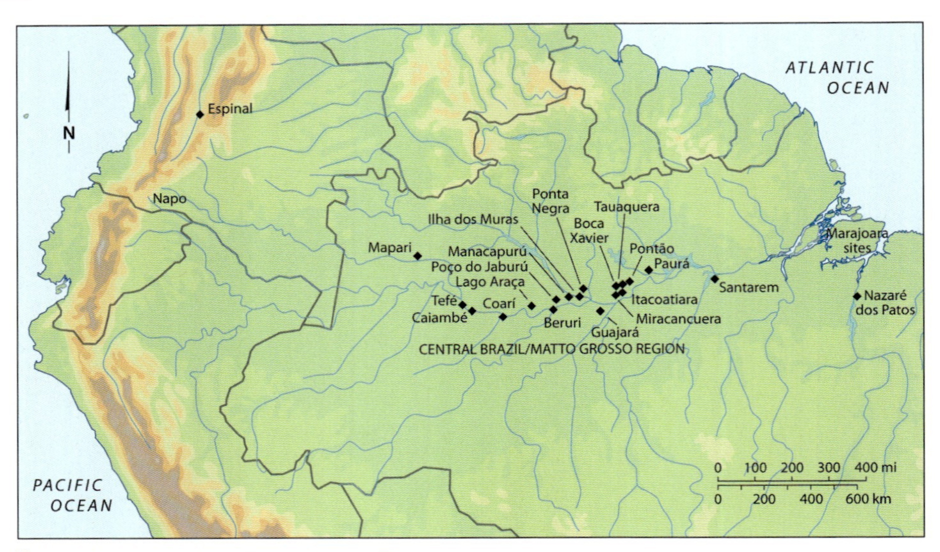

Figure 10.12 Distribution of Polychrome Tradition ceramics in Amazonia

Whatever the mechanism of their spread, the broad distribution of these intriguing ceramics is well-documented.

Polychrome decorations appear on a wide array of ceramic forms, including one of the most intriguing classes of vessels: funerary urns. These urns were used for secondary burials, in which the defleshed bones of the dead were placed inside them. As Cristina Barreto has discussed, the use of burial urns in Amazonia occurred for more than 1,200 years and was expressed in varied urn forms.[52] For example, funerary urns consisted of well-made pots shaped like cooking vessels during the Paredão phase in the Central Amazon. In contrast, the overlapping and later Guarita-phase urns included tall urns with ceramic lids, some densely decorated with fine-line motifs, others with modeled human faces, limbs, and genitalia. In other cases, the urn was essentially a ceramic sculpture of a seated human. In the Marcará region of the Lower Amazon, anthropomorphic urns 25–85 cm (approximately 10–33 inches) tall depicted individuals sitting on stools or four-legged animals.[53] The cone-shaped, removable lids were shaped as heads; eyes, eyebrows, noses, and mouths were shown. The main portion of the urn formed the body, with arms bent inward and the hands resting on the knees. The legs were thick tubes. The spinal column was indicated, as were nipples, genitalia, and navels. The urns were placed in caves, seated on the floors of caves rather than buried. The urns' flat feet plopped firmly on the cave floor (figure 10.13).

These urns from Marcará, **Vera Guapindaia** has noted, represent "just one among a series of different cultural traditions that flourished in the lower Amazon from the beginning of the second millennium AD onwards. Most of these cultural traditions are very poorly known . . . Some of them are in every sense unknown . . . and hint at what is yet to be discovered."[54]

Figure 10.13 Marcará anthropomorphic funerary urns seated in cave site, Brazil

Summary: The Amazons in Late Prehistory

These different lines of archaeological evidence—settlements, terra preta soils, defensive and other earthworks, and pottery—all suggest that Amazonia was densely occupied by AD 1000–1400. It was not an empty tropical forest incapable of supporting dense and permanent human communities.[55] The ceramics reflect extraordinary levels of craft and convey intriguing—and incompletely understood—ideas about the cosmos. The widely shared cultural traits point to long-distance exchange and trade among Amazonian peoples. The distributions of languages and mitochondrial DNA hint at complex prehistories of migration, diffusion, and interactions. Every archaeological field season results in new data, discoveries that complicate as often as clarify our vision of ancient Amazonia. Given that the region is as large as Europe and was periodically home for humans over thousands of years, many more secrets from the past undoubtedly lie hidden in Amazonia.

Colombian Chiefdoms

"Northern South America," the archaeologist **Robert Drennan** has written, "presents one of the world's richest opportunities for studying the dynamics of chiefdoms . . . The ethnohistoric documentation for the chiefdoms of northern South America provides vivid and useful snapshots of a considerable number of different chiefdoms as they existed in the sixteenth century, but only archaeology has the requisite time depth for investigating the long-term dynamics of chiefdoms . . . Northern South America gave unusually free reign to chiefdom development for several millennia, providing us with the opportunity and challenge of studying a large number of long trajectories of chiefdom development."[56]

One of the places where this occurred was in Colombia.

In a continent marked by diversity, few regions are as diverse as Colombia (figure 10.14). With coasts on the Pacific Ocean and the Caribbean, vast Amazonian tracts, a llanos region that it shares with Venezuela, high-elevation valleys and paramo, and lowland tropics, Colombia is a collision of environmental zones. The northern Andes fracture into three cordillera chains separated by major river valleys. The largest valley is drained by the enormous Rio Magdalena,which flows north nearly 950 miles from the Andes to the Caribbean; its drainage basin covers nearly one-fourth of Colombia's territory. Navigable for much of its lower extent, the Rio Magdalena is a natural corridor connecting the Caribbean Sea and the northern Andes of southern Colombia and Ecuador. This massive drainage system is a rich environment with fertile farmlands, abundant rainfall, and various minerals—most notably, gold. Not surprisingly, prehispanic societies took advantage of this river and its resources, including the **Muisca**, **Tierradentro**, **San Agustin/Alto Magdalena**, and **Tairona** chiefdoms of Colombia. In general, these chiefdoms exhibited two-tier settlement systems, composed of multiple primary centers with associated second-level communities. Based on current evidence, these primary centers shared cultural styles but retained political independence; for example, there was no single "capital" of the Muisca, Tierradentro, San Agustin/Alto Magdalena, or Tairona chiefdoms. Further, these individual chiefdoms were relatively small, sometimes less than 100 km (60 miles) across, forming a complex political mosaic in Colombia.

Muisca Chiefdom

The Muisca chiefdom emerged from earlier widely dispersed agricultural communities that, after circa 400 BC, were located on the sides of the eastern cordillera south to the Sabana de Bogota. Between circa 400 BC and AD 200, different types of economic specialization appeared, particularly in pottery production and salt extraction and trade.[57] In this early period, known as the **Herrera phase**, population density was low and there was no evidence for political centralization, with settlements consisting of either small villages or isolated homesteads. This changed in approximately AD 800–1200, during the **Early Muisca phase**, which was characterized by population growth (actually doubling in some regions) and increases in the size of communities (although the largest site covered only 3 ha [7.4 acres] and 90% of all sites were less than 1 ha [2.47 acres]). New pottery forms—such as open bowls used for serving chicha—imply an increase in feasting, alliance-building festivities correlated with increased warfare, and the need to create coalitions. Warfare is also suggested by new settlements in which communities sought refuge on islands in lakes that lacked arable land.[58]

After AD 1200 and until the arrival of Spaniards circa AD 1600, the **Late Muisca phase** was marked by substantial population compared with the Early Muisca phase (estimated at between 170% and 300% growth). A few very large

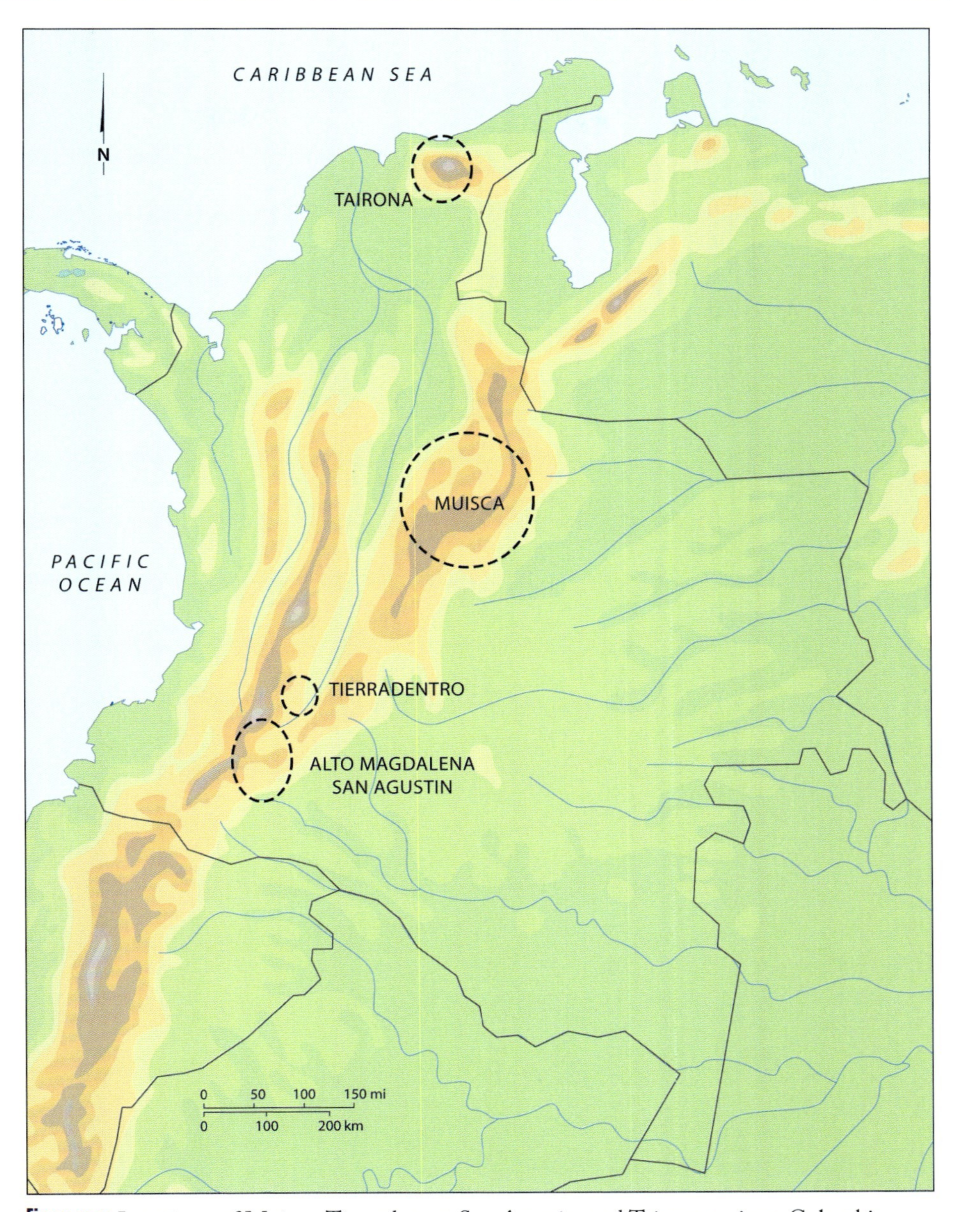

Figure 10.14 Locations of Muisca, Tierradentro, San Agustin, and Tairona regions, Colombia

settlements emerged as the seats of chiefdoms. Thus, the Late Muisca site of **Suta** was 7 ha (17.3 acres), while the vast majority of sites within its territory were less than a ha (2.47 acres). Similarly, the seat of the neighboring **Fúquene chiefdom** sprawled over 22 ha (54.3 acres), while 95 percent of its surrounding settlements were less than a hectare in size. This evidence for political centralization was accompanied by increasing evidence of long-distance trade (salt, gold, ceramics) and more feasting at larger sites (figure 10.15).

Figure 10.15 Muisca goldwork

This developmental trajectory inferred from regional settlement data has been confirmed and refined by excavations by **Ana Maria Boada Rivas** at **El Venado**, a site covering 14 ha (34.6 acres), with a stratified deposit with Late Herrera (AD 800–1000), Early Muisca (AD 1000–1300), and Late Muisca (AD 1300–1600) levels.[59] El Venado may have been founded by migrants from another community about 20 km (12 miles) away. The community of El Venado was organized as a set of wards containing multiple household groups. Wards may have begun as an individual residential group that expanded over time. While individual households were economically self-sufficient, there is evidence that different households emphasized specific types of production—one household had more large pots for boiling saltwater, another more ollas for feasts. In turn, some wards were wealthier than others and varied in the range of economic activities. Some wards had more finely decorated pottery or consumed higher-quality cuts of deer meat. Interestingly, evidence for ascribed status comes from Late Herrera burials, where select infants were buried with more grave goods than the majority of adults, suggesting they had been born into a high-status lineage. Other lines of status differences include variations in dental health: elites had better teeth than non-elites. Although ascribed status seems to have existed from the founding of El Venado, over the centuries one ward became prominent, with higher proportions of festive chicha jars, more spindles and spindle whorls suggesting textile production, and rare and highly prized imported goldwork and greenstone beads.

These different lines of evidence suggest that by the Late Muisca phase, as **Hope Henderson** and **Nicholas Osler** observe, "political authority was more centralized and organizationally complex with the formation of two-tiered regional settlement hierarchies."[60] Ethnohistoric documents suggest that chiefs maintained their power through alliances with numerous small political groups. These groups were formed from a nested set of social groups based on political and kin ties; the fundamental concept was *gue*, a Muisca term that simultaneously described a chiefly dwelling, the settlement where a chief resided, and the people affiliated with a chief. Muisca chiefdoms may have been an example of "house societies" in which residence, political affiliations, and power were conceptualized as united by a chief's "house."[61]

Although these terms and concepts are known from ethnohistoric documents, archaeological testing at the site of Suta indicates that there were variations in earlier periods. For example, the Early Muisca deposits seem to have features that might indicate a chief's dwelling, although other dwellings at Suta were found across the entire site and not clustered around the chief's house. In contrast, the Late Muisca deposits at Suta suggest that multiple gue were spread across the site. Only one of the Late Muisca gue also had Early Muisca materials, a pattern suggesting some continuity in residence and political authority. Finally, Suta apparently never had monumental architecture (e.g., mounds) or public art that proclaimed a chief's power. At most, Suta had a few unoccupied spaces—possibly plazas where leaders held feasts—and a single low platform mound that served the entire community rather than honoring a paramount chief. The survey and excavation data suggest that the elite members of Muisca society acquired and maintained their power and authority through diverse strategies, and the Muisca chiefdoms retained significant power until the Spaniards arrived.

Tierradentro

The **Tierradentro** chiefdom was located on the Paez River, a major tributary of the Upper Magdalena River.[62] The region is marked by high levels of climatic and ecological diversity. It is a mountainous region, rising from 800 m (2,624 ft) to more than 2,500 m (8,200 ft), with the highest point the 5,500-m (18,040-ft) snowcapped Nevado de Huila. The landscape is sliced by deep drainages, as rivers originating on the paramo flow into the Paez River and on to the Magdalena. Annual rainfall varies from 135 cm to 200 cm (52.7–98.4 in). Although this region has fewer archaeological adjacent zones (such as San Agustin and the Alto Magdalena to the south), it is well-known for having stone sculptures and underground crypts similar to those from the Alto Magdalena.

Initial settlements were small, dispersed homesteads established circa 1000–600 BC, slightly before the Herrera phase (discussed earlier). Population density was low, no more than one person per km^2 (2.5 persons per square mile). Homesteads were established near fertile, easily worked soils.[63] The succeeding phase, 600–300 BC, was marked by changes in ceramics but only minor changes in population density (an estimated 0.7 to 1.5 people per km^2 [2–4 people per square mile]) and settlement patterns. Between 300 BC and AD 100, there were significant changes. Many more settlements were founded and population density increased significantly, to more than 4 to 8 people per km^2 (10–20 people per square mile). New areas were farmed. Some sites emerged as distinctive centers. Based on survey data and limited excavations, some sites had numerous mounds, accompanied by stone statues, petroglyphs on boulders and cliffs, and large numbers of serving bowls and drinking vessels—suggesting that these communities were different from the average homestead. At other sites, pottery cauldrons used to boil saltwater into salt suggest specialization and exchange.

Major changes occurred in the Tierradentro region between AD 100 and 1300. Population increased significantly (more than doubling, to 23 people per km^2 [nearly 60 people per square mile]), large concentrations of settlements developed, and average site size increased. Maize agriculture was widespread. Gold-working, although rare, appeared for the first time.[64] The first stone statues were sculpted. Although the sites have been extensively looted, stone sculptures were concentrated in specific sites and regions but not necessarily those with the largest populations. Originally painted, these stone sculptures combine human and animal elements. Interestingly, at least one example of statuary depicts a "house" with columns of human faces.[65] Even the largest constructions did not require enormous workforces, although more than was commonly invested in the average dwelling.

Although the dating is less than secure, this may also be the period when underground crypts (*hypogea*) were created in Tierradentro (figure 10.16). Some of these chambers were quite elaborate, with staircases carved into bedrock leading underground to large chambers with vaulted walls. The chamber walls were carved

Figure 10.16 Tierradentro underground funeral cavern (hypogea)

with petroglyphs and painted with geometric designs and animal motifs. The dead were placed in niches, crypts, or burial urns. The tombs were communal, associated with specific communities or residential groups rather than dedicated to a single elite leader. The emergence of clear social distinctions is evident, but elite authority was apparently based as much on religion and ideology as on economic control.

San Agustin/Alto Magdalena

Moving south from Tierradentro, the most famous prehispanic Colombian chiefdom is the San Agustin culture located in the Alto Magdalena (figure 10.17). At an average elevation of 1,800 m (5,904 ft) above sea level, the main valley is a well-watered, broad drainage with fertile farmlands flanked by hilly ridges. The region sits at the nexus of natural routes and rivers connecting it to Amazonia, the Pacific Coast, the Orinoco drainage system, and north to the Caribbean by way of the Rio Magdalena. San Agustin, the archaeologist **Gerardo Reichel-Dolmatoff** wrote, "lies at the crossroads of several major natural migration and trade routes. Over these mountain passes peoples and ideas have moved back and forth for centuries, their coming and going helping to shape local cultural developments, be it by trade, migration, or invasion."[66]

Figure 10.17 (*overleaf*) Statuary and mound, San Agustin, Colombia

A 1797 account of San Agustin describes a small Colonial settlement "occupied by a few Indian families and in its vicinity are found the vestiges of an artistic and hardworking nation that no longer exists. Statues, columns, shrines, altars, animals and an enormous image of the Sun—all of stone and in prodigious numbers—indicate to us the character and strength [of] the great pueblo that once inhabited the headwaters of the Magdalena."[67]

Dating to AD 1 to 900, many of the 500 stone statues at San Agustin were upright blocks of tuff and andesite that measure between 1 m and 2 m (3.3–6.6 ft) in height. Like the Tierradentro statues, the San Agustin sculptures were originally painted (red, yellow, black, and/or white), but the pigments have eroded from any exposed statues. The statues vary, although they often follow a common design: a standing male anthropomorphic figure with a disproportionately large head, mouth filled with grimacing teeth or feline fangs, elliptical or half-moon eyes, flattened snout, and hands in front of the chest sometimes holding staffs or clubs, musical instruments, or dangling heads. Other images include more zoomorphic subjects: upright birds, squatting frogs, and lizards. As Drennan has observed, although the Alto Magdalena sculptures have been subject to various scholarly interpretations that "disagree on many points, the combination of human and animal figures and characteristics leave[s] little doubt that the subject matter is supernatural."[68] Further suggestions posit that the stones depict shamans undergoing transformations into spirit beings or secular leaders whose authority was validated by supernatural properties. Most of these sculptures are found within a 10-km (6-mile) radius of San Agustin.

San Agustin also exhibits a dense concentration of large burial chambers. They consisted of stone-slab chambers that, despite the poor preservation and general absence of preserved skeletons, apparently held a single elite individual. The burial chambers were covered by large earthen mounds, some as tall as 4 m (13 ft) and 40 m (130 ft) in diameter. These burial mounds sometimes contained stone sculptures, and the tombs were arrayed around an open area that possibly held ceremonies. At this period there is little evidence for major distinctions between households in wealth or status and scant indication for economic specialization. Houses were small elliptical structures covering less than 20 m^2 (215 ft^2). Households were spread across the countryside as isolated homesteads or small clusters of dwellings in the middle of farmlands. At the regional level, some areas had denser concentrations of houses separated from other zones by borders of unoccupied lands. Thus, the "centers" of chiefdoms in the Alto Magdalena were neither urban nor commercial centers, despite having a special ritual role indicated by the burial mounds. These features have led Drennan to conclude "that the social glue that held together the [social] hierarchies of the Alto Magdalena derived more from the realm of beliefs than the economy. This is consistent with the suggestion that monumental tombs and associated rituals were the principal currency for competition for succession at the death of a leader, in a society where leadership was incompletely institutionalized."[69]

This pattern changed after AD 900, when burial mounds were no longer built. Ironically, at this same time, population actually grew in the Alto Magdalena, a demographic increase also seen in the Tierradentro. Some settlements also grew in size and density. Additional farmlands were cleared, in some cases involving major projects that may have required coordinating large work parties. If these efforts indicate the existence of central authority—in other words, chiefs—then the basis of their authority was fundamentally different from those interred in the mounds of San Agustin.

Tairona Chiefdoms of the Sierra Nevada de Santa Marta

In northern Colombia, near the modern city of Santa Marta, the northernmost chain of the Andes extends close to the Caribbean Sea, a segment of the cordillera called the Sierra Nevada de Santa Marta. The highest peaks rise to 5,700 m (18,696 ft) only 40 km (24 miles) inland, and the Sierra Nevada de Santa Marta is a complex landscape of narrow ridges and steep river valleys. From the hot tropical coast, the environment quickly shifts to rainforest and, further up, to paramo (environments that support very different resources). Today, this area is home to the **Kaaga** (or Kogi), the descendants of the prehistoric Tairona.[70]

Archaeological investigations by **Augusto Oyuela-Caycedo** and others indicate that people began moving from the coast into the sierra sometime between AD 600 and AD 900.[71] The human presence is marked by changes in pollen cores as humans moved into the region, cutting down stands of natural forest and planting maize, agave, and avocados. The lower portions of the Sierra Nevada, 360–500 m (1,181–1,650 ft) above sea level, were first occupied in the sixth and seventh centuries and the higher zones several centuries later. One of the largest of these late settlements is the site **Ciudad Perdida** (figure 10.18)

Ciudad Perdida—also known as Teyuna and Buritaca 200—is a large set of terraces, circular dwellings, tombs, and plazas built on a web of ridges above the Rio Buritaca. The site covers about 30 ha (74 acres) and was discovered by looters in the mid-1970s. With more than 100 residential terraces, population may have been 2,000–8,000 people. Stone foundations of circular houses indicate relatively modest dwellings about 5–7 m (16.4–23 ft) in diameter, probably similar to the pole and thatch houses people still occupy in the region (see figure 10.6).

The site shows clear evidence of planning, with a major ceremonial axis of long elliptical plazas and large structures aligned on a major ridge and additional structures on lateral ridges, including stone-lined canals and retaining walls, which—remarkably—still stand (figure 10.19).

Archaeological excavations at Ciudad Perdida indicate two major phases. Between AD 1000 and 1300, ceramic styles suggest a close connection with the coast, while after AD 1300 connections shifted to the highland regions to the west. Ciudad Perdida and surrounding communities were occupied until the late 1500s, when genocidal raids by Spaniards annihilated over 90 percent of the native population, driving the survivors into even more remote refuges.[72]

Ciudad Perdida was the largest settlement in a vast network of communities connected by paved stone stairways and roads. This physical network also marked regional networks based on exchange, craft specialization, and presumably religion.

Figure 10.18 Ciudad Perdida, Colombia—plazas and terraces

What is absent on the Alto Buritaca is a neat hierarchy of settlements, the pattern often used to identify the centralized organizations of chiefdoms.[73]

Oyuela-Caycedo has written, "Decentralized political complexes coordinated the whole commercial enterprise for one or more of the mountainous valleys, as indicated for Ciudad Perdida."[74] Potatoes, sweet potatoes, and coca from higher-elevation fields were traded to the coastal zones for salt, fish, cotton, tobacco, man-

Figure 10.19 Principal ceremonial axis, Ciudad Perdida, Colombia

ioc, and shells burned to make cal for coca chewing (see chapter 5). Presumably, trading parties made these journeys depending on the season. Other evidence for trade includes gold objects from tombs placed in the floor of an abandoned dwelling at Ciudad Perdida. The jewelry included beads and earrings thought to date to AD 1385.[75] Northern Colombia is famous for its sophisticated prehispanic goldwork, but no metallurgical workshops have been found at Ciudad Perdida itself.

Religion may have been another basis for integrating communities. Based on ethnohistoric and ethnographic sources, the Kágaba have a priestly class known as the *mámas*.[76] Although it is not certain that similar religious authorities existed in pre-contact societies, modern Kágaba settlements broadly correspond to the earlier archaeological pattern. Oyuela-Caycedo writes, "The Kágaba are a society of temples, priests, sacred hamlets, sacred spaces, complex cosmology, and seasonal festivities of rituals, where religious recitation and esoteric knowledge are the bases of power. Such knowledge is the immaterial property of the *houses*."[77] By "houses," Oyuela-Caycedo means not just a dwelling but a social entity composed of people, buildings, property, and rights. In the Kágaba case, this social entity may have had an explicitly "theocratic" emphasis, as the priestly class, the mámas, had particular authority. According to Oyuela-Caycedo:

> The Kágaba priest (Máma) is the transmitter of the knowledge of the house; he is the living figure in charge of a temple that belongs to a house. At the same time, the temple building is the landmark of the house. The Máma is the only one who can learn the "Mother Laws" (the ultimate sacred propositions) . . .
>
> Knowledge is the main factor in the prestige and rank given to an individual in relation to his position in a house and between houses. Sacred knowledge is acquired mainly by avuncular descent, but common individuals can achieve status through the payment of goods, work or cash to the Máma in exchange for knowledge. If an individual wishes to be competent in knowledge, he must study throughout his life with different priests of houses that have alliances with his own. Each main house temple, with the figure of the Máma at the head, specialize [*sic*] in some aspect of knowledge . . . but no one master or temple controls the total domain of knowledge. This differential access and domain of knowledge account for the competitions and rankings between the priests and temples, as well as between the houses to which they belong.[78]

To repeat, it is not known whether late prehistoric societies in the Sierra Nevada de Santa Marta were organized along the same principles of houses, temples, and priestly savants. However, the Kágaba model would account for the archaeological patterns as currently understood. Further, these ethnographic data present an intriguing perspective on the subtle organization of chiefly societies in prehispanic Colombia.

Ecuadorian Coastal Chiefdoms: Manta

The Manteño was a cluster of chiefdoms that developed along the Ecuadorian coast, emerging from a coalition of coastal settlements involved in long-distance maritime trade.[79] The extent and richness of this trade are depicted in a 1528 account when the captain of Pizarro's ship, Bartolome de Ruiz, encountered a Manteño ocean-going raft (figure 10.20). The balsa sailing raft was manned by twenty sailors and carried a cargo of

Figure 10.20 Sailing rafts—balsas near Guayaquil, Ecuador, 1748

> many objects of silver and gold for personal ornament to barter with those with whom they were going to trade, among which were crowns and diadems and belts and bracelets and armor for the legs and breastplates and tweezers and bells and strings and masses of beads and mirrors adorned with the said silver and cups and other drinking vessels; they [also] brought many textiles of wool and cloth and shirts and tunics and capes and many other garments[,] all of them finely woven with rich detail, and of colors such as red and crimson and blue and yellow and with all the other colors and varied craftwork and figures of birds and animals and fish and trees.[80]

This luxurious cargo had been exchanged "for some sea shells from which they make colored beads like coral and white such that they came with nearly the whole vessel laden with these," undoubtedly beads and other objects made from *Spondylus* shells (figure 10.21).[81] The trade appears to have been controlled by three separate Manteño chiefdoms (*señorios*), whose major centers were located at **Jocay** (now covered by the modern city of Manta), **Picoaza** (the site **Cerro Jaboncillo**), and **Salangome** (the site of **Agua Blanca**). Each trading center was surrounded by smaller coastal towns, villages, and inland homesteads—confederations based on shared cultural practices, commerce, and political coalitions.

The richness of trade was a principal factor in the development of the Manteño chiefdoms, although not the only one (figure 10.22). The abundant marine resources have made the Ecuadorian coast attractive for human settlement since

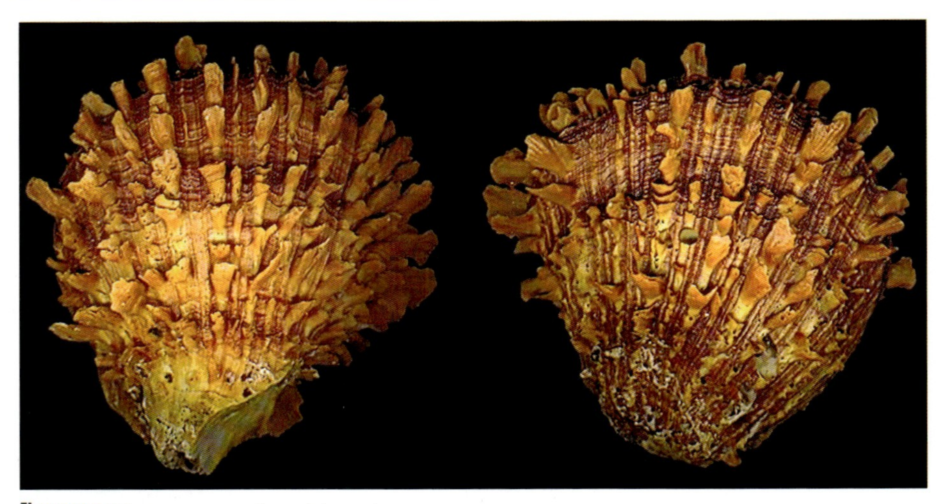

Figure 10.21 Thorny oyster, *Spondylus princeps*

the beginning of the Holocene (see chapter 4), and many Manteño settlements are underlain by or near earlier sites dating from the Formative and after. It is also possible that Manteño developed during a period of higher rainfall, as Manteño communities depended on rain-fed agriculture in areas where irrigation is essential today. The population became more concentrated during the Manteño period, especially when compared with earlier prehistoric periods, although this could be a consequence rather than a cause of socio-political changes.[82] Taking advantage of these environmental factors and demographic changes, Manteño elites employed social and religious factors to bolster their authority, creating several large constellations of settlements along 100 km (60 miles) of the Ecuadorian coast.

Manteño sites are identified by a distinctive pottery, a burnished grayish-black ceramic that is often mold-made. This results in some spectacular, nearly sculptural, anthropomorphic vessels with detailed facial features. In addition to these elaborate vessels, Manteño households also used an array of domestic vessels, such as ceramic griddles, grater plates with ring bases, cooking pots (*ollas*) with out-flaring rims, bell-rim jars, and pedestal-base plates. Some of the more elaborate vessels may have been used by elites as key objects in commensal politics, as the archaeologist **Karen Stothert** has written, in which "leaders of various social units achieved distinct goals. The corporate group adopted an aesthetic, a culture of eating, through which its members learned, practiced, and evaluated their social relationships. Formal commensal activities, repeated on numerous occasions, expressed relationships between generations, between kinfolk of different ages, and served to define the role of each person linked to the community."[83] Another type of ceramic vessel was large (more than 50 cm [19.5 in] tall) pots used as burial urns and, in turn, offerings of food and drink to the dead, a ceremony that rearticulated the connections and continuities of each Manteño community.

In addition to these ceramic assemblages, some sites have large concentrations of spindle whorls and dense deposits of worked marine shells, which sug-

Figure 10.22 Cerro Jaboncillo, Ecuador—models depicting Manteño elites

gest some of the craft activities carried out by Manteño people.[84] For example, excavations at the Manteño port of trade **Sercapez** (the modern **Puerto Lopez**) indicated a large town of more than 100 structures dating from the mid-thirteenth century. In addition to subsistence pursuits of fishing and farming and the ceremonial activities that punctuated the ancient transitions of life and death, excavations uncovered extensive evidence of "the local cottage industry production of decorative ornaments fashioned from mother-of-pearl, Spondylus, bone, copper, and, occasionally, gold. Such objects were an important component of the supply side of the long-distance exchange system known to have been engaged in by merchants along this part of the coast down through antiquity."[85] This trade was evidenced by the common presence of copper ax monies in Manteño sites, mediums of exchange that indicate the broad extent of these trade networks.[86]

Although the major Manteño center of Jotoy has been largely destroyed by the modern city of Manta, extensive portions of the sites of Picoaza at Cerro Jaboncillo and Salangome at Agua Blanca are well-preserved and are being investigated by archaeologists. Cerro Jaboncillo is a large mountain rising 600 m (1,968 ft) above the small town of Picoaza and overlooking the valley of the Rio Porto Viejo to the northwest. The area is covered with tropical dry forest of kapok (*ceiba*) and algarobbo trees, and archaeological excavations since 2006 on the northern flank of the mountain have uncovered extensive terraces over 30,000 ha (741,000 acres). Linked by steep trails and roadways, these terraces were principally for buildings rather than for agricultural fields, although some relatively small terraces

Figure 10.23 Agua Blanca, Ecuador—foundations of large Manteño structure

may have held special plants rather than being used for large-scale farming. The buildings were the rough fieldstone foundations of rectangular buildings, 8–10 m (33 ft) wide and up to 20 m (66 ft) long. Fragments of daub indicate the walls were wattle and daub. The roofs were probably thatched and steeply sloped. The dwellings were not divided into rooms, and it is easy to imagine shaded interiors of swinging hammocks and hearth smoke. Other, smaller buildings were perched on the terraces, their functions currently unknown.

The site Agua Blanca provides additional insights into the organization of Manteño society (figure 10.23). Thought to be the location of Salangome, Agua Blanca sprawls over 4 km^2 (1.5 square miles) on the foothills and ridges drained by the Rio Buenavista. Unlike Cerro Jaboncillo, where steep topography was a constraint, the relatively flat terrain at Agua Blanca provided the opportunity for some colossal constructions without extensive terracing. The traces of foundations indicate that most buildings were similar to those at Cerro Jaboncillo, but the largest buildings were significantly larger, more than 50 m (164 ft) long. The large buildings were often surrounded by ancillary buildings that formed more complex architectural patterns. One of the largest buildings at Agua Blanca seems to be oriented to the December solstice on the eastern horizon, while other buildings may form a radial pattern spatially and conceptually linking different buildings at Agua Blanca and, in turn, articulating Agua Blanca with the distant Cerro Jaboncillo.

Figure 10.24 Manteño silla de poder

The most distinctive artifacts from Cerro Jaboncillo—and one of the most distinctive objects in Manteño culture—are the large carved stone "horseshoe"-shaped seats, or *sillas de poder* (figure 10.24). These elaborate objects—the word *chair* seems too prosaic, the word *throne* too assuming—are 60–70 cm (24–27.5 in) tall. Carved from a single block of stone, a silla de poder consists of two up-curving arms that form a U perched on a lower central pedestal. In the first decades of the twentieth century, the American **Marshall Saville** collected multiple stone seats from Cerro Jaboncillo and other Manteño sites for the George Heye American Indian Museum in New York City. The British archaeologist **Colin McEwan** has carefully analyzed Saville's field notes and publications to reestablish the locations of these "seats of power," an analysis resulting in important insights into Manteño culture. Only the major Manteño settlements—such as Cerro Jaboncillo and Agua Blanca—had these carved stone seats, yet there were multiple sillas de poder within each site, often more than a dozen. Within a site, the sillas de poder tend to be clustered into groups often associated with larger buildings. Neither an imperial throne nor a folding chair, the Manteño seats of power hint at the existence of multiple elite lineages or households in Manteño society.

The Manteño chiefdoms exemplified complex social and economic factors on which wealth and prestige were based. The significance of long-distance trade is undeniable. The wealth of prestige goods linked the Ecuadorian coast to the Central Andes and, possibly, to the late prehispanic societies of the isthmus and lower Mesoamerica. That wealth, in turn, enhanced the prestige of Manteño elites but did not result in the unitary consolidation of power or the creation of a single kingdom. Wealth was not enough: prestige was displayed and perhaps validated by rituals and ceremonies that justified the power of elites.

Coastal Peruvian Kingdom: Chincha

Approximately 1,350 km (810 miles) south of Ecuador, another coastal chiefdom developed on the South Coast of Peru, the **"kingdom" of Chincha**. Chincha is the largest valley on the southern coast of Peru, a fertile valley bordered by desert and fronted by the sea. Chincha figured prominently in early Spanish accounts, which emphasize the kingdom's richness and political stature. For example, a historical document claimed that in Chincha, 30 local lords ruled over 30,000 tribute payers (essentially household heads who were taxed), of whom 12,000 were farmers, 10,000 were fishermen, and 6,000 were merchants. With this wealth based on farming, fishing, and commerce, Chincha was a rich society. The historical account unequivocally claims that "with their buying and selling they would go from Chincha to Cuzco and all of Collao [i.e., southern Peru] and others would go to Quito and Puerto Viejo [on the coast of Ecuador], from where they would bring gold beads and rich emeralds that they would sell to the lords of Ica."[87] This has led some scholars to argue that Chincha merchants traveled to the coast of Ecuador, where they traded with Manteño communities for valued items, notably objects and beads made from *Spondylus* shells.[88] Although *Spondylus* was highly prized and sacred, various archaeological excavations at late prehistoric sites in the Chincha Valley have "not yielded significant amounts of Spondylus in numerous excavated-use contexts."[89]

Regardless of whether Chincha engaged in *Spondylus* trade, there is clear evidence of the region's power, economic foundations, and religious significance. During late prehistory, extensive irrigation systems made the Chincha Valley one of the richest agricultural regions in coastal Peru. Other sources of wealth were the nearby islands, where thick layers of bird dung had accumulated over the centuries. These rich "guano islands" were an important source of natural fertilizer and may have been traded to neighboring valleys. Excavations at the fishing villages suggest a pattern of economic specialization in which farmers and fishermen were linked by exchange.[90]

The major center of the Chincha polity consists of two contiguous sites, **La Centinela** and **Tambo de Mora**, which appear to have been the locations of different sets of functions. For example, Tambo de Mora seems to have had two major zones. In one area, large quantities of food were prepared, stored, and consumed; another area had extensive evidence of metallurgy, as indicated by hearths, stone tools, ceramic molds, and a few gold, silver, and copper artifacts.[91]

In contrast, La Centinela appears to have been a political and religious center. Covering about 30 ha (74 acres), the settlement had plazas, streets, an alleyway, and a dense concentration of compounds that surrounded the site's major pyramid. The major architecture includes ten walled compounds built from *tapia*, consisting of "adobe (prepared mud) that was either poured directly into forms, much like modern concrete, or was mixed and packed in place between the forms, like modern tamped earth. Each pouring creates a fairly large rectangular block."[92] Mud, gravel, and plant fibers are mixed together into a thick slurry, slathered into layers, allowed to dry, and then additional layers of tapia are added, resulting in tall, thick walls.[93] Tapia walls delineate the Chincha-period architecture at La Centinela. These compounds surround a large 40 m (131-foot)-tall truncated pyramid that was originally painted white and glimmered in the desert sunlight. At the peak was a special chamber, its walls decorated with complex modeled reliefs deeply incised into the walls. Hidden from public view, this chamber also held a sacred boulder, "the shrine of Chinchaycamac, a branch oracle of the great Pachamamac" (discussed later).[94]

The influence of this oracle and Chincha's prestige in the neighboring Pisco and Ica Valleys seem to have been established in the early AD 1400s. The scholars **Dorothy Menzel** and **John Rowe** wrote that around AD 1400 "there was evidently a sudden increase of Chincha power . . . Pisco was brought at least partially under Chincha rule, but Ica maintained some degree of independence."[95] It seems as if Chincha enjoyed religious prestige and economic power, which underwrote centralized political power. Finally, the wealth and political order achieved at Chincha were acknowledged and sustained when the south coast—and much of Andean South America—was conquered by the expansionistic empire from the highlands: the Incas.

Ychsma/Pachacamac—an Enduring Pilgrimage Center on the Coast of Peru

A final case study from late prehistoric South America is the famous oracular shrine of **Pachacamac**, located on the Central Coast of Peru near the city of Lima (figure 10.25). Pachacamac is one of the largest and best-known sites in Peru, having been studied by archaeologists since Max Uhle (see chapter 1).[96] It has also been extensively looted. Further information about Pachacamac comes from ethnohistoric sources describing the pilgrimage center, including eyewitness accounts from Spanish conquistadors who oversaw the pillage of the temples' treasures for the failed ransom of the captured Inca emperor Atahualpa (see chapter 11). Despite this wealth of information, this section examines a rather narrow but fundamental issue: the role of Pachacamac as a pilgrimage center during late prehistory.

Covering more than 600 ha (1,482 acres), the site was a pilgrimage center from circa AD 500–600, continuing in significance over the next millennium as at least four major temple complexes were constructed at the site. When the Inca conquered the coast in the fifteenth century AD, they renamed the site from **Ychsma** and constructed a **Temple of the Sun**. Surrounded by other adobe brick compounds with mounds that have ramps and other areas—now destroyed by

Figure 10.25 Aerial view of Pachacamac, Peru

looters—that once held elite burials, the temples were the major constructions at the site.

Recent excavations directed by **Peter Eeckhout** and colleagues have dated the overall building sequence of the temples at Pachacamac, research that in turn draws on investigations by many other archaeologists.[97] The **Templo Viejo** was built between AD 500 and 600 and was used throughout late prehistory, although not continuously. The Templo Viejo was originally a shrine to a local deity associated with the Lima culture, but it was covered by a thick layer of mud that capped its painted floors during El Niño flooding circa AD 600.[98] With the arrival of the Wari, the Templo Viejo was partially refurbished and used as a burial and ritual structure before being destroyed again by El Niño flooding, after which it was not extensively used until the Incas reclaimed it.

Meanwhile, the Wari constructed the **Painted Temple**, a stepped and terraced construction about 120 m × 54 m (393 ft × 177 ft), remarkable for its various color schemes and religious artifacts. The exterior walls were originally painted red by the Wari, then covered with multiple colored paints and ultimately decorated with a variety of motifs depicting fish, agricultural crops, and anthropomorphic figures. The Templo Pintado continued in use after the Wari abandoned the coast, if anything becoming even greater in prestige and influence. The temple complex was rebuilt, with new walls controlling access to this sacred site and its deity, Ychsma. When the Inca conquered the coast and built their own **Temple of the Sun**, the Templo Pintado continued in use, as the Inca were interested in coopting—rather than destroying—the deity's prestige.

The influence of Ychsma and of the priests who interpreted his will to mortal humans was felt over a vast area of coastal Peru. The shrine attracted pilgrims from a broad area, integrating people from different regions who spoke different languages—at least temporarily—into a larger realm of belief. As the ethnographer **David Sallnow** has written of modern Andean processions, pilgrimage creates a "totemic topography" in which people journeying from distant zones move together across the landscape to a common destination, bound together by acts of faith.[99] This was certainly true of pre-Inca Pachacamac. For example, an elegantly carved wooden staff more than 2 m (6.6 ft) long was found in 1938 in the building rubble of the Painted Temple. The middle shaft displays intricately carved motifs, some recognizable Wari motifs, and others from the Central Coast of Peru. These syncretic motifs indicate that different people integrated into some larger social entity but one that was tied together not by force, commerce, or manipulation by elites but rather by a shared religious belief.

Of Ychsma's enduring importance and later integration into the Inca pantheon, Eeckhout writes, "Most authors believe that this longevity can be attributed to the divinity's burgeoning popularity from the Wari period onward. Ethnohistorical documents underscore his numerous attributes: creator of the world, oracle, healer and master of earthquakes, and, while he was associated with death, he was also connected with a fertility-related god . . . These qualities gained him widespread and long-lasting worship: the Inca conquest of the end of the fifteenth century had no destructive affect [*sic*] whatever on either the temple or the cult."[100]

Conclusion

Between AD 1000 and 1500, numerous societies developed across South America, many more than have been discussed in this chapter.[101] These societies varied enormously in population, territories, social structure, political order, and religion—a range of human experiences previously unseen in South America prehistory. Although this period witnessed the thriving existence of small-scale hunting-and-gathering societies and the emergence of states and empires—including the development and expansion of the Inca Empire (see chapter 11)—numerous regional polities developed across South America. Archaeologists sometime refer to such societies as "middle-range societies," a usefully ambiguous phrase designed to capture "the enormous organizational variation found in prestate sedentary societies."[102]

The cases discussed in this chapter exhibit some of this enormous variation. For example, various societies were integrated based on economic specialization and exchange, such as Chincha and the Manteño. Other societies developed larger coalitions in response to warfare and violence, including in the Central Amazon, the Upper Xingu, and the Muisca. Some societies developed more complex political structures and centralized power as population increased (such as during the Late Ipavu phase of the Upper Xingu), while others saw a decrease in monumental constructions and chiefly authority as population grew (such as in the later phases of the Alto Magdalena). In many cases, religious practice expressed the connections between peoples, although the results varied, from the regional theocratic networks of the Sierra Nevada de Santa Marta to the inter-regional and enduring ritual topographies anchored by the shrine at Ychsma/Pachacamac. Finally, other forms of interaction are suggested by widespread art styles—such as the broad distribution of Polychrome Ceramics across the breadth of Amazonia—although their associated meanings may have been differently understood.

In short, the complexity and diversity indicated by the archaeological record throughout South American prehistory also characterized it in the last centuries before Europeans landed on the continent, a stunning array of human creativity during the twilight of prehistory.

Notes

1. D. Yesner, M. Figuerero Torres, R. Guichon, and L. Borrero, "Stable Isotope Analysis of Human Bone and Ethnohistoric Subsistence Patterns in Tierra del Fuego," *Journal of Anthropological Archaeology* 22 (2003): 287.

2. L. Orquera and E. Piana, "Sea Nomads of the Beagle Channel in Southernmost South America: Over Six Thousand Years of Coastal Adaptation and Stability," *Journal of Island and Coastal Archaeology* 4, no. 1 (2009): 72–73.

3. Ibid., 73.

4. H. Pinto Lima, "Historia das Caretas: A Tradiçãao Borde Incisa na Amâzonia Central" (PhD diss., Muesu de Arqueologia e Etnologia, Universidade de Sao Paulo Brazil, 2008), 49, my translation.

5. E. Góes Neves, "El Formativo que nunca terminó: La larga historia de estabilidad en las ocupaciones humanas de la Amazonía central," *Boletín de Arqueología* 11 (2012): 122, my translation.

6. An eminently readable account of the European inroads and destruction in Amazonia is John Hemming, *Red Gold: The Conquest of the Brazilian Indians* (London: Macmillan, 1978).

7. R. Dixon and A. Aikhenvald, "Introduction," in *The Amazon Languages*, ed. R. Dixon and A. Aikhenvald (Cambridge: Cambridge University Press, 1999), 1.

8. There is an enormous technical literature on native South American languages. For overviews and detailed analyses, see R. Dixon and A. Aikhenvald, eds., *The Amazon Languages* (Cambridge: Cambridge University Press, 1999); L. Campbell and V. Grondona, eds., *The Indigenous Languages of South America: A Comprehensive Guide* (Boston: Walter de Gruyter, 2012).

9. F. Noelli, "The Tupi Expansion," in *Handbook of South American Archaeology*, ed. H. Silverman and W. Isbell (New York: Springer, 2008), 659, original emphasis.

10. F. Noelli, "The Tupi: Explaining the Origin and Expansions in Terms of Archaeology and Historical Linguistics," *Antiquity* 72 (1998): 649.

11. R. Walker, S. Wichmann, T. Mailund, and C. Atkisson, "Cultural Phylogenetics of the Tupi Language Family in Lowland South America," *PLOS One* 10, no. 1371 (April 10, 2012).

12. V. Ramallo, R. Bisso-Machado, C. Bravi, M. Coble, F. Salzano, T. Hünemeier, and M. Bortolin, "Demographic Expansions in South America: Enlightening a Complex Scenario with Genetic and Linguistic Data," *American Journal of Physical Anthropology* 150 (2013): 453.

13. R. Scheel-Ybert, K. Macario, A. Buarque, R. Anjos, and M. Beauclair, "A New Age to an Old Site: The Earliest Tupiguarani Settlement in Rio de Janeiro State?" *Anais da Academia Brasileira de Ciências* 80, no. 4 (2008): 763–70.

14. M. Beauclair, R. Scheel-Ybert, G. Bianchini, and A. Buarque, "Fire and Ritual: Bark Hearths in South-American Tupiguarani Mortuary Rites," *Journal of Archaeological Science* 36 (2009): 1412.

15. Noelli, "The Tupi," 660.

16. M. Heckenberger, "The Arawak Diaspora: Perspectives from South America," in *The Oxford Handbook of Caribbean Archaeology*, ed. W. Keegan, C. Hoffman, and R. Rodriguez Ramos (Oxford: Oxford University Press, 2013), 111, 115.

17. M. Heckenberger, "Rethinking the Arawakan Diaspora: Hierarchy, Regionality, and the Amazonian Formative," in *Comparative Arawakan Histories: Rethinking Language Family and Culture Area in Amazonia*, ed. J. Hill and F. Santos-Granero (Urbana: University of Illinois Press, 2002), 103.

18. J. Granberry, "Indigenous Languages of the Caribbean," in *The Oxford Handbook of Caribbean Archaeology*, ed. W. Keegan, C. Hoffman, and R. Rodriguez Ramos (Oxford: Oxford University Press, 2013), 64.

19. A. Zucchi, "A New Model of the Northern Arawakan Expansion," in *Comparative Arawakan Histories: Rethinking Language Family and Culture Area in Amazonia*, ed. J. Hill and F. Santos-Granero (Urbana: University of Illinois Press, 2002), 199–222.

20. M. Heckenberger, *The Ecology of Power: Culture, Place, and Personhood in the Southern Amazon, AD 1000–2000* (New York: Routledge, 2005), 51. Also see M. Heckenberger, J. Petersen, and E. Goés Neves, "Village Size and Permanence in Amazonia: Two Archaeological Examples from Brazil," *Latin American Antiquity* (1999): 353–76.

21. Heckenberger, "Rethinking the Arawakan Diaspora," 109.

22. Ibid., 111.

23. Ibid., 113.

24. Ibid., 112.

25. S. Tambiah, "The Galactic Polity: The Structure of Traditional Kingdoms in Southeast Asia," *Annals of the New York Academy of Sciences* 293 (1977): 69–97.

26. Heckenberger, *Ecology of Power*, 78.

27. Ibid., 167.

28. C. Barreto, "A construção social do espaço: de volta à aldeias circulares do Brasil Central" *Habitus Goiâna* 9, no. 1 (2011): 67, my translation. See also I. Wüst and C. Barreto, "The Ring Villages of Central Brazil: A Challenge for Amazonian Archaeology," *Latin American Antiquity* 10, no. 1 (1999): 3–23.

29. Wüst and Barreto, "Ring Villages of Central Brazil," 6.

30. I. Wüst, "Continuities and Discontinuities: Archaeology and Ethnoarchaeology in the Heart of the Eastern Bororo Territory, Mato Grosso, Brazil," *Antiquity* 72 (1998): 665.

31. Ibid. There is a very large archaeological and ethnographic literature regarding dualistic social structures; for an introduction see J. Moore, "The Archaeology of Dual Organization in Andean South America: A Theoretical Review and Case Study," *Latin American Antiquity* 6, no. 2 (1995): 165–81.

32. Barreto, "A construção social do espaço," 66, my translation.

33. For example, Barreto, in ibid., 64, states that there were 65 archaeological projects in the states of Mato Grosso, Goias, and Tocantins between 2005 and 2009 alone, although many of these projects were small investigations occasioned by hydroelectric projects, power transmission lines, and other development projects. For a detailed overview of archaeological projects and absolute dates obtained before 2000, see J. Eremites de Oliveira and S. Aparecida Viana, "O centro-oeste antes de cabral," *Revista USP* 44 (1999–2000): 142–89.

34. E. Neves, "Ecology, Ceramic Chronology and Distribution, Long-Term History, and Political Change in the Amazonian Floodplain," in *Handbook of South American Archaeology*, ed. H. Silverman and W. Isbell (New York: Springer, 2008), 363.

35. E. Neves, "El Formativo que nunca terminó: la larga historia de estabilidad en las ocupaciones humanas de la Amazonía central," *Boletín de Arqueología PUCP* 11 (2007): 117–42.

36. See Pinto Lima, *Historia das Caretas*.

37. This is based on C. Moraes and E. Neves, "O ano 1000: asdensamento populacional, interação e conflito no Amazônia Central," *Amazônica* 4, no. 1 (2012): 122–48.

38. Heckenberger et al., "Village Size and Permanence in Amazonia."

39. E. Góes Neves, "Warfare in Precolonial Central Amazonia: When Carneiro Meets Clastres," in *Warfare in Cultural Context: Practice, Agency, and the Archaeology of Violence*, ed. A. Nielsen and W. Walker (Tucson: University of Arizona Press, 2009), 139–64.

40. Moraes and Neves, "O ano 1000," 140.

41. Ibid., 137.

42. E. Neves, M. Heckenberger, and C. Moraes, "Super Villages, Small Towns, Garden Cities: Understanding the Large Settlements of Late Precolonial Amazonia" (paper presented, Society for American Archaeology, Honolulu, April 4, 2013).

43. H. Pinto Lima, "História das caretas: A tradição borda incisa na Amazônia central" (PhD diss., Museu de Arqueologia e Etnologia, Universidade de São Paulo, 2008).

44. Neves, "Ecology, Ceramic Chronology and Distribution," 370.

45. J. Walker, "Ceramic Assemblages and Landscape in the Mid-1st Millennium Llanos de Mojos, Beni, Bolivia," *Journal of Field Archaeology* 36, no. 2 (2011): 119–31.

46. L. Herrera, W. Bray, and C. McEwan, "Datos sobre la arqueología de Aracuara, Comisaria del Amazonas, Colombia," *Revista Colombiana de Antropología* 23 (1980–81): 183–251.

47. C. Evans and B. Meggers, *Archaeological Investigations on the Rio Napo, Eastern Ecuador* (Washington, DC: Smithsonian Institution Press, 1968). Two published dates associated with polychrome were given as 782 + 53 BP and 771 + 51 BP, which the authors interpreted as having midpoints of AD 1168 and AD 1179, respectively (81). Calibrations of these dates using the Southern Hemisphere curve for CALIB 6.0 result in cal AD 1154–1297 (two sigmas) and cal AD 1160–1297 (two sigmas).

48. G. de Saulieu and C. Duche Hidalgo, "La tradición Muitzentza y el periodo de integración (700–1500 d.C.) en la alta cuenca del río Pastaza, Amazonía ecuatoriana," *Bulletin de l'Institut Français d'Études Andines* 41, no. 1 (2012): 35–55.

49. Moraes and Neves, "O ano 1000," 137.

50. Ibid., 136, my translation.

51. Neves, "Ecology, Ceramic Chronology and Distribution," 368.

52. C. Barreto, "Meios místicos de reprodução social: arte e estilo nâ cerâmica funerária da Amazônia antiga" (PhD thesis, Universidade de Sâo Paulo, 2008), 72–99. For discussions of earlier urns from the Central Amazon, see B. Silva da Costa, A. Pye-Daniel, J. Gomes, and E. Goés Neves, "Urnas funerárias no Lago Amanã, Médio Solimões, Amazonas: contextos, gestos e processos de conservação," *Amazônica* 4, no. 1 (2012): 60–91.

53. The following is based on V. Guapindaia, "Encountering the Ancestors," in *Unknown Amazon: Culture and Nature in Ancient Brazil*, ed. C. McEwan, C. Barreto, and E. Neves (London: British Museum, 2001), 156–73.

54. Ibid, p. 169.

55. This does not mean that *all* Amazonia had dense human populations; see, for example, C. McMichael, D. Piperno, M. Bush, M. Silman, A. Zimmerman, M. Raczka, and L. Lobato, "Sparse Pre-Columbian Human Habitation in Western Amazonia," *Science* 336 (June 15, 2012): 1429–31. Although regions of Amazonia had higher prehistoric populations than once thought, it does not follow that all regions were equally populated.

56. R. Drennan, "Chiefdoms in Northern South America," *Journal of World Prehistory* 9, no. 3 (1995): 301–2.

57. There are few absolute dates for this early phase, known as the Herrera phase; estimates of its chronology range from 800 BC–AD 800 (C. Langebaek, *Arqueología*

regional en el territorio muisca: estudio de los vallesde Fúquene y Susa, Memoirs in Latin American Archaeology 9 [Pittsburgh: University of Pittsburgh, 1995], 60).

58. Ibid., 95, 97; A. Boada Rivas, *The Evolution of Social Hierarchy in a Muisca Chiefdom of the Northern Andes of Colombia* (Pittsburgh: University of Pittsburgh Memoirs in Latin American Archaeology 17, 2007), 9.

59. Boada Rivas, *Evolution of Social Hierarchy*. In addition to these levels, El Venado was occupied even earlier by hunters and gatherers. For a discussion of burial data and ancestor worship at the nearby site of Marín, see A. Boada Rivas, "Mortuary Tradition and Leadership: A Muisca Case from the Valle de Samacá, Colombia," in *Recent Advances in the Archaeology of the Northern Andes: In Memory of Gerardo Reichel-Dolmatoff*, ed. A. Oyuelo-Caycedo and J. Raymond, Monograph 39 (Los Angeles: Institute of Archaeology, University of California, 1998), 54–70. Note: the absolute dates for El Venado given by Boada Rivas are slightly different than those used by other Muisca scholars.

60. H. Henderson and N. Ostler, "Muisca Settlement Organization and Chiefly Authority at Suta, Valle de Leyva, Colombia: A Critical Appraisal of Native Concepts of House for Studies of Complex Societies," *Journal of Anthropological Archaeology* 24 (2005): 149.

61. For an archaeological discussion of house societies, see R. Joyce and S. Gillespie, eds., *Beyond Kinship: Social and Material Reproduction in House Society* (Philadelphia: University of Pennsylvania Press, 2000).

62. C. Langebaek and A. Dever, "Arqueología regional en Tierradentro, Cauca, Colombia," *Revista Colombiana de Antropología* 45, no. 2 (2009): 323–67. Brief synopses, images, and maps are available at http://www.tierradentro.info/ (accessed October 29, 2012).

63. Langebaek and Dever, "Arqueología regional en Tierradentro," 331.

64. C. Langebaek, "The Political Economy of Pre-Colombian Goldwork: Four Examples from Northern South America," in *Gold and Power in Ancient Costa Rica, Panama, and Colombia*, ed. J. Quilter and J. Hoopes (Washington, DC: Dumbarton Oaks, 2003), 248–49.

65. Langebaeck and Dever, "Arqueología regional en Tierradentro," 338.

66. G. Reichel-Dolmatoff, *San Agustín: A Culture of Colombia* (New York: Praeger, 1972), 15.

67. J. de Caldas, "Obras de Caldas," *Bibliotecas de Historia Nacional* 4 (1912): 260, quoted in K. Preuss, *Arte Monumental Prehistórico: Excavaciones en el Alto Magdalena y San Agustín*, trans. H. Walde-Waldegg (Bogota: Escuelas salesianas de tipografia y fotograbado, 1931), 18–19, my translation.

68. R. Drennan, "Chiefdoms of Southwestern Colombia," in *Handbook of South American Archaeology*, ed. H. Silverman and W. Isbell (New York: Springer, 2008), 383–84.

69. Ibid., 385.

70. Early archaeological work by J. Alden Mason defined key elements of the Tairona archaeological complex, although Mason's research did not extend into the Sierra Nevada de Santa Marta. See J. Mason, *Archaeology of Santa Marta, the Tairona Culture, Part I*, Anthropological Series 20, no. 1 (Chicago: Field Museum of Natural History, 1931).

71. A. Oyuela-Caycedo, "Late Pre-Hispanic Chiefdoms of Northern Colombia and the Formation of Anthropogenic Landscapes," in *Handbook of South American Archaeology*, ed. H. Silverman and W. Isbell (New York: Springer, 2008), 423.

72. Ibid.

73. A. Oyuela-Caycedo, "Centralización e integración en la Sierra Nevada de Santa Marta," *Boletin del Museo de Oro* 38–39 (1995): 113–132.

74. Oyuela-Caycedo, "Late Pre-Hispanic Chiefdoms of Northern Colombia," 423.

75. A. Groot de Mahecha, "Buritaca–200: una fecha de radiocarbono asociada con objetos de orfebrería Tairona," *Boletin del Museo de Oro* 3 (1980); at http://www.banrepcultural.org/blaavirtual/publicacionesbanrep/bolmuseo/1980/bol8/moma3.htm (accessed March 27, 2014). This date is cited by Groot without information about the original BP result or calibration curve employed.

76. A rich body of ethnographic data is available for the Kágaba; for an introduction, see G. Reichel-Dolmatoff, *The Sacred Mountain of Colombia's Kogi Indians* (Leiden: E. J. Brill, 1990).

77. Oyuela-Caycedo, "Centralización e integración en la Sierra Nevada," 43, emphasis added.

78. A. Oyuela-Caycedo, "Ideology, Temples, and Priests: Change and Continuity in House Societies in the Sierra Nevada de Santa Marta," in *Recent Advances in the Archaeology of the Northern Andes: In Memory of Gerardo Reichel-Dolmatoff*, ed. A. Oyuela-Caycedo and J. Raymond, Monograph 39 (Los Angeles: Institute of Archaeology, University of California, 1998), 43.

79. This discussion relies on the excellent synopsis by C. McEwan and F. Delgado-Espinoza, "Late Prehispanic Polities of Coastal Ecuador," in *Handbook of South American Archaeology*, ed. H. Silverman and W. Isbell (New York: Springer, 2008), 505–23. For other sources on Manteño culture, see K. Stothert, "Manteno," in *Encyclopedia of Prehistory*, vol. 5: *Middle America*, ed. P. Peregrine and M. Ember (New York: Kluwer, 2001), 303–27. I also benefited enormously from visits to the sites of Cerro Jaboncillo and Agua Blanca that I made in June 2011 with the archaeologist Richard Lunniss, who generously shared his extensive knowledge and insights into Manteño archaeology and the prehistoric coast of Ecuador.

80. Samano-Xerez, quoted in McEwan and Delgado-Espinoza, "Late Prehispanic Polities of Coastal Ecuador," 515.

81. Ibid.

82. A. Martin, "The Domestic Mode of Production and the Development of Sociopolitical Complexity: Evidence from the Spondylus Industry of Coastal Ecuador" (PhD diss., University of Pittsburgh, 2009), 76–79.

83. K. Stothert, "La cerámica de etiqueta de las *tolas* de Japoto (costa de Ecuador)," *Bulletin de l'Institut Français d'Études Andines* 35, no. 3 (2006): 267, my translation.

84. For an encyclopedic and detailed overview of Manteño culture and the production of objects in Spondylus, see Benjamin Carter, "Technology, Society, and Change: Shell Artifact Production among the Manteño (AD 800–1532) of Coastal Ecuador" (PhD diss., Washington University, St. Louis, MO, 2008).

85. E. Currie, *Pre-Columbian Studies, Project Grant Report 1997–1998: The López Viejo Project* (Washington, DC: Dumbarton Oaks, 1999); at http://128.103.33.14

/research/pre_columbian/doaks_pco_project_grant_reports/Currie/currie.html (accessed March 27, 2014).

86. D. Hosler, H. Lechtman, and O. Holm, *Axe-Monies and Their Relatives*, Studies in Pre-Columbian Art and Archaeology 30 (Washington, DC: Dumbarton Oaks, 1990).

87. M. Rostoworoski de Diez Canseco, "Mercaderes del valle de Chincha en la época prehispánica: un documento y unos comentarios," *Revista Española de Antropología Americana* 5 (1970): 171, my translation.

88. For example, ibid.; J. Marcos, "Cruising to Acapulco and Back with the Thorny Oyster Set: A Model for a Lineal Exchange System," *Journal of the Steward Anthropological Society* 9, no. 1–2 (1977–78): 99–132; J. Marcos, *Los Pueblos Navegantes del Ecuador Prehispánico* (Quito: Ediciones Abya-Yala, 2005), 158.

89. C. Morris and J. Santillana, "The Inka Transformation of the Chincha Capital," in *Variations in the Expression of Inka Power*, ed. R. Burger, C. Morris, and R. Matos Mendieta (Washington, DC: Dumbarton Oaks, 2007), 136. For a detailed critique of the maritime *Spondylus* trade hypothesis, see A. M. Hocquenhem, "How Did Quechua Reach Ecuador?" in *Archaeology and Language in the Andes: A Cross-Disciplinary Exploration of Prehistory*, ed. P. Heggarty and D. Beresford-Jones, Proceedings of the British Academy 173 (Oxford: Oxford University Press, 2012): 351–59.

90. See discussion in D. Sandweiss, *The Archaeology of Chincha Fishermen: Specialization and Status in Inka Peru* (Carnegie Museum of Natural History 29, 1992), 14–17, 143–48.

91. J. Alcalde Gonzales, C. del Aguila Chavez, F. Fujita Alarcon, and E. Ratamozo Rondón, "Plateros precoloniales tardíos en Tambo de Mora, valle de Chincha (siglos XIV-XVI)," *Anales del Museo de América* 10 (2002): 43–57.

92. D. Wallace, "The Inca Compound at La Centinela, Chincha," *Andean Past* 5 (1998): 11.

93. J. I. Santillana, "La Centinela: un asentamiento inka-chincha: Rasgos arquitectónicos estatales y locales," *Arqueología y Sociedad* 10 (1984): 13–32.

94. C. Morris and A. Von Hagen, *The Incas: Lords of the Four Quarters* (London: Thames and Hudson, 2011), 146.

95. D. Menzel and J. Rowe, "The Role of Chincha in Late Prehispanic Peru," *Ñawpa Pacha* 4 (1966): 67.

96. M. Uhle, *Pachacamac: Report of the William Pepper, M.D., LL.D. Peruvian Expedition of 1896* (Philadelphia: Department of Archaeology, University of Pennsylvania, 1903).

97. P. Eeckhout, "Change and Permanency on the Coast of Ancient Peru: The Religious Site of Pachacamac," *World Archaeology* 45, no. 1 (2013): 137–160; P. Eeckhout and L. S. Owens, "Human Sacrifice at Pachacamac," *Latin American Antiquity* 19, no. 4 (2008): 375–98; A. Michczincky, P. Eeckhout, A. Pazdur, and J. Pawlyta, "Radiocarbon Dating of the Temple of the Monkey: The Next Step toward Comprehensive Absolute Chronology of Pachacamac, Peru," *Radiocarbon* 49, no. 2 (2007): 565–78; T. Patterson, "Pachacamac: An Andean Oracle under Inca Rule," in *Recent Studies in Andean Prehistory and Protohistory: Papers from the Second Annual Northeast Conference on Andean Archaeology and Ethnohistory*, ed. P. D. Kvietok and D. H. Sandweis (Ithaca:

Latin American Studies Program, Cornell University, 1983), 159–76; I. Shimada, R. Segura Llanos, M. Rostworoski de Diez Canseco, and H. Watanabe, "Una nueva evaluación de la Plaza de los Peregrinos de Pacahamac: aportes de la primera campaña del Proyecto Arqueológico Pachacamac," *Bulletin de Institut Français des Etudes Andines 2004* 33, no. 3 (2004): 507–38.

98. R. Franco and Ponciano Paredes, "El Templo Viejo de Pachacamac: nuevos aportes al estudio del Horizante Medio," *Boletin de Arqueologia PUCP* 4 (2000): 607–30. For additional information regarding paleoenvironment at Pachacamac, see B. Winsborough, I. Shimada, L. A. Newsom, J. G. Jones, and R. A. Segura, "Paleoenvironmental Catastrophes on the Peruvian Coast Revealed in Lagoon Sediment Cores from Pachacamac," *Journal of Archaeological Science* 39, no. 3 (2011): 602–14.

99. D. Sallnow, *Pilgrims of the Andes: Regional Cults in Cusco* (Washington, DC: Smithsonian Institution, 1987).

100. Eeckhout, "Change and Permanency," 147.

101. For introductions to and overviews of the extensive archaeological literature for this period of Andean prehistory, see C. Conlee, J. Dulanto, C. Mackey, and C. Stanish, "Late Prehispanic Sociopolitical Complexity," in *Andean Archaeology*, ed. H. Silverman (New York: Blackwell, 2004), 209–36; R. Alan Covey, "Multiregional Perspectives on the Archaeology of the Andes during the Late Intermediate Period (c. A.D. 1000–1400)," *Journal of Archaeological Research* 16, no. 3 (2008): 287–338. For analyses of different Andean regions, see, *inter alia,* C. Conlee, "Local Elites and the Reformation of Late Intermediate Period Sociopolitical and Economic Organization in Nasca, Peru," *Latin American Antiquity* 14, no. 1 (2003): 47–65; B. Bauer and L. Kellett, "Cultural Transformations of the Chanka Homeland (Andahuaylas, Peru) during the Late Intermediate Period (AD 1000–1400)," *Latin American Antiquity* 21, no. 1 (2010), 87–111; several chapters in the indispensable H. Silverman and W. Isbell, eds., *Handbook of South American Archaeology* (New York: Springer, 2008), including articles by T. Bray, "Late Pre-Hispanic Chiefdoms of Highland Ecuador" 527–43; J. Duhlanto, "Between Horizons: Diverse Configurations of Society and Power in the Late Pre-Hispanic Central Andes," 761–82, in addition to those by A. Oyuela-Caycedo and C. McEwan and Delgado-Espinoza cited above.

102. S. Upham, "A Theoretical Consideration of Middle Range Societies," in *Chiefdoms in the Americas*, ed. R. Drennan and C. Uribe (Lanham, MD: University Press of America, 1987), 348.

Figure 11.1 Machu Picchu, Peru

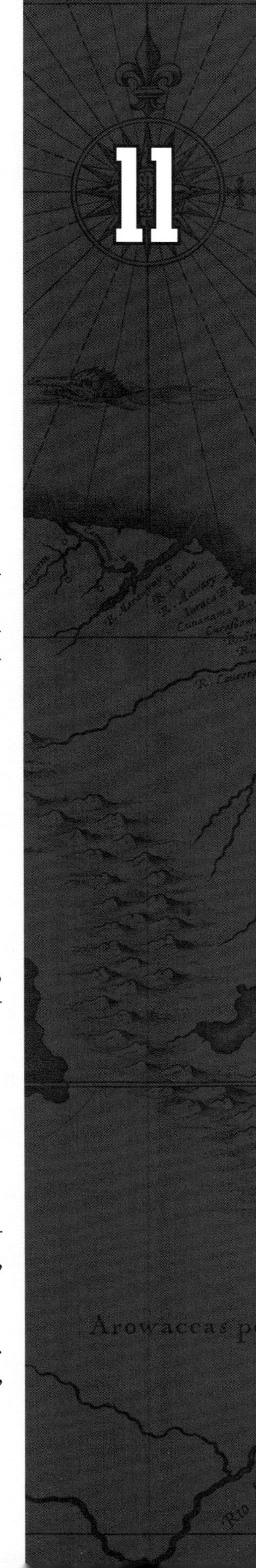

11 Empire of the Four Quarters

10.5876_9781607323334.c011

> One of the things most to be envied these rulers is how well they knew to conquer such vast lands and, with their forethought, bring them to the flourishing state in which the Spaniards found them when they discovered this new kingdom . . .
>
> In this respect they were far ahead of us, for with the order they introduced the people throve and multiplied, and arid regions were made fertile and bountiful, in the ways and goodly manner that will be told.
>
> *Pedro Cieza de Leon, circa 1550, on the Incas*

Between approximately AD 1400 and 1535, a regional chiefdom in the southern Peruvian Andes expanded throughout western South America and in the process created the largest state in the pre-Columbian Americas. Its members called their empire *Tawantinsuyu,* which means the "four (*tawa*) portions (*suyu*) that have become one (*ntin*)." They are also known as the Incas.[1]

Since previous chapters have discussed multiple prehistoric societies and their cultural achievements, one might wonder "why devote an entire chapter to the Incas?" There are several reasons. First, the Incas represent a social and political achievement several orders of magnitude larger than any other pre-contact South American society. At its peak, the Inca Empire extended from what is today northern Ecuador all the way south to central Chile, a distance of more than 4,000 km (2,400 miles) (figure 11.2). (To put that in perspective, the Aztecs, another great New World empire, controlled an area of about 1,500 km (900 miles) between central Mexico and Central America.) The Inca Empire extended over portions of the modern nations of Ecuador, Peru, Bolivia, Argentina, and Chile. With a population conservatively estimated at between 6 million and 14 million people, the Inca created one of the largest states in the Ancient World.[2]

The Inca achievement was outstanding for other reasons. Not only was it a large and populous empire, but its expansion was remarkably swift, with most of its territory gained in a century or less. Further, the Incas left their distinctive material imprint on these territories, building fortresses, roads, way stations (*tambos*), and shrines throughout their empire (figure 11.3). The Inca Empire built in stone and adobe, architectural traces of its presence. The subjects of Tawantinsuyu built bridges spanning deep river canyons in the Andes, sculpted hillsides into terraced fields, and channeled water from mountain springs to farm fields of potatoes, coca, and maize.

These material achievements were simultaneously political achievements. The Inca state mobilized an enormous workforce, organizing households, communities, and regions into a nested hierarchy of administration. This

Figure 11.2 Estimated extent of the Inca Empire and sites discussed in chapter 11

Figure 11.3 Inca stonework and fountain, Tambo Machay, Peru

labor force was directed to a vast array of projects—road building, palace construction, weaving, or warfare—with a very high percentage of success. Although not every military campaign was victorious, the Incas were remarkably effective on the battlefield and even more efficient in organizing the peoples and territories they conquered. Their strategies of empire were by turns subtle and brutal. The Incas exhibited an impressive capacity for political flexibility but always backed by the threat and exercise of force. No other prehistoric South American culture had such large-scale imperial successes as the Incas.

Another reason for devoting a chapter to the Inca Empire is the wealth of information available. There are numerous written accounts about the Incas, many authored by conquistadors or Catholic priests intent on subjugating or eliminating the Inca Empire and traditional cultural practices.[3] There are similar accounts from other regions of South America, but an enormous literature discusses the Inca Empire because its realm was such a target for Spanish conquest and Catholic conversion. Beyond this, we have an enormous amount of archaeological knowledge for the Incas, more than for any other South American culture. As discussed in chapter 1, the Incas' former realm has attracted travelers, antiquarians, and archaeologists from the eighteenth to the twentieth centuries. Even today, numerous archaeological investigations are focused on the Incas, whether in the Valley of Cusco, the northern sierra of Ecuador, or at oases in the Atacama Desert—and in most of the intervening regions.

This wealth of information allows for nuanced and detailed inquiries about the Incas. We can contrast written sources against archaeological evidence. Comparative studies can be conducted in different portions of the empire, such as in the Cuzco heartland and frontier zones. Different types of sites can be investigated:

palaces, tombs, workshops, and villages. The wealth of information permits subtle and varied explorations of the Incas and the worlds they created.

This wealth of information also shows that the Incas were not the inevitable cultural achievement in South American prehistory. The first Paleoindians did not cross into South America with the plan that one day their descendants would create the Inca Empire. Further, there is no "genetic" connection between the Incas and earlier states and empires. The parallels that exist between the Incas and earlier states and empires are broad, based on similar political systems encountering comparable environmental and social realities. All of these factors make the Incas a uniquely intriguing society in prehistoric South America.

Antecedents

Their own story was that they emerged from the womb of the Earth to create an empire. The legend states:

> At a place to the south of Cusco called Pariqtambo, there is a mountain called Tampu T'oqo (window house) in which there are three windows, or caves. At the beginning of time, a group of four brothers and their four sisters—the ancestors of the Inkas—emerged from the central window. The principal figure of this group was Manqo Qhapac, the man who was destined to become the founder-king of the empire. One of the first acts of the eight ancestors was to organize the people who were living around Tampu T'oqo into ten groups, called ayllus. The full entourage of ancestral siblings and ayllus set off from Tampu T'oqo to the north in search of fertile land on which to build their imperial capital, Cusco. At one of these stops, Manqo Qhapaq and one of his sisters, Mama Oqlluy, conceived a child whom they named Sinchi Ruq'a. After a period of wanderings filled with marvelous events, the entourage arrived at a hill overlooking the valley of Cuzco. Recognizing by miraculous signs that this was their long-sought-after home, the Inkas descended from the mountain and took possession of the valley.[4]

Not surprisingly, the archaeological data suggest more prosaic and complex origins. Archaeological surveys and test excavations directed by **Brian Bauer** in the region surrounding **Pariqtambo** (the Pauro Valley) and in the **Cusco Valley** and by **R. Alan Covey** in the adjacent **Sacred Valley** along the Vilcanota and Urubamba Rivers have resulted in a detailed vista on Inca origins (figure 11.4). These three adjacent research projects covered a combined total of 1,300 km^2 (502 square miles), with data for more than 2,000 archaeological sites from different time periods.[5]

The scenario of Inca origins began with the impact of the **Wari Empire's** expansion into the region during the mid-sixth century AD and the establishment of **Pikillacta** and other Wari colonies 25–45 km (15–27 miles) southeast of Cusco (see chapter 9). Wari presence may have been focused on the strategic control of llama caravan routes and sources of gold and coca and did not significantly influence settlement patterns. As in earlier periods, most settlements were scattered homesteads with a few larger villages 1–5 ha (2.2–11 acres) in size. There were no large Wari settlements like Pikillacta near Cusco or those in the Sacred Valley, although Wari colonists interacted with the Cusco and Sacred Valley settlements. Local elites and Wari elites may have exchanged craft products and exotic items such as obsidian. Local elites may have organized workers for the Wari. Although Wari expansion did not reorder life in Cusco and neighboring regions, it may have influenced or indirectly enhanced the power and authority of local elites, leaders who grew more powerful in the political vacuum created by the Wari Empire's decline and the abandonment of Pikillacta around AD 1000.

At this point, local polities asserted themselves, a phase marked by the presence of pre-Inca **Killke-style** pottery.[6] Killke ceramics were decorated with bands, lines, and other geometric motifs generally made with black pigment on the burnished surfaces of the pots: bowls, plates, jars, and drinking tumblers (*keros*). A visually similar and coeval pottery, the **Colcha style**, was coarser and decorated with wavy lines and dots not seen on the Killke styles. Killke and Colcha ceramics were made at the same time and were stylistically related but used in different regions, with Killke pottery predominantly at sites near Cusco and Colcha more common in the province of Paruro, about 50 km (30 miles) to the south.

The geographic distributions of Killke and Colcha ceramics, in turn, reflect regional interactions based on ethnicity and political ties. Historical sources indicate that there were at least four ethnic groups in the area: the **Incas** in the northern Valley of Cusco, the **Chillque** to the south, with two other groups—the **Masca** and the **Tambo**—occupying territories in between. These ethnic groups south of the Valley of Cusco did not form larger political systems but were organized in kin-based moieties. Their communities were relatively small, ranging from several hundred individuals (Tambo) up to fewer than 3,000 people (Masca, Chillque). As Bauer has noted, "The development of the Inca state is largely about the creation of a heartland: how the many ethnic groups of the Cusco region were forged into a single entity and how that entity was then able to expand across much of South America."[7]

The transition from Killke to Inca was marked by continuity, growth, and expansion. Excavations within the city of Cusco suggest that the Killke-period settlement covered 50 ha (110 acres), ten times the size of most settlements in the valley.[8] Cusco was surrounded by several nearby towns, resulting in a somewhat patchy urban landscape covering several square kilometers. All Killke villages continued to be inhabited during the Inca phase, and new areas were settled. By AD 1300, once-empty lands in the northern Cusco Basin were settled, large villages had been founded, steep slopes were terraced and farmed, and stream water flowed into new irrigation systems. These projects point to an increase in population and agricultural production—and also to the developing political power of the emergent Inca state.

The archaeological data indicate that a state developed in Cusco during the end of the Killke phase, with Cusco as its primary center, secondary centers established in the Sacred Valley, and villages and hamlets sprinkled across the region (figure 11.5). There is also evidence for conflict between Cusco and its neighbors.

Figure 11.4 (*overleaf*) The Sacred Valley, Urubamba, Peru

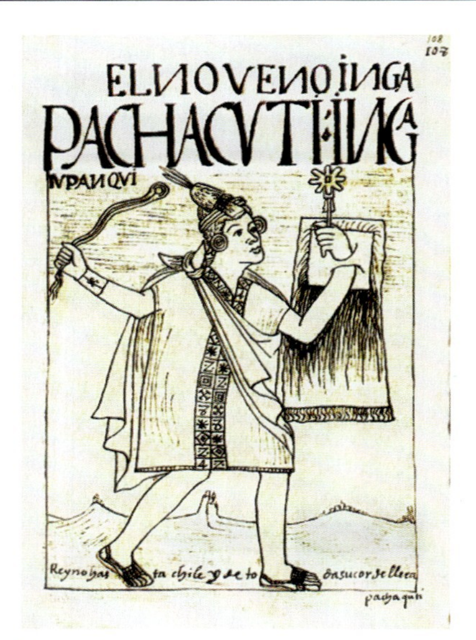

Figure 11.6 Pachacuti Inca Yupanqui, illustrated by Guaman Poma de Ayala

Some regions occupied for millennia were suddenly abandoned in the late Killke phase, becoming empty buffers between Cusco and its rivals.[9] Fortified walls protected some settlements. Other communities moved to more defensive locations on ridges. In these dangerous times, Inca Cusco was forged.

Oral histories recount that the Inca state was created by a single outstanding man in a pivotal cataclysmic moment in 1438. The Incas were attacked by the Chankas, the legend states, a rival ethnic group from Andahuaylas.[10] The Chanka attack was so fierce and overpowering that the ruler of Cusco, Viracocha Inca, and the heir apparent, Urcon, fled, leaving the city's defense in the hands of a young prince.

Outnumbered, Cusco's defenders wavered in the face of the Chanka assault, when the Inca prince shouted out that a miracle was occurring: the stones of Cusco were transformed into soldiers to defend the city. The tide of battle turned; the Incas thwarted the attack and chased the remnants of the Chanka army back to Andahuaylas. The cowardly Inca king remained in exile, the heir apparent was assassinated, and the young prince took the throne and the new name "Pachacuti" (cataclysm) and was known as **Pachacuti Inca Yupanqui** (figure 11.6).

This legend combines central elements: valiant conquests, divine endorsements, subjugation of others, construction, and veneration. Of course, political myths are seldom accurate: they are ideological justifications.

The creation of the Inca state did not occur in a single day's battle; nor was it the result of a single ruler's courage. As Bauer and Covey observe, "While Inca imperial expansion appears to have occurred quite rapidly, researchers increasingly view this as the result of antecedent and long-term regional political processes, rather than the serendipitous outcome of a single battle and the aspirations of specific individuals."[11]

More important, the political processes that resulted in the ascendancy of the Incas in the Cusco region were trial runs and templates for broader conquests. New lands were developed. Local ethnic groups were subjugated. Alliances were forged, often stabilized through inter-marriage between elites, but they could also be broken—particularly when a new leader emerged and old ties were ruptured. "The numerous rebellions, reconquests, and negotiations that took place between various groups of the region after the death of an Inca leader," Bauer and Covey write, "underscore the importance that individuals played in extending Inca control throughout the heartland."[12] In turn,

> The strategy of internal development accompanied by alliance building, intimidation, and isolation of rivals can be seen as part of the Inca imperial strategy as well. Imperial Inca expansion was based on the opportunistic manipulation of local ethnic and political relationships, and in many cases involved several

Figure 11.5 (*previous page*) View of Plaza de Armas and cathedral in Cusco; the modern plaza is located on the Haucaypata

> generations of conquest and reintegration and the establishment of more direct administration of local populations . . . Population resettlement . . . and the development of natural resources in ways that undercut local identity are also imperial strategies whose practice is seen in the Late Intermediate Period development of the early Inca state. Using the Late Intermediate Period settlement patterns and historical sources, we can now discern greater time depth to the development and practice of Inca expansion and administration.[13]

Phases of Expansion

The traditional chronology of Inca imperial expansion was established by **John Rowe** based on written sources (figure 11.7).[14] Rowe dated the initial expansion under Pachacuti at 1438, followed by consolidating the Cusco area and spreading north to the Junín region and south to the Titicaca Basin by 1463. Between 1463 and 1471, Pachacuti and his adult son and general, **Topa Inca**, expanded north, conquering the Chimú (see chapter 9). The Inca conquerors largely dismantled the Chimú state, looted its capital, Chan Chan, and established other regional centers or utterly transformed existing ones. The Inca armies rolled on into northern Peru and the highlands of Ecuador. After Pachacuti, Topa Inca continued to conquer, dominating the South Coast of Peru, Bolivia, northwest Argentina, and the northern half of Chile between 1471 and 1493. Between 1493 and 1525 the subsequent ruler, **Huayna Capac**, expanded the empire northward to the modern Ecuador-Colombia border, captured the cloud forest chiefdoms of the Chachapoyas, and responded to numerous revolts and rebellions before suddenly dying of smallpox and not naming his successor. The Inca Empire fractured into civil war, with a northern contingent led by **Atahualpa**, who had been born in Quito, vying with a southern army, led by the Cusco-born **Huascar**. Atahualpa had just emerged victorious in 1532 when he learned of the arrival of Spanish conquistadors led by Francisco Pizarro.

Some archaeological evidence suggests that this chronology may not be as accurate as it appears. As noted, research in the Cusco Basin indicates that the Inca state was consolidated and imperial expansion was under way before AD 1400, impacting neighboring ethnic groups.[15] Further, radiocarbon dates from more distant regions may suggest that the traditional chronology is incorrect. In their research in the Calchaquí region of northwest Argentina, **Terence D'Altroy** and colleagues report three radiocarbon dates associated with Inca ceramics, which they suggest may indicate an imperial expansion much earlier that the traditional chronology of circa 1470–80.[16] Thus, an earlier incursion to the south is possible but not yet proven. At the other end of Tawantinsuyu, **Dennis Ogburn** has discussed seven dates from the small Inca outpost of Chamical, located in the southern highlands of Ecuador, a region traditionally proposed to have been conquered by Topa Inca between AD 1463 and 1471. These radiocarbon dates seem to point to an earlier conquest, perhaps around AD 1450.[17]

The concern with the phases of Inca expansion reflects broader concerns. Are the historical accounts accurate depictions, or are they examples of remembered

Figure 11.7 Map showing traditional phases of imperial expansion of the Inca Empire

political propaganda glorifying the "Great Men" of the Incas? If the Incas reached northwest Argentina and Ecuador in the first half of the fifteenth century AD, what might this imply about the timing and pace of earlier developments in the Cusco heartland or elsewhere in the empire? Are these "earlier" radiocarbon dates the result of other factors, such as atmospheric variations or problems with the samples?[18] In sum, the issues of dating Inca imperial expansion require further research, but the phases of conquest may be less settled than once thought.

Cusco: City as Cosmos, City as Center

The archaeo-astronomer **Anthony Aveni** has written that Cusco was an example of the city as the "crystallized image of all the institutions that constituted the state, a lasting expression of cosmovision" (figure 11.8).[19] Located 3,400 m (11,155 ft) above sea level, the city had 20,000 residents, with several thousand more inhabitants in surrounding communities.[20] A large city by Andean standards, Cusco's impact was disproportionate to its size. Cusco was the center, the conceptual hub of Tawantinsuyu, and its name literally means "Navel of the Universe."

The four quarters of the empire—Chinchaysuyu, Antisuyu, Qollasuyu, and Kuntisuyu—converged at the large plazas, as did the four major roads that led to them. The plazas also marked the division of Cusco into upper (*hanan*) and lower (*hurin*) halves. As **Craig Morris** and **Adriana von Hagen** write, "Cusco's [urban] plan focused on a large open space, a dual plaza, rather than on a tall structure, in marked contrast to the [Catholic Church] bell towers that dominate the skyline today."[21] At this very fundamental level, Cusco's spatial order described two principles: dualism and unification.

Similar principles underlay the **ceque system**, a system of forty-one or forty-two radiating lines that spun out onto the horizon from the **Temple of the Sun**, or **Qoricancha**—"the gilded compound" (figure 11.9). **R. Thomas Zuidema** has written, "The Ceque system of Cuzco consisted of 41 *ceques*, going out from the central temple of the Sun, *Coricancha*. Together they organized 328 landmarks in the valley of Cuzco that as places of worship were considered to be *huacas* [i.e., sacred places]."[22] The ceque lines were conceptual rays that simultaneously marked the progression of time, marked the ritual cycle in which the dozen major kin-based groups within the Valley of Cuzco worshipped at their specific sacred spaces, and calibrated the agricultural cycle. The Incas created a complex cosmology in which time, ceremony, celestial events, spatial alignments, a gendered universe, and political justifications were intertwined and overlapped in their capital city, Cusco.

Thus, Cusco's dualistic and quadripartite organization reflected the division of the universe but also its unification. Similarly, the radiating axes of the ceque lines simultaneously made temporal, social, and conceptual distinctions but unified them in the Temple of the Sun. Cusco was the axis mundi of the Inca Empire. Cusco was a sacred place.

It was also home to thousands of people, although not just anyone could live there. Cusco was a sacred city, occupied by the empire's rulers, the priests of the Qoricancha, and the thousands of people who supported them. The ruler and his

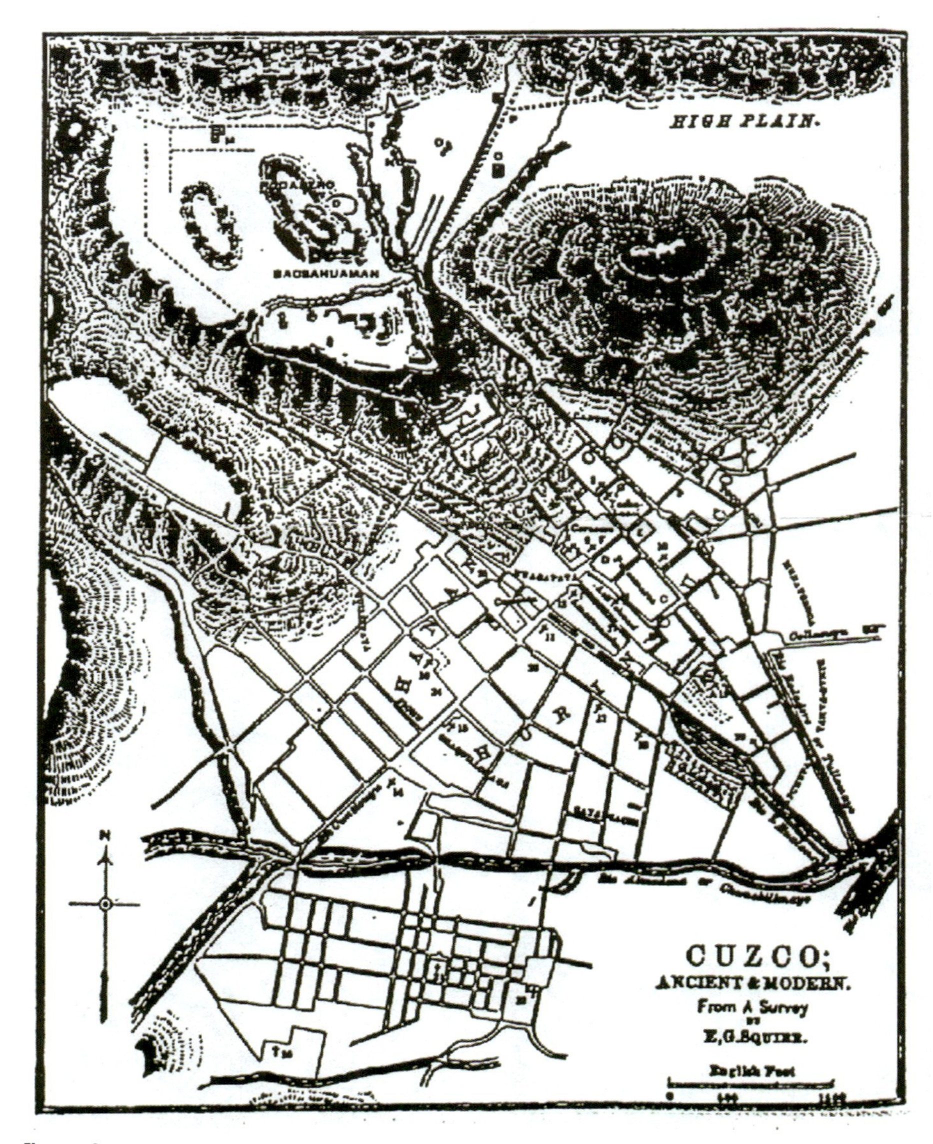

Figure 11.8 Ephraim George Squier's map of Cusco

royal family—queens, concubines, and offspring—were maintained by hundreds of servants and courtiers. The descendants of dead kings lived in the city, maintaining the royal mummy's cult and venerating the ancestors. Other compounds housed priests and their retainers. Non-royal nobles lived in Cusco—generals, administrators, and engineers—as did the "Incas-by-privilege," members of ethnic groups from the surrounding region who were granted the right to live in the capital but were not Incas by birth. The sons and daughters of conquered chiefs and rulers lived in Cusco, held as "royal hostages." Finally, the city was filled with

Figure 11.9 The Qoricancha (Temple of the Sun), Cusco

artisans—weavers, potters, chicha brewers, metalworkers, and other craftspeople—who provided the noble inhabitants with the elegant objects that physically expressed the glories of the Inca state.

These very different residents of Cusco lived in dwellings that followed shared architectural elements.[23] The **kancha** was a fundamental unit of Inca domestic architecture, a rectangular walled compound that held several rectangular buildings surrounding a central patio. The rectangular kancha was a basic element in Inca architecture, and its appearance outside the Cuzco Valley is usually interpreted as indicating either the creation of Inca colonies or the emulation of Inca architectural styles by local elites (figure 11.10).[24]

Domestic architecture had common, distinctively Inca elements, whereas other aspects varied. A common design element was the use of trapezoidal doorways, windows, and niches, openings that were wide at the base and narrow at the top (figure 11.11). Trapezoidal features were widespread, incorporated into Inca architecture in far northern Peru and in the Ecuadorian highlands.[25] Other common elements in domestic buildings were sloping roofs, drainage holes, and roof pegs.

Building materials varied enormously, material reflections of different environments and the residents' status. In more arid coastal zones, the Incas used adobe brick, while stone was preferred in the highlands. The most common stone walls were made from fieldstones, sometimes partially worked to form corners or joins, which were set into mud mortar (figure 11.12). Double-faced stone walls were also used; their finished exteriors sheathed a core of rubble fill.

Figure 11.10 Reconstructed house and residential compound (kancha) foundations, Tombebamba, Ecuador

Figure 11.11 Trapezoidal niches inside the Qoricancha, Cusco

Inca architecture was displayed throughout the empire, but Cusco was the showplace.[26] The most astounding masonry was reserved for the finest constructions, especially temples and palaces. Polygonal masonry involved cutting adjacent stones in a wall so the many edges fit together, forming a massive lithic jigsaw puzzle (figure 11.13). For example, the religious and military center of Sacsayhuaman, built on a ridge overlooking Cusco, contains some of the largest stones ever incorporated in Inca architecture.[27] Sacked by Spaniards for building materials to construct Colonial Cusco, Sacsayhuaman's most notable feature is a trio of parallel,

Figure 11.12 Reconstructed fieldstone house with grass roof, Machu Picchu, Peru

zigzagging walls whose megalithic blocks thwarted scavengers. Flanking a hillside and running for 400 m (1,312 ft), some of the walls' individual blocks are more than 8 m (26.2 ft) tall and weigh in excess of 100 tons. Many of the largest stones were quarried on the ridge itself and on surrounding outcrops, with smaller blocks of a quarry 35 km (21 miles) away.

The fact that these stones could be cut without metal tools, moved without wheeled vehicles, and transported without draft animals amazed early Spanish chroniclers (figure 11.14).[28] The chronicler **Pedro Pizarro** wrote: "On top of a hill they had a very strong fort surrounded with masonry walls of stone and with two

Figure 11.13 Massive stone walls, Sacsayhuaman, Peru

Figure 11.14 Fine Inca stonework

very high round towers. In the lower part of this wall there were stones so large and thick that it seemed impossible that human hands could have set them in place . . . They were so close together and so well fitted that the point of a pin could not have been inserted in one of the joints." **Pedro Cieza de Leon** related that 20,000 men were sent from the provinces to build Sacsayhuaman. Working on a rotating basis, with shifts of replacements, "Four thousand of them quarried and cut stones; six thousand hauled them great cables of leather and hemp; the others dug the ditch and laid the foundations . . . Overseers went around watching what they did, as did masters who were highly skilled in their work."

Even finer walls were made of equal-size blocks fitted together without mortar. To the modern eye accustomed to concrete blocks and bricks, these walls seem modest at first glance, until one realizes that every single block was made from a separate boulder that varied in its original form (figure 11.15). Each boulder was flaked, pounded with hard hammerstones, then ground with sand and other abrasives until a final block was made. Laid in elegant courses, as **John Hemming** has written, "The surface of each ashlar was allowed to bulge so that the joints were slightly countersunk. The effect of this rustication is magnificent, with each stone outlined in a frame of sharp shadow in the clear Andean air. There is a ripple of chiaroscuro over the gray or tawny beauty of the stone. It is thrilling to see the accuracy of the masonry joints. Heavy blocks of stone interlock like putty, but with the strength to resist successive earthquakes."[29]

Arguably, nowhere was the fusion of construction and setting more perfectly realized than at **Machu Picchu** (see figure 11.1). Excluding the terraces and other agricultural features, if Machu Picchu's buildings were arrayed on a flat plain, they would be a notable but relatively small set of Inca buildings covering about 550 m × 250 m (1,804 ft × 820 ft), smaller than a single royal compound at Chan Chan (see chapter 9). Without the buildings, the ridge would look like all the other ridges that tower over the Urubamba. But the combination of the buildings' elegant lines and knife-edged stone *and* the staggering location on a ridge that drops more than 450 m (1,476 ft) to the river below makes Machu Picchu one of the most beautiful sites ever built in the ancient world.

Among the numerous examples of Inca stonework, the Qoricancha contained some of the finest examples. Located at the place where the first Incas had settled, Killke pottery and architecture from below the imperial temple indicate the place's sacredness.[30] The Temple of the Sun's Quechua name reflects the fact that its walls were hung with sheets of gold. The Qoricancha sat at the center of the ceque lines and was thus the pivot of the universe.

The Qoricancha contained a walled compound of at least four religious buildings surrounding a plaza. It held numerous treasures, described by Spanish conquistadors who oversaw the ransacking of the temple. Using crowbars, the Spaniards pried the gold off the temple walls, removing 700 gold plates each weighing between 4 and 12 pounds; the gold was hauled away in 178 loads, each carried by four men. The temple also contained the Garden of the Sun. Pedro Pizarro wrote:

> Away from the room where the Sun was wont to sleep, they made a small field, which was much like a large one, where, at the proper season, they sowed maize. They sprinkled it by hand with water brought on purpose for the Sun.

Figure 11.15 (*overleaf*) Exterior of the Qoricancha, Cusco

Figure 11.16 Ushnu, Vilcashuaman, Peru

> And at the time when they celebrated their festivals, which was three times a year, that is: when they sowed the crops, when they harvested them, and when they made orejones [i.e., in a ceremony that initiated nobles], they filled this garden with cornstalks made of gold, having their ears and leaves very much like natural maize, all made of very fine gold, which they had kept in order to place them here at these times.[31]

The temple held shrines dedicated to the Sun, to the Creator God Viracocha, and to thunder and stars. The high priest of the Sun oversaw 200 male and 500 female temple servants. Morris and von Hagen write, "In the Qorikancha's central courtyard, eyewitnesses observed a stone carved in the shape of a seat covered in gold—a 'fountain' or basin—and next to it, an image shaped like a young boy, all of gold. Dressed in a tunic of fine cloth and wearing the mascay pacha, the Inca 'crown' and symbol of kingship, this image was known as the Inti Punchao. Its hollow stomach contained the ashes of deceased rulers' internal organs."[32] The idol and stone was a sacred **ushnu**, a ceremonial feature associated with the worship of the Sun, not only in the Qoricancha but also in temples to the Sun built throughout the empire (figure 11.16). The idol was offered llama meat, maize, and chicha—food and drink offered to the Sun.

Offerings of food and chicha were made to other sacred images and royal mummies, elements in an annual cycle of festivals and rites. For example, the **Haucaypata**, Cusco's main plaza, was a principal setting for the Situa ceremony, a six-day festival ridding Cuzco of illness described by **Cristobal de Molina**. During the first days of the festival, "all strangers, all whose ears were broken, and all deformed persons were sent out of the city." Four corps of 100 armed men each—representing the four suyus, with each corps composed of members of four ayllus—met in the Haucaypata, faced their respective directions, and then rushed forward to drive out evil from the city. After chasing evil forces several leagues from town, each corps stopped and bathed in "rivers of great volume, and were supposed to empty themselves into the sea and carry the evils with them."[33]

Over the next days, the Situa included processions and displays of the ancestral mummies, prayers, sacrifices, and feasting. The festival was not exclusively for nobles; at designated passages, the ceremony included poor individuals, minor lineages, and foreigners. At one point during the Situa, the images of the Sun, Viracocha and Thunder, and the royal mummies were displayed in the Haucaypata. To view these sacred icons, Molina wrote, "All the people of Cuzco came out, according to their tribes and lineages, as richly dressed as their means would allow; and having made reverence to the Creator, the Sun, and the lord Ynca, they sat down on their benches, each man according to the rank he held, the Hanan-Cuzcos being on one side, and the Hurin-Cuzcos on the other."[34]

For several days the plaza was the scene of feasts, dances, prayers and sacrifices, and vows of loyalty to the Inca. On the first day, the *yawar-sancu* (a meal of maize pudding sprinkled with sacrificial llama blood) was eaten, after all participants had sworn "never to murmur against the Creator, the Sun, or the Thunder; never to be traitors to their lord the Ynca, on pain of receiving condemnation and trouble."[35] On the final days of the Situa, representatives of conquered nations entered Cuzco, marching into the Haucaypata from the four suyus to make offerings to Viracocha, Inti, Thunder, and Huanacari, the huaca of the Inca. The Situa ended with the sacrificial burning of a llama and of "a vast quantity of clothes of many colors." The lords of distant provinces received permission to return home, carrying their huacas, gifts of servants, gold, and cloth—and with a heightened impression of their role in the Inca state. Molina concludes his description of the Situa thus: "The same feast, called Situa, was celebrated at the chief places of all the provinces, by the Ynca governors, where-ever they might be: and, although the ceremonies were less grand, and the sacrifices fewer, no part of the festival was omitted."[36] The Situa ceremonially expressed the descent of the Incas from the Sun and made rebelling against the Inca ruler a sin against the Sun.

The Situa ceremony expressed elements of the Inca worldview and political strategies on many levels. On one hand, Inca superiority over other Andean peoples was justified by their descent from the Sun. Their ability to control human labor was evident in the phases of the ritual and by the enormous quantities of food, chicha, cloth, gold, and other offerings that were the products of coordinated human effort (figure 11.17). Finally, the Situa ceremony embodied the central fulcrum of the Inca Empire's control over the provinces: loyal subjects were rewarded, rebels were destroyed.

The Incas in the Provinces

In 1959 the archaeologist **Dorothy Menzel** published a very important article.[37] Observing that "the overwhelming majority of historical documents dealing with Inca history and culture refer to events and conditions around Cuzco, the Inca

Figure 11.17 Royal Inca tunic depicting different poncho styles from provinces in Tawantinsuyu

capital," Menzel noted that "if we are interested in the cultural situation which the Incas found in the provinces they conquered and in the effect which their rule had on it we are lucky to find a few scraps of information on any one area." She went on to observe the variations in local and Inca architecture and ceramics in the Chincha, Ica, and Pisco Valleys on the South Coast of Peru. These variations pointed to different Inca political strategies, varying responses to the regional political landscapes. Commenting on the "marked differences in social and political organization among the south coast valleys at the time they were conquered by the Incas," Menzel wrote, "Chincha had a powerful centralized government, while Pisco was probably divided. Ica had a centralized organization of some kind, but we cannot be sure whether it was political or religious in nature." In responding to these local variations in political organization, "The Incas took advantage of existing centralization in Chincha and Ica, building their administrative centers at the focus of native authority. They probably ruled through the native nobility in both valleys." In regions that lacked "centralized authority . . . the Incas imposed their own, constructing an administrative center at some convenient point to serve as the focus of Inca control."[38]

Menzel's insights sparked decades of archaeological research into the impacts of the Inca Empire in the provinces, resulting in numerous archaeological investigations of the variations in imperial structure at the provincial level. In turn, these studies of the Inca Empire have contributed to comparative studies of ancient empires (figure 11.18).

The Inca encountered and responded to very different local situations. The situation in Chincha was one extreme. As Menzel noted and as demonstrated in subsequent investigations by Craig Morris, "Chincha is of particular interest because it represents a large coastal kingdom brought peacefully into Tawantinsuyu."[39] At the regional capital of **La Centinela** (see chapter 10), the Inca added a religious and administrative complex that incorporated walled enclosures made from adobe bricks, modified the existing compounds built from tapia walls, and co-opted the pyramid associated with the oracle at Chichaycamac by building a plaza and staircase that controlled access to the shrine. In this process, the Incas recognized local rulers but also constructed another palace for the Inca ruler or his representative. Just as Cusco was divided into hanan and hurin zones, a similar dual division was implemented in La Centinela. Although historical accounts emphasize the status of the king of Chincha—the only ruler allowed to be carried in a litter in the presence of the Inca emperor—in fact, his capital and authority were transformed. Morris and **Julian Santillana** write, "The Cusco elite carefully planned and executed a multilevel strategy of integration through dual control. The architectural evidence shows that it was a carefully planned attempt to influence local activities and structures—to govern in considerable depth."[40] Despite its impact on the political elites of Chincha, Inca rule had little effect on the countryside or lasting influence on local cultural traditions.

Inca control in the Upper Mantaro Valley was quite different. Located in the Central Andes at 3,150–3,400 m (10,335–11,155 ft) above sea level and flanked by puna zones at over 4,000 m (13,223 ft), the region is more than 425 km (265 miles) northwest of Cusco. Archaeological investigations by members of the Upper Mantaro Archaeological Research Project documented the changes the Inca Empire imposed.[41] In the centuries before the Inca conquest, the region was occupied by 36,000–60,000 people from two major ethnic groups—the northern Xauxas and the southern Wankas—whose members formed a handful of competing chiefdoms. D'Altroy writes that the challenge for the Incas was "not to overwhelm and divide a powerful, unified society but to centralize power within ethnic groups notable more for internal competition and instability than for unity."[42] The two large communities, **Hatunmarca** and **Tunamarca**, had about 7,000–11,000 and 8,000–13,000 inhabitants, respectively. These centers were perched on ridge tops, cordoned by defensive walls, and contained elite residences and plazas not

Figure 11.18 Inca aryballoid

seen at smaller sites. There were pronounced differences between elites and commoners. Elites ate more maize, venison, and llama meat than commoners consumed. Elites also had finer ceramics than did commoners.

This changed with the arrival of the Incas. A new Inca center, **Hatun Xauxa**, was established in the middle of the broad valley. Hatun Xauxa's exposed location indicated the Incas' self-confidence: the conquerors were not obliged to perch on defensible ridges because their power was overwhelming. The modern Peruvian city of Sausa covers most of Hatun Xauxa, but a sense of its splendor is captured by a Spanish chronicler's 1531–32 account:

> The pueblo of Xauxa is large and is in a very beautiful valley . . . It is abundant in supplies and herds; it is made in the manner of a town in Spain, tightly packed with its streets well laid out. In its view are many other subject towns, and there were so many people in said pueblo and its vicinity that it appears unlike any other town in the Indies, appearing to many Spaniards that there came together in the plaza principal each day more than 100,000 souls, and the marketplaces and plazas and other streets of said pueblo were filled with people, and this great multitude appeared a marvelous thing.[43]

The creation of Hatun Xauxa signified other changes in the Upper Mantaro Valley. For example, although local elites still lived in more elaborate dwellings than did commoners, other distinctions diminished. **Cathy Costin** and **Timothy Earle** have documented that although local elites retained certain prerogatives—they still had more fine ceramics, for example—the differences between Wanka elites and commoners were not as great as they had been before the Inca conquest.[44] Although some elites joined the Inca administration, the overall status of local elites declined while the lives of commoners improved under the Incas.

The Incas bypassed local elites in the Upper Mantaro Valley, diverting agricultural production and other resources to their own imperial project (figure 11.19). Xauxa's richness was stockpiled in nearly 2,000 storehouses totaling more than 123,716 m^3 (roughly equivalent to 3,748 shipping containers, each 20 ft long). These Inca storerooms near other settlements and along the Inca road were part of what D'Altroy and Earle have called "**staple finance**," which "generally involves obligatory payments in kind to the state of subsistence goods such as grains, livestock, and clothing. The staples form accounting units (a bushel of wheat or a head of sheep) that have established values. Staples are collected by the state as a share of commoner produce, as a specified levy, or as produce from land worked with corvée labor. This revenue in staples is then used to pay personnel attached to the state and others working for the state on a part-time basis."[45]

The thousands of Inca storerooms in the Upper Mantaro Valley are thus archaeological traces of imperial strategy, a strategy applied to multiple locations across the Inca Empire. For example, in **Cochabamba**, Bolivia, the Inca provincial center had 2,000 storehouses; **Huanuco Pampa**, in the central Peruvian Andes, was surrounded by 497 storehouses.[46] Storage was pivotal to Inca statecraft, and these storerooms contained everything from food and weapons to cloth and agricultural tools. They held items for ceremonies, the materiel of war, and provisions

Figure 11.19 Ruins of storehouses (*colcas*), Tunanmarca, Peru

for elites and workers. The creation of these storage facilities and the accumulation of goods were central to the Inca Empire's expansion.

Storage and staple finance were based on the control of labor, another fundamental of the Inca Empire. The political principle was that subjects "paid" their taxes by working for the state, even when the results were products such as cloth, pottery, or maize. This form of labor tax drew on earlier customs of reciprocal labor, in which different kin groups aided each other—helping out during planting seasons or with harvests—but with those being helped incurring the obligation to reciprocate. Known as the *mita* or *minka*, this practice could be applied to all sorts of activities—preparing chicha and food for fiestas, conducting rituals for neighboring shrines—related to imperial projects.[47]

If labor was the foundation of empire, censuses and record keeping were implements of power. The Incas used a decimal number system. The population was organized in a nested hierarchy of households, with a tribute payer in each: 10 (*chunga*), 50 (*pisca chunga*), 100 (*pachaca*), 500 (*pisca pachaca*), 1,000 (*guaranga*), 5,000 (*pisca guaranga*), and 10,000 (*huno*). As **Catherine Julien** has documented in her ethnohistoric research, this decimal administration was applied across the Inca Empire.[48] The census was a tool of empire, and the decimal administration system combined both consistency and flexibility.

Some households were relocated to be nearer to necessary raw materials or large-scale storage complexes. These relocated colonies of people were known as *mitimaes*. Mitamaes were established for economic, political, or punitive reasons, and the repercussions sometimes affected the entire Inca Empire. One of the most amazing examples occurred when the Incas conquered the Titicaca Basin.[49] The rival kingdoms, the **Colla** and the **Lupaka**, were locked in indecisive conflict when the Incas invaded. The Collas resisted the Incas and were destroyed. Acknowledging the inevitable, the Lupaka turned their kingdom over to the Incas. Nonetheless, the Incas extensively reorganized the Titicaca Basin. Locals were expelled and replaced by colonists from across Tawantinsuyu. The Incas utterly reorganized settlements on the Sacred Islands of the Sun and Moon and the nearby Copacabana Peninsula, where they drove out the local population and moved in colonists from forty-two different regions whose original homelands ranged from northern Ecuador to northern Chile. Although these mitimaes' major task was to maintain the religious shrines on the Islands of the Sun and the Moon, the replacement of a rebellious local population with intimidated colonists far from their homelands was an obvious political and punitive strategy.

The Inca Empire did not flinch in the use of power. To cite just one example, in the southern highlands of Ecuador, a number of blocks of fine Inca masonry were identified near the small town of Paquishapa, on the Inca road northward to Tombebamba (renamed Cuenca by the Spaniards). These blocks are large, well-made chunks of andesite, weighing between 200 kg and 700 kg (440–1,450 lb). Physical analyses demonstrate that the andesite blocks were originally quarried at the Rumiqolqa source, approximately 40 km (24 miles) southeast of Cusco, the same stone used in the Qoricancha. These stones, archaeologist Dennis Ogburn writes, represent

> a massive investment in labor on the part of the Inka to bring stones from such a distant quarry. The distance over which these ashlars were carried, more than 1,600 kilometers [960 miles], is the greatest known for the transport of such massive objects (of up to 700 kg [1,540 lb]) in the Andes, and possibly in the whole of the New World during pre-Columbian times. These stone blocks were carried through mountainous terrain, up and down numerous slopes, and across many rivers. This feat was accomplished strictly with human labor ... The workers employed in this project must have numbered in the thousands, and many months would have been required for the stones to reach the Saraguro region from Rumiqolqa.[50]

This extraordinary feat was motivated by two political impulses. First, the Incas wanted to solidify their northern conquests by making Tombebamba a showplace, creating a complex with the finest masonry that demonstrated the empire's power and wealth and transferring some of the sacredness of Cusco to the new provincial center (figure 11.20). The Incas also used such projects to punish rebels and display their power. The chronicler Cieza de Leon reported in 1553:

> I understand that, because of an uprising attempted by some communities around Cuzco, he [Huayna Capac] was so upset that, after beheading the leaders, he expressly ordered that the Indians of those places transport

Figure 11.20 Tombebamba (Cuenca), Ecuador

> from Cuzco the number of stones they were told to in order to build some fine buildings in Tombebamba, and that they move them with heavy ropes [cables?]; and they carried out his order. And Guaynacapa often said that, to keep the people of those realms properly subjugated when they had nothing to do or oversee, it was helpful to make them move a mountain from one place to another; and he even sent as far as Cuzco to have them bring stone blocks and slabs for buildings in Quito, which still exist in the buildings where they placed them.[51]

This exercise of naked power became a dramatic display, as literally thousands of men struggled to carry these massive stones through the highlands from Cusco to Ecuador, a sweaty political theater witnessed by tens of thousands of onlookers. It was a convincing display of the power of the Inca state and the consequences of rebellion.

The Edges of Empire

The Inca Empire was not omnipotent, and its territory was not infinite. Surprisingly, the precise frontiers of Tawantinsuyu are poorly known. **John Hyslop** argued that early historical sources overstated the extent and certainty of those frontiers: "Little time has been dedicated to the study of the external or extreme limits of the Inca Empire and no two maps of Tawantinsuyu exist that agree in their delineations."[52] For example, it is claimed that the Inca Empire extended to the modern Colombia-Ecuador border, but Hyslop argued that although the Inca army may have raided into what is now Colombia, there is little evidence that this territory was held and controlled. In contrast, numerous fortresses (*pukaras*) were built in northern Ecuador, by both the Incas and resistant local chiefdoms.[53] The **Cayambe** ethnic group in the Pambamarca region resisted Inca conquest for seventeen years, despite living only 30 km (24 miles) from Quito, which the Incas claimed was "another Cusco."[54] The Cayambe resistance was so strong that the Incas' ultimate conquest "may have been the most costly of all Inka military ventures."[55]

Although the Incas established a comprehensive imperial presence in the highlands of Ecuador, their influence on the Ecuadorian coast was indirect at best. The Incas never established roads, pukaras, or administrative centers there. Military campaigns against the coastal chiefdoms resulted in disastrous defeats for the Incas, and, after some face-saving punitive raids, they retreated to the highlands. Rather than a case of how the Incas conquered coastal Ecuadorians, it was a situation in which, as **Karen Stothert** has written, Manteños and other coastal peoples resisted and begrudgingly accommodated the Incas.[56]

Even regions with imperial infrastructure were not utterly secure. For example, excavations and survey in the department of **Tumbes** have documented a substantial Inca presence at the provincial center of **Cabeza de Vaca** (figure 11.21). Cabeza de Vaca was the northern end of the Inca coastal road, and the provincial center represented a major investment.[57] Built of large adobe bricks, the walls contained trapezoidal niches and doorways and were covered with polychrome murals. According to Spanish eyewitness accounts, Cabeza de Vaca was a walled compound that held a Temple of the Sun, a palace, and multiple workshops. Abundant Inca polychrome ceramics at Cabeza de Vaca and other nearby sites indicate a pervasive Inca presence and investment in the Tumbes region. Yet, this significant imperial investment was insufficient to protect Tumbes. In 1532, when Pizarro landed in Tumbes to begin his conquest of Peru, Tumbes had been burned to the ground. Attacked by its arch-rivals who lived on Isla Puna in the Gulf of Guayaquil, Tumbes was destroyed despite the Inca presence.

Inca control was even less certain along the eastern edge of the sierra and in the lowland jungles. According to Hyslop, "The entire eastern limit of the Inca Empire, from the Colombian-Ecuadorian border to the Bolivian-Argentinean frontier, constitutes a tremendous enigma." The limits of Inca eastern control are well-defined in only two regions: due east of Cusco and near Cochabamba. For the rest of the eastern frontier, the archaeological data are "scarce, incoherent, or historically late."[58] Traditionally, the Inca border was considered to follow the environmental boundary between the highlands and the jungle, although, as **Patricia Lyon** has noted, the scarcity of archaeological research in the montaña has reinforced this "imaginary frontier."[59]

Although it is possible that a clear definition of the Tawantinsuyu's eastern border awaits more archaeological research, it is also possible that this frontier was always permeable. In some regions, people living within the Inca Empire were linked to lowland communities by way of intermediary traders. For example, in the **Pasto region**, which straddles the Ecuador-Colombia border, local elites sponsored long-distance traders known as *mindalaes*.[60] These traders held distinctive statuses and were free from mita obligation, paying tribute to local lords in cotton cloth and beads. Beads made from marine shells were both prestige items and currency and were widely exchanged across northern South America, linking coastal, highland, and lowland zones. Gold, silver, coca, and salt were traded by mindalaes.

Figure 11.21 Inca provincial center Cabeza de Vaca, Tumbes

Early colonial documents suggest that similar intermediary trading communities existed at several points along the Andean-Amazonian border, perhaps in part reflecting earlier prehispanic patterns and suggesting a permeable frontier.[61]

Figure 11.22 Kuelap, Chachapoyas, Peru

At other locations, the eastern border was tightly held (figure 11.22). For example, the **Chachapoya**, who occupied the cloud forest region between the Marañon and Huallaga Rivers, were ultimately dominated by the Incas—but only after repeated rebellions.[62] Before the Inca conquest, the Chachapoya were divided into a number of local polities but shared similar cultural practices, including architecture, funeral practices, and ceramic styles. In the face of the Inca conquest, these disparate Chachapoya polities unified in resistance against a common enemy. The Incas responded with a heavy hand, as **Inge Schjellerup** has written: "The Incas created the infrastructure necessary to control the Chachapoya, to reorganize people, change their borders, and adjust their numbers within [the Inca] administration to enclose the Chachapoya within the Inca plan during the sixty years the occupation lasted."[63] The Incas significantly changed the Chachapoya landscape, erecting monuments and buildings that proclaimed the conquest. The Inca established administrative centers and fortresses deep within the cloud forest, with buildings that blended Inca layout and Chachapoya stonework (figure 11.23). These sites were positioned to control exchange routes along the Huallaga and Marañon Rivers and their tributaries.[64] When the Chachapoya armies were finally defeated, the Incas banished huge numbers of local people to the distant colonies in Tawantinsuyu, forcibly resettling the vanquished cloud forest dwellers as far south as Lake Titicaca.

Further south, Inca impacts on frontier regions in southern Bolivia, northern Chile, and northwest Argentina have been seen as late, brief, and shallow. These characterizations are under revision. As discussed, the Inca conquest may have occurred as early as AD 1400 and lasted a century or more. The impacts of Inca rule were extensive, not superficial. As the archaeologist **Felix Acuto** has argued, "Inka intervention in the northern **Calchaquí Valley** [northwest Argentina] disrupted native social life, albeit some communities seem to have been more affected than others."[65] Before the Incas' conquest, political power was divided between and within local communities, and differences in power, prestige, and wealth were unstratified. Skilled warriors became leaders during times of war, only to have their authority ebb when peace resumed. Local sites lacked administrative zones, elaborate monuments, and formal plazas for ceremonies or political displays. The settlements expressed "a sense of equality and sameness."[66]

This changed with the Inca conquest, at least at some Calchaquí Valley settlements. At **La Paya/Guitián**, the site grew into a large Inca center flanking two sides of a wide quebrada. The local settlement pattern of a crowded jumble of semi-subterranean circular stone houses in which "everybody carried out similar tasks in similar houses" was replaced by the Incas' "tidy spatial order where activities and functions were separated in different areas"—divided among dwellings, workshops, storerooms, plazas, and administrative and military buildings.[67] New political hierarchies were created: some communities emerged as different from their neighbors as their leaders acquired Inca ceramics and other objects, taking advantage of allegiances with Tawantinsuyu. Conversely, other communities may have engaged in subtle acts of resistance, rejecting Inca architecture for traditional homes and neighborhoods or using Inca ceramics but preferring the local and elaborately decorated pottery style as grave goods or offerings to the ancestors.

A final point along the edges of the empire was the site of **Cerro Grande de la Compañia**, Chile, about 95 km (57 miles) south of Santiago (figure 11.24).[68] Various historical sources had placed the frontier much further south, some sources hundreds of kilometers further south, to the Maule or Bio-Bio Rivers. Although the Inca launched raids into these southerly zones and their influence was undoubtedly felt, the southernmost fortress was at Cerro Grande de la Compañia. The isolated hill rises more than 670 m (2,198 ft) above the valley bottom, and the naturally defensive relief was reinforced by protective stone walls, a "walled battlement and a rectangular turret . . . protect the south hillside."[69] Sling-stones were piled on the inside of the defense walls. The hilltop site contained traces of earlier circular dwellings and later rectangular building constructed in provincial Inca style. Inca colcas dotted the hilltop. The Inca garrison at Cerro Grande de la Compañia overlooked the main Inca road heading south and strategically controlled the valley. In turn, it was one of a chain of provincial centers on the southern frontier, different types of sites not all of which were fortresses. **Jack Rossen** and colleagues have written: "The southern frontier was not merely a military outpost in the wilderness, but a layering of various military, social, and economic activities, each with a different scope and intensity. The Inkas, even at the farthest tentacles of the state, were committed to a varied strategy of settlement, consolidation, and transformation of the landscape, instead of just subjugation."[70]

Figure 11.23 Eastern facade of the wall surrounding a Kuelap fortress

Creating Worlds

The Inca achievement was not exclusively political or military, although the creation of the empire was a unique accomplishment in South American prehistory. The Inca also created sophisticated models of the universe and their place within it. Our knowledge of these conceptual worlds is fragmentary and indirect, but what is known points to creations of breathtaking concepts.

For example, the Incas and other Andean people used complex systems of knotted cords for record keeping, called *khipus* (figure 11.25).[71] Khipus consist of numbers of twisted and spun threads, known as pendant strings or cords, which dangle from a thicker primary cord. Additional secondary cords may be attached to pendant cords. The cords are usually made from cotton, although llama wool khipus are known. Approximately 750–800 khipus still exist. The earliest date to the Wari Empire, although most date to the Inca period and early Colonial period, and a few Andean communities still use khipus today. Prehistoric Inca khipus have been found from Chachapoyas to northern Chile.

Khipus are extraordinarily difficult to decode, although most seem to be administrative or calendrical in function.[72] The ability to read khipus was a skill mastered only by "scribes" (*khipukamayuq*). Although there are numerous Colonial

descriptions of khipus, there are no known descriptions of how to read them. The most illuminating documents are Spanish accounts that seem to be transcriptions of information read from khipus.[73] From these accounts, it seems as though the combinations of strings, twists, colors, and knots encode specific sets of information and were actually "read" rather than simply serving as aids for remembering.

Other glimpses into Inca cosmology come from various Colonial accounts. For example, sometime in the early 1600s, **Juan Santa Cruz Yupanqui**, a fifth-generation Christian descended from Inca nobles of Collasuyu, provided a diagram depicting the interior of the Temple of the Sun (figure 11.26).[74] According to the original text, there were three primary elements: the central image of the Creator God Viracocha—symbolized by a large disk of gold plate—flanked by the Sun (Inti) and Moon (Qilla). Across this diagram, a number of relationships were extended laterally and vertically.

The constellation of the Southern Cross (*ocorara*), which is also the model of the *chankana* (Andean cross), is labeled with the phrase "three stars all equal." Balance characterizes the image, reflecting the dual division of nature embodied in *hanan-hurin*. From left to right, the Morning Star is paired with the Evening Star, and the star-filled skies of summer are balanced against the cloudy days of winter. An X-shaped cross links four stars, two of which are named: *saramanka*,

Figure 11.24 Cerro Grande de la Compañia, Chile

cooking pot of maize, and *qura manka*, cooking pot of herbs. Lightning bolts (*catachillay*) are counterpoised against hailstorms, the hailstones splattering from a puma's mouth. A rainbow embraces *pachamama*, the Earth. A river flows from the Earth. The sea (*mamacocha*) is linked to the springs and wells where water emerges from the Earth, *puquios*.

Man and Woman stand separately and together. A set of circles with dots represents the *imay mana ñawraykunap ñawin,* "the eyes of all classes of things," the caves and springs that are the eyes of the Earth. They are contrasted with the image of a tree, which also symbolizes the ancestors (*mallkis*). The gridded square is a farm field, specifically the Colcapata, agricultural land dedicated to a deity and here perhaps representing the sacred field in the Qoricancha. More profound, the eyes of all things, the ancestral tree, and the men and women all stand on the Colcapata, which in turn is vertically opposite the Sun, Viracocha, and the Moon. All these complex images and oppositions are enclosed within the Temple of the Sun. It is a complex depiction of a subtle idea: counterpoised opposites comprise the whole. In other words, *ntin*.

It is sometimes difficult to be certain that historical accounts describe specifically Inca cosmology rather than regional Andean or post-Colonial knowledge, which often draws on broadly held Andean concepts. For example, the **Huarochiri Manuscript**—the only colonial document that describes Andean religion in an indigenous language—comes from a province on the western slope of the central Peruvian Andes drained by the Rimac and Lurin Rivers. The manuscript describes an ancient world, as **Frank Salomon** has written,

Figure 11.25 Khipu "scribe" (*khipukamayuq*) illustrated by Guaman Poma de Ayala

when cannibal deities preyed on otherwise immortal humans, of the mountain deity Paria Caca who emerged to expel the fire deities of antiquity, of the human groups that traced their victories from Paria Caca's five simultaneous

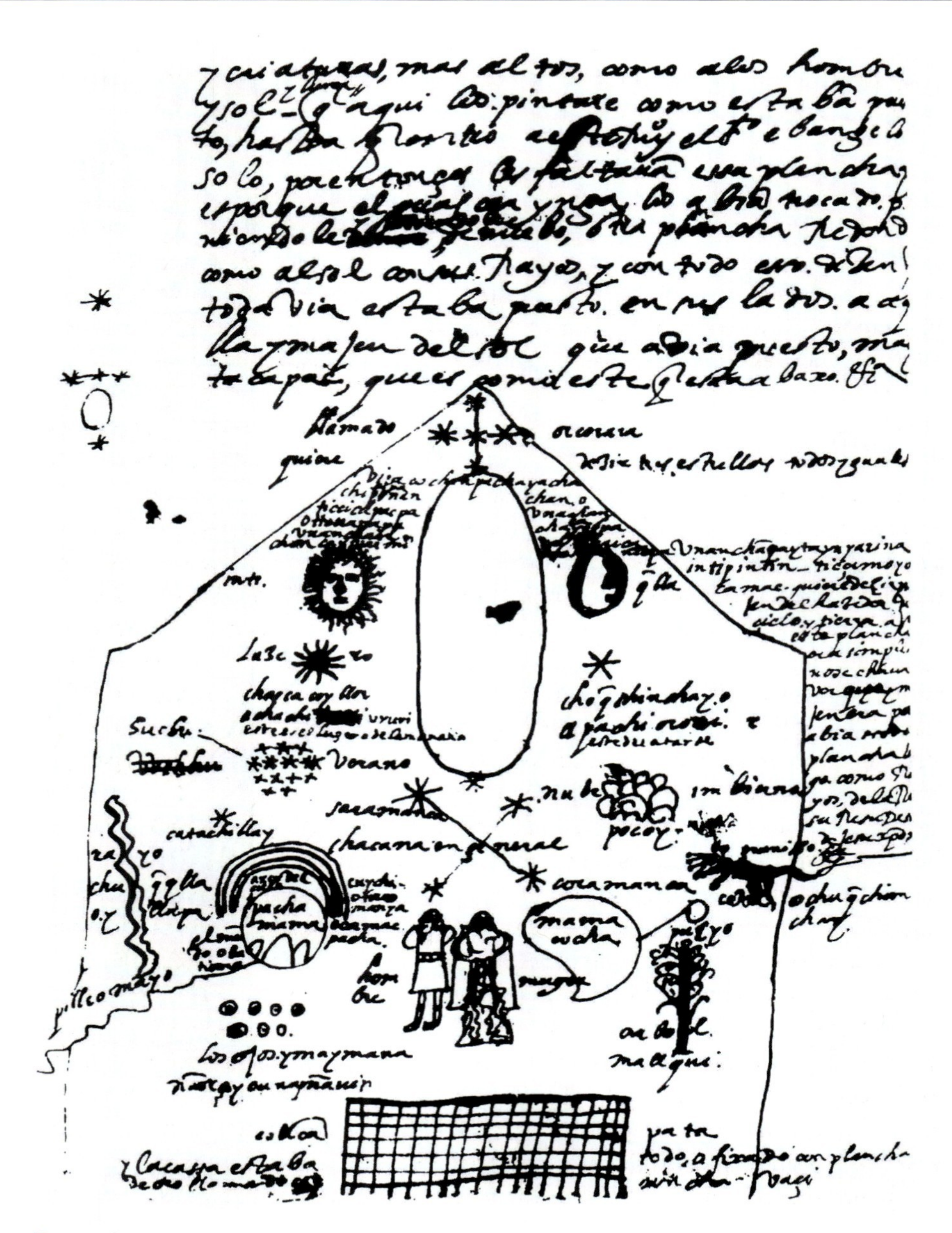

Figure 11.26 Conceptual model of the Qoricancha by Juan Santa Cruz Yupanqui

avatars, of Paria Caca's brotherhood with the fivefold female power Chaupi Ñamca, and of the society ritually organized in their names around a grand complementarity of male and female superhumans. It unfolds the splendor of ceremonies that prehispanic priests devoted to a landscape alive with the diverse sacred beings called huacas. It recalls memories of Inca rule, of how unknown invaders, the Spanish, brought new gods to displace the children of

> Paria Caca and of Chaupi Ñamca. Nothing else in all the sources from which we seek the Andean "vision of the vanquished" rivals it for immediacy, strangeness, and beauty.[75]

A number of themes and tropes embodied in the Huarochiri Manuscript probably express broadly held, but not universal, Andean beliefs.[76]

Andean religious practices were doggedly local, focused on specific shrines, landscape features, myths, and ancestral genealogies anchored in a specific region by a specific people. Unlike Islam, Buddhism, Judaism, Christianity, and other "world religions" whose broad principles and practices have a global reach, Andean religious practices were preeminently tethered to a homeland.

At various points in prehistory, inter-regional religious practices—such as Chavín (see chapter 7)—cast broad networks of belief, and more regional shrines like Cahuachi (see chapter 8) and Pachacamac (see chapter 10) could be widely venerated, yet even these devotions overlay local religious practices rather than replaced them. Further, although the Incas may have incorporated local huacas, ceremonies, and practices or established Temples of the Sun in the provinces, regional religions were not erased—as the Huarochiri Manuscript demonstrates.

But the Huarochiri Manuscript and other Colonial documents provide insights, although incomplete and fragmented, into the rich worldviews of Inca culture. Some of the most impressive accomplishments were in astronomy. For example, the Qoricancha was the pivot point from which a variety of astronomical events were observed. **Juan de Betanzos** recounts the legend of how Inca Yupanqui established solar calendars, telling "these lords that each month had thirty days and each year had three hundred and sixty days."[77] Based on his observations of the solar cycle and the phases of the moon, Yupanqui placed four pillars marking the yearly movements of the rising sun among zenith, nadir, and equinoxes and four pillars marking the variations in the setting sun. Other alignments marked the appearance of the Pleiades, the Southern Cross, and the stars Alpha and Beta Centauri, which traditional Quechua people refer to as *llamapa iiahuin* (the eyes of the llama).[78] The Andean night sky was filled with animals, as **Gary Urton** has documented.[79] Combining historical sources and ethnographic research with modern Quechua communities, Urton has documented traditional names for the stellar constellations, which were inanimate geometric and architectural forms, and the *yana phuyu* (dark clouds), animate black bodies in the Andean night sky.

When one is standing at Cusco, these dark forms of interstellar dust rise from the southeast in a curving procession. The serpent (*mach'acuay*) is followed by the toad (*hanp'atu*) and tinamou (*yutu*), a ground-dwelling pheasant-like bird. They are followed by the llama, from whose belly extends another dark form varyingly described as a baby llama (*uñallamacha*), the llama's umbilicus, or a serpent. The llama is trailed by the fox (*atoq*) and another tinamou. The living dark spaces in the sky are visible in the great river of stars, the Mayu, the "River in the Sky," which we call the Milky Way.

This folk astronomy was not just some quaint practice but a series of observations with practical consequences. The Mayu is one segment of a large hydraulic cycle. The rivers of the Andes run to the edge of the Earth, where they join the Cosmic Sea that flows around the Earth. The River in the Sky courses into the Cosmic Sea in the west, flows under the Earth, and reappears in the eastern sky. In its slow progression, the River in the Sky empties water that falls to the Earth as rain. The appearance of this pack train of dark animals announces the onset of the rainy season, and the clarity with which these animals can be seen indicates the intensity of future rainfall. If the animals are obscured by clouds, the rains will fall. If the animals are clear, little rain or a drought is foretold.

These stellar observations were vital for farming communities that depend on rain. Colonial accounts suggest that similar observations were made by Inca cosmographers and farmers, elements in a broad set of observations and insights into the nature of the Andean cosmos. Ethnographic research has shown that modern Quechua farmers observe the brightness with which the Pleiades appears in mid- to late June to predict the weather in the potato growing season, October–May.[80] Farmers scan the northeastern sky just before dawn to see how clear and large the Pleiades appears. Bright constellation and clear skies forecast early and abundant rains and thus a large potato harvest. Cloudy skies and an obscure Pleiades mean planting will be postponed and the harvest will be small. In turn, these drought years in the Southern Andes are associated with El Niño/Southern Oscillation events. Modern statistical analysis of the relationship between El Niño events and cloud cover in the southern Andean sky shows a positive correlation at 90 percent. And the Incas knew this.

Yet, the cosmic cycles were not mechanical processes indifferent to human actions. Rather, the Incas and other Andean people saw the cosmos as imbued with vital forces that required their attention and offerings. For example, the Huarochiri Manuscript repeatedly uses the Quechua verb *camay*, a complex term with no direct English counterpart.[81] Camay includes the notion of "to make," although not to create from nothingness (as in "I made a cake from scratch") but rather to take actions that cause or encourage something that already exists to express or manifest itself.

Inca water rituals express this notion. The grand hydraulic cycle linking the Cosmic Sea, the River of the Night Sky, rainfall, and the rivers and streams of the Andes required proper rituals. These human gestures did not create this cycle but re-energized and respected its flow.

For this reason, objects made from the shells of the thorny oyster, *Spondylus princeps*, were offered to highland lakes and springs (figure 11.27). The priest Bernabe Cobo observed: "These Indians were also accustomed to sacrifice seashells, especially when they made offering to the springs. They said this was a very appropriate sacrifice because the springs are the daughters of the sea, which is the mother of the waters . . . This sacrifice was offered to the above mentioned springs after the planting was done so that the springs would not dry up that year and so that these springs would flow with abundance and irrigate their sown fields as had happened in past years."[82] Offerings of *Spondylus* shell objects, referred to as *mullu*, were so pervasive that the "pagan" practice was a particular target for attacks by Catholic priests. The extirpator Father José de Arriaga instructed that priests

Figure 11.27 Necklace made from *Spondylus*

ensure that "no Indian, male or female, will have mullu."[83] The chronicler Polo de Ondegardo documented that "they sacrifice or make offerings of sea shells called Mollo [*sic*]. And they offer them to the fountains and springs, saying that the shells are the daughters of the sea, the mother of all waters."[84]

Similar offerings were also made to mountain peaks. R. Thomas Zuidema has written, "Snow-capped mountains, especially those along the coast, and mountain lakes were considered as the source of rivers of more immediate concern and the water of the former was believed to be derived from the ocean that surrounded and supported the known earth."[85] The need to placate these forces of nature and ensure the continued flow of the Cosmic Sea was expressed in **capacocha offerings** on the highest peaks of the Andes (figure 11.28).

The high-elevation archaeological sites associated with capacocha ceremonies are perhaps the most fascinating—and harrowing—the Incas created. *Capacocha*

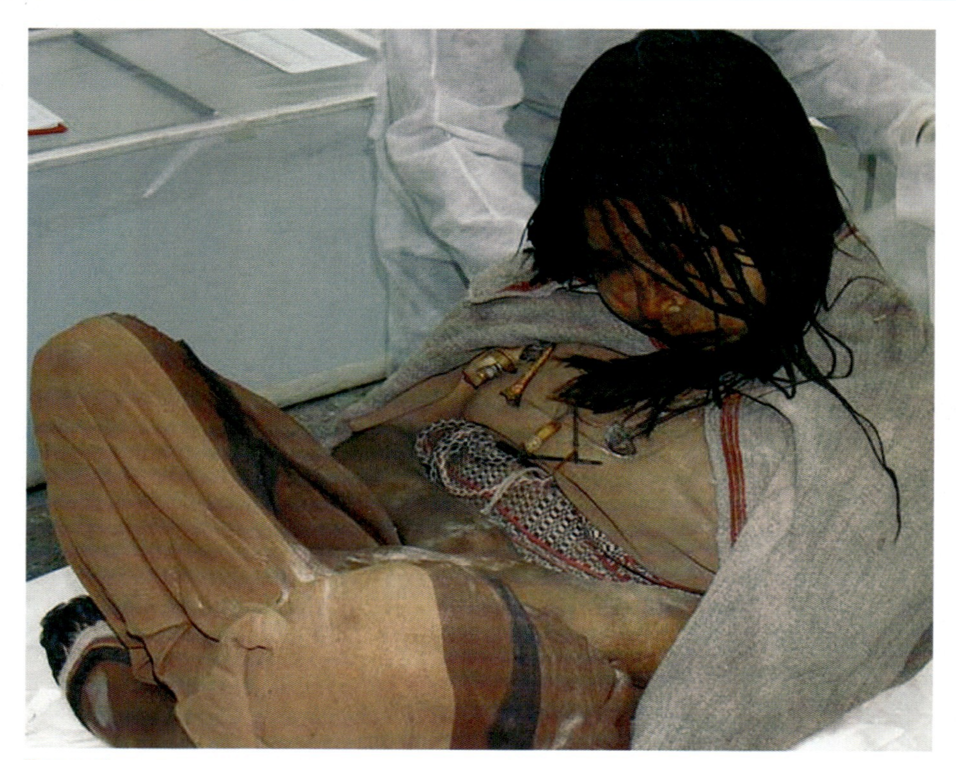

Figure 11.28 "La Doncella" (the Maiden), mummy of Inca girl sacrificed on the summit of Cerro Llullaillaco, Argentina

combines two sets of meanings: *çapay* (unique)—and thus, for example, applied to the Inca ruler as Capac Inca—and *qocha* (a lake or puddle) and, by extension, the essence of water. The distinguishing feature of the ceremony was human sacrifice, particularly the sacrifice of pure, unblemished children. The majority of the capacocha victims were children ten to fifteen years old and sometimes younger. For example, Betanzos describes how Inca Yupanqui decreed the funeral rituals for his approaching death. After an elaborate phase of public mourning and once his body was mummified, the children should be assembled:

> Then they should send out throughout the entire land and have a thousand boys and girls brought. All these children should be from five to six years of age. Some of them should be the children of caciques. They should be very well dressed, paired up male and female. As married couples they would be given all the table service, which would be of gold and silver, which a married man would have in his house.
>
> These children would be collected from all over the land and would be carried in litters together and by pairs to be buried in pairs with the table service that they had been given. They would be buried all over the land in the places where the Inca had established residence. And some of them would

> be thrown into the sea in pairs with the table service mentioned above. They called this sacrifice *capa cocha*, which means "solemn sacrifice." The Inca ordered that as these [children] were buried and sacrificed, it would be said that they were going where the Inca was in order to serve him.[86]

Capacocha sacrifices were also made on some of the tallest peaks in the Andes, including on what **Johan Rheinhard** and **Constanza Ceruti** have called "the world's highest archaeological site."[87] Located on the modern border between Chile and Argentina and rising to 6,739 m (22,110 ft) above sea level, **Mt. Llullaillaco** is the world's tallest active volcano. The mountain looms over the hyper-arid Atacama Desert to the west. Despite being permanently snow-capped, no streams flow from Mt. Llullaillaco, as normally occurs, and the name itself may mean "a place where water could not be found, even though [we] would have expected it."[88] On a flat patch ridge on the northeast side of the summit, the Incas built a shrine and offered three people as capacocha.

As Rheinhard and Ceruti insightfully observe, "A capacocha event often required a centripetal movement involving the transportation of sacrificial victims and material objects from communities in the provinces," and this was equally true for ceremonies in Cusco and on Mt. Llullaillaco.[89] It probably required several months to reach the mountain, stopping to worship at sacred places en route and walking in silence in respect to the gods. On the lower flanks of the mountain, windbreaks and tambos sheltered the pilgrims. Only a small group of priests, attendants, and victims made the final climb to the summit shrine. A two-room roofed structure sheltered the living. An exposed summit platform held the dead.

Three people were offered to the gods: a young woman age fifteen, a six-year-old girl, and a seven-year-old boy. In the months before their deaths, they were well fed, plied with rich foods and chicha, and they had eaten again shortly before they died. The children were either suffocated or buried alive, as their lungs still held air. Their bodies were accompanied by miniature ceramic vessels, llama and human figurines made from gold, silver, *Spondylus*, and precious feathers. Their bodies were wrapped in fine textiles. The boy wore a fine red tunic, leather moccasins, and anklets of white fur. The maiden wore an elaborate headdress made of snow-white feathers. The younger girl wore a silver plaque pinned to her hair, metal that attracted a lightning bolt that struck and charred her body.

These offerings on Mt. Llullaillaco exemplify many aspects of the Inca Empire. The far-flung influence is indicated by these offerings more than 1,300 km (780 miles) from Cusco. The active connections and interventions between Nature and Humanity are exemplified by the sacrifices and offerings. The profound powers of religious and political authority are exemplified by these sites and the hundreds of other sites across the length and breadth of Tawantinsuyu. Finally, the bodies of the sacrificed children and the objects that accompanied them to their deaths on these frigid peaks underscore how the archaeological sites created by the Incas and other prehistoric South American societies still hold secrets to the unknown stories of the past (figure 11.29).

The End of Prehistory

There is no way to know what might have happened to the Incas had Europeans not arrived in the early 1500s. Francisco Pizarro's conquest of Peru was a continuation of a wave of invasion, enslavement, and genocide that began as soon as Europeans arrived in the New World. On October 12, 1492, the *first day* Columbus encountered Native Americans, he wrote: "They should be good servants and intelligent, for I observed that they quickly took in what was said to them, and I believe that they would easily be made Christians, as it appeared to me that they had no religion. I, our Lord being pleased, will take hence, at the time of my departure, six natives for your Highnesses that they may learn to speak."[90] Thus, Columbus believed that native peoples were without religion, suitable for enslavement, and mute. Such assumptions governed the Spanish conquest of the Americas.

The Spanish and Portuguese conquests of the Caribbean, Central America, and South America were very fast. A year after first seeing the New World, Columbus returned and founded the European settlement of Hispaniola (today the countries of Haiti and the Dominican Republic), displacing the Arawakan Tainos in the process (see chapter 10). Despite initial setbacks, the establishment of Santo Domingo in 1496 made Hispaniola the first springboard for colonialism. From Hispaniola, other islands in the Greater Antilles were conquered (Puerto Rico, 1508; Jamaica, 1509; Cuba, 1511), explorations were sent along the Venezuelan and Colombian coasts (1509), and the first Spanish settlement in South America was founded at Santa Maria la Antigua de Darien. Cuba became the home port for explorations of the Mexican coast and the conquest of the Aztecs by Cortes (1519–21). Vasco Núñez de Balboa's 1513 crossing of the Isthmus of Panama and "discovery" of the Pacific Ocean led to the founding of the city of Panama in 1519. Pizarro's explorations of western South America and conquests of the Inca Empire were launched from Panama.

As rapid as the European advance was, another foreign agent traveled even faster: smallpox and other introduced diseases. Smallpox, measles, plague, and other infections were endemic and widespread in Africa, Asia, and Europe but unknown in the Americas until European contact. Once the ocean routes between Europe and the Americas were well-known and voyages were relatively fast, epidemics spread rapidly throughout the Americas. The results were devastating. In 1492, Hispaniola had a native population of somewhere between 200,000 and 1.2 million; by 1509, only 62,000 natives remained.[91]

The epidemics were not limited to the Caribbean. Smallpox appeared in the northern Andes by 1525, perhaps transmitted by mindalaes who traveled between the Caribbean coasts of northern South America and the Andes. Deadly viruses contributed to the collapse of the Inca Empire. Some scholars suggest that as many as three separate pandemics surged through the Andes, killing thousands—including Huayna Capac and his designated successor.

Tawantinsuyu fractured in a civil war. Two rival armies emerged, a southern army led from Cusco by the newly crowned Huascar and a northern rebel army

Figure 11.29 Gold Inca figurine

led by Atahualpa, the governor of Quito. Although Huascar's armies held most of Tawantinsuyu, Atahualpa controlled a seasoned Inca army led by outstanding generals. Atahualpa's forces captured and executed Huascar, just as messengers from the coast reported the arrival of bearded white men.

Following a template of conquest successfully used in Mexico and elsewhere, Pizarro captured Atahualpa in Cajamarca in November 1532 and demanded an extensive ransom, much of it taken from the shrines at Pachacamac (see chapter 10). Pizarro executed the Inca king anyway. One account describes that Atahualpa was given a choice: he could remain a "pagan" and be burned at the stake or become a "Christian" and be garroted. Atahualpa chose Christianity, as this would mean his body would remain intact and his mummy could join those of the ancestors in the Qoricancha, but that was not to be.

The Spaniards marched south to Cusco, where the Inca armies under **Manco Inca Yupanqui** led a strong resistance before retreating to the Vilcabamba region. Inca armies fought back Spanish incursions there for four decades, finally surrendering in 1572.

Perhaps the Inca civil war would have erupted regardless of whether epidemics had occurred or regardless of the Spanish invasion. Perhaps Tawantinsuyu had grown too large to govern, or perhaps new institutional forms would have emerged that strengthened Cusco's hold. (It is worth recalling that some of the most violent and unstable years of the Roman Republic, in which rival Roman generals struggled for supremacy, resulted in greater consolidation and centralization of the Roman Empire, not its collapse.) There is simply no way to know.

What *is* known is that over the last centuries of prehistory, an impressive set of human achievements occurred in the Andes, accomplishments that were simultaneously political and religious, military and artistic, enduring and endlessly intriguing. That achievement was known as Tawantinsuyu.

Notes

1. Scholarship on the Incas is an international endeavor, and written sources exist in many languages. Given the enormity of this literature and the audience of this book, I have emphasized sources in English, although not exclusively. One of the most influential essays on the Incas was published in 1946 by the Andeanist John H. Rowe, "Inca Culture at the Time of the Spanish Conquest," in *Handbook of South American Indians*, ed. J. Steward (Washington, DC: Smithsonian Institution, 1946), 2: 183–330; an online version is available at http://www.lib.berkeley.edu/ANTH/emeritus/rowe/pub/rowe.pdf (accessed April 28, 2013). A number of outstanding book-length overviews deal with the Incas. A partial list includes B. Bauer, *The Development of the Inca State* (Austin: University of Texas Press, 1992); T. D'Altroy, *The Incas* (Malden, MA: Blackwell, 2002); G. McEwan, *The Incas: New Perspectives* (Santa Barbara, CA: ABC-CLIO, 2006); C. Morris and A. von Hagen, *The Incas: Lords of the Four Quarters* (New York: Thames and Hudson, 2011); M. Moseley, *The Incas and Their Ancestors: The Archaeology of Peru* (London: Thames and Hudson, 1997); T. Patterson, *The Inca Empire: The Formation and Disintegration of a Pre-capitalist State* (Oxford: Berg, 1991); A. von Hagen

and C. Morris, *The Cities of the Ancient Andes* (New York: Thames and Hudson, 1998). Finally, in a narrow sense, "Incas" only refers to the members of the four lineages in Cusco whose descendants founded Tawantinsuyu rather than to all the subjects of Tawantinsuyu; however, it is common practice in English to use the term *Incas* in a broader, more generic sense.

2. G. McEwan, *The Incas*, provides a succinct overview of population estimates on 93–96.

3. The essential starting point for research into the written historical sources about the Incas and other aspects of the post-contact Andes is the magisterial three-volume J. Pillsbury, ed., *Guide to Documentary Sources for Andean Studies, 1530–1900* (Norman: University of Oklahoma Press, 2008). Recent English translations of selected principal sources include Pablo José de Arriaga, *The Extirpation of Idolatry in Peru*, trans. and ed. L. C. Keating (Lexington: University of Kentucky Press, 1968 [1621]); J. de Betanzos, *Narrative of the Incas*, trans. and ed. R. Hamilton and D. Buchanan (Austin: University of Texas Press, 1996 [1557]); B. Cobo, *History of the Inca Empire*, trans. R. Hamilton (Austin: University of Texas Press, 1979 [1653]); B. Cobo, *Inca Religions and Customs*, trans. R. Hamilton (Austin: University of Texas Press, 1990 [1653]); S. de Gamboa, *The History of the Incas*, trans. and ed. B. Bauer and V. Smith (Austin: University of Texas Press, 2007 [1572]); C. de Molina, *Account of the Fables and Rites of the Incas*, trans. and ed. B. Bauer, V. Smith, and G. Cantarutti (Austin: University of Texas Press, 2011 [1576–76]); G. de la Vega, *Royal Commentaries of the Incas*, trans. H. V. Livermore (Austin: University of Texas Press, 1965 [1609]).

4. Gary Urton's lucid paraphrase draws on several sources, including Sarmiento de Gamboa; see G. Urton, *The History of a Myth: Paqariqtambo and the Origin of the Inkas* (Austin: University of Texas Press, 1990), 13–14.

5. This discussion is based on B. Bauer, *The Development of the Inca State* (Austin: University of Texas Press, 1992); B. Bauer and R. Covey, "Processes of State Formation in the Inca Heartland (Cusco, Peru)," *American Anthropologist* 104 (2002): 846–64; R. Covey, *How the Incas Built Their Heartland: State Formation and the Innovation of Imperial Strategies in the Sacred Valley, Peru* (Ann Arbor: University of Michigan Press, 2009). It is amazing that although scientific archaeology in the Cusco region occurred in the first half of the twentieth century, as indicated by J. Rowe, "An Introduction to the Archaeology of Cuzco," Papers of the Peabody Museum of American Archaeology and Ethology 27, no. 2 (1944), there were no systematic archaeological surveys in the region until 1982–2000.

6. Bauer, *Development of the Inca State*, 72–94.

7. B. Bauer, *Ancient Cuzco: Heartland of the Inca* (Austin: University of Texas Press, 2004), 15.

8. Bauer and Covey, "Processes of State Formation," 852; Covey, *How the Incas Built Their Heartland*, 123–25.

9. Bauer and Covey, "Processes of State Formation," 857–58.

10. For an important cautionary analysis of the term *Chanka* and its association with an ethnic group, see B. Bauer and L. Kellett, "Cultural Transformation of the Chanka Homeland (Andahuaylas, Peru) during the Late Intermediate Period (A.D. 1000–1400)," *Latin American Antiquity* 21, no. 1 (2010): 87–111.

11. Bauer and Covey, "Processes of State Formation," 849.

12. Ibid., 860.

13. Ibid.

14. Rowe, "Inca Culture at the Time of the Spanish Conquest," 203–9. Rowe based the dates on the 1586 account of Miguel Cabello Valboa, as in Valboa, "Inga Yupanqui Began to Reign Peacefully throughout the Year 1438," in *Miscelánea Antártica*, ed. I. Lerner (Madrid: Fundación Jose Manuel Lara, 2011), 406, my translation.

15. Bauer and Covey, "Processes of State Formation."

16. T. D'Altroy, A. Lorandi, V. Williams, M. Calderari, C. Hastorf, E. DeMarrais, and M. Hagstrum, "Inka Rule in the Northern Calchaquí Valley, Argentina," *Journal of Field Archaeology* 27, no. 1 (2000): 1–26. These dates (QL–4708 550 ± 30 cal, AD 1409–36; QL–4714 486 ± 30 cal, AD 1436–58; and QL–4709 453 ± 20 cal, AD 1447–78) appear earlier than expected when calibrated and reported at a single sigma (i.e., 68% confidence). The situation is less clear when the dates are calibrated at two sigmas (i.e., 95% confidence): cal AD 1399–1446, cal AD 1415 –86, and cal AD 1441–97. In a subsequently published discussion, D'Altroy, Williams, and Lorandi cite additional dates that might suggest "that the southern Andes may have first come under Inca rule in the first half of the fifteenth century, not midway through the second half"; T. D'Altroy, V. Williams, and A. Lorandi, "The Inkas in the Southlands," in *Variations in the Expression of Inka Power*, ed. R. Burger, C. Morris, and R. Matos (Washington, DC: Dumbarton Oaks, 2007), 93.

17. D. E. Ogburn, "Reconceiving the Chronology of Inca Imperial Expansion," *Radiocarbon* 54, no. 2 (2012): 219–37.

18. These issues are considered and discussed by Ogburn and by D'Altroy and colleagues.

19. A. Aveni, *Empires of Time: Calendars, Clocks, and Cultures* (New York: Basic Books, 1989), 164.

20. Bauer, *Ancient Cuzco: Heartland of the Inca*, 3. Other estimates are much higher; for example, C. Morris and A. von Hagen, in *The Incas* (New York: Thames and Hudson, 2007), 113, estimate a total population of around 100,000 in "greater Cusco," based on historical accounts.

21. Morris and von Hagen, *The Incas*, 104.

22. R. T. Zuidema, "The Inca Calendar, the Ceque System, and Their Representation in Exsul Immeritus" (2007), 80, at http://amsacta.unibo.it/2350/7/Cap2.pdf (accessed March 28, 2014).

23. The following discussion is based on J. Hyslop, *Inka Settlement Planning* (Austin: University of Texas Press, 1990); G. Gasparini and L. Margolies, *Inca Architecture*, trans. P. Lyon (Bloomington: Indiana University Press, 1980).

24. For example, see C. Costin and T. Earle, "Status Distinction and Legitimation of Power as Reflected in Changing Patterns of Consumption in Late Prehispanic Peru," *American Antiquity* 54, no. 4 (1989): 691–714; K. Wise, "Late Intermediate Period Architecture of Lukurmata," in *Domestic Architecture, Ethnicity, and Complementarity in the South-Central Andes*, ed. M. Aldenderfer (Iowa City: University of Iowa Press, 1993), 103–13. For an excellent overview, see D. Nash, "Household Archaeology in the Andes," *Journal of Archaeological Research* 17, no. 3 (2009): 205–61.

25. See, for example, M. Uhle, *Las ruinas de Tomebamba* (Quito: Editorial Sáenz Rebolledo, 1923); J. Idrovo, *Tomebamba: Arqueología e Historia de una Ciudad Imperial* (Quito: Banco Central de Ecuador, 2000). Trapezoidal niches and doorways are also present at the Inca provincial center of Cabeza de Vaca, department of Tumbes, Peru, located on the far northern terminus of the Inca coastal road.

26. There are a number of outstanding sources on Inca stonework and masonry architecture. Among them are J. P. Protzen and R. Batson, *Inca Architecture and Construction at Ollantaytambo* (New York: Oxford University Press, 1993); S. Nair, "Inca Architecture and the Conquest of the Countryside," in *Architecture–Design Methods–Inca Structures: Festschrift for Jean-Pierre Protzen*, ed. J. Dehlinger and H. Dehlinger (Kassel, Germany: Kassel University Press, 2009), 114–25; S. Niles, "Inca Architecture and Sacred Landscape," in *The Ancient Americas: Art from Sacred Landscapes*, ed. R. Townsend (Chicago: Art Institute of Chicago, 1992), 346–57; S. Niles, *The Shape of Inca History: Narrative and Architecture in an Andean Empire* (Iowa City: University of Iowa Press, 1999). In addition, two very different and intriguing considerations of Inca architecture and cultural landscapes are C. Dean, *A Culture of Stone: Inka Perspectives on Rock* (Durham, NC: Duke University Press, 2010); C. Pasternosto, *The Stone and the Thread: Andean Roots of Abstract Art*, trans. E. Allen (Austin: University of Texas Press, 1996).

27. Morris and von Hagen, *The Incas*, 124.

28. The quotes from Pizarro and Cieza de Leon are from Bauer 2007: 102–3, my translation.

29. J. Hemming, *Monuments of the Incas* (Boston: Little, Brown, 1982), 26; this book is illustrated with stunning photographs by Edward Ranney.

30. Betanzos, *Narrative of the Incas*, 16; Bauer, *Ancient Cuzco: Heartland of the Inca*, 157.

31. P. Pizarro (1921 [1571]), *Relation of the Discovery and Conquest of the Kingdoms of Peru* (no. 4), trans. P. Means. Kraus Reprint Co., 255.

32. Morris and von Hagen, *The Incas*, 120.

33. C. de Molina, "An Account of the Fables and Rites of the Yncas," in *Narratives of the Rites and Laws of the Yncas*, trans. and ed. C. Markham (New York: Burt Franklin, 1964 [ca. 1570–84]), 3–64; the account of the Situa ceremony is on 20–34.

34. Ibid., 26.

35. Ibid., 32.

36. Ibid., 34.

37. D. Menzel, "The Inca Occupation of the South Coast of Peru," *Southwestern Journal of Anthropology* 15, no. 2 (1959): 125–42.

38. Ibid., 140.

39. C. Morris and J. Santillana, "The Inka Transformation of the Chincha Capital," in *Variations in the Expression of Inka Power*, ed. R. Burger, C. Morris, and R. Matos Mendieta (Washington, DC: Dumbarton Oaks, 2007), 135–36.

40. Ibid., 157–58.

41. This research project was directed by Timothy Earle, Terence D'Altroy, Christine Hastorf, and Cathy Scott, beginning in 1977 and continuing over several field seasons until 1986, when violence and political instability associated with the Shining

Path guerilla movement made fieldwork impossible. A number of scholars participated in this research, and numerous publications resulted. A sample includes C. Costin, "From Chiefdom to Empire State: Ceramic Economy among the Prehispanic Wanka of Highland Peru" (PhD diss., University of California, University Microfilms, Ann Arbor, 1986); C. Costin, T. Earle, B. Owen, and G. Russell, "Impact of Inka Conquest on Local Technology in the Upper Mantaro Valley, Peru," in *What's New: A Closer Look at the Process of Innovation*, ed. S. E. van der Leeuw and R. Torrence (London: Unwin and Allen, 1989), 107–39; C. Costin and M. Hagstrum, "Standardization, Labor Investment, Skill, and the Organization of Ceramic Production in Late Prehispanic Highland Peru," *American Antiquity* (1995): 619–39; T. D'Altroy, "Empire Growth and Consolidation: The Xauxa Region of Peru under the Incas" (PhD diss., University of California, University Microfilms, Ann Arbor, 1981); T. D'Altroy, "Transitions in Power: Centralization of Wanka Political Organization under Inka Rule," *Ethnohistory* 34 (1987): 78–103; T. D'Altroy, *Provincial Power in the Inka Empire* (Washington, DC: Smithsonian Institution, 1992); T. D'Altroy and T. Earle, "Staple Finance, Wealth Finance, and Storage in the Inka Political Economy," *Current Anthropology* 25 (1985): 187–206; T. D'Altroy, C. Hastorf, and associates, *Empire and domestic economy* (New York: Kluwer/Plenum, 2001); C. A. Hastorf and S. Johannessen, "Pre-Hispanic Political Change and the Role of Maize in the Central Andes of Peru," *American Anthropologist* 95, no. 1 (1993): 115–38.

42. D'Altroy, *Provincial Power in the Inka Empire*, 47.

43. Original quote in ibid., 236n14, my translation.

44. C. Costin and T. Earle, "Status Distinction and Legitimation of Power as Reflected in Changing Patterns of Consumption in Late Prehispanic Peru," *American Antiquity* 54, no. 4 (1989): 691–714.

45. T. D'Altroy and T. Earle, "Staple Finance, Wealth Finance, and Storage in the Inka Political Economy," *Current Anthropology* 26, no. 2 (1985): 188.

46. Hyslop, *Inka Settlement Planning*, 297C; Morris and D. Thompson, "Huanuco Viejo: An Inca Administrative Center," *American Antiquity* 35, no. 3 (1970): 344–62.

47. There is a large literature on this Andean practice, which continues in use in rural communities. The same term was applied to the Colonial labor tax that forced Indians to labor in the mines of Potosi; a classic study of the Colonial system is J. Cole, *The Potosi Mita, 1573–1700: Compulsory Indian Labor in the Andes* (Palo Alto: Stanford University Press, 1985).

48. C. Julien, "How Inca Decimal Administration Worked," *Ethnohistory* 35, no. 3 (1988): 267.

49. B. Bauer and C. Stanish, *Ritual and Pilgrimage in the Ancient Andes: The Islands of the Sun and Moon* (Austin: University of Texas Press, 2001); C. Stanish, "Nonmarket Imperialism in the Prehispanic Americas: The Inka Occupation of the Titicaca Basin," *Latin American Antiquity* 8, no. 3 (1997): 195–216.

50. D. Ogburn, "Evidence for Long-Distance Transportation of Building Stones in the Inka Empire, from Cuzco, Peru to Saraguro, Ecuador," *Latin American Antiquity* 15, no. 4 (2004): 432.

51. Quoted in D. Ogburn, "Power in Stone: The Long-Distance Movement of Building Blocks in the Inca Empire," *Ethnohistory* 51, no. 1 (2004), 114–15.

52. J. Hyslop, "Las fronteras estateles extremas de Tawantinsuyo," in *La frontera del estado inca*, ed. T. Dillehay and P. Netherly (Quito: Fundación Alexander von Humboldt / Ediciones Abya-Yala, 1998), 33.

53. R. Lippi and A. Gudiño, "Inkas and Yumbos in Palmitopamba in Northwestern Ecuador," in *Distant Provinces in the Inka Empire: Toward a Deeper Understanding of Inka Imperialism*, ed. M. Malpass and S. Alconini (Iowa City: University of Iowa Press, 2010), 260–78.

54. S. Connell, C. Gifford, A. González, and M. Carpenter, "Hard Times in Ecuador: Inka Troubles at Pambamarca," Antiquity Project Gallery, *Antiquity Journal* 338 (2003). Regarding "other Cuzcos," see L. Coben, "Other Cuzcos: Replicated Theaters of Inka Power," in *Archaeology of Performance: Theaters of Power, Community, and Politics*, ed. T. Inomata and L. Coben (New York: Altamira, 2006), 223–59.

55. J. Hyslop, *The Inka Road System* (Orlando: Academic Press, 1984), 21. See also T. Bray, "The Effects of Inka Imperialism on the Northern Frontier" (PhD diss., SUNY-Binghamton, 1991); T. Bray, "The Panzaleo Puzzle: Non-Local Pottery in Northern Highland Ecuador," *Journal of Field Archaeology* 22, no. 2 (1995): 137–48; T. Bray, "Late Pre-Hispanic Chiefdoms of Highland Ecuador," in *Handbook of South American Archaeology*, ed. H. Silverman and W. Isbell (New York: Springer, 2008), 527–43.

56. K. Stothert, "The Peoples of the Coast of Ecuador Accommodate the Inca State," *Ñawpa Pacha* 33, no. 1 (2013): 71–102.

57. C. Astahuaman, "Inka Settlements in the Sierra de Piura, Northern Peru" (PhD diss., University College London, 2008); A. Hocquenhem, "Los Españoles en los Caminos del Extremo Norte del Perú en 1532," *Bulletin de L'Institut Francais d'Etudes Andines* 23, no. 1 (1994): 1–67; J. Murra, "The Historic Tribes of Ecuador," in *Handbook of South American Indians*, ed. J. Steward, Bulletin of American Ethnology 143, no. 2 (1948): 785–822; C. Vilchez, *Diseño Arquitectónico y Secuencia Constructiva de la Huaca Cabeza de Vaca: Valle de Tumbes*, Proyecto de Investigación para Optar el Título de Licenciado en Arqueología (Universidad Nacional de Trujillo, Trujillo, 1999); C. Vilchez, *Camino Inka de la Costa–Tramo Tumbes,* Proyecto Qhapaqñan del INC-Lima (2003); C. Vilchez, *Informe Final, Proyecto de Investigación Arqueológica Cabeza de Vaca, Temporada 2009*, Programa Qhapaq Ñan, INC-Lima (2010).

58. Hyslop, "Las fronteras estateles extremas de Tawantinsuyo," 35.

59. P. Lyon, "An Imaginary Frontier: Prehistoric Highland-Lowland Interchange in the Southern Peruvian Andes," in *Networks of the Past: Regional Interaction in Archaeology*, ed. P. Francis, F. Kense, and P. Duke (Proceedings of the Twelfth Annual Conference, Archaeological Association of the University of Calgary, Alberta, 1981), 3–18.

60. F. Salomon, "A North Andean Status Trader Complex under Inka Rule," *Ethnohistory* 34, no. 1 (1987): 63–77; F. Salomon, *Native Lords of Quito in the Age of the Incas* (Cambridge: Cambridge University Press, 1986), 97–115.

61. M. Reeve, "Regional Interaction in the Western Amazon: The Early Colonial Encounter and the Jesuit Years: 1538–1767," *Ethnohistory* 41, no. 1 (1994): 106–38.

62. W. Church and A. von Hagan, "Chachapoyas: Cultural Development in an Andean Cloud Forest Crossroads," in *Handbook of South American Archaeology*, ed. H. Silverman and W. Isbell (New York: Springer, 2008), 903–26.

63. I. Schjellerup, "Reflexiones sobre los Chachapoya en el Chinchaysuyu," *Boletín de Arqueología PUCP* 67 (2002): 52, my translation.

64. A. Ruiz Estrada, "Purumllacta: un centro administrativo incaico en Chachapoyas," *Inestigaciones Sociales* 8, no. 13 (Lima: Universidad Nacional Mayor de San Marcos, 2004): 73–84.

65. F. Acuto, "Living under the Imperial Thumb in the Northern Calchaquí Valley, Argentina," in *Distant Provinces in the Inka Empire: Toward a Deeper Understanding of Inka Imperialism*, ed. M. Malpass and S. Alconini (Iowa City: University of Iowa Press, 2010), 123.

66. Ibid., 121.

67. F. Acuto, "Experiencing Inca Domination in Northwestern Argentina and the Southern Andes," in *Handbook of South American Archaeology*, ed. H. Silverman and W. Isbell (New York: Springer, 2008), 852.

68. The site is also known as Cerro del Inga. The following discussion is based on J. Rossen, M. Planella, and R. Stehberg, "Archaeobotany of Cerro del Inga, Chile, at the Southern Inka Frontier," in *Distant Provinces in the Inka Empire: Toward a Deeper Understanding of Inka Imperialism*, ed. M. Malpass and S. Alconini (Iowa City: University of Iowa Press, 2010), 14–43; M. Planella and R. Stehberg, "Etnohistoria y arqueología en el estudio de la fortaleza indígena de Cerro Grande de la Compañía," *Chungará: Revista de Antropología Chilena* 26 (1994): 65–78.

69. Rossen et al., "Archaeobotany of Cerro del Inga," 21.

70. Ibid., 42.

71. For an introduction to khipus and their study, see Harvard University's Khipu Database Project, directed by G. Urton, at http://khipukamayuq.fas.harvard.edu/. Other sources include M. Ascher and R. Ascher, *Mathematics of the Incas: Code of the Quipu* (Mineola, NY: Courier Dover, 1997); J. Quilter and G. Urton, eds., *Narrative Threads: Accounting and Recounting in Andean Khipu* (Austin: University of Texas Press, 2002); G. Urton, *Signs of the Inka Khipu: Binary Coding in the Andean Knotted-String Records* (Austin: University of Texas Press, 2003). For ethnographic accounts of recent khipu use in the Andes, see C. Mackey, "Knot records in ancient and modern Peru" (PhD diss., University of California at Berkeley, 1970); F. Salomon, *The Cord Keepers: Khipus and Cultural Life in a Peruvian Village* (Durham, NC: Duke University Press, 2004).

72. R. T. Zuidema, "Bureaucracy and Systematic Knowledge in Andean Civilization," in *The Inca and Aztec States, 1400–1800*, ed. G. Collier, R. Rosaldo, and J. Wirth (New York: Academic Press, 1982), 419–58; R. T. Zuidema, "A Quipu Calendar from Ica, Peru, with a Comparison to the Ceque Calendar from Cuzco," in *World Archaeoastronomy*, ed. A. F. Aveni (Cambridge: Cambridge University Press, 1989), 341–51.

73. G. Urton, "From Knots to Narratives: Reconstructing the Art of Historical Record Keeping in the Andes from Spanish Transcriptions of Inka Khipus," *Ethnohistory* 45, no. 3 (1998): 409–38; see also J. Murra, "Las etno-categorias de un khipu estatal," in *Formaciones económicas y politicas del mundo andino* (Lima: Instituto de Estudios Peruanos, 1975 [1973]), 244–54.

74. There have been numerous commentaries on this image. An early English translation is J. Santa Cruz Yupanqui, "An account of the antiquities of Peru," in *Rites*

and Narratives of the Incas, trans. and ed. C. Markham (London: Hakylut Society, n.d.), 65–120. An excellent commentary and bibliographic overview is P. Duviols, "Pachacuti Yamqu Salcamaygua, Joan de Santa Cruz (seventeenth century)," in *Guide to Documentary Sources for Andean Studies, 1530–1900*, ed. J. Pillsbury (Norman: University of Oklahoma Press, 2008), 3: 488–96. I also drew on the excellent essay by Rita Fink (2001), "La cosmología en el dibujo del altar del Quri Kancha según don Joan de Santa Cruz Pachacuti Yamqui Salca Maygu," *Revista Histórica* [Universidad Católica del Perú] 25, no. 1: 9–75.

75. F. Salomon, "Introductory Essay: The Huarochiri Manuscript," in *The Huarochiri Manuscript: A Testament of Ancient and Colonial Andean Religions* (Austin: University of Texas Press, 1991), 1.

76. Ibid., 4.

77. Betanzos, *Narrative of the Incas*, 68.

78. R. Zuidema, "Catachillay: The Role of the Pleiades and of the Southern Cross and α and β Centauri in the Calendar of the Incas," *Annals of the New York Academy of Sciences* 385 (1982): 203–29.

79. G. Urton, "Animals and Astronomy in the Quechua Universe," *Proceedings of the American Philosophical Society* 125, no. 2 (1981): 110–27.

80. B. Orlove, J. Chiang, and M. Cane, "Forecasting Andean Rainfall and Crop Yield from the Influence of El Niño on Pleiades Visibility," *Nature* 403 (January 6, 2000): 68–71.

81. Salomon, "Introductory Essay," 16; see also T. Bray, "An Archaeological Perspective on the Andean Concept of Camaquen: Thinking through Late Pre-Columbian Ofrendas and Huacas," *Cambridge Archaeological Journal* 19, no. 3 (2009): 357–66.

82. B. Cobo, *Inca Religion and Customs*, trans. and ed. R. Hamilton (Austin: University of Texas Press, 1990 [1653]), 117.

83. Arriaga, *Extirpation of Idolatry in Peru*, 174, my translation.

84. J. Polo de Ondegardo, *Informaciones a cerca de la religión y gobierno de los incas* (Lima: Imprenta y Libreria Sanmarti, 1916 [1554]), 39, my translation.

85. R. T. Zuidema, "Shafttombs and the Inca Empire," *Journal of the Steward Anthropological Society* 9, no. 1–2 (1978): 134.

86. Betanzos, *Narrative of the Incas*, 132.

87. J. Rheinhard and C. Ceruti, *Inca Rituals and Sacred Mountains: A Study of the World's Highest Archaeological Sites* (Los Angeles: Cotsen Institute of Archaeology, 2010), xi.

88. Ibid., 23.

89. Ibid., 121.

90. *The Journal of Christopher Columbus (during His First Voyage, 1492–93) and Documents Relating to the Voyages of John Cabot and Caspar Corte Real*, ed. C. Markham (London: Hakluyt Society, 1893), 38, at https://archive.org/stream/journalchristop-01markgoog#page/n10/mode/2up (accessed March 30, 2014).

91. For a brief overview of the population collapse in Hispaniola, see N. Cook, "Sickness, Starvation, and Death in Early Hispaniola," *Journal of Interdisciplinary History* 32, no. 3 (2002): 349–86.

Figure 12.1 A 1575 map of South America

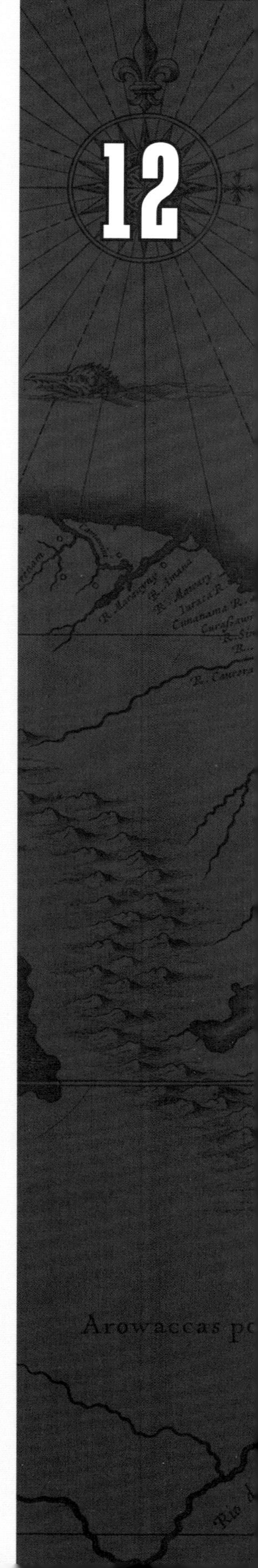

After Prehistory

10.5876_9781607323334.c012

> The empire of Guiana is directly east from Peru towards the sea, and lieth under the equinoctial line; and it hath more abundance of gold than any part of Peru, and as many or more great cities than ever Peru had when it flourished most.
>
> . . . And I have been assured by such of the Spaniards as have seen Manoa, the imperial city of Guiana, which the Spaniards call El Dorado, that for the greatness, for the riches, and for the excellent seat, it far exceedeth any of the world.
>
> *Sir Walter Raleigh, 1596,* The Discovery of Guiana

Within a decade of Columbus's voyages to the Indies, Europe's attempt to understand the native people of South America began, an effort deeply entangled with the goals of conquest, subjugation, and domination. It was neither a dispassionate intellectual quest nor a particularly well-informed one. The 1494 papal edict, **The Treaty of Tordesillas**, established a line between Spanish and Portuguese colonial interests, one that ceded eastern South America and Africa to Portugal and much of the Americas to Spain. The expansion of Spain and Portugal into South America, tentatively begun with Columbus's third voyage in 1498, increased in tempo in 1510 as **Vasco Nunez de Balboa** established the first Spanish settlement on the South American mainland at Santa Maria de la Darien, a colony that succumbed to Indian raids and tropical fevers and was abandoned by 1524. In 1513 Balboa crossed the Isthmus of Panama and "discovered" the South Sea (Pacific Ocean), and the city of Panama was established. In 1519, the Portuguese navigator **Ferdinand Magellan**, exploring for the King of Spain, sailed along the southern Atlantic Coast of South America, through the straits that bear his name in Tierra del Fuego and into the Pacific Ocean. The pace of Spanish exploration quickened. Subsequent explorations were launched from Panama, including the several voyages led by **Francisco Pizarro** that ultimately led to the conquest of the Inca Empire in 1532–35 and the establishment of Spanish control of the Andes.

The European encounter with the native peoples of South America was not an encounter between the "Other" and the "Modern." Rather, it was a complex confrontation between remarkably diverse indigenous societies and a medieval European worldview—partly shaped by Catholicism, the encounter with Islam, and the *reconquista* of the Iberian peninsula and influenced by the accounts of distant peoples derived from classical sources (figure 12.2).

Many explorers were "adventure capitalists," treasure-hunting entrepreneurs who raised funds for ships, soldiers, weapons, and horses and obtained

Figure 12.2 (*overleaf*) Ruins of the Catedral de São Miguel Arcanjo das Missões, Brazil

royal permissions to conquer, with the personal objective of gaining great wealth. With only limited knowledge of the lands and peoples they hoped to rule, these explorers credulously grasped the legends describing the great wealth of South America's native kingdoms.

And the greatest of these was **the legend of El Dorado** (figure 12.3). Few legends have been so seductive.

Neil Whitehead described the legend:

> In essence the European El Dorado myth refers to the existence of a "Golden One"—that is a "king" or "high chief"—who once a year was anointed by the sprinkling of gold dust onto his body. He was then paddled to the centre of a vast lake where he would deposit votive offerings of gold work. A further subsidiary element in this tale concerns the names of this lake—variously given as Paytiti, Parime, or Rupununi—and the great and golden city which stood on its edge called Manoa. This city was held to lie in an upland area, perhaps recalling locations such as Tenochtitlan and Cuzco, and so it was that, in the high sierras of the upper Amazon, Colombia, Venezuela and Guyana, the El Dorado legend came successively to rest.[1]

The legend of El Dorado was the most powerful of the myths of conquest, more enticing than the nation of the Amazons or the existence of the Kingdom of Cinnamon. Yet, the actual achievements of native peoples of South America were, if anything, more spectacular and awe-inspiring than any of these legends claimed—as the previous chapters in *A Prehistory of South America* have shown.

Prehistory, History, and Archaeology in the Post-Columbian World

In a narrow but important sense, South America's prehistory ended with the arrival of written words.[2] As historical documents, administrative records, and travelers' accounts accumulated, the burden of evidence shifted from the material traces of the past to the notations in ink on parchment and paper. The shift to a historical record was not abrupt, synchronous, nor impermeable. The earliest writings describing the Caribbean and the Atlantic Coast of South America were written between 1492 and 1510, but some native societies living in inland regions largely were undocumented for another 400 years. One of the earliest accounts of Amazonian societies is by **Friar Gaspar de Carvajal**, who accompanied the remarkable and miserable expedition down the Rio Napo and then on down the length of the Amazon in 1540–42, but other Amazonian societies living away from major navigable rivers were not written about until nineteenth and twentieth centuries.[3] And if, for example, aspects of indigenous society and culture were mentioned by early explorers—such as Charles Darwin's shocked descriptions of the Fuegians in 1830, more nuanced and detailed writings about Yamaná ritual, cosmology, and life would not appear for another century or more, with the writings of the Jesuit ethnographer Martin Gusinde and the Franco-American anthropologist Anne Chapman.

Well into the eighteenth century, historical accounts principally were written by men from Spain and Portugal, as the epigraphs that open each of the chap-

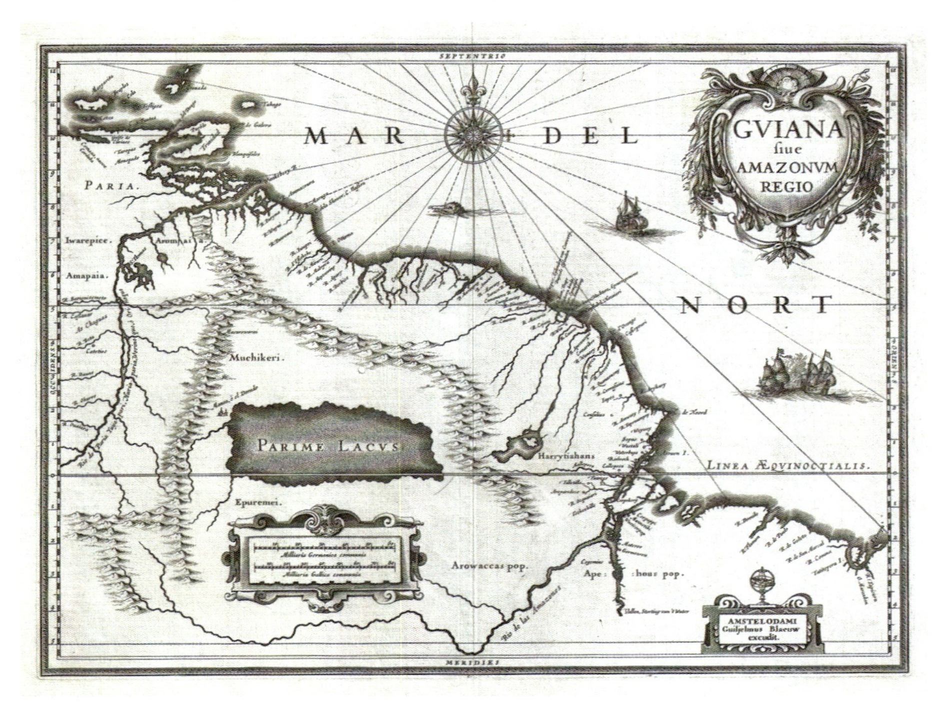

Figure 12.3 1635 map of northeastern South America showing the location of "Manoa o El Dorado" on the northwestern shore of Lake Parime

ters in this book suggest.[4] Given the limited literacy—not even the conquistador Francisco Pizarro could sign his name, leaving a mark instead—many accounts were written by clerics, notaries, and scribes, whose documents were motivated by conquest, conversion, or the Inquisition.[5]

Even writings that took a less aggressive stance against native societies were mediated by the acts of translating language and culture. For example, **Juan Diez de Betanzos** (? – d. 1576) wrote his *Suma y Narración de los Incas* within twenty-five years of the Spanish conquest. Betanzos, a leading translator of Quechua, had the additional advantage of having as a source of information his wife, Cuxirimay Ocllo, an Inca noblewoman who had been Atahualpa's primary wife and later Francisco Pizarro's mistress. Nonetheless, the *Suma y Narración de los Incas*, as Bruce Mannheim writes, "were themselves the very stuff of political contention, both among the Inca elites before the European invasion and among their colonial descendants. These accounts were necessarily partisan, reflecting both earlier contention for power and legitimacy and later claims to fiscal privileges and lands."[6] In a similar way, the great volume *Nueva Corónica y Buen Gobierno*, 1,190 pages of text and drawings sent to the King of Spain by the Spanish-literate Andean mestizo **Felipe Guaman Poma de Ayala** (b. ca. 1535–50, d. 1616), contained a wealth of detailed information about traditional Andean life but was motivated by political and personal objectives.

Therefore, the appearance of the written record in South America did not eliminate the importance of knowledge gained through archaeology. Rather, archaeology may serve as a counterpoint to the ways we understand the past.[7] The archaeologist **Charles Orser Jr.** has defined three overlapping emphases of archaeology as it intersects with post-contact cultures. Since the 1930s, **historical archaeology** has tended to encompass "two related, but actually distinctive, ways: methodologically—as the combination of excavated and textual information—and as archaeology that is exclusively focused on post-Columbian history."[8] In South America, this involves either (a) archaeology that uses Spanish and Portuguese documents as sources for the interpretation of late prehistoric or contact period indigenous sites or (b) the archaeology of post-contact sites, whether their occupants were Europeans, indigenous peoples, Africans, or others. A second emphasis, Orser suggests, is **global historical archaeology**, which is designed to draw attention to "the many inter- and intra-territorial and trans-cultural connections that had extended through time and across space after about [AD] 1500 or so."[9] This approach emphasizes the interconnections among different regions, peoples, and societies as empire and capitalism linked people into global systems of commerce, politics, religion, language, and worldviews. Again, archaeology can illuminate these interconnections in ways distinct from the historical record. Finally, Orser discusses the related emphasis of **modern-world archaeology**, referencing "a post-Columbian archaeology that openly searches for global connections."[10]

Ross Jamieson has written that initial forays into historical archaeology were the accidental by-products of archaeological investigations principally focused on pre-contact materials that unintentionally encountered Colonial period burials, artifacts, or features.[11] However, beginning in the 1970s more focused excavations on historical sites were increasingly common as efforts to document cultural patrimony became central elements in research projects dealing with the post-Colonial world.

For example, archaeological investigations directed by **Prudence Rice**, **Gregory Smith**, **Susan de France**, and **Mary Van Buren** in the Moquegua Valley on the southern coast of Peru examined changing settlement patterns imposed on native communities as Colonial policies shifted from grants of labor (*encomiendas*) to the forced resettlement and concentration of people in towns and villages (*reducciones*).[12] Such policies were accompanied by new forms of urban design as Spaniards moved native communities into settlements that were laid out on a grid (figure 12.4).

With its central plaza flanked by church, governmental buildings (*alcaldía*), and the homes of Colonial elites, the gridded Spanish town plan was "a visual manifestation of the divine order of Augustine's City of God," the art historian **Tom Cummins** has observed, with the central plazas surrounded by "places of the secular and religious power of the colonial order."[13] Other archaeological evidence of post-Colonial realities in Moquegua include the presence of ceramics imported from Panama and Spain, the manufacture of large jars for holding olive oil and wine, and the introduction of new domesticates such as chickens, pigs, and grapes—all indicated by the material record in historic archaeological sites (figure 12.5).

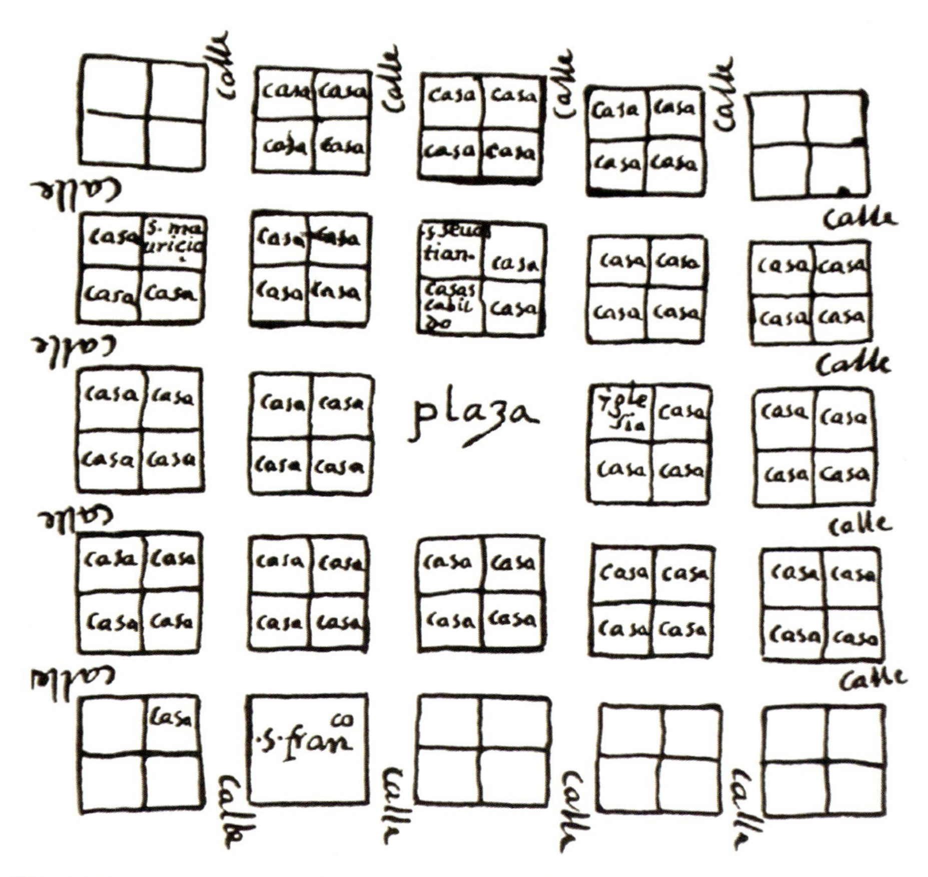

Figure 12.4 First map of Caracas, Venezuela, in 1578, showing grid town plan

The post-contact materialization of Christianity has been studied by **Steven Wernke** in the southern Peruvian highlands, in the province of Collagua in the Department of Arequipa.[14] With rich agricultural lands in the Colca Valley and expansive altiplano grazing lands for llamas, Collagua was a rich and populous zone under the Inca Empire. Extensive agricultural terraces were built between AD 500 and 1000, and the Inca Empire expropriated the region and its people between AD 1450 and 1532, imposing its own modes of settlement, architecture, and political order, including the consolidation of regional centers. Christian conversion began with the arrival of Franciscan friars in 1540. The Franciscans' first step was the exorcism of place, planting crosses on mountain peaks and sacking huacas of idols and ancestral mummies. Crowds of local people were baptized, often without significant instruction in Christian doctrine. Rustic chapels were built in each of the four major settlements that had been established by the Inca Empire. Catholic priests expropriated significant places, Wernke writes, as "the friars intentionally associated their space of conversion with the former space of Inka state integration."[15] These early conversions occurred in the open plazas that previously

Figure 12.5 Colonial wine and olive oil jars from southern Peru

held Inca rituals and processions; the Franciscans, Wernke argues, intentionally drew on those associations. Rather than being simply a matter of one-sided imposition, initially "colonial and indigenous actors created new hybrid social fields and spaces that were the creation of both but not controlled entirely by either."[16] Although these negotiated interactions would be replaced in 1570, when Indian communities were forced into *reducciones* and open plazas were replaced by the interior spaces of more formal chapels, the initial contacts between Franciscans and Andeans were marked by more subtle interactions, which ironically are indicated by the archaeological record and unrecorded in the triumphant historical accounts written by Franciscans.

The evolution of the city of **Buenos Aires**, on the other side of the continent, has been studied by a number of archeologists, most prominently by Argentine archaeologist **Daniel Schávelzon** (figure 12.6).[17]

Covering 3,680 km^2 (1,420 mi^2) and with a population of around 3 million people surrounded by a metropolitan area of approximately 14 million inhabitants, Buenos Aires is a city with a history that has both surface and subterranean domains. Schávelzon explains:

> The city of Buenos Aires is known to the majority of its inhabitants, as in any other city, as being everything that is above the earth: its architecture, its streets, its citizens, the visible traits of lives public and private, and all that occurs daily: love, hate, work, pleasure, feelings, culture, life and death. And logically this includes its patrimony, in all its forms and expressions. To a great extent, life occurs above the earth, which is to say "history." Although this part of life may appear complex, underneath the earth another domain of life also occurs, much about the death of persons and objects—the "discards" we call them—which we usually overlook. . . .

Figure 12.6 Satellite image showing modern Buenos Aires, Argentina, on the right bank of the Rio de la Plata

> A slightly different vista is one that looks at the level of the earth and below it, with the intent of understanding the nature of soil and subsoil, an archaeological interpretation that does not overlook their nature, and that allows us to comprehend the present as a historical act. . . . Buenos Aires is—and in this it is different from many other cities—an enormous, gigantic cultural construction in which humans and nature have come together at a scale like only a few other places in the world.[18]

In his book *The Historical Archaeology of Buenos Aires: A City at the End of the World*, Schávelzon details the historical trajectory of the city, beginning in 1580 as an ephemeral and tenuous Spanish settlement clinging to the Atlantic Coast. As its erstwhile conquistadores were wracked by indolence, incompetence, and starvation, Buenos Aires was dwarfed in significance by Asunción (today the capital of Paraguay), which was founded inland on the Rio de la Plata and nearer the anticipated riches of the Andes. Buenos Aires held on as a small Spanish colonial town, although never achieving the size or glories of Lima, Cartagena, or Potosí. In an area without permanent native settlements, the early European inhabitants of Buenos Aires divided the city into square blocks 140 *varas* (approximately 115 m [377 ft]) on a side, established a fortress on a nearby hill and a plaza near the river, and constructed modest churches and marketplaces around the plaza. Each city block was divided into four square lots, and the principal Spaniard residents (men known as *vecinos*) received two lots.[19]

The archaeological record for these initial centuries shows that early residents' houses were built from wattle and daub walls with log posts supporting a straw-thatched roof, eventually replaced with tapia walls and tiled roofs. The houses had two to three long rooms and were roomy but modest with little difference between the residences of rich and poor.

The archaeological and historical records of early Buenos Aires suggest a city and community focused on Europe rather than on South America. A trash pit dated to 1630–1640 contained a majority of objects manufactured in Europe—an English knife, Spanish pottery, fragments of imported glass—and only a small percentage of native or mestizo ceramics. Schávelzon writes that within the center of Buenos Aires "family tableware would include 88% of objects brought from Europe."[20] In 1619, a settlement of 200 vecinos included mostly Spaniards, with only forty-two Portuguese, two Flemish, and a Florentine and a Greek. This European and Eurocentric core was surrounded, in essence, by concentric bands of interaction, with the European giving way to the indigenous. As new towns were established in the interior of Argentina, lands were taken from their native inhabitants, and yet Buenos Aires remained focused across the Atlantic. The city only boomed in the late nineteenth century, as European immigrants swelled the city's populations and transformed the city into "the Paris of the South."

Even after 1800, when the historical documents from Buenos Aires are more abundant, archaeology uncovers new elements of this South American city. Although written documents and oral histories classify the residents as "whites," "blacks," and "Indians," the reality was more complex. By the late nineteenth century, Schávelzon observes, "Europe was represented by Spaniards, Portuguese, Italians, Walloons, Flemish, Irish, and Germans among others; by Jewish immigrants from faraway places in central Europe who left their home lands through Spain; and finally by the criollos or whites born" in South America. "Consequently there never was such a thing as an ethnically homogenous population, although, actually, it was mostly white."[21] Yet, the archaeological record of historic Buenos Aires indicates that "the city, even though it could cast the image of being European-like, white and Catholic, was instead multicultural, multinational, pluriethnic, and, above all, marginal. It was the *ciudad del fin del mundo*, the city at the end of the world, one that stubbornly refused to accept its reality."[22]

Archaeologies of Resistance

The European invasions of South America triggered a complex series of consequences with global impacts. A wide array of species—humans, plants, animals, viruses, and bacteria—were transferred between Europe, Africa, Asia, and the Americas, and to islands around the globe.[23] New systems of political and economic order were imposed across South America with varying degrees of success. One of the most fundamental changes was **the creation of the trans-Atlantic slave trade**, as workers were forced to toil in mines and on ranches and plantations for Spanish, Dutch, English, French, and Portuguese overseers. Initial efforts to enslave native South Americans were undermined by the demographic collapse of indigenous populations from introduced diseases such as smallpox, influenza, and the plague. Theological debates, such as the 1550 debate between Dominican friar

Bartolome de las Casas and theologian **Juan Ginés de Sepulveda** in Valladolid, led the Spanish Crown to determine that Indians could be exploited but not enslaved. This theological nicety did not apply to Africans.

The trans-Atlantic slave trade was initiated by Christopher Columbus on his 1493–94 second voyage, when he loaded 500 Indians on his ships to export to Spain. Two hundred natives died as the ships approached Spain, and their bodies were cast into the sea.[24] Rather quickly the flow of humans was reversed, as Africans were captured and sold largely in African zones claimed by Portugal and then shipped to the Americas. Although there are debates about the volume of the African slave trade between 1500 and 1830, the evidence suggests that more than 9.5 million people were transported across the Atlantic Ocean. Nearly half of them, approximately 4.7 million people, were taken to South America. Of those, approximately 85 percent to 90 percent of slaves were taken to Brazil.[25]

The plantation economies based on the enslavement of Africans left behind an extensive archaeological record.[26] For example, in the **Mato Grosso** region of western Brazil, the discovery of gold in 1719 led to the establishment of communities, including the regional capital of Cuiabá.[27] Slaves worked the mines, but in less than a century the gold mines were exhausted. The discovery of diamonds in the early 1800s did not resuscitate the mining economy. As mining collapsed, local plantations increased. Slaves were sold to cattle ranches and plantations. The ranches and plantations produced beef, sugar, and *cachaça* (a distilled liquor made from fresh sugarcane juice) for the inhabitants of Cuiabá and the surrounding region. As in the mines, the hard work in the cane fields, ranchos, and *engenhos* (sugar mills) was done by slaves from Africa or of African descent.

The men and women enslaved in Mato Grosso came from different parts of Africa, off-loaded in Brazil via either the northern port of Rio de Janeiro or the southern coastal city of Salvador. Most of the slaves transported to Rio de Janeiro were originally from Central Africa; those passing through Salvador were from West Africa. They were members of tremendously varied nations, speaking distinct languages—the Central African Bantu languages of Kikongo, Umbundu, and Ovimbundu and the West African Yoruba and Gbe languages such as Ewe, Fon, and Allada—and including both Muslim and non-Muslim groups. In short, the category of "slave" was a complex, varied mix of ethnicities united only in their loss of freedom.

Historical archaeologists working at sites associated with slave communities initially expected to see aspects of "African" culture reflected in the archaeological record. This has proven a somewhat naïve expectation, given the complexities of slavery and Brazilian plantation society. This does not mean that no elements of African cultures were sustained in the Americas. For example, in the late 1600s or early 1700s an adult male buried in a plantation cemetery in the British colony of Barbados was interred with a number of artifacts of African origins: a tobacco pipe of African manufacture; a necklace of cowry shells, fish vertebrates, and dog teeth; and a distinctive ceramic bead from India. The artifacts indicate that the man was a traditional healer or diviner, his status respected and recognized by his fellows.[28]

But the overwhelming pattern was more complex than simple retention of cultural practices, as Africans interacted and created new identities within plantation societies in the Americas (figure 12.7).

The archaeologists **Marcos André Torres de Souza** and **Luís Cláudio Pereira Symanski** have described the historical archaeology of several plantations and associated settlements in the county of **Chapada dos Guimarães**, located in western Brazil. Their excavations focused on different portions of the plantation: the plantation owner's house, the overseer's house, slaves' houses and barracks, and the villages of runaway slaves. Torres de Souza and Pereira Symanski have analyzed the pottery associated with the different settlements in Chapada dos Guimarães, and the results are intriguingly complex. First, there were few differences between plantation houses and the houses of slaves in the forms of ceramic vessels. The pottery used for cooking, serving, eating, and storage were essentially the same, although there were some minor differences in the ratios of different types of vessels. Second, over time the varieties of ceramic vessels decreased, especially after 1840, as glasswares replaced earlier serving bowls, but this was true for both overseers and slaves. Third, the types of decorations changed. Earlier ceramics (ca. 1797–1840) were decorated with incised lines, zigzags, and diamonds, a decorative treatment rarely used on Portuguese or the indigenous pre-contact pottery of western Brazil but extremely common in sub-Saharan Africa. Torres de Souza and Pereira Symanski write:

> [W]ith the exception of corrugated decorations, all other decorative techniques present in the Chapada dos Guimarães' pottery assemblages may be found in sub-Saharan Africa's archaeological assemblages from both the end of the Iron Age and the colonial period. In addition, designs such as waves, diamonds, and zigzags are employed generically in pottery from Africa, appearing in a number of compositions. This evidence suggests that slaves were probably using a repertoire of knowledge from their experience in Africa for building these vessels. The evidence does not mean, however, that they were reproducing African pottery decorations. In fact, there are clear stylistic differences between the pottery from the Chapada dos Guimarães and those from different regions of Africa, indicating that slaves who lived in Chapada did significant adaptations in creating these decorative motifs.[29]

Other ceramic forms used at Chapada dos Guimarães drew on local indigenous pottery traditions, such as the corrugated ceramic griddles used to toast manioc flour. Another transformation occurred in the last half of the nineteenth century, when slave households began acquiring a wider variety of earthenware vessels from local markets. This suggests that slave households had become somewhat more independent. Slave households had their own gardens and plots where they raised crops to feed themselves and to sell in local markets, "thus generating earnings that permitted them to become more active consumers."[30] Concurrently, as slave households gained greater economic autonomy, the number of runaway slaves (known as *quilombos*) also increased.

Communities of fugitive slaves were established in various portions of the Americas.[31] Called *cimarrones* in Spanish (literally, "people or animals who have run

Figure 12.7 Indians visiting a Brazilian farm plantation in Minas Gerais, 1824. Painting by Johann Moritz Rugendas

away to live on a mountain peak," or *cima*) and *maroon* communities in Suriname and Jamaica, **quilombo** communities were established in Brazil. Frequently joining local Native American populations, who were also trying to avoid domination, fugitive slave communities are often difficult to find in the archaeological record as they were intentionally hidden in swamps or other inaccessible areas and often abandoned as fugitives escaped their pursuers. Further, the artifacts may not be markedly different from those found in other multiethnic sites. Finally, many acts of resistance are subtle, seen by dominant culture as acts of thievery, malingering, or lawlessness but constituting acts of resistance that have been called "the weapons of the weak."[32]

A remarkably robust archaeological record is associated with **Palmares**, an organized "fugitive polity" established in the 1600s in eastern Brazil and covering some 27,000 km^2 (10,425 mi^2).[33] Established among the palm-forested foothills (or *palmares*) about 80 km (50 mi) inland, the Palmares polity consisted of nine to eleven communities united under a quilombo leader called the Ganga Zumba, or "Great Lord." The total population was approximately 20,000–30,000 people, and the capital **Macaco** was as large as most settlements in colonial Brazil. In 1694 an army of slave raiders from the south (known as "Paulistas" or "*bandeirantes*") invaded Palmares, destroyed Macaco, and executed its leaders.

Macaco has been studied by the archaeologists **Pedro Paulo Funari** and Charles Orser Jr. Although Macaco was documented in historical sources, archaeological research in the 1990s resulted in a slightly different perspective on this important settlement. "Palmares was a community at war, fighting for its very existence, and the state of continuous warfare strongly influenced every aspect of life in the villages."[34] Macaco consisted of a string of homesteads, strategically placed on a bluff overlooking a river from which bandeirantes would attack. Ceramics were a mix of unglazed pottery drawing on local Tupinamba styles (and perhaps made by Amerindian women married to maroons), European glazed wares obtained through trade, and glazed ceramics similar to Dutch and Portuguese styles but locally made for trade with non-elites of European and mixed descent living on the coast. "The material world of Palmares," Orser and Funari write, "was not native, European or African; it was specific, forged in their fight for freedom."[35]

The archaeology of slavery and the African diaspora results in a perspective on the complexities of this historical experience, as Africans, Europeans, Creoles, and Native Americans interacted in complex ways. "This approach provides a potential way to escape from generalizing misconceptions about an African monolithic culture," Torres de Souza and Symanski write, "focusing on the diversified cultural backgrounds of these groups and on the ways through which they kept, modified, recontextualized, and reinvented their cultural practices and worldviews in the multicultural environments [of the Americas]."[36]

A final example of the archaeology of resistance comes from southern Chile, where the **Mapuche** successfully resisted domination until the late 1800s. Speakers of one of the five Araucanian languages of central and southern Chile, the Mapuche were established in the Southern Andes between AD 1100 and 1200, their presence marked by the construction of mounds (*kuel*) (figure 12.8).

The archaeologist **Tom Dillehay** has conducted extensive research on the Mapuche, writing, "Mounds or *kuel* (*cuel*) in the native language are perceived by people as living kindred who participate in public ceremony, converse with priestly shamans about the well-being and future of the community, and thus have powerful influence over people."[37] Relatively small mounds were built between AD 1200 and 1500. Simultaneously, the introduction of agriculture to this region led to population growth, competition between kin-based social groups or patrilineages, and shifting power relations as some groups became dominant over others. Between 1500 and 1600, there was an explosive increase in mound building, as the Araucanians expanded and new agricultural villages were founded.

At this time, the Inca Empire attempted to conquer Chile, entering territory held by northern Araucanians. Tawantinsuyu's cultural influence was felt further south, even among the unconquered Mapuche. Simultaneously, the Mapuche developed a political system referred to by Spanish speakers as the *estado*. Rather than a centralized political system, the Mapuche *estado* consisted of four territories held by different patrilineages whose leaders had religious, military, and economic power, what Dillehay has called a "confederated regional polity." Although the Araucanian *estado* was not a result of the Spanish invasion—as it originated *before* the Spaniards' expeditions into Chile—it was an extraordinarily effective instru-

Figure 12.8 A historic Mapuche ceremonial mound, or *kuel*

ment of resistance. "This polity became the stronghold of Araucanian resistance between 1550 and 1700 and had lasting political and spiritual effects on resisting populations through the Araucania until the early twenty-first century. In the late seventeenth century, the *estado* expanded eastward from Andean mountain passes into Argentina and was second only to the Inka Empire in terms of its geopolitical expanse and cultural influence in South America."[38] The Araucanians continued to resist domination, fighting against Chilean forces until 1860–1880, just as Argentina's War of the Desert subjugated neighboring groups on the eastern side of the Andes. Today more than 1 million Mapuche live in Chile, maintaining distinctive cultural practices that are anchored in the vital forces of the mounds (figure 12.9).

Archaeology does not become irrelevant once history is written. The material record of the past illuminates the lives of people who did not write history books, whether they were African slaves, maroons, or Mapuche. These three examples of the archaeology of resistance show only a few ways that archaeology illuminates the recent past.

Unwritten Histories

Archaeology has exposed other harrowing aspects of recent South American history. During the late twentieth century, military dictatorships developed in Brazil (1964–1985), Uruguay (1973–1985), Argentina (1976–1983), and Chile (1973–1990), regimes that used violent methods to squelch protest and repress opposition. These actions included imprisonments, torture, executions, and anonymous burials in clandestine cemeteries. Archaeologists and forensic anthropologists have documented these abuses of human rights. For example, the archaeologists Pedro Paulo Funari and **Nanci Viera de Olivera** describe their excavations of a clandestine

Figure 12.9 Mapuche wooden ancestral statues, male (*left*) and female (*right*)

graveyard containing the skeletons of *desaparecidos* (literally, "the disappeared") in a portion of the Ricardo de Albuquerque cemetery in Rio de Janeiro. Rather than an orderly interment of individual corpses, the *desaparecidos* had been mixed among the bones of ordinary graves and homeless people, and the skeletons of victims of political violence were intentionally disarticulated and damaged, the corpses burned and bashed apart with pickaxes. The conditions of the skeletons, Funari and Viera de Olivera write, "were a result of intentional actions aimed at preventing the identification of *desaparecidos*."[39]

Similar injustices occurred in Uruguay. The archaeologist **Jose María López Mazz** explains: "The physical disappearance of prisoners is a central theme of repression. On the one hand, it diminishes the rights of victims and threatens the resolution of legal cases on the basis of people's absence. On the other hand, permanent disappearance represents an open wound for missing people's relatives and friends. Repression indirectly affects them in an extratemporal dimension."[40]

The violent erasure of human existence occurred among different regimes, ancient and modern (figure 12.10). One horrific case occurred near the mining town of **Calama** in the Atacama Desert in northern Chile.[41] On October 19, 1974, a group of twenty-eight miners and labor organizers deemed "subversive" were captured by a military unit known as La Guarda de la Muerte and executed. Their bodies were dumped in a large sandy pit in the desert. Sticks of dynamite were placed among the corpses and detonated, blasting the bodies into unrecognizable bits. This brutal effort to deny existence was foiled, as the families of the disappeared paid for a forensic investigation to identify the dead using teeth and dental records. In commemoration, these relatives and their supporters erected the Park for the Preservation of Historical Memory, an exceedingly sad "archaeological" monument commemorating a dark moment in South American history.

Figure 12.10 Park for the Preservation of Historical Memory, Calama, Chile

The archaeology of repression is not limited to skeletons and graves. The objects and places of imprisonment and torture have been studied by archaeologists. **Andrés Zarankin** and **Claudio Niro** describe the extensive and systematic use of clandestine detention centers by the Argentinean military dictatorship between 1976 and 1983.[42] Unlike police stations or military barracks, the clandestine detention centers were not formally recognized and given innocuous names such as the Club Atlético ("Athletic Club") and the Azopardo Garage. Simultaneously, the interrogations and tortures stripped prisoners of identity and existence, as they were hooded, shackled, beaten, and degraded. Archaeological investigations in 2003 at the Club Atlético documented the material traces and architecture of this detention center, comparing those results to survivors' descriptions and drawings of the prison. Zarankin and Niro write, "[A]rchaeology gives us the opportunity to discuss some of the discourses and ideologies in the walls of the detention centers. . . . Clandestine detention centers are at the same time power devices aimed at destroying prisoners' bodies and souls, and material metaphors codifying authoritarian discourses. Their analysis reveals a systematic plan of the military government to annihilate all dissidence."[43] These brutal erasures of human existence have been recovered, in part, through the archaeology of the recent past.

The Past in the Present

In a fundamental sense, the past is in the present. Across all of South America, people regularly interact with the material record of earlier societies. The nature of these interactions is varied, ranging from unthinking and violent destructions to subtle engagements with cultural heritage.

In many South American countries archaeological sites are considered essential elements in national identity, although not equally so. Table 12.1 lists current (2013) data on the number of **UNESCO World Heritage sites** in South America, natural and cultural properties classified as having global significance. For example, Machu Picchu is the most iconic image of the Peru, recognizable internationally and a source of tremendous national pride. In South America, however, most World Heritage sites are preserved because of their natural properties, such as Ecuador's Galapagos Islands. Of those sites that are cultural properties, most are examples of architecture and cultural landscapes created *after* Europeans arrived in South America; only 14 percent are prehistoric cultural properties. The nations with the largest percentage of prehistoric cultural heritage sites—such as Peru, Bolivia, and Colombia—also incorporate to varying extents their indigenous traditions into modern discussions of national identity. (In contrast, Mexico has forty-three World Heritage properties of which twenty-one are prehispanic and thirteen are historic or modern cultural properties, reflecting that nation's emphasis on *mestizaje*, in which native and Spanish traditions are blended to create modern Mexico's cultural and national identity.)

Archaeological sites and museums are also economic resources. Although Machu Picchu is Peru's top tourist destination, receiving 2,500 visitors daily and generating about $40 million to the economy, other archaeological sites such as the Huacas de la Luna y del Sol and Chan Chan also attract a steady stream of tourists.[44] Such sites have economic impacts, directly employing archaeologists, workers, and guards and indirectly stimulating other businesses such as tour agencies, restaurants, hotels, and taxi companies. Tiwanaku is one of Bolivia's major tourist attractions. Even more modest archaeological developments have important economic effects for local communities. For example, in the Sierra Nevada de Santa Marta, guided trekking tours make the several-day hike to visit the site of Ciudad Perdida. The route leads through areas once contested by guerillas, *narcotraficantes*, and the Colombian army, a zone now pacified and safe. With the support of USAID and the Global Heritage Fund, a series of modest camps have been established along the route, places where trekkers and guides can prepare meals and eat, shower, and sleep in mosquito-net-covered hammocks. Other small businesses have sprouted along the route, such as small stores and stands that sell drinks and snacks. The route to Ciudad Perdida has become a lineal economic enterprise zone, with modest investments that have major consequences for the local economy anchored to the Parque Arqueológico.[45]

In many Latin American cities, museums with archaeological collections are sources of national pride and tourist revenue. The Museo de la Nación and Museo Larco Hoyle in Lima, the Museo del Oro in Bogotá (the largest of six archaeological museums located across Colombia),[46] the Museo de Arqueología e Arte Contemporaneo in Guayaquil, the Museo del Banco Central in Quito, and the Museo del Arte Precolombino in Santiago are just a few places where pre-Columbian objects are displayed. And yet, modern interest in the ancient past varies among South American nations. For example, the metropolis of Buenos Aires has more museums focusing on modern and European art, in

Table 12.1 The number of UNESCO World Heritage sites in South America

Country	*Total World Heritage Sites*	*Cultural Sites: Historic or Modern*	*Cultural Sites: Prehistoric*	*% of World Heritage Sites that are Prehistoric Cultural Monuments*
Argentina	8	3	1	12.5
Bolivia	6	3	2	33.3
Brazil	18	10	1	5.5
Chile	4	4	0	0.0
Colombia	7	3	2	28.6
Ecuador	4	2	0	0.0
Paraguay	1	1	0	0.0
Peru	11	2	6	54.5
Suriname	2	1	0	0.0
Uruguay	1	1	0	0.0
Venezuela	3	2	0	0.0
Totals	65	32	12	—

keeping with a national identity that looks to Europe rather than to its indigenous foundations.

Finally, the past and the present interact as archaeological sites become implicated in cultural creation. For example, every October the Parque Arqueológico at Ciudad Perdida is closed to outsiders as the indigenous Kaaga (Kogi) reoccupy the site and conduct ceremonies among the places built by their ancestors (figure 12.11).

Near Cusco, the normally empty Inca fortress of Sacsayhuaman is reoccupied by tens of thousands of people on the winter solstice (approximately June 21)—people from Cusco and the surrounding villages as well as Peruvian and foreign tourists—to witness the ceremony of **Inti Raymi** (figure 12.12).

It is a spectacular pageant that glorifies the Inca Empire. Dancers dressed in elaborate costumes depicting the regional garb of the four quarters of Tawantinsuyu dance into the open plaza, where a replica of an ushnu has been built. A man dressed as an Inca priest awaits the royal entries. A young woman chosen to be the Inca queen for this year's celebration is brought in on a litter carried by a dozen men and accompanied by drummers and the deep-throated roar of conch-shell trumpets. An even more elaborate litter conveys a young man portraying the Inca king, and his entrance is duly royal.

The Inca priest waits as six men carry a llama onto the ushnu. A bottle of cane alcohol is poured down the animal's throat. The priest raises a tumi knife, which he then plunges into the llama's chest and cuts out the heart. Seeing this reenacted gesture of sacrifice, the crowd falls silent.[47]

Conclusion

In the opening paragraph of his influential book, *The Past Is a Foreign Country*, David Lowenthal wrote: "The past is everywhere. All around us lie features which,

Figure 12.11 A Kogi/Kaaga house at Ciudad Perdida, Colombia

like ourselves and our thoughts[,] have more or less recognizable antecedents. Relics, histories, memories suffuse human experience. Each particular trace of the past ultimately perishes, but collectively they are immortal. Whether it is celebrated or rejected, attended to or ignored, the past is omnipresent."[48]

The principal goal of *A Prehistory of South America* is to introduce a reader to the accomplishments of people who settled South America at the end of the Pleistocene and to the achievements of their descendants, whether living in impermanent camps, small villages, independent homesteads, towns, or cities. These people managed to survive and thrive in challenging natural environments—arid deserts, windswept headlands, dense jungles, and oxygen-thin mountains—and create cultural traditions that continue to amaze us. Whether creating objects of aching beauty or engaging in acts of brutal violence, the different peoples of ancient South America present us with a panorama of human experience. In the process, the prehistory of South America shows us a basic truth: that we humans are similar in fundamentally different ways.

This incredibly diverse array of the human experience is largely known through archaeology. While historical documents and ethnographic descriptions are essential sources of information, the prehistory of South America and the lives of its peoples are known principally through the material record. It is through the careful study of the material record—artifacts, plant and animal remains, features, and sites—that we know about the people who inhabited the past. Archaeology is a broad and diverse field dedicated to rescuing the unsaid, the unwritten, the un-

Figure 12.12 Inti Raymi at Sacsayhuaman, Cusco, Peru

known, and the hidden. Whether archaeologists are discovering the earliest traces of human presence in Patagonia or recovering the existence of modern victims of political repression, archaeology is dedicated to the study of the material evidence of human existence to make those past lives part of the consultable record of the human experience.

Finally, there is much more to be learned about the prehistory of South America. One of the purposes of this book is not only to describe what is known but also to discuss the gaps in current knowledge. New finds are made daily. Enormous gaps in our understanding remain. *A Prehistory of South America* was written to inform but also to encourage new archaeological investigations into the cultural diversity of the least known continent.

Discoveries await you.

Notes

1. N. L. Whitehead, "El Dorado, Cannibalism and the Amazons: European Myth and Amerindian Praxis in the Conquest of South America," *Beeld en Verbeelding van Amerika*, ed. W. Pansters and J. Weerdenberg (Utrecht: University of Utrecht Press, 1992), 53–70, 55.

2. There is an enormous literature regarding the European colonization of South America. For overviews, see P. J. Bakewell and P. Bakewell, *A History of Latin America: c. 1450 to the Present* (Malden, MA: Blackwell, 2004); and J. Moya, ed., *The Oxford Handbook of Latin American History* (New York: Oxford, 2011). The reader should consult appropriate entries in B. Tennenbaum, ed., *The Encyclopedia of Latin American Culture and History* (New York: Scribner's, 1996). For contacts between Europeans and indigenous peoples of Brazil, see J. Melatti, *Índios do Brasil* (Sao Paulo: Editora da Univer-

sidade de Sao Paulo, 2007), and the eminently readable classic by John Hemming, *Red Gold: The Conquest of the Brazilian Indians* (Cambridge, MA: Harvard University Press, 1978).

3. For an English translation of Gaspar de Carvajal's amazing account of this voyage, see B. Lee and H. Heaton, trans. and ed., *The Discovery of the Amazon According to the Account of Friar Gaspar de Carvajal, and Other Documents*, Special Publication 17 (New York: American Geographical Society, 1934).

4. For example, the authoritative three-volume *Guide to Documentary Sources for Andean Studies, AD 1530–1900*, ed. J. Pillsbury (Washington, DC: Center for the Advanced Study of the Visual Arts, National Gallery, 2008), discusses some 186 writers and documents. Among these, only one is a woman, the Basque nun Catalina de Erauso (ca. 1592–1650), who shed her vows and nun's habit to travel to South America as a man, where she soldiered for two decades in the Spanish conquests of Chile and Peru and gained a reputation for violent fearlessness, at one point actually killing her own brother in a case of mistaken identity; see L. De Leonardis, "Erauso, Catalina de (ca. 1592–1650)," in volume 2: 197–200.

5. On literacy among the conquistadores, see J. Lockhart's classic *The Men of Cajamarca: A Social and Biographical Study of the First Conquerors of Peru* (Austin: University of Texas Press, 1972), 33–35, 72.

6. B. Mannheim, "Diez de Betanzos, Juan (?–1576)," *Guide to Documentary Sources for Andean Studies, AD 1530–1900*, ed. J. Pillsbury, vol. 3 (Washington, DC: Center for the Advanced Study of the Visual Arts, National Gallery, 2008), 186–190, 187.

7. For English-language discussions of historical archaeology in South America, see P. Funari, "A Report on Historical Archaeology Publications in Latin America," *International Journal of Historical Archaeology* 11, no. 2 (2007): 183–191; F. Gómez Romero, "A Brief Overview of the Evolution of Historical Archaeology in Argentina," *International Journal of Historical Archaeology* 9, no. 3 (2005): 135–141; J. Martín, A. Brooks, and T. Andrade Lima, "Crossing Borders and Maintaining Identities: Perspectives on Current Research in South American Historical Archaeology," *Historical Archaeology* 46, no. 3 (2012): 1–15; M. Van Buren, "The Archaeological Study of Spanish Colonialism in the Americas," *Journal of Archaeological Research* 18 (2010): 151–201; and A. Zarankin and M. Salerno, "Looking South: Historical Archaeology in South America," *Historical Archaeology* 42, no. 4 (2008): 38–58.

8. C. Orser Jr., "Historical Archaeology as Modern-World Archaeology in Argentina," *International Journal of Historical Archaeology* 12 (2008): 181–194, 182.

9. Ibid., 182.

10. Ibid., 184.

11. R. Jamieson, "Colonialism, Social Archaeology and *lo Andino*: Historical Archaeology in the Andes," *World Archaeology* 37, no. 3 (2005): 352–372, 354.

12. P. Rice, "Order (and Disorder) in Early Colonial Moquegua, Peru," *International Journal of Historical Archaeology* 15 (2011): 481–501. For additional references, see S. de France, "Iberian Foodways in the Moquegua and Torata Valleys of Southern Peru," *Historical Archaeology* 30, no. 3 (1996): 20–48; P. Rice, "Wine and Brandy Production in Colonial Peru: A Historical and Archaeological Investigation," *Journal of Interdisciplinary History* 27 (1996): 455–479; P. Rice, "The Archaeology of Wine:

The Wine and Brandy Haciendas of Moquegua, Peru," *Journal of Field Archaeology* 23 (1996): 187–204; P. Rice, "Tin-Enameled Ceramics of Moquegua, Peru," in *Approaches to the Historical Archaeology of Mexico, Central and South America*, ed. J. Gasco, G. Smith, and P. Fournier-García (Los Angeles: Institute of Archaeology, University of California, 1997), 167–175; P. Rice, "Volcanoes, Earthquakes, and the Spanish Colonial Wine Industry of Moquegua, Peru," in *Andean Civilization: A Tribute to Michael E. Moseley*, ed. J. Marcus and P. R. Williams (Los Angeles: Cotsen Institute of Archaeology, 2009), 379–392; P. Rice, *Vintage Moquegua: History, Wine, and Archaeology in a Colonial Peruvian Periphery* (Austin: University of Texas Press, 2011); G. Smith, "Heard It through the Grapevine: Andean and European Contributions to Spanish Colonial Culture and Viticulture in Moquegua, Peru" (PhD diss., University of Florida, 1991); M. Van Buren, "Community and Empire in Southern Peru: The Site of Torata Alta under Spanish Rule" (PhD diss., University of Arizona, Tucson, 1993); and M. Van Buren, M. Bürgi, and P. Rice, "Torata Alta: A Late Highland Settlement in the Osmore Drainage," in *Domestic Architecture, Ethnicity, and Complementarity in the South-Central Andes*, ed. M. Aldenderfer (Iowa City: University of Iowa Press, 1993), 136–152.

13. T. Cummins, "Forms of Andean Colonial Towns, Free Will, and Marriage," in *The Archaeology of Colonialism*, ed. C. Lyons and J. Papadopoulos (Los Angeles: Getty Research Institute, 2002), 199–240, 205, 206.

14. S. Wernke, "The Politics of Community and Inka Statecraft in the Colca Valley, Peru," *Latin American Antiquity* 17, no. 2 (2006): 177–208; S. Wernke, "Analogy or Erasure? Dialectics of Religious Transformation in the Early *Doctrinas* of the Colca Valley, Peru," *International Journal of Historical Archaeology* 11, no. 2 (2007): 152–182; S. Wernke, "Spatial Network Analysis of a Terminal Prehispanic and Early Colonial Settlement in Highland Peru," *Journal of Archaeological Science* 39 (2012): 1111–1122.

15. Wernke, "Analogy or Erasure?," 162.

16. Ibid., 179.

17. Schávelzon and colleagues have produced an extensive body of archaeological research regarding historical Buenos Aires. D. Schávelzon's *The Historical Archaeology of Buenos Aires: A City at the End of the World* (New York: Springer, 1999) is an outstanding overview, while for more focused analyses, see D. Schávelzon, "Arqueología urbana e imaginario: El supuesto polvorín colonial en el Jardín Botánico de Buenos Aires," *Arqueología Iberoamericana* 15 (2012): 13–26; D. Schávelzon, "Argentina and Great Britain: Studying an Asymmetrical Relationship through Domestic Material Culture," *Historical Archaeology* 47, no. 1 (2013): 10–25; M. Carminati and D. Schávelzon, "Arqueología en una plaza metropolitan: Recoleta, Buenos Aires," *Arqueologia Iberoamericana* 3 (2009): 37–47. Also see Schávelzon's website at http://www.danielschavelzon.com.ar/.

18. D. Schávelzon, "Naturaleza y desarrollo urbano: Una Mirada arqueológica a Buenos Aires," *Declamatoria de Buenos Aires: Patrimonio Natural y Cultural de la Humanidad* (2009): 2, my translation.

19. Schávelzon, *The Historical Archaeology of Buenos Aires*, 153.

20. Ibid., 28.

21. Ibid., 117.

22. Ibid., 160.

23. A starting point for this topic is W. Crosby, *The Columbian Exchange: Biological and Cultural Consequences of 1492* (Westport, CT: Greenwood Press, 1972). See also W. McNeill, *Plagues and Peoples* (New York: Random House Digital, 2010). For a recent treatment focusing on the economic consequences of the Columbian exchange, see N. Nunn and N. Qian, "The Columbian Exchange: A History of Disease, Food, and Ideas," *The Journal of Economic Perspectives* 24, no. 2 (2010): 163–188. For post-contact population decline among native South Americans, see N. Cook, *Demographic Collapse: Indian Peru, 1520–1620* (Cambridge: Cambridge University Press, 2004); and N. Cook and W. G. Lovell, eds., *Secret Judgments of God: Old World Disease in Colonial Spanish America* (Norman: University of Oklahoma Press, 2001).

24. J. Rawley, *The Transatlantic Slave Trade: A History* (New York: W.W. Norton, 1981), 3. A WorldCat search for "Transatlantic Slave Trade" results in a citation of some 300 nonfiction books dealing with the slave trade and its impacts in the Americas. For book-length overviews of this complex topic, see P. Curtin, *The Atlantic Slave Trade: A Census* (Madison: University of Wisconsin Press, 1972); D. Elitis, *The Rise of African Slavery in the Americas* (Cambridge: Cambridge University Press, 2000); H. Thomas, *The Slave Trade: The Story of the Atlantic Slave Trade, 1440–1870* (New York: Simon and Schuster, 1997). Also see more specific studies, such as L. Newson and S. Minchin, *From Capture to Sale: The Portuguese Slave Trade to Spanish South America in the Early Seventeenth Century* (Leiden: Brill, 2007); and F. Bowser, *The African Slave in Colonial Peru, 1524–1650* (Stanford, CA: Stanford University Press, 1974).

25. Rawley, *The Transatlantic Slave Trade*, 18–19.

26. C. E. Orser Jr., "The Archaeology of the African Diaspora," *Annual Review of Anthropology* 27 (1998): 63–82; P. Funari, "Conquistadors, Plantations, and Quilombo: Latin America in Historical Archaeological Context," in *Historical Archaeology*, ed. M. Hall and S. Silliman (Malden, MA: Blackwell Publishing, 2006), 209–229.

27. M. Torres de Souza and L. Pereira Symanski, "Slave Communities and Pottery Variability in Western Brazil: The Plantations of Chapada dos Guimarães," *International Journal of Historical Archaeology* 13 (2009): 513–548.

28. J. Handlers, "An African-Type Healer/Diviner and His Grave Goods: A Burial from a Plantation Slave Cemetery in Barbados, West Indies," *International Journal of Historical Archaeology* 1, no. 2 (1997): 91–130.

29. M. Torres de Souza and L. Pereira Symanski, "Slave Communities and Pottery Variability," 533.

30. Ibid., 537.

31. For overviews, see E. Kofi Agorsah, "Archaeology and Resistance History in the Caribbean," *The African Archaeological Review* 11 (1993): 175–195; and the excellent doctoral dissertation examining maroons in Suriname, C. Ngwenyama, "Material Beginnings of Saramaka Maroons: An Archaeological Investigation" (PhD diss., University of Florida, Gainesville, 2007). For an introduction to the literature, see P. Funari, "A Report on Historical Archaeology Publications in Latin America," *International Journal of Historical Archaeology* 11 (2007): 183–191.

32. The phrase comes from the influential work of anthropologist and political scientist James C. Scott, *Weapons of the Weak: Everyday Forms of Peasant Resistance* (New Haven, CT: Yale University Press, 1985).

33. Brazilian archaeologist Pedro Paulo A. Funari has written extensively about Palmares and historical archaeology in Brazil. In addition to publications cited elsewhere, see P. Funari, "Maroon, Race and Gender: Palmares Material Culture and Social Relations in a Runaway Settlement," in *Historical Archaeology: Back from the Edge*, ed. P. Funari, M. Hall, and S. Jones (London: Routledge, 1999), 308–327; "Conflicto e interpretación en Palmares," in *Arqueología Histórica en América del Sur: Los Desafíos del Siglo XXI*, ed. A. Zarakin and P. Funari (Bogota: Ediciones Uniandes, 2004), 11–28; and P. Funari, N. Vieria de Oliveira, and E. Tamaninin, "Archaeology to the Lay Public in Brazil: Three Experiences," in *Past Meets Present: Archaeologists Partnering with Museum Curators, Teachers, and Community Groups*, ed. J. Jameson Jr. and S. Baugher (New York: Springer, 2007), 217–228.

34. C. Orser and P. Funari, "Archaeology and Slave Resistance and Rebellion," *World Archaeology* 33 (2001): 61–72, 68–69.

35. Ibid., 67.

36. M. Torres de Souza and L. Pereira Symanski, "Slave Communities and Pottery Variability," 543.

37. T. Dillehay, *Monuments, Empires, and Resistance: The Araucanian Polity and Ritual Narratives* (Cambridge: Cambridge University Press, 2007), 1.

38. Ibid., 31.

39. P. Funari and N. Viera de Olivera, "The Archaeology of Conflict in Brazil," in *Memories from Darkness: Contributions to Global Historical Archaeology*, ed. P. Funari, A. Zarankin, and M. Salerno (New York: Springer, 2009), 5–31, 29. This volume contains a dozen essays and case studies describing this harrowing period of South American history.

40. J. López Mazz, "An Archaeological View of Political Repression in Uruguay (1971–1985)," in *Memories from Darkness: Contributions to Global Historical Archaeology*, ed. P. Funari, A. Zarankin, and M. Salerno (New York: Springer, 2009), 33–43, 35.

41. This description is based on personal observations and photographs on October 21, 2009.

42. A. Zarankin and C. Niro, "The Materialization of Sadism: Archaeology of Architecture in Clandestine Detention Centers (Argentinean Military Dictatorship, 1976–1983)," in *Memories from Darkness: Contributions to Global Historical Archaeology*, ed. P. Funari, A. Zarankin, and M. Salerno (New York: Springer, 2009), 57–77.

43. Ibid., 75.

44. http://smithsonianmag.com/ist/?next=/people-places/machu.html/?c=y&page=2.

45. Personal observation, June 2012.

46. http://www.banrepcultural.org/blaavirtual/revistas/bolet-n-de-arqueolog-fian-o-6-no-1-1991.

47. Personal observation, June 1984.

48. D. Lowenthal, *The Past Is a Foreign Country* (Cambridge: Cambridge University Press 1985), xv.

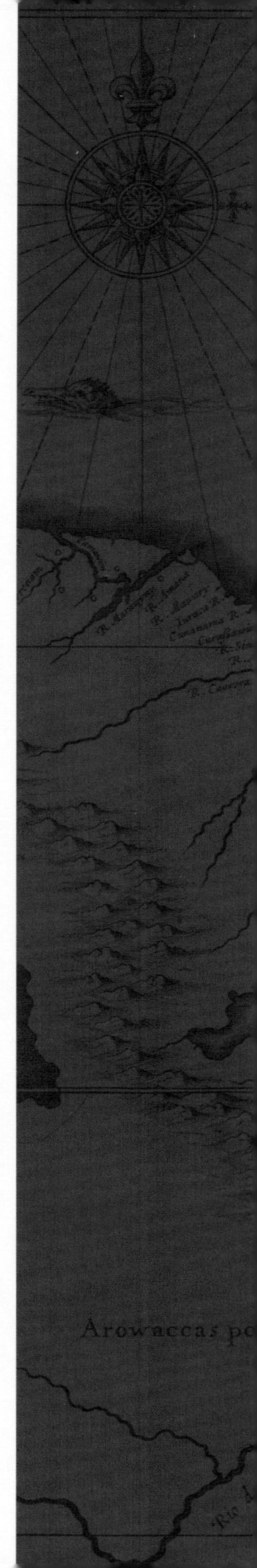

Acknowledgments

Any text that attempts to summarize the prehistory of a continent is necessarily based on the kindness of strangers and friends. First, I thank the hundreds of scholars who conducted the archaeological investigations discussed in *A Prehistory of South America*. Too numerous to name here, their names and works are listed in the notes following each chapter. After consulting these references, I hope the reader will appreciate the vast, international, and collective enterprise that South American archaeology represents. I thank my fellow archaeologists for their contributions to our knowledge of South American prehistory.

Second, I thank the archaeologists who shared photographs documenting their research and gave permission to publish them in *A Prehistory of South America*. Some of these archaeologists are dear friends; others I have never met. I thank all of them for their generosity: Mark Aldenderfer, Paulo de Blasis, Brenda Bowser, Daniel Contreras, Tom Dillehay, Clark Erickson, Peter Fuchs, Eduardo Góes Neves, Michael Heckenberger, José Iriarte, Augusto Oyuela-Caycedo, John Patton, Gustavo Politis, Elsa Redmond, Anna C. Roosevelt, Sanna Saunaluoma, Daniel Sandweiss, Denise Schaan, Charles Spencer, Karen Stothert, Carolina Vilchez, and Karen Wise.

My personal knowledge of South American archaeology has come not only from my own investigations in Peru but also from visiting archaeological sites in Peru, Bolivia, Chile, Argentina, Ecuador, and Colombia. I thank the archaeologists who over the years have taken the time to show me sites and share their research: Robin Beck, Brian Billman, Alicia Boswell, Jesus Briceño, Luis Jaime Castillo, Nicole Couture, Christopher Donnan, George Gummerman III, Richard Lunnis, Carol Mackey, Bernardino Olaya Olaya, Shelia Pozorski, Thomas Pozorski, Wilson Puell Mendoza, Karen Stothert, Mathilde Temme, Santiago Uceda, Francisco Valdez, Carolina Vilchez, and Alexi Vranich. I also thank my traveling companions who have shared these journeys, including Doug Bryant (Colombia), Bill Fox (Chile), Patrick Kehoe (Peru), Andrew Stewart (Argentina), and my wife and son, Janine Gasco and Nathan Moore (Peru and Ecuador).

At the University Press of Colorado, I express my deep thanks to Darrin Pratt for asking me to write this book and for guiding the manuscript to publication. Darrin is an ideal editor—supportive, full of useful suggestions, and committed to a successful book. Also at the University Press of Colorado, I thank Bill Nelson for producing the maps, Laura Furney for managing the publication process, and Jessica d'Arbonne for transforming manuscript into book and for coordinating the illustration program. Five peer reviewers read the manuscript, made suggestions, and were uniformly supportive of the text. Two of these reviewers have shared their names—Mark Aldenderfer and Elizabeth Klarich—and I thank them and the three anonymous reviewers for their helpful comments.

Finally, I dedicate this book to two archaeologists who first took me to South America, Carol J. Mackey and A. M. Ulana Klymyshyn. Our 1981 field season in Peru literally changed my life. I first studied South American archaeology under Carol's and Ulana's tutelage, but they also taught me—by their personal examples—about the thrill of scientific discovery and the profound pleasure of conducting archaeological research in South America. If I can convey a sense of that excitement to the reader, it is due to Carol Mackey and Ulana Klymyshyn and the opportunity they gave me. I dedicate *A Prehistory of South America* to them as a small token of my enduring gratitude.

Illustration Credits

Figure 0.1 Illustration from Wikimedia Commons contributors, "Big Blue Marble," *Wikimedia Commons, the free media repository*, http://upload.wikimedia.org/wikipedia/commons/6/66/Big_Blue_Marble.jpg (accessed May 15, 2014).

Figure 1.1 Photograph from Wikimedia Commons contributors, "Map South America," *Wikimedia Commons, the free media repository*, http://upload.wikimedia.org/wikipedia/commons/0/08/Map_South_America.jpg (accessed May 15, 2014).

Figure 1.2 Illustration from Wikimedia Commons contributors, "Musei Wormiani Historia," *Wikimedia Commons, the free media repository*, http://upload.wikimedia.org/wikipedia/commons/f/f5/Musei_Wormiani_Historia.jpg (accessed May 15, 2014).

Figure 1.3 Illustration from Wikimedia Commons contributors, "Alexandre Humboldt," *Wikimedia Commons, the free media repository*, http://upload.wikimedia.org/wikipedia/commons/d/db/Alexandre_humboldt.jpg (accessed May 15, 2014).

Figure 1.4 Illustration from Wikimedia Commons contributors, "EGeoSquier," *Wikimedia Commons, the free media repository*, http://commons.wikimedia.org/wiki/File:EGeoSquier.png (accessed May 15, 2014).

Figure 1.5 Squier's map of Chankillp from *Incidents of Travel and Exploration in the Land of the Incas*, published 1877; public domain.

Figure 1.6 Photograph from NASA, "Chankillo Observatory, Peru," *Earth Observatory: Where every day is Earth Day*, http://eoimages.gsfc.nasa.gov/images/imagerecords/7000/7606/chankillo_iko_2002013_lrg.jpg (accessed May 15, 2014).

Figure 1.7 Illustration from Wikimedia Commons contributors, "Tiahuanaco Gate EG Squier 1877," *Wikimedia Commons, the free media repository*, http://en.wikipedia.org/wiki/File:TiahuanacoGateEGSquier1877.jpg (accessed May 15, 2014).

Figure 1.8 Illustration from Wikimedia Commons contributors, "Georges B. Von Grumbkow-Alphons Stübel at the Portal of the Sun, Tiahuanaco," *Wikimedia Commons, the free media repository*, http://commons.wikimedia.org/wiki/File:Georges_B._Von_Grumbkow_-_Alphons_St%C3%BCbel_at_the_Portal_of_the_Sun,_Tiahuanaco_-_Google_Art_Project.jpg (accessed May 15, 2014).

Figure 1.9 Illustration from Wikimedia Commons contributors, "2Wiener-Tintin-Dieu Soleil," *Wikimedia Commons, the free media repository*, http://commons.wikimedia.org/wiki/File:2Wiener-Tintin-Dieu_Soleil.jpg (accessed May 15, 2014).

Figure 1.10 From A. Bandelier's *Indians and Aboritial Ruins near Chachapoyas in Northern Peru* (1893); public domain.

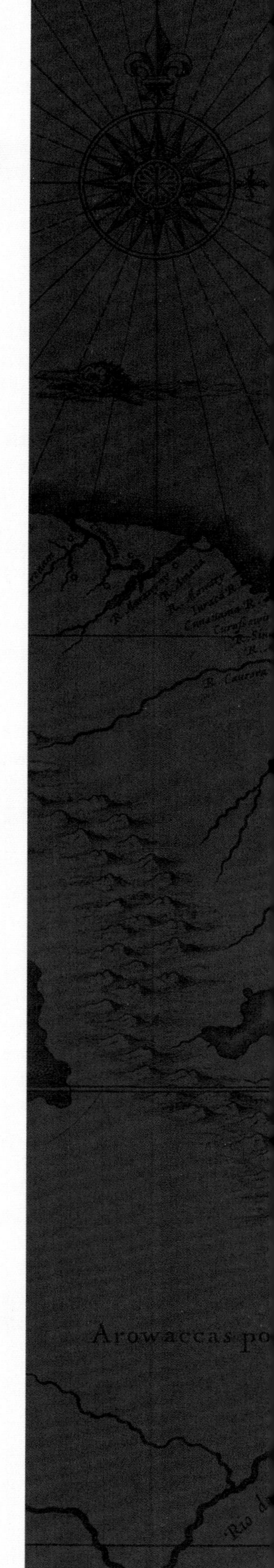

Figure 1.11 Archivo de la Marina de Guerra, Peru; public domain.

Figure 1.12 Photograph from Penn Museum, "Penn Museum Image #18588," http://www.penn.museum/blog/wp-content/uploads/2013/10/18588.jpg (accessed May 15, 2014).

Figure 1.13 From M. Uhle's "Types of Culture in Peru," 1902; public domain.

Figure 1.14 Photograph from Wikimedia Commons contributors, "Tello en Nunamarka Chillia 1937," *Wikimedia Commons, the free media repository*, http://upload.wikimedia.org/wikipedia/commons/1/12/Tello_en_Nunamarka_Chillia_1937.jpg (accessed May 15, 2014).

Figure 2.1 Illustration from Wikimedia Commons contributors, "South America—Blue Marble Orthographic," *Wikimedia Commons, the free media repository*, http://upload.wikimedia.org/wikipedia/commons/5/54/South_America_-_Blue_Marble_orthographic.jpg (accessed May 15, 2014).

Figure 2.2 Map by Bill Nelson.

Figure 2.3 Photograph from Wikimedia Commons contributors, "Anden2," *Wikimedia Commons, the free media repository*, http://upload.wikimedia.org/wikipedia/commons/7/76/Anden2.JPG (accessed May 15, 2014).

Figure 2.4 Map by Bill Nelson.

Figure 2.5 Photograph from NASA, "ISS027-E-011058," *Earth Observatory: Where every day is Earth Day*, http://eoimages.gsfc.nasa.gov/images/imagerecords/50000/50385/ISS027-E-011058_lrg.jpg (accessed May 15, 2014).

Figure 2.6 Photograph from Wikimedia Commons contributors, "Manus Amazon NASA," *Wikimedia Commons, the free media repository*, http://upload.wikimedia.org/wikipedia/commons/9/94/Manaus-Amazon-NASA.jpg (accessed May 15, 2014).

Figure 2.7 Map by Bill Nelson.

Figure 2.8 Photograph by author.

Figure 2.9 Photograph by author.

Figure 2.10 Photograph from Wikimedia Commons contributors, "Patagonian Steppe," *Wikimedia Commons, the free media repository*, http://upload.wikimedia.org/wikipedia/commons/7/74/Patagonian_Steppe_%2832608429 62%29.jpg (accessed May 15, 2014).

Figure 2.11 Photograph from Wikimedia Commons contributors, "Lake Titicaca (4094294277)," *Wikimedia Commons, the free media repository*, http://commons.wikimedia.org/wiki/File:Lake_Titicaca_(4094294277).jpg (accessed May 15, 2014).

Figure 2.12 Photograph from NASA, "ITCZ GOES 11," *Earth Observatory: Where every day is Earth Day*, http://eoimages.gsfc.nasa.gov/images/imagerecords/0/703/itcz_goes11_lrg.jpg (accessed May 15, 2014).

Figure 2.13 Map by Bill Nelson.

Figure 2.14 Photograph by author.

Figure 2.15 Photograph from NASA "ISS010-E-5194," *Earth Observatory Where every day is Earth Day*, http://eoimages.gsfc.nasa.gov/images/imagerecords/5000/5001/ISS010-E-5194_lrg.jpg (accessed May 15, 2014).

Figure 2.16 Map by Bill Nelson.

Figure 2.17 Photograph from Wikimedia Commons contributors, "Forest, Santa Criz Dept, Bolivia," *Wikimedia Commons, the free media repository*, http://upload.wikimedia.org/wikipedia/commons/9/93/Forest%2C_Santa_Criz_Dept%2C_Bolivia.jpg (accessed May 15, 2014).

Figure 2.18 Photograph by author.

Figure 2.19 Photograph from Wikimedia Commons contributors, "Antarctic beech trees, Patagonia," http://upload.wikimedia.org/wikipedia/commons/8/8f/Nothofagus.jpg (accessed May 21, 2014).

Figure 3.1 Photograph from Wikimedia Commons contributors, "Selknam playa 1930," *Wikimedia Commons, the free media repository*, http://commons.wikimedia.org/wiki/File:Selknam_playa_1930.jpg (accessed May 15, 2014).
Figure 3.2 Photograph from Denver Museum of Nature and Science.
Figure 3.3 Photograph from National Park Service.
Figure 3.4 Map by Bill Nelson
Figure 3.5 Photograph from Wikimedia Commons contributors, "Cueva Fell exterior," *Wikimedia Commons, the free media repository*, http://commons.wikimedia.org/wiki/File%3ACueva_Fell_exterior.jpg (accessed May 15, 2014).
Figure 3.6 Photograph from Wikimedia Commons contributors, "Puntas cola de pescado Cueva Fell," *Wikimedia Commons, the free media repository*, http://en.wikipedia.org/wiki/File:Puntas_cola_de_pescado_Cueva_Fell.jpg (accessed May 15, 2014).
Figure 3.7 Photograph courtesy of Tom Dillehay.
Figure 3.8 Photograph courtesy of Tom Dillehay.
Figure 3.9 Photograph courtesy of John Douglass and Anna Roosevelt.
Figure 3.10 Photograph by author.
Figure 3.11 Map by Bill Nelson.
Figure 4.1 Photograph from Wikimedia Commons contributors, "Selknam cazando," *Wikimedia Commons, the free media repository*, http://commons.wikimedia.org/wiki/File:Selknam_cazando.jpg (accessed May 15, 2014).
Figure 4.2 Map by Bill Nelson.
Figure 4.3 Photograph courtesy of Karen Stothert.
Figure 4.4 Photograph courtesy of Karen Stothert.
Figure 4.5 Photograph courtesy of Karen Stothert.
Figure 4.6 Photograph by author.
Figure 4.7 Photograph courtesy of Augusto Oyuela-Caycedo.
Figure 4.8 Photograph courtesy of Gustavo Politis.
Figure 4.9 Photograph courtesy of Gustavo Politis.
Figure 4.10 Photograph courtesy of Gustavo Politis.
Figure 4.11 Photograph courtesy of Daniel Sandweiss.
Figure 4.12 Photograph courtesy of Daniel Sandweiss.
Figure 4.13 Photograph courtesy of Daniel Sandweiss.
Figure 4.14 Photograph courtesy of Daniel Sandweiss.
Figure 4.15 Photograph courtesy of Daniel Sandweiss.
Figure 4.16 Photograph from Wikimedia Commons contributors, "Momia cultura chincorra año 3000," *Wikimedia Commons, the free media repository*, http://upload.wikimedia.org/wikipedia/commons/a/af/Momia_cultura_chinchorro_a%C3%B10_3000_AC.jpg (accessed May 15, 2014).
Figure 4.17 Photograph from Wikimedia Commons contributors, "Chinchorro mummy, south coast of Peru or north coast of Chile, 5000–2000 BC, San Diego Museum of Man," *Wikimedia Commons, the free media repository*, http://upload.wikimedia.org/wikipedia/commons/e/ea/Chinchorro_mummy%2C_south_coast_of_Peru_or_north_coast_of_Chile%2C_5000-2000_BC_-_San_Diego_Museum_of_Man_-_DSC06921.JPG (accessed May 15, 2014).
Figure 4.18 Photograph courtesy of Karen Wise.
Figure 4.19 Photograph courtesy of Paulo De Blassis.
Figure 4.20 Photograph © Pichugin Dmitry / Shutterstock.

Figure 4.21 Photograph from Wikimedia Commons contributors, "Parincota volcano," *Wikimedia Commons, the free media repository*, http://upload.wikimedia.org/wikipedia/commons/a/a7/Parinacota_volcano.jpg (accessed May 15, 2014).

Figure 4.22 Photograph courtesy of Mark Aldenderfer.

Figure 5.1 Photograph from Wikimedia Commons contributors, "Quinua," *Wikimedia Commons, the free media repository*, http://commons.wikimedia.org/wiki/File:Quinua.JPG (accessed May 15, 2014).

Figure 5.2 Photograph from Wikimedia Commons contributors, "Petroglyph atacama," *Wikimedia Commons, the free media repository*, http://upload.wikimedia.org/wikipedia/commons/8/8c/Petroglifo_atacama.jpg (accessed May 15, 2014).

Figure 5.3 Photograph © Katarzyna Citko / Shutterstock.

Figure 5.4 Photograph by author.

Figure 5.5 Photos courtesy of José Iriarte.

Figure 5.6 Map by Bill Nelson.

Figure 5.7 Photograph © Morphart Creation / Shutterstock.

Figure 5.8 Photograph © YanaG / Shutterstock.

Figure 5.9 Photograph from Wikimedia Commons contributors, "Racine de yucca (manioc)," *Wikimedia Commons, the free media repository*, http://commons.wikimedia.org/wiki/File:Racine_de_yucca_(manioc).jpg (accessed May 15, 2014).

Figure 5.10 Photograph © Hann Leon Stock / Shutterstock.

Figure 5.11 Photograph © Mark Skalny / Shutterstock.

Figure 5.12 Photograph © pisaphotography / Shutterstock.

Figure 5.13 Photograph © Alexandra Gl / Shutterstock.

Figure 5.14 Photograph © kccullenPhoto / Shutterstock.

Figure 5.15 Photograph © joloei / Shutterstock.

Figure 5.16 Photograph Courtesy of Brenda Bowser and John Patton.

Figure 5.17 Photograph © Eduardo Rivero / Shutterstock.

Figure 5.18 Photograph © Dr. Morley Read / Shutterstock.

Figure 5.19 Photograph from Wikimedia Commons contributors, "Cactus San Pedro," *Wikimedia Commons, the free media repository*, http://upload.wikimedia.org/wikipedia/commons/4/48/Cactus_san_pedro.jpg (accessed May 15, 2014).

Figure 5.20 Photograph © Photographer unknown / Shutterstock.

Figure 5.21 Photograph © Ammit Jack / Shutterstock.

Figure 5.22 Photograph from Wikimedia Commons contributors, "Cactus San Pedro," *Wikimedia Commons, the free media repository*, http://upload.wikimedia.org/wikipedia/commons/4/48/Cactus_san_pedro.jpg (accessed May 15, 2014).

Figure 5.23 Photograph from Wikimedia Commons contributors, "Fires along the Rio Xingu, Brazil," *Wikimedia Commons, the free media repository*, http://upload.wikimedia.org/wikipedia/commons/c/cb/Fires_along_the_Rio_Xingu%2C_Brazil.JPG (accessed May 15, 2014).

Figure 5.24 Photograph courtesy of John Patton and Brenda Bowser.

Figure 5.25 Photograph courtesy of Clark Erickson.

Figure 5.26 Photograph courtesy of Clark Erickson.

Figure 5.27 Photograph © Jennifer Stone / Shutterstock.

Figure 5.28 Photograph © ckchiu / Shutterstock.

Figure 5.29 Photograph from Wikimedia Commons contributors, "Terrace farming in the Andes mountains Pisac Peru," *Wikimedia Commons, the free media repository*, http://commons.wikimedia.org/wiki/File:Terrace_farming_in_the_Ande_mountains_Pisac_Peru.jpg (accessed May 19, 2014).

Figure 5.30 Photograph by author.

Figure 5.31 Photograph from Wikimedia Commons contributors, "Guamán Poma 1615–1141 abril," *Wikimedia Commons, the free media repository*, http://upload.wikimedia.org/wikipedia/commons/d/d9/Guam%C3%A1n_Poma_1615_1141_abril.png (accessed May 19, 2014).

Figure 6.1 Photograph courtesy of Carolina Vílchez.

Figure 6.2 Map by Bill Nelson.

Figure 6.3 Photograph by author.

Figure 6.4 Photograph from Wikimedia Commons contributors, "Ecuadorian—Figure of a Pregnant Woman—Walters 482771—Three Quarter," *Wikimedia Commons, the free media repository*, http://upload.wikimedia.org/wikipedia/commons/8/80/Ecuadorian_-_Figure_of_a_Pregnant_Woman_-_Walters_482771_-_Three_Quarter.jpg (accessed May 19, 2014).

Figure 6.5 Photograph by author.

Figure 6.6 Photograph by author.

Figure 6.7 Photograph by author.

Figure 6.8 Photograph by author.

Figure 6.9 Photograph by author.

Figure 6.10 Photograph by author.

Figure 6.11 Photograph by author.

Figure 6.12 Photograph by author.

Figure 6.13 Photograph by author.

Figure 6.14 Photograph by author.

Figure 6.15 Photograph courtesy of Denise Schaan.

Figure 6.16 Photograph courtesy of Sanna Sanaluoma.

Figure 6.17 Photograph courtesy of Sanna Sanaluoma.

Figure 6.18 Photograph courtesy of José Iriarte.

Figure 6.19 Photograph courtesy of José Iriarte.

Figure 6.20 Photograph courtesy of José Iriarte.

Figure 7.1 Photograph by author.

Figure 7.2 Map by Bill Nelson.

Figure 7.3 Photograph © Christian Vinces / Shutterstock.

Figure 7.4 Photograph by John Collier, reprinted by permission from the America Museum of Natural History.

Figure 7.5 Photograph from Wikimedia Commons contributors, "PeruCaral11," *Wikimedia Commons, the free media repository*, http://commons.wikimedia.org/wiki/File:PeruCaral11.jpg (accessed May 19, 2014).

Figure 7.6 Photograph from Wikimedia Commons contributors, "Caral-Supe in Peru," *Wikimedia Commons, the free media repository*, http://upload.wikimedia.org/wikipedia/commons/5/55/Caral-Supe_in_Peru.jpg (accessed May 19, 2014).

Figure 7.7 Photograph courtesy of Peter Fuchs.

Figure 7.8 Photograph courtesy of Peter Fuchs.

Figure 7.9 Photograph from Wikimedia Commons contributors, "Sechín Archaeological site-relief (heads)," *Wikimedia Commons, the free media repository*, http://upload.wikimedia.org/wikipedia/commons/5/5b/Sech%C3%ADn_Archaeological_site_-_relief_%28heads%29.jpg (accessed May 19, 2014).

Figure 7.10 Photograph from Wikimedia Commons contributors, "Sechín Archaeological site-relief (head profile left)," *Wikimedia Commons, the free media repository*, http://upload.wikimedia.org/wikipedia/commons/9/92/Sech%C3%ADn_Archaeological_site_-_relief_%28head_profile_left%29.jpg (accessed May 19, 2014).

Figure 7.11 Photograph by author.

Figure 7.12 Photograph by author.

Figure 7.13 Photograph courtesy of Daniel Contreras.

Figure 7.14 Photograph from Wikimedia Commons contributors, "Chavin-Août 2007," *Wikimedia Commons, the free media repository*, http://upload.wikimedia.org/wikipedia/commons/5/52/Chavin_-_Ao%C3%BBt_2007.jpg (accessed May 19, 2014).

Figure 7.15 Photograph by author.

Figure 7.16 Photograph from Wikimedia Commons contributors, "Raimondi Stela (Chavin de Huantar)," *Wikimedia Commons, the free media repository*, http://upload.wikimedia.org/wikipedia/commons/a/af/Raimondi_Stela_%28Chavin_de_Huantar%29.svg (accessed May 19, 2014).

Figure 7.17 Photograph from Wikimedia Commons contributors, "Chavín-Stirrup Vessel with Incised Designs—Walters 482823—Side A," *Wikimedia Commons, the free media repository*, http://upload.wikimedia.org/wikipedia/commons/f/f0/Chav%C3%ADn_-_Stirrup_Vessel_with_Incised_Designs_-_Walters_482823_-_Side_A.jpg (accessed May 19, 2014).

Figure 7.18 Photograph from Wikimedia Commons contributors, "Lago Menor o Huiñamarca Perú Bolivia Satelital map 68.85829W 16," *Wikimedia Commons, the free media repository*, http://upload.wikimedia.org/wikipedia/commons/8/8e/Lago_Menor_o_Hui%C3%B1amarca_Per%C3%BA_Bolivia_Satelital_map_68.85829W_16.png (accessed May 19, 2014).

Figure 7.19 Map by Bill Nelson.

Figure 8.1 Reprinted from Princeton University Library, "Inhabitants of Tierra del Fuego [Hawkesworth, vol. 2, plate 1]," *library.princeton.edu*, http://libweb5.princeton.edu/visual_materials/maps/websites/pacific/cook1/cook-fuegians.jpg (accessed May 19, 2014).

Figure 8.2 Map by Bill Nelson.

Figure 8.3 Photograph from Wikimedia Commons contributors, "Isla Gable, Tierra del Fuego," *Wikimedia Commons, the free media repository*, http://upload.wikimedia.org/wikipedia/commons/6/66/Isla_Gable%2C_Tierra_del_Fuego.jpg (accessed May 19, 2014).

Figure 8.4 Photograph from Wikimedia Commons contributors, "Sea Lions in the Beagle Channel 5524709929," *Wikimedia Commons, the free media repository*, http://upload.wikimedia.org/wikipedia/commons/a/a1/Sea_Lions_in_the_Beagle_Channel_%285524709929%29.jpg (accessed May 19, 2014).

Figure 8.5 Photograph from Wikimedia Commons contributors, "Aerial view of the Lower Paraná Delta, 2009-03-25," *Wikimedia Commons, the free media repository*, http://upload.wikimedia.org/wikipedia/commons/9/9e/Aerial_view_of_the_Lower_Paran%C3%A1_Delta%2C_2009-03-25.jpg (accessed May 19, 2014).

Figure 8.6 Photograph from Wikimedia Commons contributors, "Ratao do banhado 1 REFON," *Wikimedia Commons, the free media repository*, http://upload.wikimedia.org/wikipedia/commons/0/02/Ratao_do_banhado_1_REFON_.jpg (accessed May 19, 2014).

Figure 8.7 Map by Bill Nelson.

Figure 8.8 Photograph from Wikimedia Commons contributors, "Mouths of Amazon Geocover 1990," *Wikimedia Commons, the free media repository*, http://upload.wikimedia.org/wikipedia/commons/6/6f/Mouths_of_amazon_geocover_1990.png (accessed May 19, 2014).

Figure 8.9 Map by Bill Nelson.

Figure 8.10 Photograph from Wikimedia Commons contributors, "Cylindrical vessel Collection H Law 170 n1," *Wikimedia Commons, the free media repository*, http://upload.wikimedia.org/wikipedia/commons/f/f6/Cylindrical_vessel_Collection_H_Law_170_n1.jpg (accessed May 19, 2014).

Figure 8.11 Photograph from Wikimedia Commons contributors, "Funerary vessel Collection H Law 172 n1," *Wikimedia Commons, the free media repository*, http://upload.wikimedia.org/wikipedia/commons/d/dd/Funerary_vessel_Collection_H_Law_172_n1.jpg (accessed May 19, 2014).

Figure 8.12 Map by Charles Spencer, courtesy of Charles Spencer and Elsa Redmond.

Figure 8.13 Photograph from NASA Cnazca_IKO_2005015_lrger; public domain.

Figure 8.14 Photograph from Wikimedia Commons contributors, "Mantle, plain weave of camelid fiber and cotton, early Nasca style, Ica, Peru—Peruvian fabric in the American Museum of Natural History—DSC06128," *Wikimedia Commons, the free media repository*, http://commons.wikimedia.org/wiki/File:Mantle,_plain_weave_of_camelid_fiber_and_cotton,_early_Nasca_style,_Ica,_Peru_-_Peruvian_fabric_in_the_American_Museum_of_Natural_History_-_DSC06128.JPG (accessed May 19, 2014).

Figure 8.15 Photograph from Brooklyn Museum, "38.121 border figure03 IMLS," *brooklynmuseum.org*, http://cdn2.brooklynmuseum.org/images/opencollection/objects/size4/38.121_border_figure03_IMLS.jpg (accessed May 19, 2014).

Figure 8.16 Photograph from Wikimedia Commons contributors, "NazcaLinesMonkey," *Wikimedia Commons, the free media repository*, http://commons.wikimedia.org/wiki/File:NazcaLinesMonkey.jpg (accessed May 19, 2014).

Figure 8.17 Photograph from Wikimedia Commons contributors, "Bridge-spouted Bottle with Anthropomorphic Mythical Being—warrior, 100-300 AD, Nasca culture, south coast Peru, earthenware with colored slips—Gardiner Museum, Toronto—DSC01301," *Wikimedia Commons, the free media repository*, http://commons.wikimedia.org/wiki/File%3ABridge-spouted_Bottle_with_Anthropomorphic_Mythical_Being_-_warrior%2C_100-300_AD%2C_Nasca_culture%2C_south_coast_Peru%2C_earthenware_with_colored_slips_-_Gardiner_Museum%2C_Toronto_-_DSC01301.JPG (accessed May 19, 2014).

Figure 8.18 Photograph from Wikimedia Commons contributors, "Cahuachi 10," *Wikimedia Commons, the free media repository*, http://commons.wikimedia.org/wiki/File:Cahuachi_10.jpg (accessed May 19, 2014).

Figure 8.19 Photograph from Wikimedia Commons contributors, "62 Nazca (22)," *Wikimedia Commons, the free media repository*, http://commons.wikimedia.org/wiki/File%3A62_Nazca_(22).jpg (accessed May 19, 2014).

Figure 8.20 Photograph from Wikimedia Commons contributors, "Nazca—Stirrup-spouted Bottle—Walters 20092028," *Wikimedia Commons, the free media repository*, http://upload.wikimedia.org/wikipedia/commons/b/b6/Nazca_-_Stirrup-spouted_Bottle_-_Walters_20092028.jpg (accessed May 19, 2014).

Figure 8.21 Photograph from Wikimedia Commons contributors, "Nazca—Stirrup-spouted Bottle—Walters 20092028—Top," *Wikimedia Commons, the free media repository*, http://upload.wikimedia.org/wikipedia/commons/f/f4/Nazca_-_Stirrup-spouted_Bottle_-_Walters_20092028_-_Top.jpg (accessed May 19, 2014).

Figure 9.1 Photograph from Wikimedia Commons contributors, "Peruvian—Funerary Mask—Walters 20092017," *Wikimedia Commons, the free media repository*, http://upload.wikimedia.org/wikipedia/commons/4/4e/Peruvian_-_Funerary_Mask_-_Walters_20092017.jpg (accessed May 19, 2014).

Figure 9.2 Map by Bill Nelson.

Figure 9.3 Map by Bill Nelson.

Figure 9.4 Photograph from Wikimedia Commons contributors, "Huaca de la Luna y Huaca del Sol," *Wikimedia Commons, the free media repository*, http://commons.wikimedia.org/wiki/File:Huaca_de_la_Luna_y_Huaca_del_Sol.jpg (accessed May 19, 2014).

Figure 9.5 Photograph from Wikimedia Commons contributors, "Moche—Portrait Vessel—Walters 482827," *Wikimedia Commons, the free media repository*, http://commons.wikimedia.org/wiki/File:Moche_-_Portrait_Vessel_-_Walters_482827.jpg (accessed May 19, 2014).

Figure 9.6 Photograph from Wikimedia Commons contributors, "Moche—Feline Effigy Stirrup Vessel—Walters 482843—Three Quarter," *Wikimedia Commons, the free media repository*, http://commons.wikimedia.org/wiki/File:Moche_-_Feline_Effigy_Stirrup_Vessel_-_Walters_482843_-_Three_Quarter.jpg (accessed May 19, 2014).

Figure 9.7 Photograph from Wikimedia Commons contributors, "Tumba Sr Sipan Huaca Rajada," *Wikimedia Commons, the free media repository*, http://commons.wikimedia.org/wiki/File:Tumba_Sr_Sipan_Huaca_Rajada.jpg (accessed May 19, 2014).

Figure 9.8 Photograph from Wikimedia Commons contributors, "Cerro Blanco and Huaca de la Luna," *Wikimedia Commons, the free media repository*, http://commons.wikimedia.org/wiki/File:Cerro_Blanco_and_Huaca_de_la_Luna.jpg (accessed May 19, 2014).

Figure 9.9 Photograph by author.

Figure 9.10 Photograph by author.

Figure 9.11 Photograph by author.

Figure 9.12 Photograph from Wikimedia Commons contributors, "Personally signed adobe bricks made 1500 years ago for Huaca de la Luna," *Wikimedia Commons, the free media repository*, http://upload.wikimedia.org/wikipedia/commons/9/96/Personally_signed_adobe_bricks_made_1500_years_ago_for_Huaca_de_la_Luna.JPG (accessed May 19, 2014).

Figure 9.13 Photograph from Wikimedia Commons contributors, "RPM Peru 080," *Wikimedia Commons, the free media repository*, http://upload.wikimedia.org/wikipedia/commons/9/91/RPM_Peru_080.jpg (accessed May 19, 2014).

Figure 9.14 Photograph from Wikimedia Commons contributors, "Unknown (Lambayeque style)—Funerary shirt ML600141," *Wikimedia Commons, the free media repository*, http://upload.wikimedia.org/wikipedia/commons/b/b1/Unknown_%28Lambayeque_style%29_-_Funerary_shirt_ML600141_-_Google_Art_Project.jpg (accessed May 19, 2014).

Figure 9.15 Photograph from Wikimedia Commons contributors, "Ethnologisches Museum Dahlem Berlin Mai 2006 002," *Wikimedia Commons, the free media repository*, http://upload.wikimedia.org/wikipedia/commons/4/4c/Ethnologisches_Museum_Dahlem_Berlin_Mai_2006_002.jpg (accessed May 19, 2014).

Figure 9.16 Photograph from Wikimedia Commons contributors, "The Valleys of Túcume (Peru)," *Wikimedia Commons, the free media repository*, http://upload.wikimedia.org/wikipedia/commons/d/d0/The_Valleys_of_T%C3%BAcume_%28Peru%29.jpg (accessed May 19, 2014).

Figure 9.17 Photograph from Wikimedia Commons contributors, "Chan chan view1," *Wikimedia Commons, the free media repository*, http://commons.wikimedia.org/wiki/File:Chan_chan_view1.jpg (accessed May 19, 2014).

Figure 9.18 Photograph from Wikimedia Commons contributors, "Chan Chan Model," *Wikimedia Commons, the free media repository*, http://upload.wikimedia.org/wikipedia/commons/d/d6/Chan_Chan_Model.jpg (accessed May 19, 2014).

Figure 9.19 Photograph © Yolka / Shutterstock.

Figure 9.20 Photograph from Wikimedia Commons contributors, "Chimú—Beaker—Walters 572307—Three Quarter Right," *Wikimedia Commons, the free media repository*, http://upload.wikimedia.org/wikipedia/commons/1/10/Chim%C3%BA_-_Beaker_-_Walters_572307_-_Three_Quarter_Right.jpg (accessed May 19, 2014).

Figure 9.21 Photograph from Wikimedia Commons contributors, "Ceremonial Knife (Tumi) A.D. 1100-1550 Peru, Chimú," *Wikimedia Commons, the free media repository*, http://upload

.wikimedia.org/wikipedia/commons/1/19/Ceremonial_Knife_%28Tumi%29_A.D._1100-1550_Peru%2C_Chim%C3%BA.jpg (accessed May 19, 2014).

Figure 9.22 Photograph from Wikimedia Commons contributors, "Inca Figurine EthnM," *Wikimedia Commons, the free media repository*, http://upload.wikimedia.org/wikipedia/commons/5/50/Inka_Figurine_EthnM.jpg (accessed May 19, 2014).

Figure 9.23 May by Bill Nelson.

Figure 9.24 Photograph from Wikimedia Commons contributors, "Peru Huari Standing Dignitary 1 Kimbell," *Wikimedia Commons, the free media repository*, http://commons.wikimedia.org/wiki/File%3APeru_Huari_Standing_Dignitary_1_Kimbell.jpg (accessed May 19, 2014).

Figure 9.25 Photograph from Wikimedia Commons contributors, "Piquillacta Archaeological site—street," *Wikimedia Commons, the free media repository*, http://upload.wikimedia.org/wikipedia/commons/3/36/Piquillacta_Archaeological_site_-_street.jpg (accessed May 19, 2014).

Figure 9.26 Photograph from Wikimedia Commons contributors, "Wari Würdenträger Museum Rietberg RPB 320," *Wikimedia Commons, the free media repository*, http://commons.wikimedia.org/wiki/File%3AWari_W%C3%BCrdentr%C3%A4ger_Museum_Rietberg_RPB_320.jpg (accessed May 19, 2014).

Figure 9.27 Photograph from Wikimedia Commons contributors, "Huari style—Unku with designs of stylized figures—Google Art Project," *Wikimedia Commons, the free media repository*, http://commons.wikimedia.org/wiki/File%3AHuari_style_-_Unku_with_designs_of_stylized_figures_-_Google_Art_Project.jpg (accessed May 19, 2014).

Figure 9.28 Photograph from Wikimedia Commons contributors, "Hand with figure of captive, Wari, 600-1100 AD, central Peru—Staatliches Museum für Völkerkunde München—DSC08565," *Wikimedia Commons, the free media repository*, http://upload.wikimedia.org/wikipedia/commons/d/dc/Hand_with_figure_of_captive%2C_Wari%2C_600-1100_AD%2C_central_Peru_-_Staatliches_Museum_f%C3%BCr_V%C3%B6lkerkunde_M%C3%BCnchen_-_DSC08565.JPG (accessed May 19, 2014).

Figure 9.29 Photograph from Wikimedia Commons contributors, "Huari style—Cotton and feather standard ML600003—Google Art Project," *Wikimedia Commons, the free media repository*, http://upload.wikimedia.org/wikipedia/commons/2/28/Huari_style_-_Cotton_and_feather_standard_ML600003_-_Google_Art_Project.jpg (accessed May 19, 2014).

Figure 9.30 Photograph © David Hlavacek / Shutterstock.

Figure 9.31 Photograph © Eduardo Rivero / Shutterstock.

Figure 9.32 Photograph from Wikimedia Commons contributors, "Monolito Fraile y Pirámide de Akapana al fondo," *Wikimedia Commons, the free media repository*, http://commons.wikimedia.org/wiki/File:Monolito_Fraile_y_Pir%C3%A1mide_de_Akapana_al_fondo.jpg (accessed May 19, 2014).

Figure 9.33 Photography by author.

Figure 9.34 Photograph from Wikimedia Commons contributors, "RPM Peru 068," *Wikimedia Commons, the free media repository*, http://upload.wikimedia.org/wikipedia/commons/6/6a/RPM_Peru_068.jpg (accessed May 19, 2014).

Figure 10.1 Photograph from Wikimedia Commons contributors, "TITLE," *Wikimedia Commons, the free media repository*, URL.jpg (accessed May 19, 2014).

Figure 10.2 Map by Bill Nelson.

Figure 10.3 Map by Bill Nelson.

Figure 10.4 Map by Bill Nelson.

Figure 10.5 Courtesy of Michael Heckenberger.

Figure 10.6 Photograph from Wikimedia Commons contributors, "Parque Indígena do Xingu," *Wikimedia Commons, the free media repository*, http://commons.wikimedia.org/wiki/File:Parque_Ind%C3%ADgena_do_Xingu.jpg (accessed May 19, 2014).
Figure 10.7 Photograph courtesy of Eduardo Góes Neves.
Figure 10.8 Photograph courtesy of Eduardo Góes Neves.
Figure 10.9 Photograph courtesy of Eduardo Góes Neves.
Figure 10.10 Courtesy of Eduardo Góes Neves.
Figure 10.11 Photograph by author.
Figure 10.12 Map by Bill Nelson.
Figure 10.13 Photograph courtesy of Eduardo Góes Neves.
Figure 10.14 Map by Bill Nelson.
Figure 10.15 Photograph © gary yim / Shutterstock.
Figure 10.16 Photograph from Wikimedia Commons contributors, "Tombs in Tierra Dentro—access to the hypogeum by spiral stairs," *Wikimedia Commons, the free media repository*, http://commons.wikimedia.org/wiki/File:Tombs_in_Tierra_Dentro_-_access_to_the_hypogeum_by_spiral_stairs.jpg (accessed May 19, 2014).
Figure 10.17 Photograph from Wikimedia Commons contributors, "San Agustin," *Wikimedia Commons, the free media repository*, http://commons.wikimedia.org/wiki/File%3ASan_Agustin.jpeg (accessed May 19, 2014).
Figure 10.18 Photograph by author.
Figure 10.19 Photograph by author.
Figure 10.20 Photograph from Wikimedia Commons contributors, "Balsa del Corregimiento de Guayaquil y sus contigüedades—AHG," *Wikimedia Commons, the free media repository*, http://upload.wikimedia.org/wikipedia/commons/2/29/Balsa_del_Corregimiento_de_Guayaquil_y_sus_contig%C3%BCedades_-_AHG.jpg (accessed May 19, 2014).
Figure 10.21 Photograph by author.
Figure 10.22 Photograph by author.
Figure 10.23 Photograph by author.
Figure 10.24 Photograph by author.
Figure 10.25 Photograph courtesy of James Nations.
Figure 11.1 Photograph © Christian Vinces / Shutterstock.
Figure 11.2 Map by Bill Nelson.
Figure 11.3 Photograph from Wikimedia Commons contributors, "Tambo Machay Archaeological site—overview," *Wikimedia Commons, the free media repository*, http://upload.wikimedia.org/wikipedia/commons/3/3c/Tambo_Machay_Archaeological_site_-_overview.png (accessed May 19, 2014).
Figure 11.4 Photograph © aquatic creature / Shutterstock.
Figure 11.5 Photograph © Goodluz / Shutterstock.
Figure 11.6 Photograph from Wikimedia Commons contributors, "Pachacutec-small," *Wikimedia Commons, the free media repository*, http://upload.wikimedia.org/wikipedia/commons/5/53/Pachacutec-small.png (accessed May 19, 2014).
Figure 11.7 Map by Bill Nelson.
Figure 11.8 Map by Ephraim George Squier from Wikimedia Commons contributors, *Wikimedia Commons, the free media repository*, http://upload.wikimedia.org/wikipedia/commons/b/b9/Cuzco1860.jpg (accessed May 21, 2014).
Figure 11.9 Photograph © Christian Vinces / Shutterstock.
Figure 11.10 Photograph by author.
Figure 11.11 Photograph by author.

Figure 11.12 Photograph by author.
Figure 11.13 Photograph © 3plusX / Shutterstock.
Figure 11.14 Photograph © D.O.F. / Shutterstock.
Figure 11.15 Photograph © Christopher Kolaczan / Shutterstrock.
Figure 11.16 Photograph from Wikimedia Commons contributors, "Willkawaman ushnu," *Wikimedia Commons, the free media repository*, http://upload.wikimedia.org/wikipedia/commons/3/30/Willkawaman_ushnu.jpg (accessed May 19, 2014).
Figure 11.17 Photograph from Wikimedia Commons contributors, "Tupa inca tunic," *Wikimedia Commons, the free media repository*, http://upload.wikimedia.org/wikipedia/commons/a/a2/Tupa-inca-tunic.png (accessed May 19, 2014).
Figure 11.18 Photograph from Wikimedia Commons contributors, "Cuzco MAP P1100897," *Wikimedia Commons, the free media repository*, http://upload.wikimedia.org/wikipedia/commons/4/44/Cuzco_MAP_P1100897.JPG (accessed May 19, 2014).
Figure 11.19 Photograph from Wikimedia Commons contributors, "Tunanmarca Archaeological site—storehouse," *Wikimedia Commons, the free media repository*, http://upload.wikimedia.org/wikipedia/commons/3/39/Tunanmarca_Archaeological_site_-_storehouse.jpg (accessed May 19, 2014).
Figure 11.20 Photograph by author.
Figure 11.21 Photograph courtesy of Carolina Vílchez.
Figure 11.22 Photograph from Wikimedia Commons contributors, "Kuelap," *Wikimedia Commons, the free media repository*, http://upload.wikimedia.org/wikipedia/commons/0/0b/Kuelap.jpg (accessed May 19, 2014).
Figure 11.23 Photograph from Wikimedia Commons contributors, "Kuelap—Août 2007—0," *Wikimedia Commons, the free media repository*, http://upload.wikimedia.org/wikipedia/commons/e/e1/Kuelap_-_Ao%C3%BBt_2007_-_09.jpg (accessed May 19, 2014).
Figure 11.24 Photograph from Wikimedia Commons contributors, "Pucará de La Compañía 01," *Wikimedia Commons, the free media repository*, http://commons.wikimedia.org/wiki/File:Pucar%C3%A1_de_La_Compa%C3%B1%C3%ADa_01.JPG (accessed May 19, 2014).
Figure 11.25 Illustration by Felipe Guaman Poma de Ayala Nueva Crónica y Buen Gobierno; public domain.
Figure 11.26 Illustration from J. Santa Cruz Yupanqui, "An account of the antiquities of Peru," in *Rites and Narratives of the Incas*, trans. and ed. C. Markham (London: Hakylut Society, n.d.); public domain
Figure 11.27 Photograph from Wikimedia Commons contributors, "Cuzco MAP P1100675," *Wikimedia Commons, the free media repository*, http://commons.wikimedia.org/wiki/File:Cuzco_MAP_P1100675.JPG (accessed May 19, 2014).
Figure 11.28 Photograph from Wikimedia Commons contributors, "Llullaillaco mummies in Salta city, Argentina," *Wikimedia Commons, the free media repository*, http://upload.wikimedia.org/wikipedia/commons/9/9f/Llullaillaco_mummies_in_Salta_city%2C_Argentina.jpg (accessed May 19, 2014).
Figure 11.29 Photograph from Wikimedia Commons contributors, "Gold figure, Inca, 1450-1532, Peru—Staatliches Museum für Völkerkunde München—DSC08497," *Wikimedia Commons, the free media repository*, http://commons.wikimedia.org/wiki/File:Gold_figure,_Inca,_1450-1532,_Peru_-_Staatliches_Museum_f%C3%BCr_V%C3%B6lkerkunde_M%C3%BCnchen_-_DSC08497.JPG (accessed May 19, 2014).
Figure 12.1 Illustration from Wikimedia Commons contributors, "Map of South America 1575," *Wikimedia Commons, the free media repository*, http://upload.wikimedia.org/wikipedia/commons/c/cb/Map_of_South_america_1575.jpg (accessed May 19, 2014).

Figure 12.2 Photograph from Wikimedia Commons contributors, "Catedral de Sao Miguel Arcanjo," *Wikimedia Commons, the free media repository*, http://upload.wikimedia.org/wikipedia/commons/4/4b/Catedral.de.S%C3%A30.Miguel.Arcanjo.jpg (accessed May 19, 2014).

Figure 12.3 Map from Wikimedia Commons contributors, "Gviana siue Amazonvm Regio" by G. Blaeu, *Wikimedia Commons, the free media repository*, http://upload.wikimedia.org/wikipedia/commons/5/53/1635_Blaeu_Map_Guiana,_Venezuela,_and_El_Dorado_-_Geographicus_-_Guiana-blaeu-1635.jpg

Figure 12.4 Photograph from Wikimedia Commons contributors, "First Map of Caracas, 1578," *Wikimedia Commons, the free media repository*, http://commons.wikimedia.org/wiki/File:First_Map_of_Caracas,_1578.jpg (accessed May 19, 2014).

Figure 12.5 Photograph by author.

Figure 12.6 Photograph from Wikimedia Commons contributors, "Rio de la Plata BA 2," *Wikimedia Commons, the free media repository*, http://upload.wikimedia.org/wikipedia/commons/0/0b/Rio_de_la_Plata_BA_2.JPG (accessed May 19, 2014).

Figure 12.7 Illustratoin from Wikimedia Commons contributors, "Índios emu ma fazenda," *Wikimedia Commons, the free media repository*, http://upload.wikimedia.org/wikipedia/commons/2/23/%C3%8Dndios_em_uma_fazenda.jpg (accessed May 19, 2014).

Figure 12.8 Photograph courtesy of Tom Dillehay.

Figure 12.9 Photograph courtesy of Tom Dillehay.

Figure 12.10 Photograph by author.

Figure 12.11 Photograph by author.

Figure 12.12 Photograph by author.

Index

Page numbers in italics indicate illustrations.

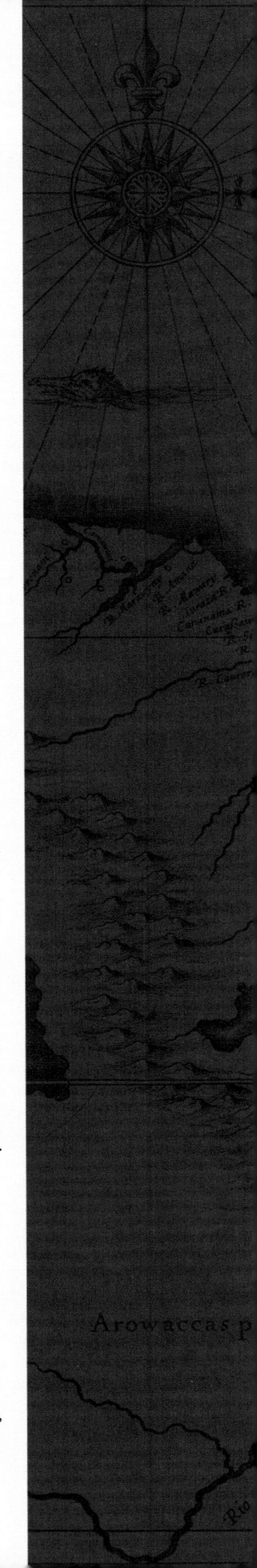